Object Oriented Programming with C++

Revised First Edition

REEMA THAREJA

Assistant Professor

Department of Computer Science

University of Delhi

OXFORD

UNIVERSITY PRESS

OXFORD
UNIVERSITY PRESS

Oxford University Press is a department of the University of Oxford. It furthers the University's objective of excellence in research, scholarship, and education by publishing worldwide. Oxford is a registered trade mark of Oxford University Press in the UK and in certain other countries.

Published in India by
Oxford University Press
22 Workspace, 2nd Floor, 1/22 Asaf Ali Road, New Delhi 110 002

First Edition published in 2015
Revised First Edition published in 2018
Seventh impression 2023

ISBN-13: 978-0-19-948567-3
ISBN-10: 0-19-948567-4

Typeset in Times New Roman
by Ideal Publishing Solutions, Delhi
M P Printer (a unit of D B Corp. Ltd.), Noida 201 305

Cover image: Mmaxer / Shutterstock

For product information and current price, please visit www.india.oup.com

I dedicate this book to my family and my uncle, Mr B.L. Theraja, who is a well-known author

Features of

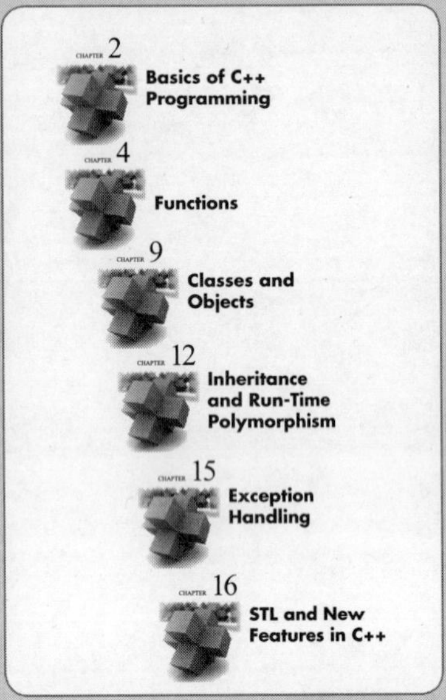
CHAPTER 2 Basics of C++ Programming

CHAPTER 4 Functions

CHAPTER 9 Classes and Objects

CHAPTER 12 Inheritance and Run-Time Polymorphism

CHAPTER 15 Exception Handling

CHAPTER 16 STL and New Features in C++

Span of Coverage

The book provides wider span of coverage of topics, starting from basic concepts of object oriented programming (OOP) including discussion on Arrays, Functions, Strings, and Pointers, details on all the important concepts such as Classes, Inheritance, Operator Overloading, File Management, and Exception Handling. It also includes separate chapters on Standard Library Template (STL) and Object Oriented Systems. This will help readers have a thorough knowledge of the subject.

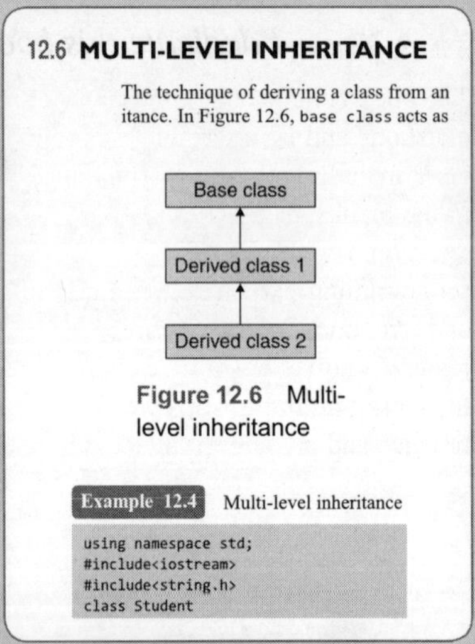
12.6 MULTI-LEVEL INHERITANCE

The technique of deriving a class from an itance. In Figure 12.6, base class acts as

Figure 12.6 Multi-level inheritance

Example 12.4 Multi-level inheritance

```
using namespace std;
#include<iostream>
#include<string.h>
class Student
```

Approach

The book adopts bottom-up and example-based approach for explaining concepts. It first introduces the concept using simple language, examples and illustrations, and then delves into its intricacies and implementation aspects. This makes the text easier to comprehend for the readers.

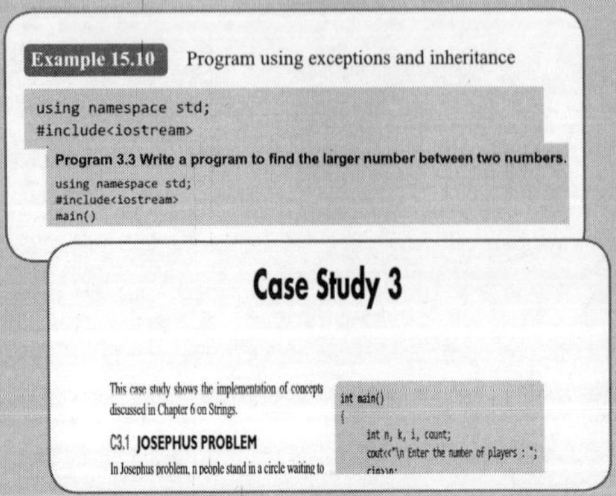
Example 15.10 Program using exceptions and inheritance

```
using namespace std;
#include<iostream>
```

Program 3.3 Write a program to find the larger number between two numbers.

```
using namespace std;
#include<iostream>
main()
```

Case Study 3

This case study shows the implementation of concepts discussed in Chapter 6 on Strings.

C3.1 JOSEPHUS PROBLEM

In Josephus problem, n people stand in a circle waiting to

```
int main()
{
    int n, k, i, count;
    cout<<"\n Enter the number of players : ";
```

Programming Examples and Case Studies

Plenty of programming examples (close to 520) along with their outputs and descriptions are provided in support of text. These examples are arranged in a simple-to-complex format. Case-studies illustrating the applications of concepts studied in different scenarios are also included in the book. These will help readers understand the concept, logic, and syntax used while developing a program, thereby transforming them into efficient programmers.

the Book

Notes and Programming Tips

Every chapter includes 'notes' mentioning the important concepts to remember and 'programming tips' stating the do's and don'ts while developing a program. This will help readers keep the critical points in mind and create error-free programs.

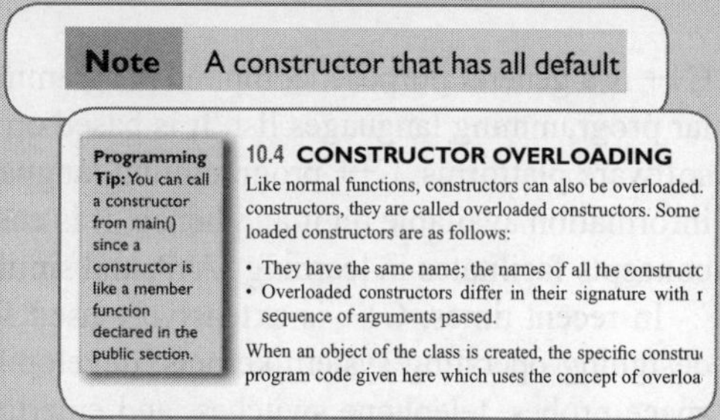
Note A constructor that has all default

Programming Tip: You can call a constructor from main() since a constructor is like a member function declared in the public section.

10.4 CONSTRUCTOR OVERLOADING

Like normal functions, constructors can also be overloaded. constructors, they are called overloaded constructors. Some loaded constructors are as follows:

- They have the same name; the names of all the constructc
- Overloaded constructors differ in their signature with r sequence of arguments passed.

When an object of the class is created, the specific constru program code given here which uses the concept of overloa

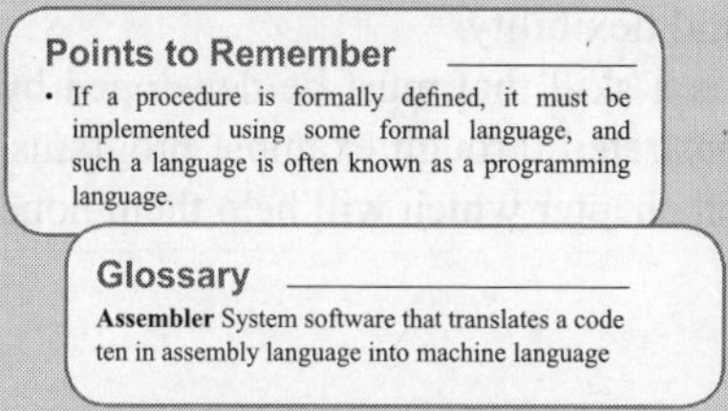
Points to Remember

- If a procedure is formally defined, it must be implemented using some formal language, and such a language is often known as a programming language.

Glossary

Assembler System software that translates a code ten in assembly language into machine language

Glossary and Points to remember

A point-wise summary and glossary of terms are provided at the end of each chapter to help readers quickly recollect and memorize the important concepts explained in that chapter.

Test Your Skills

The book contains numerous (close to 1880) questions and a variety of chapter-end exercises including objective-type questions (fill in the blanks, true/false, and multiple choice questions) with answers, review questions, programming exercises, and find the output and error questions. These are provided to test readers' knowledge of the concepts, improve their programming skills as also help them practice and prepare for their examinations.

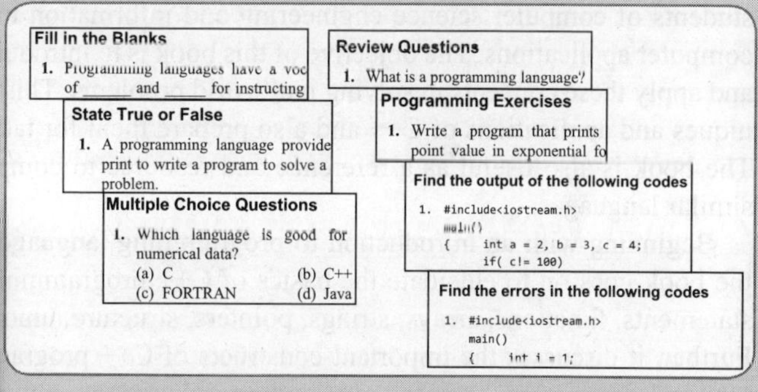
Fill in the Blanks

1. Programming languages have a voc of ___ and ___ for instructing

State True or False

1. A programming language provide print to write a program to solve a problem.

Multiple Choice Questions

1. Which language is good for numerical data?
(a) C (b) C++
(c) FORTRAN (d) Java

Review Questions

1. What is a programming language?

Programming Exercises

1. Write a program that prints point value in exponential fo

Find the output of the following codes

```
1. #include<iostream.h>
   main()
   {  int a = 2, b = 3, c = 4;
      if( c!= 100)
```

Find the errors in the following codes

```
1. #include<iostream.h>
   main()
   {  int i = 1;
```

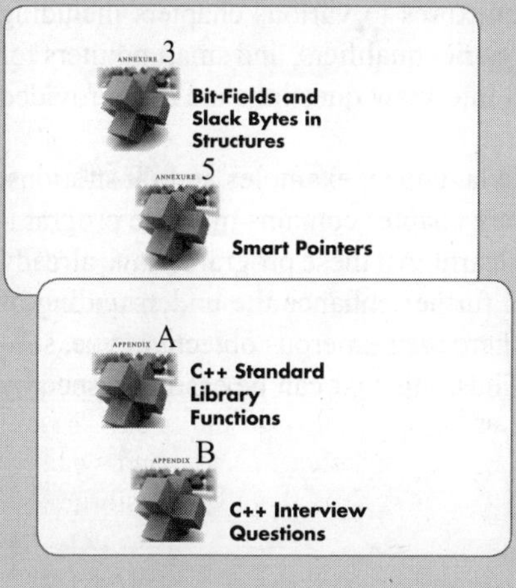
ANNEXURE 3 Bit-Fields and Slack Bytes in Structures

ANNEXURE 5 Smart Pointers

APPENDIX A C++ Standard Library Functions

APPENDIX B C++ Interview Questions

Annexures and Appendices

The annexures linked to various chapters of the book details some of the important concepts discussed in that particular chapter to further enhance the knowledge of the readers. Appendices on library functions and interview questions will help readers get better understanding and hands-on knowledge of the C++ concepts.

Preface

C++ is a general purpose, compiled programming language that stands second (only to C) in the most popular programming languages list. It is based on object-oriented concepts and can be used on several different software platforms. C++ programming language has been in use for a long time. Therefore there is a lot of information available on it and hence, it is easier to comprehend. Moreover, a sound understanding of C++ concepts facilitates in learning JAVA and similar programming languages.

In recent times, C++ is extensively used for implementing desktop applications, system programming, designing operating system kernels, developing embedded systems and web search engines, SQL servers, space probes, telephone switches, and entertainment software, to name a few. The important features that make C++ so exciting to use include its high performance, efficiency, and flexibility.

No student can learn to program just by reading a book; rather it is a skill that must be developed by practice. After learning the C++ concepts and their applications demonstrated through example programs, students will find a number of programming exercises at the end of each chapter which will help them hone their programming skills.

About the Book

Object Oriented Programming with C++ is designed as a textbook for undergraduate degree and diploma students of computer science engineering and information technology as well as postgraduate students of computer applications. The objective of this book is to introduce the concepts of C++ programming language and apply these concepts in solving real world problems. This will help readers get acquainted with the techniques and applications of C++ and also prepare them for taking up programming-based challenging tasks. The book is also useful as a reference and resource to computer professionals working in C++ and other similar languages.

Beginning with an introduction to programming languages and object-oriented programming concepts; the book goes on to elucidate the basics of C++ programming. It explains the various control and looping statements, functions, arrays, strings, pointers, structure, union and enumeration in the subsequent chapters. Further, it discusses the important constructs of C++ programming, namely, classes and objects, constructors and destructors, operator overloading, inheritance, polymorphism, templates, generics, and exception handling in detail. Finally, standard template library and object oriented analysis, design and development are discussed in separate chapters. The book also contains useful annexures to various chapters including user-defined header files, pointer declarations, bit-fields, volatile and restrict qualifiers, and smart pointers for additional information. Case studies, important library functions, and interview questions are also provided to supplement the text.

The book first explains the fundamentals of a concept using simple language, examples and illustrations, and then delves into its complexities and implementation aspects. Every chapter contains multiple programming examples to impart practically sound knowledge of the concepts learnt. All these programs have already been implemented and tested using Dev C++ and g++ compilers. To further enhance the understanding of the subject and the application and analytical ability of the students, there are numerous objective type, subjective type, and programming exercises at the end of each chapter. Thus, this text can be easily grasped by the readers.

Salient Features

The salient features of the book include:

- *Simple and lucid explanations* for important C++ concepts using block diagrams and examples for easy understanding.
- All programs in this book compiled on Dev C++ and g++ compilers.
- Plenty of *example programs provided along with their outputs* to help readers hone their programming skills.
- *Notes* and *Programming tips* to help readers keep in mind the critical concepts and develop error-free programs.
- *Case studies* interspersed within the text include programs which demonstrate the implementation of the concepts learnt in the various chapters.
- Abundant and variety of chapter-end exercises including *objective-type questions* (fill in the blanks, true/false, and multiple choice questions) *with answers, review questions, programming exercises,* and *find the error and output type questions* for self-check and practice.
- *Glossary* of key terms and point-wise *summary* at the end of each chapter to help readers quickly revise and memorize the important concepts learnt.
- *Interview questions* at the end of the book to help readers prepare for competitive examinations.

Organization of the Book

The book is divided into 17 chapters, 6 case studies, 5 annexures, and 2 appendices.

Chapter 1 provides an introduction to programming languages, different programming paradigms, concepts of OOP along with merits and demerits of object oriented programming languages. The chapter also gives a comparative study of some OOP languages and highlights the difference between C and C++.

Chapter 2 discusses the building blocks of the C++ programming language. The chapter includes identifiers, constants, variables, operators, type conversion, and casting supported by the C++ language.

Annexure 1 given at the end of this chapter covers user-defined header files.

Chapter 3 deals with the different types of decision control statements in C++ such as conditional branching statement, iterative statement, break statement, control statement, and jump statement.

Case Study 1 including representation of roman numbers and calculation of day and date of birth using a program illustrates the implementation of concepts discussed in Chapters 2 and 3.

Chapter 4 deals with declaring, defining, and calling functions. The chapter also discusses the storage classes, variable scope in C++, inline functions, and function overloading. It ends with an important concept of recursive functions.

Chapter 5 provides a detailed explanation of arrays that includes one, two, and multi-dimensional arrays. The operations that can be performed on such arrays are also explained.

Case Study 2 shows the applications of concepts discussed in Chapters 4 and 5 with the help of merge sort and quick sort examples.

Chapter 6 unleashes the concept of strings which are better known as character arrays. The chapter not only focuses on reading and writing strings but also explains various operations that can be used to manipulate the strings.

Chapter 7 presents a detailed overview of pointers, pointer variables, pointer arithmetic, so and so forth. The chapter also relates the use of pointers with arrays, strings and functions for writing better and efficient programs. The chapter ends with the discussions on dynamic memory management.

Annexure 2 on the process of deciphering pointer declarations is given after Chapter 7.

Chapter 8 deals with the two user-defined data types—structure and union. The chapter includes the use of structures and unions with pointers, arrays and functions so that the inter-connectivity between the programming techniques can be well understood. Enumerated data types are also explained in this chapter.

Annexure 3 discuss bit-fields and slack bytes in structures followed by ***Case Study 3*** on Josephus Problem shows the implementation of string operations.

Chapter 9 introduces the concept of classes and objects. It explains dynamic allocation of objects, static data members, nested, inline and friend functions, constant members, this pointer, empty and local classes.

Chapter 10 goes a step beyond declaration and definition of user defined classes. It unleashes the use of constructors and destructors. It also explains overloading of constructors and creating anonymous objects.

Case Study 4 covering the examples of Interpolation Search and Selection Sort presents the implementation of concepts covered in Chapters 9 and 10.

Chapter 11 is all about overloading unary and binary operators. It also discusses the conversion of a variable from one class type to another and from basic type to class type and vice versa.

Case Study 5 illustrates the concept of operator overloading discussed in Chapter 11.

Chapter 12 introduces inheritance in its various forms—single, hierarchical, hybrid, multi-level, and multiple. It provides a detailed explanation for different access specifiers, virtual functions, abstract classes, and object slicing. It also throws light on polymorphism and run time polymorphism through virtual functions. Abstract base classes, pure virtual functions, and virtual constructors and destructors are also covered in this chapter.

Chapter 13 discusses how data can be stored in files. The chapter explains the different types of files, and opening, processing and closing of files through a C++ program. These files are handled in text mode as well as binary mode for better clarity of the concepts. It also discusses sequential I/O functions and error handling during file operations.

Case Study 6 demonstrates the implementation of concepts discussed in Chapters 12 and 13.

Chapter 14 is about generic programming through templates. In this chapter, function and class templates have been discussed. It also gives a combo effect of templates and overloading, templates and inheritance, templates and static functions, templates and friends to name a few.

Chapter 15 presents the concepts of exception handling that can be used to make robust programs. The chapter demonstrates the application of exception handling in overloaded classes and functions, inherited classes, constructors or destructors. It also discusses various advantages and disadvantages of exception handling.

Chapter 16 elucidates the features of the standard template library. It also introduces some new features that have been added to the C++ language. These concepts include containers, iterators, algorithms, the string class, data type Boolean, keywords—mutable and explicit, namespaces, and finally the run time type identifiers.

Annexures 4 and 5 following this chapter briefs about the restrict and volatile qualifiers and smart pointers, respectively.

Chapter 17, the last chapter of the book, co-relates the use of objects and classes with the software development methodology. The chapter also gives an introduction of unified modelling language (UML).

The two appendices, namely, *Appendix A* discusses some of the important library functions in C++ and *Appendix B* provides frequently asked interview questions with answers and certain programming tips.

Online Resources

To aid teachers and students, the book is accompanied with online resources that are available at http://oupinheonline.com/book/thareja-object-oriented-programming-with-C/9780199459636. The content for the online resources are as follows.

For Faculty

- Chapter-wise PPTs
- Solutions Manual

For Students

- Projects
- MCQ test generator
- Model Question Papers (with answers)
- Introduction to graphics programming
- Solution to find the output and error questions
- Algorithms for basic programs
- Source codes of the programs given in the book
- Additional case studies on data structures and sorting
- Extra reading material on algorithms and flowcharts, slack bytes, bit level programming, macros, and ASCII chart

Acknowledgments

The writing of this textbook was a mammoth task for which a lot of help was required from many people. Fortunately, I have had wholehearted support of my family, friends, and fellow members of the teaching staff at Shyama Prasad Mukherji College, New Delhi.

My special thanks would always go to my parents, Mr Janak Raj Thareja and Mrs Usha Thareja, and my siblings, Pallav, Kimi, and Rashi, who were a source of abiding inspiration and divine blessings for me. I am especially thankful to my son, Goransh, who has been very patient and cooperative in letting me realize my dreams. My sincere thanks goes to my uncle, Mr B.L. Theraja, for his inspiration and guidance in writing this book. I would like to acknowledge Er Udit Chopra for his technical assistance in designing and testing the programs.

I would like to express my gratitude to the following reviewers of this revised edition as well as the previous edition for their valuable suggestions and constructive feedback that helped in improving the book.

Ms Preeti Rai Jain
Miranda House, University of Delhi

Ms Seema Rani
Shyama Prasad Mukherji College, University of Delhi

Ms Pratibha Yadav
Shyama Prasad Mukherji College, University of Delhi

Mr Soumen Swarnakar
Netaji Subhash Engineering College, Garia, Kolkata

CH.V.K.N.S.N. Moorthy
Institute of Aeronautical Engineering (Autonomous), Hyderabad

Dr Anthonisan Arockiasamy
Saveetha School of Engineering, Saveetha University, Chennai

Nithya E.
Dr Ambedkar Institute of Technology, Bangalore

Last but not the least I would like to thank the editorial team at Oxford University Press, India for their help and support.

Comments and suggestions for the improvement of the book are welcome. Please send to me at reemathareja@gmail.com.

Reema Thareja

Detailed Contents

11. Operator Overloading and Type Conversions 474

12. Inheritance and Run-Time Polymorphism 529

13. File Handling 592

17. Object-Oriented System Analysis, Design, and Development 757

CHAPTER 1

Introduction to Object Oriented Programming (OOP)

KEY Concepts

Generation of programming languages • Programming paradigms • Concepts of OOP • Merits, demerits, and applications of OOP • Differences between C and C++

INTRODUCTION

A programming language is a language specifically designed to express computations that can be performed by the computer. Programming languages are used to create programs that control the behaviour of a system, to express algorithms, or can be used as a mode of human communication.

Usually, programming languages have a vocabulary of syntax and semantics for instructing a computer to perform specific tasks. The term 'programming language' usually refers to high-level languages such as BASIC, C, C++, COBOL, FORTRAN, ADA, and PASCAL, to name a few. All these languages have a unique set of keywords (words that the language understands) and a special syntax for organizing program instructions.

While high-level programming languages are easy for us to read and understand, the computer understands the machine language that consists only of numbers. Different types of central processing unit (CPU) have their own unique machine languages.

Assembly language is a type of language that exists in between machine languages and high-level languages. Assembly languages are similar to machine languages, but are much easier to program in because they allow a programmer to substitute names for numbers.

However, irrespective of what language the programmer uses, the program written using any programming language has to be converted into machine language so that the computer can understand the same. There are two ways to do this—compile the program or interpret the program.

The determination of the language is dependent on the following factors:

- The type of computer (microcontroller, microprocessor, etc.) on which the program has to be executed.
- The type of program (system program, application program, etc.).

- The expertise of the programmer. That is, the proficiency level of a programmer in a particular language.

For example, FORTRAN is particularly good for processing numerical data but it does not lend itself very well to organizing large programs. Pascal can be used for writing well-structured and readable programs but it is not as flexible as C language. C++ goes one step ahead of C by incorporating powerful object oriented features but it is complex and difficult to learn.

These programming languages have slowly evolved with time to be more user-friendly and task-oriented. In the next section, we will study the different generations of programming languages to understand their distinguishing features.

1.1 GENERATION OF PROGRAMMING LANGUAGES

We now know that programming languages are the primary tools for creating software. As of now, hundreds of programming languages exist in the market, some more used than others and each claiming to be the best. However, in the 1940s when computers were being developed, there was just one language—machine language.

The concept of generations of programming languages (also known as levels) is closely connected to the advances in technology. The five generations of programming languages include machine language, assembly language, high-level language (also known as the third generation language or 3GL), very high-level language (also known as the fourth generation language or 4GL), and fifth generation language that includes artificial intelligence.

1.1.1 First Generation: Machine Language

The first program was programmed using the machine language. This is the lowest level of programming language and is the only language that a computer understands. All the commands and data values are expressed using 0s and 1s, corresponding to the *off* and *on* electrical states in a computer.

In the 1950s, each computer had its own native language, and programmers had primitive systems for combining numbers to represent instructions such as *add* and *subtract*. Although there were similarities between each of the machine languages, a computer could not understand programs written in another machine language (refer to Fig. 1.1).

In machine language, all instructions, memory locations, numbers, and characters are represented in strings of ones and zeroes.

In machine language, all instructions, memory locations, numbers, and characters are represented in strings of 0s and 1s. Although machine language programs are typically displayed with the *binary* numbers represented in *octal* (base 8) or *hexadecimal* (base 16) number systems, these programs are not easy for humans to read, write, or debug.

The main advantage of machine language is that the execution of the code is very fast and efficient since it is directly executed by the CPU. However, on the downside, machine language is difficult to learn and is far more difficult to edit if errors occur. Moreover, if we want to store some instructions in the memory at some location, then all the instructions after the insertion point would have to be moved down to make room in the memory to accommodate the new instructions. In addition, the code written in machine language is not portable, and to transfer the code to a different computer, it needs to be completely rewritten since the machine language for one computer could be significantly different from that for another computer. Architectural considerations make portability a tough issue to resolve. Table 1.1 lists the advantages and disadvantages of first generation language.

This is an example of a machine language program that will add two numbers and find their average. It is in hexadecimal notation instead of binary notation because that is how the computer presented the code to the programmer. The program was run on a VAX/VMS computer, a product of the Digital Equipment Corporation.

```
                                           000 0000A    0000
                                           000 0000F    0008
                                           000 0000B    0008
                                                        0008
                                                        0058
                                                        00Θ0
FF55   CF   FF54   CF   FF53   CF   C1                  00A9
       FF24   CF   FF27   CF   D2   C7                  00CC
                                                        00E4
                                                        010D
                                                        013D
```

Figure 1.1 A machine language program

Table 1.1 Advantages and disadvantages of first generation language

Advantages	Disadvantages
• Code can be directly executed by the computer. • Execution is fast and efficient. • Programs can be written to efficiently utilize memory.	• Code is difficult to write. • Code is difficult to understand by other people. • Code is difficult to maintain. • There is more possibility for errors to creep in. • It is difficult to detect and correct errors. • Code is machine dependent and thus non-portable.

1.1.2 Second Generation: Assembly Language

Second-generation programming languages (2GLs) comprise the assembly languages. Assembly languages are symbolic programming languages that use symbolic notations to represent machine language instructions. These languages are closely connected to machine language and the internal architecture of the computer system on which they are used. Since it is close to machine language, assembly language is also a low-level language. Nearly all computer systems have an assembly language available for use.

Assembly language developed in the mid-1950s was a great leap forward. It used symbolic codes, also known as *mnemonic* codes, which are easy-to-remember abbreviations, rather than numbers. Examples of these codes include ADD for add, CMP for compare, and MUL for multiply.

Assembly language programs consist of a series of individual statements or instructions to instruct the computer what to do. Basically, an assembly language statement consists of a label, an operation code, and one or more *operands*.

Labels are used to identify and refer instructions in the program. The operation code (opcode) is a mnemonic that specifies the operation to be performed, such as *move*, *add*, *subtract*, or *compare*. The operand specifies the register or the location in the main memory where the data to be processed is located.

However, like machine language, the statement or instruction in assembly language will vary from machine to machine, because the language is directly related to the internal architecture of the computer and is not designed to be machine independent. This makes the code written in assembly language less portable, as the code written to be executed on one machine will not run on machines from a different manufacturer or sometimes even the same manufacturer.

Nevertheless, the code written in assembly language will be very efficient in terms of execution time and main memory usage, as the language is similar to computer language.

Programs written in assembly language need a translator, often known as the assembler, to convert them into machine language. This is because the computer will understand only the language of 0s and 1s. It will not understand mnemonics such as ADD and SUB.

The following instructions are part of an assembly language code to illustrate addition of two numbers:

```
MOV AX,4      Stores the value 4 in the AX register of CPU
MOV BX,6      Stores the value 6 in the BX register of CPU
ADD AX,BX     Adds the contents of AX and BX registers; stores the result in AX register
```

Although it is much easier to work with assembly language than with machine language, it still requires the programmer to think on the machine's level. Even today, some programmers use assembly language to write those parts of applications where speed of execution is critical; for example, videogames, but most programmers have switched to 3GL or 4GL even to write such codes. Table 1.2 lists the advantages and disadvantages of using second generation language.

Table 1.2 Advantages and disadvantages of second generation language

Advantages	Disadvantages
• It is easy to understand. • It is easier to write programs in assembly language than in machine language. • It is easy to detect and correct errors. • It is easy to modify. • It is less prone to errors.	• Code is machine dependent and thus non-portable. • Programmers must have a good knowledge of the hardware and internal architecture of the CPU. • The code cannot be directly executed by the computer.

Assembler

Since computers can execute only codes written in machine language, a special program, called the assembler, is required to convert the code written in assembly language into an equivalent code in machine language, which contains only 0s and 1s. The working of an assembler is shown in Fig. 1.2; it can be seen that the assembler takes an assembly language program as input and gives a code in machine language (also called object program) as output. There is a one-to-one correspondence between the assembly language code and the machine language code. However, if there is an

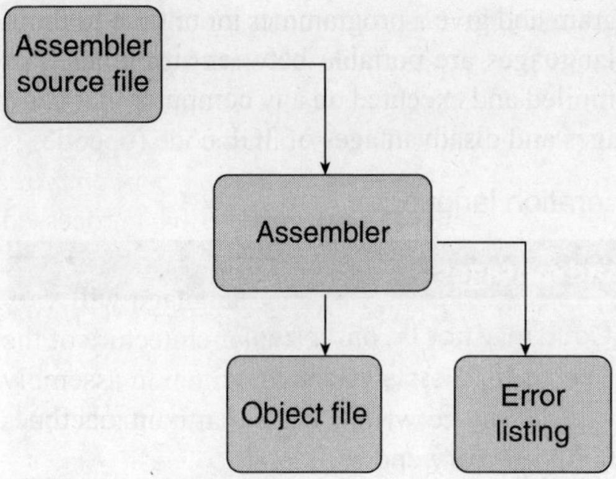

Figure 1.2 Assembler

error, the assembler gives a list of errors. The object file is created only when the assembly language code is free from errors. The object file can be executed as and when required.

1.1.3 Third Generation: High-level Language

Third-generation programming languages are a refinement of 2GLs. The second generation brought logical structure to software. The third generation was introduced to make the languages more programmer friendly.

The 3GLs spurred the great increase in data processing that occurred in the 1960s and 1970s. In these languages, the program statements are not closely related to the internal characteristics of the computer. Hence, these languages are often referred to as high-level languages.

Note An assembler only translates an assembly program into machine language. The result is an object file that can be executed. However, the assembler itself does not execute the object file.

In general, a statement written in a high-level programming language will expand into several machine language instructions. This is in contrast to assembly languages, where one statement would generate one machine language instruction. 3GLs made programming easier, efficient, and less prone to errors.

High-level languages fall somewhere between natural languages and machine languages. 3GLs include FORTRAN and COBOL, which made it possible for scientists and entrepreneurs to write programs using familiar terms instead of obscure machine instructions.

The widespread use of high-level languages in the early 1960s changed programming into something quite different from what it had been. Programs were written in languages that were more English-like, making them more convenient to use and giving the programmer more time to address a client's problems.

Although 3GLs relieve the programmer of demanding details, they do not provide the flexibility available in low-level languages. However, a few high-level languages such as C and FORTH combine some of the flexibility of assembly languages with the power of high-level languages, but these languages are not well suited to programmers at the beginner level.

Some high-level languages were specifically designed to serve a specific purpose (such as controlling industrial robots or creating graphics), whereas other languages were flexible and considered to be general purpose. Most programmers preferred to use general-purpose high-level languages such as BASIC, FORTRAN, Pascal, COBOL, C++, or Java to write the code for their applications.

Again, a translator is needed to translate the instructions written in a high-level language into the computer-executable machine language. Such translators are commonly known as interpreters and compilers. Each high-level language has many compilers, and there is one for each type of computer.

For example, the machine language generated by one computer's C compiler is not the same as the machine language of some other computer. Therefore, it is necessary to have a C compiler for each type of computer on which the C programs are to be executed.

The 3GLs make it easy to write and debug a program and give a programmer more time to think about its overall logic. Programs written in such languages are portable between machines. For example, a program written in standard C can be compiled and executed on any computer that has a standard C compiler. Table 1.3 provides the advantages and disadvantages of 3GLs.

Table 1.3 Advantages and disadvantages of third generation languages

Advantages	Disadvantages
• The code is machine independent. • It is easy to learn and use the language. • There are few errors. • It is easy to document and understand the code. • It is easy to maintain the code. • It is easy to detect and correct errors.	• Code may not be optimized. • The code is less efficient. • It is difficult to write a code that controls the CPU, memory, and registers.

Compiler

A compiler is a special type of program that transforms the source code written in a programming language (the *source language*) into machine language, which uses only two digits—0 and 1 (the *target language*). The resultant code in 0s and 1s is known as the object *code*. The object code is used to create an executable program.

Therefore, a compiler (refer to Fig. 1.3) is used to translate the source code from a high-level programming language to a lower-level language (e.g., assembly language or machine code). There is a one-to-one correspondence between the high-level language code and machine language code generated by the compiler.

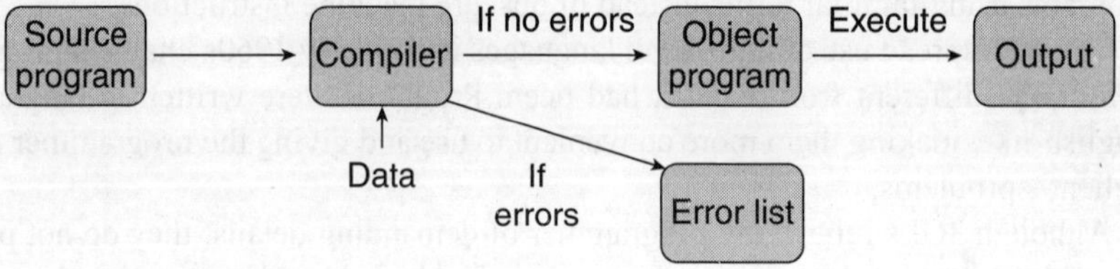

Figure 1.3 Compiler

If the source code contains errors, then the compiler will not be able to do its intended task. Errors that limit the compiler in understanding a program are called syntax errors. Examples of syntax errors are spelling mistakes, typing mistakes, illegal characters, and use of undefined variables. The other type of error is the logical error, which occurs when the program does not function accurately. Logical errors are much harder to locate and correct than syntax errors. Whenever errors are detected in the source code, the compiler generates a list of error messages indicating the type of error and the line in which the error has occurred. The programmer makes use of this error list to correct the source code.

The work of a compiler is only to translate the human-readable source code into a computer-executable machine code. It can locate syntax errors in the program (if any) but cannot fix it. Unless the syntactical error is rectified, the source code cannot be converted into the object code.

Each high-level language has a separate compiler. A compiler can translate a program in one particular high-level language into machine language. For a program written in some other programming language, a compiler for that specific language is needed.

How compilers work?

Compilers like other programs reside on the secondary storage. To translate a source code into its equivalent machine language code, the computer first loads the compiler and the source program from the secondary memory to the main memory. The computer then executes the compiler along with the source program as its input. The output of this execution is an object file which is also stored on the secondary storage. Whenever the program has to be executed, the computer loads the object file into memory and executes it. This means that it is not necessary to compile the program every time it has to be executed. Compilation will be needed only the source is modified.

Interpreter

Like the compiler, the interpreter executes instructions written in a high-level language. Basically, a program written in a high-level language can be executed in any of the two ways—by compiling the program or by passing the program through an interpreter.

The compiler translates instructions written in a high-level programming language directly into machine language; the interpreter, on the other hand, translates the instructions into an intermediate form, which it then executes. The interpreter takes one statement of high-level code, translates it into the machine level code, executes it, and then takes the next statement and repeats the process until the entire program is translated.

Note An interpreter not only translates the code into machine language but also executes it.

Figure 1.4 Interpreter

Figure 1.4 shows an interpreter that takes a source program as its input and gives the output. This is in contrast with the compiler, which produces an object file as the output of the compilation process. Usually, a compiled program executes faster than an interpreted program. Moreover, since there is no object file saved for future use, users will have to reinterpret the entire program each time they want to execute the code.

Overall, compilers and interpreters both achieve similar purposes, but they are inherently different as to how they achieve that purpose. The differences between compilers and interpreters are given in Table 1.4.

Table 1.4 Differences between compiler and an interpreter

Compiler	Interpreter
• It translates the entire program in one go. • It generates error(s) after translating the entire program. • Execution of code is faster. • An object file is generated. • Code need not be recompiled every time it is executed. • It merely translates the code. • It requires more memory space (to save the object file).	• It interprets and executes one statement at a time. • It stops translation after getting the first error. • Execution of code is slower as every time reinterpretation of statements has to be done. • No object file is generated. • Code has to be reinterpreted every time it is executed. • It translates as well as executes the code. • It requires less memory space (no object file).

Linker

Software development in the real world usually follows a modular approach as given in structured programming (discussed in Section 1.2.3). In this approach, a program is divided into various (smaller) modules as it is easy to code, edit, debug, test, document, and maintain them. Moreover, a module written for one program can also be used for another program. When a module is compiled, an object file of that module is generated.

Once the modules are coded and tested, the object files of all the modules are combined together to form the final executable file. Therefore, a linker, also called a link editor or binder, is a program that combines the object modules to form an executable program (refer to Fig.1.5). Usually, the compiler automatically invokes the linker as the last step in compiling a program.

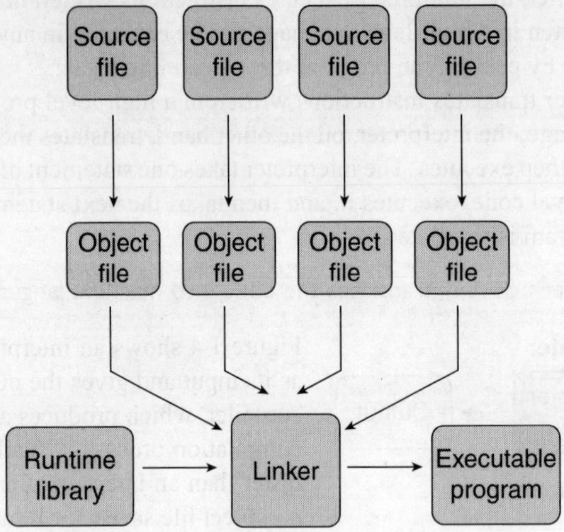

Figure 1.5 Role of linker

Loader

A loader is a special type of program that copies programs from a storage device to the main memory, where they can be executed. The functionality and complexity of most loaders are hidden from the users.

1.1.4 Fourth Generation: Very High-level Languages

With each generation, programming languages started becoming easier to use and more similar to natural languages. 4GLs are a little different from their prior generation because they are non-procedural. While writing a code using a procedural language, the programmer has to tell the computer how a task is done—add this, compare that, do this if the condition is true, and so on—in a very specific step-by-step manner. In striking contrast, while using a non-procedural language, programmers define what they want the computer to do but they do not supply all the details of how it has to be done. For example, in a procedural language like C++, to show the details of all the students we write programs that contains instructions specifying how the details are to be fetched and displayed but the same task in SQL (a non procedural language) can be written in a single sentence (select * from Students)

Although there is no standard rule that defines a 4GL, certain characteristics of such languages include the following:

- The instructions of the code are written in English-like sentences.
- They are non-procedural, so users concentrate on the 'what' instead of the 'how' aspect of the task.

- The code written in a 4GL is easy to maintain.
- The code written in a 4GL enhances the productivity of programmers, as they have to type fewer lines of code to get something done. A programmer supposedly becomes 10 times more productive when he/she writes the code using a 4GL than using a 3GL.

A typical example of a 4GL is the query language, which allows a user to request information from a database with precisely worded English-like sentences. A query language is used as a database user interface and hides the specific details of the database from the user. For example, when working with structured query language (SQL), the programmer just needs to remember a few rules of *syntax* and *logic*, and therefore, it is easier to learn than COBOL or C.

Let us take an example in which a report needs to be generated. The report displays the total number of students enrolled in each class and in each semester. Using a 4GL, the request would look similar to the following:

```
TABLE FILE ENROLLMENT
SUM STUDENTS BY SEMESTER BY CLASS
```

Therefore, we see that a 4GL is very simple to learn and work with. The same task if written in C or any other 3GL would require multiple lines of code.

The 4GLs are still evolving, which makes it difficult to define or standardize them. The only downside of a 4GL is that it does not make efficient use of a machine's resources. However, the benefit of executing a program quickly and easily far outweighs the extra costs of running it.

1.1.5 Fifth Generation Programming Language

Fifth-generation programming languages (5GLs) are centred on solving problems using the constraints given to a program rather than using an algorithm written by a programmer. Most constraint-based and logic programming languages and some declarative languages form a part of the 5GLS. These languages are widely used in artificial intelligence research. Another aspect of a 5GL is that it contains visual tools to help develop a program. Typical examples of 5GLs include Prolog, OPS5, Mercury, and Visual Basic.

Therefore, taking a forward leap, 5GLs are designed to make the computer solve a given problem without the programmer. While working with a 4GL, programmers have to write a specific code to do a work, but with a 5GL, they only have to worry about what problems need to be solved and what conditions need to be met, without worrying about how to implement a routine or an algorithm to solve them.

In general, 5GLs were built upon LISP, many originating on the LISP machine such as ICAD. There are also many frame languages such as KL-ONE.

In the 1990s, 5GLs were considered the wave of the future, and some predicted that they would replace all other languages for system development (except the low-level languages). During the period ranging from 1982 to 1993, Japan carried out extensive research on and invested a large amount of money into their fifth-generation computer systems project, hoping to design a massive computer network of machines using these tools. However, when large programs were built, the flaws of the approach became more apparent. Researchers began to observe that given a set of constraints defining a particular problem, deriving an efficient algorithm to solve it is itself a very difficult problem. All factors could not be automated and some still require the insight of a programmer.

However, today the fifth-generation languages are pursued as a possible level of computer language. Software vendors across the globe currently claim that their software meets the visual 'programming' requirements of the 5GL concept.

Knowing about the evolution of programming languages is just not enough until and unless we have a sound background knowledge about structure and style of writing of programs. The next section therefore talks about programming paradigms so that you can have an insight into how object oriented programming is better than the traditional paradigms.

1.2 PROGRAMMING PARADIGMS

A programming paradigm is a fundamental style of programming that defines how the structure and basic elements of a computer program will be built. The style of writing programs and the set of capabilities and limitations that a particular programming language has depends on the programming paradigm it supports. While some programming languages strictly follow a single paradigm, others may draw concepts from more than one. The sweeping trend in the evolution of high-level programming languages has resulted in a shift in programming paradigm. These paradigms, in sequence of their application, can be classified as follows:

- Monolithic programming—emphasizes on finding a solution
- Procedural programming—lays stress on algorithms
- Structured programming—focuses on modules
- Object-oriented programming—emphasizes on classes and objects
- Logic-oriented programming—focuses on goals usually expressed in predicate calculus
- Rule-oriented programming—makes use of 'if-then-else' rules for computation
- Constraint-oriented programming—utilizes invariant relationships to solve a problem

Each of these paradigms has its own strengths and weaknesses and no single paradigm can suit all applications. For example, for designing computation intensive problems, procedure-oriented programming is preferred; for designing a knowledge base, rule-based programming would be the best option; and for hypothesis derivation, logic-oriented programming is used. In this book, we will discuss only first four paradigms. Among these paradigms, object oriented paradigms supersede to serve as the architectural framework in which other paradigms are employed.

1.2.1 Monolithic Programming

Programs written using monolithic programming languages such as assembly language and BASIC consist of global data and sequential code. The global data can be accessed and modified (knowingly or mistakenly) from any part of the program, thereby, posing a serious threat to its integrity.

A sequential code is one in which all instructions are executed in the specified sequence. In order to change the sequence of instructions, jump statements or 'goto' statements are used. Figure 1.6 shows the structure of a monolithic program.

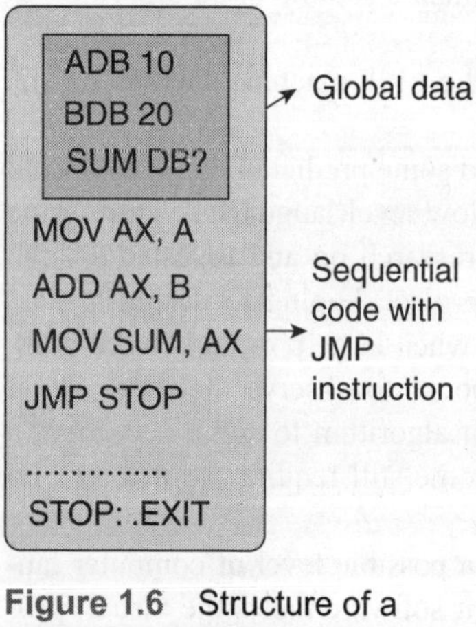

Figure 1.6 Structure of a monolithic program

As the name suggests, monolithic programs have just one program module as such programming languages do not support the concept of subroutines. Therefore, all the actions required to complete a particular task are embedded within the same application itself. This not only makes the size of the program large but also makes it difficult to debug and maintain.

For all these reasons, monolithic programming language is used only for very small and simple applications where reusability is not a concern.

1.2.2 Procedural Programming

In procedural languages, a program is divided into *n* number of subroutines that access global data. To avoid repetition of code, each subroutine

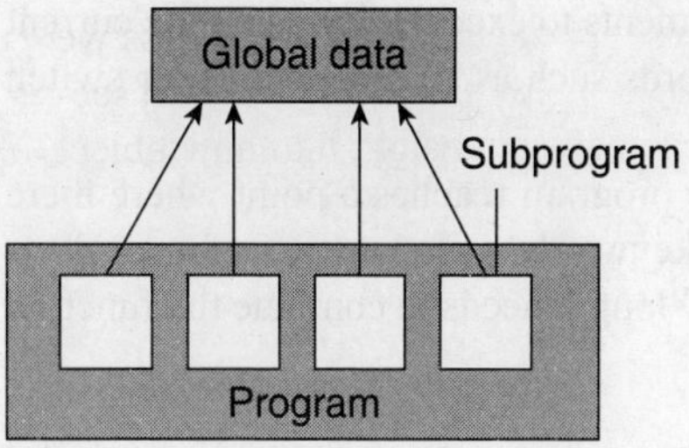

Figure 1.7 Structure of a procedural program

performs a well-defined task. A subroutine that needs the service provided by another subroutine can call that subroutine. Therefore, with 'jump', 'goto', and 'call' instructions, the sequence of execution of instructions can be altered. Figure 1.7 shows the structure of a procedural language.

FORTRAN and COBOL are two popular procedural programming languages.

Advantages

- The only goal is to write correct programs
- Programs were easier to write as compared to monolithic programming

Disadvantages

- Writing programs is complex.
- No concept of reusability.
- Requires more time and effort to write programs.
- Programs are difficult to maintain.
- Global data is shared and therefore may get altered (mistakenly).

1.2.3 Structured Programming

Structured programming, also referred to as modular programming, was first suggested by mathematicians, Corrado Bohm and Guiseppe Jacopini. It was specifically designed to enforce a logical structure on the program to make it more efficient and easier to understand and modify. Structured programming was basically defined to be used in large programs that require large development team to develop different parts of the same program.

Structured programming employs a top-down approach in which the overall program structure is broken down into separate modules. This allows the code to be loaded into memory more efficiently and also be reused in other programs. Modules are coded separately and once a module is written and tested individually, it is then integrated with other modules to form the overall program structure (refer to Fig.1.8).

Structured programming is, therefore, based on modularization which groups related statements together into modules. Modularization makes it easier to write, debug, and understand the program.

Ideally, modules should not be longer than a page. It is always easy to understand a series of 10 single-page modules than a single 10-page program.

For large and complex programs, the overall program structure may further require the need to break the modules into subsidiary pieces. This process continues until an individual piece of code can be written easily.

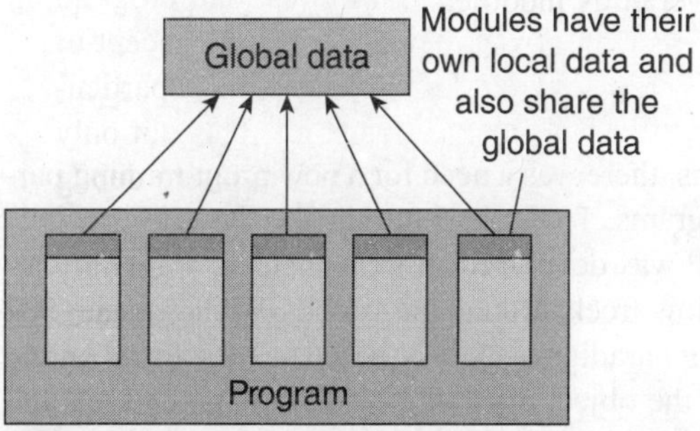

Figure 1.8 Structured program

Almost every modern programming language similar to C, Pascal, etc. supports the concepts of structured programming. Even OOP can be thought of as a type of structured programming. In addition to the techniques of structured programming for writing modules, it also focus on structuring its data.

In structured programming, the program flow follows a simple sequence and usually avoids the use of 'goto' statements. Besides sequential flow, structured programming also supports selection and repetition as mentioned here.

- Selection allows for choosing any one of a number of statements to execute, based on the current status of the program. Selection statements contain keywords such as if, then, end if, or switch that help to identify the order as a logical executable.
- In repetition, a selected statement remains active until the program reaches a point where there is a need for some other action to take place. It includes keywords such as repeat, for, or do… until. Essentially, repetition instructs the program as to how long it needs to continue the function before requesting further instructions.

Advantages

- The goal of structured programming is to write correct programs that are easy to understand and change.
- Modules enhance programmer's productivity by allowing them to look at the big picture first and focus on details later.
- With modules, many programmers can work on a single, large program, with each working on a different module.
- A structured program takes less time to be written than other programs. Modules or procedures written for one program can be reused in other programs as well.
- Each module performs a specific task.
- Each module has its own local data.
- A structured program is easy to debug because each procedure is specialized to perform just one task and every procedure can be checked individually for the presence of any error. In striking contrast, unstructured programs consist of a sequence of instructions that are not grouped for specific tasks. Their logic is cluttered with details and, therefore, difficult to follow.
- Individual procedures are easy to change as well as understand. In a structured program, every procedure has meaningful names and has clear documentation to identify the task performed by it. Moreover, a correctly written structured program is self-documenting and can be easily understood by another programmer.
- More emphasis is given on the code and the least importance is given to the data.
- Global data may get inadvertently changed by any module using it.
- Structured programs were the first to introduce the concept of functional abstraction.

Note Functional abstraction allows a programmer to concentrate on what a function (or module) does and not on how it does.

Disadvantages

- Structured programming is not data-centered.
- Global data is shared and therefore may get inadvertently modified.
- Main focus is on functions.

1.2.4 Object Oriented Programming

With the increase in size and complexity of programs, there was a need for a new programming paradigm that could help to develop maintainable programs. To implement this, the flaws in previous paradigms had to be corrected. Consequently, OOP was developed. It treats data as a critical element in the program development and restricts its flow freely around the system. We have seen that monolithic, procedural, and structured programming paradigms are task-based as they focus on the actions the software should accomplish. However, the object oriented paradigm is task-based and data-based. In this paradigm, all the relevant data and tasks are grouped together in entities known as objects (refer to Fig. 1.9).

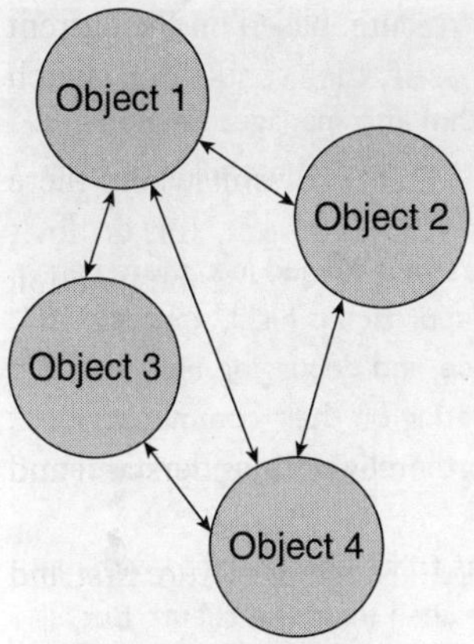

Objects of a program interact by sending messages to each other

Figure 1.9 Object oriented paradigm

For example, consider a list of numbers stored in an array. The procedural or structured programming paradigm considers this list as merely a collection of data. Any program that accesses this list must have some procedures or functions to process this list. For example, to find the largest number or to sort the numbers in the list, we needed specific procedures or functions to do the task. Therefore, the list was a passive entity was it is maintained by a controlling program rather than having the responsibility of maintaining itself.

However, in the object oriented paradigm, the list and the associated operations are treated as one entity known as an object. In this approach, the list is considered an object consisting of the list, along with a collection of routines for manipulating the list. In the list object, there may be routines for adding a number to the list, deleting a number from the list, sorting the list, etc.

The striking difference between OOP and traditional approaches is that the program accessing this list need not contain procedures for performing tasks; rather, it uses the routines provided in the object. In other words, instead of sorting the list as in the procedural paradigm, the program asks the list to sort itself.

Therefore, we can conclude that the object oriented paradigm is task-based (as it considers operations) as well as data-based (as these operations are grouped with the relevant data).

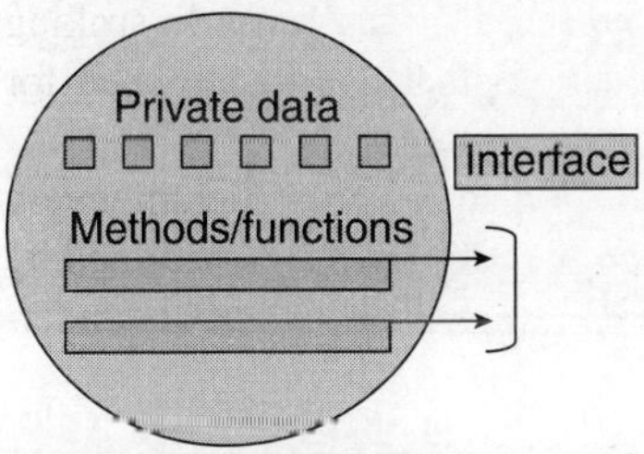

Figure 1.10 Object

Figure 1.10 represents a generic object in the object oriented paradigm. Every object contains some data and the operations, methods, or functions that operate on that data. While some objects may contain only basic data types such as characters, integers, floating types, the other object, the other objects on the other hand may incorporate complex data types such as trees or graphs.

Programs that need the object will access the object's methods through a specific interface. The interface specifies how to send a message to the object, that is, a request for a certain operation to be performed.

For example, the interface for the list object may require that any message for adding a new number to the list should include the number to be added. Similarly, the interface might also require that any message for sorting specify whether the sort should be ascending or descending. Hence, an interface specifies how messages can be sent to the object.

Note OOP is used for simulating real world problems on computers because real world is made of objects.

The striking features of OOP include the following:

- The programs are data-centered.
- Programs are divided in terms of objects and not procedures.
- Functions that operate on data are tied together with the data.
- Data is hidden and not accessible by external functions.
- New data and functions can be easily added as and when required.
- Follows a bottom-up approach for problem solving.

Top-down vs Bottom-up approach

While top-down approach follows a stepwise refinement by decomposing the algorithm into manageable modules, the bottom-up approach on the other hand defines a module and then groups together several modules to form a new higher level module.

In a top-down approach, we start from an abstract design and then at each step, this design is refined into more concrete levels until a level is reached that requires no further refinement Therefore, this approach is highly appreciated for ease in documenting the modules, generation of test cases, implementation of code, and debugging. However, it is also criticized because the sub-modules are analysed in isolation without concentrating on their communication with other modules or on reusability of components and little attention is paid to data, thereby ignoring the concept of information hiding.

While the bottom-up approach allows information hiding as it first identifies what has to be encapsulated within a module and then provides an abstract interface to define the module's boundaries as seen from the clients. But all this is difficult to be done in a strict bottom-up strategy. Some top-down activities need to be performed for this. Whether the top-down strategy should be followed or a bottom-up is a question that can be answered depending on the application at hand.

1.3 FEATURES OF OBJECT ORIENTED PROGRAMMING

The object oriented language must support mechanisms to define, create, store, manipulate objects, and allow communication between objects. In this section, we will read about the underlying concepts of OOP. These are as follows:

- Classes
- Objects
- Methods
- Message passing
- Inheritance
- Polymorphism
- Containership
- Genericity
- Reusability
- Delegation
- Data Abstraction and Encapsulation

1.3.1 Classes

Almost every language has some basic data types such as int, float, long, and so on, but not all real world objects can be represented using these built-in types. Therefore, OOP, being specifically designed to solve real world problems, allows its users to create user defined data types in the form of classes.

A class is used to describe something in the world, such as occurrences, things, external entities, and so on. A class provides a template or a blueprint that describes the structure and behaviour of a set of similar objects. Once we have the definition for a class, a specific instance of the class can be easily created. For example, consider a class student. A student has attributes such as roll number, name, course, and marks. The operations that can be performed on its data may include 'get_details', 'set_details', 'edit_details', and so on (refer to Fig. 1.11). Therefore, we can say that a class describes one or more similar objects.

```
class student
{
    private:
        int roll_no;
        char name[20];
        float marks;
    public:
        get_details();
        show_details();
};
```

Figure 1.11 A sample student class

It must be noted that this data and the set of operations that we have given here can be applied to all students in the class. When we create an instance of a student, we are actually creating an object of class student. Therefore, once a class is declared, a programmer can create any number of objects of that class.

Note Classes define properties and behaviour of objects.

Therefore, a class is a collection of objects of similar type. It is a user-defined data type that behaves same as the built-in data types. This can be realized by ensuring that the syntax of creating an object is same as that of creating an int variable. For example, to create an object (`stud`) of class student, we write

```
student stud;
```

> **Note** Defining a class does not create any object. Objects have to be explicitly created by using the syntax as follows:
> `class-name object-name;`

1.3.2 Objects

In the previous section, we have taken an example of student class and have mentioned that a class is used to create instances, known as objects. Therefore, if student is a class, then all the 60 students in a course (assuming there are maximum 60 students in a particular course) are the objects of the student class. Therefore, all students such as Aditya, Chaitanya, Deepti, and Esha are objects of the class.

Hence, a class can have multiple instances.

Every object contains some data and functions (also called methods) as shown in Fig. 1.12. These methods store data in variables and respond to messages that they receive from other objects by executing their methods (procedures).

> **Note** While a class is a logical structure, an object is a physical actuality.

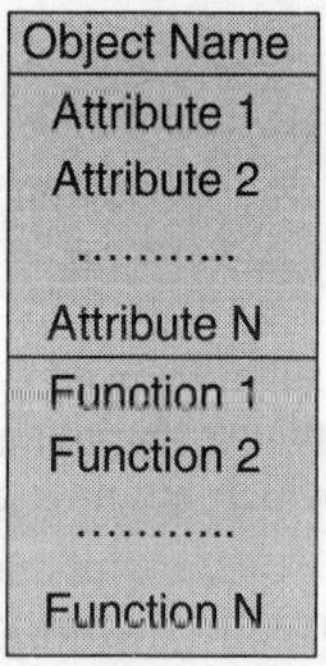

Figure 1.12 Representation of an object

1.3.3 Method and Message Passing

A method is a function associated with a class. It defines the operations that the object can execute when it receives a message. In object oriented language, only methods of the class can access and manipulate the data stored in an instance of the class (or object). Figure 1.13 shows how a class is declared using its data members and member functions.

Every object of the class has its own set of values. Therefore, two distinguishable objects can have the same set of values. Generally, the set of values that the object takes at a particular time is known as the *state* of the object. The state of the object can be changed by applying a particular method. Table 1.5 shows some real world objects along with their data and operations.

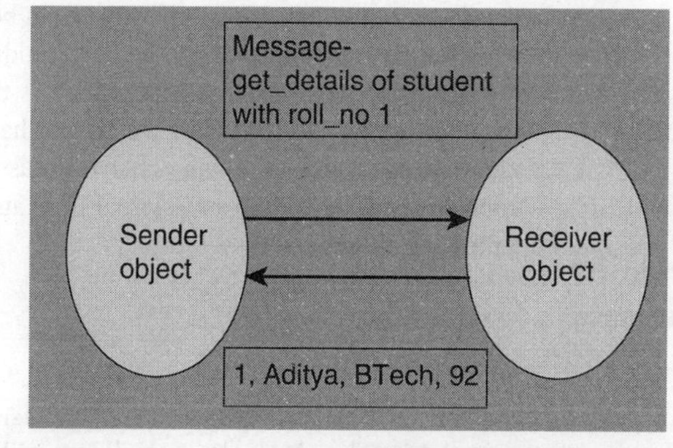

Figure 1.13 Objects sending messages

Table 1.5 Objects with data and functions

Object	Data or attributes	Functions or methods
Person	Name, age, sex	Speak(), walk(), listen(), write()
Vehicle	Name, company, model, capacity, colour	Start(), stop(), accelerate()
Polygon	Vertices, border, colour	Draw(), erase
Account	Type, number, balance	Deposit(), withdraw(), enquire()
City	Name, population, area, literacy rate	Analyse, data(), display()
Computer	Brand, resolution, price	Processing(), display(), printing()

Note An object is an instance of a class which can be uniquely identified by its name. Every object has a state which is given by the values of its attributes at a particular time.

Two objects can communicate with each other through messages. An object asks another object to invoke one of its methods by sending it a message. In Fig. 1.13 in which a sender object is sending a message to the receiver object to get the details of a student. In reply to the message, the receiver sends the results of the execution to the sender.

In the figure, sender has asked the receiver to send the details of student having `roll_no 1`. This means that the sender is passing some specific information to the receiver so that the receiver can send the correct and precise information to the sender. The data that is transferred with the message is called parameters. Here, `roll_no 1` is the parameter.

Therefore, we can say that messages that are sent to other objects consist of three aspects—the receiver object, the name of the method that the receiver should invoke, and the parameters that must be used with the method.

1.3.4 Inheritance

Inheritance is a concept of OOP in which a new class is created from an existing class. The new class, often known as a sub-class, contains the attributes and methods of the parent class (the existing class from which the new class is created).

The new class, known as sub-class or derived class, inherits the attributes and behaviour of the pre-existing class, which is referred to as super-class or parent class (refer to Fig. 1.14). The inheritance relationship of sub- and super classes generates a hierarchy. Therefore, inheritance relation is also called 'is-a' relation. A sub-class not only has all the states and behaviours associated with the super-class but has other specialized features (additional data or methods) as well.

The main advantage of inheritance is the ability to reuse the code. When we want a specialized class, we do not have to write the entire code for that class from scratch. We can inherit a class from a general class and add the specialized code for the sub-class. For example, if we have a class student with following members:

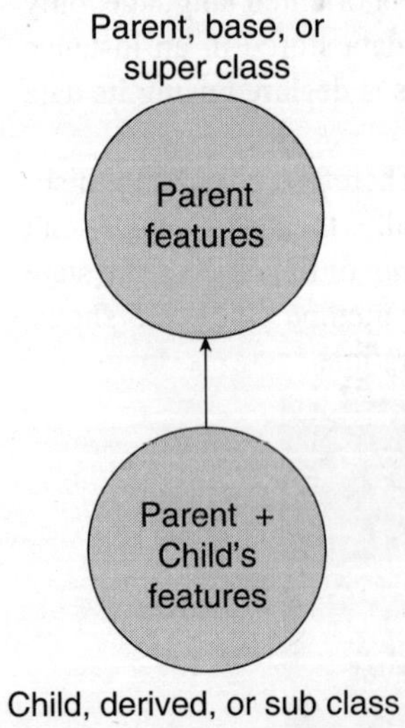

Figure 1.14 Inheritance

```
Properties: roll_number, name, course, and marks
Methods:    get_details, set_details
```

We can inherit two classes from the class `student`, namely, `under_graduate` students and `post_graduate` students (refer to Fig. 1.15). These two classes will have all the properties and methods of class students and in addition to that, will have even more specialized members.

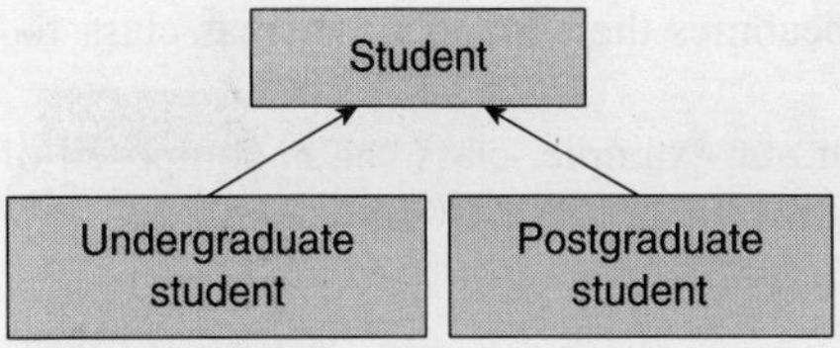

Figure 1.15 Example for Inheritance

When a derived class receives a message to execute a method, it finds the method in its own class. If it finds the method, then it simply executes it. If the method is not present, it searches for that method in its super class. If the method is found, it is executed, otherwise, an error message is reported. A sub class can inherit properties and methods from multiple parent classes. This is called multiple inheritance.

Note A sub class can inherit properties and methods from multiple parent classes. This is called multiple inheritance.

1.3.5 Polymorphism: Static Binding and Dynamic Binding

Polymorphism, one of the essential concepts of OOP, refers to having several different forms. While inheritance is related to classes and their hierarchy, polymorphism, on the other hand, is related to methods.

Polymorphism is a concept that enables the programmers to assign a different meaning or usage to a variable, function, or an object in different contexts.

When polymorphism is applied on variables, the variable with a given name may be allowed to have different forms. The program will then decide which form to use. For example, variable '`roll_no`' of a class student may be an integer (number) or an alphanumeric character (combination of numbers and alphabets). The program can be coded to distinguish between the two forms of the variable so that it can be handled in its own way.

Polymorphism can also be applied to a function in such a way that depending on the parameters it is given, a particular form of the function can be selected for execution. For example, if the roll number of the student is an integer, then its corresponding function will be executed. In case it consists of alphanumeric characters, another function having the same name will be executed. This type of polymorphism is called function overloading.

Polymorphism can also be applied to operators. For example, we know that operators can be applied only on basic data types that the programming language supports. Therefore, `a + b` will give the result of adding `a` and `b`. If `a = 2` and `b = 3`, then `a + b = 5`. When we overload the `+` operator to be used with strings, then `str1 + str2` gives the result `str2` concatenated with `str1`. Therefore, if `str1 = "Oxford"` and `str 2 = "University"` then `str1 + str2 = "Oxford University"`.

All types of polymorphism we have discussed so far are better known as compile time polymorphism or static binding. Dynamic binding or late binding, also known as run time polymorphism, is a feature that enables programmers to associate a function call with a code at the execution (or run) time. For example, if we have a function `print_result()` in class student, then both the inherited classes, under graduate and post graduate students will also have the same function implemented in their respective classes. Now, when there is a call to `print_result()`,

```
ptr_to_student-> print_result();
```

then, the decision regarding which version to call—the one in under graduate class or the one in post graduate class—will be taken at the execution time. Hence, the name.

Note Binding means associating a function call with the corresponding function code to be executed in response to the call.

1.3.6 Containership

The ability of a class to contain object(s) of one or more classes as member data. For example, class `One` can have an object of class `Two` as its data member. This would allow the object of class `One` to call the public functions of class Two. Here, class One becomes the container, whereas class Two becomes the contained class.

Containership is also called composition because as in our example, class One is composed of class Two. In OOP, containership represents a 'has-a' relationship.

1.3.7 Genericity

To reduce code duplication and generate short, simpler code, C++ supports the use of generic codes (or templates) to define the same code for multiple data types. This means that a C++ function or a class can perform similar operations on different data types like integers, float, and double. This means that a generic function can be invoked with arguments of any compatible type.

Generic programs, therefore, act as a model of function or class that can be used to generate functions or classes. During program compilation, C++ compiler generates one or more functions or classes based on the specified template. Figure 1.16(a) and (b) clarifies this concept.

This discussion states that generic programming is a technique of programming in which a general code is written first. The code is instantiated only when need arises for specific types (provided as parameters).

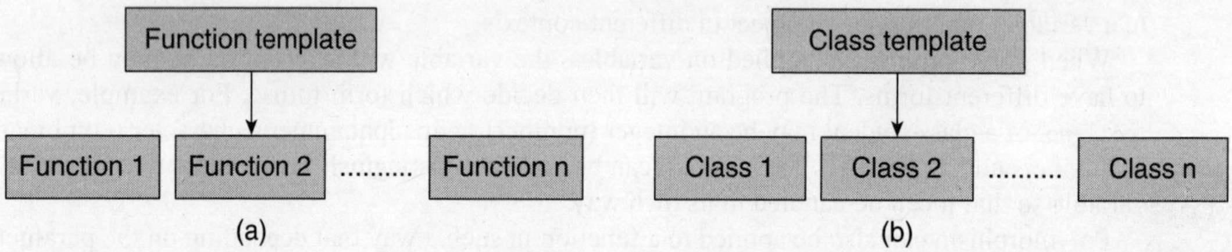

Figure 1.16 (a) Generated functions (b) Generated classes

Reusability

Reusability means developing codes that can be reused either in the same program or in different programs. C++ gives due importance to building programs that are reusable. Reusability is attained through inheritance, containership, polymorphism, and genericity.

1.3.8 Delegation

To provide maximum flexibility to programmers and to allow them to generate a reusable code, object oriented languages also support delegation, also known as composition or containership. In composition, an object can be composed of other objects and thus, the object exhibits a 'has-a' relationship.

In delegation, more than one object is involved in handling a request. The object that receives the request for a service, delegates it to another object called its delegate. The property of delegation emphasizes on the ideology that a complex object is made of several simpler objects. For example, our body is made up of brain, heart, hands, eyes, ears, etc., the functioning of the whole body as a system rests on correct functioning of the parts it is composed of. Similarly, a car has a wheel, brake, gears, etc. to control it.

Delegation differs from inheritance in that two classes that participate in inheritance share an 'is-a' relationship; however, in delegate, they have a 'has-a' relationship.

1.3.9 Data Abstraction and Encapsulation

Data abstraction refers to the process by which data and functions are defined in such a way that only essential details are revealed and the implementation details are hidden. The main focus of data abstraction is to separate the interface and the implementation of a program. For example, as users of television sets, we can switch it on or off, change the channel, set the volume, and add external devices such as speakers and CD or DVD players without knowing the details about how its functionality has been implemented. Therefore, the internal implementation is completely hidden from the external world.

Similarly, in OOP languages, classes provide public methods to the outside world to provide the functionality of the object or to manipulate the object's data. Any entity outside the world does not know about the implementation details of the class or that method.

Data encapsulation, also called data hiding, is the technique of packing data and functions into a single component (class) to hide implementation details of a class from the users. Users are allowed to execute only a restricted set of operations (class methods) on the data members of the class. Therefore, encapsulation organizes the data and methods into a structure that prevents data access by any function (or method) that is not specified in the class. This ensures the integrity of the data contained in the object.

Encapsulation defines three access levels for data variables and member functions of the class. These access levels specify the access rights, explained as follows.

- Any data or function with access level as public can be accessed by any function belonging to any class. This is the lowest level of data protection.
- Any data or function with access level protected can be accessed only by that class or by any class that is inherited from it.
- Any data or function with access level private can be accessed only by the class in which it is declared. This is the highest level of data protection

Note Creating a new data type using encapsulated items that is well suited for an application is called data abstraction.

1.4 MERITS AND DEMERITS OF OBJECT ORIENTED PROGRAMMING LANGUAGE

OOP offers many benefits to program developers and users. It not only provides a solution for many problems associated with software development and its quality but also enhances programmer productivity and reduces maintenance cost. Some key advantages of OOP include the following:

- Elimination of redundant code through inheritance (by extending existing classes)
- Higher productivity and reduced development time due to reusability of the existing modules
- Secure programs as data cannot be modified or accessed by any code outside the class
- Real world objects in the problem domain can be easily mapped objects in the program
- A program can be easily divided into parts based on objects
- The data-centred design approach captures more details of a model in a form that can be easily implemented
- Programs designed using OOP are expandable as they can be easily upgraded from small to large systems
- Message passing between objects simplifies the interface descriptions with external systems
- Software complexity becomes easily manageable
- With polymorphism, behaviour of functions, operators, or objects may vary depending upon the circumstances
- Data abstraction and encapsulation hides implementation details from the external world and provides it a clearly defined interface
- OOP enables programmers to write easily extendable and maintainable programs
- OOP supports code reusability to a great extent

However, the down side of OOP include the following:

- Programs written using object oriented languages have greater processing overhead as they demand more resources
- Requires more skills to learn and implement the concepts
- Beneficial only for large and complicated programs
- Even an easy to use software when developed using OOP is hard to be build
- OOP cannot work with existing systems
- Programmers must have a good command in software engineering and programming methodology

1.5 APPLICATIONS OF OBJECT ORIENTED PROGRAMMING

No doubt, the concepts of object oriented technology have changed the way of thinking, analyzing, planning, and implementing software. Software or applications developed using this technology are not only efficient but also easy to upgrade. Therefore, programmers and software engineers all over the world have shown their keen interest in developing applications using OOP. As a result, there has been a constant increase in areas where OOP has been successfully implemented. Some of these areas include the following:

- Designing user interfaces such as work screens, menus, windows, and so on
- Real-time systems
- Simulation and modelling
- Compiler design
- Client server system
- Object oriented databases
- Object oriented distributed database
- Artificial intelligence—expert systems and neural networks
- Parallel programming
- Decision control systems
- Office automation systems
- Networks for programming routers, firewalls, and other devices
- Computer-aided design (CAD) systems
- Computer-aided manufacturing (CAM) systems
- Computer animation
- Developing computer games
- Hypertext and hypermedia

1.6 DIFFERENCES BETWEEN PROGRAMMING LANGUAGES

Most of you have learnt programming in C. To appreciate the power of C++, let us first compare C++ with C language which is not an object oriented language and then try to understand how C++ is different from other object oriented languages.

Table 1.6 summarizes the differences between C and C++ and Table 1.7 highlights the differences between commonly used object oriented languages.

Table 1.6 Differences between C and C++

C	C++
• Procedural language • Does not support virtual functions • Does not support polymorphism • Does not support operator overloading	• Uses top-down approach to build complex programs • Does not support namespaces • Object oriented language

(Contd)

Table 1.6 (*Contd*)

C	C++
• Supports virtual functions • Supports polymorphism • Supports operator overloading • Uses bottom-up approach to build complex programs • Supports namespaces • Can have multiple declarations for global variables • Printf() and scanf() functions in stdio.h file are used for I/O • Difficult to determine which function can and cannot modify data • Allows main() to be called through other functions • All variables must be defined at the beginning of the function (or scope) • Does not support inheritance • Does not support exception handling • Uses malloc(), calloc(), and free() for dynamically allocating or de-allocating memory	• A character constant is automatically elevated to an integer • Identifiers cannot start with two or more consecutive underscores, but may contain them in other positions. • Cannot have multiple declarations for global variables • Objects cin and cout of iostream are used for input or output • Easy mapping between data and functions • Does not allow main() to be called through other functions • Variables can be defined at any location but before their first use. • Supports inheritance • Supports exception handing • Uses new and delete operators for dynamically allocating or de-allocating memory • A character constant is not elevated to integer • Identifiers are not allowed to contain two or more consecutive underscores in any position

Table 1.7 Comparison between commonly used object oriented languages

Attributes	EIFFEL	C++	JAVA	SMALLTALK
Static typing	Statically typed	Statically typed but supports C-style 'casts' which may lead to violation of type rules	Statically typed but needs dynamic typing for generic container structures	Dynamically typed
Proprietary status	Open and standardized	Open, ANSI standard	Licensed from Sun	Not standardized
Compilation technology	Combination of interpretation and compilation	Compiled	Interpreted and on the fly compilation	Initially interpreted but currently mix of interpretation and compilation
Efficiency of code	Fast executable	Fast executable	Performance problems	Executables require a 'Smalltalk image'

(*Contd*)

Table 1.7 (*Contd*)

Attributes	EIFFEL	C++	JAVA	SMALLTALK
Multiple inheritance	Supported and widely used	Supported but not widely used because of performance problems	Single inheritance	Single inheritance
Understandability	Clear and simple	Complex syntax	Complex syntax	In between simple and complex
Garbage collection	Supported automatically	Not supported	Supported automatically	Supported automatically
Encapsulation	Supported	Supported	Poor support	Supported
Binding (early or late)	Early	Both	Late	Late

1.7 C++ COMPILERS

In this section we will discuss some C++ compilers that are widely used today.

Clang Clang is a C++ compiler developed primarily by Apple. It supports various ISO (International Standards Organization) C++ language standards. This compiler has been released under the BSD license.

MinGW-w64 MinGW-w64 provides the library files, header files, and runtime support needed for the GNU C++ compilers to run on a Windows system. The w64 means that the project support files that allow users to create 64-bit programs in addition to 32-bit ones. Another appealing feature of MinGW-w64 is that it provides cross-compilers that allows users to compile a Windows program from a Linux system or vice versa. Applications generated using MinGW are faster than those generated by the Cygwin32 system and are free from the encumbrances of the GNU license.

Microsoft Visual Studio Express 2013 Visual Studio Express 2013 can be used on Windows desktop as well as on Windows Phone. Visual Studio Express is a package that has an integrated development environment (IDE), compilers for C++, C# and Visual Basic. However, the Express version does not include all the tools and features of the full Visual Studio, like the full MSDN library, resource editor, macro assembler, etc.

x86 Open64 compiler system It is a high performance code generation tool designed for high performance parallel computing workloads. It is a version of the Open64 compiler suite that requires Linux and has been tuned for AMD processors. The C++ compiler conforms to the ISO C++ 98 standards and supports 32-bit and 64-bit code generation, vector and scalar code generation. It also comprises of an optimizer that supports a huge variety of optimizations (global, loop transformation, vectorization, feedback-directed, inter-procedural analysis, etc), multi-threading. The compiler creates a strong foundation for building robust, high performance parallel code. It also has an optimized AMD Core Math Library and documentation.

Open Source Watcom/OpenWatcom C/C++ Compiler An open source and free compiler which generates code for Win32, Windows 3.1 (Win16), OS/2, Netware NLM, MSDOS (16-bit and 32-bit protected mode), etc. The compiler includes support for C++ Standard Template Library.

Digital Mars C/C++ Compiler (Symantec C++ Replacement) Digital Mars C++ supports compiling programs for Win32, Windows 3.1, MSDOS, and 32-bit extended MSDOS. If the target machine does not have a floating point processor the programmers can still link the floating point emulation into their programs. The compiler supports the C++ definition specified in The Annotated C++ Reference Manual (ARM) and the enhanced language features of AT&T version 3.0. Features like templates, nested classes, nested types, exception handling, and runtime type identification, command line and GUI versions, tutorials, sample code, online updates, and much more all are supported by this compiler.

Bloodshed Dev-C++ Compiler A Win32 IDE that includes the egcs C++ compiler and GNU debugger from the Mingw32 environment along with an editor and other facilities to make program development using the Mingw32 gcc compiler easier on Windows. This compiler also comprises of an installer for application programs.

DJGPP C++ Compilers It is a development system based on GNU C++ compiler that generates 32-bit MSDOS executables. It is a complete system that comprises of IDEs, graphics libraries, lexical analyser generators (flex), parser generators (bison), text processing utilities (like grep, sed), a program maintenance utility (i.e. make), a dos extender, etc.

Cygwin C++ Compilers The compiler generates Win32 GUI and console applications. It comes with source code for the compiler, libraries, and tools. The compiler makes it easy for programmers to distribute their source code (while compiling and linking with their libraries).

Sun Studio It is a high-performance, optimizing compiler for the Solaris OS on SPARC and ×86/×64 platforms. It provides multi platform support and comprises of command-line tools plus a NetBeans-based Integrated Development Environment (IDE) for application performance analysis and debugging of mixed source language applications.

Borland C++ provides a programming environment for MS-DOS and Microsoft Windows. It has an IDE and is considered as a successor to Turbo C++. Borland has a library that contains a set of classes to make it easier to develop professional graphical Windows applications as DOS applications.

Turbo C++ Turbo C++ is a utility tool that helps programmers to code their C++ programs easily and effectively. Although Turbo C++ lacks some of the advanced features but it includes all features that any user might need to execute their programs. On the positive side, it is a free software which is simple to use and has an intuitive interface. However, on the downside it has very few advanced features.

Points to Remember

- If a procedure is formally defined, it must be implemented using some formal language, and such a language is often known as a programming language.
- Programming languages are used to create programs that control the behaviour of a system, to express algorithms, or used as a mode of human communication.
- Machine language was used to program the first stored-program computer systems. This is the lowest level of programming language.
- Assembly languages are symbolic programming languages that use symbolic notation to represent machine-language instructions.
- 5GLs are centred on solving problems using constraints given to the program.
- Object oriented programming (OOP) emphasizes on classes and objects.
- Programs written using monolithic programming languages such as assembly language and BASIC consist of global data and sequential code.
- In procedural languages, a program is divided into *n* number of subroutines that access global data.
- Structured programming employs a top-down approach in which the overall program structure is broken down into separate modules.
- OOP treats data as a critical element in the program development and restricts its flow freely around the system.
- A class provides a template or a blueprint that describes the structure and behaviour of a set of similar objects.

Glossary

Assembler System software that translates a code written in assembly language into machine language

Compiler A special type of program that transforms source code written in a third programming language into machine language

Data abstraction Creating a new data type using encapsulated items that is well suited for an application

Data encapsulation It is also called data hiding, and is the technique of packing data and functions into a single component (class) to hide implementation details of a class from users

Functional abstraction A technique that allows a programmer to concentrate on what a function (or module) does and not on how it does

Inheritance A concept of object oriented programming in which a new class is created from an existing class

Linker A program that combines object modules to form an executable program

Loader A program that copies programs from a storage device to main memory, where they can be executed

Method Function associated with a class

Multiple inheritance A technique that allows a sub class to inherit properties and methods from multiple parent classes

Object An instance of a class

Polymorphism A concept that enables programmers to assign a different meaning or usage to a variable, function, or an object in different contexts

Programming language A language specifically designed to express computations that can be performed the computer

Programming paradigm A fundamental style of programming that defines how the structure and basic elements of a computer program will be built

Repetition A technique that allows a selected statement to remain active until the program reaches a point where there is a need for some other action to take place

Sequential code Code in which all the instructions are executed in the specified sequence one by one

Selection A technique that allows for choosing any one of a number of statements to execute, based on the current status of the program

Exercises

Fill in the Blanks

1. Programming languages have a vocabulary of _____ and _____ for instructing a computer to perform specific tasks.
2. Assembly language uses _____ to write programs.
3. An assembly language statement consists of a _____, _____, and _____.
4. _____ are used to identify and reference instructions in the program.
5. The output of an assembler is a _____ file.
6. A typical example of a 4GL is the _____.
7. Examples of a 5GL include _____, _____, and _____.
8. _____ defines the structure of a program.
9. _____ programming emphasizes on classes and objects.
10. Logic-oriented programming focus on _____ expressed in _____.
11. Two examples of languages that support monolithic programming paradigm are ____ and _____.
12. _____ and _____ statements are used to change the sequence of execution of instructions.
13. FORTRAN and COBOL are two popular _____ programming languages.
14. Functional abstraction was first supported by _____ programming.
15. An object contains _____ and _____.
16. _____ paradigm supports bottom-up approach of problem solving.
17. _____ provides a template that describes the structure and behaviour of an object.
18. While _____ is a logical structure, _____ is a physical actuality.
19. State defines the _____.
20. The data that is transferred with the message is called _____.
21. A message consists of _____, _____, and _____.

22. Inheritance relation is also called as ______ relation.
23. ______ is related to classes and their hierarchy.
24. Polymorphism is related to ______.
25. Any data or function with access level ______ can be accessed by any function belonging to any class.

State True or False

1. A programming language provides a blueprint to write a program to solve a particular problem.
2. Machine language is the lowest level of language.
3. Code written in machine language is not portable.
4. Compiler not only translates the code into machine language but also executes it.
5. An interpreted program executes faster than a compiled program.
6. Nonprocedural code that illustrates the 'how' aspect of the task is a feature of 3GL.
7. Constraint-based programming is used for hypothesis derivation.
8. In monolithic paradigm, global data can be accessed and modified from any part of the program.
9. Monolithic program has two modules.
10. Monolithic programs are easy to debug and maintain.
11. Structured programming is based on modularization.
12. Object oriented programming supports modularization.
13. Structured programming heavily used goto statements.
14. Modules enhance the programmer's productivity.
15. A structured program takes more time to be written than other programs.
16. The interface specifies how to send a message to the object.
17. OOP does not support modularization.
18. A class is a user-defined data type.
19. Once a class is declared, a programmer can create maximum 10 objects of that class.
20. Polymorphism means several different forms.
21. Any data or function with access level private can be accesses only by that class or by any class that is inherited from it.
22. OOP helps to develop secure programs.
23. It is difficult to manage software complexity in object oriented programs.
24. Programs written using object oriented languages have greater processing overhead.

Multiple Choice Questions

1. Which language is good for processing numerical data?
   (a) C (b) C++
   (c) FORTRAN (d) Java
2. Which is the fastest and the most efficient language?
   (a) Machine level
   (b) Assembly
   (c) High level
   (d) Artificial intelligence
3. FORTRAN, COBOL, and Pascal are examples of which generation language?
   (a) First (b) Second
   (c) Third (d) Fourth
4. In which generation language does the code comprise instructions written in English-like sentences?
   (a) First (b) Second
   (c) Third (d) Fourth
5. Which feature is affected by programming paradigm?
   (a) Style of programming
   (b) Capabilities
   (c) Limitations
   (d) All of these
6. Which programming paradigm utilizes invariant relationships to solve a problem?
   (a) Rule-based
   (b) Constraint-based
   (c) Structured
   (d) Object oriented
7. Which is the preferred paradigm for designing a knowledge base?
   (a) Rule-based
   (b) Constraint-based
   (c) Structured
   (d) Object oriented
8. Which type of programming does not support sub routines?
   (a) Monolithic (b) Structured
   (c) Rule-based (d) Object oriented

9. C and Pascal belong to which type of programming language?
(a) Monolithic (b) Structured
(c) Logic-oriented (d) Object oriented
10. Which paradigm holds data as a priority?
(a) Monolithic (b) Structured
(c) Logic-oriented (d) Object oriented
11. Two objects can communicate with each other through ____
(a) Classes (b) Objects
(c) Methods (d) Messages
12. Which concept enables programmers to assign a different meaning or usage to a variable, function, or an object in different contexts?
(a) Inheritance
(b) Message passing
(c) Polymorphism
(d) Abstraction
13. Which access level allows data and functions to be accessed only by the class in which it is declared?
(a) Public (b) Private
(c) Protected (d) None of these
14. In which of these applications is OOP applied?
(a) CAD (b) CAM
(c) Compiler design (d) All of these

Review Questions

1. What is a programming language?
2. Write a short note on generation of programming languages.
3. Differentiate between a compiler and an interpreter.
4. Differentiate between syntax errors and logic errors.
5. What do you understand by the term 'programming paradigm'?
6. Discuss any three programming paradigms in detail.
7. How is structured programming better than monolithic programming?
8. Describe the special characteristics of monolithic programming.
9. Explain how functional abstraction is achieved in structured programming.
10. Which programming paradigm is data-based and why?
11. Explain the concepts of OOP.
12. Differentiate between a class and an object.
13. How is a message related with a method?
14. Inheritance helps to make reusable code. Justify.
15. What do you understand by the term 'polymorphism'?
16. Why is data abstraction and encapsulation called the building blocks of OOP?
17. Explain the three levels of data protection.
18. What are the merits and demerits of OOP?

Answers

Fill in the Blanks

1. Syntax, semantics; **2.** Mnemonic codes; **3.** Label, an operation code, and one or more operands; **4.** Labels; **5.** Object; **6.** Query language; **7.** Prolog, OPS5, and Mercury; **8.** Programming paradigm; **9.** Object oriented; **10.** Goals, predicate; **11.** assembly language and BASIC; **12.** goto and call; **13.** 3GL; **14.** Structured; **15.** Data and methods; **16.** OOP; **17.** Class; **18.** Class, object; **19.** values of its attributes at a particular time; **20.** parameter; **21.** the receiver object, the name of the method that the receiver should invoke, and the parameters that must be used with the method; **22.** Is-a; **23.** Inheritance; **24.** methods; **25.** public

True or False

1. False	**2.** True	**3.** True	**4.** False	**5.** False	**6.** False	**7.** False	**8.** True
9. False	**10.** False	**11.** True	**12.** True	**13.** False	**14.** True	**15.** False	**16.** True
17. False	**18.** True	**19.** False	**20.** True	**21.** False	**22.** True	**23.** False	**24.** True

Multiple Choice Questions

1. (c); **2.** (a); **3.** (c); **4.** (d); **5.** (d); **6.** (b); **7.** (a); **8.** (a); **9.** (b); **10.** (d); **11.** (d); **12.** (c); **13.** (b); **14.** (d)

CHAPTER 2

Basics of C++ Programming

KEY Concepts

Introduction to C++ • Structure of C++ programs • Files in a C++ program • Writing C++ programs • Keywords • Identifiers • Data types • Operators • Type conversion and type casting

INTRODUCTION TO C++

C++ is a general purpose programming language developed by Bjarne Stroustrup in 1979 at Bell Labs. Similar to C programming, C++ is also considered as an intermediate level language because it includes the features of both high-level and low-level languages.

C++ is a very popular programming language that can be implemented on a wide variety of hardware and operating system platforms. It is a powerful language for high-performance applications, including writing operating systems, system software, application software, device drivers, embedded software, high-performance client and server applications, software engineering, graphics, games, and animation software. C++ is a superset of the C language; it supports all features of C language and adds other new features such as classes, objects, polymorphism, inheritance, data abstraction, encapsulation, single-line comments using two forward slashes, strong type checking, and so on.

C++ is an object oriented programming (OOP) language and facilitates design, reuse, and maintenance for complex software. It has an extensive library to enable programmers to reuse the existing code. Generally, the number of instructions required to perform a task in C++ is comparatively less than those required to be written in other high-level languages. The code written in C++ is easy to write, debug, and modify.

2.1 HISTORY OF C++

In 1979, Bjarne Stroustrup, while working for his Ph D thesis, used a language called Simula, which was specifically designed for simulations. It was the first language to support the features of OOP. Though the language was very powerful, it was too slow for practical use. Therefore, Stroustrup started working on 'C with Classes', with an aim to integrate OOP features such as classes, inheritance, inline functions, and default arguments with the C language. This new language was easily portable and fast, provided low-level functionality, and included OOP concepts. In the same period, C front (the first C with classes compiler) was developed to translate C with classes code to ordinary C. Most of the code for C front was written in C with classes, making it a self-hosting compiler. A self-hosting compiler compiles itself. However, the use of this compiler was abandoned in 1993 after it became difficult to integrate new features such as exceptions into it.

In 1983, the name of the language was changed to C++, where ++ refers to adding new features in the C language. At this time, some more features such as virtual functions, function overloading, references with the `&` symbol, `const` keyword, and single-line comments were added. In 1985, though C++ was not officially standardized, it was implemented as a commercial product. In 1989, C++ was again updated to include protected members, static members, and multiple inheritance. In 1990, Turbo C++ compiler was released and added additional libraries. In 1998, the first international standard for C++ that included the standard template library, called the C++98, was published. However, this version had some problems which were addressed in the version released in 2003. It was called C++03.

The latest version of C++ known as C++11 was released in 2011. It added new features such as support for regular expression, a new C++ time library, atomics support, a standard threading library, a new `for` loop syntax (similar to `for each` loop), the auto keyword, new container classes, and better support for unions and array-initialization.

2.2 STRUCTURE OF C++ PROGRAM

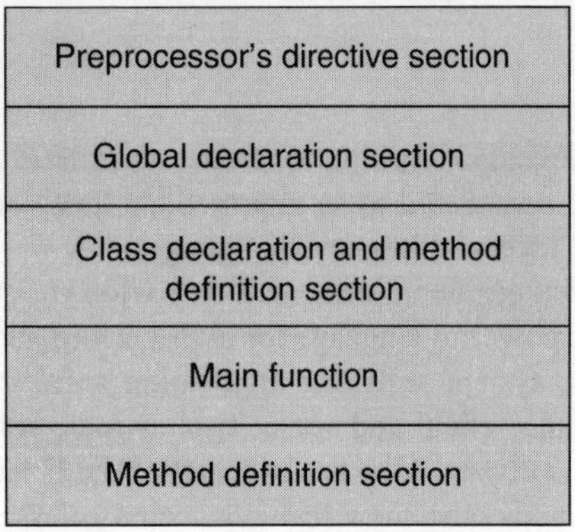

Figure 2.1 Structure of a C++ program

A C++ program is composed of a preprocessor directives section, global declaration section, class declaration and method definition section, and a main function as shown in Fig. 2.1.

The preprocessor directives contain special instructions that indicate how to prepare the program for compilation. One of the most important and commonly used preprocessor commands is 'include', which informs the compiler that some information is needed from the specified header file to execute the program.

In this section, we will omit the global declaration part and revisit it in the chapter on 'Functions'. Usually, it is used to declare data (variables), functions, and structures that have global scope.

The class declaration and method definition section can be considered as a part of global declaration section that is used to declare classes. A class consists of data and methods. The methods or functions of the class are also defined in this section.

A C++ program may contain any number of functions. A function is defined as a group of C++ statements that are executed together and written in a logical sequence to perform a specific task. The 'main()' function is the most important function and is a part of every C++ program. Rather, the execution of a C++ program begins at this function as the operating system automatically calls it main(). This means that main() is the entry point for all the functions. All other functions, if present in the program, are called from main().

The method definition section is optional and required only if there are functions other than class methods in the program. This section was also added to support C++ programs.

2.3 WRITING THE FIRST C++ PROGRAM

To write a C++ program, we need to write the code. We need to open a text editor. If you are a Windows user, you may use Notepad and if you prefer working on UNIX or Linux, you can use emacs or vi. Once the text editor is opened on your screen, type the following statements.

```
1.//  My first program
2.  using namespace std;
3.  #include<iostream>
4.  main()
5.  {
6.    cout<<"\n Welcome to the World of C++";
7.    return 0;
8.  }
```

Note The cout and return statements have been indented or moved away from the left side. This is done to make the code more readable.

After writing this code, save the file with any name with a `.cpp` extension. For example, let us save this file with the name, '`first.cpp`'. Once Turbo C++ is installed in your computer and if you are using Windows, open the command prompt by clicking 'Start->Run', type 'command', and click Ok.

Using the command prompt, change to the directory in which you had saved your file and then type the following:

```
C:\>tcc first.cpp
```

This command is used to compile your C++ program. If there are any mistakes in the program, the compiler point out the mistake and the line on which it was done. In case of errors, you need to reopen your `.cpp` file and correct those mistakes. However, if everything is correct, no errors will be reported and the compiler will create an exe file for your program. This `.exe` file can be directly run by typing the following:

```
C:\>first.exe or simply C:\>first
```

Linux users should write `$ g++ first.cpp` to compile the program, and then type `$./a.out` to execute it.

This will give you the following output on the screen:

```
Welcome to the World of C++
```

Let us now try to understand the meaning of each line of the program.

```
Line 1. // My first program
```

The statement begins with two slash signs to indicate that the rest of the line is a comment. A comment is specifically inserted by the programmer to include short explanations concerning the code. This makes the programs more readable and understandable by the users. These comments have no effect on execution of the program. In the program mentioned here, comment has been simply included to give a brief introductory description of the program.

```
Line 2. using namespace std;
```

Let us take an analogy if a team has four members then you can either refer to each person individually or just say the entire team. When you use the word 'team' it means every individual member. Same is the case with namespaces. We will read about namespaces in the latter chapters but for now just understand that namespace is a collection of important functions and classes. There can be many namespaces. So, every namespace is identified by a specific name. If you are using any particular thing from a namespace, then you have to write the statement

```
using namespace name;
```

The statement using namespace std; makes all the names from the namespace std available in the current program. std is an abbreviation of standard. It is the standard namespace in C++. cout, cin and a lot of other things are defined in it.

If you don't write the using namespace std; then the compiler will not be able to understand which classes or functions you are trying to access and will thus, generate a compiler error.

```
Line 3. #include<iostream>
```

Programming Tip: If you will not place a parenthesis after 'main', a compiler error will be generated.

This is a preprocessor command that comes as the first statement in our code. All preprocessor commands start with a hash symbol (#). The preprocessor commands are not executed by the compiler. Rather, they are read and interpreted by the preprocessor. It is a special line interpreted before the commencement of the compilation of the program. The `#include` statement tells the compiler to include the standard input or output library or header file `(iostream)` in the program. This file has some in-built functions. By including this file in our code, we can use these functions directly. The standard input or output header file contains functions for input and output of data such as reading values from the keyboard and printing the results on the screen.

```
Line 4. int main()
```

`int` is the return value of the main function. After all the statements in the program have been written, the last statement of the program will return an integer value (zero for successful execution and a non-zero value for any abnormal termination) to the operating system. The statement `int main()` is basically the function declaration. We will read more on function declaration in chapter 4.

Note By default the return type of main() function is int. So, writing main() or int main() is equivalent.

```
Lines 5&8. { }
```

The two curly brackets are used to group all related statements of the function main. All statements between the braces form the function body. The function body contains a set of instructions to perform the given task.

```
Line 6. cout<<"\n Welcome to the World of C++";
```

The `cout` function is defined in the `iostream.h` file and is used to print text on the screen. The message that has to be displayed on the screen is enclosed within double quotes. The '\n' is an escape sequence and represents a newline character. It is used to print the message on a new line on the screen.

An *escape sequence* is a combination of characters that is translated into another character or a sequence of characters that may be difficult or impossible to represent directly. Similar to the newline character, the other escape sequences supported by C++ are shown in Table 2.1. The end of the statement is marked with semicolon (;).

Programming Tip: Placing a semi-colon after the parenthesis of main will generate a compiler error.

Note
1. Escape sequences are actually non-printing control characters that begin with a backslash (\).
2. statement in the main function ends with a semi-colon (;).

Table 2.1 Escape sequences

Escape sequence	Purpose	Escape sequence	Purpose
\a	Audible signal	\?	Question mark
\b	Backspace	\\	Back slash
\t	Tab	\’	Single quote
\n	Newline	\”	Double quote
\v	Vertical tab	\0	Octal constant
\f	New page\Clear screen	\x	Hexadecimal constant
\r	Carriage return		

```
Line 7. return 0;
```

This is a return command that is used to return the value `0` to the operating system to give an indication that there were no errors during the execution of the program.

2.4 FILES USED IN C++ PROGRAM

Every C++ program has four kinds of files associated with it (refer to Fig. 2.2).

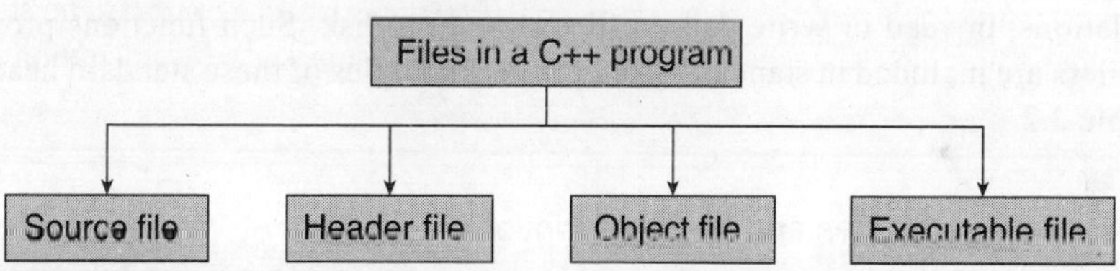

Figure 2.2 Files in a C++ program

2.4.1 Source Code File

The source code file contains the source code of the program. The file extension of any C++ source code file is `.cpp`. This file contains the C++ source code that defines the main function and other functions as well. The `main()` is the starting point of execution when you successfully compile and run the program. A C++ program, in general, may include even other source code files (with the file extension `.cpp`).

2.4.2 Header Files

When working with large projects, it is often desirable to separate certain sub routines from the `main()` of the program. There may be a case that the same subroutine has to be used in different programs. In the latter case, one option is to copy the code of the desired subroutine from one program to another. However, copying the code is often tedious, error-prone, and makes maintainability more difficult.

Therefore, another option is to make subroutines and store them in a different file known as the header file. The advantage of header files can be realized in the following situations:

- If the programmer wants to use the same subroutines in different programs, he has to compile the source code of the subroutines once, and then link with the resulting object file with any program that requires the functionalities of these subroutines.

Programming Tip: Missing the inclusion of appropriate header file in the C++ program will generate an error. Such a program may compile but the linker will give an error message as it will not be able to find the functions used in the program.

- The programmer wants to change or add subroutines, and have those changes reflected in all other programs. In this case, he just needs to change the source file for the subroutines, recompile its source code, and recompile and relink programs that use them. In this manner, enormous time can be saved as compared to editing the subroutines in each program that uses them.

Therefore, we see that using a header file produces the same results as copying the header file into each source file that needs it. When a header file is included, the related declarations appear in only one place. If we need to modify the subroutines, we just need to make the changes in one place, and the programs that include the header file will automatically use the new version when they are recompiled subsequently. There is no need to find and change all copies of the subroutine that have to be changed.

Conventionally, header files names end with a `'dot h'` (`.h`) extension and the name must include only letters, digits, dashes, and underscores. Although some standard header files are automatically available to C++ programmers, in addition to those header files, the programmer may have his own user defined header files.

Standard Header Files

In C++programs, there are functions which are used without coding. These functions are already written and compiled for ease of programmers. We just need to link the desired library function's code with our code. These functions may provide the functionality to manage the memory for our programs, perform input or output operations, do complex mathematical calculations, or read or write data to files stored on disk. Such functions provided by all C++ compilers are included in standard header files. Examples of these standard header files are given in Table 2.2.

Table 2.2 Header files and their description

Header files	Description
`string.h`	Used for string handling functions
`time.h`	Used for manipulating time and date
`stdlib.h`	Used for functions such as random numbers and converting numbers to text
`stdio.h`	Used for standard input and output functions
`math.h`	Used for mathematical functions
`complex.h`	Used for complex math functions
`assert.h`	Used for adding diagnostics that helps in program debugging

All header files are referenced at the start of the source code file that uses one or more functions from that file.

2.4.3 Object Files

Object files are generated by the compiler after processing the source code file. Object files contain a compact binary code of the function definitions. The linker uses this object file to produce an executable file (.exe file) by combining the object files together. Object files have an .obj extension; however, some operating systems such as Windows and MS-DOS have .obj extension for the object file.

2.4.4 Binary Executable File

The binary executable file is generated by the linker. The linker links the various object files to produce a binary file that can be directly executed. On Windows operating system, the executable files have .exe extension.

2.5 COMPILING AND EXECUTING C++ PROGRAMS

C++ is a compiled language. Therefore, once the C++ program is written, you must run it through a C++ compiler that can create an executable file to be run by the computer. While the C++ program can be read by us, the executable file, on the other hand, is a machine-readable file available in an executable form.

The mechanical part of running a C++ program begins with one or more program source files, and ends with an executable file, which can be run on a computer.

The programming process starts with creating a source file that consists of the statements of the program written in C++ language. This source file usually contains ASCII characters and can be produced with a text editor, such as Windows notepad, or in an integrated design environment like the one we have in Borland C++.

The source file is then processed by a special program called a compiler.

Note Every programming language has its own compiler.

The compiler translates the source code into an object code. The object code contains the machine instructions for the central processing unit (CPU).

However, even the object file is not an executable file. Therefore, in the next step, the object file is processed with another special program called a linker. While there is a different compiler for each language, the same linker is used for object files, regardless of the original language in which the new program was written. The output of the linker is an executable or runnable file. The process is shown in Fig. 2.3.

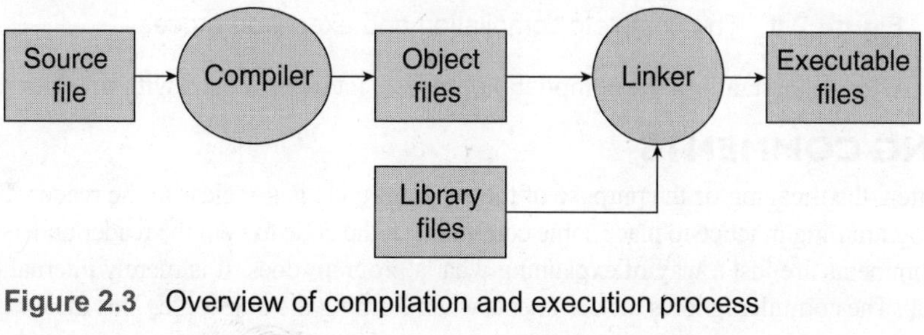

Figure 2.3 Overview of compilation and execution process

In C++ language programs, there are two kinds of source files. In addition to the main (*.cpp*) source file that contains executable statements, there are also header (*.h*) source files. As input and output in C++ programs are executed through library functions, every C++ program, therefore, uses standard header files. These header files should be written as part of the source code for modular C++ programs as shown in Fig. 2.3.

The compilation process in Fig. 2.4 is done in two steps. In the first step, the preprocessor program reads the source file as text, and produces another text file as the output. Source code lines that begin with the hash symbol are actually not written in C++ but in the preprocessor language. The output of the preprocessor is a text file and does not contain any preprocessor statements. This file is ready to be processed by the compiler. The linker combines the object file with library routines, supplied with the compiler, to produce the final executable file.

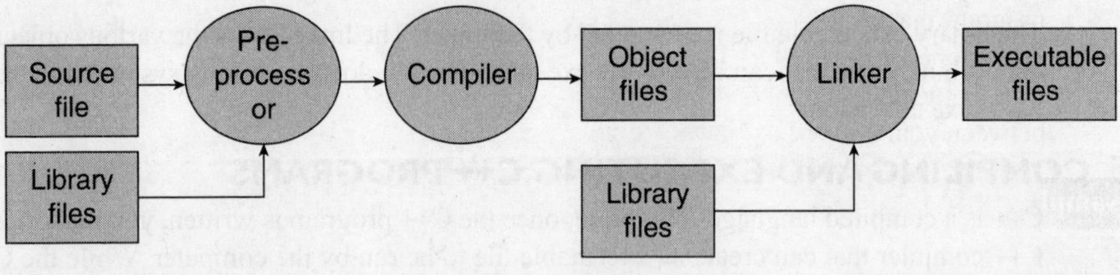

Figure 2.4 Elaborate compilation before execution

When modular programming is used, the source code is divided into two or more source files. All these source files are compiled separately, thereby, producing multiple object files. These object files are combined by the linker to produce an executable file (refer to Fig. 2.5).

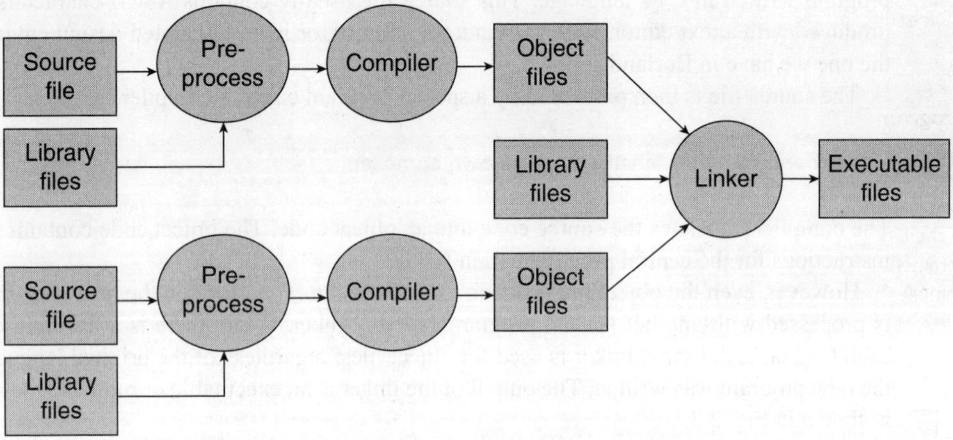

Figure 2.5 The complete compilation and execution process

After understanding the compilation process, let us now start with programming details.

2.6 USING COMMENTS

Often, the meaning or the purpose of the program code is not clear to the reader. Therefore, it is a good programming practice to place some comments in the code to help the reader understand the code clearly. Comments are just a way of explaining what a program does. It is merely internal program documentation. The compiler ignores the comments when forming the object file. This means that the comments are non-executable statements. C++ supports two types of commenting.

- // is used to comment a single statement. This is known as a line comment. A line comment can be placed anywhere on the line and it does not require to be specifically ended as the end of the line automatically ends the line. This means that a line comment discards everything from where the pair of slash signs (//) are found up to the end of that same line.

- `/*` is used to comment multiple statements. A `/*` is ended with `*/` and all statements that lie within these characters are commented. This type of comment is known as block comment. This is mostly used for multiline comments.

Note that commented statements are not executed by the compiler. Rather, they are ignored by the compiler as they are simply added in the program to make the code understandable by the programmer as well as other people who read it. It is a good habit to put a comment at the beginning of a program that tells you what the program does. This will help in defining the usage of the program as you open it.

Commented statements can be used anywhere in the program. You can also use comments in between your code to explain a piece of code that is a bit complicated.

Example 2.1 To show the way in which we can make use of comments in our first program given below

```
/* Author: Reema Thareja
Description: To print "Welcome to the world of C++" on the screen */
using namespace std;
#include<iostream>
int main()
{
    cout<<"\n Welcome to the world of C++ "; //prints message
    return 0; // returns a value 0 to the operating system
}
```

OUTPUT

```
Welcome to the world of C++
```

Programming Tip: Not putting the */ after the termination of the block comment is a compiler error.

As comments are not executed by the compiler, they do not affect the execution speed and the size of the compiled program. Therefore, use comments liberally in your programs so that other users can understand the operations of the program and serve as an aid to debugging and testing.

2.7 TOKENS IN C++

Tokens are the basic buildings blocks in C++ language. You may think of a token as the smallest individual unit in a C++ program. This means that a program is constructed using a combination these tokens. There are six main types of tokens in C++. They are shown in the Fig. 2.6.

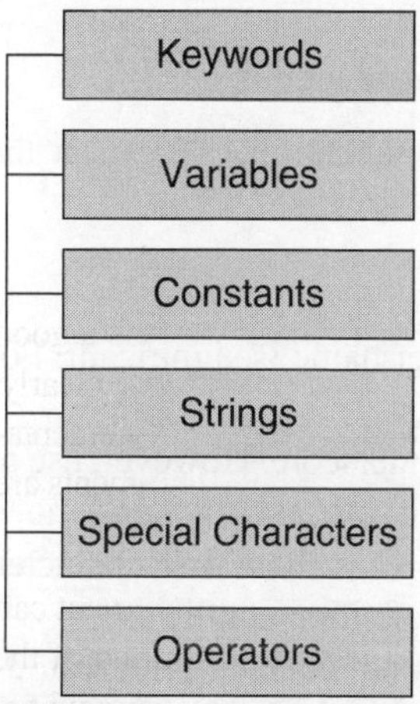

Figure 2.6 Tokens in C++

2.8 CHARACTER SET

Similar to human natural languages, computer languages also use a character set that defines the fundamental raw material used to represent information. In C++, a character means any alphabet, digit, or special symbols used to represent information. These characters when combined together forms a token that acts as the basic building block of a C++ program. The character set of C++ can, therefore, be given as:

- Alphabets include both lower case (a – z) as well as upper case (A – Z) characters.
- Digits include numerical digits from 0 to 9.

- Special characters include symbols like ~, @, %, ^, &, *,{, }, <. >, =, _, +, –, $, /, , (,), \, ;, :, [,], ', ", ?, ., !,.
- White space characters are used to print a blank space on the screen.
- Escape sequences have already been discussed in Section 2.8. They include- \\, \', \", \n, \a, \0, \?.

2.9 KEYWORDS

Similar to every computer language, C++ has a set of reserved words, often known as keywords that cannot be used as an identifier. All keywords are basically a sequence of characters that have a fixed meaning. The meaning of a keyword cannot be changed by the programmer. Conventionally, all keywords must be written in lowercase. Table 2.3 contains a list of keywords that are common to C and C++. Table 2.4 lists some C++-specific keywords.

Table 2.3 Keywords common to C and C++ languages

auto	break	case	char	const	continue	default	Do
double	else	enum	extern	Float	for	goto	if
int	long	register	return	Short	signed	sizeof	static
struct	switch	typedef	union	unsigned	void	volatile	while

Table 2.4 Keywords specific to C++ language

asm	new	template	catch	operator	this	class	private
throw	delete	protected	try	friend	public	virtual	inline

As you read this book, the meaning and utility of each keyword will become clearer to you.

2.10 IDENTIFIER

Identifiers, as the name suggests, helps us to identify data and other objects in the program. Identifiers are basically the names given to program elements such as variables, arrays, and functions. An identifier may consist of an alphabet, digit, or an underscore.

Rules for Forming Identifier Name

The following are some rules to be followed while naming an identifier:

> **Programming Tip:** C++ is a case-sensitive language. Therefore, if by mistake, you type printf function as Printf then an error will be generated.

- The name cannot include any special characters or punctuation marks, except the underscore"_".
- There cannot be two successive underscores.
- Keywords cannot be used as identifiers.
- The case of alphabetic characters that form the identifier name is significant. For example, "FIRST" is different from "first" and "First".
- The identifier name must begin with an alphabet or an underscore. However, use of underscore as the first character must be avoided because several complier-defined identifiers in the standard C++ library have underscore as their first character. Therefore, inadvertently duplicated names may cause definition conflicts.
- Identifiers can be of any reasonable length. They should not contain more than 31 characters. They can be longer than 31; however, the compiler looks at only the first 31 characters of the name.

Although it is not compulsory, it is a good practice to use meaningful identifier names. Good identifiers are descriptive but short. To cut short the identifier, you may use abbreviations. C++ allows identifiers (names) to be up to 63 characters long. If a name is longer than 63 characters, then only the first 63 characters are used.

As a general practice, if the identifier is a little long (more than 4-5 characters), then you may use an underscore to separate the parts of the name or you may use capital letters for each part.

Examples of valid identifiers include the following:

```
roll_number, marks, name, emp_number, basic_pay, HRA, DA, dept_code, DeptCode, RollNo,
EMP_NO
```

Examples of invalid identifiers include the following:

```
23_student, %marks, @name, #emp_number, basic.pay, -HRA, (DA), &dept_code, auto
```

Note C++ is a case-sensitive language. Therefore, rno, Rno, RNo, and RNO are different identifiers.

2.11 DATA TYPES IN C++

Data are used to represent information. They can be classified into different categories or types as shown in Fig. 2.7.

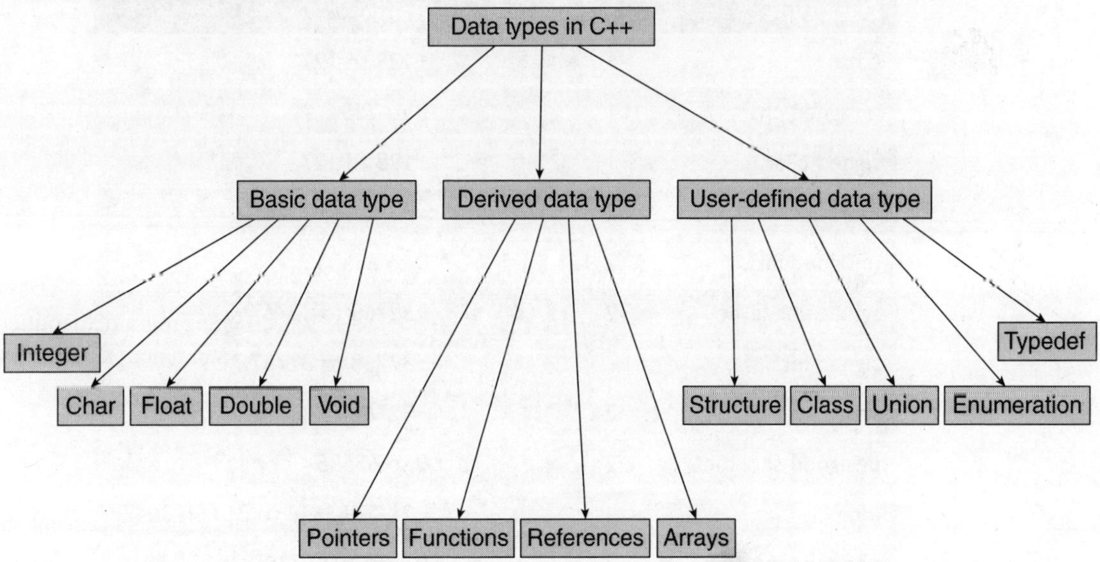

Figure 2.7 Data types in C++

In this section, we will read only about the basic data types in C++. The complex data types will be taken up in subsequent chapters.

C++ language provides very few basic data types. Table 2.5 lists the data types, their keywords, size, range, and usage for a C++ programmer on a 16-bit computer.

In addition to this, we also have variants of `char`, `int`, and `double` data types.

The char data type is one byte and is used to store single characters. Note that C++ does not provide any data type for storing text. This is because the text is made up of individual characters.

Generally, char is supposed to store characters not numbers; however, the range of char is given as `-128` to `127` here. The reason for this change is that in memory, characters are stored in their

Table 2.5 Basic data types in C++

Data type	Keyword used	Size in bytes	Range	Use
Character	char	1	−128 to 127	To store characters
Integer	int	2	−32768 to 32767	To store integers
Floating point	float	4	3.4E-38 to 3.4E+38	To store floating point numbers
Double	double	8	1.7E-308 to 1.7E+308	To store big floating point numbers
Valueless	void	0	Valueless	–

ASCII codes. For example, the character 'A' has the ASCII code 65. In memory, we will not store 'A' but 65 in binary format.

Table 2.6 shows the variants of basic data types in detail.

Table 2.6 Detailed list of data types

Data type	Size in bytes	Range
Char	1	−128 to 127
unsigned char	1	0 to 255
signed char	1	−128 to 127
Int	2	−32768 to 32767
unsigned int	2	0 to 65535
signed short int	2	−32768 to 32767
signed int	2	−32768 to 32767
short int	2	−32768 to 32767
unsigned short int	2	0 to 65535
long int	4	−2147483648 to 2147483647
unsigned long int	4	0 to 4294967295
signed long int	4	−2147483648 to 2147483647
Float	4	3.4E-38 to 3.4E+38
Double	8	1.7E-308 to 1.7E+308
long double	10	3.4E-4932 to 1.1E+4932

In Table 2.6, we have unsigned char and signed char, but do not have negative characters. The reason for having negative data types is because we use signed and unsigned char to ensure portability of programs that store non-character data as char.

While the smaller data types occupy less memory, the larger types incur a performance penalty. Although the data type we use for our variables does not have a big impact on the speed or memory usage of the application, we should always try to use int, unless there is a special need to use any other data type.

Last but not the least, the void type holds no value. It is primarily used in three cases as follows:

- To specify the return type of a function (when the function returns no value)
- To specify the parameters of the function (when the function accepts no arguments from the caller)
- To create generic pointer

We will study about void in detail in subsequent chapters.

Note Unsigned int/char liberates the sign bit and makes the entire word available for storage of the non-negative numbers.

2.12 VARIABLES

A variable is defined as a meaningful name given to the data storage location in computer memory. When using a variable, we actually refer to address of the memory where the data is stored. C++ language supports two basic kinds of variables.

Numeric variables Numeric variables can be used to store either integer values or floating point values. While an integer value is a whole numbers without a fraction part or decimal point in them, a floating point number, on the other hand, can have a decimal point in them.

Numeric values may also be associated with modifiers such as short, long, signed, and unsigned. The difference between signed and unsigned numeric variables is that signed variables can be either negative or positive but unsigned variables can only be positive. Therefore, by using an unsigned variable, we can increase the maximum positive range. When we omit the signed/unsigned modifier, C++ language automatically makes it a signed variable. To declare an unsigned variable, the unsigned modifier must be explicitly added during the declaration of the variable.

Character variables Character variables can include any letter from the alphabet or from the ASCII chart and numbers 0 – 9 inserted between single quotes. In C++, a number that is put in single quotes is not the same as a number without them.

2.12.1 Declaring Variables

Each variable to be used in the program must be declared. To declare a variable, specify the data type of the variable, followed by its name. The syntax for declaring a variable can therefore be given as

```
data_type variable_name;
```

The data type indicates the kind of data that the variable will store. Variable names should always be meaningful and must reflect the purpose of their usage in the program. Practically speaking, where the variable is located in memory is not our concern; it is a concern only for the compiler. Programmers must only be concerned with accessing data through their symbolic names. In C++, variable declaration always ends with a semicolon. For example,

```
int emp_num;
float salary;
char grade;
double balance_amount;
unsigned short int acc_no;
```

Programming Tip: A variable cannot be of type void.

In C++,variables can be declared at any place in the program; however, two things must be kept in mind. First, variables should be declared before using them. Second, variables should be declared closest to their first point of use so that the source code is easier to maintain.

C++ allows multiple variables of the same type to be declared in one statement. Therefore, the following statement is absolutely legal in C++.

```
float temp_in_celsius, temp_in_farenheit;
```

In C++, variables are declared at three basic places as follows:

- First, when a variable is declared inside a function it is known as a local variable.
- Second, when a variable is declared in the definition of function parameters, it is known as formal parameter (we will study this in Chapter 4).
- Third, when the variable is declared outside all functions, it is known as a global variable.

Variable declaration in C and C++

Difference In C, all variables are declared at the beginning of a scope. For example, as soon as the `main()` function starts. In contrast, C++ allows declaration anywhere in the scope even at the point where it is used for the first time

Advantage Makes program more understandable and readable

Disadvantage May lead to multiple declarations of the same variable and it is difficult to see the variables in the scope at a glance

2.12.2 Initializing Variables

While declaring the variables, we can also initialize them with some value. For example,

```
int emp_num = 7;
float salary = 5000;
char grade = 'A';
double balance_amount = 100000000;
```

Note that the initializer applies only to the variable defined immediately before it. Therefore, the statement

```
int count, flag = 1;
```

initializes the variable flag and not count. If you want both the variables to be declared in a single statement, then write

```
int count = 0, flag = 1;
```

Remember that when variables are declared but not initialized, they usually contain garbage values. There is exceptions to the rule, which will be dealt with in Chapter 4.

2.12.3 Reference Variables

Reference variable is a new feature added to C++. A reference variable basically assigns an alternative name (alias) to an existing variable. The syntax of creating a reference variable is as follows:

```
data_type & reference_name = variable_name
```

Programming Tip: References must be initialized at the time of declaration; otherwise, the compiler will give an error. Therefore, writing int & num; is an error.

For example, if we want a variable num to be a reference to the variable n, then n and num can be interchangeably used to represent that variable. This is same as if someone calls us by our nick name or by our formal name, both names refer to the same person. Therefore, if we write

```
int n = 10;
int &num = n;
```

Then, both n and num are of type integers and refer to the same data. Therefore,

```
cout<<num; // will print 10    and    cout<<num; // will print 10
```

Therefore, if we write num = 100; Then

```
cout<<num; // will print 100    and    cout<<num; // will print 100
```

2.13 CONSTANTS

Constants are identifiers whose value does not change. While variables can change their value at any time, constants can never change their value. Constants are used to define fixed values such as Pi or the charge on an electron so that their value does not get changed in the program even by mistake.

A constant is an explicit data value specified by the programmer. The value of the constant is known to the compiler at the compile time. C++ allows the programmer to specify constants of integer type, floating point type, character type, and string type (refer to Fig. 2.9).

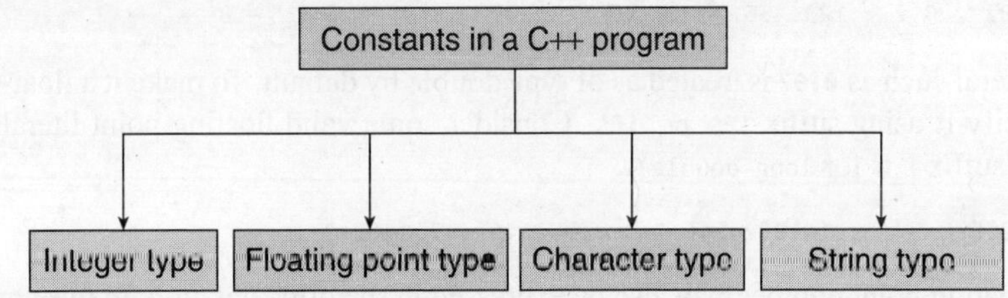

Figure 2.9 Constants in C++

2.13.1 Integer Constant

A constant of integer type consists of a sequence of digits. For example, 1, 34, 567, and 8907 are valid integer constants. A literal (constant) integer such as 1234 is of type int by default. For a long integer constant, the literal is succeeded with either 'L' or 'l' (such as 1234567L). Similarly, an unsigned int literal is written with a 'U' or 'u' suffix (ex, 12U). Therefore,

```
1234L  1234l  1234U  1234u  1234LU   1234ul are all valid integer constants.
```

Literal integers can be expressed in decimal, octal, or hexadecimal notation. By default, an integer is expressed in decimal notation. Decimal integers consist of a set of digits from 0 through 9, preceded by an optional - or + sign. Examples of decimal integer constants include 123   -123   +123   0

While writing integer constants, embedded spaces, commas and non-digit characters are not allowed. Therefore, integer constants given below are totally invalid in C++.

```
123  456   12, 34, 567   $123   123.456
```

An integer constant preceded by a zero (0) is an octal number. Octal integers consist of a set of digits, 0 through 7. Example of octal integers include

```
012    0    01234
```

Similarly, an integer constant is expressed in hexadecimal notation if it is preceded by 0x or 0X. Hexadecimal numbers contain digits from 0-9 and alphabets from A through F. The alphabets A through F represent numbers 10 through 15. For example, decimal 72 is equivalent to 0110 in octal notation and 0x48 in hexadecimal notation. Example of octal integers include

```
0X12   0x7F   0xABCD    0X1A3B
```

Note A decimal integer constant is treated as an unsigned long if its magnitude exceeds that of signed long. An octal or hexadecimal integer that exceeds the limit of int is taken to be unsigned. If even this limit is exceeded, it is taken as long; and in case this limit is exceeded, it is treated as unsigned long.

2.13.2 Floating Point Constant

Integer numbers are inadequate to express numbers that have a fractional part. A floating point constant, therefore, consists of an integer part, a decimal point, a fractional part, and an exponent field, containing an e or E (e means exponent) followed by an integer where the fraction part and integer part are sequence of digits. However, it is not necessary that every floating point constant must contain all these parts. Some floating point numbers may have certain parts missing. Some valid examples of floating point numbers are as follows:

```
0.02  -0.23  123.456    +0.34    123.  .9    -.7    +.8
```

A literal such as 0.07 is treated as of type double by default. To make it a float-type literal, you must specify it using suffix 'F' or 'f'. Consider some valid floating point literals given below. (Note that suffix L is for long double)

```
0.02F 0.34f 3.141592654L    0.002146   2.146E-3
```

A floating point number may also be expressed in scientific notation. In this notation, the mantissa is either a floating point number or an integer and exponent is an integer with an optional plus or minus sign. Therefore, the numbers given below are valid floating point numbers.

```
0.5e2 14E-2 1.2e+3     2.1E-3     -5.6e-2
```

Hence, we see that scientific notation is used to express numbers that are either very small or very large. For example,

```
120000000 = 1.2E8 and -0.000000025 = -2.5E-8:
```

2.13.3 Character Constant

A character constant consists of a single character enclosed in single quotes. For example, 'a', '@' are character constants. In computers, characters are stored using machine's character set for example using ASCII codes. Note that all escape sequences mentioned in Table 2.6 are also character constants.

2.13.4 String Constant

A string constant is a sequence of characters enclosed in double quotes. Hence, 'a' is not the same as "a". The characters comprising the string constant are stored in successive memory locations.

When a string constant is encountered in a C++ program, the compiler records the address of the first character and appends a null character (`'\0'`) to the string to mark the end of the string. Therefore, the length of a string constant is equal to number of characters in the string plus `1` (for the null character). In the same manner, the length of string literal `"hello"` is `6`.

2.13.5 Declaring Constants

To declare a constant, precede the normal variable declaration with const keyword and assign it a value.
For example,

```
const data_type const_name = value;
```

The const keyword specifies that the value of pi cannot change.

```
const float PI = 3.14;
```

However, another way to designate a constant is to use the preprocessor command `define`. Similar to other preprocessor commands, define is preceded with a `#` symbol. Although `#define` statements can be placed anywhere in a C program, it is always recommended that these statements be placed at the beginning of the program to make them easy to find and modify at a later stage. Look at the example given here which defines the value of `PI` using define.

```
#define PI 3.14159
#define service_tax 0.12
```

In these examples, though the value of `PI` will never change, service tax may change. Whenever the value of the service tax is altered, it can be corrected only in the define statement.

When the preprocessor reformats the program to be compiled by the compiler, it replaces each defined name (such as `PI and service_tax`) with its corresponding value, wherever it is found in the source program. Hence, it just works similar to the Find and Replace command available in a text editor.

Let us have a look at some rules that needs to be applied to a #define statement which defines a constant.

Rule 1 Constant names are usually written in capital letters to visually distinguish them from other variable names which are normally written in lower case characters. Note that this is just a convention and not a rule.

Rule 2 No blank spaces are permitted in between the `#` symbol and define keyword.

Rule 3 Blank space must be used between `#define` and constant name and between constant name and constant value.

Rule 4 `#define` is a preprocessor compiler directive and not a statement. Therefore, it does not end with a semi-colon.

2.14 INPUT AND OUTPUT STATEMENTS IN C++

Before performing input and output in C++ programs, let us first understand the concepts. This section deals with the basic understanding of the phenomena involved in accepting input and printing output in C++ programs.

2.14.1 Streams

Basically, a stream involves transfer of information as a sequence of bytes. A stream acts in two ways. It is the source as well as the destination of data. C++ programs input data and output data from a stream. Streams are associated with a physical device such as the monitor or with a file stored on the secondary memory. C++ uses two forms of streams as shown in the Fig. 2.10.

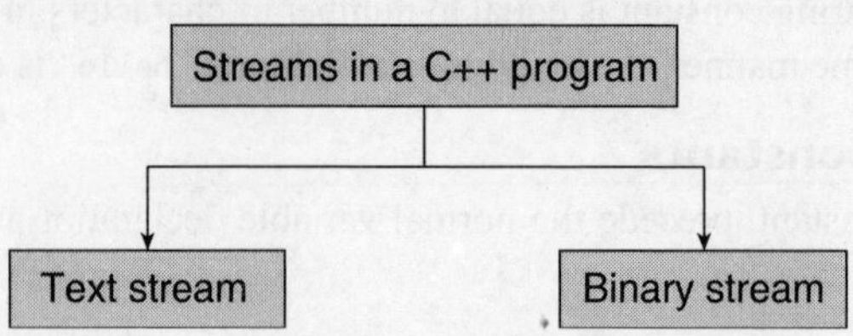

Figure 2.10 Streams in C++

In a text stream, the sequence of characters is divided into lines, with each line being terminated with a new-line character (`\n`). On the other hand, a binary stream contains data values using their memory representation.

Although we can input or output from the keyboard, monitor, or from any file, in this chapter, we will assume that the source of data is the keyboard and destination of the data is the monitor (refer to Fig. 2.11). In Chapter 13 on file handling, handling of the input and output values via C++ programs will be discussed.

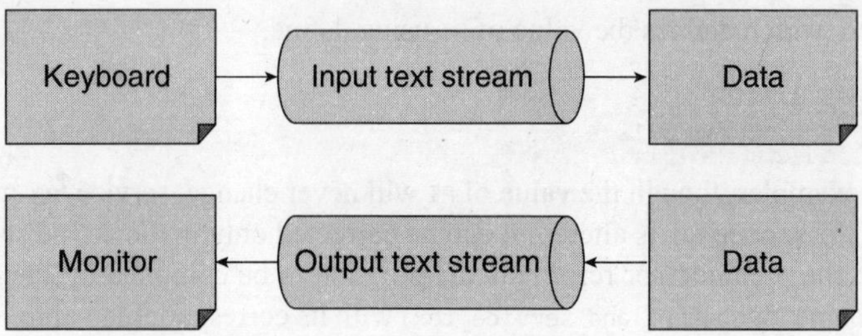

Figure 2.11 Input and output streams in C++

Note A stream is an entity where a program can either insert or extract characters to or from. The stream can be associated with a disk file, a program, or a computer on the network. We need not know details about the media associated to the stream or any of its internal specifications.

The standard C++ library defines the following stream objects to access the standard sources and destinations of characters during program execution:

```
cin: standard input stream (usually the keyboard)
cout: standard output stream (usually the screen)
cerr: standard error stream, it is the same as the output stream
clog: standard logging stream, it is the same as the output stream
```

Programming Tip: You can also use printf() to display data in C++ programs.

Standard Output

The statement `cout<<"Welcome to the world of C++";` makes use of two new features of C++. First, `cout` (pronounced as `C out`) is a predefined object (of `ostream`) that represents the standard output stream that is the screen. Second, the operator `<<` also known as the insertion operator or the put to operator transfers the content of the variable on its right to the object on its left.

Standard Input

The statement `cin<<number;` waits for the user to type a number on the keyboard followed by an Enter key. Once the user enters a number, its value is assigned to the variable `number`. The statement makes use of `cin` (pronounced as `C in`), a predefined object (of `istream`) that represents the standard input stream that is the keyboard. The operator `>>`, also known as the extraction operator or the get from operator, retrieves the content from the keyboard and assigns it to the variable on the right.

Cascading of Input or Output Operators

We can use the << operator multiple times in the same line. This is called cascading. For example, if we write,

```
cout<<"\n"<<" First Name - "<<"Jian";
```

Programming Tip: String literals to be printed on screen are placed within double quotes as they are to be printed as it is. Identifiers are not placed in double quotes because their value has to be printed.

Here, a new line character is sent to `cout` that will print the next output on a new line. The `First Name -` will be printed followed by `Jian`. We could have done the same task using three separate `cout` statements.

Similar to `cout, cin` can also be cascaded. For example,

```
cout<<"\n Enter the marks obtained in English and Hindi";
cin>>marks_Hindi>>marks_English;
```

Here, the user needs to input two numbers. When the user enters two numbers, the values are assigned from left to right. If the user enters `80` and `90`, the first value (`80`) will be assigned to `marks_Hindi` and the second value (`90`) will be assigned to `marks_English`.

2.14.2 Reading and Writing Characters and Strings

C++ has functions such as `get()` and `put()` are used to input and output a single character. These functions are discussed in detail in Chapter 6.

There are two ways of using the `get` function as shown here.

```
char grade;
cin.get(grade); //The value for grade is read
OR
grade = cin.get();    // A character is read and assigned to grade
```

Similarly, if we write `cout.put(grade)`, the value of grade will be displayed on the screen.

`cin` can also be used to read strings (a series of characters) as it is used to read value for other basic data types. For example, if we write,

```
string mesg;
cin>>mesg;
```

The statement will read a single word form the keyboard. The extraction of characters will terminate as soon as space (e.g., a white, tab, new-line, etc.) is encountered. To read a phrase, sentence or a paragraph, users must use the `getline()`, which takes information about the string variable and its size.

For example, if we want user to enter his full name (which may consist of a first name, middle name, and last name), then we will use the `getline()` as given below.

```
string name;
cin.getline(name,20);
cout<<"\n Welcome"<<name;
```

The `getline()` will terminate in two conditions if either the user has entered a newline character or if `size - 1` characters have been read. When the user enters a `newline` character, it is read but not saved in the string. The string is then terminated with a `null` character.

`write()` is used to print an entire line on the screen. The function takes two types of information. First, the `line` to be printed and second, the `size` of the line which implies the number of characters.

The function will not stop displaying the characters on the screen even if the `null` character has been encountered. It will keep printing until `size` characters are printed. The statement `cout.write(name, 20);` will print `20` characters of string name. However, if the name entered had only `12` characters, then the user will see some extra characters printed on the screen.

Note Two strings can be concatenated and then displayed using *write*() by typing

```
cout.write(string1, m).write(string2, n);
```

2.14.3 Formatted Input and Output Operations

In C++, users can print input and output in two ways as shown in Fig. 2.12.

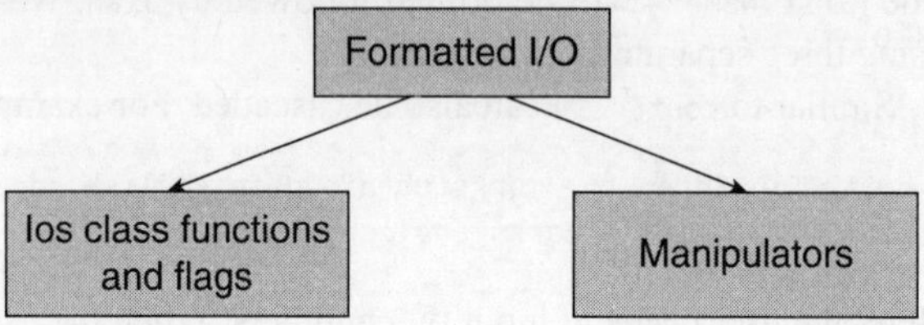

Figure 2.12 Formatted I/O

In this section, we will first discuss the functions and flags in the `iosclass`. Basically, the `ios` class is the base class for all stream classes including the `iostream.h` header file. We will read more about it later in Chapter13 but for now, let us understand some of its important functions. Table 2.7 gives a list of some I/O functions, their syntax, purpose, and usage.

Table 2.7 Functions for Input/Output

Function	Purpose	Syntax	Usage	Result	Comment
width()	Specifies field size (no. of columns) to display the value	cout. width(w)	cout.width(6);cout<<1239;	1239	It can specify field width for only one value
precision()	Specifies no. of digits to be displayed after the decimal point of a float value	cout. precision(d)	cout. precision(3);cout<<1.234567;	1.234	It retains the setting in effect until it is reset
fill()	Specify a character to fill the unused portion of a field	cout.fill(ch)	cout.fill('#');cout. width(6);cout<<1239;	##1239	It retains the setting in effect until it is reset

Example 2.2 To print the value of PI using the formatted I/O functions given in Table 2.7.

```
using namespace std;
#include<iostream>
#define PI 3.14159
main()
{   cout.precision(3);
    cout.width(10);
    cout.fill('#');
    cout<<PI;
}
```

OUTPUT

```
#####3.142
```

Explanation: In the above program, specified width for displaying PI is 10 but it requires only 4. Therefore, rest of spaces are filled with '#'

Formatting with Flags

The `setf()` is a member function of the `ios` class that is used to set flags for formatting output. The syntax for `setf` function that stands for set flags can be given as

```
cout.setf(flag, bit-field)
```

Here, `flag` defined in the `ios` class specifies how the output should be formatted and `bit-field` is a constant (defined in `ios`) that identifies the group to which the formatting flag belongs to. There are two types of `setf()`—one that takes both `flag` and `bit-fields` and the other that takes only the `flag`. Table 2.8 lists the types of `setf()`.

Table 2.8 Types of `setf()`

Flag	Bit-field	Usage	Purpose	Comment
ios :: left	ios :: adjustifield	cout.setf(ios :: left, ios :: adjustifield)	For left justified output	If no flag is set, then by default, the output will be right justified.
ios :: right	ios:: adjustifield	cout.setf(ios :: right, ios :: adjustifield)	For right justified output	
ios :: internal	ios:: adjustifield	cout.setf(ios :: internal, ios :: adjustifield)	Left-justify sign or base indicator, and right-justify rest of number	
ios :: scientific	ios:: floatifield	cout.setf(ios :: scientific, ios :: floatifield)	For scientific notation	If no flag is set then any of the two notations can be used for floating point numbers depending on the decimal point
ios :: fixed	ios :: floatifield	cout.setf(ios :: fixed, ios :: floatifield)	For fixed point notation	

(*Contd*)

Table 2.8 (*Contd*)

Flag	Bit-field	Usage	Purpose	Comment
ios :: dec	ios :: basefield	cout.setf(ios :: dec, ios :: basefield)	Displays integer in decimal	If no flag is set, then the output will be in decimal.
ios :: oct	ios :: basefield	cout.setf(ios :: oct, ios :: basefield)	Displays integer in octal	
ios :: hex	ios :: basefield	cout.setf(ios :: hex, ios :: basefield)	Displays integer in hexadecimal	
ios :: showbase	Not applicable	cout.setf(ios :: showbase)	Show base when displaying integers	
ios :: showpoint	Not applicable	cout.setf(ios :: showpoint)	Show decimal point when displaying floating point numbers	
ios :: showpos	Not applicable	cout.setf(ios :: showpos)	Show + sign when displaying positive integers	
ios :: uppercase	Not applicable	cout.setf(ios :: uppercase)	Use uppercase letter when displaying hexadecimal (OX) or exponential numbers (E)	
ios :: boolalpha	Not applicable	cout.setf(ios :: boolalpha)	Use text rather than integer to read and write boolean values (TRUE and FALSE instead of 1 and 0)	
ios :: skipws	Not applicable	cout.setf(ios :: skipws)	To skip whitespace on input	
ios :: unitbuf	Not applicable	cout.setf(ios :: unitbuf)	To flush output buffer after each insertion	

Before using the `setf()`, you must remember that when the user has not set any flag, then by default, `ios::skipws` and `ios::dec` are set. At any point of time, if required, you may unset the flags by using `unsetf()`. For example, if you write `cout.unsetf(ios::left)`; then the output will no longer be left justified.

Example 2.3 To enter a number and display its hex and octal equivalent and its square root.

```
using namespace std;
#include<iostream>
#include<math.h>
main()
{   int num;
    cout<<"\n Enter a number : ";
    cin>>num;
    // To display hexadecimal of 64
    cout.setf(ios::left );
    cout<<"\n hexadecimal of" <<num;
    // To display *************40
    cout.fill('*');
    cout.unsetf(ios::left);
```

```
    cout.width(15);
    cout.setf(ios::hex);
    cout<<num;
    // To display octal of 64
    cout.setf(ios::left);
    cout.unsetf(ios::hex);
    cout<<"\n Octal of "<<num;
    // To display *************100
    cout.unsetf(ios::left);
    cout.width(20);
    cout.setf(ios::oct);
    cout<<num;
    // To Display Square root
    cout.setf(ios::left | ios :: showpoint | ios::showpos);
    cout.unsetf(ios::oct);
    cout<<"\n Square Root of "<<num;
    // **********+8.000
    cout.unsetf(ios::left);
    cout.precision(3);
    cout.width(20);
    cout<<sqrt(num);
}
```

OUTPUT

```
Enter a number : 64
HeaxaDecimal of 64*************40
Octal of 64*****************100
Square Root of +64**************+8.000
```

Formatted Output Using Manipulators

C++ has a header file `iomanip.h` that contains certain manipulators to format the output. Though you can do the same formatting using `ios` class `flags`, formatting with manipulators is easier to learn and convenient to use. Table 2.9 lists some commonly used manipulators along with their alternatives defined in `ios`.

Table 2.9 Different types of manipulators

Manipulator	Purpose	Usage	Result	Alternative
setw(w)	Specifies field size (number of columns) to display the value	cout<<setw(6) <<1239;	1 2 3 9	width()
setprecision(d)	Specifies number of digits to be displayed after the decimal point of a float value	cout<<setprecision(3) <<1.234567;	1.235	precision()
setfill(c)	Specify a character to fill the unused portion of a field	cout<<setfill('#') <<setwidth(6) <<1239;	# # 1 2 3 9	fill()

Example 2.4 Using manipulators obtain the same output as given in Example 2.3.

> **Programming Tip:** endl is a manipulator that add a newline. Instead of using "\n", you can also write coutt<<endl;.

```
using namespace std;
#include<iostream>
#include<iomanip>
#include<math.h>
int main()
{   int num;
    cout<<"\n Enter a number : ";
    cin>>num;
    // To display HeaxaDecimal of 64
    cout<<"\n HeaxaDecimal of "<<num;
    cout<<setw(10)<<setfill('*')<<hex<<num;
    // To display octal of 64
    cout<<"\n Octal of "<<dec<<num;
    cout<<setw(20)<<setfill('*')<<oct<<num;
    // To display Square root of
    cout<<"\n Square root of "<<dec<<num;
    cout.setf(ios::showpoint | ios::showpos);
    cout<<setw(20)<<setfill('*')<<setprecision(3)<<dec<<sqrt(num);
}
```

OUTPUT

```
Enter a number : 64
HeaxaDecimal of 64************40
Octal of 64*****************100
Square Root of +64**************+8.000
```

Explanation: It can be seen that with the use of manipulators, the above code has become very small and readable.

Note C++ allows programmers to use mix of I/O manipulators and functions.

Program 2.1 Write a program to print values of variables of different data types.

```
using namespace std;
#include<iostream>
main()
{   // Declare and initialize variables
    int num = 7;
    float amt = 123.45;
    char code = 'A';
    double pi = 3.1415926536;
    long int population_of_India = 10000000000;
    char msg[] = "Hi";
    // Print the values of variables
    cout<<"\n NUM = "<< num <<"\t AMT = "<< amt <<"\t CODE = "<< code << "\t
    POPULATION OF INDIA = "<< population_of_India<< "\t MESSAGE = "<< msg;
    return 0;
}
```

OUTPUT

```
NUM = 7AMT - 123.45000CODE = API = 3.141590e+00
POPULATION OF INDIA = 10000000000MESSAGE = Hi
```

Program 2.2 Write a program to read and print values of variables of different data types.

```
using namespace std;
#include<iostream>
main()
{
    int num;
    float amt;
    char code;
    double pi;
    long int population_of_India;
    char msg[10];
    cout<<"\n Enter the value of num : ";
    cin>>num;
    cout<<"\n Enter the value of amt : ";
    cin>>amt;
    cout<<"\n Enter the value of pi : ";
    cin>>pi;
    cout<<"\n Enter the population of India : ";
    cin>>population_of_India;
    cout<<"\n Enter the value of code : ";
    cin>>code;
    cout<<"\n Enter the message : ";
    cin>>msg;
    // Print the values of variables
    cout<<"\n NUM = "<< num <<"\t AMT = "<< amt <<"\t CODE = "<< code << "\t POPULATION
OF INDIA = "<< population_of_India<< "\t MESSAGE = "<< msg;
    return 0;
}
```

OUTPUT

```
Enter the value of num : 5
Enter the value of amt : 123.45
Enter the value of pi : 3.14159
Enter the population of India : 12345
Enter the value of code : c
Enter the message : Hello
NUM = 5AMT = 123.45000PI = 3.141590e+00
POPULATION OF INDIA = 12345CODE = c MESSAGE = Hello
```

Program 2.3 Write a program to calculate area of a triangle using Heron's formula. (Hint: Heron's formula is given as: `area = sqrt(S*(S-a)*(S-b)*(S-c)))`

```
using namespace std;
#include<iostream>
#include<math.h>
int main()
 {
      float a, b, c, area, S;
      cout<<"\n Enter the three sides of the triangle : ";
      cin>>a>>b>>c;
      S = (a + b + c)/2;
      // sqrt is a mathematical function defined in math.h header file
      area = sqrt(S*(S-a)*(S-b)*(S-c));
      cout<<"\n Area = "<<area;
```

```
        return 0;
}
```

OUTPUT

```
Enter the three sides of the triangle : 12 16 20
Area = 96
```

Program 2.4 Write a program to calculate the distance between two points.

```
using namespace std;
#include<iostream>
#include<math.h>
int main()
{
        int x1, x2, y1, y2;
        float distance;
        cout<<"\n Enter the x and y coordinates of the first point : ";
        cin>>x1>>y1;
        cout<<"\n Enter the x and y coordinates of the second point : ";
        cin>>x2>>y2;
        // sqrt and pow are mathematical functions defined in math.h header file
        distance = sqrt(pow((x2-x1), 2) + pow ((y2-y1), 2));
        cout.precision(2);
        cout<<"\n Distance = "<<distance;
        return 0;
}
```

OUTPUT

```
Enter the x and y coordinates of the first point : 2 5
Enter the x and y coordinates of the second point : 3 7
Distance = 2.24
```

Unformatted output is done without use of I/O manipulators and functions. (For example, the value of PI will be displayed as 3.14285714285... if printed without formatted I/O options but the same value will be printed as 3.14 with I/O manipulators and functions).

2.15 OPERATORS IN C++

An operator is defined as a symbol that specifies the mathematical, logical, or relational operation to be performed. C++ language supports a lot of operators to be used in expressions. These operators can be categorized into the following major groups:

- Arithmetic operators
- Relational operators
- Equality operators
- Logical operators
- Unary operators
- Conditional operators
- Bitwise operators
- Assignment operators
- Comma operator
- Sizeof operator

In this section, we will read about all these operators.

2.15.1 Arithmetic Operators

Consider three variables declared as,

```
int a=9, b=3, result;
```

We will use these variables to explain arithmetic operators. Table 2.10 shows the arithmetic operators, their syntax, and usage in C++ language.

In Table 2.10, a and b (on which the operator is applied) are called operands. Arithmetic operato can be applied to any integer or floating-point number. Addition, subtraction, and multiplication -, and *) operators perform the usual arithmetic operations in C++ programs. Therefore, you already familiar with these operators.

Table 2.10 Use of arithmetic operators

Operation	Operator	Syntax	Comment	Result
Multiply	*	a * b	result = a * b	27
Divide	/	a / b	result = a / b	3
Addition	+	a + b	result = a + b	12
Subtraction	-	a - b	result = a - b	6
Modulus	%	a % b	result = a % b	0

However, the operator % must be new to you. The modulus operator (%) finds the remainder of an integer division. This operator can be applied only to integer operands and cannot be used on float or double operands. Therefore, the code given below generates a compiler error.

```
using namespace std;
#include<iostream>
int main()
{
      float c = 20.0;
      cout<<"\n Result = "<<c % 5;
      // WRONG. Modulus operator is being applied to a float operand
      return 0;
}
```

While performing modulo division, the sign of the result is always the sign of the first operand (the dividend). Therefore,

```
16 % 3 = 1        -16 % 3 = -1       16 % -3 = 1        -16 % -3 = -1
```

When both operands of the division operator (/) are integers, the division is performed as an integer division. Integer division always results in an integer result. Therefore, the result is always rounded-off by ignoring the remainder. Therefore,

```
9/4 = 2    and    -9/4 = -3
```

From the observation, we can conclude that if op1 and op2 are integers and the quotient is not an integer, then

- If op1 and op2 have the same sign, then op1/op2 is the largest integer less than the true quotient
- If op1 and op2 have opposite signs, then op1/op2 is the smallest integer greater than the true quotient

...le to divide any number by zero. This is an illegal operation that results in a run-...sion-by-zero exception', thereby, terminating the program.

Except for modulus operator, all other arithmetic operators can accept a mix of integers and floating point numbers. If both operands are integers, the result will be an integer; if one or both operands are floating point numbers, the result would also be a floating point number.

All the arithmetic operators bind from left to right. As in mathematics, multiplication, division, and modulus operators have higher precedence over the addition and subtraction operators. If an arithmetic expression consists of a mix of operators, then multiplication, division, and modulus operations will be carried out first in a left to right order, before any addition and subtraction could be performed. For example,

```
3 + 4 * 7
= 3 + 28
= 31
```

Program 2.5 Write a program to perform addition, subtraction, multiplication, division, integer division, and modulo division on two integer numbers.

```
using namespace std;
#include<iostream>
int main()
{	int num1, num2;
	int add_res=0, sub_res=0, mul_res=0, idiv_res=0, modiv_res=0;
	float fdiv_res=0.0;
	cout<<"\n Enter the two numbers : ";
	cin>>num1>>num2;
	add_res = num1+num2;
	sub_res = num1 - num2;
	mul_res = num1 * num2;
	idiv_res = num1/num2;
	modiv_res = num1%num2;
	fdiv_res = (float)(num1/num2);
	cout<<"\n"<<num1<<" + "<<num2<<" = "<<add_res;
	cout<<"\n"<<num1<<" - "<<num2<<" = "<<sub_res;
	cout<<"\n"<<num1<<" * "<<num2<<" = "<<mul_res;
	cout<<"\n"<<num1<<" / "<<num2<<" = "<<idiv_res<<" (Integer Division)";
	cout<<"\n"<<num1<<" % "<<num2<<" = "<<modiv_res<<" (Modulo Division)";
	cout<<"\n"<<num1<<" / "<<num2<<" = "<<fdiv_res<<" (Normal Division)";
	return 0;
}
```

OUTPUT

```
Enter the two numbers : 9 7
9 + 7 = 16
9 - 7 = 2
9 * 7 = 63
9 / 7 = 1 (Integer division)
9 % 7 = 2 (Modulus division)
9 / 7 = 1.29 (Normal division)
```

Program 2.6 Write a program to perform addition, subtraction, division, and multiplication on two floating point numbers.

```
using namespace std;
#include<iostream>
int main()
{     float num1, num2;
      cout<<"\n Enter the two numbers : ";
      cin>>num1>>num2;
      cout.precision(2);
      cout<<"\n "<<num1 << " + "<<num2 <<" = "<< num1 + num2;
      cout<<"\n "<<num1 << " - "<<num2 <<" = "<< num1 - num2;
      cout<<"\n "<<num1 << " / "<<num2 <<" = "<< num1 / num2;
      cout<<"\n "<<num1 << " * "<<num2 <<" = "<< num1 * num2;
      return 0;
}
```

Assignment Perform all the arithmetic operators on double and long int values.

OUTPUT

```
Enter the two numbers : 3.5 1.2
3.5 + 1.2 = 4.70
3.5 - 1.2 = 2.30
3.5 * 1.2 = 4.20
3.5 / 1.2 = 2.20
```

2.15.2 Relational Operators

A relational operator, also known as a comparison operator, is an operator that compares two values. Expressions that contain relational operators are called relational expressions. Relational operators return true or false values, depending on whether the conditional relationship between the two operands holds true or not.

For example, to test the expression, if x is less than y, relational operator `<` is used as `x<y`. This expression will return `TRUE` value if the x is less than y; otherwise, the value of the expression will be `FALSE`.

Relational operators can be used to determine the relationships between operands. These relationships are illustrated in Table 2.11.

Table 2.11 Relational operators

Operator	Meaning	Example
<	Less than	3 < 5 gives 1
>	Greater than	7 > 9 gives 0
<=	Less than or equal to	100 <= 100 gives 1
>=	Greater than equal to	50 >=100 gives 0

Relational operators are evaluated from left to right. The operands of a relational operator must evaluate to a number. Characters are considered valid operands as they are represented by numeric values in the computer system. Therefore, if we say `'A' < 'B'`, then the result would be `1` as `65 < 66`.

When arithmetic expressions are used on either side of a relational operator, the first the arithmetic expression will be evaluated and then the result will be compared. This is because arithmetic operators have a higher priority over relational operators.

However, relational operators should not be used for comparing strings as this will result in comparing the address of the string and not their contents. The answer to this question will be clear to you in the later chapters.

```
Example of relational operators
If x=1, y=2, z=4 and a=3, then

Expressions that evaluate to true        Expressions that evaluate to false
(a)                                      (x - y)
(x + y)                                  (!(z))
(z * 9)                                  (0 * y)
(z + 10 - 5 * a)                         (y == 1)
(z - x + y)                              (y % 2)
```

Note Although blank spaces are allowed between an operand and an operator, no space is permitted between the components of an operator (e.g., > = is not allowed, it should be >=).

2.15.3 Equality Operators

C++ supports two kinds of equality operators to compare their operands for strict equality or inequality. They are equal to (`==`) and not equal to (`!=`) operator. The equality operators have lower precedence than relational operators.

The equal-to operator (`==`) returns `true (1)` if operands on both the side of the operator have the same value; otherwise, it returns `false (0)`. On the contrary, the not-equal-to operator (`!=`) returns `true(1)` if the operands do not have the same value; else it returns `false (0)`. Table 2.12 summarizes the different types of equality operators.

Table 2.12 Equality operators

Operator	Meaning
==	Returns 1 if both operands are equal, 0 otherwise
!=	Returns 1 if operands do not have the same value, 0 otherwise

2.15.4 Logical Operators

C++ supports three logical operators—logical AND (&&), logical OR (||), and logical NOT (!). As in case of arithmetic expressions, the logical expressions are evaluated from left to right.

Logical AND (&&)

Logical AND operator is used to simultaneously evaluate two conditions or expressions with relational operators. If expressions on both the sides (left and right side) of the logical operator are true, then the whole expression is true. The truth table of logical AND operator is given in Table 2.13.

Example,

```
(a < b) && (b > c)
```

Table 2.13 Truth table of logical AND

A	B	A && B
0	0	0
0	1	0
1	0	0
1	1	1

The expression to the left is `a < b` and that on the right is `b > c`. The whole expression is true only if both expressions are true—if `b` is greater than `a` and `c`.

Logical OR (||)

Logical `OR` operator is used to simultaneously evaluate two conditions or expressions with relational operators. If one or both the expressions on the left side and right side of the logical operator is true, then the whole expression is true. The truth table of logical `OR` operator is given in Table 2.14.

Table 2.14 Truth table of logical OR

A	B	A || B
0	0	0
0	1	1
1	0	1
1	1	1

Example,

```
(a < b) || (b > c)
```

The expression to the left is `a < b` and that on the right is `b > c`. The whole expression is true if either `b` is greater than `a` or `b` is greater than `c`.

Logical NOT (!)

The logical not operator takes a single expression and negates the value of the expression. Logical NOT produces a `zero` if the expression evaluates to a non-zero value and produces a `1` if the expression produces a `zero`. In other words, it just reverses the value of the expression. The truth table of logical `NOT` operator is given in Table 2.15.

Table 2.15 Truth table of logical NOT

A	!A
0	1
1	0

For example,

```
int a = 10, b;
b = !a;
```

Now, the value of `b = 0`. This is because the value of `a = 10. !a = 0`. The value of `!a` is assigned to `b`, hence, the result.

Note logical expressions operate in a short-cut fashion and stop the evaluation when it knows the final outcome for sure. For example, in a logical expression involving logical AND, if the first operand is false, then the second operand is not evaluated as it is certain that the result will be false. Similarly, for a logical expression involving logical OR, if the first operand is true, then the second operand is not evaluated as it is certain that the result will be true.

However, this approach has a side-effect. For example, consider the following expression:

```
(x > 9) && (y++ > 0)        OR       (x > 9) || (y++ > 0)
```

Here, it is logical AND expression if the first operand is false and the entire expression will not be evaluated; thus, the value of `y` will never be incremented. Same is the case with the logical `OR` expression. If the first expression is true, then the second will never be evaluated and the value of `y` will never be incremented.

Program 2.7 Write a program that demonstrates the use of relational operators.

```
using namespace std;
#include<iostream>
int main()
{     int x=10, y=20;
      cout<<"\n "<<x<< " < "<< y<< " = "<< (x<y);
      cout<<"\n "<<x<< " == "<< y<< " = "<< (x==y);
```

```
    cout<<"\n "<<x<< " ! "<< y<< " = "<< (x!=y);
    cout<<"\n "<<x<< " > "<< y<< " = "<< (x>y);
    cout<<"\n "<<x<< " >= "<< y<< " = "<< (x>=y);
    cout<<"\n "<<x<< " <= "<< y<< " = "<< (x<=y);
    return 0;
}
```

OUTPUT

```
10 < 20 = 1 (true because 10 is less than 20 is true)
10 == 20 = 0 (false because 10 is not equal to 20)
10 != 20 = 1 (true because 10 is not equal to 20)
10 > 20 = 0 (false because 10 is not greater than 20)
10 >= 20 = 0 (false because 10 is neither greater nor equal than 20)
10 <= 20 = 1 (true because 10 is less than 20)
```

2.15.5 Unary Operators

Unary operators act on single operands. C++ supports three unary operators—minus, increment, and decrement operators.

Unary Minus (–)

Unary minus operator is strikingly different from the binary arithmetic operator that operates on two operands and subtracts the second operand from the first operand. When an operand is preceded by a minus sign, the unary operator negates its value.

For example, if a number is positive, it becomes negative when preceded with a unary minus operator. Similarly, if the number is negative, it becomes positive after applying the unary minus operator, For example,

```
int a, b = 10;
a = -(b);
```

The result of this expression, is `a = -10`, because a variable b has a positive value. After applying unary minus operator `(-)` on the operand b, the value becomes `-10`, which indicates it as a negative value.

Increment Operator (++) and Decrement Operator (––)

The increment operator is a unary operator that increases the value of its operand by `1`. Similarly, the decrement operator decreases the value of its operand by `1`. For example, `--x` is equivalent to writing `x = x - 1`.

The increment/decrement operators have two `variants–prefix` or `postfix`. In a prefix expression `(++x or --x)`, the operator is applied before an operand is fetched for computation; thus, the altered value is used for the computation of the expression in which it occurs. On the contrary, in a postfix expression `(x++ or x--)`, an operator is applied after an operand is fetched for computation. Therefore, the unaltered value is used for the computation of the expression in which it occurs.

Therefore, an important point to note about unary increment and decrement operators is that `++x` is not the same as `x++`. Similarly, `--x` is not the same as `x--`. Although `++x` and `x++` both increment the value of `x` by `1`, in the second case, the value of `x` is returned before it is incremented, while, in the first case, the value of `x` is returned after it is incremented. For example,

```
int x = 10, y;
y = x++;
is equivalent to writing
```

```
y = x;
x = x + 1;
whereas, y = ++x;
is equivalent to writing
x = x + 1;
y = x;
```

The same principle applies to unary decrement operators. Note that unary operators have a higher precedence than binary operators. In an expression, if we have more than one unary operator, unlike arithmetic operators, they are evaluated from right to left.

When applying the increment or decrement operator, the operand must be a variable. In no case can this operator be applied to a constant or an expression. Therefore, the following codes will generate a compiler error.

```
using namespace std;
#include<iostream>
int main()
{
      int a = 3;
      cout<<"\n ++(a - 3) = "<< ++(a - 3);
}
```

```
using namespace std;
#include<iostream>
int main()
{
      cout<<"\n ++3 = "<< (++3);
}
```

Note When postfix ++ or –– is used with a variable in an expression, then the expression is evaluated first using the original value of the variable and then the variable is incremented or decremented by one.
Similarly, when prefix ++ or –– is used with a variable in an expression, then the variable is first incremented or decremented and then the expression is evaluated using the new value of the variable.

Program 2.8 Write a program to illustrate the use of unary prefix increment and decrement operators.

```
using namespace std;
#include<iostream>
main()
{     int num = 3;
      // Using unary prefix increment operator
      cout<<"\n The value of num = "<< num;
      cout<<"\n The value of ++num = "<< ++num;
      cout<<"\n The new value of num = "<< num;
      // Using unary prefix decrement operator
      cout<<"\n\n The value of num = "<< num;
      cout<<"\n The value of --num = "<< --num;
      cout<<"\n The new value of num = "<< num;
}
```

OUTPUT

```
The value of num = 3
The value of ++num = 4
```

```
The new value of num = 4
The value of num = 4
The value of --num = 3
The new value of num = 3
```

Program 2.9 Write a program to illustrate the use of unary postfix increment and decrement operators.

```
using namespace std;
#include<iostream>
main()
{       int num = 3;
        // Using unary postfix increment operator
        cout<<"\n The value of num = "<<num;
        cout<<"\n The value of num++ = "<< num++;
        cout<<"\n The new value of num = "<< num;
        // Using unary postfix decrement operator
        cout<<"\n\n The value of num = "<< num;
        cout<<"\n The value of num = "<< num--;
        cout<<"\n The new value of num = "<< num;
        return 0;
}
```

OUTPUT

```
The value of num = 3
The value of num++ = 3
The new value of num = 4
The value of num = 4
The value of num-- = 4
The new value of num = 3
```

2.15.6 Conditional Operators

The conditional operator or the ternary `(?:)` is just similar to an `if ... else` statement that can be within expressions. Such an operator is useful in situations in which there are two or more alternatives for an expression. The syntax of the conditional operator is as follows:

```
exp1 ? exp2 : exp3
```

`exp1` is evaluated first. If it is true, then `exp2` is evaluated and becomes the result of the expression; otherwise, `exp3` is evaluated and it becomes the result of the expression. For example,

```
large = (a > b) ? a : b
```

The conditional operator is used to find largest of two given numbers. First, `exp1`, that is `a > b` is evaluated. If `a` is greater than `b`, then `large = a`, else `large = b`. Hence, large is equal to either `a` or `b` but not both.

Therefore, conditional operator is used in certain situations, replacing `if-else` condition phrases. Conditional operators make the program code more compact, more readable, and safer to use as it is easier both to check and guarantee that the arguments that are used for evaluation.

Conditional operator is also known as ternary operator as it is neither a unary nor a binary operator; it takes three operands.

As a conditional operator is itself an expression, it can be used as an operand of another conditional operation. That means C++ allows you to have nested conditional expressions. Consider the expression given below which illustrates this concept.

```
int a = 5, b = 3, c= 7, small;
small = (a < b ? (a < c ? a : c) : (b < c ? b : c));
```

Program 2.10 Write a program two find largest of two numbers using ternary operator.

```
using namespace std;
#include<iostream>
int main()
{       int num1, num2, large;
        cout<<"\n Enter the two numbers : ";
        cin>>num1>>num2;
        large = num1>num2?num1:num2;
        cout<<"\n The largest number is : "<< large;
        return 0;
}
```

OUTPUT

```
Enter the two numbers : 23 34
The largest number is : 34
```

Program 2.11 Write a program two find largest of three numbers using ternary operator.

```
using namespace std;
#include<iostream>
int main()
{       int num1, num2, num3, large;
        cout<<"\n Enter the three numbers : ";
        cin>>num1>>num2>>num3;
        large = num1>num2?(num1>num3?num1:num3):(num2>num3?num2:num3);
        cout<<"\n The largest number is : "<< large;
        return 0;
}
```

OUTPUT

```
Enter the three numbers : 12 34 23
The largest number is : 34
```

2.15.7 Bitwise Operators

As the name suggests, bitwise operators perform operations at bit level. These operators include `bitwise AND`, `bitwise OR`, `bitwise XOR`, and `shift` operators. Bitwise operators expect their operands to be of integers and treat them as a sequence of bits.

Bitwise AND

The bitwise AND operator (&) is a small version of the boolean AND (&&) as it performs operation on bits instead of bytes, chars, integers, etc. When we use the bitwise AND operator, the bit in the first operand is `ANDed` with the corresponding bit in the second operand. The truth table is same as we had seen in logical AND operation. Therefore, the bitwise AND operator compares each bit of its first operand with the corresponding bit of its second operand. If both bits are `1`, the corresponding bit in the result is `1` and `o` otherwise.

For example,

```
10101010 & 01010101 = 00000000
```

In a C++ program, the `&` operator is used as follows:

```
int a = 10, b = 20, c = 0; c = a&b;
```

Bitwise OR

The bitwise OR operator (|) is a small version of the boolean OR (||) as it performs operation on bits instead of bytes, chars, integers, etc. When we use the bitwise OR operator, the bit in the first operand is ORed with the corresponding bit in the second operand. The truth table is same as we had seen in logical OR operation. The bitwise OR operator compares each bit of its first operand with the corresponding bit of its second operand. If one or both bits are `1`, the corresponding bit in the result is `1` and `0` otherwise.

For example,

```
10101010 & 01010101 = 11111111
```

In a C++ program, the | operator is used as follows:

```
int a = 10, b = 20, c = 0;
c = a|b
```

Bitwise XOR

The bitwise XOR operator (^) performs operation on individual bits of the operands. The truth table of bitwise XOR operator can be given as shown in Table 2.16. When we use the bitwise XOR operator, the bit in the first operand is XORed with the corresponding bit in the second operand. That is, the bitwise-XOR operator compares each bit of its first operand with the corresponding bit of its second operand. If one of the bits is `1`, the corresponding bit in the result is `1` and `0` otherwise.

For example,

Table 2.16 Truth table of bitwise XOR

A	B	A ^ B
0	0	0
0	1	1
1	0	1
1	1	0

```
10101010 ^ 01010101 = 11111111
```

In a C++ program, the ^ operator is used as follows:

```
int a = 10, b = 20, c = 0;
c = a^b
```

Bitwise NOT (~)

The bitwise NOT, or complement, is a unary operation, performs logical negation on each bit of the operand. By performing negation of each bit, it actually produces the ones' complement of the given binary value. Bitwise NOT operator sets the bit to 1, if it was initially 0 and sets it to 0 if it was initially 1. For example,

```
~10101011 = 01010100
```

Shift Operators

C++ supports two bitwise shift operators. They are shift left (<<) and shift right (>>). These operations are simple to and are responsible for shifting bits to the left or to the right.

The syntax for a shift operation can be given as follows:

```
operand op num
```

where the bits in operand are shifted left or right depending on the operator (left if the operator is << and right if the operator is >>) by number of places denoted by num.

For example, if we have x = 0001 1101, then

```
x << 1 gives result = 0011 1010
```

When we apply a left shift, every bit in x is shifted to the left by one place. Therefore, the MSB (most significant bit) of x is lost, the LSB of x is set to 0.

Therefore, if we have x = 0001 1101, then

```
x << 4 gives result = 1010 0000
```

If you observe carefully, you will notice that shifting once to the left multiplies the number by 2 Hence, multiple shifts of 1 to the left, results in multiplying the number by 2 over and over again.

On the contrary, when we apply a right shift, every bit in x is shifted to the right by one place. Therefore, the LSB (least significant bit) of x is lost, the MSB of x is set to 0. For example, if we have x = 0001 1101, then

```
x >> 1 gives result = 0000 1110.
```

Similarly, if we have x = 0001 1101, then

```
x << 4 gives result = 0000 0001,
```

If you observe carefully, you will notice that shifting once to the right divides the number by 2. Hence, multiple shifts of 1 to the right, results in dividing the number by 2 over and over again.

Note Bitwise operators are used for testing the bits or shifting them left or right. Always remember that bitwise operators cannot be applied to float or double variables.

2.15.8 Assignment Operators

The assignment operator is responsible for assigning values to the variables. While the equal sign (=) is the fundamental assignment operator, C++ language also supports other assignment operators that provide shorthand ways to represent common variable assignments.

When an equal sign is encountered in an expression, the compiler processes the statement on the right side of the sign and assigns the result to the variable on the left side. For example,

```
x;
x = 10;
= assigns the value 10 to variable x.
if we have,
int x = 2, y = 3, sum = 0;
sum = x + y;
then, sum = 5.
```

The assignment operator has right-to-left associativity, so the expression

```
a = b = c = 10;
```

is evaluated as

```
(a = (b = (c = 10)));
```

First, 10 is assigned to c, then the value of c is assigned to b. Finally, the value of b is assigned to a.

Note that the operand to the left of the assignment operator must be a variable name. C++ does not allow any expression, constant or function to be placed to the left of the assignment operator. Therefore, the statement `a + b = 0`, is invalid in C++ language.

To the right of the assignment operator, you may have an arbitrary expression. In that case, the expression would be evaluated and the result would be stored in the location denoted by the variable name.

Note An expression is a combination of operand(s) and operators to specify a computation.

Program 2.12 Write a program to demonstrate the use of assignment operators.

```
using namespace std;
#include<iostream>
main()
{   int num1 = 3, num2 = 5;
    cout<<"\n Initial value of num1 = "<<num1<<" and num2 = "<<num2;
    num1 += num2 * 4 - 7;//
    cout<<"\n After the evaluation of the expression num1 = "<<num1<<" and num2 = "<<
    num2;
    return 0;
}
```

OUTPUT

```
Initial value of num1 = 3 and num2 = 5
After the evaluation of the expression num1 = 16 and num2 = 5
```

2.15.9 Comma Operator

The comma operator in C++ takes two operands. It works by evaluating the first and discarding its value, and then evaluates the second and returns the value as the result of the expression. Comma separated operands, when chained together, are evaluated in a left-to-right sequence with the right-most value yielding the result of the expression. Among all the operators, the comma operator has the lowest precedence.

Therefore, when a comma operator is used, the entire expression evaluates to the value of the right expression.

For example, the following statement assigns the value of `b` to `x`, then increments `a`, and then increments `b`:

```
int a=2, b=3, x=0;
x = (++a, b+=a);
Now, the value of x = 6.
```

2.15.10 Sizeof Operator

The `sizeof` is a unary operator used to calculate the sizes of data types. It can be applied to all data types. When using this operator, the keyword '`sizeof`' is followed by a type name, variable, or expression. The operator returns the size of the variable, data type, or expression in bytes. Therefore, the `sizeof` operator is used to determine the amount of memory space that the variable, expression, or data type will take.

When a type name is used, it is enclosed in parentheses; however, in case of variable names and expressions, they can be specified with or without parentheses. A `sizeof` expression returns an unsigned value that specifies the size the space in bytes required by the data type, variable, or expression. For example,

```
sizeof(char) returns 1, that is the size of a character data type
```

If we have,

```
int a = 10;
unsigned int result;
result = sizeof(a);
```

then the result = 2, that is, space required to store the variable a in memory. Since a is an integer, it requires 2 bytes of storage space.

2.15.11 Operator Precedence and Associativity

C++ operators have two properties—priority and associativity. When an expression has more than one operator, then it is the relative priorities of the operators with respect to each other that determine the order in which the expression will be evaluated. Associativity defines the direction in which the operator having the same precedence acts on the operands. It can be either left-to-right or right-to-left. Therefore, priority is applied before associativity to determine the order in which thc expressions are evaluated. Associativity is then applied, if need arises.

Table 2.17 lists the operators that C++ language supports in the order of their *precedence* (highest to lowest). The associativity indicates the order in which the operators of equal precedence in an expression are evaluated.

Table 2.17 Operator precedence and associativity chart

Operator	Associativity
() [] . −> ++ −− (Postfix increment and decrement)	left-to-right
++ −− (Prefix increment and decrement) Unary + and − ! ~ (*type*) * & sizeof new delete	right-to-left
* / %	left-to-right
+ −	left-to-right
<< >>	left-to-right
< <= > >=	left-to-right
== !=	left-to-right
&	left-to-right
^	left-to-right
|	left-to-right
&&	left-to-right
||	left-to-right
?:	right-to-left
= += −= *= /= %= &= ^= |= <<= >>=	right-to-left
,	left-to-right

Note Some of the operators mentioned in the chart will be discussed in later chapters.

The priority of the assignment operator is so low is because the action of assignment is performed only when the entire computation is done. It is not uncommon for a programmer to forget the priority of the operators while writing any program. In that case, it is recommended that you use the parentheses operator to override default priorities. From Table 2.17, you can see that parenthesis operator has the highest priority. Any operator placed within the parenthesis will be evaluated before any other operator.

Examples of Expressions Using the Precedence Chart

```
1. x = 3 * 4 + 5 * 6
     = 12 + 5 * 6
     = 12 + 30
     = 42
2. x = 3 * (4 + 5) * 6
     = 3 * 9 * 6
     = 27 * 6
     = 162
3. x = 3 * 4 % 5 / 2
     = 12 % 5 / 2
     = 2 / 2
     = 1
4. x = 3 * (4 % 5) / 2
     = 3 * 4 / 2
     = 12 / 2
     = 6
5. x = 3 * 4 % (5 / 2)
     = 3 * 4 % 2
     = 12 % 2
     = 0
6. x = 3 * ((4 % 5) / 2)
     = 3 * (4 / 2)
     = 3 * 2
     = 6
   Take the following variable declarations,
   int a = 0, b = 1, c = -1;
   float x = 2.5, y = 0.0;
   If we write,
   a = b = c = 7;
   Since the assignment operator works from right-to-left, therefore
   c = 7. Then since b = c, therefore b = 7. Now a = b, so a = 7.
7. a += b -= c *= 10
   This is expanded as
   a = a + (b = b - (c = c * 10))
     = a + ( b = 1 - (-10))
     = a + ( b = 11)
     = 0 + 11
     = 11
8. --a * ( 5 + b) / 2 - c++ * b
     =--a * 6 / 2 - c++ * b
     = --a * 6 / 2 - -1 * b
   (Value of c has been incremented but its altered value will not be visible for the
   evaluation of this expression)
     = -1 * 6 / 2 - -1 * 1
```

```
(Value of a has been incremented and its altered value will be used for the evalu-
ation of this expression)
   = -1 * 3 - -1 * 1
   = -3 - -1 * 1
   = -3 - -1
   = -2
9. a * b * c
   = (a * b) * c (because associativity of * is from left-to-right)
   = 0
10. a && b = 0
11. a < b && c < b = 1
12. b + c || ! a= ( b + c) || (!a)= 0 ||1 = 1
13. x * 5 && 5 || ( b / c)= ((x * 5) && 5) || (b / c) = (12.5 && 5) || (1/-1)= 1
14. a <= 10 && x >= 1 && b = ((a <= 10) && (x >= 1)) && b= (1 && 1) && 1= 1
15. !x || !c || b + c = ((!x) || (!c)) || (b + c)= (0 || 0) || 0 = 0
16. x * y < a + b || c = ((x * y) < (a + b)) || c= (0 < 1) || -1 = 1
17. (x > y) + !a || c++ = ((x > y) + (!a)) || (c++)= (1 + 1) || 0 = 1
```

Program 2.13 Write a program to calculate area of a circle.

```
using namespace std;
#include<iostream>
int main()
{   float radius;
    double area, circumference;
    cout<<"\n Enter the radius of the circle : ";
    cin>>radius;
    area = 3.14 * radius * radius;
    circumference = 2 * 3.14 * radius;
    cout.precision(2);
    cout<<"\n AREA = "<<area<<"\t CIRCUMFERENCE = "<<circumference;
    return 0;
}
```

OUTPUT

```
Enter the radius of the circle : 7
Area = 153.86 CIRCUMFERENCE = 43.96
```

Program 2.14 Write a program to print the ASCII value of a character.

```
using namespace std;
#include<iostream>
#include<iomanip>
int main()
{   char ch;
    cout<<"\n Enter any character : ";
    cin>>ch;
    cout<<"\n The ascii value of "<<ch<<" is : "<<(int)ch;
}
```

OUTPUT

```
Enter any character : A
The ascii value of A is : 65
```

Program 2.15 Write a program to read a character in upper case and then print it in lower case.

```
using namespace std;
#include<iostream>
#include<ctype.h>  // For character functions- here to lower
int main()
{   char ch;
    cout<<"\n Enter any character in upper case : ";
    cin>>ch;

    /*to lower converts a character in its lower case. Since it returns an integer,
    the result must be converted to char */

    cout<<"\n The character in lower case is : "<<(char)tolower(ch);
}
```

OUTPUT

```
Enter any character : A
The character in lower case is : a
```

Program 2.16 Write a program to print the digit at one's place of a number.

```
using namespace std;
#include<iostream>
main()
{   int num, digit_at_ones_place;
    cout<<"\n Enter any number : ";
    cin>>num;
    digit_at_ones_place = num % 10;
    cout<<"\n The digit at ones place of "<<num<<" is "<<digit_at_ones_place;
}
```

OUTPUT

```
Enter any number : 123
The digit at ones place of 123 is 3
```

Program 2.17 Write a program to swap two numbers using a temporary variable.

```
using namespace std;
#include<iostream>
int main()
{   int num1, num2, temp;
    cout<<"\n Enter the two numbers : ";
    cin>>num1>>num2;
    temp = num1;
    num1=num2;
    num2=temp;
    cout<<"\n The first number is = "<<num1<<" and the second number = "<< num2;
}
```

OUTPUT

```
Enter the two numbers : 3 5
The first number is 5 and the second number = 3
```

Program 2.18 Write a program to swap two numbers without using a temporary variable.

```
using namespace std;
#include<iostream>
int main()
{   int num1, num2;
    cout<<"\n Enter the two numbers : ";
    cin>>num1>>num2;
    num1 = num1 + num2;
    num2= num1 - num2;
    num1 = num1 - num2;
    cout<<"\n The first number is = "<<num1<<" and second number = "<<num2;
}
```

OUTPUT

```
Enter the two numbers : 3 5
The first number is = 5 and second number = 3
```

Program 2.19 Write a program to calculate average of two numbers. Print their deviation.

```
using namespace std;
#include<iostream>
main()
{   int num1, num2;
    float avg, dev1, dev2;
    cout<<"\n Enter the two numbers : ";
    cin>>num1>>num2;
    avg = (num1 + num2) / 2;
    dev1 = num1 - avg;
    dev2 = num2 - avg;
    cout.precision(2);
    cout<<"\n AVERAGE = "<<avg;
    cout<<"\n Deviation of first number = "<< dev1;
    cout<<"\n Deviation of second number = "<< dev2;
}
```

OUTPUT

```
Enter the two numbers : 45 32
AVERAGE = 38.00
Deviation of first number = 7.00
Deviation of first number = -6.00
```

Program 2.20 Write a program to convert degrees fahrenheit into degrees celsius.

```
using namespace std;
#include<iostream>
#include<iomanip>
intmain()
{   float fahrenheit, celsius;
    cout<<"\n Enter the temperature in fahrenheit : ";
    cin>>fahrenheit;
    celsius = (0.56) * (fahrenheit - 32);
    cout<<setprecision(2);
    cout<<"\n Temperature in degrees celsius = "<<celsius;
}
```

OUTPUT

```
Enter the temperature in fahrenheit : 273
Temperature in degrees celsius = 134.96
```

Program 2.21 Write a program that displays the size of every data type.

```
using namespace std;
#include<iostream>
int main()
{   cout<<"\n The size of short integer is : "<< sizeof(short int);
    cout<<"\n The size of unsigned integer is : "<< sizeof(unsigned int);
    cout<<"\n The size of signed integer is : "<< sizeof(signed int);
    cout<<"\n The size of integer is : "<<sizeof(int);
    cout<<"\n The size of long integer is : "<< sizeof(long int);
    cout<<"\n The size of character is : "<< sizeof(char);
    cout<<"\n The size of unsigned character is : "<< sizeof(unsigned char);
    cout<<"\n The size of signed character is : "<< sizeof(signed char);
    cout<<"\n The size of floating point number is : "<< sizeof(float);
    cout<<"\n The size of double number is : "<< sizeof(double);
}
```

OUTPUT

```
The size of short integer is : 2
The size of unsigned integer is : 4
The size of signed integer is : 4
The size of integer is : 4
The size of long integer is : 4
The size of character is : 1
The size of unsigned character is : 1
The size of signed character is : 1
The size of floating point number is : 4
The size of double number is : 8
```

Program 2.22 Write a program to calculate the total amount of money in the piggybank, given the coins of Rs 10, Rs 5, Rs 2, and Re 1.

```
using namespace std;
#include<iostream>
intmain()
{   int num_of_10_coins, num_of_5_coins, num_of_2_coins, num_of_1_coins;
    float total_amt = 0.0;
    cout<<"\n Enter the number of 10Rs, 5Rs, 2Rs and 1 Re coins in the piggybank : ";
    cin>>num_of_10_coins>>num_of_5_coins>>num_of_2_coins>>num_of_1_coins;
    total_amt = num_of_10_coins * 10 + num_of_5_coins * 5 + num_of_2_coins * 2 + num_
of_1_coins;
    cout.precision(2);
    cout<<"\n Total amount in the piggybank = "<< total_amt;
}
```

OUTPUT

```
Enter the number of 10Rs coins in the piggybank : 10
Enter the number of 5Rs coins in the piggybank : 23
Enter the number of 2Rs coins in the piggybank : 43
Enter the number of 1Re coins in the piggybank : 6
Total amount in the piggybank = 307
```

Program 2.23 Write a program to calculate the bill amount for an item given its quantity sold, value, discount, and tax.

```
using namespace std;
#include<iostream>
main()
{  float total_amt, amt, sub_total, discount_amt, tax_amt, qty, val, discount, tax;
   cout<<"\n Enter the quantity of item sold : ";
   cin>>qty;
   cout<<"\n Enter the value of item : ";
   cin>>val;
   cout<<"\n Enter the discount percentage : ";
   cin>>discount;
   cout<<"\n Enter the tax : ";
   cin>>tax;
   amt = qty * val;
   discount_amt = (amt * discount)/100.0;
   sub_total = amt - discount_amt ;
   tax_amt = (sub_total * tax) /100.0;
   total_amt = sub_total + tax_amt;
   cout<<"\n\n\n *************BILL****************";
   cout<<"\n\n Quantity Sold : \t "<< qty;
   cout<<"\n Price per item : \t "<< val;
   cout<<"\n \t \t ----------";
   cout<<"\n Amount : \t\t"<<amt;
   cout<<"\n Discount : \t\t- "<< discount_amt;
   cout<<"\n \t \t ----------";
   cout<<"\n Discounted Total : \t "<<sub_total;
   cout<<"\n Tax : \t\t\t + "<< tax_amt;
   cout<<"\n \t \t ----------";
   cout<<"\n Total Amount to be paid "<< total_amt;
}
```

OUTPUT

```
Enter the quantity of item sold : 20
Enter the value of item : 300
Enter the discount percentage : 10
Enter the tax : 12
************* BILL **************"
Quantity Sold :              20
Price per item :            300
                     -------------
Amount :                   6000
Discount :                - 600
Discounted Total :         5400
Tax :                     + 648
                     -------------
Total Amount to be paid 6048
```

2.16 TYPE CONVERSION AND TYPE CASTING

Till now, we have assumed that all expressions involved data of the same type. However, we need to analyze what happens when expressions involving two different data types such as multiplying a floating point number and an integer is involved. Such type of situation is handled either through type conversion or type casting.

Type conversion or typecasting of variables refers to changing a variable of one data type into another. While type conversion is done implicitly, casting has to be done explicitly by the programmer. We will discuss these concepts.

2.16.1 Type Conversion

Type conversion is done when the expression has variables of different data types. To evaluate the expression, the data type is promoted from lower to higher level where the hierarchy of data types (from higher to lower) can be given as—`double, float, long, int, short` and `char`. Figure 2.13 shows the conversion hierarchy of data types.

Type conversion is automatically done when we assign an integer value to a floating point variable. Consider the code given below in which an integer data type is promoted to float. This is known as promotion (when a lower level data type is promoted to a higher type).

Note Implicit type conversions are also called silent conversion as the programmers' are unaware about them.

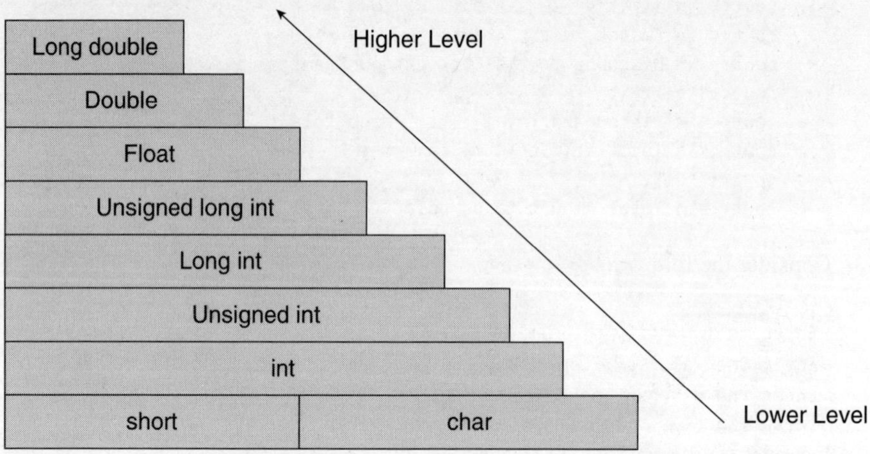

Figure 2.13 Conversion hierarchy of data types

Now, x = 3.0, as automatically the integer value is converted into its equivalent floating point representation. In some cases, when an integer is converted into a floating point number, the resulting floating point number may not exactly match the integer value. This is because the floating point number format used internally by the computer cannot accurately represent every possible integer number. Therefore, even if the value of x = 2.99999995, there is no need to worry. The loss of accuracy because of this feature would be always insignificant for the final result. Let us summarize how promotion is done:

```
float x;
int y = 3;
x = y;
```

- `float` operands are converted to `double`.
- `char or short` operands whether `signed or unsigned` are converted to `int`.
- If anyone operand is `double`, the other operand is also converted to `double`. Hence, the result is also of type `double`.
- If any one operand is `long`, the other operand is also converted to `long`. Hence, the result is also of type `long`.

Type conversion in an expression is exhibited in Fig. 2.14.

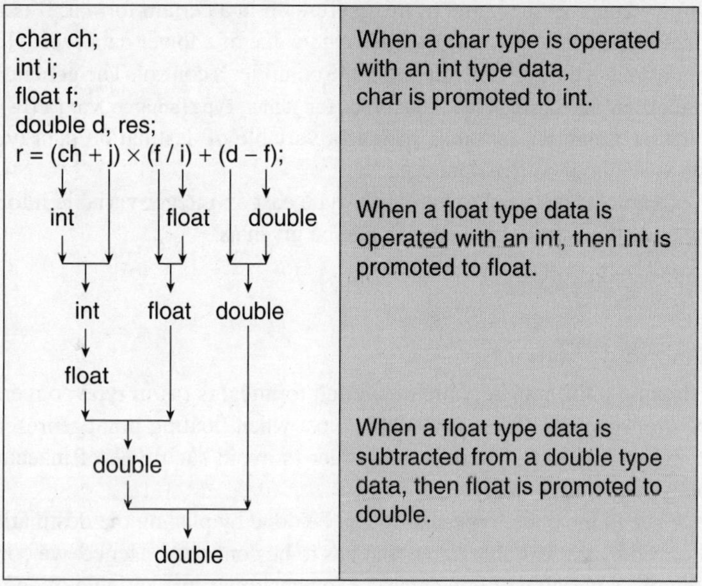

Figure 2.14 Type conversion

Consider the following group of statements.

```
float f = 3.5;
int i;
i = f;
```

The statement `i = f` results in f to be demoted to type `int`. That is, the fractional part of `f` will be lost and `I` will contain `3 (not 3.5)`. in this case demotion takes place. A higher level data type is converted into a lower type. Whenever demotion occurs, some information is lost. For example, in this case the fractional part of the floating point number is lost.

Similarly, if we convert an integer to a short integer or a `long int` to `int;` or `int` to `char`, the compiler just drops the extra bits (refer to Fig. 2.15). Note that no compile time warning message is generated when information is lost while demoting the type of data.

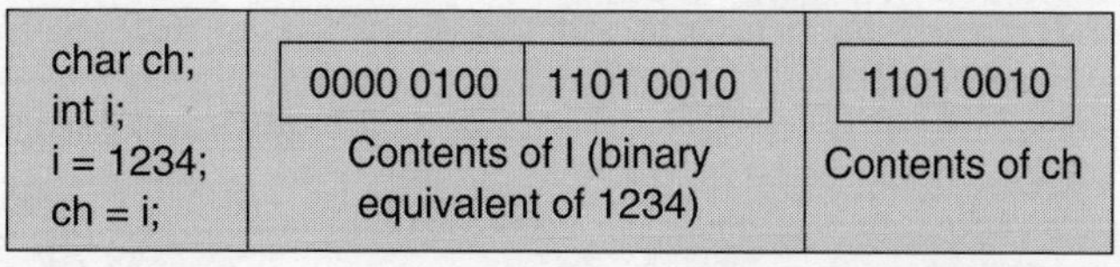

Figure 2.15 Implicit conversion example

Therefore, we can observe the following changes that are unavoidable when performing type conversions. These changes may cause incorrect results.

- When a `float` value is converted to an `integer` value, the fractional part is truncated.
- When a `double` value is converted to a `float` value, rounding of digits is done.
- When a `long int` is converted into `int`, the excess higher order bits are dropped.

2.16.2 Type Casting

Type casting is also known as forced conversion. Type casting an arithmetic expression tells the compiler to represent the value of the expression in a certain format. It is done when the value of a higher data type has to be converted into the value of a lower data type. However, this cast is under the programmer's control and not under the compiler's control. The general syntax for type casting is

`destination_variable_name = destination_data_type(source_variable_name);`

where the `destination_variable_name` is a variable of destination data type and `source_variable_name` is a variable of source data type.

For example, if we need to explicitly type cast an integer variable into a floating point variable, then the code to perform type casting can be given as,

```
float salary = 10000.00;
int sal;
sal = int(salary);
```

When floating point numbers are converted to integers (as in type conversion), the digits after the decimal are truncated. Therefore, data is lost when floating-point representations are converted to integral representations. Therefore, in order to avoid such type of inaccuracies, int type variables must be type cast to float type.

As we see in the code, typecasting can be done by placing the destination data type in parentheses, followed by the variable name that has to be converted. Hence, we conclude that typecasting is done to make a variable of one data type to act similar to a variable of another type.

We can also typecast integer values to its character equivalent (as per ASCII code) and vice versa. Typecasting is also done for arithmetic operation to get correct results. For example, when dividing two integers, the result can be of floating type. When multiplying two integers, the result can be a long int. Therefore, to get correct precision value, typecasting can be done. For example,

```
int a = 500, b = 70 ;
float res;
res = float (a/b);
```

Let us look at some more examples of type casting:

```
• res = int(9.5);
  9.5 is converted to 9 by truncation and then assigned to res
• res = int(12.3) / int(4.2);
  evaluated as 12/4 and the value 3 is assigned to res
• res = double(total/n);
  total is converted to double and then division is done in floating point mode
• res = int(a+b);
  the value of a+b is converted to integer and then assigned to res
• res = int(a + b);
  a is converted to int and then added with b
• res = cos(double(x));
converts x to double before finding its cosine value
```

Differences In C, the syntax for type casting is the `(type_name)expression`. In C++, the syntax is `type_name(expression)`. However, to support C features, C++ supports both the styles.

Program 2.24 Write a program to convert a floating point number into the corresponding integer.

```
#include<iostream.h>
int main()
{    float f_num;
     int i_num;
     cout<<"\n Enter any floating point number: ";
     cin>>f_num;
     i_num = int(f_num);
     cout<<"\n The integer variant of "<<f_num<<" = "<<i_num;
}
```

OUTPUT

```
Enter any floating point number: 23.45
The integer variant of 23.45 is = 23
```

Program 2.25 Write a program to convert an integer into the corresponding floating point number.

```
using namespace std;
#include<iostream>
int main()
{    float f_num;
     int i_num;
     cout<<"\n Enter any integer: ";
     cin>>i_num;
     f_num = float(i_num);
     cout.setf(ios::showpoint);
     cout.precision(2);
     cout<<"\n The floating point variant of "<<i_num<< " is = "<<f_num;
}
```

OUTPUT

```
Enter any integer: 12
The floating point variant of 12 is = 12.00
```

Program 2.26 Write a program to calculate a student's result based on two examinations, 1 sports event and 3 activities conducted. The weightage of activities = 30 per cent, sports = 20 per cent, and examination = 50 per cent.

```
using namespace std;
#include<iostream>
#define ACTIVITIES_WEIGHTAGE 30
#define SPORTS_WEIHTAGE 20
#define EXAMS_WEIGHTAGE 50
#define EXAMS_TOTAL 200
#define ACTIVITIES_TOTAL 60
#define SPORTS_TOTAL 50
main()
{   int exam_score1, activities_score1, sports_score;
```

```
    int exam_score2, activities_score2, activities_score3;
    float exam_total, activities_total;
    float total_percent, exam_percent, sports_percent, activities_percent;
    cout<<"\n Enter the score obtained in two examination (out of 100) : ";
    cin>>exam_score1>>exam_score2;
    cout<<"\n Enter the score obtained in sports events (out of 50) : ";
    cin>>sports_score;
    cout<<"\n Enter the score obtained in three activities (out of 20) : ";
    cin>>activities_score1>>activities_score2>>activities_score3;
    exam_total = exam_score1 + exam_score2;
    activities_total = activities_score1 + activities_score2 + activities_score3;
    exam_percent = float(exam_total * EXAMS_WEIGHTAGE / EXAMS_TOTAL);
    sports_percent = float(sports_score * SPORTS_WEIHTAGE / SPORTS_TOTAL);
    activities_percent = float(activities_total * ACTIVITIES_WEIGHTAGE / ACTIVITIES_
TOTAL);
    total_percent = exam_percent + sports_percent + activities_percent;
    cout<<"\n\n ********************** RESULT *************************";
    cout<<"\n Total percent in examination :      "<< exam_percent;
    cout<<"\n Total percent in activities  :      "<< activities_percent;
    cout<<"\n Total percent in sports      :      "<< sports_percent;
    cout<<"\n ---------------------------------------------------------";
    cout<<"\n Total percentage             :      "<< total_percent;
}
```

OUTPUT

```
Enter the score obtained in two examination (out of 100) : 78 89
Enter the score obtained in sports events (out of 50) : 34
Enter the score obtained in three activities (out of 20) : 19 18 17
********************** RESULT *************************
Total percent in examination : 41.75
Total percent in activities : 27
Total percent in sports     : 13
-------------------------------------------------------
Total percentage            : 82%
```

Points to Remember

- C++ was developed in the early 1980s by Bjarne Stroustrup.
- A function is defined as a group of C++ statements that are executed together. The execution of a C++ program begins at this function.
- Every word in a C++ program is either a keyword or an identifier. C++ has a set of reserved words often known as keywords that cannot be used as an identifier.
- A variable is defined as a meaningful name given to the data storage location in computer memory. When using a variable, we actually refer to address of the memory where the data is stored.
- The difference between signed and unsigned numeric variables is that signed variables can be either negative or positive but unsigned variables can only be positive. By default, C++ makes a signed variable.
- Return 0, returns the value 0 to the operating system to give an indication that there were no errors during the execution of the program.
- The conditional operator or the ternary (?:) is just similar to an if … else statement that can be within expressions. Conditional operator is also known as ternary operator as it is neither a unary nor a binary operator; it takes *three* operands.
- The bitwise NOT, or complement, produces the ones' complement of the given binary value.
- The comma operator evaluates the first expression and discards its value, and then evaluates the second and returns the value as the result of the expression.
- sizeof is a unary operator used to calculate the sizes of data types. This operator can be applied to all data types.

- While type conversion is done implicitly, casting has to be done explicitly by the programmer. Type casting is done when the value of a higher data type has to be converted in to the value of a lower data type.

Glossary

Constant A value that cannot be changed

Data type Definition of the data. For example, *int, char, and float*

Escape sequence Control codes that comprises of combinations of a backslash followed by letters or digits which represent non printing characters

Expression A sequence of operators and operands that may yield a single value as the result of its computation

Executable program Program which will run in the environment of the operating system or within an appropriate run time environment

Floating-point number Number that comprises a decimal place and exponent

Identifier The names used to refer to stored data values as in case of *constants, variables* or *functions*

Integer A number that has no fractional part

Keyword A word which has a predefined meaning to a 'C++' compiler and therefore must not be used for any other purpose

Library file The file which comprises of compiled versions of commonly used functions that can be linked to an object file to make an executable program

Library function A function whose source code is stored in the external *library file*

Linker The tool that connects object code and libraries to form a complete, executable program

Operator precedence The order in which operators are applied to operands during the evaluation of an expression

Preprocessor A processor which manipulates the initial directives of the source file which contains instructions that specifies how the source file shall be processed and compiled

Preprocessor directive Instructions in the source file that specifies how the file shall be processed and compiled

Program A text file that contains the source code to be compiled

Run time error A program that is encountered when a program is executed

Keywords A word which has a predefined meaning to a C++ compiler. Such words cannot be used for any other purpose

Source code A text file that contains the source code to be compiled

Statement A simple statement in C++ language that is followed by a semicolon

Syntax error An error or mistake in the source code that prevents the compiler from converting it into object code

Variable An identifier (and storage) for a data type. The value of a variable may change as the program runs.

Exercises

Fill in the Blanks

1. C++ was developed by ______.
2. ______ is a group of C++ statements that are executed together.
3. Execution of the C++ program begins at ______.
4. In memory, characters are stored as ______.
5. Return 0, returns 0 to the ______.
6. ______ finds the remainder of an integer division.
7. ______ operator reverses the value of the expression.
8. sizeof is a ______ operator used to calculate the sizes of data types.
9. ______ is also known as forced conversion.
10. endl is a ______.
11. ______ operator prints data on the monitor.
12. ______ establishes the original value for a variable.

13. Character constants are quoted using ______.
14. A C++ program ends with a ______.
15. ______ file contains mathematical functions.
16. ______ causes the cursor to move to the next line.
17. Floating point values denote ______ values by default.
18. A variable can be made constant by declaring it with the qualifier ______ at the time of initialization.
19. The sign of the result is positive in modulo division if ______.
20. Associativity of operators defines ______.
21. ______ can be used to change the order of evaluation expressions.
22. ______ operator returns the number of bytes occupied by the operand.

State True or False

1. We can have only one function in a C++ program.
2. Header files are used to store program's source code.
3. Keywords are case sensitive.
4. Variable first is same as First.
5. An identifier can contain any valid printable ASCII character.
6. Signed variables can increase the maximum positive range.
7. Commented statements are not executed by the compiler.
8. $amount is a valid identifier in C++.
9. Comments cannot be nested.
10. The equality operators have higher precedence than the relational operators.
11. Shifting once to the left multiplies the number by 2.
12. 1,234 is a valid integer constant.
13. A cout statement can generate only one line of output.
14. iostream.h is used to store the source code of the program.
15. the closing brace of main() is the logical end of the program.
16. The declaration section gives instructions to the computer.
17. Any valid printable ASCII character can be used for a variable name.
18. Declaration of variables can be done anywhere in the program.
19. Underscore can be used anywhere in the variable name.
20. amt is same as AMT in C++.
21. Void is a data type in C++.
22. cin can be used to read only one value at a time.
23. All arithmetic operators have same precedence.
24. The modulus operator can be used only with integers.
25. The expression containing all integer operands is called an integer expression.

Multiple Choice Questions

1. The operator which compares two values is
   (a) Assignment (b) Relational
   (c) Unary (d) Equal
2. Which operator is used to simultaneously evaluate two expressions with relational operators?
   (a) AND (b) OR
   (c) NOT (d) All of these
3. On how many operands does the ternary operator operate on?
   (a) 1 (b) 2
   (c) 3 (d) 4
4. Which operator produces the ones' complement of the given binary value?
   (a) Logical AND (b) Bitwise AND
   (c) Logical OR (d) Bitwise NOT
5. Which operator has the lowest precedence?
   (a) Sizeof (b) Unary
   (c) Assignment (d) Comma
6. Which of the following is not a character constant?
   (a) 'A' (b) 'bb'
   (c) "A" (d) ' '
   (e) '*'
7. Which of the following is not a floating-point constant?
   (a) 20 (b) –4.5
   (c) 'a' (d) "1"
   (e) pi
8. Identify the invalid variable names.
   (a) Initial.Name (b) A+B
   (c) $amt (d) Floats
   (e) 1st_row
9. Which operator cannot be used with float operands?
   (a) + (b) –
   (c) % (d) *
   (e) /
10. Identify the erroneous expression.
   (a) x = y = 2, 4; (b) res = ++a * 5;
   (c) res = /4; (e) res = a++ –b *2

Review Questions

1. What are header files? Why are they important? Can we write a C++ program without using any header file?
2. What are variables?
3. Explain the difference between declaration and definition.
4. How memory is reserved using a declaration statement?
5. What does the data type of a variable signify?
6. Give the structure of a C++ program.
7. What do you understand by identifiers and keywords?
8. Write a short note on basic data types that the C++ language supports.
9. Why do we need signed and unsigned char?
10. Explain the terms 'variables' and 'constants'? How many types of variables are supported by C++?
11. Why do we include `<iostream.h>` in our programs?
12. Write a short note on operators available in C++ language.
13. Give the operator precedence chart.
14. Evaluate the expression: (x > y) + ++a || !c
15. Differentiate between type casting and type conversion
16. Write a program to read an integer. Display the value of that integer in decimal, octal and hexadecimal notation.
17. How can we get formatted output in C++ programs?
18. Explain the utility of #define and #include statements.

Programming Exercises

1. Write a program that prints the a floating point value in exponential format with the following specifications:
   (a) correct to two decimal places;
   (b) correct to four decimal places; and
   (c) correct to eight decimal places.
2. Write a program to read 10 integers. Display these numbers by printing three numbers in a line separated by commas.
3. Write a program to print the count of even numbers between 1–200 and print their sum.
4. Write a program to count number of vowels in a text.
5. Write a program to read the address of a user. Display the result by breaking it in multiple lines.
6. Write a program to read two floating point numbers. Add these numbers and assign the result to an integer. Finally display the value of all the three variables.
7. Write a program to read a floating point number. Display the rightmost digit of the integral part of the number.
8. Write a program to calculate simple interest and compound interest.
9. Write a program to calculate salary of an employee given his basic pay (to be entered by the user), HRA = 10 per cent of basic pay, TA = five per cent of basic pay. Define HRA and TA as constants and use them to calculate the salary of the employee.
10. Write a program to prepare a grocery bill. For that enter the name of the items purchased, quantity in which it is purchased and its price per unit. Then display the bill in the following format.

```
**************** B I L L ****************
Item        Quantity      Price        Amount
_____________________________________________


_____________________________________________
Total Amount to be paid


_____________________________________________
```

11. Write a program using cout statement to print BYE in the following format.

```
BBB     Y   Y    EEEE
B  B     Y Y     E
BBB       Y      EEEE
B  B      Y      E
BBB       Y      EEEE
```

Find errors in the following declaration statements

```
1. int n;
2. float a b;
3. double = a, b;
4. complex a b;
5. a,b : INTEGER
6. long int a;b;
```

Find the errors in the following codes

1.
```
int a = 9;
float y = 2.0;
a = b % a;
cout<<a;
```

2.
```
int main()
{   int a = 4;
    cout<<"\n", 10 + ++a++;
    cout<<"\n"<< 10 + ++a;
    return 0;
}
```

3.
```
int main()
{   cout<<"\n", 10++;
    return 0;
}
```

Find the output of the following codes

1.
```
using namespace std;
#include<iostream>
main()
{   int x=3, y=5, z=7;
    int a, b;
        a = x * 2 + y / 5 - z * y;
    b = ++x * (y - 3) / 2 - z++ * y;
    cout<<"\n a = "<<a;
    cout<<"\n b = "<< b;
    return 0;
}
```

2.
```
using namespace std;
#include<iostream>
main()
{   int a, b =3;
    char c = 'A';
    a = b + c;
    cout<<"\n a = "<<a;
    return 0;
}
```

3.
```
using namespace std;
#include<iostream>
main()
{   int a = 4, b = 5, c= 6;
    a = b == c;
    cout<<"\n a = "<< a;
    return 0;
}
```

4.
```
using namespace std;
#include<iostream>
main()
{   int a=1, b=2, c=3, d=4, e=5, res;
    res = a + b /c - d * e;
    cout<<"\n The value of the expression a
    + b /c - d * e = "<<res;
    res = (a + b) /c - d * e;
    cout<<"\n The value of the expression (a
    + b) /c - d * e = "<<res;
    res = a + ( b / (c -d)) * e;
    cout<<"\n The value of the expression a
    +( b / (c - d)) * e = %d"<<res;
    return 0;
}
```

5.
```
using namespace std;
#include<iostream>
int main()
{   int a = 4, b = 12, c= -3, res;
    res = a > b && a < c;
    cout<<"\n"<< res;
    res = a == c || a < b;
    cout<<"\n"<< res;
    res = b >10 b && c < 0 || a > 0;
    cout<<"\n"<< res;
    res = (a/2.0 == 0.0 && b/2.0 != 0.0) ||
    c < 0.0;
    cout<<"\n "<< res;
    return 0;
}
```

6.
```
using namespace std;
#include<iostream>
int main()
{   int a = 20, b = 5, result;
    float c = 20.0, d= 5.0;
    cout<<"\n 10 + a / 4 * b = "<< 10 + a /
    4 * b;
    cout<<"\n c / d * b + a % b = "<< c / d
    * b + a % b;
    return 0;
}
```

7.
```
using namespace std;
#include<iostream>
int main()
{   int a, b;
    cout<<"\n a = "<<a<<"\t b = "<<b<<" \t a
    + b = "<<a+b;
    return 0;
}
```

8.
```
using namespace std;
#include<iostream>
int main()
{   cout<<"\n "<<'F';
}
```

9.
```
using namespace std;
#include<iostream>
 int main()
{   int n = 2;
```

```
    n = !n;
    cout<<"\n = "<< n;
  }
```

10.
```
using namespace std;
#include<iostream>
 int main()
 { int a = 100, b = 3;
   float c;
   c = a/b;
   cout<<"\n c = "<< c;
 }
```

11.
```
using namespace std;
#include<iostream>
 int main()
 { int a = 2, b = 3, c, d;
   a++;
   ++b;
   cout<<"\n a =<<a<<"b = "<<b;
 }
```

12.
```
using namespace std;
#include<iostream>
 int main()
 { int a = 2, b = 3;
   cout<<"\n "<< ++a - b;
 }
```

13.
```
using namespace std;
#include<iostream>
 int main()
 { int a = 2;
   a = a + 3*a++;
   cout<<"\n a= "<< a;
 }
```

14.
```
using namespace std;
#include<iostream>
 int main()
 { int result;
   result = 3 + 5 - 1 * 17 % -13;
   cout<<result;
   result = 3 * 2 + ( 15 / 4 % 7);
   cout<<result;
   result = 18 / 9 / 3 * 2 * 3 * 5 % 10 / 4;
   cout<<result;
 }
```

15.
```
using namespace std;
#include<iostream>
 int main()
 { int n = 2;
   cout<<"\n "<<n++<<n<<++n;
 }
```

Hint: *The arguments in the function call will be pushed from left to right. However, these arguments are evaluated from right to left.*

16.
```
using namespace std;
#include<iostream>
 main()
 { int a = -21, b = 3;
   Cout<<"\n "<< a/b + 10;
   b = -b;
   cout<<"\n "<< a/b + 10);
 }
```

17.
```
using namespace std;
#include<iostream>
main()
{  int a;
   float b;
   cout<<"\n Enter any four digit number :
   ";
   cin>>a;
   cout<<"\n Enter any floating point number
   : ";
   cin>>b;
   cout<<"\n The numbers are : <<a<<" and
   "<<b;
 }
```

18.
```
using namespace std;
#include<iostream>
 main()
 { char a, b, c;
   cout<<"\n Enter three characters : ";
   cin>>a>>b>>c;
   a++; b++; c==;
   cout<<"\n a = "<<a<<" b = "<<b<<"c = "<<c;
 }
```

19.
```
using namespace std;
#include<iostream>
 { int x=10, y=20, res;
   res = y++ + x++;
   res += ++y + ++x;
   cout<<"\n x = "<<x<<" y = "<<y<<" RESULT
   = "<<res);
 }
```

20.
```
using namespace std;
#include<iostream>
 { int x=10, y=20, res;
   res = x+++y;
   cout<<"\n x = "<<x<<" y = "<<y<<" RESULT
   = "<<res;
 }
```

21.
```
using namespace std;
#include<iostream>
main()
 { int a;
   out<<"\n"<< 1/3 + 1/3);
   cout<<"\n"<< 1.0/3.0 + 1.0/3.0);
   a = 15/10.0 + 3/2;
```

```
    cout<<"\n"<<a;
    return 0;
}
```

22.
```
using namespace std;
#include<iostream>
int main()
{  int a = 4);
   cout<<"\n", 10 + a++;
cout<<"\n"<< 10 + ++a;
return 0;
}
```

23.
```
using namespace std;
#include<iostream>
main()
{  int a = 4, b = 5;
   cout<< (a > b)? a: b);
   return 0;
}
```

24.
```
using namespace std;
#include<iostream>
int main()
{  int n = -2;
   cout<<"\n = "<< -n;
}
```

25.
```
using namespace std;
#include<iostream>
int main()
{  int a = 2, b = 3, c, d;
   c = a++;
   d = ++b;
   cout<<"\n c = <<c<<" d = "<<d);
}
```

26.
```
using namespace std;
#include<iostream>
int main()
{ int _ = 30;
  cout<<"\n _ = "<< _;
}
```

27.
```
using namespace std;
#include<iostream>
int main()
{ int a = 2, b = 3;
  cout<<"\n "<< ++(a - b);
}
```

28.
```
using namespace std;
#include<iostream>
int main()
{ int a = 2, b = 3;
  cout<<"\n a * b = "<< a*b;
  cout<<"\n a / b = "<< a/b;
  cout<<"\n a % b = "<< a%b;
  cout<<"\n a && b = "<< a*&&b;
}
```

29.
```
using namespace std;
#include<iostream>
int main()
{ int a = 2, b = 3, c=4;
  a=b==c;
  cout<<"\n a = "<<a;
}
```

30.
```
using namespace std;
#include<iostream>
#include<iomanip>
int main()
{ int num = 070;
  cout<<"\n num = "<<num;
  cout<<"\n num = "<<oct<<num;
  cout<<"\n num = "<<hex<<num;
}
```

Answers

Fill in the Blanks

1. Bjarne Stroustrup; **2.** function; **3.** main() ; **4.** ASCII codes; **5.** operating system; **6.** modulus operator; 7. Logical NOT; **8.** unary; **9.** type casting; **10.** number of values that are successfully read **11.** cout; **12.** abs() in math.h; **13.** single quotes; **14.** closing bracket; **15.** math.h; **16.** \n; **17.** double; **18.** const; **19.** the sign of the first operand is positive; **20.** the direction in which the operator having the same precedence acts on the operands; **21.** parenthesis; **22.** sizeof

State True or False

1. false	**2.** false	**3.** true	**4.** false	**5.** true	**6.** false	**7.** true	**8.** false
10. false	**11.** true	**12.** true	**13.** false	**14.** false	**15.** false	**16.** true	**17.** true
18. false	**19.** false	**20.** false	**21.** true	**22.** false	**23.** false	**24.** true	**25.** true

Multiple Choice Questions

1. (b); **2.** (a); **3.** (c); **4.**(d); **5.** (d); **6.** (c); **7.** (c) and (e); **8.** (d); **9.** (c); **10.** (c)

ANNEXURE 1

User-Defined Header Files

INTRODUCTION

At times, the programmer may need a function that provides additional processing capabilities and may want to create a separate source code file to contain that function. This would help to segregate the function from rest of the main source code. In such a situation, the user may create a user-defined header file so that the compiler knows how to call this function.

For example, if we want the factorial function to be stored in a user defined header file, then write the code of the factorial function in a file and save it as `fact.h`. Then, in the main program file, we will include the `fact.h` file and call the function in the same way as we call other functions. Look at the code given below which illustrates this concept.

```
int factorial(int num)
{
      long int f=1;
      for(;num>= 1;num--)
            f = f * num;
      return f;
}

// Contents for the main file
```

Example A1.1 Using user-defined header file

```
using namespace std;
#include<iostream>
#include "fact.h"
main()
{
      int num, f;
      cout<<"\n Enter any number : ";
      cin>>num;
      f = factorial(num);
      cout<<"\n FACTORIAL of "<<num<<" = "<<f;
```

```
    return 0;
}
```

OUTPUT

```
Enter any number : 5
Factorial of 5 is 120
```

In the code, a user-defined header file-`fact.h` has been used. The name of the header file has been enclosed within quotes to tell the compiler not to look along the standard library path, but to look in the same path as the source file.

Note that you will compile the file that contains the source code, that is the file contains the `main()`. The compiler will compile it into object code. As long as the `C++` program is syntactically correct, the object code will be created.

The linker will combine the object code, library files, and create the executable. It is the header file that links the definition of the function with the implementation.

CHAPTER 3

Decision Control and Looping Statements

KEY Concepts

If statement • If-else statement • If-else-if statement • Switch statement • While loop • Do-while loop • For loop • Nested loops • Break, continue, and goto

INTRODUCTION TO DECISION CONTROL STATEMENTS

We know that the code in a C++ program is executed sequentially from the first line of the program to the last line. The second statement is executed after the first, the third statement is executed after the second, so on, and so forth.

Although this is true in general, in some cases, we want only the selected statements to be executed. This type of conditional processing extends the usefulness of programs. It allows programmers to build a program that determines which statements of the code should be executed and which should be ignored.

C++ supports two types of decision control statements that can alter the flow of a sequence of instructions. These include conditional type branching and unconditional type branching. Figure 3.1 shows the categorization of decision control statements in C++ language.

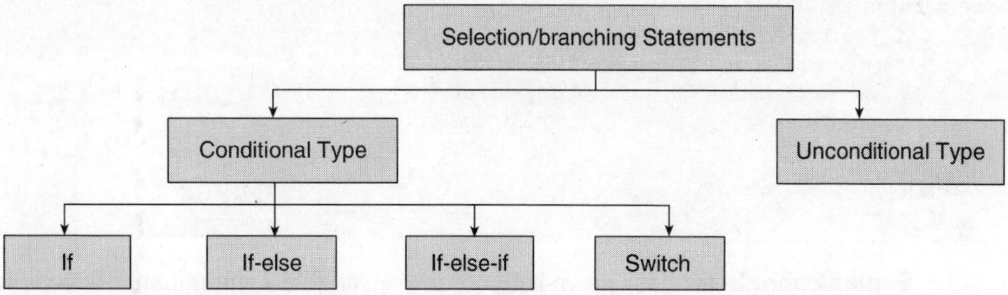

Figure 3.1 C++ decision control statements

3.1 CONDITIONAL BRANCHING STATEMENTS

Conditional branching statements help to jump from one part of the program to another depending on whether a particular condition is satisfied or not. These decision control statements include the following:

- `If` statement
- `If` else statement
- `If else if` statement
- `Switch` statement

3.1.1 If Statement

The `if` statement is the simplest form of decision control statements, frequently used in decision-making. The general form of a simple `if` statement is shown in Fig. 3.2.

```
Syntax of if statement

if(test expression 1)
{
        statement 1;
         .......
        statement n;
}
Statement x;
```

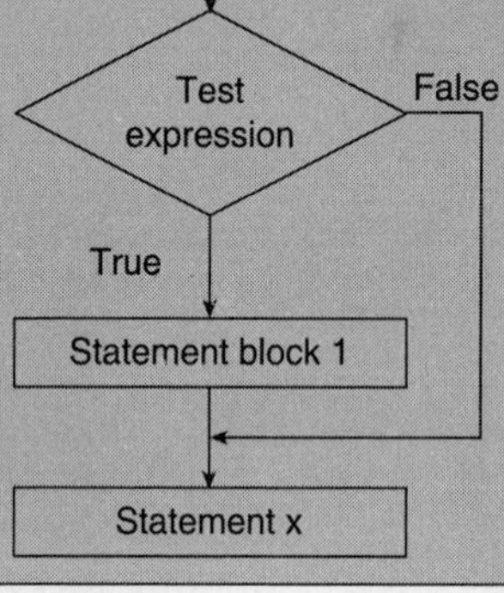

Figure 3.2 If statement construct

Programming Tip: Indent the statements that are dependent on the previous statements properly.

The `if` structure may `include 1` statement or `n` statements enclosed within curly brackets. First, the test expression is evaluated. If the test expression is true, the statement of `if` block (statement `1` to `n`) is executed; otherwise, these statements will be skipped and the execution will jump to statement `x`.

The statement in an `if` construct is any valid C++ language statement and the test expression is any valid C++ language expression that may include logical operators. Note that there is no semicolon after the test expression. This is because the condition and statement should be put together as a single statement.

Example 3.1 To check and increment a number if it is positive

```
using namespace std;
#include<iostream>
int main()
{     int x = 10;                    // Initialize the value of x
        if(x > 0)                  // Test the value of x
            x++;                     // Increment the value of x if it is > 0
        cout<<"\n x = "<<x;          // Print the value of x
}
```

OUTPUT

```
x = 11
```

Explanation: In the code given here, we take a variable `x` and initialize it to `10`. In the test expression, we check if the value of `x` is greater than `0`. If the test expression is evaluated to be true, the value of `x` is incremented. Then, the value of `x` is printed on the screen. The output of this program is as follows:

```
x = 1
```

It can be observed that the `cout` statement will be executed even if the test expression is false.

Note In case the statement block contains only one statement, putting curly brackets becomes optional. If there are more than one statement in the statement block, putting curly brackets becomes mandatory.

Program 3.1 Write a program to determine whether a person is eligible to vote.

```
using namespace std;
#include<iostream>
main()
{   int age;
    cout<<"\n Enter the age : ";
    cin>>age;
    if(age >= 18)
    cout<<"\n You are eligible to vote";
}
```

OUTPUT

```
Enter the age : 28
You are eligible to vote
```

Program 3.2 Write a program to determine the character entered by the user.

```
using namespace std;
#include<iostream>
#include<ctype.h>
main()
{       char ch;
        cout<<"\n Press any key : ";
        cin>>ch;
        if(isalpha(ch) > 0)
            cout<<"\n The user has entered a character";
        if(isdigit(ch) > 0)
            cout<<"\n The user has entered a digit";
        if(isprint(ch) > 0)
            cout<<"\n The user has entered a printable character";
        if(ispunct(ch) > 0)
            cout<<"\n The user has entered a punctuation mark";
        if(isspace(ch) > 0)
            cout<<"\n The user has entered a white space character";
}
```

OUTPUT

```
Press any key : 2
The user has entered a digit
```

3.1.2 If-Else Statement

We have studied that using the `if` statement plays a vital role in conditional branching. Its usage is very simple; the test expression is evaluated, if the result is true, the statement(s) followed by the expression is executed. If the expression is false, the statement is skipped by the compiler.

When you want a separate set of statements to be executed and the expression returns a zero value, we use an `if-else` statement rather than using a simple `if` statement. The general form of a simple `if-else` statement is shown in Fig. 3.3.

Syntax of if-else statement

```
if(test expression)
{
        statement block 1;
}
else
{
        statement block 2;
}
Statement x;
```

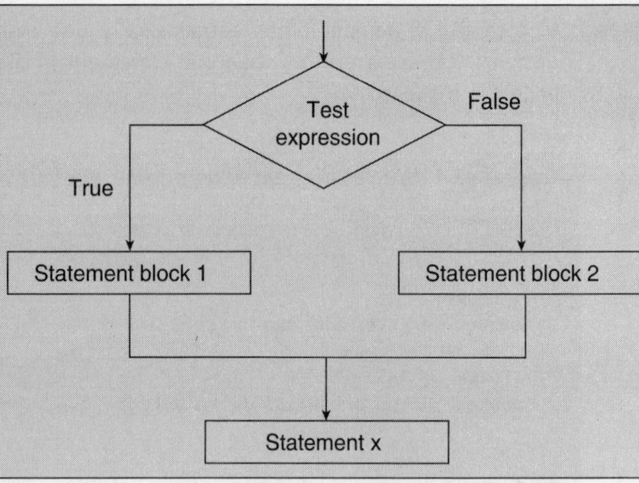

Figure 3.3 If-else statement construct

> **Programming Tip:** Align the matching `if-else` clause vertically.

In the syntax given here, we have written a statement block. A statement block may include one or more statements. According to the `if-else` construct, first, the test expression is evaluated. If the expression is true, `statement block 1` is executed and `statement block 2` is skipped. If the expression is false, `statement block 2` is executed and `statement block 1` is ignored. Now, in any case after the `statement block 1 or 2` gets executed, the control will pass to `statement x`. Therefore, `statement x` is executed in every case.

Program 3.3 Write a program to find the larger number between two numbers.

```
using namespace std;
#include<iostream>
main()
{   int a, b, large;
    cout<<"\n Enter the value of a and b : ";
    cin>>a>>b;
        if(a>b)
            large = a;
        else
            large = b;
    cout<<"\n LARGE = "<<large;
}
```

OUTPUT

```
Enter the value of a and b : 12 32
LARGE = 32
```

Program 3.4 Write a program to find whether the given number is even or odd.

```
using namespace std;
#include<iostream>
main()
{       int num;
        cout<<"\n Enter any number : ";
        cin>>num;
        if(num%2 == 0)
        cout<<"\n"<<num<<" is an even number";
        else
```

```
        cout<<"\n"<<num<<" is an odd number";
}
```

OUTPUT

```
Enter any number : 11
11 is an odd number
```

Program 3.5 Write a program to enter any character. If the entered character is in lower case, convert it into upper case. If it is a lower case character, then convert it into upper case.

```
using namespace std;
#include<iostream>
int main()
{       char ch;
        cout<<"\n Enter any character : ";
        cin>>ch;
        if(ch >='A' && ch <= 'Z')
    {       ch = ch+32;
        cout<<"\n The entered character was in upper case. In lower case it is : "<<ch;
    }
    else
    {   ch = ch-32;
        cout<<"\n The entered character was in lower case. In upper case it is : "<<ch;
    }
}
```

OUTPUT

```
Enter any character : a
The entered character was in lower case. In upper case it is A
```

Note ASCII value of A = 32 and a = 97. In order to convert a character from upper case to lower case, add 32 to it. Similarly, to convert a character from lower case to upper case, subtract 32 from it.

Program 3.6 A company decides to give bonus to all its employees on Diwali. A five per cent bonus on salary is given to male workers and 10 per cent bonus on salary to female workers. Write a program to enter the salary and sex of the employee. If the salary of the employee is less than ₹10,000 then the employee gets an extra two per cent bonus on salary. Calculate the bonus that has to be given to the employee and display the salary that the employee will get.

```
using namespace std;
#include<iostream>
main()
{   char ch;
    float sal, bonus, amt_to_be_paid;
    cout<<"\n Enter the sex of the employee (m or f): ";
    cin>>ch;
    cout<<"\n Enter the salary of the employee : ";
    cin>>sal;
    if(ch == 'm')
        bonus = 0.05 * sal;
    else
        bonus = 0.10 * sal;
    if (sal < 10000)
        bonus += 0.20 * sal;
    amt_to_be_paid = sal + bonus;
    cout<<"\n Salary = "<<sal;
```

```
    cout<<"\n Bonus = "<<bonus;
    cout<<"\n ***************************";
    cout<<"\n Amount to be paid : "<<amt_to_be_paid;
}
```

OUTPUT

```
Enter the sex of the employee (m or f): f
Enter the salary of the employee : 12000
Salary = 12000
Bonus = 1200
***************************
Amount to be paid : 13,200
```

Programming Tip: Do not use floating point numbers for checking for equality in the test expression.

Pitfall

A very common pitfall is to use assignment operator (=) instead of comparison operator (==). For example, consider the statement:

```
if(a = 10)
    cout<<a;
```

Here, the statement does not test whether a is equal to 10 or not. Rather, the value 10 is assigned to a and the value is returned to the if construct for testing. As the value of a is non-zero, the if construct returns a 1.

The compiler cannot detect such kinds of errors; hence, the programmer should use the operators carefully. The program code given in Fig. 3.4 shows the outcome of mishandling the assignment and the comparison operators.

```
using namespace std;
#include<iostream>
main()
{     int x = 2, y = 3;
      if(x = y)
            cout<<"\n EQUAL";
      else
            cout<<"\n NOT EQUAL";
}
```

OUTPUT

EQUAL

```
using namespace std;
#include<iostream>
main()
{     int x = 2, y = 3;
      if(x == y)
            cout("\n EQUAL");
      else
            cout("\n NOT EQUAL");
}
```

OUTPUT

NOT EQUAL

Figure 3.4 Outcome of mishandling the assignment and the comparison operators

Programming Tip: Braces must be placed on separate lines so that the block of statements can be easily identified

3.1.3 If-Else-If Statement

C language supports if-else-if statements to test additional conditions apart from the initial test expression. The if-else-if construct works in the same way as a normal if statement. The if-else-if construct is also known as a nested if construct. Its construct is given in Fig. 3.5.

It is not necessary that every if statement should have an else block as C++ supports simple if statements. After the first test expression or the first if branch, the programmer can have as many else if branches as he wants depending on the expressions that have to be tested.

Syntax of if-else-if statement

```
if(test expression 1)
{
        statement block 1;
}
else if(test expression 2)
{
        statement block 2;
}
.....................
else if(test expression N)
{
        statement block N;
}
else
{
        statement Block X;
}
Statement Y;
```

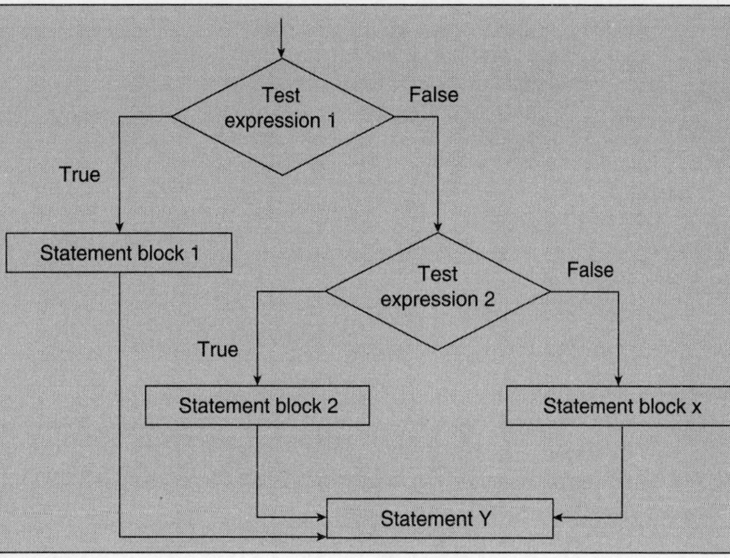

Figure 3.5 If-else-if statement construct

Example 3.2 To test whether a number entered by the user is negative, positive or equal to zero

> **Programming Tip:** Keep the logical expressions simple and short. For this, you may use nested if statements.

```
using namespace std;
#include<iostream>
main()
{      int num;
       cout<<"\n Enter any number : ";
       cin>>num;
       if(num == 0)
            cout<<"\n The value is equal to zero";
       else if(num > 0)
            cout<<"\n The number is positive";
       else
            cout<<"\n The number is negative";
}
```

OUTPUT

```
Enter any number: 0
The number is zero
```

Explanation: In this program, if the first test expression evaluates a true value, then rest of the statements in the code will be ignored and after executing the cout statement, it displays `'The value is equal to zero'`, the control will jump to `return 0` statement.

Example 3.3 To show the usage of the `if-else-if` statement for finding the division of a student

```
using namespace std;
#include<iostream>
main()
{      int marks;
       cout<<"\n Enter the marks obtained : ";
       cin>>marks;
   if (marks >= 75)
       cout<<"\n DISTINCTION";
```

```
        else if (marks >= 60 && marks < 75)
        cout<<"\n FIRST DIVISION";
        else if (marks >= 50 && marks < 60)
        cout<<"\n SECOND DIVISION";
        else if (marks >= 40 && marks < 50)
        cout<<"\n THIRD DIVISION";
    else
        cout<<"\n FAIL";
}
```

OUTPUT

```
Enter the marks obtained : 55
SECOND DIVISION
```

Note Use the AND operand (&&) to form a compound relation expression. In C++, the following expression is invalid.

```
if (60 ≤ marks ≤ 75)
```

The correct way is to write

```
if ((marks ≥ 60) && (marks ≤ 75)
```

Program 3.7 Write a program to demonstrate the use of nested `if` structure.

```
using namespace std;
#include<iostream>
{   int x, y;
    cout<<"\n Enter two numbers : ";
    cin>>x>>y ;
    if(x == y)
        cout<<"\n The two numbers are equal";
    else if(x > y)
        cout<<"\n "<<x<<" is greater than "<<y;
    else
        cout<<"\n "<<y<<" is less than "<<y;
}
```

OUTPUT

```
Enter two numbers : 12 23
12 is less than 23
```

Program 3.8 Write a program to find whether a given year is leap year or not.

```
using namespace std;
#include<iostream>
int main()
{   int year;
    cout<<"\n Enter any year : ";
    cin>>year;
    if((year%4 == 0 && year%100 != 0) || (year%400 == 0))
        cout<<"\n Leap Year";
    else
        cout<<"\n Not A Leap Year";
}
```

OUTPUT

```
Enter any year : 1996
Leap Year
```

Program 3.9 Write a program to calculate tax given the following conditions.
If income is less than ₹1,50,000, then no tax
if taxable income is ₹1,50,001 - ₹300,000, then charge 10 per cent tax
if taxable income is ₹3,00,001 - ₹500,000, then charge 20 per cent tax
if taxable income is above ₹5,00,001, then charge 30 per cent tax

```
using namespace std;
#include<iostream>
#define MIN1 150001
#define MAX1 300000
#define RATE1 0.10
#define MIN2 300001
#define MAX2 500000
#define RATE2 0.20
#define MIN3 500001
#define RATE3 0.30
main()
{   double income, taxable_income, tax;
    cout<<"\n Enter the income : ";
    cin>>income;
    taxable_income = income - 150000;
    if(taxable_income <= 0)
        cout<<"\n NO TAX";
    else if(taxable_income >= MIN1 && taxable_income < MAX1)
        tax = (taxable_income - MIN1) * RATE1;
    else if(taxable_income >= MIN2 && taxable_income < MAX2)
        tax = (taxable_income - MIN2) * RATE2;
    else
        tax = (taxable_income - MIN3) * RATE3;
    cout<<"\n TAX = "<<tax;
}
```

OUTPUT

```
Enter the income : 900000
TAX = 74999.70
```

Program 3.10 Write a program to find the greatest number from three numbers.

```
using namespace std;
#include<iostream>
int main()
{   int num1, num2, num3, big = 0;
    cout<<"\n Enter the three numbers : ";
    cin>>num1>>num2>>num3;
    if(num1 > num2)
    {
        if(num1 > num3)
            cout<<"\n"<<num1<<" is greater than "<<num2<<" and "<<num3;
        else
            cout<<"\n"<<num3<<" is greater than "<<num1<<" and "<<num2;
    }
        else if(num2 > num3)
            cout<<"\n"<<num2<<" is greater than "<<num1<<" and "<<num3;
        else
            cout<<"\n The three numbers are equal";
}
```

OUTPUT

```
Enter the three numbers : 12 23 9
23 is greater than 12 and 9
```

Program 3.11 Write a program to take input from the user and then check whether it is a number or a character. If it is a character, determine whether it is in upper case or lower case.

```
using namespace std;
#include<iostream>
int main()
{   char ch;
    cout<<"\n Enter any character : ";
    cin>>ch;
    if(ch >= 'A' && ch <= 'Z')
        cout<<"\n Upper case character was entered";
    if(ch >= 'a' && ch <= 'z')
        cout<<"\n Lower case character was entered";
    else if(ch >= '0' && ch <= '9')
        cout<<"\n You entered a number";
    return 0;
}
```

OUTPUT

```
Enter any character : C
Upper case character was entered
```

Program 3.12 Write a program to enter the marks of a student in four subjects. Then calculate the total, aggregate, and display the grade obtained by the student. If the student scores aggregate is greater than 75 per cent, then the grade is Distinction. If aggregate is 60 >= and < 75, then the grade is First Division. If aggregate is 50 >= and < 60, then the grade is Second Division. If aggregate is 40 >= and ω 50, then the grade is Third Division. Else the grade is Fail.

```
using namespace std;
#include<iostream>
main()
{   int marks1, marks2, marks3, marks4, total = 0;
    float avg = 0.0;
        cout<<"\n Enter the marks in Mathematics, Science, Social Science and Computers : ";
        cin>>marks1>>marks2>>marks3>>marks4;
        total = marks1 + marks2 + marks3 + marks4;
        avg = (float)total/4;
        cout<<"\n Total = "<<total<<"\t Aggregate = "<<avg;
        if(avg >= 75)
            cout<<"\n DISTINCTION";
        else if(avg >= 60 && avg<75)
            cout<<"\n FIRST DIVISION";
        else if(avg >= 50 && avg<60)
            cout<<"\n SECOND DIVISION";
        else if(avg >= 40 && avg < 50)
            cout<<"\n THIRD DIVISION";
        else
            cout<<"\n FAIL";
}
```

OUTPUT

```
Enter the marks in Mathematics, Science, Social Science and Computers : 90 91 92 93
TOTAL = 366 AGGREGATE = 91.00
DISTINCTION
```

Program 3.13 Write a program to calculate roots of a quadratic equation.

```
using namespace std;
#include<iostream>
#include<math.h>
int main()
{   int a, b, c;
    float D, deno, root1, root2;
    cout<<"\n Enter the values of a, b and c :";
            cin>>a>>b>>c;
                D = (b * b) - (4 * a * c);
                deno = 2 * a;
                if(D > 0)
                { cout<<"\n REAL ROOTS";
                    root1 = (-b + sqrt(D)) / deno;
                    root2 = (-b - sqrt(D)) / deno;
                    cout<<"\n ROOT1 = "<<root1<<"\t ROOT 2 = "<<root2;
                }
        else if(D == 0)
        {
            cout<<"\n EQUAL ROOTS";
            root1 = -b/deno;
            cout<<"\n ROOT1 = "<<root1<<"\t ROOT 2 = "<< root2;
        }
        else
            cout<<"\n IMAGINARY ROOTS";
}
```

OUTPUT

```
Enter the values of a, b and c : 3 4 5
IMAGINARY ROOTS
```

Programming Tip: The opening and closing braces must be aligned properly.

Let us now summarize the rules for using `if`, `if-else`, and `if-else-if` statements.

- **Rule 1** The expression must be enclosed in parentheses.
- **Rule 2** No semicolon is placed after the `if/if-else/if-else-if` statement. Semicolon is placed only at the end of statements in the statement block.
- **Rule 3** A statement block begins and ends with a curly brace. No semicolon is place after the opening or closing braces.

Dangling Else Problem

With nesting of `if-else` statements, we often encounter a problem known as dangling else problem. This problem is created when there is no matching `else` for each `if` statement. In such cases, C++ always pairs an `else` statement to the most recent unpaired `if` statement in the current block. Consider the code given here which shows such a scenario.

```
if(a > b)
    if(a > c)
        cout<<"\n a is greater than b and c";
    else
        cout<<"\n a is not greater than b and c";
```

Programming Tip: While forming the conditional expression, try to use positive statements rather than using compound negative statements.

The problem is that both the outer `if` statement and the inner `if` statement might conceivably own the `else` clause. The C++ solution to pair the if-construct with the nearest `if` may not always be correct. Therefore, the programmer must always see that every `if` statement is paired with an appropriate else statement.

Comparing floating point numbers

Never test floating point numbers for exact equality. This is because floating point numbers are just approximations; it is always better to test floating point numbers for 'approximately equal' rather than testing for exactly equal.

We can test for approximate equality by subtracting two floating point numbers (that are to be tested) and comparing their absolute value of the difference against a very small number, **epsilon**. For example, consider the code given here which compares two floating point numbers. Note that epsilon is chosen by the programmer to be small enough so that the two numbers can be considered equal.

```
using namespace std;
#include<iostream>
#define EPSILON 1.0e-5
main()
{   double num1 = 10.0, num2 = 9.5;
    double res1, res2;
    res1 = num2 / num1 * num1;
    res2 = num2;
    /*fabs() is a C++ library function that returns the floating point absolute value */
    if(fabs(res2 - res1) < EPSILON)
        cout<<"EQUAL";
    else
        cout<<"NOT EQUAL";
}
```

Adding a very small floating point value to a very large floating point value or subtracting floating point numbers of widely differing magnitudes may not have any effect on the result (or on the original number). This is because adding or subtracting two floating point numbers that differ in magnitude by more than the precision of the data type used will not affect the larger number.

3.1.4 Switch Case Statement

A `switch case` statement is a multi-way decision statement that is a simplified version of an `if-else` block that evaluates only one variable. The general form of a `switch` statement is shown in Fig. 3.6. Table 3.1 compares the general form of a `switch` statement with that of an `if-else` statement

Note Statement block 1, statement block 2, and so on, are statement lists that may contain zero or more statements. These statements in the block are not enclosed within opening and closing braces.

Programming Tip: It is always recommended to use default label in a `switch` statement.

Table 3.1 Comparison between `switch` case and `if-else` constructs

Generalized form of `switch case` statement	Generalized form of `if-else` statement

switch(x) {
case 1: // do this
case 2: // do this
case 3: // do this
....
default:
//do this
}
	if(exp1) {
	// do this
	} else if(exp2) {
	// do this
	} else if(exp3) {
	// do this
	}

syntax of switch case statement

```
switch (variable)
{
   case  value1:
      Statement Block 1;
      break;
   case  value2:
      Statement Block 2;
      break;
      .......
   case  value N:
      Statement Block N;
      break;
   default:
      Statement Block D;
      break;
}
Statement X;
```

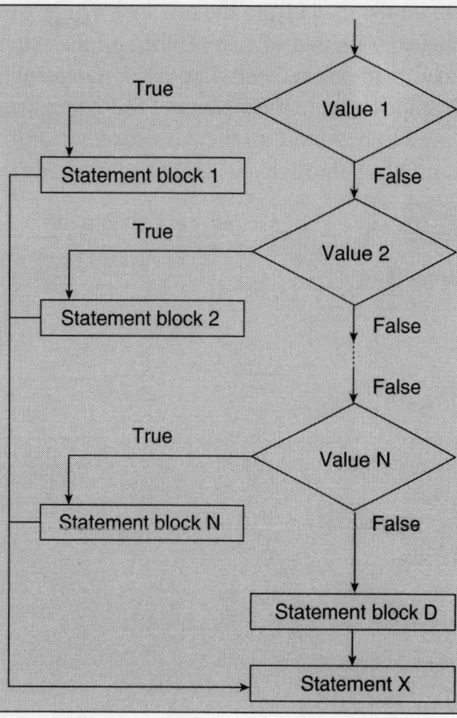

Figure 3.6 The switch case statement construct

The power of a nested `if-else` statement lies in the fact that it can evaluate more than one expression in a single logical structure. Switch statements are mostly used in two situations as follows:

- When there is only one variable to evaluate in the expression
- When many conditions are being tested for

> **Programming Tip:** C++ supports decision control statements that can alter the flow of a sequence of instructions. A `switch case` statement is a multi-way decision statement that is a simplified version of an `if-else` block that evaluates only one variable.

When there are many conditions to test, using the `if` and `else if` constructs becomes a bit complicated and confusing. Therefore, `switch` case statements are often used as an alternative to long `if` statements that compare a variable to several integral values. Integral values are those values that can be expressed as an integer, such as the value of a char. `Switch` statements are also used to handle the input given by the user.

We have already seen the syntax of the `switch` statement. The `switch case` statement compares the value of the variable given in the `switch` statement with the value of each case statement that follows it. This happens when the value of the switch and the `case` statement matches the statement block of that particular case is executed.

There is a keyword default in the syntax of the `switch case` statement. `Default` is also a case that is executed when the value of the variable does not match with any of the values of the case statement. Therefore, default case is executed when there is no match found between the values of `switch` and `case` statements and there are no statements to be executed. Although the `default case` is optional, it is always recommended to include it as it handles any unexpected cases.

In the syntax of the `switch case` statement, we have used another keyword, `break`. The `break` statement must be used at the end of each case because if it were not used, then all the cases from the one met will be executed. For example, if the value of `switch` statement matched with that of `case 2`, then all the statements in `case 2` as well as rest of the cases including default will be executed. The `break` statement tells the compiler to jump out of the `switch case` statement and execute the statement following the `switch case` construct. Therefore, the keyword `break` is used to break out of the `case` statements. It indicates the end of a case and prevents the program from falling through and executing the code in all the rest of the `case` statements.

Example 3.4 Usage of `switch case` statement

```
using namespace std;
#include<iostream>
void main()
{
char grade = 'C';
switch(grade)
{   case 'O':     cout<<"\n Outstanding";
                   break;
    case 'A':     cout<<"\n Excellent";
                   break;
    case 'B':     cout<<"\n Good";
                   break;
    case 'C':     cout<<"\n Fair";
                   break;
    case 'F':     cout<<"\n Fail";
                   break;
    default:     cout<<"\n Invalid Grade";
                   break;
}
}
```

OUTPUT

```
Fair
```

Example 3.5 To demonstrate the use of `switch` statement without a break

```
using namespace std;
#include<iostream>
main()
{   int option = 1;
    switch(option)
        {   case 1: cout<<"\n In case 1";
            case 2: cout<<"\n In case 2";
            default: cout<<"\n In case default";
        }
}
```

OUTPUT

```
In case 1
In case 2
In case default
```

If the value of option had been 2, then the output would have been

```
In case 2
In case default
```

If the option was equal to 3 or any other value, then only the default case would have been executed thereby printing the following:

```
In case default
```

Programming Tip: Keep the logical expressions simple and short. For this, you may use nested `if` statements.

To summarize the `switch case` construct, let us go through the following rules:

- The control expression that follows the keyword `switch` must be of integral type. It can either be an integer or any value that can be converted to an integer.
- Each `case` label should be followed with a constant or a constant expression.
- Every `case` label must evaluate to a unique constant expression value.
- `Case` labels must end with a colon.
- Two `case` labels may have the same set of actions associated with them.
- The default label is optional and is executed only when the value of the expression does not match with any labelled constant expression. It is recommended to have a `default case` in every `switch case` statement.
- The `default` label can be placed anywhere in the `switch` statement. However, the most appropriate position of the `default case` is at the end of the `switch case` statement.
- There can be at most one `default` label in a `switch` statement.
- C++ permits nested `switch` statements, that is, `switch` statement within another `switch` statement. ….

Program 3.14 Write a program to determine whether an entered character is a vowel or not.

```
using namespace std;
#include<iostream>
int main()
{   char ch;
    cout<<"\n Enter any character : ";
    cin>>ch;
    switch(ch)
        {   case 'A':
            case 'a':
            case 'E':
            case 'e':
            case 'I':
            case 'i':
            case 'O':
            case 'o':
            case 'U':
            case 'u':
                cout<<"\n "<<ch<<" is VOWEL";
                break;
            default: cout<< "\n "<<ch<<" is not a vowel";
        }
}
```

Assignment Try the same program using if-else statement.

Programming Tip: `default` is also a case that is executed when the value of the variable does not match with any of the values of the case statement.

OUTPUT

```
Enter any character : E
E is a VOWEL
```

Note In this program, if there is no `break` statement and if the character 'A' is entered, then control will execute the statements given in case 'a'.

Program 3.15 Write a program to enter a number from 1–7 and display the corresponding day of the week using `switch case` statement.

```
using namespace std;
#include<iostream>
int main()
{   int day;
    cout<<"\n Enter any number from 1 to 7 : ";
    cin>>day;
    switch(day)
    {   case 1 : cout<<"\n SUNDAY";      break;
        case 2 : cout<<"\n MONDAY";      break;
        case 3 : cout<<"\n TUESDAY";     break;
        case 4 : cout<<"\n WEDNESDAY";     break;
        case 5 : cout<<"\n THURSDAY";    break;
        case 6 : cout<<"\n FRIDAY";      break;
        case 7 : cout<<"\n SATURDAY";    break;
        default: cout<<"\n Wrong Number";
    }
}
```

OUTPUT

```
Enter any number from 1 to 7 : 5
THURSDAY
```

Program 3.16 Write a program that accepts a number from 1–10. Print whether the number is even or odd using a `switch-case` construct.

```
using namespace std;
#include<iostream>
main()
{   int num;
    cout<<"\n Enter any number from 1 to 10 : ";
    cin>>num;
    switch(num)
    {   case 1:
        case 3:
        case 5:
        case 7:
        case 9:   cout<<"\n ODD";     break;
        case 2:
        case 4:
        case 6:
        case 8:
        case 10:   cout<<"\n EVEN";     break;
        default : cout<<"\n INVALID INPUT";
    }
}
```

OUTPUT

```
Enter any number from 1 to 10 : 7
ODD
```

Advantages of Using a Switch Case Statement

Switch case statement is preferred by programmers for the following reasons:

- Easy to debug
- Easy to read and understand

- Ease of maintenance as compared to its equivalent `if-else` statements
- Like `if-else` statements, switch statements can also be nested
- Execute faster than its equivalent `if-else construct`

Note C++ allow programmers to use nested `switch case` statements.

3.2 ITERATIVE STATEMENTS

Iterative statements are used to repeat the execution of a list of statements, depending on the value of an integer expression. C++ language supports three types of iterative statements. These statements are also known as looping statements. They are as follows:

- While loop
- Do-while loop
- For loop

In this section, we will discuss all these statements.

3.2.1 While Loop

The `while` loop provides a mechanism to repeat one or more statements if a particular condition is true. Figure 3.7 shows the syntax and general form of representation of a `while` loop.

Programming Tip: Iterative statements are used to repeat the execution of a list of statements, depending on the value of an integer expression.

Syntax of while loop

```
Statement X;
while(condition)
{
        Statement Block;
}
Statement y;
```

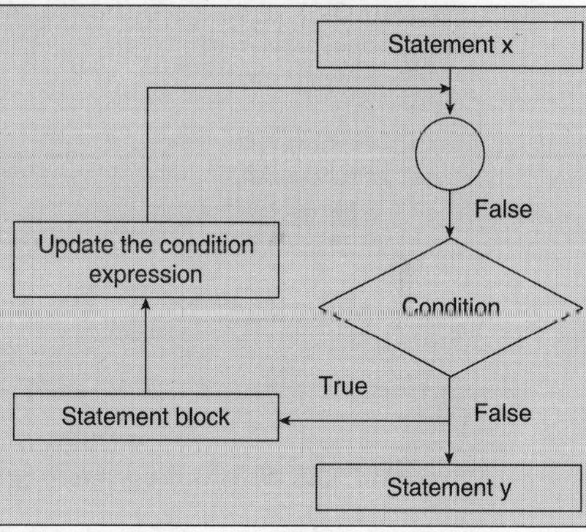

Figure 3.7 The `while` loop construct

Note In the `while` loop, the condition is tested before any of the statements in the statement block is executed. If the condition is true, only then the statements will be executed. If the condition is false, the control will jump to statement `y`, that is the immediate statement outside the `while` loop block.

Programming Tip: Check that the relational operator is not mistyped as an assignment operator.

In the flow diagram, it is clear that we need to constantly update the condition of the `while` loop. This condition determines the end of the loop. The `while` loop will execute as long as the condition is true. If the condition is never updated and the condition never becomes false, the computer will run into an infinite loop, which is never desirable.

A `while` loop is also referred to as a top-checking loop since control condition is placed as the first line of the code. If the control condition evaluates to false, then the statements enclosed in the loop are never executed.

Example 3.6 To print first 10 numbers using a `while` loop

```
using namespace std;
#include<iostream>
int main()
{   int i = 0;  // initialize loop variable
    while(i <= 10) // test the condition
    {           // execute the loop statements
            cout<<"\t"<<i;
            i = i + 1;          // condition updated
    }
}
```

OUTPUT

```
0  1  2  3  4  5  6  7  8  9  10
```

Explanation: In the program given here, initially, `i = 0` and is less than 10, and if the condition is true, in the `while` loop, the value of `i` is printed and the condition is updated so that with every execution of the loop, the condition becomes more approachable.

Let us look at some more programming examples that illustrate the use of `while` loop.

Program 3.17 Write a program to calculate the sum of first 10 numbers.

```
using namespace std;
#include<iostream>
int main()
{   int i = 0, sum = 0;
    while(i <= 10)
    {   sum = sum + i;
        i = i + 1;          // condition updated
    }
        cout<<"\n SUM = "<<SUM;
}
```

OUTPUT

```
SUM = 55
```

Program 3.18 Write a program to print 20 horizontal asterisks (*).

```
using namespace std;
#include<iostream>
main()
{   int i = 1;
    while(i <= 20)
    {   cout<<"*";
        i++;
    }
}
```

OUTPUT

```
********************
```

Program 3.19 Write a program to calculate the sum of numbers from m to n.

```
using namespace std;
#include<iostream>
int main()
{   int n, m, sum = 0;
```

```
    cout<<"\n Enter the value of m and n : ";
    cin>>m>>n;
// m is now the starting limit and n is the ending limit
    while(m <= n)
    {   sum = sum + m;
        m = m + 1;
    }
        cout<<"\n SUM = "<<sum;
}
```

OUTPUT

```
Enter the value of m and n : 7 11
SUM = 45
```

Program 3.20 Write a program to display the largest of 10 numbers using ternary operator.

```
using namespace std;
#include<iostream>
int main()
{   int i = 0, large = -1, num;
    while(i <= 10)
    {   cout<<"\n Enter the number : ";
        cin>>num;
        large = num>large?num:large;
        i++;
    }
    cout<<"\n The largest of ten numbers entered is : "<<large;
}
```

SAMPLE OUTPUT

```
Enter the number : 72
..............................
Enter the number : 108
The largest of ten numbers entered is : 108
```

Program 3.21 Write a program to read the numbers until –1 is encountered. Count the negative, positive, and zeroes entered by the user.

```
using namespace std;
#include<iostream>
int main()
{   int num;
    int negatives = 0, positives = 0, zeroes = 0;
    cout<<"\n Enter -1 to exit….";
    cout<<"\n\n Enter any number : ";
    cin>>num;
//The program will accept numbers until -1 is entered
    while(num != -1)
    {   if(num > 0)
            positives++;
        else if(num < 0)
            negatives++;
        else
            zeroes++;
        cout<<"\n\n Enter any number : ";
        cin>>num;
    }
```

```
    cout<<"\n Count of positive numbers entered = "<< positives;
    cout<<"\n Count of negative numbers entered = "<< negatives;
    cout<<"\n Count of zeroes entered = "<<zeroes;
}
```

SAMPLE OUTPUT

```
Count of positive numbers entered = 10
Count of negative numbers entered = 4
Count of zeroes entered = 3
```

Program 3.22 Write a program to calculate the average of numbers entered by the user.

```
using namespace std;
#include<iostream>
int main()
{    int num, sum = 0, count = 0;
 float avg;
 cout<<"\n Enter any number. Enter -1 to STOP";
 cin>>num;
 while(num != -1)
 {   count++;
     sum = sum + num;
     cout<<"\n Enter any number. Enter -1 to STOP";
     cin>>num;
 }
 avg = (float)sum/count;
 cout<<"\n SUM = "<< sum<<"\t AVERAGE = "<<avg;
}
```

SAMPLE OUTPUT

```
SUM = 250     AVERAGE = 2.5
```

Programming Tip: Placing a semicolon after the `while`/`for` loop in not a syntax error. So it will not be reported by the compiler. However, it is considered to be a logical error as it changes output of the program.

Therefore, we see that the `while` loop is very useful for designing interactive programs in which the number of times the statements in loop has to be executed is not known in advance. The program will execute until the user wants to stop by entering `-1`.

Now, look at the code given here which hangs the computer up in an infinite loop. The code is supposed to calculate average of first `10` numbers; however, since the condition never becomes `false`, the output will not be generated and the intended task will not be performed.

Example 3.7 To demonstrate an infinite loop

```
using namespace std;
#include<iostream>
int main()
{   int i = 0, sum =0;
    float avg = 0.0;
    while(i <= 10)
        sum = sum + i;
        avg = sum/10;
        cout<<"\n The sum of first 10 numbers = "<<sum;
        cout<<"\n The average of first 10 numbers = "<<avg;
}
```

SAMPLE OUTPUT

ERROR

Explanation: The above program will not give the desired output but will enter in an infinite loop.

3.2.2 Do-while Loop

The `do-while` loop is similar to the `while` loop. The only difference is that in a `do-while` loop, the test condition is tested at the end of the loop. This clearly means that the body of the loop gets executed at least one time (even if the condition is false). Figure 3.8 shows the syntax and general form of representation of a `do-while` loop.

```
Syntax of do-while loop

Statement X;
do
{
        Statement Block;
} while(condition)
Statement y;
```

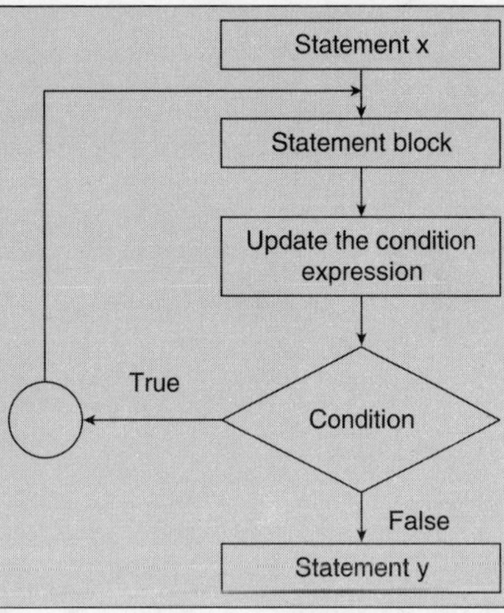

Figure 3.8 Do-while construct

The test condition is enclosed in parentheses and is followed by a semicolon. The statements in the statement block are encapsulated within a curly bracket. The curly bracket is optional if there is only one statement in the body of the `do-while` loop.

Like the `while` loop, the `do-while` loop continues to execute while a condition is `true`. There is no choice whether to execute the loop or not because the loop will be executed at least once irrespective of whether the condition is true or false. Hence, entry in the loop is automatic there is only a choice to continue it further or not. The `do while` loop will continue to execute while the condition is `true` and when the condition becomes `false,` the control will jump to statement following the `do-while` loop.

Similar to the `while` loop, the `do-while` is an indefinite loop as the loop can execute until the users want to stop. The number of times the loop has to be executed can be determined at the run time. However, unlike the `while` loop, the `do-while` loop is a bottom-checking loop, as the control expression is placed after the body of the loop.

The major disadvantage of using a `do-while` loop is that it always executes at least once; therefore, even if the user enters some invalid data, the loop will be executed. However, `do-while` loops are widely used to print a list of options for a menu driven program.

For example, look at the code given here.

```
using namespace std;
#include<iostream>
int main()
{   int i = 0;
    do
    {   cout<<"\n "<<i;
```

```
        i = i + 1;
    } while(i <= 10);
}
```

What do you think will be the output? The code will print numbers from `0 to 10`.

Program 3.23 Write a program to calculate the average of first n numbers.

Programming Tip: Do not forget to place a semicolon at the end of the do-while statement.

```
using namespace std;
#include<iostream>
int main()
{ int n, i = 0, sum = 0;
  float avg = 0.0;
  cout<<"\n Enter the value of n : ";
  cin>>n;
  do
  {   sum = sum + i;
      i = i + 1;
  } while(i <= n);
      avg = sum/n;
      cout<<"\n The sum of first n numbers = "<<sum;
      cout<<"\n The average of first "<<n<<" numbers = "<<avg;
}
```

OUTPUT

```
Enter the value of n : 18
The sum of first n numbers = 171
The average of first %d numbers = 9.00
```

Program 3.24 Write a program using `do-while` loop to display the square and cube of first n natural numbers.

Programming Tip: Avoid using do-while loop for implementing pre-test loops and prefer to use the do-while loop for post-test loops.

```
using namespace std;
#include<iostream>
#include<math.h>
int main()
{ int i = 1, n;
      cout<<"\n Enter the value of n : ";
      cin>>n;
      cout<<"\n ---------------------------------";
      do
  {   cout<<"\n | \t "<<i<<" \t | \t "<<pow(i,2)<<" \t | \t "<<pow(i,3)<<" \t |";//
      i++;
  } while(i <= n);
      cout<<"\n ---------------------------------";
}
```

SAMPLE OUTPUT

```
Enter the value of n : 5
```

1	1	1
2	4	8
3	9	27
4	16	64
5	25	125

Program 3.25 Write a program to list all the leap years from 1900 to 2100.

```
using namespace std;
#include<iostream>
int main()
{   int m = 1900, n = 2100,i;
//
    do
    {   if(i%4 == 0)
            cout<<"\n "<<m<<" is a leap year";
        else
            cout<<"\n "<<m<<" is not a leap year";
                m = m + 1;
        }while(m <= n);
}
```

Programming Tip: If you want that the body of the loop must get executed at least once, then use the do-while loop.

OUTPUT

```
2010 is not a leap year
2011 is not a leap year
2012 is a leap year
2013 is not a leap year
..............
```

Program 3.26 Write a program to read a character until a * is encountered. Count the number of upper case, lower case, and numbers entered by the users.

```
using namespace std;
#include<iostream>
int main()
{   char ch;
    int lowers = 0, uppers = 0, numbers = 0;
    cout<<"\n Enter any character : ";
    cin>>ch;
    do
    {   if(ch >= 'A' && ch <= 'Z')
            uppers++;
        if(ch >= 'a' && ch <= 'z')
            lowers++;
        if(ch >= '0' && ch <= '9')
            numbers++;
            cout<<"\n Enter another character. Enter * to exit.";
            cin>>ch;
    } while(ch != '*');
    cout<<"\n Total count of lower case characters entered = "<< lowers;
    cout<<"\n Total count of upper case characters entered = "<< uppers;
    cout<<"\n Total count of numbers entered = "<< numbers;
}
```

OUTPUT

```
Enter any character : O
Enter another character. Enter * to exit. x
Enter another character. Enter * to exit. F
Enter another character. Enter * to exit. o
Enter another character. Enter * to exit.R
Enter another character. Enter * to exit. d
Enter another character. Enter * to exit. *
Total count of lower case characters entered = 3
Total count of upper case characters entered = 3
Total count of numbers entered = 0
```

Program 3.27 Write a program to read the numbers until −1 is encountered. Calculate the sum and mean of all positive numbers entered and the sum and mean of all negative numbers entered separately.

```
using namespace std;
#include<iostream>
int main()
{   int num;
    int sum_negatives = 0, sum_positives = 0;
    int positives = 0, negatives = 0;
    float mean_positives = 0.0, mean_negatives = 0.0;
    cout<<"\n Enter -1 to exit…";
    cout<<"\n\n Enter any number : ";
    cin>>num;
    do
    {   if(num > 0)
        {   sum_positives += num;
            positives++;
        }
    else if(num < 0)
        {   sum_negatives += num;
            negatives++;
        }
        cout<<"\n\n Enter any number : ";
        cin>>num;
    } while(num != -1);
cout<<"sum of all positive numbers entered = "<<sum_positives;
mean_positives = sum_positives/positives;
cout<<"mean of all positive numbers entered = "<<mean_positives;
cout<<"sum of all negative numbers entered = "<<sum_negatives;
mean_negatives = sum_negatives/negatives;
cout<<"mean of all negative numbers entered = "<<mean_negatives;
}
```

SAMPLE OUTPUT

```
Sum of all positive numbers entered = 45
Mean of all positive numbers entered = 5
Sum of all negative numbers entered = -14
Mean of all negative numbers entered = 0
```

3.2.3 For LOOP

Like the `while` and `do-while` loop, the `for` loop provides a mechanism to repeat a task until a particular condition is true. The `for` loop is usually known as a determinate or definite loop because the programmer knows exactly how many times the loop will be repeated. The number of times the loop has to be executed can be determined mathematically checking the logic of the loop. The syntax and general form of a `for` loop is given in Fig. 3.9.

```
for (initialization; condition; increment/decrement/update)
{
    statement block;
}
Statement Y;
```

When a `for` loop is used, the loop variable is initialized only once. With every iteration of the loop, the value of the loop variable is updated and the condition is checked. If the condition is `true`, the statement block of the loop is executed else, the statements comprising the statement block of the `for` loop are skipped and the control jumps to the immediate statement following the `for` loop body.

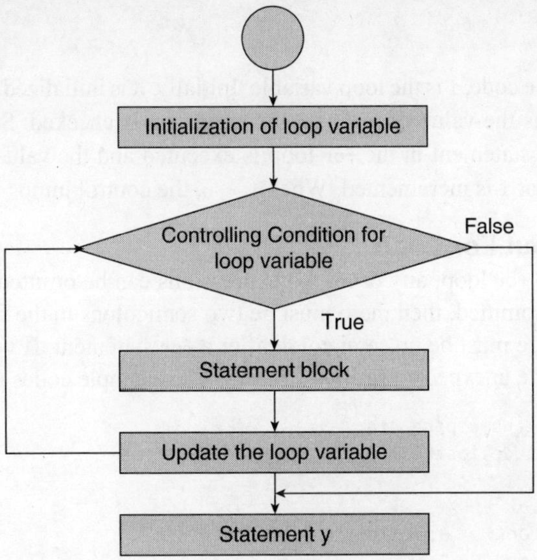

Figure 3.9 For loop construct

In the syntax of the `for` loop, the initialization of the loop variable allows the programmer to give it a value. Second, the condition specifies that while the conditional expression is true, the loop should continue to repeat itself. Every iteration of the loop must make the condition near to approachable. Therefore, with every iteration, the loop variable must be updated. Updating the loop variable may include incrementing the loop variable, decrementing the loop variable or setting it to some other value like, `i += 2`, where `i` is the loop variable.

Note that every section of the `for` loop is separated from the other with a semicolon. It is possible that one of the sections may be empty, though the semicolons still have to be inserted. However, if the condition is empty, it is evaluated as true and the loop will repeat until something else stops it.

The `for` loop is widely used to execute a single or a group of statements a limited number of times. Another point to consider is that in a `for` loop, condition is tested before the statements contained in the body are executed. If the condition does not hold true, then the body of the `for` loop may never get executed.

Example 3.8 To print the first n numbers using `for` loop

```
using namespace std;
#include<iostream>
int main()
{  int i, n;
   cout<<"\n Enter the value of n :";
   cin>>n;
   for(i = 0;i <= n;i++)
```

```
        cout<<"\t "<<i;
}
```

OUTPUT

```
Enter the value of n : 10
1    2    3    4    5    6    7    8    9    10
```

Explanation: In the code, `i` is the loop variable. Initially, it is initialized with the value zero. Suppose the user enters `10` as the value of `n`. Then, the condition is checked. Since the condition is true as `i` is less than `n`, the statement in the `for` loop is executed and the value of `i` is printed. After every iteration, the value of `i` is incremented. When `i = n`, the control jumps to the `return 0` statement.

Key Points about For Loop

- In a `for` loop, any or all the expressions can be omitted. In case all the expressions are omitted, then there must be two semicolons in the for statement
- There must be no semi colon after a `for` statement. If you do so, you are sure to get some unexpected results. Consider the example codes given here.

Programming Tip: It is a logical error to update the loop control variable in the body of the for loop as well as in the for statement.

```
using namespace std;
#include<iostream>
main()
{   int i;
    for(i = 0;i < 10;i++);
    cout<"   "<<i;
}
```

In this code, the loop is initialized from `i` to 0 and increments its value. Since a semicolon is placed after the loop, it means that loop does not contain any statement. Even if the condition is true, no statement is executed. The loop continues till `i` becomes 10 and the moment `i = 10`, the statement following the `for` loop is executed and the value of `i` that `10` is printed on the screen.

When we place a semicolon after the `for` statement, the compiler will not generate any error message. Rather, it will treat the statement as a null statement. Usually, such type of null statement is used to generate some time delays. For example, the code given here produces no output and simply delays further processing.

Programming Tip: Although we can place the initialization, testing and updating the loop control variable outside the for loop, try to avoid it as much as possible.

```
using namespace std;
#include<iostream>
main()
{         int i;
          for(i = 10000;i > 0;i--);
          cout<<"   "<<i;
}
```

- Multiple initializations must be separated with a comma operator as shown here:

```
using namespace std;
#include<iostream>
main()
{ int i, sum;
          for(i = 0, sum = 0;i < 10;i++)
                sum += i;
          cout<<" "<< sum;
}
```

- If there is no initialization to be done, the initialization statement can be skipped by giving only a semicolon. This is shown in the code here.

```
using namespace std;
#include<iostream>
main()
{   int i = 0;
    for(;i < 10;i++)
        cout<<"    "<<i;
}
```

- Multiple conditions in the test expression can be tested by using the logical operator `&&` or `||`.
- If the loop controlling variable is updated within the statement block, then the third part can be skipped. This is shown in the code given here.

```
using namespace std;
#include<iostream>
main()
{
    int i = 0;
    for(;i < 10;)
    {      cout<<"   "<<i;
        i = i + 1;
    }
}
```

- Multiple statements can be included in the third part of the `for` statement by using the comma operator. For example, the `for` statement given here is valid in `C`.

```
for(i = 0, j = 10;i < j; i++, j--)
```

- The controlling variable can be incremented or decremented by any value other than one. This is shown in the code here, which prints all odd numbers from `0 to 10`.

```
using namespace std;
#include<iostream>
main()
{   int i;
    for(i = 0;i <= 10;i += 2)
        cout<<"  "<<i;
}
```

- If the `for` loop contains nothing but two semicolons, it does not denote initialization, condition testing, and updating of the loop control variable. The `for` loop may become an infinite loop if no stopping condition is specified in the body of the loop. For example, the following code will infinitely print `C++ Programming` on the computer screen.

```
using namespace std;
#include<iostream>
main()
{   for(;;)
        cout<<"C++ Programming";
}
```

Programming Tip: Although placing an arithmetic expression in initialization and updating section of the `for` loop is permissible, but try to avoid them as they may cause some round-off and/ or truncation errors.

- Never use a floating point variable as the loop control variable. This is because floating point values are just approximations and may result in imprecise values and are an inaccurate test for termination. For example, the code given here will result in an infinite loop because of inaccuracies of floating point numbers.

```
using namespace std;
#include<iostream>
main()
{   float i;
    for(i = 100;i >= 10)
    {     cout<<"  "<<i;
        i = (float)i/10;
    }
}
```

3.2.4 Selecting an Appropriate Loop

Loops can be entry-controlled (also known as pre-test) or exit-controlled (also known as post-test). While in entry-controlled loop, condition is tested before the loop starts, the exit-controlled loop, on the other hand, tests the condition after the loop is executed. If the condition is not met in the entry-controlled loop, the loop will never be executed. However, in case of post-test, the body of the loop is executed unconditionally for the first time.

If you want to have a pre-test loop, then choose either `for` loop `or` `while` loop. In case you need to have a post-test loop, go for `do-while` loop.

Table 3.2 shows a comparison between a pre-test loop and a post test loop.

Table 3.2 Comparison between pre-test and post-test loops

Feature	Pre-test loop	Post-test loop
Initialization	1	1
Number of tests	n+1	n
Statements executed	N	n
Loop control variable update	N	n
Minimum Iterations	0	1

When we know the number of times the loop should be executed in advance, we use a counter-controlled loop. The counter is a variable that must be initialized, tested, and updated for performing loop operations. Such a counter-controlled loop in which the counter is assigned a constant or a value is also known as a definite repetition loop.

When we do not know the number of times the loop will be executed in advance, we use a sentinel controlled loop. In such a loop, a special value called the sentinel value is used to change the loop control expression from true to false. For example, when data is read from the user, the user may be notified that when they want the execution to stop, they may enter `-1`. Here, `-1` is called the sentinel value. A sentinel controlled loop is often useful for indefinite repetition loop.

If you want to have a counter-controlled loop, choose `for` loop. If you need to have a sentinel-controlled loop, then go for either `while` loop or `do-while` loop. Although a sentinel-controlled loop can be used `for` loop, `while` and `do-while` loop offer better options.

3.3 NESTED LOOPS

C++ allows users to have nested loops. These are loops that can be placed inside other loops. Although this feature will work with any loop such as `while loop`, `do-while loop`, and `for loop`, it is most commonly used with for loop, because this is the easiest to control. A `for` loop can be used to control the number of times that a particular set of statements will be executed. Another outer loop could be used to control the number of times that a whole loop is repeated.

In C++, loops can be nested to any desired level. However, the loops should be properly indented in order to enable the reader to easily determine which statements are contained within each for statement. To analyse the benefit of nesting loops, we will go through some programs that exhibit the use of nested for, while, and do-while loops.

Program 3.28 Write a program to print the following pattern.

Pass 1– 1 2 3 4 5
Pass 2– 1 2 3 4 5
Pass 3– 1 2 3 4 5
Pass 4– 1 2 3 4 5
Pass 5– 1 2 3 4 5

```
using namespace std;
#include<iostream>
main()
{   int i, j;
    for(i = 1;i <= 5;i++)
    {   cout<<"\n Pass "<<i<<" - ";
        for(j = 1;j <= 5;j++)
        cout<<" "<< j;
    }
}
```

Program 3.29 Write a program to print the following pattern.

```
**********
**********
**********
**********
**********
```

```
using namespace std;
#include<iostream>
main()
{   int i, j;
    for(i = 1;i <= 5;i++)// for rows
    {   cout<<"\n";
        for(j = 1;j <= 5;j++)// for columns
        cout<<"*";
    }

}
```

Program 3.30 Write a program to print the following pattern.

```
*
**
```

```
***
****
*****
```

```
using namespace std;
#include<iostream>
main()
{   int i, j;
    for(i = 1;i <= 5;i++)
    {   cout<<"\n";
        for(j = 1;j <= i;j++)
        cout<<"*";
    }
}
```

Program 3.31 Write a program to print the following pattern.

1
12
123
1234
12345

```
using namespace std;
#include<iostream>
main()
{   int i, j;
    for(i = 1;i <= 5;i++)
    {   cout<<"\n";
        for(j = 1;j <= i;j++)
            cout<<""<< j;
    }
}
```

Program 3.32 Write a program to print the following pattern.

1
22
333
4444
55555

```
using namespace std;
#include<iostream>
main()
{   int i, j;
    for(i = 1;i <= 5;i++)
    {   cout<<"\n";
        for(j = 1;j <= i;j++)
            cout<<""<<i;
    }
}
```

Program 3.33 Write a program to print the following pattern.

0
12
345
6789

```
using namespace std;
#include<iostream>
```

```
main()
{   int i, j, count = 0;
    for(i = 1;i <= 5;i++)
    {   cout<<"\n";
        for(j = 1;j <= i;j++)
            cout<<""<<count++;
    }
}
```

Program 3.34 Write a program to print the following pattern.

A
AB
ABC
ABCD
ABCDE
ABCDEF

```
using namespace std;
#include<iostream>
main()
{   char i, j;
    for(i = 65;i <= 70;i++)
     {  cout<<"\n";
        for(j = 65;j <= i;j++)
            cout<<char(j);
    }
}
```

Program 3.35 Write a program to print the following pattern.

```
          1
         12
        123
       1234
      12345
```

```
using namespace std;
#include<iostream>
#define N 5
main()
{   int i, j, k;
    for(i = 1;i <= N;i++)
    {   for(k = N;k >= i;k--)
        cout<<" ";
        for(j = 1;j <= i;j++)
                cout<<""<<j;
        cout<<"\n";
     }
}
```

Program 3.36 Write a program to print the following pattern.

```
        1
       121
      12321
     1234321
    123454321
```

```
using namespace std;
#include<iostream>
```

```
#define N 5
main()
{   int i, j, k, l;
    for(i = 1;i <= N;i++)
    {   for(k = N;k >= i;k--)
        cout<<" ";
    for(j = 1;j <= i;j++)
    cout<<""<<j;
    for(l = j-2;l > 0;l--)
    cout<<""<<l;
    cout<<"\n";
    }
}
```

Program 3.37 Write a program to print the following pattern.

```
    1
   2 2
  3 3 3
 4 4 4 4
5 5 5 5 5
```

```
using namespace std;
#include<iostream>
#define N 5
main()
{   int i, j, k, count = 5;
    for(i = 1;i <= N;i++)
    {   for(k = 1;k <= count;k++)
            cout<<" ";
        for(j = 1;j <= i;j++)
        {   cout.width(2);
            cout<<i;
        }
            cout<<"\n";
            count--;
    }
}
```

Program 3.38 Write a program to print the multiplication table of n, where n is entered by the user.

```
using namespace std;
#include<iostream>
int main()
{   int n, i;
    cout<<"\n Enter any number : ";
    cin>>n;
    cout<<"\n Multiplication table of "<<n;
    cout<<"\n ************************";
    for(i = 0;i <= 20;i++)
    cout<<"\n "<<n<<i<<" X "<<" = "<<(n * i);
}
```

OUTPUT

```
Enter any number : 2
Multiplication table of 2
************************
2 X 0 = 0
```

```
2 X 1 = 2
…..
2 X 20 = 40
```

Program 3.39 Write a program using `for` loop to print all the numbers from m – n thereby classifying them as even or odd.

```
using namespace std;
#include<iostream>
int main()
{   int i, m, n;
    cout<<"\n Enter the value of m and n : ";
    cin>>m>>n;
    for(i = m;i <= n;i++)
    {   if(i%2 == 0)
            cout<<"\n "<<i<<" is even";
        else
            cout<<"\n "<<i<<" is odd";
    }
}
```

OUTPUT

```
12 is even
13 is odd
14 is even
15 is odd
```

Program 3.40 Write a program using `for` loop to calculate the average of first n natural numbers.

```
using namespace std;
#include<iostream>
int main()
{   int n, i, sum = 0;
    float avg = 0.0;
    cout<<"\n Enter the value of n : ";
    cin>>n;
    for(i = 1;i <= n;i++)
        sum = sum + i;
    avg = sum/n;
    cout<<"\n The sum of first n natural numbers = "<<sum;
    cout<<"\n The average of first n natural numbers = "<<avg;
}
```

OUTPUT

```
Enter the value of n : 10
The sum of first n natural numbers = 55
n The average of first n natural numbers = 5.500
```

Program 3.41 Write a program using `for` loop to calculate factorial of a number.

```
using namespace std;
#include<iostream>
int main()
{   int fact = 1, num, i;
    cout<<"\n Enter the number : ";
    cin>>num;
    if(num == 0)
        fact = 1;
    else
```

```
    {   for(i = 1; i <= num;i++)
            fact = fact * i;
    }
    cout<<"\n Factorial of "<<num<<" is : "<<fact;
}
```

OUTPUT

```
Enter the number : 5
Factorial of is : 120
```

Program 3.42 Write a program to classify a given number as prime or composite.

```
using namespace std;
#include<iostream>
int main()
{   int flag = 0, i, num;
    cout<<"\n Enter any number : ";
    cin>>num;
    for(i = 2; i < num/2;i++)
    {   if(num%i == 0)
        {   flag = 1;
                break;
        }
    }
        if(flag == 1)
            cout<<"\n "<<num<<" is not a composite number";
        else
            cout<<"\n "<<num<<" is a prime number";
}
```

OUTPUT

```
Enter the number : 5
5 is a prime number
```

Program 3.43 Write a program using `do-while` loop to read the numbers until −1 is encountered. Count the number of prime numbers and composite numbers entered by the user.

```
using namespace std;
#include<iostream>
int main()
{   int num, i;
    int primes = 0, composites = 0, flag = 0;
        cout<<"\n Enter -1 to exit…";
        cout<<"\n\n Enter any number : ";
        cin>>num;
        do
        { for(i = 2;i <= num%2;i++)
        {   if(num%i == 0)
            {       flag = 1;
                    break;
            }
        }
        if(flag == 0)
            primes++;
        else
            composites++;
        flag = 0;
        cout<<"\n\n Enter any number : ";
        cin>>num;
```

```
        }   while(num != -1);
        cout<<"\n Count of prime numbers entered = "<<primes;
        cout<<"\n Count of composite numbers entered = "<<composites;
}
```

SAMPLE OUTPUT

```
Count of prime numbers entered = 4
Count of composite numbers entered = 7
```

Program 3.44 Write a program to calculate pow(x,n).

```
using namespace std;
#include<iostream>
int main()
{   int i, num, n;
    long int result = 1;
    cout<<"\n Enter the number : ";
    cin>>num;
    cout<<"\n Till which power to calculate : ";
    cin>>n;
    for(i = 1;i <= n;i++)
        result = result * num;
    cout<<"\n pow("<<num<<","<<n<<") = "<<result;
}
```

OUTPUT

```
Enter the number : 2
Till which power to calculate : 5
pow(2, 5) = 32
```

Program 3.45 Write a program to print the reverse of a number.

```
using namespace std;
#include<iostream>
int main()
{   int num, temp;
        cout<<"\n Enter the number : ";
        cin>>num;
        cout<<"\n The reversed number is : ";
        while(num != 0)
        {   temp = num%10;
            cout<<temp;
            num = num/10;
        }
}
```

OUTPUT

```
Enter the number : 123
The reversed number is : 321
```

Program 3.46 Write a program to enter a number and then calculate the sum of its digits.

```
using namespace std;
#include<iostream>
int main()
{   int num, temp, sumofdigits = 0;
    cout<<"\n Enter the number : ";
    cin>>num;
    while(num != 0)
    {   temp = num%10;
```

```
        sumofdigits += temp;
        num = num/10;
    }
    cout<<"\n The sum of digits = "<<sumofdigits;
}
```

OUTPUT

```
Enter the number : 123
The sum of digits = 6
```

Program 3.47 Write a program to enter a decimal number. Calculate and display the binary equivalent of this number.

```
using namespace std;
#include<iostream>
#include<math.h>
int main()
{   int decimal_num, remainder, binary_num = 0,
    i = 0;
    cout<<"\n Enter the decimal number : ";
    cin>>decimal_num;
    while(decimal_num != 0)
    {   remainder = decimal_num%2;
        binary_num += remainder*pow(10,i);
        decimal_num = decimal_num/2;
        i++;
    }
        cout<<"\n The binary equivalent = "<<binary_num;
}
```

Assignment WAP to convert a decimal no. into octal and hexadecimal. Hint: Instead of dividing by 2, divide by 8 and 16 respectively.

OUTPUT

```
Enter the decimal number : 7
The binary equivalent = 111
```

Program 3.48 Write a program to enter a binary number. Calculate and display the decimal equivalent of this number.

```
using namespace std;
#include<iostream>
#include<math.h>
int main()
{   int decimal_num = 0, remainder, binary_num, i = 0;
    cout<<"\n Enter the binary number : ";
    cin>>binary_num;
    while(binary_num != 0)
    {   remainder = binary_num%10;
        decimal_num += remainder*pow(2,i);
        binary_num = binary_num/10;
        i++;
    }
    cout<<"\n The decimal equivalent of = "<<decimal_num;
}
```

Assignment WAP to convert an octal and hexadecimal no. into decimal. Hint: Instead of finding pow(2,i) find pow(8,i) and pow(16,i) respectively.

OUTPUT

```
Enter the binary number : 111
The decimal equivalent = 7
```

Program 3.49 Write a program to calculate GCD of two numbers.

```
using namespace std;
#include<iostream>
int main()
{   int num1, num2, temp;
    int dividend, divisor, remainder;
    cout<<"\n Enter the two numbers : ";
    cin>>num1>>num2;
    if(num1>num2)
    {   dividend = num1;
        divisor = num2;
    }
    else
    {   dividend = num2;
        divisor = num1;
    }
        while(divisor)
        {   remainder = dividend%divisor;
            dividend = divisor;
            divisor = remainder;
        }
    cout<<"\n GCD of "<<num1<<" and "<<num2<<" is = "<<dividend;
}
```

OUTPUT

```
Enter the first number : 64
Enter the second number : 14
GCD of 64 and 14 is = 2
```

Program 3.50 Write a program to sum the series – 1 + 1/2 + . . . +1/n.

```
using namespace std;
#include<iostream>
main()
{   int n;
    float sum = 0.0, a, i;
    cout<<"\n Enter the value of n : ";
    cin>>n;
    for(i = 1.0;i <= n;i++)
    {   a = 1/i;
        sum = sum +a;
    }
    cout<<"\n The sum of series 1/1 + 1/2 + .... + 1/"<<n<<" = "<<sum;
}
```

OUTPUT

```
Enter the value of n : 10
The sum of series 1/1 + 1/2 + .... + 1/10 = 2.928968
```

Program 3.51 Write a program to sum the series – $1/1^2 + 1/2^2 + \ldots 1/n^2$.

```
using namespace std;
#include<iostream>
#include<math.h>
main()
{   int n;
    float sum = 0.0, a, i;
    cout<<"\n Enter the value of n : ";
    cin>>n;
```

```
    for(i = 1.0;i <= n;i++)
    {   a = 1/pow(i,2);
        sum = sum +a;
    }
    cout<<"\n The sum of series 1/1² + 1/2² + …. 1/n² = "<<sum;
}
```

OUTPUT

```
Enter the value of n : 10
The sum of series 1/1¹ + 1/2²+ .... + 1/n² = 1.549768
```

Program 3.52 Write a program to sum the series — 1/2 + 2/3 + . . . n/(n+1).

```
using namespace std;
#include<iostream>
main()
{   int n;
    float sum = 0.0, a, i;
    cout<<"\n Enter the value of n : ";
    cin>>n;
    for(i = 1.0;i <= n;i++)
    {   a = i/(i + 1);
        sum = sum + a;
    }
    cout<<"\n The sum of series 1/2 + 2/3 + .... + "<<n<<" / "<<n + 1<<" = "<<sum;
}
```

OUTPUT

```
Enter the value of n : 3
The sum of series 1/2 + 2/3 + .... + 3/4 = 1.91667
```

Program 3.53 Write a program to sum the series — $1/1 + 2^2/2 + 3^3/3 + \ldots$

```
using namespace std;
#include<iostream>
#include<math.h>
main()
{   int n, NUM;
    float i,sum = 0.0;
    cout<<"\n Enter the value of n : ";
    cin>>n;
    for(i = 1.0;i <= n;i++)
    {   NUM = pow(i,i);
        sum += (float)NUM/i;
    }
    cout<<"\n 1/1 + 4/2 + 27/3 + .... = "<<sum;
}
```

OUTPUT

```
Enter the value of n : 3
1/1 + 4/2 + 27/3 + .... = 12
```

Program 3.54 Write a program to calculate sum of cubes of numbers from 1 – n.

```
using namespace std;
#include<iostream>
#include<math.h>
main()
{   int i, n;
    int term, sum = 0;
```

```
    cout<<"\n Enter the value of n : ";
    cin>>n;
    for(i = 1;i <= n;i++)
    {   term = pow(i,3);
        sum += term;
    }
    cout<<"\n 1³ + 2³ + 3³ + ...... = "<<sum;
}
```

OUTPUT

```
Enter the value of n : 5
1³ + 2³ + 3³ + ...... = 25
```

Programming Tip: It is a logical error to skip the updating of loop control variable in the while/do-while loop. Without an update statement, the loop will become an infinite loop.

Program 3.55 Write a program to sum of squares of even numbers.

```
using namespace std;
#include<iostream>
#include<math.h>
main()
{   int i, n;
 int term, sum = 0;
 cout<<"\n Enter the value of n : ";
 cin>>n;
 for(i = 1;i <= n;i++)
 {  if(i%2 == 0)
        term = pow(i,2);
    else
        term = pow(i,3);
        sum += term;
 }
    cout<<"\n 2² + 4² + 6² + ...... = "<<sum;
}
```

OUTPUT

```
Enter the value of n : 5
2² + 4² + 6² + ...... = 173
```

Program 3.56 Write a program to find whether the given number is an Armstrong number or not.

```
using namespace std;
#include<iostream>
#include<math.h>
main()
{   int num, sum = 0, r, n;
    cout<<"\n Enter the number : ";
    cin>>num;
        n = num;
    while(n > 0)
    {   r = n%10;
        sum += pow(r,3);
        n = n/10;
    }
    if(sum == num)
    cout<<"\n "<<num<<" is an Armstrong number";
    else
    cout<<"\n "<<num<<" is not an Armstrong number";
}
```

OUTPUT

```
Enter the number : 432
432 is not an armstrong number
```

Program 3.57 Write a program using `for` loop to calculate the value of an investment. (*Hint: Given an initial value for investment and the annual interest, calculate the value of investment over time.*)

```
using namespace std;
#include<iostream>
main()
{
    double initVal, futureVal, ROI;
    int yrs, i;
    cout<<"\n Enter the investment value : ";
    cin>>initVal;
    cout<<"\n Enter the rate of interest: ";
    cin>>ROI;
    cout<<"\n Enter the number of years for which investment has to be done : ";
    cin>>yrs;
    futureVal = initVal;
    cout<<"\n YEAR \t\t VALUE";
    cout<<"\n ________________________";
    for(i = 1;i <= yrs;i++)
    {   futureVal = futureVal * (1 + ROI/100.0);
        cout<<"\n " <<i<<" \t "<<futureVal;
    }
}
```

OUTPUT

```
Enter the investment value : 20000
Enter the rate of interest: 12
Enter the number of years for which investment has to be done : 5
YEAR    VALUE
______________________
1       22400.00
2       25088.00
3       28098.56
4       31470.38
5       35246.83
```

Program 3.58 Write a program to generate calendar of a month given the start_day and the number of days in that month.

```
using namespace std;
#include<iostream>
main()
{   int i, j, startDay, num_of_days;
    cout<<"\n Enter the starting day of the week (1 to 7): ";
    cin>>startDay;
    cout<<"\n Enter the number of days in that month : ";
    cin>>num_of_days;
    cout<<" Sun Mon Tue Wed Thurs Fri Sat\n";
    cout<<"\n ________________________________";
    for(i = 0;i < startDay - 1;i++)
        cout<<" ";
```

```
        for(j = 1;j <= num_of_days;j++)
        {   if(i>6)
            {   cout<<"\n";
                i = 1;
            }
            else
                i++;
                cout.width(2);
                cout<<j;
        }
    }
```

EXPECTED OUTPUT

```
Calendar of the month entered
```

3.4 BREAK STATEMENT

The `break` statement is used to terminate the execution of the nearest enclosing loop in which it appears. We have already seen its usage in the `switch` statement. The `break` statement is widely used with `for` loop, `while` loop, and `do-while` loop. When a compiler encounters a `break` statement, the control passes to the statement that follows the loop in which the `break` statement appears. Its syntax is quite simple, just type keyword `break` followed with a semicolon.

```
break;
```

In `switch` statement, if the `break` statement is missing, then every case from the matched `case` label to the end of the `switch`, including the `default`, is executed.

Example 3.9 Manner in which `break` statement is used to terminate the statement in which it is embedded

```
using namespace std;
#include<iostream>
int main()
{       int i = 0;
      while(i <= 10)
      {       if (i == 5)
                  break;
            cout<<"\n "<<i;
            i = i + 1;
      }
}
```

OUTPUT

```
0
1
2
3
4
```

Explanation: The code given here is meant to print the first `10` numbers using a `while` loop, but it will actually print only numbers from `0` to `4`. As soon as `i` becomes equal to `5`, the `break` statement is executed and the control jumps to the statement following the `while` loop.

Hence, the `break` statement is used to exit a loop from any point within its body, bypassing its normal termination expression. When the `break` statement is encountered inside a loop, the loop is immediately terminated, and program control is passed to the next statement following the loop. Figure 3.10 shows the transfer of control when the `break` statement is encountered.

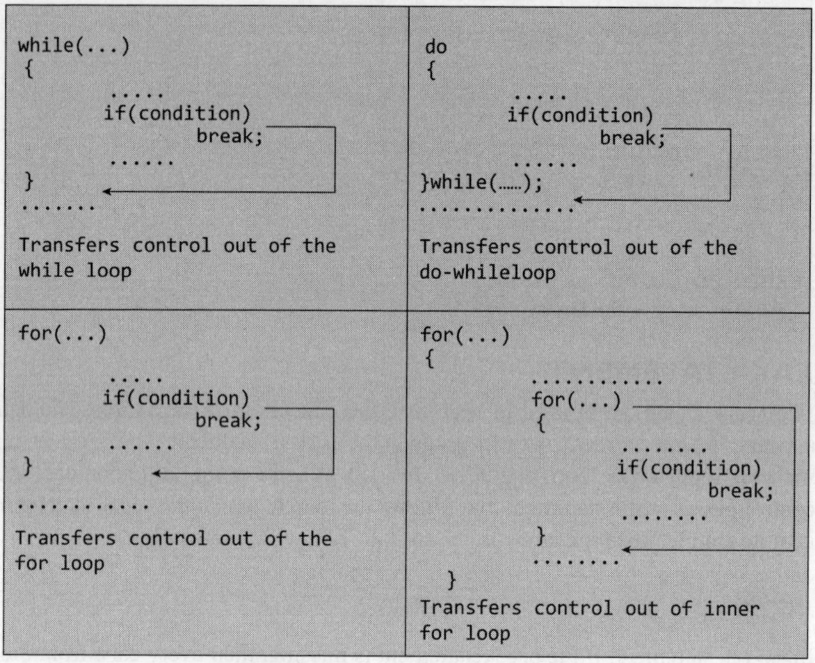

Figure 3.10 The `break` statement

> **Programming Tip:** When the compiler encounters a continue statement, then the rest of the statements in the loop are skipped and the control is unconditionally transferred to the continuation portion of the nearest enclosing loop.

3.5 CONTINUE STATEMENT

Like the `break` statement, the `continue` statement can only appear in the body of a loop. When the compiler encounters a `continue` statement, the rest of the statements in the loop are skipped and the control is unconditionally transferred to the loop-continuation portion of the nearest enclosing loop. Its syntax is quite simple; just type keyword `continue`, followed by a semicolon as shown here.

```
continue;
```

Like the `break` statement, the `continue` statement cannot be used without an enclosing `for`, `while`, or `do while` statement. When the `continue` statement is encountered in the `while` and in the `do-while` loop, the control is transferred to the code that tests the controlling expression. However, if placed with a `for` loop, the `continue` statement causes a branch to the code that updates the loop variable.

Example 3.10 Using `continue` statement

```
using namespace std;
#include<iostream>
int main()
{  int i;
   for(i = 0; i <= 10; i++)
   {  if (i == 5)
```

```
            continue;
            cout<<"\t "<<i;
            i = i + 1;
        }
}
```

OUTPUT

```
0  1  2  3  4  6  7  8  9  10
```

Programming Tip: Try not to use goto, break, and continue statement.

Explanation: This code is meant to print numbers from `0 to 10`. As soon as `i` becomes equal to `5`, the continue statement is encountered, and the rest of the statements in the `for` loop are skipped and the control passes to the expression that increments the value of `i`. The output of this program would print numbers from 0 to 10.

Note There is no 5... 5 could not be printed as continue caused early increment of i and skipping of statement that printed the value of i on screen.

Figure 3.11 illustrates the use of continue statement in loops.

Hence, we conclude that the `continue` statement is almost the opposite of the `break` statement. It forces the next iteration of the loop to take place, skipping any code in between itself and the test condition of the loop. The continue statement is usually used to restart a statement sequence when an error occurs. Look at the program code given here that demonstrates the use of `break` and `continue` statement.

```
while(...)
{
        .....
        if(condition)
                continue;
        ......
}
......

Transfers control to the condition
expression of the while loop
```

```
do
{
        .....
        if(condition)
                continue;
        ......
}while(......);
..............

Transfers control to the condition
expression of the do-while loop
```

```
for(...)
{
        .....
        if(condition)
                continue;
        ......
}
..............

Transfers control to the condition
expression of the for loop
```

```
for(...)
{
        ............
        for(...)
        {
                ........
                if(condition)
                        continue;
                ........
        }
        .......
}
Transfers control to the condition
expression of the inner for loop
```

Figure 3.11 The `continue` statement

Program 3.59 Write a program to calculate square root of a number.

```
using namespace std;
#include<iostream>
#include<math.h>
main()
{   int num;
    do
    {   cout<<"\n Enter any number. Enter 999 to stop : ";
        cin>>num;
            if(num == 999)
                break;              // quit the loop
            if (num < 0)
        {   cout<<"\n Square root of negative numbers is not defined";
                    continue;       // skip the statements following
        }
        cout<<"\n The square root of "<<num<< "is "<<sqrt(num);
    }while(1);
}
```

SAMPLE OUTPUT

```
The square root of 4 is 2
```

3.6 GOTO STATEMENT

The `goto` statement is used to transfer control to a specified `label`. However, the `label` must reside in the same function and can appear before only one statement in the same function. The syntax of `goto` statement can be given as shown in Fig. 3.12.

Here, `label` is an identifier that specifies the place where the branch is to be made. `Label` can be any valid variable name that is followed by a colon (:). The `label` is placed immediately before the statement where the control has to be transferred.

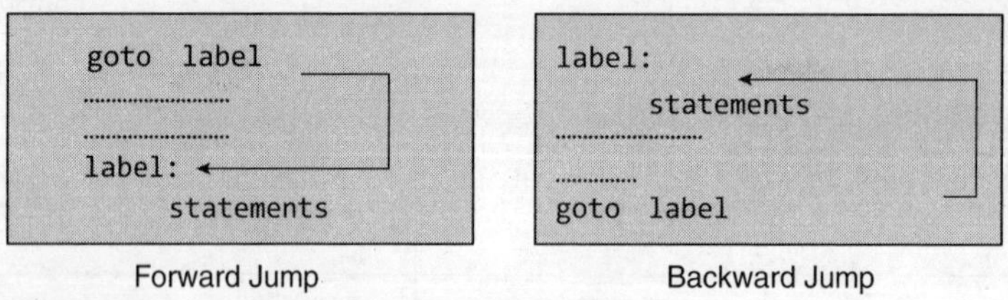

Figure 3.12 The `goto` statement

The `label` can be placed anywhere in the program either before or after the `goto` statement. Whenever the `goto` statement is encountered, the control is immediately transferred to the statements following the `label`. Therefore, `goto` statement breaks the normal sequential execution of the program. If the `label` is placed after the `goto` statement, it is called a forward jump; if it is located before the `goto` statement, it is said to be a backward jump.

The `goto` statement is often combined with the `if` statement to cause a conditional transfer of control.

```
IF condition THEN goto Label
```

In this book, we will not use the `goto` statement because computer scientists usually avoid this statement in favour of the structured programming paradigm. Some scientists think that the `goto` statement should be abolished from higher-level languages because it complicates the task of analysing and verifying the correctness of programs, particularly those involving loops.

> **Programming Tip:** Follow proper indentation for better clarity, readability, and understanding of the loops.

Moreover, structured program proves that the availability of the `goto` statement is not necessary to write programs as combination of sequence, selection, and repetition constructs are sufficient to perform any computation.
`using namespace std;`

Example 3.11 To calculate the sum of all positive numbers entered by the user by using `goto` statement

```
#include<iostream>
main()
{   int num, sum = 0;
    read:        // label for go to statement
        cout<<"\n Enter the number. Enter 999 to end : ";
        cin>>num;
        if (num != 999)
        {       if(num < 0)
            goto read;       // jump to label- read
            sum += num;
            goto read;              // jump to label- read
        }
        cout<<"\n Sum of the numbers entered by the user is = "<<sum;
}
```

SAMPLE OUTPUT

```
Sum of the numbers entered by the user is = 28
```

3.6.1 Key Points about Goto Statement

- It is not necessary to use `goto` statement as it can always be eliminated by rearranging the code.
- Using the `goto` statement violates the rules of structured programming.
- It is a good programming style to use the `break`, `continue`, and `return` statement, in preference to `goto` whenever possible.
- `Goto` statements make the program code complicated and render the program unreadable.

3.7 AVOIDING USAGE OF BREAK, CONTINUE, AND GOTO STATEMENTS

Note that one must avoid using `break`, `continue`, and `goto` statements as much as possible as they are techniques used in unstructured programming. In structured programming, you must prefer to use if and if-else construct to avoid such statements.

Example 3.12 Consider the code given here to calculate the sum of numbers entered by the user. The first version uses the `break` statement. The second version replaces `break` by `if-else` construct.

```
// Using break statement
using namespace std;
#include<iostream>
main()
{   int num, sum = 0;
    while(1)
              {cout<<"\n Enter any number. Enter 999 to stop : ";
```

```
        cin>>num;
        if(num == 999)
            break;       // quit the loop
            sum += num;
    }
    cout<<"\n SUM = "<<sum;
}
// same program without using break statement
using namespace std;
#include<iostream>
main()
{   int num, sum = 0, flag = 1;
    // flag will be used to exit from the loop
    while(flag == 1)      // loop control variable
    {       cout<<"\n Enter any number. Enter 999 to stop : ";
            cin>>num;
            if(num != 999)
                sum += num;
            else
                flag = 0;        // set the variable to quit the loop
    }
            cout<<"\n SUM = "<<sum;
}
```

SAMPLE OUTPUT

```
SUM = 55
```

Explanation: Now let us also see how we can eliminate `continue` statement from our programs.

Example 3.13 Let us first write a program to calculate the average of all non-zero numbers entered by the user using the `continue` statement. The second program will do the same job but without using `continue`.

```
//Using continue construct
using namespace std;
#include<iostream>
main()
{   int num, sum = 0, flag = 1, count = 0;
    float avg;
    // flag will be used to exit from the loop
    while(flag == 1)
    {   cout<<"\n Enter any number. Enter 999 to stop : ";
        cin>>num;
        if(num == 0)
            continue;      // skip the following statements
        if(num != 999)
        {       sum += num;
                count++;
        }
        else
                flag = 0;
                // set loop cntl variable to jump out of the loop
    }
    cout<<"\n SUM = "<<sum;
    avg = (float) sum/count;
    cout<<"\n Average = "<<avg;
```

```
}
// same program without using continue statement
using namespace std;
#include<iostream>
main()
{   int num, sum = 0, flag = 1, count = 0;
    float avg;
    // flag will be used to exit from the loop
    while(flag == 1)
    {   cout<<"\n Enter any number. Enter 999 to stop : ";
        cin>>num;
        if(num != 0)
        {   if(num != 999)
            {   sum += num;
            count++;
        }
        else
            flag = 0;
    }
    }
        cout<<"\n SUM = "<<sum;
        avg = (float) sum/count;
        cout<<"\n Average = "<<avg;
}
```

SAMPLE OUTPUT

```
SUM = 55
Average = 7
```

Points to Remember

- The conditional branching statements help to jump from one part of the program to another depending on whether a particular condition is satisfied or not
- C++ language supports `if else if` statements to test additional conditions apart from the initial test expression.
- The power of nested `if-else` statement's lies in the fact that it can evaluate more than one expression in a single logical structure.
- `Default case` is executed when there is no match found between the values of `switch` and `case` statements and thus there are no statements to be executed.
- The `break` statement tells the compiler to jump out of the `switch case` statement and execute the statement following the `switch case` construct.
- A `while` loop is also referred to as a top-checking loop since control condition is placed as the first line of the code.
- The only difference is that in a `do-while` loop, the test condition is tested at the end of the loop
- The major disadvantage of using a `do while` loop is that it always executes at least once, so even if the user enters some invalid data, the loop will execute.
- Every section of the `for` loop is separated from the other with a semi-colon. It is possible that one of the sections may be empty, though the semicolons still have to be there.
- When the continue statement is encountered in the `while` loop and in the `do-while`, the control is transferred to the code that tests the controlling expression. However, if placed with a `for` loop, the continue statement causes a branch to the code that updates the loop variable
- The `goto` statement is used to transfer control to a specified label. It is often combined with the `if` statement to cause a conditional transfer of control.

Glossary

Break statement Statement is used to terminate the execution of the nearest enclosing loop in which it appears

Conditional branching Conditional branching statements are used to jump from one part of the program to another, depending on whether a particular condition is satisfied or not

Continue statement Statement that can appear in the body of a loop. When the compiler encounters a continue statement then the rest of the statements in the loop are skipped and the control is unconditionally transferred to the loop-continuation portion of the nearest enclosing loop.

Dangling else problem Problem encountered with nesting of `if-else` statements created when there is no matching else for every `if` statement

Do while loop The `do-while` loop is similar to the while loop. The only difference is that in a `do-while` loop, the test condition is tested at the end of the loop.

For loop The mechanism used to repeat a task until a particular condition is true. `For` loop is usually known as a determinate or definite loop because the programmer knows exactly how many times the loop will repeat.

Go to statement The `goto` statement is used to transfer control to a specified `label`. However, the `label` must reside in the same function and can appear before only one statement in the same function.

If statement The simplest form of decision control statements that is frequently used in decision-making

If-else statement Decision control statement in which first the test expression is evaluated. If the expression is true, statement block 1 is executed and statement block 2 is skipped. Otherwise, if the expression is false, statement block 2 is executed, and statement block 1 is ignored.

If-else-if statement Decision control statement that works in the same way as a normal if statement. It is also known as nested `if` construct.

Iterative statement Statements used to repeat the execution of a list of statements, depending on the value of an integer expression

Nested loop Loops placed inside other loops

Switch case statement A switch case statement is a multi-way decision statement that is a simplified version of an `if-else` block that evaluates only one variable

While loop The mechanism used to repeat one or more statements while a particular condition is true

Exercises

Fill in the Blanks

1. `Dangling` else problem occurs when ______.
2. The `switch case` control expression must be of ______ type.
3. In a `do-while` loop, if the body of the loop is executed n times, the test condition is evaluated ______ times.
4. The ______ statement is used to skip statements in a loop.
5. A loop that always satisfies the test condition is known as a ______ loop.
6. In a counter-controlled loop, ______ variable is used to count the number of times the loop will execute.
7. ______ statements help to jump from one part of the program to another depending on whether a particular condition is satisfied or not.
8. ______ statements are used to repeat the execution of a list of statements.
9. In ______ loop, the entry is automatic as there is only a choice to continue it further or not.
10. When we do not know the number of times the loop will be executed in advance, we use a ______ loop.
11. The ______ statement is used to transfer control to a specified `label`.
12. ____ statement violates the rules of structured programming.

State True or False

1. Decision control statements are used to repeat the execution of a list of statements.
2. The expression in a selection statement can have no side effects.
3. An expression in an `if` statement must be enclosed within parentheses.
4. No two case labels can have the same value.
5. The case labeled constant can be a constant or a variable.
6. `If-else` statement requires integral values in its expressions.
7. There can be only one default case in the `switch-case` statement.
8. The `do-while` loop checks the test expression and then executes the statements placed within its body.
9. In a `while` loop, if the body is executed n times, then the test expression is executed n + 1 times.
10. The number of times the loop control variable is updated is equal to the number of times the loop iterates.
11. In the `for` loop, the value of the loop control variable must be less than that of its ending value.
12. It is necessary to have initialization, testing, and updating expressions within the for statement.
13. In a pre-test loop, the test condition is checked after the body of the loop.
14. Post-test loops get executed at least for one time.
15. In a `while` loop, the loop control variable is initialized in the body of the loop.
16. The loop control variable may be updated before or after the loop iterates.
17. The number of times the loop control variable is updated is equal to the number of times the loop is executed.
18. Counter-controlled loops must be designed as pre-test loops.
19. `Do-while` loop is a post-test loop.
20. `For` loop and `while` loop are pre-test loops.
21. Every case label must evaluate to a unique constant expression value.
22. Two case labels may have the same set of actions associated with it.
23. The default label can be placed anywhere in the switch statement.
24. C++ does not permit nested switch statements.
25. When we place a semicolon after the for statement, then the compiler will generate an error message.

Multiple Choice Questions

1. Which type of statement helps to jump from one part of the program to another depending on whether a particular condition is satisfied or not?
   (a) Conditional branching
   (b) loops
   (c) Iterative
   (d) None of these
2. A statement block consists of how many statements?
   (a) 0 (b) 1
   (c) N (d) None of these
3. Dangling else problem can arise in which of the following statement(s)?
   (a) Conditional branching
   (b) loops
   (c) Iterative
   (d) None of these
4. Which among the following is a multi-way decision statement?
   (a) `If-else` (b) `If-else-if`
   (c) `Switch` (d) `Do while loop`
5. Case labels must end with which token?
   (a) , (b) :
   (c) ; (d) /
6. The default label can be placed at which position in the `switch` statement?
   (a) Beginning (b) End
   (c) Middle (d) anywhere
7. The statements in the statement block are encapsulated within a __________?
   (a) () (b) {}
   (c) [] (d) <>
8. Which statement is used to terminate the execution of the nearest enclosing loop in which it appears?
   (a) Break (b) Continue
   (c) Default (d) case
9. When the __________ statement is encountered then the rest of the statements in the loop are skipped.
   (a) Break (b) Continue
   (c) Default (d) case

Review Questions

1. What are decision control statements? Explain in detail
2. Compare the use of `if-else` construct with that of ternary operator.

3. Explain the importance of a `switch case` statement. In which situations is a `switch case` desirable? Give its limitations.
4. How is comma operator useful in a `for` loop? Explain with the help of relevant examples.
5. Write a short note on `Goto` statement. As a programmer, would you prefer to use this statement? Justify your answer.
6. Explain the dangling `if-else` problem with an example.
7. Why should floating point numbers not be used for equality in expressions?
8. Explain the usefulness of default statement in `switch case` statement.
9. When will you prefer to work with a `switch` statement?
10. Describe the similarities and differences between a `while` loop and a `do-while` loop.
11. Distinguish between the `break` and the `continue` statement.
12. What is a null statement? How can it be useful in our programs?
13. When will you use prefer to use `for, while, and do while` loop?
14. Write a short not on iterative statements that C++ language supports.

Programming Exercises

1. Write a program to read a floating point number and an integer. If the value of the floating point number is greater than 4.14, add 10 to the integer.
2. Enter two integers as dividend and divisor. If the divisor is greater than zero, divide the dividend by the divisor. Assign their result to an integer variable rem and their quotient to a floating point number quo.
3. Write a program to print the prime factors of a number.
4. Write a program to test if a given number is a power of 2.
   Hint: *A number x is a power of 2 if x != 0 and x & (x - 1)) == 0*
5. Write a program to print the Floyd's triangle.
   1
   2 3
   4 5 6
   7 8 9 10
   11 12 13 14 15
6. Write a program to read two numbers. Find out whether the first number is a multiple of the second number.
7. Write a program using switch case to display a menu that offers five options—read three numbers, calculate total, calculate average, display the smallest value, and display the largest value
8. Write a program to display the sin(x) value, where x ranges from 0 to 360 in steps of 15.
9. Write a program to display the value of cos(x) and tan(x) where x ranges from 0 to 360 in steps of 15.
10. Write a program to calculate electricity bill based on following information:

Consumption unit	Rate of charge
0 – 150	₹3 per unit
151 – 350	₹100 plus ₹3.75 per unit exceeding 150 units
301 – 450	₹250 plus ₹4 per unit exceeding 350 units
451 – 600	₹300 plus ₹4.25 per unit exceeding 450 units
Above 600	₹400 plus ₹5 per unit exceeding 600 units

11. Write a program to read an angle from the user and display its quadrant.
12. Write a program that accepts the current date and the date of birth of the user. Then calculate the age of the user and display it on the screen. Note that the date should be displayed in the format specified as dd/mm/yy.
13. A class has 50 students. Every student is supposed to give three examinations. Write a program to read the marks obtained by each student in all three examinations. Calculate and display the total marks and average of each student in the class.
14. Write a program in which the control variable is updated in the statements of the for loop.
15. Write a program which demonstrates the use of goto, break, and continue statements.
16. Can we use a for loop when the number of iterations is not known in advance? If yes, give a program that illustrates how this can be done.
17. Write a program that displays all the numbers from 1–100 that are not divisible 2 as well as by 3.

18. Write a program to calculate parking charges of a vehicle. Enter the type of vehicle as a character (like c for car, b for bus, etc) and number of hours then calculate charges as given here:
    Truck/bus – ₹20 per hour
    Car – ₹10 per hour
    Scooter/ Cycle/ Motor cycle – ₹5 per hour
19. Modify the previous program to calculate the parking charges. Read the hours and minutes when the vehicle enters the parking lot. When the vehicle is leaving, enter its leaving time. Calculate the difference between the two timings to calculate the number of hours and minutes for which the vehicle was parked. Finally, calculate the charges based on following rules and then display the result on the screen.

Vehicle	Rate till three hours	Rate after three hours
Truck or bus	20	30
Car	10	20
Cycle, motor cycle, or scooter	5	10

20. Write a program to read month of the year as an integer. Display the name of the month.
21. Write a program to print the sum of all odd numbers from 1 to 100.
22. Write an interactive program to read an integer. If it is positive, display the corresponding binary representation of that number. The user must enter 999 to stop. In case the user enters a negative number then ignore that input and ask the user to re-enter any different number.
23. Write a program to print 20 asterisks.
24. Change the following for loop in to a while loop. Convert the for loop into a do-while loop.

```
int i;
for(i = 10;i > 0;i--)
  cout<<i;
```

25. Change the following do while loop into a for loop. Rewrite the code by changing the do-while loop into a for loop.

```
int num;
cout<<"\n Enter any number. Enter 999 to
stop : ";
cin>>num;
do
{ cout<<x;
  cout<<"\n Enter any number. Enter 999 to
  stop : ";
  cin>>num;
}while(num != 999);
```

26. Write a program that accepts any number and prints the number of digits in that number.
27. Change the following while loop in to a do-while loop. Convert the `while` loop into a `for` loop.

```
int num;
cout<<"\n Enter any number. Enter 999 to
stop : ";
cin>>num;
while(num != 999)
{ cout<<x;
  cout<<"\n Enter any number. Enter 999 to
  stop : ";
  cin>>num;
}
```

28. The following for loops are written to print numbers from 1 to 10. Are these loops correct? Justify your answer.

```
int i;
for(i = 0;i < 10;i++)
      cout<<i;
int i, num;
for(i = 0;i < 10;i++)
{      num = i+1;
      cout<<num;
}
int i;
for(i = 1;i <= 10;i++)
{      cout<<i;
      i++;
}
```

29. Write a program to generate the following pattern.

```
* * * * *
*       *
*       *
*       *
* * * * *
```

30. Write a program to generate the following pattern.

```
$ * * * *
* $     *
*   $   *
*     $ *
* * * * $
```

31. Write a program to generate the following pattern.

```
$ * * * $
* $   $ *
*   $   *
* $   $ *
$ * * * $
```

32. Write programs to implement the following sequence of numbers.

1, 8, 27, 64,…

–5, –2, 0, 3, 6, 9, 12, …

–2, –4, –6, –8, –10, –12, …

1, 4, 7, 10, …

33. Write a program that reads integers until the user wants to stop. When the user stops entering numbers, display the largest of all the numbers entered.

34. Write a program to print the sum of the following series.

–x + x2 – x3 + x4 +…

1 + (1+2) + (1+2+3) +…

1 – x + x2/2! – x3/3! + …

35. Write a program to print the following pattern.

```
*
* *
* * *
* * * *
* * * * *
* * * *
* * *
* *
*
```

36. Write a program to print the following pattern.

```
1
2 1 2
3 2 1 2 3
```

Find the functionality of the loops given below

- ```
  int i = 1, sum = 0;
  while(i != 10)
  {     sum += i;
        i = i+2;
  }
  ```
- ```
  int i, sum = 0;
  for (i = 1;i <= 10)
    sum += i;
  ```
  ```
  int i;
  ```
- ```
  for (i = 1;i <= 10;i++)
        i--;
  ```
- ```
  int i = 10;
  do
  {     cout<<i;
  } while(i > 0);
  ```
- ```
  int i = 10;
  do
  {     cout<<i;
  } while(i < 5);
  ```
- ```
  int i = 1, n = 10, sum = 0;
  while(i <= n)
  {     sum += i;
        i--;
  }
  ```
- ```
  int i, sum = 0;
  for (i = 1;;i++)
        sum += i;
  ```
- ```
  int i = 10;
  while(i --> 0)
        cout<<i;
  ```
- ```
  int i;
  for (i = 10;i > 5;i- = 2)
        cout<<i;
  ```
- ```
  int i;
  for (i = 10;i > 5;)
        cout<<i;
  ```

Find the errors in the following codes

1. ```
   using namespace std;
   #include<iostream>
   main()
   {     int i = 1;
         while(i <= 10)
         {     i = 1;
               cout<<i;
               i++;
         }
   }
   ```
2. ```
   using namespace std;
   #include<iostream>
   main()
   {     int i;
         for(i = 0,i <= 10;i++)
               cout<<i;
   }
   ```
3. ```
   using namespace std;
   #include<iostream>
   main()
   {     int i = 1;
         do
         {     cout<<i;
               i++;
   ```
   ```

```
        }while(i = 10)
    }
```

4.
```
using namespace std;
#include<iostream>
main()
{       int i,j;
        for(i = 1,j = 0;i + j <= 10;i++)
        cout<<i;
        j += 2;
}
```

Find the output of the following codes

1.
```
using namespace std;
#include<iostream>
main()
{       int a = 2, b = 3, c = 4;
        if(c!= 100)
                a = 10;
        else
                b = 10;
        if(a + b > 10)
        c = 12;
        a = 20;
        b = ++c;
        cout<<"\n a = "<<a<<" \t b = "<<b<< "
        \t c = "<<c;
}
```

2.
```
using namespace std;
#include<iostream>
main()
{       int a = 2, b = 3, c = 4;
        if(b == 2)
                a = 10;
        else
                c = 10;
        cout<<"\n a = "<<a<< " \t b = "<<b<<"
        \t c = "<<c;
}
```

3.
```
using namespace std;
#include<iostream>
main()
{       int a = 2, b = 3, c = 4;
        if(a&&b)
                c = 10;
        else
                c = 20;
        cout<<"\n a = "<<a<<" \t b = "<<b<<"
        \t c = "<<c;
}
```

4.
```
using namespace std;
#include<iostream>
main()
{       int a = 2, b = 3, c = 4;
        if(a || b || c)
                c = 10;
        else
                c = 20;
        cout<<"\n a = "<<a<<" \t b = "<<b<< "
        \t c = "<<c;
}
```

5.
```
using namespace std;
#include<iostream>
main()
{       int a = 2, b = 3, c = 4;
        if(a)
                if(b)
                c = 10;
        else
                c = 20;
        cout<<"\n a = "<<a<< " \t b = "<<b<<"
        \t c = "<<c;
}
```

6.
```
using namespace std;
#include<iostream>
main()
{       int a = 2, b = 3, c = 4;
        if(a == 0 || b >= c && c > 0)
                if(a && b)
                c = 10;
        else
                c = 20;
        cout<<"\n a = "<<a<<" \t b = "<<b<<"
        \t c = "<<c;
}
```

7.
```
using namespace std;
#include<iostream>
main()
{       int a = 2, b = 3, c = 4;
        if( a = b)
                c++;
        cout<<"\n a = "<<a<<" \t b = "<<b<< "
        \t c = "<<c;
}
```

8.
```
using namespace std;
#include<iostream>
main()
{       int a = 2, b = 3, c = 4;
        if( a = b < c)
        {       c++;
                a--;
        }
        ++b;
```

```
        cout<<"\n a = "<<a<<"\t b = "<<b<<" \t
        c = "<<c;
    }
```

9. using namespace std;
```
    #include<iostream>
    main()
    {   int num = 10;
        cout<<"\n "<<(num > 100);
    }
```

10. using namespace std;
```
    #include<iostream>
    main()
    {   cout<<"HELLO";
        if(-1)
            cout<<"WORLD";
    }
```

11. using namespace std;
```
    #include<iostream>
    main()
    {   int a = 3;
        if(a < 10)
            cout<<"\n LESS";
        if(a < 20)
            cout<<"\n LESS";
        if(a < 30)
            cout<<"\n LESS";
    }
```

12. using namespace std;
```
    #include<iostream>
    main()
    {   int a = 10, b = 20, c = 30, d = 40;
        if(c < d)
            if ( c < b)
                cout<<"\n c";
            else if(a < c)
                cout<<"\n a";
            if(a > b)
                cout<<"\n b";
            else
                cout<<"\n d";
    }
```

13. using namespace std;
```
    #include<iostream>
    main()
    {   char ch = 'Y';
        switch(ch)
        {   default:
                cout<<"\n YES OR NO";
            case 'Y':
                cout<<"YES";
                break;
            case 'N':
                cout<<"NO";
                break;
        }
    }
```

14. using namespace std;
```
    #include<iostream>
    main()
    {   int num = 10;
        for(num++;num++;num++)
            cout<<num;
    }
```

15. using namespace std;
```
    #include<iostream>
    main()
    {   int num = 10;
        for(;--num;)
            cout<<num;
    }
```

16. using namespace std;
```
    #include<iostream>
    main()
    {   int num = 10;
        for(;!num;num++)
            cout<<num;
    }
```

17. using namespace std;
```
    #include<iostream>
    main()
    {   float PI = 3.14, area;
        int r = 7;
        while(r >= 0)
        {   area = PI * r * r;
            cout<<"\n Area = "<<area;
        }
    }
```

18. using namespace std;
```
    #include<iostream>
    main()
    {   int i = 0, n = 10;
        while(i == 0)
        {   if(n < 10)
                break;
            n--;
        }
        cout<<"\n i = "<<i<<" and n="<<n;
    }
```

19. using namespace std;
```
    #include<iostream>
    main()
    {   int i = 0;
        do
```

```
    {     cout<<"\n "<<i;
          i++;
    }while(i <= 0);
    cout<<"\n STOP";
}
```

20.
```
using namespace std;
#include<iostream>
main()
{     int i, j;
      for(i = 0;i <= 10;i++)
      {     cout<<"\n";
            for(j = 0;j <= i0;j++)
      cout<<" ";
            cout<<"\n "<<j;
      }
}
```

21.
```
using namespace std;
#include<iostream>
int main()
{     int num = 10;
      cout<<"\n "<< (num > 10);
}
```

22.
```
using namespace std;
#include<iostream>
main()
{     cout<<"HELLO";
      if (!1)
            cout<<"WORLD";
}
```

23.
```
using namespace std;
#include<iostream>
main()
{     int x = -1;
      unsigned int y = 1;
      if(x < y)
            cout<<<"\n SMALL";
      else
            cout<<"\n LARGE";
}
```

24.
```
using namespace std;
#include<iostream>
main()
{     char ch = -63;
      int num = -36;
      unsigned int unum = -18;
      if(ch > num)
      {     cout<<"A";
            if(ch > unum)
                  cout<<"B";
            else
                  cout<<"C";
      }
      else
      {
            cout<<"D";
            if(num < unum)
                  cout<<"E";
            else
                  cout<<"F";
      }
}
```

25.
```
using namespace std;
#include<iostream>
main()
{     int num = 10;
      for(;++num;num -= 2)
            cout<<num;
}
```

26.
```
using namespace std;
#include<iostream>
main()
{     int num = 10;
      for(;;)
            cout<<"HI";
      return 0;
}
```

27.
```
using namespace std;
#include<iostream>
main()
{
      int num = 10;
      for(num++; num <= 100; num = 100)
            cout<<num;
}
```

28.
```
using namespace std;
#include<iostream>
main()
{     while(1);
      cout<<"Hi";
}
```

29.
```
using namespace std;
#include<iostream>
main()
{     int i = 0;
      char c = '0';
      while(i < 10)
      {     cout<<char(c + i);
            i++;
      }
}
```

30.
```
using namespace std;
#include<iostream>
```

```
main()
{     int i = 0;
      do
      {     if(i > 10)
                  continue;
            i++;
      }while(i < 20);
      cout<<"\n i = "<<i;
}
```

31.
```
using namespace std;
#include<iostream>
main()
{     int i = 1;
      for(;i <= 1;i++)     {
            cout<<"\n "<<i;
      cout<<"\n STOP";
}
```

32.
```
using namespace std;
#include<iostream>
main()
{     int i, j;
      for(i = 10;i >= 0;i--)
      {     cout<"\n";
            for(j = i;j >= 0;j--)
                  cout<<j;
      }
}
```

Answers

Fill in the Blanks

1. there is no matching else; **2.** integral; **3.** n; **4.** break/continue; **5.** infinite; **6.** loop; **7.** decision control; **8.** iterative; **9.** post test loops; **10.** sentinel controlled; **11.** goto; **12.** goto

True or False

1. False	**2.** False	**3.** True	**4.** True	**5.** True	**6.** True	**7.** True	**8.** False
9. True	**10.** True	**11.** True	**12.** False	**13.** False	**14.** True	**15.** False	**16.** True
17. False	**18.** True	**19.** True	**20.** True	**21.** True	**22.** True	**23.** False	**24.** False
25. False							

Multiple Choice Questions

1. (a); **2.** (c); **3.** (a); **4.** (b) and (c); **5.** (b); **6.** (d); **7.** (b); **8.** (a); **9.** (b)

Case Study 1

This case study shows the implementation of concepts discussed in Chapters 1 and 2 on Introduction to OO Programming and Basics of C++ Programming.

C1.1 ROMAN REPRESENTATION OF A NUMBER

Roman numerals are written as combinations of seven letters. These letters include the following:

I = I	C = 100
V = 5	D = 500
X = 10	M = 1,000
L = 50	

If smaller numbers follow larger numbers, the numbers are added. If a smaller number precedes a larger number, the smaller number is subtracted from the larger number.

Example C1.1 To convert 1,100 into Roman numerals, you would write M for 1,000 and then a C after it for 100 (as shown in Table C1.1). Therefore, 1100 = MC in Roman numerals.

Some morc cxamples are listed here:

VII = 5 + 2 = 7
IX = 10 – 1 = 9
XL = 50 – 10 = 40
CX = 100 + 0 = 11
MCMLXXXIV = 1000 + (1000 – 100) + 50 + 30 + (5 – 1) = 1984

Table C1.1 Roman numeral table

1	I	14	XIV	27	XXVII	150	CL
2	II	15	XV	28	XXVIII	200	CC
3	III	16	XVI	29	XXIX	300	CCC
4	IV	17	XVII	30	XXX	400	CD
5	V	18	XVIII	31	XXXI	500	D
6	VI	19	XIX	40	XL	600	DC
7	VII	20	XX	50	L	700	DCC
8	VIII	21	XXI	60	LX	800	DCCC
9	IX	22	XXII	70	LXX	900	CM
10	X	23	XXIII	80	LXXX	1000	M
11	XI	24	XXIV	90	XC	1600	MDC
12	XII	25	XXV	100	C	1700	MDCC
13	XIII	26	XXVI	101	CI	1900	MCM

Program C1.1 Display the Roman number representation of a given number.

```
using namespace std;
#include<iostream>
main()
{
int number;
int ones, tens, hundreds, thousand;
cout<<"\n Enter any number (1-3000): ";
cin>>number;
if(number==0||number>3000)
//check for a valid number
            cout<<"\n INVALID NUMBER";
thousand = (number/1000)*1000;
// extract the digit at thousand's place
hundreds = ((number/100)%10)*100;
// extract the digit at hundred's place
tens = ((number/10)%10)*10;
// extract the digit at ten's place
ones = ((number/1)%10)*1;
// extract the digit at one's place
if (thousand ==1000)
            cout<<"M";
else if (thousand ==2000)
            cout<<"MM";
else if (thousand ==3000)
            cout<<"MMM";
if (hundreds == 100)
            cout<<"C";
else if (hundreds == 200)
            cout<<"CC";
else if (hundreds == 300)
            cout<<"CCC";
else if (hundreds == 400)
            cout<<"CD";
else if (hundreds ==500)
            cout<<"D";
else if (hundreds == 600)
            cout<<"DC";
else if (hundreds == 700)
            cout<<"DCC";
else if (hundreds ==800)
            cout<<"DCCC";
else if (hundreds == 900)
            cout<<"CM";
if (tens == 10)
            cout<<"X";
else if (tens == 20)
            cout<<"XX";
else if (tens == 30)
            cout<<"XXX";
else if (tens == 40)
            cout<<"XL";
else if (tens ==50)
            cout<<"L";
else if (tens == 60)
            cout<<"LX";
else if (tens == 70)
            cout<<"LXX";
else if (tens ==80)
            cout<<"LXXX";
else if (tens == 90)
            cout<<"XC";
if (ones == 1)
            cout<<"I";
else if (ones == 2)
            cout<<"II";
else if (ones == 3)
            cout<<"III";
else if (ones == 4)
            cout<<"IV";
else if (ones ==5)
            cout<<"V";
else if (ones == 6)
            cout<<"VI";
else if (ones == 7)
            cout<<"VII";
else if (ones ==8)
            cout<<"VIII";
else if (ones == 9)
            cout<<"IX";
}
```

OUTPUT

```
Enter any number (1-3000): 1881
MDCCCLXXXI
```

C1.2 FIND YOUR DAY OF BIRTH BASED ON YOUR DATE OF BIRTH

An algorithm to calculate the day of the week

- Find the century. Use the centuries table given below to calculate the century.
- Find the year. We know that there are 365 days in a year, that is, 52 weeks plus one day. Each year starts on the day of the week after the first day of

the preceding year. Each leap year has one more day than a common year.

If we know on which day a century starts (from the above) and we add the number of years elapsed since the start of the century, plus the number of leap years that have elapsed since the start of the century, we get the day of the week on which the year starts, where year is the last two digits of the year.

- Find the month. Use the months' table to find the day of the week when a month starts.
- Find the day of the month. Once we know on which day of the week the month starts, we simply add the day of the month to find the final result.

Centuries table

Century	Value
1700-1799	4
1800-1899	2
1900-1999	0
2000-2099	6
2100-2199	4
2200-2299	2
2300-2399	0
2400-2499	6
2500-2599	4
2600-2699	2

Months Table

Month	Value
January	0 (in leap year 6)
February	3 (in leap year 2)
March	3
April	6
May	1
June	4
July	6
August	2
September	5
October	0
November	3
December	5

Days Table

Day	Value
Sunday	0
Monday	1
Tuesday	2
Wednesday	3
Thursday	4
Friday	5
Saturday	6

Example C1.2 Consider the following algorithm to calculate the day of 24 April 1982

- Find the century value of 1900s from the centuries table 0
- Last two digits give the value of year 82
- Divide the 82 by 4, 82/4 = 20.5 and drop the fractional part 20
- Find the value of April in the months table 6
- Add all numbers from steps 1–4 to the day of the month (in this case, 24) 0 + 82 + 20 + 6 + 24 = 132
- Divide the result of step 5 by 7 and find the remainder: 132/7 = 18 remainder 6
- Look up the day's table for the remainder obtained 6 = Saturday

Program C1.2 Calculate the day of birth on entering the date of birth.

```
using namespace std;
#include<iostream>
#include<stdlib.h>
main()
```

```
{
int dd,mm,yy,year,month,day,i,n;
cout<<"\n Enter the date :      ";
cin>>dd>>mm>>yy;
if( dd>31 || mm>12)
// check for valid date
{
cout<<"\n INVALID INPUT ";
exit(0);
}
year = yy-1900;       //find year
year = year/4;
year = year+yy-1900;
switch(mm)      // find month
{
case 1:
case 10:
                      month = 1;
                      break;
case 2:
case 3:
case 11:
                      month = 4;
                      break;
case 7:
case 4:
                     month = 0;
                     break;
case 5:
                     month = 2;
                     break;
case 6:
                     month = 5;
                     break;
case 8:
                     month = 3;
                     break;
case 9:
case 12:
                     month = 6;
                     break;
}
year = year+month;
year = year+dd;
day  = year%7;
switch(day)      // find day
{
case 0:
                    cout<<"\n  SATURDAY";
                    break;
case 1:
                    cout<<"\n SUNDAY";
                    break;
case 2:
                    cout<<"\n MONDAY";
                    break;
case 3:
                    cout<<"\n TUESDAY";
                    break;
case 4:
                    cout<<"\n WEDNESDAY";
                    break;
case 5:
                    cout<<"\n THURSDAY";
                    break;
case 6:
                    cout<<"\n FRIDAY";
                    break;
}
return 0;
}
```

OUTPUT

```
Enter the date :       29 10 1981
THURSDAY
```

CHAPTER 4

Functions

KEY Concepts

Function declaration, definition, and call • Return statement Passing parameters • Using default arguments • Returning reference variables • Functions with variable arguments • Storage classes • Variable scope • Inline functions • Function overloading • Recursive functions

INTRODUCTION

C++ enables programmers to break up a program into segments commonly known as functions. Each function can be written more or less independently of the others. Every function in the program is supposed to perform a well-defined task. Therefore, the program code of one function is completely insulated from that of other functions.

Every function interfaces to the outside world in terms of how information is transferred to it and how results generated by the function are transmitted back from it. This interface is basically specified by the function name. For example, look at Fig. 4.1 which explains how the `main()` calls another function to perform a well-defined task.

In Fig. 4.1, we see that `main()` calls function named `func1()`. Therefore, `main()` is known as the calling function and `func1()` is known as the called function. The moment the compiler encounters a function call, instead of executing the next statement in the calling function, the control jumps to the statements that are a part of the called function. After the called function is executed, the control is returned back to the calling program.

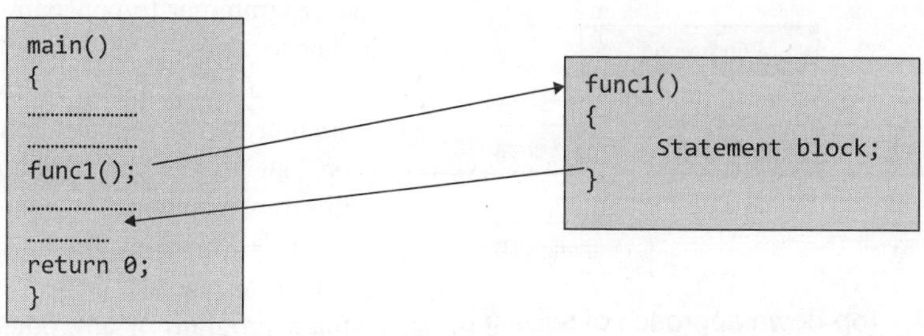

Figure 4.1 main() and func1()

It is not necessary that the `main()` can call only one function. It can call as many functions as it wants and as many times as it wants. For example, a function call placed within a `for` loop, `while` loop, or `do-while` loop may call the same function multiple times until the condition holds true.

Another point to note here is that it is not that only the `main()` can call another functions. Any function can call any other function. For example, look at Fig. 4.2 which shows one function calling another, and the other function, in turn, calling some other function.

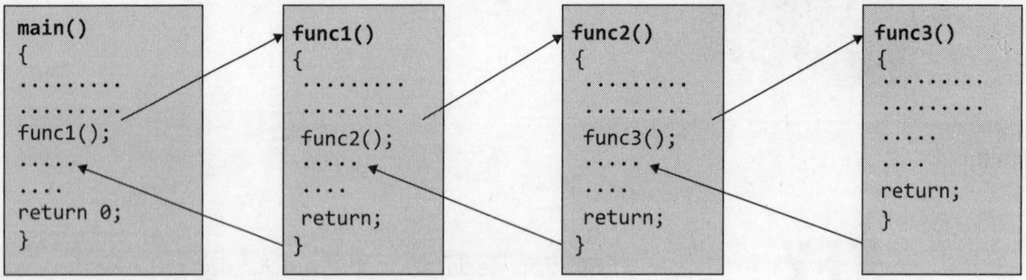

Figure 4.2 Function calling another function

Therefore, we see that every function encapsulates a set of operations and when called, it returns information to the calling program.

4.1 NEED FOR FUNCTIONS

Analysing the reasons for segmenting a program into manageable chunks is an important aspect of programming.

- Dividing the program into separate well-defined functions facilitates each function to be written and tested separately. This simplifies the process of getting the total program to work. Figure 4.3 shows that the `main()` calls other functions for dividing the entire code into smaller sections (or functions).
- Understanding, coding, and testing multiple separate functions are far easier than doing the same for one huge function.
- If a big program has to be developed without using any function other than `main()`, there will be many lines in the `main()`. Maintaining the program will be a big mess. A large program is a serious issue in micro-computers where memory space is limited.
- All libraries in C++ contain a set of functions that programmers are free to use in their programs. These functions have been prewritten and pretested. Therefore, programmers use them without worrying about their code details. This speeds up program development, by allowing the programmer to concentrate only on the code that he has to write.
- When a big program is broken into comparatively smaller functions, different programmers working on that project can divide the workload by writing different functions.
- Like C++ libraries, programmers can also make their functions and use them from different points in the main program or any other program that needs its functionalities.

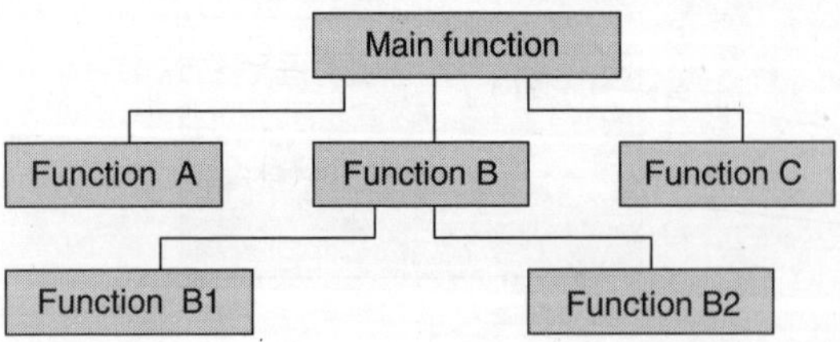

Figure 4.3 Top-down approach of solving a problem

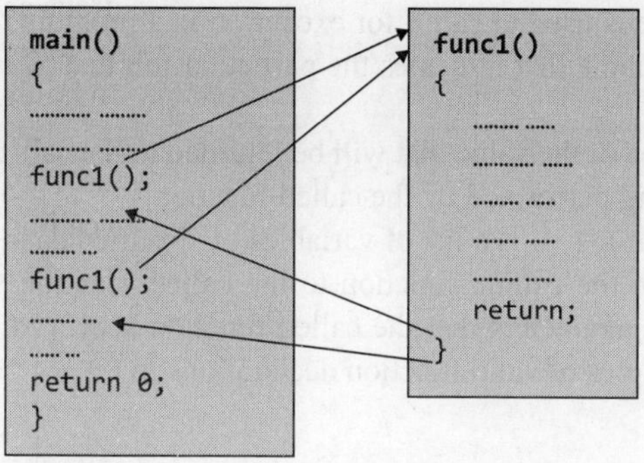

Figure 4.4 Function func1() called twice from the main()

Consider a program that executes a set of instructions repeatedly `n` times, though not continuously. In case the instructions had to be repeated continuously for `n` times, they can better be placed within a loop. However, if these instructions have to be executed abruptly from anywhere within the program code, instead of writing these instructions in all areas where they are required, it is better to place these instructions in a function and call that function wherever required. Figure 4.4 explains this concept.

4.2 USING FUNCTIONS

In the first chapter, we have mentioned that while executing a C++ program, the operating system calls the `main()` function which marks the entry point for execution of the program. When the program is executed, the `main()` returns some value to the operating system.

Any function, including `main`, can be compared to a black box that takes in input, processes it, and spits out the result. However, we may also have a function that does not take any inputs at all or that does not return anything at all.

While using functions, we will use the terminology as follows.

- A function, `f`, that calls another function g, is known as the calling function and `g` is known as the called function.
- The inputs that the function takes are known as arguments or parameters.
- When a called function returns some result back to the calling function, it is said to return that result.
- The calling function may or may not pass parameters to the called function. If the called function accepts the arguments, the calling function will pass parameters, otherwise, it will not do so.
- Function declaration is a declaration statement that identifies a function with its name, a list of arguments that it accepts, and the type of data it returns.
- Function definition consists of a function header that identifies the function, followed by the body of the function containing the executable code for that function

4.3 FUNCTION DECLARATION OR FUNCTION PROTOTYPE

Before using the function, the compiler must know about the number and types of parameters that the function expects to receive and the data type of value that it will return to the calling program. For this, we need to declare a function (or give the function prototype). Placing the function declaration statement prior to its use enables the compiler to make a check on the arguments used while calling that function.

The general format for declaring a function that accepts some arguments and returns some value as result can be given as follows:

```
return_data_type function_name(data_type variable1, data_type variable2,..);
```

We must note the following here.

- `function_name` is a valid name for the function. Naming a function follows the same rules that naming variables follows. A function should have a meaningful name that must clarify the task

> **Programming Tip:** Not placing a semicolon after the function declaration is an error.

that it will perform. The function name is used to call it for execution in a program. Every function must have a different name that indicates the particular job that the function does.

- `return_data_type` specifies the data type of the value that will be returned to the calling function as a result of the processing performed by the called function.
- `data_type variable1, data_type variable2, ...` is a list of variables of specified data types. These variables are passed from the calling function to the called function. They are also known as arguments or parameters that the called function accept to perform its task. Table 4.1 shows examples of valid function declarations in C++.

Table 4.1 Valid function declarations

Function declaration	Use of the function
`char convert_to_uppercase(char ch);` (Return Data Type)	Converts a character to upper case. The function receives a character as an argument, converts it into upper case, and returns the converted character back to the calling program.
`float avg(int a, int b);` (Function Name)	Calculates average of two numbers a and b received as arguments. The function returns a floating point value.
`int find_largest(int a, int b, int c);` (Data Type of Variable)	Finds the largest of three numbers a, b, and c received as arguments. An integer value which is the largest number of the three numbers is returned to the calling function.
`double multiply(float a, float b);` (Variable 1)	Multiplies two floating point numbers a and b that are received as arguments and returns a double value.
`void swap(int a, int b);`	Swaps or interchanges the value of integer variables a and b received as arguments. The function returns no value; therefore, the data type is void.
`void print(void);`	The function is used to print information on screen. The function neither accepts any value as argument nor returns any value. Therefore, the return type is void and the argument list contains void.

The following are the key points to remember about function declaration:

- After the declaration of every function, there is a semicolon. If the semicolon is missing, the compiler will generate an error message.
- The name of the function is global. Therefore, the declared function can be called from any point in the program.
- Use of argument names in the function declaration statement is optional. Both declaration statements are valid in C++.

> **Programming Tip:** Though optional, use argument names in the function declaration.

```
int func(int, char, float); or
int func(int num, char ch, float fnum);
```

- No function can be declared within the body of another function.
- A function having `void` as its `return type` cannot return any value.
- A function having `void` as its parameter list cannot accept any value. A function is declared as

```
void print(void);          OR       void print()
```

does not accept any input/arguments from the calling function.
- If the function declaration does not specify any return type, by default, the function returns an integer value. Therefore, when a function is declared as

```
sum(int a, int b);
```

the function sum accepts two integer values from the calling function and, in turn, returns an integer value to the caller.
- Some compilers make it compulsory to declare the function before its usage while other compilers make it optional. However, it is always good to declare the function before its usage as it allows error checking on the arguments in the function call.

4.4 FUNCTION DEFINITION

When a function is defined, space is allocated for that function in the memory. A function definition comprises two parts as follows:

- Function header
- Function body

Programming Tip: It is an error to place a semicolon after the function header in the function definition.

The syntax of a function definition can be given as

```
return_data_type function_name(data_type variable1, data_type variable2,..)
{ ............
  statements
  ............
  return( variable);
}
```

Note The number of arguments and the order of arguments in the function header must be same as that given in function declaration statement.

Programming Tip: The parameter list in the function definition as well as function declaration must match with each other.

While `return_data_type function_name(data_type variable1, data_type variable2,..)` are known as the function header, the rest of the portion comprising program statements within `{ }` is the function body which contains the code to perform the specific task.

The function header is same as that of function declaration. The only difference between the two terms is that a function header is not followed by a semicolon. The list of variables in the function header is known as the formal parameter list. The parameter list may have zero or more parameters of any data type. The function body contains instructions to perform the desired computation in a function.

Programming Tip: A function can be defined either before or after the main().

The function definition itself can act as an implicit function declaration. Therefore, the programmer may skip the function declaration statement if the function is defined before being used.

Note The argument names in the function declaration and function definition need not be the same. However, the data types of the arguments must match with that specified in function declaration and function definition.

4.5 FUNCTION CALL

The function call statement invokes the function. When a function is invoked, the compiler jumps to the called function to execute the statements that are a part of that function. Once the called function is executed, the program control passes back to the calling function.

A function call statement has the following syntax:

```
function_name(variable1, variable2, …);
```

When the function declaration is present before the function call, the compiler can check for the correct number and type of arguments used in the function call and that the returned value, if any, is being used reasonably.

Function definitions are often placed in a separate header file which can be included in other C++ source files that wish to use the functions. For example, the header file `math.h`, contains the definition of `pow` and `sqrt` functions. We simply include this file and straightaway call these functions without worrying about the code to implement their functionality.

Note List of variables used in function call is known as actual parameter list. The actual parameter list may be variable names, expressions, or constants.

Programming Tip: It is a logical error if the arguments in the function call are placed in a wrong order.

The following are the key points to remember while calling the function:

- Function name and the number and type of arguments in the function call must be the same as that given in the function declaration and function header of the function definition
- If, by mistake, the parameters passed to a function are more than specified to accept, then the extra arguments will be discarded.
- If, by mistake, the parameters passed to a function are less than specified to accept, then the unmatched argument will be initialized to some garbage value (i.e. arbitrary meaningless value).
- Names, and not the types, of variables in function declaration, function call, and header of function definition may vary.
- If the data type of the argument passed does not match with that specified in the function declaration, then depending on the compiler being used, either the unmatched argument will be initialized to some garbage value or there will be some compile time error.
- Arguments may be passed in the form of expressions to the called function. In such cases, arguments are first evaluated and converted to the type of formal parameter and the body of the function gets executed.
- The parameter list must be separated by commas.
- If the return type of the function is not `void`, then the value returned by the called function may be assigned to some variable as follows.

```
variable_name = function_name(variable1, variable2, …);
```

Let us now try a program using function.

Example 4.1 To add two integers using functions

```
using namespace std;
#include<iostream>
int sum(int a, int b);    // FUNCTION DECLARATION
int main()
{   int num1, num2, total = 0;
    cout<<"\n Enter two numbers : ";
    cin>>num1>>num2;
    total = sum(num1, num2);        // FUNCTION CALL
    cout<<"\n Total = "<<total;
}
// FUNCTION DEFNITION
int sum (int a, int b)      // FUNCTION HEADER
{         // FUNCTION BODY
    int result;
    result = a + b;
    return result;
}
```

OUTPUT

```
Enter the two numbers : 20   30
Total = 50
```

Programming Tip: It is an error to use void as the return type when the function is expected to return a value to the calling function.

Note that the variables declared within the function as well as its parameters are local to that function. The programmer may use the same names for variables in other functions. This prevents him to think of and keep unique names for variables in case there are several functions in the program.

In the `sum()`, we have declared a variable result just like any other variable. Variables declared within a function are called automatic local variables because of the following reasons.

- First, they are local to the function. Therefore, their effect in terms of scope, lifetime, or accessibility, is limited to the function. Any change made to these variables is visible only in that function.
- Second, they are automatically created whenever the function is called and they cease to exit at the end of the function.

Note A function cannot be used on the right side of an assignment statement. Therefore, writing func(10) = 100; is invalid in C++, where func is a function that accepts an integer value.

4.6 RETURN STATEMENT

The `return` statement is used to terminate the execution of a function and return control to the calling function. When the `return` statement is encountered, the program execution resumes in the calling function at the point immediately following the function call. Refer Fig. 4.2 in which the control passes from the called function to the calling function when the return statement is encountered.

A `return` statement may or may not return a value to the calling function. The syntax of `return` statement can be given as follows:

```
return <expression>;
```

Programming Tip: It is an error to use a `return` statement in a function that has void as its return type.

Here, expression is placed in between angular brackets because specifying an expression is optional. The value of expression, if present, is returned to the calling function. However, in case the expression is omitted, the return value of the function is undefined.

The expression, if present, is converted to the type returned by the function. A function that has `void` as its return type cannot return any value to the calling function. Therefore, a function that has been declared with return type `void, a return statement` containing an expression generates a warning and the expression is not evaluated.

For functions that have no `return` statement, the control automatically returns to the calling function after the last statement of the called function is executed. An implicit return takes place after completion of the last statement of the called function, and control automatically returns to the calling function.

Note The programmer may or may not place the expression within parentheses. By default, the return type of a function is `int`.

A function may have more than one `return` statement as explained by the following program.

Example 4.2 Using more than one `return` statement

Programming Tip: When the value returned by a function is assigned to a variable, then the returned value is converted to the type of the variable receiving it.

Programming Tip: An error is generated when the function does not return data of the specified type.

```
using namespace std;
#include<iostream>
int check_relation(int a, int b);          // FUNCTION DECALARATION
main()
{   int a = 3, b = 5, res;
    res = check_relation(a, b);            // FUNCTION CALL
    if(res == 0)                           // Test the returned value
        cout<<"\n EQUAL";
    if(res == 1)
        cout<<"\n a is greater than b";
    if(res == -1)
        cout<<"\n a is less than b";
}
int check_relation(int a, int b)           // FUNCTION DEFINITION
{   if(a == b)
        return 0;
if(a > b)
        return 1;
else if (a < b)
        return -1;
}
```

OUTPUT

```
a is less than b
```

Explanation: In this program, there are multiple return statements. Note that only one of them will get executed, depending upon the condition. Like the `break` statement, `return` statement is also used to cause a premature termination of the function.

An expression appearing in a `return` statement is converted to the return type of the function in which the statement appears. If no implicit conversion is possible, the `return` statement is invalid. This means that since the return type of the function `check_relation()` is `int`, the result either `0, 1, or -1` is evaluated as an integer.

Recall that the variables declared inside the function cease to exist after the last statement of the function is executed. We need to examine how to return the value of sum in the program that adds two integers using function. A copy of the value being returned is made automatically and this copy is available to the return point in the program.

4.7 PASSING PARAMETERS TO THE FUNCTION

Programming Tip: A function that does not return any value cannot be placed on the right side of the assignment operator.

When a function is called, the calling function may have to pass some values to the called function. Although we have already been doing this in the programming examples given earlier, now, we will learn the technicalities involved in passing arguments or parameters to the called function.

Basically, there are two ways in which arguments or parameters can be passed to the called function. They include the following:

- Call-by-value, in which values of the variables are passed by the calling function to the called function. The programs that we have written so far call the function using call-by-value method of passing parameters
- Call-by-address, in which the address of the variables is passed by the calling function to the called function.
- Call-by-reference in which a reference of the variable is passed by the calling function to the called function.

In this section, we will read about these types in detail.

4.7.1 Call-by-Value

Programming Tip: It is legal to have multiple return statements in C++.

Till now, we had been calling the functions and passing arguments to them by using call-by-value method. In this method, the called function creates new variables to store the value of the arguments passed to it. Therefore, the called function uses a copy of the actual arguments to perform its intended task.

If the called function is supposed to modify the value of the parameters passed to it, then the change will be reflected only in the called function. In the calling function, no change will be made to the value of the variables. This is because all the changes were made to the copy of the variables and not on the actual variables. The following program explains this concept.

Example 4.3 Program to call a function with a parameter

```
using namespace std;
#include<iostream>
void add(int n);  // FUNCTION DECLARATION
int main()
{   int num = 2;
    cout<<"\n The value of num before calling the function = "<<num;
    add(num);  // FUNCTION CALL
    cout<<"\n The value of num after calling the function = "<<num;
}
void add(int n)   // FUNCTION DEFINITION
{   n = n + 10;
    cout<<"\n The value of num in the called function = "<<n;
}
```

OUTPUT

```
The value of num before calling the function = 2
```

```
The value of num in the called function = 20
The value of num after calling the function = 2
```

The function `add()` accepts an integer variable `num` and adds `10` to it. In the calling function, the value of `num = 2`. In `add()`, the value of `num` is modified to `20` but in the calling function the change is not reflected.

Note that since the called function uses a copy of num, the value of num in the calling function remains untouched. This concept can be more clearly understood from Fig. 4.5.

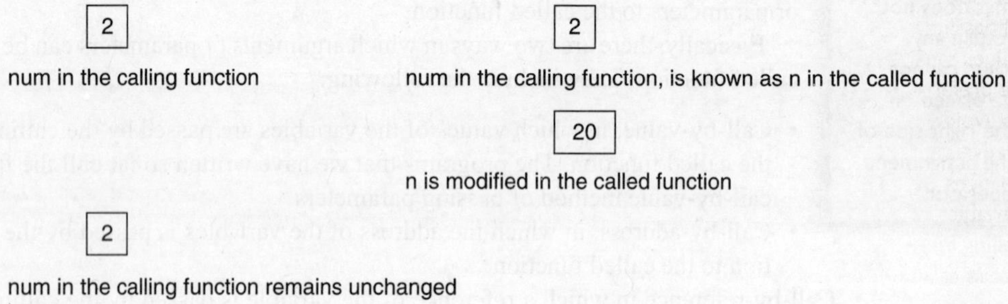

Figure 4.5 Call-by-value method of argument passing

It can be observed in the program that the called function could not directly modify the value of the argument that was passed to it. In this case, the value has to be changed then the programmer may use the return statement. This is shown in the modified code given next.

Example 4.4 Consider another program given here that calls a function with a parameter. The modified value of the parameter is returned to effect changes in the calling function.

```
using namespace std;
#include<iostream>
int add(int n);    // FUNCTION DECLARARTION
int main()
{  int num = 2;
   cout<<"\n The value of num before calling the function = "<<num;
   num = add(num);                    // FUNCTION CALL
   cout<<"\n The value of num after calling the function = "<<num;
}
int add(int n)                        // FUNCTION DEFINITION
{  n = n + 10;
   cout<<"\n The value of num in the called function = "<<n;
   return n;
}
```

OUTPUT

```
The value of num before calling the function = 2
The value of num in the called function = 20
The value of num after calling the function = 20
```

The following are the key points to remember while passing arguments to a function using call-by-value method.

- When arguments are passed by value, the called function creates new variables of the same data type as the arguments passed to it.

- The values of the arguments passed by the function are copied into the newly created variables.
- Arguments are called by value when the function does not need to modify the values of the original variables in the calling program.
- Values of the variables in the calling functions remain unaffected when the arguments are passed using call-by-value technique.

Programming Tip: Using call-by-value method of passing values must be preferred to avoid inadvertent changes to variables of the calling function in the called function.

Therefore, call-by-value method of passing arguments to a function must be used only in the following two cases:

- When the called function does not modify the value of the actual parameter. It simply uses the value of the parameters to perform its task.
- When you want that the called function should only temporarily modify the value of the variables and not permanently. Therefore, although the called function may modify the value of the variables, these variables remain unchanged in the calling program.

Pros and Cons of Call-by-Value

While the biggest advantage of using call-by-value technique to pass arguments to the called function is that arguments can be variables (e.g., `x`), literals (e.g., `6`), or expressions (e.g., `x+1`), the main side effect is that copying data consumes additional storage space. In addition, it can take a lot of time to copy, thereby, resulting in performance penalty, especially if the function is called many times.

4.7.2 Call-by-Address

The call-by-pointer or call-by-address method of passing arguments to a function copies the address of an argument into the formal parameter. The function then uses the address to access the actual argument. This means that any changes made to the value stored at a particular address will be reflected in the calling function also.

The called function uses pointers to access the data. In other words, the dereferencing operator is used to access the variables in the called function. Though we will read about the pointer in the coming chapters, for now, we must understand that when we writes `variable`, it refers to the address of the variable, and when we write `*variable`, it refers to the value of the variable.

Example 4.5 Program that uses call-by-address method to pass arguments to the called function

```
using namespace std;
#include<iostream>
void add(int *n);
int main()
{   int num = 2;
    cout<<"\n The value of num before calling the function = "<<num;
    add(&num);
    cout<<"\n The value of num after calling the function = "<<num;
        return 0;
}
void add( int *n)
{   *n = *n + 10;
    cout<<"\n The value of num in the called function = "<<*n;
}
```

OUTPUT

```
The value of num before calling the function = 2
The value of num in the called function = 12
The value of num after calling the function = 12
```

Explanation: In the program, the statement `add(&num)` assigns address of `num` to `n`. Therefore, now, `n = address of num`. To use the contents of `n` or `num` which now means the same, we use dereferencing operator (*). Therefore, `*n` means the contents (value) of `n`.

Pros and Cons of Call-by-Address

The advantages of using call-by-address technique of passing arguments include the following:

- Since arguments are not copied into new variables, it provides greater time and space efficiency.
- The function can change the value of the argument and the change is reflected in the caller.
- A function can return only one value. In case, we need to return multiple values, we have to pass those arguments by reference, so that modified values are visible in the calling function.

However, the side effect of using this technique is that when an argument is passed using call-by-address, it becomes difficult to tell whether that argument is meant for input, output, or both.

4.7.3 Call-by-Reference

When the calling function passes arguments to the called function using call-by-value method, the only way to return the modified value of the argument to the caller is by using the return statement explicitly. A better option when a function can modify the value of the argument is to pass arguments using call-by-reference technique. In call-by-reference, we declare the function parameters as references rather than normal variables. When this is done, any changes made by the function to the arguments it received are visible by the calling program.

To indicate that an argument is passed using call-by-reference, an ampersand sign (`&`) is placed after the type in the parameter list. In this way, changes made to that parameter in the called function body will be reflected in its value in the calling program.

Hence, in a call-by-reference method, a function receives an implicit reference to the argument, rather than a copy of its value. Therefore, the function can modify the value of the variable and that change will be reflected in the calling function as well. The following program explains this concept.

Note The reference type parameters are accessed in the same way as other normal variables are accessed.

Example 4.6 Program that uses call-by-reference method to pass arguments to the called function

```
using namespace std;
#include<iostream>
void add(int &n);
int main()
{   int num = 2;
    cout<<"\n The value of num before calling the function = "<<num;
    add(num);
    cout<<"\n The value of num after calling the function = "<<num;
}
void add(int &n)
{   n = n + 10;
    cout<<"\n The value of num in the called function = "<<n;
}
```

OUTPUT

```
The value of num before calling the function = 2
The value of num in the called function = 12
The value of num after calling the function = 12
```

Pros and Cons of Call-by-Reference

The advantages of using call-by-reference technique of passing arguments include the following:

- Since arguments are not copied into new variables, it provides greater time and space efficiency
- The function can change the value of the argument and the change is reflected in the caller.
- A function can return only one value. In case, we need to return multiple values, pass those arguments by reference, so that modified values are visible in the calling function.

Note We will make a comparison between call-by-reference and call-by-address in Chapter 7, where we will read about pointer variables and using address in detail.

Example 4.7 Program to swap the values of two variables using call-by-value and call-by-reference mechanisms. Note the value of integers in the calling function and the called function

```
using namespace std;
#include<iostream>
void swap_call_by_val(int, int);
void swap_call_by_add(int *, int *);
void swap_call_by_ref(int &, int &);
int main()
{   int a = 1, b = 2, c = 3, d = 4;
    cout<<"\n In main(), a = "<<a<<" and b = "<<b;
    swap_call_by_val(a, b);
    cout<<"\n In main(), a = "<<a<<" and b = "<<b;
    cout<<"\n\n In main(), c = "<<c<<" and d = "<<d;
    swap_call_by_add(&c, &d);
    cout<<"\n In main(), c = "<<c<<" and d = "<<d;
    swap call by ref(c, d);
    cout<<"\n In main(), c = "<<c<<" and d = "<<d;
}
void swap_call_by_val(int a, int b)
{   int temp;
    temp = a;
    a = b;
    b = temp;
    cout<<"\n In function (Call-By-Value Method) - a = "<<a<<" and b = "<<b;
}
void swap_call_by_add(int *c, int *d)
{   int temp;
    temp = *c;   // *operator used to refer to the value
    *c = *d;
    *d = temp;
    cout<<"\n In function (Call-By-Address Method) - c = "<<*c<<" and d = "<<*d;
}
void swap_call_by_ref(int &c, int &d)
{
    int temp;
    temp = c;
    c = d;
    d = temp;
    cout<<"\n In function (Call-By-Reference Method) - c = "<<c<<" and d = "<<d;
}
```

OUTPUT

```
In main(), a = 1 and b = 2
In function (Call-By-Value Method) - a = 2 and b = 1
In main(), a = 1 and b = 2
```

```
In main(), c = 3 and d = 4
In function (Call-By-Reference Method) - c = 4 and d = 3
In main(), c = 4 and d = 3
In main(), c = 3 and d = 4
In function (Call-By-Address Method) - c = 4 and d = 3
In main(), c = 4 and d = 3
```

Program 4.1 Write a program to find the biggest of three integers using functions.

```
using namespace std;
#include<iostream>
int larger(int a, int b, intc);
int main()
{   int num1, num2, num3, large;
    cout<<"\n Enter the three numbers : ";
    cin>>num1>>num2>>num3;
    large = larger(num1, num2, num3);
    cout<<"\n Largest number = "<<large;
}
int larger(int a, int b, int c)
{   if(a>b && a>c)
        return a;
    if(b>a && b>c)
        return b;
    else
        return c;
}
```

OUTPUT

```
Enter the three numbers : 45 23 34
Largest number = 45
```

Program 4.2 Write a program to calculate the area of a circle using functions.

```
using namespace std;
#include<iostream>
float cal_area(float r);
int main()
{   float area, radius;
    cout<<"\n Enter the radius of the circle : ";
    cin>>radius;
    area = cal_area(radius);
    cout.precision(2);
    cout<<"\n Area of the circle with radius "<<radius<<" = "<< area;
}
float cal_area(float radius)
{   return (3.14 * radius * radius);
}
```

OUTPUT

```
Enter the radius of the circle : 7
Area of the circle with radius 7 = 153.83
```

Program 4.3 Write a program to find whether a number is even or odd using functions.

```
using namespace std;
#include<iostream>
int evenodd(int);
int main()
```

```
{   int num, flag;
    cout<<"\n Enter the number : ";
    cin>>num;
    flag = evenodd(num);
    if (flag == 1)
        cout<<"\n"<<num<<" is EVEN";
    else
        cout<<"\n"<<num<<" is ODD";
}
int evenodd(int a)
{   if(a%2 == 0)
        return 1;
    else
        return 0;
}
```

OUTPUT

```
Enter the number : 42
EVEN
```

Program 4.4 Write a program to convert time into minutes.

```
using namespace std;
#include<iostream>
int convert_time_in_mins(int hrs, int minutes);
main()
{   int hrs, minutes, total_mins;
    cout<<"\n Enter the hours and minutes : ";
    cin>>hrs>>minutes;
    total_mins = convert_time_in_mins(hrs, minutes);
    cout<<"\n Total minutes = "<<total_mins;
}
int convert_time_in_mins(int hrs, int minutes)
{   int mins;
    mins = hrs*60 + minutes;
    return mins;
}
```

OUTPUT

```
Enter the hours and minutes : 4 30
Total minutes = 270
```

Program 4.5 Write a program to calculate P(n/r).

```
using namespace std;
#include<iostream>
int Fact(int num);
main()
{   int n, r;
    float result;
    cout<<"\n Enter the value of n and r : ";
    cin>>n>>r;
    result = (float)Fact(n)/Fact(n-r);
    cout<<"\n P(n/r) - P("<<n<<")/("<<r<<") = "<<result;
}
int Fact(int num)
{   int f = 1, i;
    for(i = num;i >= 1;i--)
        f = f*i;
```

```
    return f;
}
```

OUTPUT

```
Enter the value of n and r : 4 2
P(n/r) - P(4)/(2) = 12.00
```

Program 4.6 Write a program to calculate C(n/r).

```
using namespace std;
#include<iostream>
int Fact(int num)
main()
{   int n, r;
    float result;
    cout<<"\n Enter the value of n and r : ";
    cin>>n>>r;
    result = (float)Fact(n)/(Fact(r)*Fact(n-r));
    cout.precision(2);
    cout<<"\n C(n/r) - C("<<n<<"/"<<r<<") = "<<result;
}
int Fact(int num)
{   int f = 1, i;
    for(i = num;i >= 1;i--)
        f = f*i;
    return f;
}
```

OUTPUT

```
Enter the value of n and r: 4 2
C(n/r) - C(4)/(4) = 6.00
```

Program 4.7 Write a program to sum the series 1/1! + ½! + 1/3! +   + 1/n!.

```
using namespace std;
#include<iostream>
int Fact(int);
main()
{   int n, f, i;
    float result = 0.0;
    cout<<"\n Enter the value of n : ";
    cin>>n;
    for(i = 1;i <= n;i++)
    {   f = Fact(i);
        result += 1/(float)f;
    }
    cout<<"\n The sum of the series 1/1! + 1/2! + 1/3!… = "<< result;
}
int Fact(int num)
{   int f = 1, i;
    for(i = num;i >= 1;i--)
        f = f*i;
    return f;
}
```

OUTPUT

```
Enter the value of n : 5
The sum of the series 1/1! + 1/2! + 1/3!… = 1.716667
```

Program 4.8 Write a program to sum the series 1/1! + 4/2! + 27/3! +

```
using namespace std;
#include<iostream>
#include<math.h>
int Fact(int);
main()
{   int n, i, NUM, DENO;
    float sum = 0.0;
    cout<<"\n Enter the value of n : ";
    cin>>n;
    for(i = 1;i <= n;i++)
    {   NUM = pow(i,i);
        DENO = Fact(i);
        sum += (float)NUM/DENO;
    }
    cout<<"\n 1/1! + 4/2! + 27/3! +  ·= "<<sum;
}
int Fact(int n)
{   int f = 1, i;
    for(i = n;i >= 1;i--)
        f = f*i;
    return f;
}
```

OUTPUT

```
Enter the value of n : 5
1/1! + 4/2! + 27/3! +    = 44.208332
```

4.8 DEFAULT ARGUMENTS

Till now we have studied that when a function is called, all its arguments must be passed to it in totality. However, C++ gives little freedom to programmers by providing default arguments. When a function is specified with default arguments, the function can be called with missing arguments. When a function is called with a missing argument, the function assigns a default value to the parameter. This default value is specified by the programmer in the function declaration statement.

While specifying the default values during function declaration, the programmer must keep the following in mind:

- Only trailing arguments can have default values; therefore, specify them from right to left.
- No argument specified in the middle can have default values.

Let us analyse some function declarations with default arguments to understand which declaration is correct.

```
int my_func(int a, int b, int c = 10);              //Correct
int my_func(int a, int b = 5, int c = 10);          //Correct
int my_func(int a = 1, int b = 5, int c = 10);      //Correct
int my_func(int a, int b = 5, int c);               //Wrong
```

Note Default arguments are used when arguments usually have the same value (with or without some exceptional cases).

Some example codes which demonstrate the usage of default arguments are as follows.

Programming Tip: Arguments explicitly specified in function call override the default values given during function declaration.

Program 4.9 Write a program to calculate the volume of a cuboid using default arguments.

```
using namespace std;
#include<iostream>
int Volume( int length, int width = 3, int height = 4 );
int main()
{ cout<<"\n Volume = "<<Volume(4, 6, 2);
  cout<<"\n\n Volume = "<<Volume(4, 6);
  cout<<"\n\n Volume = "<<Volume(4);
}
int Volume(int length, int width, int height)
{       cout<<"\n Length = "<<length<<" Width = "<<width<<" and Height
        = "<<height;
    return length * width * height;
}
```

OUTPUT

```
Length = 4 Width = 6 and Height = 2
Volume = 48
Length = 4 Width = 6 and Height = 4
Volume = 96
Length = 4 Width = 3 and Height = 4
Volume = 48
```

Program 4.10 Write a program to calculate simple interest. Suppose the customer is a senior citizen. He is being offered 12 per cent rate of interest; for all other customers, the ROI is 10 per cent.

```
using namespace std;
#include<iostream>
float interest(float principle, int years, int r = 10);
main()
{   float p;
    int n;
    char senior_citizen;
    cout<<"\n Enter the principal and number of years : ";
    cin>>p>>n;
    cout<<"\n Is the customer a senior citizen? (y/n) ";
    cin>>senior_citizen;
    if(senior_citizen == 'y')
        cout<<"\n Interest = "<<interest(p,n,12);
    else
        cout<<"\n Interest = "<<interest(p,n);
}
float interest(float principle, int years, int r)
{   return(principle*years*r/100);
}
```

OUTPUT

```
Enter the principal and number of years : 10000 5
Is the customer a senior citizen? (y/n)y
Interest = 6000
```

Program 4.11 Write a program to print the following pattern using default arguments.

```
%%%%%
^^^^^^
^^^^^^^^^^
^^^^^^^^^^^^^^^
^^^^^^^^^^^^^^^
```

```
using namespace std;
#include<iostream>
void print(char c='%', int n = 6, int r = 1);
main()
{   char c;
    int num_rows, num_cols;
    cout<<"\n Enter the character, number of rows and columns : ";
    cin>>c>>num_rows>>num_cols;
    print();
    print(c);
    print(c,10);
    print(c,15,2);
}
void print(char c, int n, int r)
{   cout<<"\n";
    for(int i = 0;i < r;i++)
    {   cout<<"\n";
        for(int j = 0;j < n;j++)
        cout<<c;
    }
}
```

4.9 RETURN BY REFERENCE

Similar to call-by-reference, a C++ program can also return a value by reference. This allows a function to be used on the left side of an assignment statement.

The following are the key points to remember while returning by reference:

- The function should not return a local variable by reference as it will go out of scope immediately as soon as the function ends. The code given below illustrates this concept. Though the compiler will not generate any error but will definitely issue a warning stating "reference to local variable 'x' returned"

```
int &my_func(int num)
{ int x = num*2;
return x; //x is a local variable, you should not return it as reference
}
```

- The function may return a reference to a static variable. Therefore, the code given here is permissible in C++.

```
#include<iostream>
#include<cstring>
using namespace std;
int &my_func()
{ static int x=10;
return x;
}
main()
{
    int x;
    x = my_func();
    cout<<x;
}
```

OUTPUT

```
10
```

- Variables passed by reference can be returned by reference.
- Return by reference is extensively used to return structure variables and objects of classes.

Note Values returned by reference must be variables. Returning a reference to a literal or an expression is not allowed.

Example 4.8 To return value using reference

```
using namespace std;
#include<iostream>
int &larger(int &x, int &y)
{   if(x>y)
        return x;
    else
        return y;
}
main()
{   int num1, num2, large;
    cout<<"\n Enter two numbers : ";
    cin>>num1>>num2;
    cout<<"\n Two numbers are : "<<num1<<" "<<num2;
    large = larger(num1, num2);
    cout<<"\n Large = "<<large;
    larger(num1,num2) = -1;
    cout<<"\n Two numbers are : "<<num1<<" "<<num2;
}
```

OUTPUT

```
Enter two numbers : 5 2
Two numbers are : 5 2
Large = 5
Two numbers are : -1 2
```

Explanation: In the given here, variables `num1` and `num2` are passed by reference to `greater()`. The function will make a reference to variable x or y whichever is greater and return it to the caller. When we write

```
greater(num1,num2) = -1;
```

the statement will assign `-1` to the variable having greater value. Therefore, the output is obtained.

4.10 PASSING CONSTANTS AS ARGUMENTS

When parameters are passed by reference parameter, the called function may intentionally or inadvertently modify the actual parameters. However, at times, the programmer may strictly want the actual parameters not to be modified by the called function. In such cases, a constant parameter must be passed.

We have seen that pass by reference is a preferred technique of passing arguments to a function due to performance reasons. Therefore, using the const keyword allows programmers to achieve performance benefits while ensuring that the actual parameter is not modified. The following program explains this concept.

Example 4.9 To demonstrates the use of a constant argument

```
using namespace std;
#include<iostream>
void add_2(int const &x)
{   x = x + 2;   // ERROR, cannot modify a constant
    cout<<"\n The numbers is now : "<<x;
}
```

```
main()
{   int num1;
    cout<<"\n Enter a number : ";
    cin>>num1;
    add_2(num1);
}
```

OUTPUT

```
Error
```

Explanation: The program given here will not execute and give a compiler error as the function cannot modify a constant. The function can use it but cannot alter it.

4.11 VARIABLES SCOPE

Programming Tip: It is an error to use the name of a function argument as the name of a local variable.

In C++, all constants and variables have a defined scope. By scope, we mean the accessibility and visibility of variables at different points in the program. A variable or a constant in C++ has four types of scope—block, function, file, and program scope.

4.11.1 Block Scope

As discussed earlier, a statement block is a group of statements enclosed within an opening and closing curly brackets ({ }). If a variable is declared within a statement block, as soon as the control exits that block, the variable will cease to exist. Such a variable also known as a local variable is said to have a *block scope.*

Example 4.10 Code which illustrates the block scope concept

```
using namespace std;
#include<iostream>
int main()
{   int x = 10;
    int i=0;
    cout<< "\n The value of x outside the while loop is "<<x;
    while (i<3)
    {
        int x = i;
        cout<<"\n The value of x inside the while loop is "<<x;
    i++;
    }
    cout<<"\n The value of x outside the while loop is "<< x;
}
```

OUTPUT

```
The value of x outside the while loop is 10
The value of x inside the while loop is 0
The value of x inside the while loop is 1
The value of x inside the while loop is 2
The value of x outside the while loop is 10
```

Programming Tip: Try to avoid variable names that hide variables in outer scope.

Note In order to avoid error, a programmer must prefer to use different names for variables not common to inner as well as outer blocks.

4.11.2 Function Scope

Function scope indicates that a variable is active and visible from the beginning to the end of a function. In C++, only the `goto` label has function scope.

4.11.3 Scope of the Program

Till now, we have studied that variables declared within a function are local variables. These local variables, also known as internal variables, are automatically created when they are declared in the function and are usable only in that function. The local variables are unknown to other functions in the program. Such variables cease to exist after the last statement in the function in which they are declared and are recreated each time the function is called.

However, if you want the functions to be able to access some variables which are not passed to them as arguments, declare those variables outside any function blocks. Such variables are commonly known as *global variables*. Global variables are those variables that can be accessed from any point in the program.

Lifetime

Global variables are created at the beginning of program execution and remain in existence throughout the period of execution of the program. These variables are known to all the functions in the program and are accessible to them for usage. Global variables are not limited to a particular function so that they exit even if a function calls another function. These variables retain their value so that they can be used from every function in the program.

Programming Tip: The value of a global variable can be used from anywhere in the program while the local variable ceases to exist outside the function in which it is declared.

Place of Declaration

The global variables are declared outside all the functions, including `main()`. Although there is no specific rule that states where the global variables must be declared, it is always recommended to declare them on top of the program code.

Name Conflict

If we have a variable declared in a function that has the same name as that of the global variable, the function will use the local variable declared within it and ignore the global variable. However, the programmer must use names of global variables as the names of local variables may lead to confusion and erroneous results.

Note If a global variable is not initialized during its initialization, it is automatically initialized to zero by default.

Example 4.11 Code to illustrate the concept of program scope

```
using namespace std;
#include<iostream>
int x = 10;
void print();
int main()
{   cout<<"\n The value of x in the main() = "<<x;
    int x = 2;
    cout<<"\n The value of local variable x in the main() = "<<x;
    print();
}
void print()
{   cout<<"\n The value of x in the print() = "<<x;

}
```

```
OUTPUT
The value of x in the main() = 10
The value of local variable x in the main() = 2
The value of x in the print() = 10
```

Note Functions are considered to be self-contained and independent modules. Therefore, they need to be isolated from the rest of the code; however, using global variables lose this idea behind making functions.

4.11.4 File Scope

When a global variable is accessible until the end of the file, the variable is said to have file scope. To allow a variable to have file scope, declare that variable with the static keyword before specifying its data type as follows:

```
static int x = 10;
```

A global static variable can be used anywhere from the file in which it is declared but it is not accessible by any other files. Such variables are useful when the programmer writes his own header files.

4.12 STORAGE CLASSES

The storage class of a variable defines the scope or visibility and life time of variables and/or functions declared within a C++ program. Additionally, the storage class gives the following information about the variable or the function:

- The storage class of a function or a variable determines the part of memory where storage space will be allocated for that variable or function (whether the variable/function will be stored in a register or in `RAM`).
- It specifies how long the storage allocation will continue to exist for that function or variable.
- It specifies the scope of the variable or function. The storage class indicates the part of the C++ program in which the variable name is visible, or the part in which it is accessible. In other words, whether the variable or function can be referenced throughout the program or only within the function, block, or source file where it has been defined is given.
- It specifies whether the variable or function has internal, external, or no linkage.
- It specifies whether the variable will be automatically initialized to zero or to any indeterminate value.

C++ supports four storage classes—`automatic`, `register`, `external`, and `static` which have been discussed in the following sections. The general syntax for specifying the storage class of a variable can be given as follows:

```
<storage_class_specifier> <data type> <variable name>
```

4.12.1 Auto Storage Class

The `auto` storage class specifier is used to explicitly declare a variable with automatic storage. It is the default storage class for variables declared inside a block.

For example, if we write

```
auto int x;
```

then, x is an integer that has automatic storage. It is deleted on exiting the block in which x was declared exits.

The auto storage class can be used to declare variables in a block or to the names of function parameters. However, since the variable names or names of function parameters have automatic storage by default, the auto storage class specifier is, therefore, treated as redundant while declaring data.

Example 4.12 Code which uses an auto integer that is local to the function in which it is defined

```
using namespace std;
#include<iostream>
void func1()
{   int a=10;
    cout<<"\n a = "<<a;    // auto integer local to func1()
}
void func2()
{   int a=20;
    cout<<"\n a = "<<a;    // auto integer local to func2()
}
int main()
{   int a=30;              // auto integer local to main()
    func1();
    func2();
    cout<<"\n a = "<<a;
}
```

OUTPUT

```
a = 10
a = 20
a = 30
```

4.12.2 register Storage Class

When a variable is declared using register as its storage class, it is stored in a CPU register instead of RAM. Since the variable is stored in the RAM, the maximum size of the variable is equal to the register size. One drawback of using a register variable is that it cannot be operated using the unary '&' operator because it does not have a memory location associated with it. A register variable is declared in the following manner:

```
register int x;
```

Register variables are used when there is a need for quick access to the variable. It is not always necessary that the register variable will be stored in the register. Rather, the register variable might be stored in a register depending on the hardware and implementation restrictions.

Hence, programmers can only suggest the compiler to store those variables in the registers which are used repeatedly or whose access times are critical. However, for the compiler, it is not an obligation to always accept such requests. In case the compiler rejects the request to store the variable in the register, the variable is treated as having the storage class specifier auto.

Example 4.13 Program that uses a register variable

```
using namespace std;
#include<iostream>
```

```
int exp(int a, int b);    // FUNCTION DECLARATION
main()
{   int a = 3, b = 5, res;
    res = exp(a, b);     // FUNCTION CALL
    cout<<"\n "<<a<<" to the power of "<<b<<" = "<<res;
}
int exp(int a, int b)    // FUNCTION DEFINITION
{   register int res = 1;
    int i;
    for(i = 1;i <= b;i++)
        res = res*b;
    return res;
}
```

OUTPUT

```
3 to the power of 5 = 243
```

4.12.3 extern Storage Class

A large C++ program can be broken down into smaller programs. When these smaller programs are compiled, they are joined together to form a large program. However, these smaller programs may need to share certain variables for processing. For such situations, C++ language provides an external storage class that is specified using the keyword `extern`.

`extern` is used to give a reference of a global variable that is visible to all the program files. Such global variables are declared like any other variable in one of the program files. When there are multiple files in a program and you need to use a particular function or variable in a file apart from which it is declared, then use the keyword `extern`. To declare a variable `x` as `extern` write

```
extern int x;
```

External variables may be declared outside any function in a source code file as any other variable is declared. However, usually, external variables are declared and defined at the beginning of a source file.

Example 4.14 Program code using `extern` keyword

```
// FILE1.CPP
using namespace std;
#include<iostream>
#include<FILE2.CPP    // Programmer's own header file
int x;
void print(void);
int main()
{   x = 10;
    cout<<"\n x in FILE1 = "<<x;
    print();
}
// END OF FILE1.CPP
// FILE2.CPP
using namespace std;
#include<iostream>
extern int x;
void print()
{   cout<<"\n x in FILE 2 = "<<x;
```

```
}
main()
{
    // Statements
}
// END OF FILE2.CPP
```

OUTPUT

```
x in FILE1 = 10
x in FILE2 = 10
```

Explanation: In this program, we have used two files—`File1` and `File2`. `File1` has declared a global variable `x`. `File1` also includes `File2` which has a print function that uses the external variable `x` to print its value on the screen. The extern specifier tells the compiler that the variable `(x)` has already been declared elsewhere and therefore, it should not allocate storage space for that variable again. During compilation of the program, the linker will automatically resolve the reference problem.

In a multi-file program, the global variable must be declared only once in any one of the files without using the extern keyword. Otherwise, the linker will have a conflict as to which variable to use; therefore, in such a situation, it raises a warning message.

4.12.4 Static Storage Class

While `auto` is the default storage class for all local variables, `static` is the default storage class for all global variables. Static variables have a lifetime (is visible) over the entire program. This means that memory for the `static` variables is allocated when the program begins running and is freed when the program terminates. To declare an integer x as `static`, write

```
static int x = 10;
```

Here, `x` is a local static variable. The difference between an `auto` variable and a static variable is that the static variable when defined within a function is not re-initialized when the function is called repeatedly. It is initialized just once and further calls of the function share the value of the static variable. Hence, the static variable inside a function retains its value during various calls.

When a `static` variable is not explicitly initialized by the programmer, then it is automatically initialized to zero when memory is allocated for them. Although `static` automatic variables exist even after the block in which they are defined is terminated, their scope is local to the block in which they are defined.

`Static` storage class can be specified for `auto` as well as `external` variables. For example, we can write

```
static extern int x;
```

When we declare a variable as `external static` variable, then that variable is accessible from all functions in this source file.

Note that `static` variables can be initialized while they are being declared. However, this initialization is done only once at the compile time when memory is being allocated for the `static` variable. The value with which the static variable is initialized must be a constant expression.

Example 4.15 Program to clearly differentiate a static variable from a normal variable

```
using namespace std;
#include<iostream>
void print(void);          // FUNCTION DECLARATION
int main()
{   cout<<"\n First call of print()";
    print();                   // FUNCTION CALL
    cout<<"\n\n Second call of print()";
    print();                   // FUNCTION CALL
    cout<<"\n\n Third call of print()";
    print();                   // FUNCTION CALL
}
void print()               // FUNCTION DEFINITION
{   static int x;
    int y = 0;
    cout<<"\n Static integer variable, x = "<<x;
    cout<<"\n Integer variable, y = "<<y;
    x++;   y++;
}
```

OUTPUT

```
First call of print()
Static integer variable, x = 0
Integer variable, y = 0
Second call of print()
Static integer variable, x = 1
Integer variable, y = 0
Third call of print()
Static integer variable, x = 2
Integer variable, y = 0
```

4.12.5 Comparison of Storage Classes

The comparison between the key features of the four types of storage classes are discussed in Table 4.2.

Table 4.2 Comparison of storage classes

Feature	Storage class			
	Auto	**Extern**	**Register**	**Static**
Accessibility	Accessible within the function or block in which it is declared	Accessible within all program files that are a part of the program	Accessible within the function or block in which it is declared	Local Accessible within the function or block in which it is declared Global: Accessible within the program in which it is declared

(Contd)

Table 4.2 (*Contd*)

Feature	Storage class			
	Auto	Extern	Register	Static
Storage	Main memory	Main memory	CPU register	Main memory
Existence	Exists when the function or block in which it is declared is entered. Ceases to exist when the control returns from the function or the block in which it was declared	Exists throughout the execution of the program	Exists when the function or block in which it is declared is entered. Ceases to exist when the control returns from the function or the block in which it was declared	Local Retains value between function calls or block entries Global Preserves value in program files
Default value	Garbage	Zero	Garbage	Zero

4.13 INLINE FUNCTIONS

C++ provides a very useful feature of `inline` functions that is commonly used with classes. The major difference between an ordinary function and an `inline` function is that when an `inline` function is called, the compiler places a copy of its code at each point of call. As in case of an ordinary function, the compiler does not have to jump to the called function. This saves the function call overhead and results in faster execution of the code. We can make a function `inline` by taking caring of two aspects as follows.

- First, write the keyword `inline` before the function name.
- Second, define that function before any calls are made to it.

However, the programmer must not forget that keyword inline just makes a request to the compiler to make the function inline (and place its code at each point of call), the compiler may ignore the request if the function has too many lines.

Note Inline functions work best with short functions that are executed frequently.

Let us see two programs that use the concept of inline functions.

Example 4.16 To find the larger number using an inline function

Programming Tip: `main()` cannot be used as an inline function.

```
using namespace std;
#include<iostream>
inline int larger(int x, int y) // Function definition
{ return (x > y)? x : y; // Function returning larger of the two nos
}
int main( )
{    int num1, num2;
cout << "\n Enter two numbers : ";
cin>>num1>>num2;
   cout<<"\n The larger number is : "<<larger(num1,num2);      // Function call
}
```

OUTPUT

```
Enter two numbers : 5 9
The larger number is : 9
```

Example 4.17 To find square of a number using inline function

```
using namespace std;
#include<iostream>
inline int sqr(int x)
{return (x*x);
}
int main()
{  int num;
   cout<<"\n Enter a number : ";
   cin>>num;
   cout<<"\n Square of "<<num<<" = "<<sqr(num);
}
```

OUTPUT

```
Enter a number : 9
Square of 9 = 81
```

4.13.1 Advantages and Disadvantages of Inline Functions

The advantages of using inline function are as follows:

- An inline function generates faster code as it saves the time required to execute function calls.
- Small inline functions (three lines or less) create less code than the equivalent function call as the compiler does not have to generate code to handle function arguments and a return value.
- Inline functions are subject to code optimizations that are usually not available to normal functions as the compiler does not perform inter-procedural optimizations.
- Inline function avoids function call overhead. As a result, we need to save variables and other program parameters on the system stack.
- Since there are no function calls, the overhead of returning from a function is also avoided.
- It allows the compiler to apply intra-procedural optimization

The disadvantages of using inline function are as follows:

- Size of the program increases.
- Large programs may take longer time to be executed.
- At times, the program may not fit in the cache memory.
- There may be a problem in making efficient use of CPU registers if the inline function has many register variables.
- If the code of the inline function is modified, the entire program needs to be re-compiled.
- Inline functions should not be used for designing embedded systems due to memory size constraints.

4.13.2 Comparison of Inline Functions with Macros

The concept of inline functions is similar to that of macros (refer Annexure 5). However, inline functions have a good blend of flexibility and power offered by macros as well as an ordinary function. Therefore, inline functions should be preferred over macros that were extensively used in C language due to the following reasons:

- Macro invocations skip the job of type checking; this is a must-to-do work in function calls.
- Macros cannot return a value while a function can return a value.
- Macros use mere textual substitution which can give unintended results due to inaccurate reevaluation of arguments and order of operations.
- Debugging of compiler errors in case of macros is more difficult than debugging functions.
- All constructs cannot be expressed using macros; however, with functions, they can be expressed with ease.
- Macros have a slightly difficult syntax while the syntax of writing function is similar to that of a normal function.

Example 4.18 To show why the use of inline function is better than macros

```
using namespace std;
#include<iostream>
#define SQUARE(x) x * x
inline int sqr(int x)
{return (x*x);
}
int main()
{   int num, n;
    cout<<"\n Enter a number : ";
    cin>>num;
    n = num;
    cout<<"\n Square of "<<num<<" using Inline function = "<<sqr(++num);
    cout<<"\n Square of "<<n<<" using Macros = "<<SQUARE(++n);
}
```

OUTPUT

```
Enter a number : 6
Square of 7 using Inline function = 49
Square of 8 using Macros = 64
```

Explanation: In this program, you will find that due to wrong evaluation of arguments, macros give wrong results.

Inline functions cannot be used with the following:

- Recursive functions
- Functions having static variables
- Functions that return a value and also have go to statements, switch statements, or iterative statements
- Functions that do not return a value but have a return statement

4.14 FUNCTION OVERLOADING

Function overloading, also known as method overloading, is a feature in C++ that allows creation of several methods with the same name but with different parameters. For example, print(), print(int), and print("Hello") are overloaded methods. While calling `print()`, no arguments are passed to the function; however, when calling `print(int)` and `print("Hello")`, an integer and a string arguments are passed to the called function.

Note Function overloading allows one function to perform different tasks.

Function overloading is a type of polymorphism. Basically, there are two types of polymorphism—compile time (or static) polymorphism and run-time (or dynamic) polymorphism. Function overloading falls in the category of static polymorphism which calls a function using the best match technique or overload resolution.

According to this technique, the compiler compares the arguments in terms of number and type used in function call with the parameters specified in function definition to determine the most appropriate definition to use.

4.14.1 Matching Function Calls with Overloaded Functions

When an overloaded function is called, one of the following cases occurs:

`Case 1`: A direct match is found, and there is no confusion in calling the appropriate overloaded function.

`Case 2`: If a match is not found, a linker error will be generated. However, if a direct match is not found, then, at first, the compiler will try to find a match through the type conversion or type casting. For example, char, unsigned char, and short are promoted to an int; unsigned short can be promoted to int or unsigned int; float is promoted to double; and enum is promoted to int. Hence, the following function call will be matched with the given declaration.

```
void print(int);    // Function declaration
print('R');         // Function call
```

Note To find a suitable match, C++ compiler also tries user-defined conversions, which we will discuss later in this book. If nothing is possible, then a no match, linker error is generated.

`Case 3`: If an ambiguous match is found, that is, when the arguments match more than one overloaded function, a compiler error will be generated. This usually happens because all standard conversions are treated equal. For example, consider the function declarations and function call given here.

Example 4.19 To demonstrate the ambiguity in function call

```
using namespace std;
#include<iostream>
void print(int n){ cout<<n;}
void print(char c){ cout<<c; }
void print(float f){ cout<<f;}
main()
{   print(5);   //Function call
    print((float)98.7);
    print('R');
}
```

OUTPUT

```
Error
```

Explanation: When you execute this code, you will get a compile time error as there two function declarations are valid for `print(5);` the function call can invoke either `int` or `float` version because all standard conversions are treated equal. Therefore, `5` can be treated as an `int` as well as a `float`.

Note All floating literals are treated as double unless they have the 'f' suffix.

4.14.2 Key Points about Function Overloading

- In function overloading, there are multiple definitions for the same function name in the same scope.
- The definitions of these functions vary according to the types and/or the number of arguments in the argument list.
- Data type of the return value is not considered while writing overloaded functions because the appropriate function is called at the compile time while the return value will be obtained only when the function is called and executed.

Example 4.20 To compute the volume of different shapes using function overloading concept

```
using namespace std;
#include<iostream>
int volume(int side)
{   return side*side*side; // cube
}
float volume(float radius, float height)
{   return 3.14+radius*radius*height; //cylinder
}
long int volume(int length, int breadth, int height)
{   return length*breadth*height; //cuboid
}
main()
{  int s,l,b,height;
   float r, h;
   cout<<"\n Enter the side of the cube : ";
   cin>>s;
   cout<<"\n Volume of cube with side "<<s<<" = "<<volume(s);
   cout<<"\n \n\n Enter the radius and height of the cylinder : ";
   cin>>r>>h;
   cout<<"\n Volume of cylinder with radius "<<r<<" and height "<<h<<" = "<<volume(r,h);
   cout<<"\n Enter the length, breadth and height of the cuboid : ";
   cin>>l>>b>>height;
   cout<<"\n Volume of cuboid with length "<<l<<" breadth "<<b<<" and height
   "<<height<<" = "<<volume(l,b,height);
}
```

OUTPUT

```
Enter the side of the cube : 3
Volume of cube with side 3 = 27
Enter the radius and height of the cylinder : 3 4
Volume of cylinder with radius 3 and height 4 = 39.13
Enter the length, breadth and height of the cuboid : 2 3 4";
Volume of cuboid with length 2 breadth 3 and height 4 = 24
```

Note Function overloading is a form of compile time or static polymorphism (to be discussed in detail in Inheritance).

Program 4.12 Write a program to display values of different data types using compile time polymorphism.

```
using namespace std;
#include<iostream>
void print(float num)
```

```
{   cout<<"\n The number is : "<<num;
}
void print(char str[])
{   cout<<"\n The string is : "<<str;
}
main()
{
   print(9);
   print(3.78);
   print("Hello");
}
```

OUTPUT

```
The number is : 9
The number is : 3.78
The string is : Hello
```

Program 4.13 Write a program to add two values of different data types using static polymorphism.

```
#include<string.h>
using namespace std;
#include<iostream>
int add(int a, int b)
{   return a + b;
}
double add(double a, float b)
{   return a + b;
}
void add(string str1, string str2)
{
   cout<<"\n The concatenated string is : "<<(str1 + str2);
}
main()
{
   cout<<"\n 5 + 7 = "<<add(5,7);
   cout<<"\n 123.678 + 25.97 = "<<add(123.678, 25.97);
   add("Oxford", "University");
}
```

OUTPUT

```
5 + 7 = 12
123.678 + 25.97 = 149.647
The concatenated string is : OxfordUniversity
```

Program 4.14 Write a program that finds the absolute value of a number.

```
#include<string.h>
using namespace std;
int abs(int n)
{   return n > 0?n : -n;
}
double abs(double n)
{   return n > 0?n : -n;
}
main()
{  cout<<"\n Absolute value of 1234 = "<<abs(-1234);
   cout<<"\n Absolute value of 1234.5678 = "<<abs(1234.5678);
}
```

```
OUTPUT
Absolute value of 1234 = 1234
Absolute value of 1234.5678 = 1234.5678
```

4.14.3 Functions that Cannot be Overloaded

- Functions that differ only in the return type. For example, the program given here will give compile time error.

```
using namespace std;
#include<iostream>
int my_func()    { return 1; }
char my_func()   { return 'E'; }
main()
{ int num = my_func();
 char c = my_func();
}
```

- Parameter declarations that differ only in a pointer * versus an array [] are equivalent. A program with the following declarations will give a compilation error as both declarations are equivalent. The reason why they are equivalent will be clear in the chapter on Pointers.

```
int my_func(int *ptr);
int my_func(int ptr[]);
```

- If parameters in two functions differ only in the presence or absence of const and/or volatile, then those functions are considered to be equivalent. For example, the program having following declarations will not compile.

```
int my_func(int n);
int my_func(const int n;
```

- Using typedef does not introduce a new type, therefore, the following two function declarations are equivalent and this cannot be overloaded. (Use of `typedef` will be studied in chapter on Structures).

```
typedef int integer;
int my_func(int n);
int my_func(integer n;
```

- Function declarations that differ only in their default arguments are equivalent. Therefore, the program having function declarations given below will not compile.

```
int my_func(int n);
int my_func(int n = 10);
```

- Function declarations that differ only in a reference parameter and a normal parameter cannot be overloaded. Therefore, the program having function declarations given here will not compile.

```
int my_func(int n);
int my_func(int &n);
```

4.15 RECURSIVE FUNCTIONS

A recursive function is defined as a function that calls itself to solve a smaller version of its task until a final call is made which does not require a call to itself. Every recursive solution has two major cases which are given as follows:

- Base case, in which the problem is simple enough to be solved directly without making any further calls to the same function
- Recursive case, in which first the problem at hand is divided into simpler sub parts. Second, the function calls itself but with sub parts of the problem obtained in the first step. Third, the result is obtained by combining the solutions of simpler sub-parts.

Therefore, recursion involves defining large and complex problems in terms of a smaller and more easily solvable problem. In recursive function, a complicated problem is defined in terms of simpler problems and the simplest problem is given explicitly.

To understand recursive functions, let us take an example of calculating factorial of a number. To calculate `n!`, what we have to multiply the number with the factorial of the number that is 1 less than that number. In other words, `n! = n X (n-1)!`

Let us say we need to find the value of `5!`...

```
5! = 5 X 4 X 3 X 2 X 1
   = 120
```

This can be written as

```
5! = 5 X 4!, where
 4!= 4 X 3!
Therefore,
5! = 5 X 4 X 3!
Similarly, we can also write,
5! = 5 X 4 X 3 X 2!
Expanding further,
5! = 5 X 4 X 3 X 2 X 1!
We know, 1! = 1
```

Therefore, the series of problems and solutions can be given as shown in Fig. 4.6

```
     Problem                          Solution
     5!                               5 X 4 X 3 X 2 X 1!
=    5 X 4!                      =    5 X 4 X 3 X 2 X 1
=    5 X 4 X 3!                  =    5 X 4 X 3 X 2
=    5 X 4 X 3 X 2!              =    5 X 4 X 6
=    5 X 4 X 3 X 2 X 1!          =    5 X 24
                                 =    120
```

Figure 4.6 Recursive factorial function

If you look at the problem carefully, you can see that we can write a recursive function to calculate the factorial of a number. Note that we have said every recursive function must have a base case and a recursive case. For the factorial function,

- Base case is when `n=1`, because if `n = 1`, the result is known to be `1` as `1!` = `1`.
- Recursive case of the factorial function will call itself but with a smaller value of `n`, this case can be given as

```
factorial(n) = n X factorial (n-1)
```

Example 4.21 To calculate the factorial of a number recursively

> **Programming Tip:** Every recursive function must have at least one base case. Otherwise, the recursive function will generate an infinite sequence of calls, thereby resulting in an error condition known as an infinite stack.

```
using namespace std;
#include<iostream>
int Fact(int);    // FUNCTION DECLARATION
main()
{ int num;
  cout<<"\n Enter the number : ";
  cin>>num;
  cout<<"\n Factorial of "<<num<<" = "<<Fact(num);// FUNCTION CALL
}
int Fact( int n)    // FUNCTION DEFINITION
{   if(n==1)
      return 1;
   return (n * Fact(n-1));    // FUNCTION CALL
}
```

OUTPUT

```
Enter the number : 5
Factorial of 5 = 120
```

Explanation: From this example, let us analyse the basic steps of a recursive program.

Step 1 Specify the base case which will stop the function from making a call to itself.

Step 2 Check to see whether the current value being processed matches with the value of the base case. If yes, process and return the value.

Step 3 Divide the problem into a smaller or simpler sub-problem.

Step 4 Call the function on the sub-problem.

Step 5 Combine the results of the sub-problems.

Step 6 Return the result of the entire problem.

> **Note** The base case of a recursive function acts as the terminating condition. Therefore, in the absence of an explicitly defined base case, a recursive function would call itself indefinitely.

4.15.1 Greatest Common Divisor

The greatest common divisor (GCD) of two numbers (integers) is the largest integer that divides both the numbers. We can find GCD of two numbers recursively by using Euclid's algorithm that states the following:

$$\text{GCD}(a, b) = \begin{cases} b, & \text{if } b \text{ divides } a \\ \text{GCD}(b, a \bmod b) & \text{otherwise} \end{cases}$$

GCD can be implemented as a recursive function because if b does not divide a, then we call the same function (GCD) with another set of parameters that are smaller and simpler than the original ones. Here, we assume that `a > b`. However, if `a < b`, then interchange `a` and `b` in the formula given.

```
Assume a = 62 and b = 8
GCD(62, 8)
   rem = 62 % 8 = 6
   GCD(8, 6)
      rem = 8 % 6 = 2
      GCD(6, 2)
      rem = 6 % 2 = 0
      Return 2
   Return 2
Return 2
```

Program 4.15 Write a program to calculate GCD using recursive functions.

```
using namespace std;
#include<iostream>
int GCD(int, int);    // FUNCTION DECLARATION
main()
{   int num1, num2, res;
    cout<<"\n Enter the two numbers : ";
    cin>>num1>>num2;
    res = GCD(num1, num2);    // FUNCTION CALL
    cout<<"\n GCD of "<<num1<<" and "<<num2<<" = "<<res;
}
int GCD(int x, int y)    // FUNCTION DEFINITION
{   int rem;
    rem = x%y;
    if(rem == 0)
       return y;
    else
       return (GCD(y, rem));    // FUNCTION CALL
}
```

OUTPUT

```
Enter the two numbers : 96 6
GCD of 96 and 6 = 6
```

4.15.2 Finding Exponents

We can find a solution to find exponent of a number using recursion. To find x^y, the base case would be when `y = 0`, as we know that any number raise to the power `0` is `1`. Therefore, the general formula to find x^y can be given as

```
EXP(x, y) = { 1, if y == 0
            { x * EXP(x^(y-1)) otherwise
```

```
exp_rec(2, 4) = 2 * exp_rec( 2, 3)
    exp_rec(2, 3) = 2 * exp_rec( 2, 2)
      exp_rec(2, 2) - 2 * exp_rec( 2, 1)
         exp_rec(2, 1) = 2 * exp_rec( 2, 0)
              exp_rec( 2, 0) = 1
         exp_rec( 2, 1) = 2 * 1 = 2
      exp_rec( 2, 2) = 2 * 2 = 4
```

```
   exp_rec( 2, 3) = 2 * 4 = 8
exp_rec( 2, 4) = 2 * 8 = 16
```

Program 4.16 Write a program to calculate exp(x,y) using recursive functions.

```
using namespace std;
#include<iostream>
int exp_rec(int, int);
main()
{   int num1, num2, res;
    cout<<"\n Enter the two numbers : ";
    cin>>num1>>num2;
    res = exp_rec(num1, num2);
    cout<<"\n RESULT = "<<res;
}
int exp_rec(int x, int y)
{   if( y == 0)
      return 1;
    else
      return (x * exp_rec(x, y-1));
}
```

OUTPUT

```
Enter the two numbers : 3 5
RESULT = 243
```

4.15.3 Fibonacci Series

The Fibonacci series can be given as follows:

```
0   1   1   2   3   5   8   13   21   34   55...
```

The third term of the series is the sum of the first and second terms. On similar grounds, the fourth term is the sum of second and third terms, so on, and so forth. Now, we will design a recursive solution to find the nth term of the Fibonacci series. The general formula to do so can be given as follows:

```
FIB(n) = { 1, if n<=2
         { FIB (n - 1) + FIB (n - 2), otherwise
```

As per the formula, `FIB(1) = 1` and `FIB(2) = 1`. Therefore, we have two base cases. This is necessary because every problem is divided into two smaller problems (Refer to Fig. 4.7).

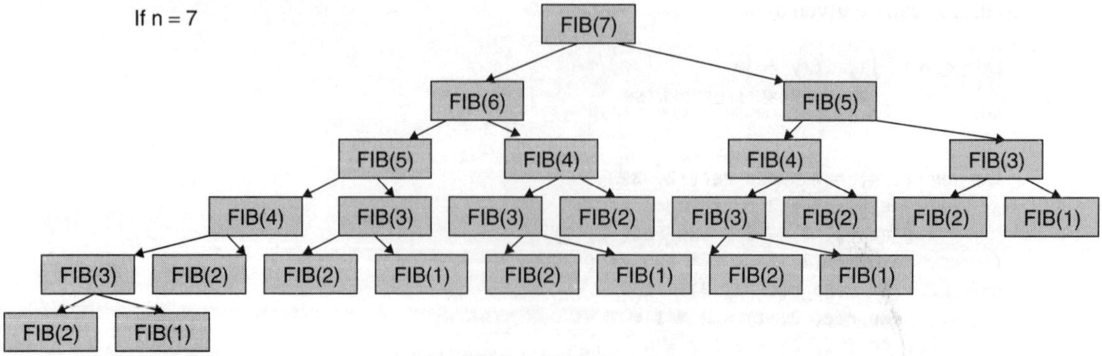

Figure 4.7 Recursion structure of Fib function

Program 4.17 Write a program to print the Fibonacci series using recursion.

```
using namespace std;
#include<iostream>
int Fibonacci(int);
main()
{   int n;
    cout<<"\n Enter the number of terms in the series : ";
    cin>>n;
    for(int i = 0;i < n;i++)
       cout<<"\n Fibonacci ("<<i<<") = "<<Fibonacci(i);
}
int Fibonacci(int num)
{   if(num <= 2)
      return 1;
   return (Fibonacci (num - 1) + Fibonacci(num - 2));
}
```

OUTPUT

```
Enter the number of terms in the series : 3
Fibonacci(0) = 1
Fibonacci(1) = 1
Fibonacci(2) = 1
```

4.16 RECURSION VERSUS ITERATION

Recursion is more of a top-down approach to problem solving in which the original problem is divided into smaller sub-problems. On the contrary, iteration follows a bottom-up approach that begins with what is known and then constructing the solution step by step.

Recursion is an excellent way of solving complex problems especially when the problem can be defined in recursive terms. For such problems, a recursive code can be written and modified in a much simpler and clearer manner.

However, recursive solutions are not always the best solutions. In some cases, recursive programs may require substantial amount of run-time overhead. Therefore, when implementing a recursive solution, there is a trade-off involved between the time spent in constructing and maintaining the program and the cost incurred in running time and memory space required for the execution of the program.

Whenever, a recursive function requires some amount of overhead in the form of a run-time stack is always involved. Before jumping to the function with a smaller parameter, the original parameters, the local variables, and the return address of the calling function are all stored on the system stack. Therefore, while using recursion, a lot of time is needed to first push all the information on the stack when the function is called and then, time is again involved in retrieving the information stored on the stack once the control passes back to the calling function.

To conclude, one must use recursion only to find solution to a problem for which no obvious iterative solution is known. To summarize the concept of recursion, let us briefly discuss the pros and cons of recursion.

Pros and Cons of using a Recursive Program

The benefits of using a recursive program are as follows:

- Recursive solutions often tend to be shorter and simpler than non-recursive ones.
- Code is clearer and easier to use.

- Recursion represents like the original formula to solve a problem.
- Follows a divide and conquer technique to solve problems.
- In some (limited) instances, recursion may be more efficient.

The drawbacks of using a recursive program are as follows:

- For some programmers and readers, recursion is a difficult concept.
- Recursion is implemented using system stack. If the stack space on the system is limited, recursion to a deeper level will be difficult to implement.
- Aborting a recursive process in midstream is slow and sometimes nasty.
- Using a recursive function takes more memory and time to execute as compared to its non-recursive counter part.
- It is difficult to find bugs, particularly, when using global variables

Therefore, the benefits of recursion pay-off for the extra overhead involved in terms of time and space required.

4.17 FUNCTIONS WITH VARIABLE NUMBER OF ARGUMENTS

We have seen that while declaring a function, the data type and the number of arguments are specified and they are fixed at compile time. However, in case we need a function that should accept a variable number of arguments, we have to design a function that accepts the data-type and/or number of arguments at the run-time while execution and not during compilation.

Let us take a sample program that accepts any number of values and then return the average. In this program, the programmer is unaware about the number of arguments that will be passed to the function. To write such a program, we must include the `cstdarg` header file to use the following macros:

- `va_list` that stores the list of arguments.
- `va_start` to initialize the list. It is a macro from which we can begin reading arguments from it. It accepts two arguments—`va_list` and a last named argument. After the last named argument, the number of arguments read is stored.
- `va_arg` returns the next argument in the list. It helps in accessing the individual arguments in the list. For this, you must just need to specify the type of argument to retrieve.
- `va_end` is used to clean up the variable argument list once we are done with it.

A function that is supposed to accept variable number of arguments must be declared in a special way. Instead of writing the last argument, you must put an ellipsis (like '…'). Therefore, `int my_func( int x, … );` means that `my_func` accepts any number of arguments.

Example 4.22 Using variable number of arguments

```
#include<stdarg.h>
using namespace std;
#include<iostream>
float avg(int argc, ...)
{   va_list args;
    int i, sum = 0;
    va_start(args, argc);
    for(i = 0;i < argc;i++)
        sum += va_arg(args, int); // Adds next value in args to sum
    va_end(args);
    return( (float) sum/argc);
}
```

```
main()
{   float result;
    result = avg(7,8,9,10,4,5,10,10,10,9,7,8,9,10,10);
    cout.precision(2);
    cout<<"\n AVERAGE = "<<result;
}
```

OUTPUT

```
AVERAGE = 8.00
```

Explanation: In the program, the following are important points to be noted.

- The name of the list is `args`.
- `va_start` accepts two arguments—the list `(args)` and name of the variable that directly precedes the ellipsis `(…)`. Here, the name of the variable is `argc` that stores the number of arguments passed to the function.
- `va_arg` takes `args` and a data type in which the next argument in the list will be returned.
- The for loop is executed till `argc` (number of arguments).
- Each time the `for loop` executes, the next argument is fetched from the list and added to sum.

Points to Remember

- Every function in the program is supposed to perform a well defined task. The moment the compiler encounters a function call, the control jumps to the statements that are a part of the called function. After the called function is executed, the control is returned back to the calling program.
- All the libraries in C++ contain a set of functions that have been prewritten and pre-tested, so the programmers use them without worrying about their code details. This speeds up program development.
- While function declaration statement identifies a function with its name, a list of arguments that it accepts and the type of data it returns, the function definition, on the other hand, consists of a function header that identifies the function, followed by the body of the function containing the executable code for that function
- main() is the function that is called by the operating system and therefore, it is supposed to return the result of its processing to the operating system.
- Placing the function declaration statement prior to its use enables the compiler to make a check on the arguments used while calling that function.
- A function having void as its return type cannot return any value. Similarly, a function having void as its parameter list cannot accept any value
- When a function defined, space is allocated for that function in the memory. A function definition comprises of two parts: function header and a Function body.
- Call-by-value method passes values of the variables to the called function. Therefore, the called function uses a copy of the actual arguments to perform its intended task. This method is used when the function does not need to modify the values of the original variables in the calling program.
- In call-by-reference method address of the variables are passed by the calling function to the called function. Hence, in this method, a function receives an implicit reference to the argument, rather than a copy of its value. This allows the function to modify the value of the variable and that change will be reflected in the calling function as well.
- Scope means the accessibility and visibility of the variables at different points in the program. A variable or a constant in C++ has four types of scope: block, function, file and program scope.
- The storage class of a variable defines the scope (visibility) and life time of variables and/or functions declared within a C++ Program.
- The auto storage class is the default storage class for variables declared inside a block. The scope of the variable is local to the block in which it is declared. When a variable is declared using register as its storage class, it is stored in a CPU register instead of RAM. Extern is used to give a reference

of a global variable that is visible to all the program files. Static is the default storage class for global variables.

- A recursive function is defined as a function that calls itself to solve a smaller version of its task until a final call is made which does not require a call to itself. They are implemented using system stack

Glossary

Argument A value passed to the called function by the calling function

Block A sequence of definitions, declarations, and statements, enclosed within curly brackets {}

Divide and conquer Solving a problem by dividing it into two or more smaller instances. Each of these smaller instances is recursively solved, and the solutions are combined to produce a solution for the original problem.

Iteration Solving a problem by repeatedly working on successive parts of the problem

Recursion An algorithmic technique where a function calls itself with a smaller of the task in order to solve that task

Recursion termination The point at which the base condition is met and a recursive algorithm stops calling itself and begins to return values

Recursion tree Technique to analyse the complexity of an algorithm by diagramming the recursive function calls

Exercises

Fill in the Blanks

1. ______ provides an interface to use the function.
2. After the function is executed, the control passes back to the ________.
3. A function that uses another function is known as the _____.
4. The inputs that the function takes are known as _____.
5. `Main()` is called by the ______.
6. Function definition consist of _______ and _____.
7. In ______ method, address of the variable is passed by the calling function to the called function.
8. Function scope is applicable only with ________.
9. Function that calls itself is known as a _____ function.
10. Recursive functions are implemented using ______.
11. _______ function is defined as a function that calls itself.
12. `int func();` takes ___ arguments.
13. ___ variables can be accessed from all functions in the program.
14. The execution of a program starts at ___.
15. By default, the return type of a function is ____.
16. Parameters used in function call are called ____.
17. Variable declared inside a function is known as ____.

State True or False

1. The calling function must pass parameters to the called function.
2. Function header is used to identify the function.
3. The name of function is global.
4. No function can be declared within the body of another function.
5. The function call statement invokes the function.
6. Auto variables are stored inside CPU registers.
7. Extern variables are initialized by default.
8. The default storage class of local variables is extern.
9. Recursion follows a divide-and-conquer technique to solve problems.
10. Local variables overwrite the value of global variables.
11. A C++ function can return only one value.
12. A function must have at least one argument.
13. A function can be declared and defined before the main().
14. A function can be defined in the main().
15. Variable names in the function definition must match with those specified in function declaration.
16. Specifying variable names in the function declaration is optional.
17. main() is a user-defined function.

Multiple Choice Questions

1. The function that is invoked is known as
(a) Calling function
(b) Caller function
(c) Called function
(d) Invoking function
2. Function declaration statement identifies a function with its
(a) Name
(b) Arguments
(c) Data type of return value
(d) All of these
3. Which return type cannot return any value to the caller?
(a) int (b) float
(c) void (d) double
4. Memory is allocated for a function when the function is
(a) declared (b) defined
(c) called (d) returned
5. Which keyword allows a variable to have file scope?
(a) auto (b) static
(c) register (d) extern
6. The default storage class of global variables is
(a) auto (b) static
(c) register (d) extern
7. Which variable retain its value in-between function calls?
(a) auto (b) static
(c) register (d) extern
8. The default storage class of a local variable is
(a) auto (b) static
(c) register (d) extern

Review Questions

1. Define a function. What is the need for functions?
2. Explain the concept of making function calls.
3. Differentiate between function declaration and function definition.
4. Differentiate between formal parameters and actual parameters
5. How many types of storage classes does C++ language support? Why do we need different types of such classes?
6. Give the features of each storage class.
7. Explain the concept of recursive functions with examples.
8. Differentiate between an iterative function and a recursive function. Which one will you prefer to use in which circumstances?
9. What will happen when the actual parameters are less than formal parameters in a function?
10. What will happen when data type of a variable in the function declaration does not match with the corresponding variable in the function header?
11. What will happen when a function returns a value that does not match with the return type of the function?
12. Explain the tower of Hanoi problem.
13. Differentiate between call-by-value and call-by-reference using suitable examples.
14. What do you understand by scope of a variable? Explain in detail with suitable examples.
15. What is function overloading? How is it a desirable feature of C++?
16. How can we pass default arguments to a function? Explain with the help of an example.
17. How is a reference variable passed as well returned from a function? Explain its significance.
18. Why is a function declaration statement placed prior to function definition?

Programming Exercises

1. Write a function to reverse a string using recursion.
2. Write a function is_prime() that returns a 1 if the argument passed to it is a prime a number and a 0 otherwise.
3. Write a function that accepts an integer between 1 and 12 to represent the month number and displays the corresponding month of the year (For example, if month = 1, then display JANUARY)
4. Write a function is_leap_year which takes the year as its argument and checks whether the year is a leap year or not and then displays an appropriate message on the screen.
5. Write a program to concatenate two strings using recursion.
6. Write a program to read an integer number. Print the reverse of this number using recursion.
7. Write a program to swap two variables that are defined as global variables.
8. Write a program to compute F(x, y) where
```
F(x, y) = F(x-y, y) + 1 if y ≤ x
And F(x, y) = 0 if x < y.
```
9. Write a program to compute F(n, r) where F(n, r) can be recursively defined as
```
F(n, r) = F(n-1, r) + F(n-1, r-1).
```

10. Write a program to compute Lambda(n) for all positive values of n where Lambda(n) can be recursively defined as
`Lambda(n) = Lambda(n/2) + 1 if n > 1`
`AND Lambda(n) = 0 if n = 1.`
11. Write a program to compute F(M, N) where F(M,N) can be recursively defined as
`F(M,N) = 1 if M = 0 or M ≥ N ≥ 1`
`AND F(M,N) = F(M-1,N) + F(M-1, N-1) otherwise.`
12. Write a menu driven program to add, subtract, multiply, and divide two integers using functions.
13. Write a program to calculate factorial of a number using recursion. Write a non-recursive procedure to do the same job.
14. Write a program using function that calculates the hypotenuse of a right-angled triangle.
15. Write a function that accepts a number n as input and returns the average of numbers from 1 to n.
16. Write a program to find the biggest of three integers using functions.
17. Write a program to calculate the area of a triangle using function.
18. Write a program to find whether a number is even or odd using functions.
19. Write a program to illustrate call-by-value technique of passing arguments to a function.
20. Write a program to illustrate call-by-reference technique of passing arguments to a function.
21. Write a program to swap two integers using call-by-value method of passing arguments to a function.
22. Write a program using function to calculate x to the power of y, where y an be either negative or positive.
23. Write a program using function to calculate compound interest given the principal, rate of interest, and number of years
24. Write a program to swap two integers using call-by-reference method of passing arguments to a function.
25. Write a program to reverse a string using recursion.
26. Write a program to reverse a string without using recursion.
27. Write a program to calculate exp(x,y) using recursion.
28. Write a program to calculate exp(x,y) without using recursion.
29. Write a program to print the Fibonacci series using recursion.
30. Write a program to print the Fibonacci series without using recursion.
31. Write a program using functions to perform calculator operations.
32. Write a function that converts temperature given in Celsius into Fahrenheit.
33. Write a function to draw the following pattern on the screen

```
********
!      !
!      !
!      !
********
```

34. Write a function to print a table of binomial coefficients which is given by the formula:
`B(m, x) = m!/ (x! (m-x)!) where m > x`
Hint: `B (m,0) = 1, B(0,0) = 1 and`
`B(m,x) = B(m, x-1) * [(m - x + 1)/x]`
35. Write a program to evaluate f(x) = x − x^3/3! + x^5/5! − x^7/7! +.....
36. Write a program to add two long integers and two floating point numbers using compile time polymorphism.
37. Write a program using static polymorphism to calculate the area of a circle, rectangle, triangle and a square.

Which function prototypes given here are correct?

(a) void func(int);
(b) int func(void);
(c) int func(a);
(d) void func(int, int b);
(e) void func(void, int);
(f) float average(int x, int y);
(g) int power(int x, int y-1);
(h) int mul(int num, 2);
(i) int min(int x; int y;);
(j) int min(int x, y);

Find the errors in the following codes

1.
```
using namespace std;
#include<iostream>
main()
{   cout<<func();
}
void func()
{   cout<<"\n Hello";   }
```

2.
```
using namespace std;
#include<iostream>
void func(int);
```

```
void func(char);
main()
{   cout<<func(2);
    cout<<func('B');
}
void func(int num)
{   cout<<"\n Hello";   }
void func(char ch)
{   cout<<"\n Hello";   }
```

3.
```
using namespace std;
#include<iostream>
void func();
main()
{   void func()
{   cout<<"\n Hello";   }
}
```

4.
```
using namespace std;
#include<iostream>
int func();
int counter;
main()
{   cout<<func();
    cout<<func();
}
int func()
{   return counter++;
}
```

Find the output of the following codes

1.
```
using namespace std;
#include<iostream>
int func();
main()
{   cout<<func();
    cout<<func();
    cout<<func();
    cout<<func();
}
int func()
{   int counter = 0;
    return counter;
}
```

2.
```
using namespace std;
#include<iostream>
int func();
int counter = 5;
main()
{   cout<<func();
    cout<<func();
    cout<<func();
    cout<<func();
}
int func()
{   return counter++;
}
```

3.
```
using namespace std;
#include<iostream>
int add(int, int);
main()
{   int a = 2, b = 3;
    cout<<a<<b<<add(a, b));
}
int add(int a, int b)
{   int c;
    c = a+b
}
```

4.
```
using namespace std;
#include<iostream>
int func(int);
main()
{   int a = 2;
    cout<<func(a);
}
int func(int a)
{   if(a > 1)
      return func(--a) + 10;
    else
      return 0;
}
```

5.
```
using namespace std;
#include<iostream>
void func(int);
main()
{   int a = 127;
    cout<<a;
    func(a);
}
void func(int a)
{
    a++;
    cout<<a;
}
```

6.
```
using namespace std;
#include<iostream>
void func(int);
auto int a;
main()
{   int a = 10;
    cout<<a;
    func(a);
}
```

```
void func(int a)
{   a++;
    cout<<a;
}
```

7.
```
using namespace std;
#include<iostream>
static int add(int val)
{ static int sum;
    sum += val;
    return sum;
}
main()
{   int i, n = 10;
    for(i = 0;i < 10;i++)
    add(i);
    cout<<"\n SUM = "<<func(0);
}
```

8.
```
using namespace std;
#include<iostream>
void print(double)
{ cout<<"\n DOUBLE"; }
  void print(int)
{ cout<<"\n int"; }
main()
{ print(3.14);
  print('A');
  print(123);
}
```

9.
```
using namespace std;
#include<iostream>
int func();
main()
{   cout<<func();
    cout<<func();
    cout<<func();
    cout<<func();
}
int func()
{   static int counter = 0;
    return counter;
}
```

10.
```
using namespace std;
#include<iostream>
int add(int, int);
main()
{   int a = 2, b = 3;
    cout<<a<<b<<add(a, b);
}
int add(int a, int b)
{   int c;
    c = a + b
    return;
}
```

11.
```
using namespace std;
#include<iostream>
int func(int);
main()
{   int a = 2;
   cout<<func(a);
}
int func(int a)
{ {
     ;
  }
  { { ;
    }
     return a;
  }
}
```

12.
```
using namespace std;
#include<iostream>
void func(int);
int a = 10;
main()
{   int a = 2;
    cout<<a;
    func(a);
    cout<<a;
}
void func(int a)
{
   a = 20;
}
```

13.
```
using namespace std;
#include<iostream>
void func(char);
main()
{   char ch = 256;
    func(ch);
}
void func(char a)
{
 cout<< a;
}
```

14.
```
using namespace std;
#include<iostream>
int a;
static int func()
```

```
{ return a++;
}
main()
{   a = 10;
 cout<<func();
 a *= 10;
 cout<<func();
}
```

15.
```
using namespace std;
#include<iostream>
int prod(int x, int y)
{   return (x*y);
}
main()
{   int x = 2, y = 3, z;
    z = prod(x,prod(x,y));
    cout<<z;
}
```

16.
```
using namespace std;
#include<iostream>
int c = 10;
main()
{ int c = 20;
 {
 int c = 3 * ::c;
 cout<<" c = "<<c;
 cout<<"\n c = "<<::c;
 }
 cout<<" c = "<<c;
 cout<<"\n c = "<<::c;
}
```

Answers

Fill in the Blanks

1. function name; **2.** calling function; **3.** calling function; **4.** arguments/parameters; **5.** operating system; **6.** function header and function body; **7.** call-by-reference; **8.** goto label; **9.** recursive; **10.** system stack; **11.** recursive; **12.** zero or no; **13.** global; **14.** main(); **15.** int; **16.** arguments; **17.** local variable

State True or False

1. false	**2.** true	**3.** true	**4.** true	**5.** true	**6.** false	**7.** true	**8.** false
9. true	**10.** true	**11.** true	**12.** false	**13.** true	**14.** false	**15.** false	**16.** true
17. true							

Multiple Choice Questions

1. (c); **2.** (d); **3.** (c); **4.** (b); **5.** (b); **6.** (d); **7.** (b); **8.** (a)

CHAPTER 5

Arrays

KEY Concepts

Declaration • Accessing elements • Storing values • Calculating the length of an array • 2D Arrays • Multi-dimensional arrays • Operations on arrays • Arrays with functions • Sparse matrices

INTRODUCTION

Consider a situation in which we have 20 students in a class. We have to write a program that reads and prints the marks of these 20 students. In this program, we will need 20 integer variables with different names, as shown in Fig. 5.1.

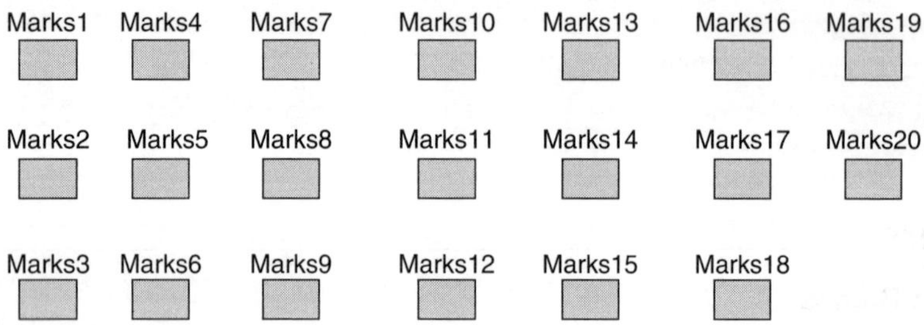

Figure 5.1 Twenty variables

In order to read values for these 20 different variables, we must have 20 read statements. Similarly, to print the value of these variables, we need 20 write statements. If it is just a matter of 20 variables, then it might be acceptable for the user to follow this approach. However, if we had to read and print marks of the students

- in the entire course (say 100 students)
- in the entire college (say 500 students)
- in the entire university (say 10,000 students),

then, it is definitely impossible. To process large amount of data, we need a data structure known as an array.

Programming Tip: In an array of size n, the index ranges from 0 to n-1.

An array is a collection of similar data elements. These data elements have the same data type. The elements of the array are stored in consecutive memory locations and are referenced by an index, also known as the subscript. The subscript indicates an ordinal number of the element, counting from the beginning of the array. Some examples where the concept of an array can be used are as follows:

- List of temperatures recorded on every day of the month
- List of employees in a company
- List of students in a class
- List of products sold
- List of customers

5.1 DECLARATION OF ARRAYS

We have already discussed that every variable must be declared before it is used. The same concept is true in case of array variables as well. An array must be declared before it is used. Declaring an array refers to specifying three aspects:

- The data type—what kind of values it can store ex, int, char, float, and double
- Name—to identify the array
- The size—the maximum number of values that the array can hold

Arrays are declared using the following syntax:

```
type name[size];
```

Here, the type can be either int, float, double, char, or any other valid data type. The number within brackets indicates the size of the array, that is, maximum number of elements that can be stored in the array. The size of the array is a constant and must have a value at compilation time. For example, if we write,

```
int marks[10];
```

Programming Tip: To declare and define an array, you must specify its name, type, and size.

The statement declares a `marks` to be an array containing `10` elements. In C++, the array `index`, also known as subscripts, starts from `zero`. This means that the array marks will contain `10` elements in all. The first element will be stored in `marks[0]`, second element in `marks[1]`, and so on. Therefore, the last element—the 10th element—will be stored in `marks[9]`. Note that `0, 1, 2, and 3` written within square brackets are subscripts or index. In memory, the array will be stored as shown in Fig. 5.2.

1st element	2nd element	3rd element	4th element	5th element	6th element	7th element	8th element	9th element	10th element
marks[0]	marks[1]	marks[2]	marks[3]	marks[4]	marks[5]	marks[6]	marks[7]	marks[8]	marks[9]

Figure 5.2 Memory representation of an array of 10 elements

Key Points to Remember about Arrays

- C++ does not allow declaring an array whose number of elements is not known at the time of compilation. Therefore, the following array declarations are illegal:

```
int arr[];
int n, arr[n];
```

- Generally, it is a good programming practice to define the size of an array as a symbolic constant as shown in the code given here.

```
using namespace std;
#include<iostream>
#define N 100
main()
{  int arr[N];
   ..........
}
```

- The size of the array can be specified using an expression. However, the components of the expression must be available for evaluation of the expression when the program is compiled. Therefore, the following array declarations are valid in C++.

```
using namespace std;
#include<iostream>
#define N 100
main()
{  int i = 10;
   int arr[N + 10], my_arr[i-5*10];
   ..........
}
```

Note C++ array indices start from 0. For an array with `N` elements, the index of the last element is `N-1`.

- C++ never checks the validity of the array index—neither at compile time nor at run time. Therefore, even if you declare an array as

```
int arr[N];
```

The C++ compiler will not raise any error but the result of running such a code is totally unpredictable. Even if you declare an array of 10 elements and later on, by mistake, try to access the 11th element, no error will be generated. However, the results will be unpredictable as the memory occupied by the so-called 11th element may be storing data of another object.

Programming Tip: To access all the elements of the array, you must use a loop. There is no single statement that can do the work.

5.2 ACCESSING ELEMENTS OF THE ARRAY

For accessing an individual element of the array, the array subscript must be used. For example, to access the fourth element of the array, you must write `arr[3]`. The subscript or index must be an integral value or an expression that evaluates to an integral value.

Although storing the related data items in a single array enables programmers to develop concise and efficient programs, there is no single operation that can operate on all the elements of the array. To access all the elements of the array, a loop must be used. In this way, we can access all elements of the array by varying the value of the subscript into the array. It must be noted that the subscript must be an integral value or an expression that evaluates to an integral value. As shown in Fig. 5.2, the first element of the array `marks[0]` can be accessed by writing, `marks[0]`. In order to process all the elements of the array, we will use a loop as shown in Fig. 5.3. Figure 5.4 shows the result of the code shown in Fig. 5.3.

```
// Set each element of the array to -1

int i, marks[10];
for(i = 0;i < 10;i++)
      marks[i] = -1;
```

Figure 5.3 Code to initialize each element of the array to -1

The code accesses each element of the array and sets its value to `-1`. In the `for` loop, the value of `marks[0]` is set to `-1`, the value of the index (i) is incremented, and the next value—marks[1] – is set to -1. The procedure is continued until all the 10 elements of the array are set to -1.

–1	–1	–1	–1	–1	–1	–1	–1	–1	–1
[0]	[1]	[2]	[3]	[4]	[5]	[6]	[7]	[8]	[9]

Figure 5.4 The array marks after executing the code given in Fig. 5.4

Note There is no single statement that can read, access, or print all the elements of the array. To do this, we have to do it using a for, while, or do while loop to execute the same statement with different index values.

5.2.1 Calculating the Address of Array Elements

C++ identifies where an individual element of the array is located in the memory as the array name is a symbolic reference for the address to the first byte of the array. When we use the array name, we are actually referring to the first byte of the array.

The subscript or the index represents the offset from the beginning of the array to the element being referenced. That is, with just the array name and the index, C++ can calculate the address of any element in the array.

An array stores all its data elements in consecutive memory location. Therefore, storing just the base address—the address of the first element in the array—is sufficient. The address of other data elements can simply be calculated using the base address. The formula for doing this calculation is as follows: The salient features of this array are as follows:

```
Address of data element, A[k] = BA(A) + w( k - lower_bound)
```

- A is the array.
- k is the index of the element of which we have to calculate the address.
- BA is the base address of the array A.
- w is the word size of one element in memory, for example, size of int is 2.
- lower_bound is the index of the first element in the array.

Example 5.1 Given here is an array int marks[] = {99,67,78,56,88,90,34,85}. Calculate the address of marks[4] if base address = 1000.

99	67	78	56	88	90	34	85
marks[0]	marks[1]	marks[2]	marks[3]	**marks[4]**	marks[5]	marks[6]	marks[7]
1000	1002	1004	1006	**1008**	1010	1012	1014

We know that storing an integer value requires two bytes; therefore, word size is two bytes.

```
Marks[4] = 1000 + 2(4 - 0)
         = 1000 + 2(4) = 1008
```

Example 5.2 Given here is an array float avg[] ={99.0, 67.0, 78.0, 55.0, 88.0, 90.0, 34.0, 85.0}. Calculate the address of avg [4] if base address = 1000.

99.0	67.0	78.0	55.0	**88.0**	90.0	34.0	85.0
avg[0]	avg[1]	avg[2]	avg[3]	**avg[4]**	avg[5]	avg[6]	avg[7]
1000	1004	1008	1012	**1016**	1020	1024	1028

We know that storing a floating point number requires four bytes, therefore, word size is four bytes.

```
Avg[4] = 1000 + 4(4 - 0)
       = 1000 + 4(4) = 1016
```

Note When we write `arr[i]`, the compiler interprets it as the contents of memory slot, which is i slots away from the beginning of the array `arr`.

5.3 STORING VALUES IN ARRAYS

Programming Tip: By default, the elements of the array are not initialized. They may contain some garbage value, so before using the array you must initialize the array or read some meaningful data into it.

When we declare and define an array, we are just allocating space for the elements; no values are stored in the array. To store values in the array, there are three ways—first, to initialize the array elements; second, to input value for every individual element; and third to assign values to the elements. This is shown in Fig. 5.5.

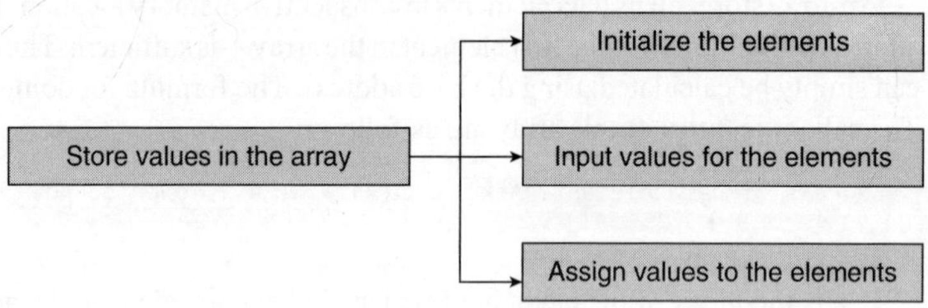

Figure 5.5 Storing values in an array

5.3.1 Initialization of Arrays

Elements of the array can also be initialized at the time of declaration as every other variable. When an array is initialized, we need to provide a value for every element in the array. Arrays are initialized by writing,

```
type array_name[size] = {list of values};
```

The values are written with curly brackets and every value is separated by a comma. It is a compiler error to specify more values than there are elements in the array. When we write,

```
int marks[5] = {90, 82, 78, 95, 88};
```

an array with name `marks` is declared that has enough space to store 5 elements. The first element, that is, `marks[0]` is assigned with the value `90`. Similarly, the second element of the array, that is, `marks[1]` has been assigned `82`, so on, and so forth. This is shown in Fig. 5.6.

marks[0]	90
marks[1]	82
marks[2]	78
marks[3]	95
marks[4]	88

Figure 5.6 Initialization of array `marks[5]`

While initializing the array at the time of declaration, the programmer may omit to mention the size of the array. For example,

```
int marks[] = { 98, 97, 90};
```

The statement is absolutely legal. Here, the compiler will allocate sufficient space for all initialized elements. If the number of values provided is less than the number of elements in the array, the unassigned elements are filled with zeros. Figure 5.7 shows the initialization of arrays.

Programming Tip: In order to initialize all the elements of array to zero, just initialize its first element with zero.

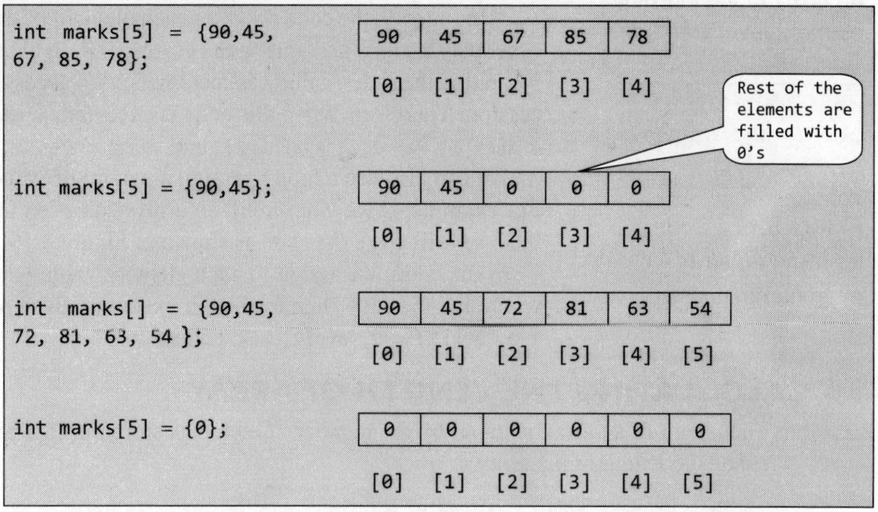

Figure 5.7 Initialization of array elements

Note If we have more initializers than the declared size of the array, then a compile time error will be generated. For example, the following statement will result in a compiler error.

```
int marks[3] = {1,2,3,4};
```

5.3.2 Inputting Values

```
// Input value of each element of the array

int i, marks[10];
for(i = 0;i < 10;i++)
      cin>>&marks[i]);
```

Figure 5.8 Code for inputting each element

An array can be filled by inputting values from the keyboard. In this method, a `while/do-while` or a `for` loop is executed to input the value for each element of the array. For example, look at the code shown in Fig. 5.8.

In this code, we start at the index `i` at `0` and input the value for the first element of the array. Since the array can have `10` elements, we must input values for elements whose index varies from `0` to `9`. Therefore, in the `for` loop, we test for condition (`i<10`) which means the number of elements in the array.

5.3.3 Assigning Values

The third way to assign values to individual elements of the array is by using the assignment operator. Any value that evaluates to an appropriate data type as that of the array can be assigned to the individual array element. A simple assignment statement can be written as,

```
marks[3] = 100;
```

```
int i, arr1[10], arr2[10];
for(i = 0;i < 10;i++)
        arr2[i] = arr1[i];
```

Figure 5.9 Code to copy an array at the individual element level

Here, `100` is assigned to the fourth element of the array which is specified as `marks[3]`.

We cannot assign one array to another array, even if the two arrays have the same type and size. To copy an array, you must copy the value of every element of the first array into the element of the second array. Figure 5.9 illustrates the code to copy an array.

In Fig. 5.9, the code accesses each element of the first array and simultaneously assigns its value to the corresponding element of the second array. Finally, the index value `i` is incremented to access the next element in succession. Therefore, when this code is executed, `arr2[0] = arr1[0]`, `arr2[1] = arr1[1]`, `arr2[2] = arr1[2]`, and so on.

```
int i, arr[10];
for(i = 0;i < 10;i++)
        arr[i] = i*2;
```

Figure 5.10 Code for filling an array with even numbers

We can also use a loop to assign a pattern of values to the array elements. For example, if we want to fill an array with even integers starting (from `0`), then we will write the code as shown in Figure 5.10.

In the code, we assign to each element value equal to twice of its index, where index starts Therefore, after executing this code, we will have `arr[0] = 0`, `arr[1] = 2`, `arr[2] = 4`, and so on.

5.4 CALCULATING THE LENGTH OF ARRAY

The length of an array is given by the number of elements stored in it. The general formula to calculate the length of the array is

```
Length = upper_bound - lower_bound + 1
```

where `upper_bound` is the `index` of the last element and `lower_bound` is the index of the first element in the array

Usually, `lower_bound` is zero; however, this is not a compulsion as we can have an array whose index may start from any non-zero value.

Example 5.3 Let age be an array of integers such that

`Age[0] = 2   Age[1] = 5   Age = 3   Age[4] = 1   Age[5] = 7`

Show the memory representation of the array and calculate its length.

Memory representation of the array `Age` is given as follows:

2	5	3	1	7
`Age[0]`	`Age[1]`	`Age[2]`	`Age[3]`	`Age[4]`

`Length = upper_bound - lower_bound + 1`

Here, `lower_bound = 0, upper_bound = 4`

Therefore, `length` = 4 − 0 + 1 = 5

5.5 OPERATIONS THAT CAN BE PERFORMED ON ARRAYS

There are several operations that can be preformed on arrays. These operations are as follows:

- Traversal
- Search
- Merging
- Insertion
- Deletion
- Sorting

We will study all these operations in detail in this section.

5.5.1 Traversal

As discussed earlier while reading about accessing array elements, traversing the array element means accessing each element of the array for a specific purpose.

If `A` is an array of homogeneous data elements, then traversing the data elements can include printing every element, counting the total number of elements, or performing any process on these elements. As an array is a linear data structure because all its elements form a sequence, traversing its elements is very simple and straightforward. The algorithm for array traversal is given in Fig. 5.11.

```
Step 1: [Initialization] Set I = lower_bound
Step 2: Repeat steps 3 to 4 while I <= upper_bound
Step 3: Apply Process to A[I]
Step 4: Set I = I + 1
        [End of Loop]
Step 5: Exit
```

Figure 5.11 Alogrithm for array traversal

In Step 1, we initialize index to the `lower bound` of the array. In Step 2, a `while` loop is executed. Steps 3 and 4 form a part of the loop. Step 3 processes the individual array element as specified by the array name and index vale. Step 4 increments the index value so that the next array element could be processed. The `while` loop in Step 2 is executed until all the elements in the array are processed. In other words, until `I` is less than or equal to the `upper bound` of the array.

Example 5.4 Assume that there is an array `Marks[]`, such that the index of the array specifies the roll number of the student and the value of a particular element denotes the marks obtained by the student. For example, if it is given `Marks[4] = 78`, then the student whose roll number is 4 has obtained 78 marks in the examination. Now, write an algorithm to

- Find the total number of students who have secured 80 or more marks
- Print the roll number and marks of all the students who have got distinction

```
Step 1: [Initialization] Set I = I + 1
Step 2: Repeat for I = lower_bound to upper_bound
    If Marks[I] >= 80, then : Set Count = Count + 1
    [End of Loop]
Step 3: Exit
    b) Step 1: [Initialization] Set I = I + 1
Step 2: Repeat for I = lower_bound to upper_bound
                If Marks[I] >= 75,  Write: I , Marks[I]
      [End of Loop]
Step 3: Exit
```

Program 5.1 Write a program to read and display n numbers using an array.

```
using namespace std;
#include<iostream>
int main()
{   int i = 0, n, arr[20];
    cout<< "\n Enter the number of elements : ";
    cin>>n;
    for(i = 0;i < n;i++)
```

```
    {   cout<<"\n Arr["<<i<<"] = ";
        cin>>arr[i];
    }
    cout<<"\n The array elements are \n";
    for(i = 0;i < n;i++)
    cout<<"\t Arr["<<i<<"] = "<<arr[i];
}
```

OUTPUT

```
Enter the number of elements : 5
1 2 3 4 5
The array elements are
Arr[0] = 1 Arr[1] = 2 Arr[2] = 3 Arr[3] = 4 Arr[4] = 5
```

Program 5.2 Write a program to read and display n random numbers using an array.

```
using namespace std;
#include<iostream>
#include<stdlib.h>
#define MAX 10
main()
{   int arr[MAX], i,RandNo;
    for(i = 0;i < MAX;i++)
    {   // Scale the random number in the range 0 to MAX-1
        RandNo = rand() % MAX;
    arr[i] = RandNo;
    }
    cout<<"\n The contents of the array are :- ";
    for(i = 0;i < MAX;i++)
        cout<<"\t"<<arr[i];
}
```

OUTPUT

```
The contents of the array are :-7  0  1  2  4  6  5  4   8  3
```

Program 5.3 Write a program to find largest of n numbers using arrays.

```
using namespace std;
#include<iostream>
int main()
{   int i, n, arr[20], large = 0;
    cout<<"\n Enter the number of elements in the array : ";
    cin>>n;
    cout<<"\n Enter the elements :\n";
    for(i = 0;i < n;i++)
        cin>>arr[i];
    large = arr[0];
    for(i = 1;i < n;i++)
    {   if(arr[i] > large)
        large = arr[i];
    }
    cout<<"\n The largest number is : "<<large;
}
```

OUTPUT

```
Enter the number of elements : 5
1 2 3 4 5
The largest number is : 5
```

Program 5.4 Write a program to interchange the largest and the smallest number in the array.

```
using namespace std;
#include<iostream>
int main()
{   int i, n, arr[20], temp;
    int small, small_pos = 0, large, large_pos = 0;
    cout<<"\n Enter the number of elements in the array : ";
    cin>>n;
    cout<<"\n Enter the elements :\n";
    for(i = 0;i < n;i++)
        cin>>arr[i];
    small = large = arr[0];
    for(i = 0;i < n;i++)
    {   if(arr[i] < small)
        {   small = arr[i];
            small_pos = i;
        }
        if(arr[i] > large)
        {   large = arr[i];
        large_pos = i;
        }
    }
    cout<<"\n The smallest of these numbers is : "<<small;
    cout<<"\n The position of the smallest number in the array is : "<<small_pos;
    cout<<"\n The largest of these numbers is : "<<large;
    cout<<"\n The position of the largest number in the array is : "<<large_pos;
    temp = arr[large_pos];
    arr[large_pos] =arr[small_pos];
    arr[small_pos] = temp;
    cout<<"\n The new array is : ";
    for(i = 0;i < n;i++)
        cout<<" \n arr["<<i<<"] = "<<arr[i];
}
```

OUTPUT

```
Enter the number of elements : 5
1 2 3 4 5
The smallest number is : 1
The position of the smallest number in the array is : 0
The largest number is : 5
The position of the largest number in the array is : 4
The new array is
5 4 3 2 1
```

Program 5.5 Write a program to find the second largest number using an array of n numbers.

```
using namespace std;
#include<iostream>
int main()
{   int i, n, arr[20], large, second_large;
    cout<<"\n Enter the number of elements in the array : ";
    cin>>n;
    cout<<"\n Enter the elements :\n";
```

```
    for(i = 0;i < n;i++)
        cin>>arr[i];
    large = second_large = arr[0];
    for(i = 0;i < n;i++)
    {   if(arr[i]>large)
            large = arr[i];
    }
    for(i = 0;i < n;i++)
    {   if(arr[i] != large)
        {
            if(arr[i]>second_large)
                second_large = arr[i];
        }
    }
    cout<<"\n The numbers you entered are : ";
    for(i = 0;i < n;i++)
        cout<<arr[i];
        cout<<"\n The largest of these numbers is : "<<large;
        cout<<"\n The second largest of these numbers is : "<<second_large;
}
```

OUTPUT

```
Enter the number of elements : 5
1 2 3 4 5
The numbers you entered are :
1 2 3 4 5
The largest of these numbers is : 5
The second largest of these numbers is : 4
```

Program 5.6 Write a program to enter n number of digits and then form a number using these digits.

```
using namespace std;
#include<iostream>
#include<math.h>
int main()
{   int number = 0, digit[10], numofdigits,i;
    cout<<"\n Enter the number of digits : ";
    cin>>numofdigits;
    for(i = 0;i < numofdigits;i++)
    {   cout<<"\n Enter the "<<i<<" th digit : "<<i;
        cin>>digit[i];
    }
    i = 0;
    while(i < numofdigits)
    {   number = number + digit[i] * pow(10,i);
        i++;
    }
    cout<<"\n The number is : "<<number;
}
```

OUTPUT

```
Enter the number of digits : 3
Enter the 0th digit : 3
Enter the 1th digit : 4
Enter the 2th digit : 5
The number is : 543
```

Program 5.7 Write a program to find whether the array of integers contain a duplicate number.

```
using namespace std;
#include<iostream>
int main()
{   int array1[10], i, n, j, flag = 0;
    cout<<"\n Enter the number of elements in the array : ";
    cin>>n;
    cout<<"\n Enter the elements :\n";
    for(i = 0;i <n ;i++)
        cin>>array1[i];
    for(i = 0;i < n;i++)
    {   for(j = i + 1;j < n;j++)
    {   if(array1[i] == array1[j] && i!=j)
        { flag = 1;
          cout<<"\n Duplicate number "<<array1[i]<<" found at location "<<i<<" and "<<j;
        }
    }
    }
    if(flag = 0)
    cout<<"\n No Duplicate";
}
```

OUTPUT

```
Enter the number of elements : 5
1 2 3 4 5
No Duplicate
```

Program 5.8 Write a program to read marks of 50 students in the range of 0–100. Then make 10 groups such as 0-10, 10-20, 10-20, and so on. Count the number of values that falls in each group. And display the result.

```
using namespace std;
#include<iostream>
main()
{   int marks[50], i;
    int group[10] = {0};
    cout<<"\n Enter the marks of 50 students : \n";
    for(i = 0;i < 50;i++)
    {   cout<<"\n MARKS["<<i<<"] = ";
        cin>>marks[i];
        ++group[(int)(marks[i])/10];
    }
    cout<<"\n\n ************************";
    cout<<"\n GROUP \t\t FRQUENCY";
    for(i=0;i<10;i++)
    cout<<"\n "<<i<<" \t\t "<<group[i];
}
```

SAMPLE OUTPUT

```
*************************
GROUP   FRQUENCY
0         4
1         2
2         6
```

```
3        5
4        10
5        22
6        18
7        9
8        5
9        4
10       0
```

Program 5.9 Modify the previous program to display frequency histograms of each group.

```
using namespace std;
#include<iostream>
main()
{   int marks[50], i;
    int group[10] = {0};
    cout<<"\n Enter the marks of 50 students : \n";
    for(i = 0;i < 50;i++)
    {   cout<<"\n MARKS["<<i<<"] = ";
    cin>>marks[i];
    ++group[(int)(marks[i])/10];
    }
    cout<<"\n\n ************************";
    cout<<"\n GROUP \t\t FREQUENCY";
    for(i = 0;i < 10;i++)
        cout<<"\n "<<i<<" \t\t "<<group[i];
    cout<<"\n\n FREQUENCY HISTOGRAM";
    for(i = 0;i < 10;index++)
    cout<<"\n GROUP "<<i<<" | ";
    for(i = 0;i < group[i];i++)
    cout<<" *";
}
```

SAMPLE OUTPUT

```
GROUP   FREQUENCY
0   ****
1   **
2   ******
3   *****
```

Program 5.10 Write a program to read a sorted list of floating point values and then calculate and display the median of the values.

```
using namespace std;
#include<iostream>
main()
{   int i, j, n;
    float median, values[10];
    cout<<"\n Enter the size of the array : ";
    cin>>n;
    cout<<"\n Enter the values : ";
    for(i = 0;i<n;i++)
        cin>>values[i];
    if(n%2 == 0)
        median = (values[n/2] + values[n/2+1])/2.0;
    else
```

```
        median = values[n/2 + 1];
    cout<<"\n MEDIAN = "<<median;
}
```

OUTPUT

```
Enter the size of the array : 5
Enter the values :
12 34 56 78 89
MEDIAN = 55.00
```

5.5.2 Insertion

Inserting an element in the array means adding a new data element in an already existing array. If the element has to be inserted at the end of the existing array, then the task of inserting is quite simple. We just have to add 1 to the `upper_bound` and assign the value. Here, we assume that the memory space allocated for the array is still available. For example, if an array is declared to contain 10 elements, but is currently having only 8 elements, then, obviously, there is space to accommodate two more elements. However, if it already has `10` elements, then we will not be able to add another element to it.

However, if we have to insert an element in the middle of the array, for example, in an array whose elements are arranged in ascending order then we have to first find the location where the new element will be inserted and then move all the elements that have a value greater than that of the new element one space to the right, so that space can be created to store the new value.

Program 5.11 Write a program to insert a number at a given location in an array.

```
using namespace std;
#include<iostream>
int main()
{   int i, n, num, pos, arr[10];
    cout<<"\n Enter the number of elements in the array : ";
    cin>>n;
    cout<<"\n Enter the elements :\n";
    for(i = 0;i < n;i++)
        cin>>arr[i];
    cout<<"\n Enter the number to be inserted : ";
    cin>>num;
    cout<<"\n Enter the position at which the number has to be added : ";
    cin>>pos;
    for(i = n;i >= pos;i--)
        arr[i + 1] = arr[i];
        arr[pos] = num;
    cout<<"\n The array after insertion of "<<num<<" is : ";
    for(i = 0;i < n+1;i++)
        cout<<"\n Arr[:"<<i<<"] = "<<arr[i];
}
```

OUTPUT

```
Enter the number of elements in the array : 5
Enter the values :
1 2 3 4 5
```

```
Enter the number to be inserted : 7
Enter the position at which the number has to be added :3
The array after insertion of 7 is :
1 2 3 7 4 5
```

Program 5.12 Write a program to insert a number in an array that is already sorted in ascending order.

```
using namespace std;
#include<iostream>
int main()
{   int i, n, j, num, arr[10];
    cout<<"\n Enter the number of elements in the array : ";
    cin>>n;
    cout<<"\n Enter the elements :\n";
    for(i = 0;i < n;i++)
        cin>>arr[i];
    cout<<"\n Enter the number to be inserted : ";
    cin>>num;
    for(i = 0;i < n;i++)
    {   if(arr[i] > num)
        {   for(j = n-1; j >= i; j--)
                arr[j+1] = arr[j];
            arr[i] = num;
            break;
        }
    }
    cout<<"\n The array after insertion of "<<num<<" is : ";
    for(i = 0;i < n+1;i++)
    cout<<"\n Arr["<<i<<"] = "<<arr[i];
}
```

OUTPUT

```
Enter the number of elements in the array : 5
1 2 3 4 5
Enter the number to be inserted : 6
The array after insertion of 6 is :
1 2 3 4 5 6
```

5.5.3 Deletion

Deleting an element from the array means removing a data element from an already existing array. If the element has to be deleted from the end of the existing array, then the task of deletion is quite simple. We just have to subtract 1 from the `upper_bound`.

However, if we have to delete the element from the middle of the array, then this task is not trivial. As on an average, we might have to move as much as half of the elements from its position in order to occupy the space of the deleted element.

For example, consider an array whose elements are arranged in ascending order. If an element has to be deleted probably from somewhere middle in the array, find the location from where the element has to be deleted and then move all the elements that have a value greater than that of the element one space towards the left so that space vacated by the deleted element be occupied by rest of the elements.

5.5.4 Merging

Merging two arrays in a third array means first copying the contents of the first array into the third array and then copying the contents of the second array into the third array. Hence, the merged array contains contents of the first array followed by the contents of the second array.

If the arrays are unsorted, then merging the arrays is very simple as one just needs to copy the contents of one array into another. However, merging is not a trivial task when two arrays are sorted and the merged array also needs to be sorted. Let us first discuss the merge operation on unsorted arrays. This operation is shown in Fig. 5.12.

Array 1	90	56	89	77	69							
Array 2	45	88	76	99	12	58	81					
Array 3	90	56	89	77	69	45	88	76	99	12	58	81

Figure 5.12 Merging of two unsorted arrays

Program 5.13 Write a program to merge two unsorted arrays.

```
using namespace std;
#include<iostream>
main()
{   int arr1[10], arr2[10], arr3[20];
    int i, n1, n2, m, index=0;
    cout<<"\n Enter the number of elements in array1 : ";
    cin>>n1;
    cout<<"\n\n Enter the Elements of the first array";
    cout<<"\n ***************************************\n";
    for(i = 0;i < n1;i++)
        cin>>arr1[i];
    cout<<"\n Enter the number of elements in array2 : ";
    cin>>n2;
    cout<<"\n\n Enter the Elements of the second array";
    cout<<"\n ***************************************\n";
    for(i = 0;i < n2;i++)
        cin>>arr2[i];
    m = n1 + n2;
    for(i = 0;i < n1;i++)
    {   arr3[index] = arr1[i];
        index++;
    }
    for(i = 0;i < n2;i++)
    {   arr3[index] = arr2[i];
        index++;
    }
    cout<<"\n\n The merged array is";
    cout<<"\n ********************";
    for(i = 0;i < m;i++)
        cout<<"\n Arr["<<i<<"] = "<<arr3[i];
}
```

OUTPUT

```
Enter the number of elements in array1 : 3
Enter the Elements of the first array :
**************************************
1  2  3
Enter the number of elements in array2 : 4
Enter the Elements of the second array
**************************************
4  5  6  7
The merged array is
*******************
1   2 3 4 5 6 7
```

If we have two sorted arrays and the resultant merged array also needs to be a sorted one, then the task of merging the arrays becomes a little difficult. The task of merging can be explained using Fig. 5.13.

Array 1	20	30	40	50	60

Array 2	15	22	31	45	56	62	78

Array 3	15	20	22	30	31	40	45	50	56	60	62	78

Figure 5.13 Merging of two sorted arrays

The figure shows how the merged array is formed using two sorted arrays. Here, we first compare the first element of array 1 with the first element of `array 2`, and put the smaller element in the merged array. Since `20>15`, we put `15` as the first element in the merged array. We then compare the second element of the second array with the first element of the first array. Since `20<22`, now `20` is stored as the second element of the merged array. Next, second element of the first array is compared with the second element of the second array. Since `30>22`, we store `22` as the third element of the merged array. Now, we will compare the second element of the first array with `third` element of the second array. As `30<31`, we store `30` as the fourth element of the merged array. This procedure will be repeated until elements of both the arrays are placed in the right location in the merged array.

Program 5.14 Write a program to merge two sorted arrays.

```
using namespace std;
#include<iostream>
main()
{   int arr1[10], arr2[10], arr3[20];
    int i, n1, n2, m, index=0;
    int index_first = 0, index_second = 0;
    cout<<"\n Enter the number of elements in array1 : ";
    cin>>n1;
    cout<<"\n\n Enter the Elements of the first array";
    for(i = 0;i < n1;i++)
        cin>>arr1[i];
    cout<<"\n Enter the number of elements in array2 : ";
    cin>>n2;
    cout<<"\n\n Enter the Elements of the second array";
    for(i = 0;i < n2;i++)
```

```
        cin>>arr2[i];
    m = n1 + n2;
    while(index_first < n1 && index_second < n2)
    {       if(arr1[index_first]<arr2[index_second])
        {   arr3[index] = arr1[index_first];
            index_first++;
        }
        else
        {   arr3[index] = arr2[index_second];
            index_second++;
        }
        index++;
    }
    // if elements of the first array is over and the second array has some elements
        if(index_first == n1)
        {   while(index_second<n2)
            {   arr3[index] = arr2[index_second];
                index_second++;
                index++;
            }
        }
// if elements of the second array is over and the first array has some elements
    else if(index_second == n2)
    {   while(index_first<n1)
        {   arr3[index] = arr1[index_first];
            index_first++;
            index++;
        }
    }
    cout<<"\n\n The contents of the merged array are-";
    cout<<"\n ****************************************";
    for(i = 0;i < m;i++)
        cout<<"\n Arr["<<i<<"] = "<<arr3[i];
}
```

OUTPUT

```
Enter the number of elements in array1 : 3
Enter the Elements of the first array : 1   2   3
Enter the number of elements in array2 : 4
Enter the Elements of the second array : 4   5   6   7
The merged array is: 1 2 3 4 5 6 7
```

5.5.5 Searching the Array Elements

Searching refers to find whether a particular value is present in the array or not. If the value is present in the array, then searching is said to be successful and the searching process gives the location of that value in the array. Otherwise, if the value is not present in the array, the searching process displays the appropriate message and in this case searching is said to be unsuccessful.

There are two popular methods for searching the elements of an array such as linear search and binary search. The algorithm that should be used depends entirely on how the values are organized in the array. For example, if the elements of the array are arranged in the ascending order, then binary search should be used as it is more efficient for sorted list in terms of complexity. We will discuss these two methods in detail in this section.

Linear Search

Linear search, also called sequential search, is a very simple method used for searching an array for a particular value. It works by comparing every element of the array one by one in sequence until a match is found. Linear search is mostly used to search an unordered list of elements. This refers to an array in which data elements are not sorted. For example, if an array `A[]` is declared and initialized as

```
int A[] = { 10, 8, 2, 7, 3, 4, 9, 1, 6, 5};
```

and `VAL = 7`, then searching means to find out whether the value '7' is present in the array or not. If yes, then returns the position of its occurrence. Here, the `POS = 3` (index starting from 0). Figure 5.14 illustrates this concept.

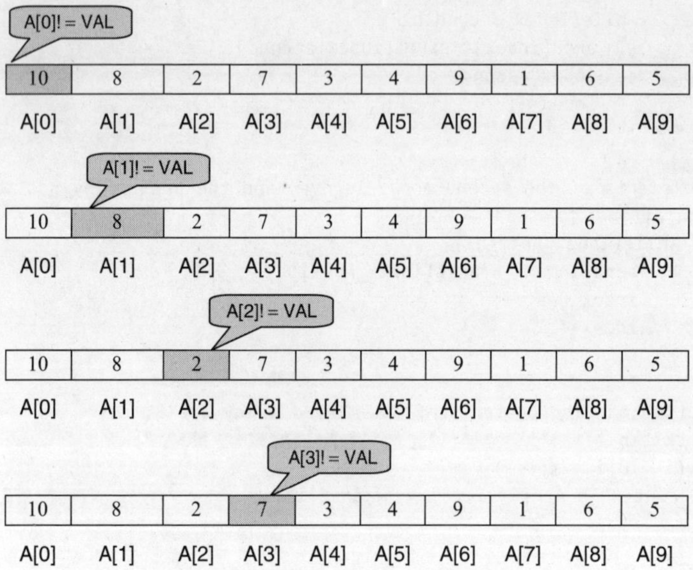

Figure 5.14 Linear search

The algorithm to perform linear search is given in Fig. 5.15.

```
LINEAR_SEARCH(A, N, VAL, POS)

Step 1: [INITIALIZE] SET POS = -1
Step 2: [INITIALIZE] SET I = 0
Step 3: Repeat Step 4 while I<N
Step 4:         IF A[I] = VAL, then
                              SET POS = I
                              PRINT POS
                              Go to Step 6
                [END OF IF]
        [END OF LOOP]
Step 5: PRINT "Value Not Present In The Array"
Step 6: EXIT
```

Figure 5.15 Algorithm for linear search

In Steps 1 and 2 of the algorithm, we initialize the value of `POS` and `I`. In Step 3, a `while` loop is executed that would be executed until `I` is less than `N` (total number of elements in the array). In Step 4, a check is made to see if a match is found between the current array element and the `VAL`. If a match is found, then the position of the array element is printed else the value of `I` is incremented to match the next element with `VAL`. However, if all the arrays elements have been compared with `VAL`, and no match is found, then it means that the `VAL` is not present in the array.

Program 5.15 Write a program to implement linear search in any given array.

```
using namespace std;
#include<iostream>
main()
{   int arr[10], num, i, n, found = 0, pos = -1;
    cout<<"\n Enter the number of elements in the array : ";
    cin>>n;
    cout<<"\n Enter the elements :";
    for(i = 0;i < n;i++)
        cin>>arr[i];
    cout<<"\n Enter the number that has to be searched : ";
    cin>>num;
    for(i = 0;i < n;i++)
    {   if(arr[i] == num)
        {   found = 1;
            pos = i;
            cout<<"\n "<<num<<" is found in the array at position = "<<i;
            break;
        }
    }
    if (found == 0)
        cout<<"\n"<<num<<" DOES NOT EXIST in the array";
}
```

OUTPUT

```
Enter the number of elements in the array : 5
Enter the elements : 1 2 3 4 5
Enter the number that has to be searched 7
7DOES NOT EXIST in the array
```

Binary Search

We have seen that the linear search algorithm is very slow. If we have an array with one million entries, then to search a value from that array, we would need to make one million comparisons at the maximum. However, if the array is sorted, we have a better and efficient alternative, known as binary search.

Binary search refers to searching an algorithm that works efficiently with a sorted list. The algorithm finds out the position of a particular element in the array. The mechanism of binary search can be better understood by an analogy of a telephone directory. When we are searching for a particular name in the directory, we will first open the directory from the middle and decide whether to look for the name in the first part of the directory or in the second part of the directory. We will open some page in the middle and the whole process will be repeated until we finally find the name.

Take another analogy. In order to find words in a dictionary, we open the dictionary somewhere in the middle, compare the first word on that page with the desired word whose meaning has to be found. If the word comes before the word that appears on the page, we will look in the first half of the dictionary; else, we will look in the second half. Again, we will open up some page in the first half of the dictionary's pages, compare the first word on that page with the desired word, and repeat the same procedure until we finally get the word. The same mechanism is applied in binary search.

Now, let us consider how this mechanism will be applied to search for a value in a sorted array. Given an array that is declared and initialized as,

```
int A[] = {0, 1, 2, 3, 4, 5, 6, 7, 8, 9, 10};
```

and `VAL = 9`, the algorithm will proceed in the following manner.

```
BEG = 0, END = 10, MID = (0 + 10)/2 = 5
```

Now, `VAL = 9 and A[MID] = A[5] = 5`

`A[5]` is less than `VAL`, therefore, we will now search for the value in the later half of the array. So, we change the values of `BEG` and `MID`.

Now, `BEG = MID + 1 = 6, END = 10, MID = (6 + 10)/2 =16/2 = 8`

Now, `VAL = 9 and A[MID] = A[8] = 8`

`A[8]` is less than `VAL`, therefore, we will now search for the value in the later half of the array. So, again we change the values of `BEG` and `MID`.

Now, `BEG = MID + 1 = 9,    END = 10,    MID = (9 + 10)/2 = 9`

Now `VAL = 9 and A[MID] = 9.`

Now `VAL = 9 and A[MID] = 9.`

In this algorithm, we see that `BEG` and `END` are the beginning and ending positions of the segment that we are looking to search for the element. `MID` is calculated as `(BEG + END)/2`. Initially, `BEG = lower_bound` and `END = upper_bound`. The algorithm will terminate when `A[MID] = VAL`. When the algorithm ends, we will set `POS = MID`. `POS` is the position at which the value is present in the array.

However, if `VAL` is not equal to `A[MID]`, then the values of `BEG`, `END`, and `MID` will change, depending on whether the `VAL` is smaller or greater than `A[MID]`.

- If `VAL < A[MID]`, then `VAL` will be present in the left segment of the array. Therefore, the value of `END` will be changed as, `END = MID - 1`
- If `VAL > A[MID]`, then `VAL` will be present in the right segment of the array. So, the value of `BEG` will be changed as, `BEG = MID + 1`

Finally, if the `VAL` is not present in the array, then eventually, `END` will be less than `BEG`. When this happens, the algorithm should terminate as it will indicate that the element is not present in the array and the search will be unsuccessful.

Let us consider another example.

```
int A[] = {0,1, 2, 3, 4, 5, 6, 7, 8, 9, 10}; and VAL = 2
Step 1: BEG = 0, END = 10, MID = 5
                A[MID] > VAL
Step 2: BEG = 0, END = MID - 1 = 4, MID = 2
                A[MID] = VAL
```

Figure 5.16 shows an algorithm for binary search.

```
BINARY_SEARCH(A, lower_bound, upper_bound, VAL, POS)
Step 1: [INITIALIZE] SET BEG = lower_bound, END = upper_bound,
POS =  -1
Step 2: Repeat Step 3 and Step 4 while BEG <= END
Step 3:             SET MID = (BEG + END)/2
Step 4:             IF A[MID] = VAL, then
                          POS = MID
                          PRINT POS
                          Go to Step 6
                    IF A[MID] > VAL then;
                          SET END = MID   - 1
                    ELSE
                          SET BEG = MID +   1
                    [END OF IF]
      [END OF LOOP]
Step 5: IF POS =   -1, then
             PRINTF "VAL IS NOT PRESENT IN THE ARRAY"
      [END OF IF]
Step 6: EXIT
```

Figure 5.16 Algorithm for binary search

In Step 1, we initialize the value of variables, `BEG`, `END`, and `POS`. In Step 2, a `while` loop is executed until `BEG` is less than or equal to `END`. In Step 3, the value of `MID` is calculated. In Step 4, we check if the value of `MID` is equal to `VAL`, the item to be searched in the array. If a match is found, value of the `POS` is printed and the algorithm exits. However, if a match is not found, and if the value of `A[MID]` is greater than `VAL`, then the value of `END` is modified; otherwise, if `A[MID]` is greater than `VAL`, then the value of `BEG` is altered. In Step 5, if the value of `POS = -1`, then it means `VAL` is not present in the array and an appropriate message is printed on the screen before the algorithm exits.

Program 5.16 Write a program to implement binary search.

```
using namespace std;
#include<iostream>
main()
{   int arr[10], num, i, n, beg, end, mid, found = 0;
    cout<<"Enter the number of elements in the array";
    cin>>n;
    cout<<"\n Enter the elements :";
    for(i = 0;i < n;i++)
        cin>>arr[i];
    cout<<"\n Enter the number that has to be searched :";
    cin>>num;
    beg = 0, end = n - 1;
    while(beg <= end)
    {   mid = (beg + end)/2;
        if (arr[mid] == num)
        {   cout<<"\n"<<num<<" is present in the array at position = "<<mid;
            found = 1;
            break;
        }
```

```
        if (arr[mid]>num)
            end = mid-1;
        else if (arr[mid] < num)
            beg = mid + 1;
        }
        if ( beg > end && found == 0)
            cout<<"\n"<<num<<" DOES NOT EXIST IN THE ARRAY";
}
```

OUTPUT

```
Enter the number of elements in the array : 5
Enter the elements : 1 2 3 4 5
Enter the number that has to be searched 7
7   DOES NOT EXIST in the array
```

5.6 ONE-DIMENSIONAL ARRAYS FOR INTER FUNCTION COMMUNICATION

Like variables of other data types, we can also pass an array to a function. In some situations, you may want to pass individual elements of the array, and in other situations you may want to pas the entire array. In this section, we will discuss both these cases. Figure 5.17 makes the concept easier to understand.

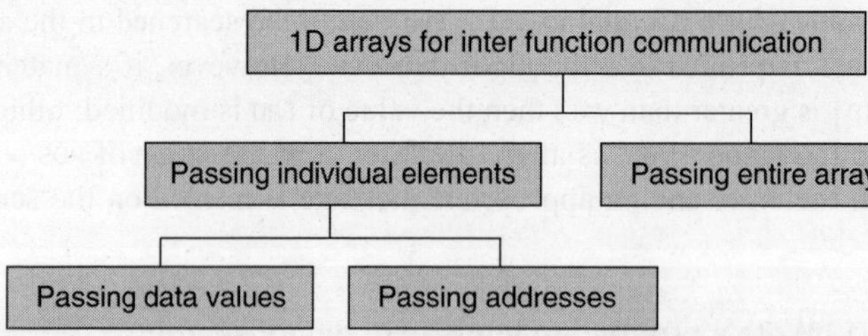

Figure 5.17 One-dimensional arrays for inter function communication

5.6.1 Passing Individual Elements

The individual elements of an array can be passed to a function either by passing their addresses or the data values.

Passing Data Values

The individual elements can be passed in the same manner as we pass variable of any other data type. The condition is just that data type of the array element must match the type of function parameter. Figure 5.18 shows the code to pass an individual array element by passing data value.

In the example, only one element of the array is passed to the called function. This is done by using the index expression. Therefore, `arr[3]` actually evaluates to a single integer value. The called function hardly bothers whether a normal integer variable is passed to it or an array value is passed.

Calling function

```
main()
{
	int arr[5] = {1, 2, 3, 4, 
5};
	func(arr[3]);
}
```

Called function

```
void func(int num)
{
	cout<<num;
}
```

Figure 5.18 Passing individual array elements to function

Passing Addresses

Like ordinary variables, we can pass the address of an individual array element by preceding the address operator to the element's indexed reference. Therefore, to pass the address of the fourth element of the array to the called function, we will write `&arr[3]`.

However, in the called function, the value of the array element must be accessed using the indirection `(*)` operator. Examine the code shown in Fig. 5.19. We will read more about this technique in the following sections.

Calling function

```
main()
{
	int arr[5] = {1, 2, 3, 4, 
5};
	func(&arr[3]);
}
```

Called function

```
void func(int *num)
{
	cout<<num;
}
```

Figure 5.19 Passing individual array elements to function

5.6.2 Passing the Entire Array

We have studied that in C++, the array name refers to the first byte of the array in memory. The address of rest of the elements in the array can be calculated using the array name and the index value of the element. Therefore, when we need to pass an entire array to a function, we can simply pass the name of the array. Figure 5.20 illustrates the code which passes the entire array to the called function.

If we want that the called function should not make any changes to the array, the array must be received as a constant array by the called function. This prevents any type of un-intentional modifications of the array elements. To declare the array as a constant array, simply add the keyword 'cconst' before the data type of the array.

Programming Tip: When an entire array is to be sent to the called function, the calling function just need to pass the name of the array.

Calling function

```
main()
{
	int arr[5] = {1, 2, 3, 4, 
5};
	func(arr);
}
```

Called function

```
void func(int arr[5])
{
	int i;
	for(i = 0;i < 5;i++)
		cout<<num;
}
```

Figure 5.20 Passing entire array to function

Program 5.17 Write a program to read an array of n numbers and then find out the smallest number.

```
using namespace std;
#include<iostream>
void read_array( int arr[], int);
int find_small(int arr[], int n);
int main()
{   int num[10], n, smallest;
    cout<<"\n Enter the size of the array : ";
    cin>>n;
    read_array(num, n);
    smallest = find_small(num, n);
    cout<<"\n The smallest number in the array is = "<<smallest;
}
void read_array( int arr[10], int n)
{   int i;
    for(i = 0;i < n;i++)
        cin>>arr[i];
}
int find_small(int arr[10], int n)
{   int i, small = arr[0];
    for(i = 0;i < n;i++)
    {   if(arr[i] < small)
            small = arr[i];
    }
    return small;
}
```

OUTPUT

```
Enter the size of the array : 5
1 2 3 4 5
The smallest number in the array is = 1
```

Program 5.18 Write a program to merge two integer arrays. Display the merged array in reverse order.

```
using namespace std;
#include<iostream>
void read_array(int arr1[], int);
void display_array(int arr3[], int);
void merge_array(int arr3[], int, int arr1[], int arr2[], int );
void reverse_array(int my_array[], int);
int main()
{   int arr1[10], arr2[10], arr3[20], n, m, t;
    cout<<"\n Enter the size of the first array : ";
    cin>>m;
    read_array(arr1, m);
    cout<<"\n Enter the size of the second array : ";
    cin>>n;
    read_array(arr2, n);
    t = m + n;
    merge_array(arr3, m, arr1, arr2, n);
    cout<<"\n The merged array is : ";
    display_array(arr3, t);
    cout<<"\n The merged array in reverse order is : ";
    reverse_array(arr3, t);
}
```

```
void read_array( int my_array[10], int n)
{   int i;
    for(i = 0;i < n;i++)
    cin>>my_array[i];
}
void merge_array(int my_array1[], int m, int my_array2[], int my_array3[], int n)
{   int i, j = 0;
    for(i = 0; i < m; i++)
    {   my_array1[j] = my_array2[i];
        j++;
    }
    for(i = 0; i < n; i++)
    {   my_array1[j] = my_array3[i];
        j++;
    }
}
void display_array( int my_array[], int n)
{   int i;
    for(i = 0;i < n;i++)
        cout<<"\n array["<<i<<"d] = "<<my_array[i];
}
void reverse_array(int my_array[], int m)
{   int i, j;
    for(i = m-1, j = 0;i >= 0;i--, j++)
        cout<<"\n array["<<i<<"] = "<<my_array[i];
}
```

OUTPUT

```
Enter the number of elements in array1 : 3
Enter the Elements of the first array : 1   2   3
Enter the number of elements in array2 : 4
Enter the Elements of the second array : 4   5   6   7
The merged array is: 1 2 3 4 5 6 7
The merged array in reverse order is: 7 6 5 4 3 2 1
```

Program 5.19 Write a program to interchange the biggest and the smallest number in the array using functions.

```
using namespace std;
#include<iostream>
void read_array(int arr[], int);
void display_array(int arr[], int);
void interchange(int arr[], int);
int find_biggest_pos(int my_array[10], int n);
int find_smallest_pos(int my_array[10], int n);
int main()
{   int arr[10], n;
    cout<<"\n Enter the size of the array : ";
    cin>>n;
    read_array(arr, n);
    interchange(arr, n);
}
void read_array( int my_array[10], int n)
{   int i;
    for(i = 0;i < n;i++)
        cin>>my_array[i];
}
```

```
void display_array( int my_array[10], int n)
{   int i;
    for(i = 0;i < n;i++)
        cout<<"\n array["<<i<<"] = "<<my_array[i];
}
void interchange(int my_array[10], int n)
{   int temp, big_pos, small_pos;
    big_pos = find_biggest_pos(my_array, n);
    small_pos = find_smallest_pos(my_array,n);
    temp = my_array[big_pos];
    my_array[big_pos] = my_array[small_pos];
    my_array[small_pos] = temp;
    display_array(my_array,n);
}
int find_biggest_pos( int my_array[10], int n)
{   int i, large, pos = -1;
    large = my_array[0];
    for(i = 1;i < n;i++)
    {   if (my_array[i] > large)
        {   large = my_array[i];
            pos = i;
        }
    }
    return pos;
}
int find_smallest_pos( int my_array[10], int n)
{   int i, small , pos = 0;
    small = my_array[0];
    for(i = 1;i < n;i++)
    {   if (my_array[i] < small)
        {   small = my_array[i];
            pos = i;
        }
    }
    return pos;
}
```

OUTPUT

```
Enter the number of elements in array1 : 5
Enter the Elements of the first array : 1  2 3 4 5
5 2 3 4 1
```

Note If a function receives an array that does not change it, then the array should be received as a constant array. This would ensure that the contents of the array are not accidentally changed. To declare an array as constant, prefix its type with the const keyword, as.

```
int sum(const int arr[], int n);
```

5.7 TWO-DIMENSIONAL ARRAYS

Till now, we have read only about one-dimensional arrays. A one-dimensional array is organized linearly in only in one direction. At times, we need to store data in the form of matrices or tables. Here, the concept of single dimension arrays is extended to incorporate two-dimensional data structures. A two-dimensional array is specified using two subscripts where one subscript denotes row and the

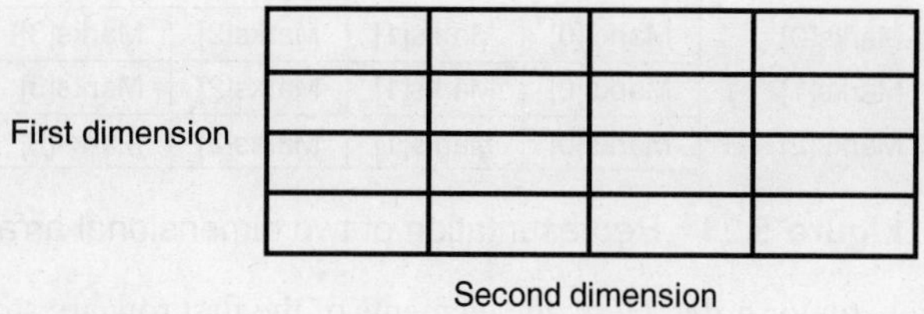

Figure 5.21 Two-dimensional array

other denotes column. A two-dimensional array is an array of a one-dimensional array. Figure 5.21 shows a 2D array which can be viewed as array of arrays.

5.7.1 Declaration of Two-dimensional Arrays

Like one-dimensional array, two-dimensional arrays must be declared before being used. The declaration statement tells the compiler the name of the array, the data type of each element in the array, and the size of each dimension. A 2D array is declared as follows:

```
data_type array_name[row_size][column_size];
```

Therefore, a two-dimensional m × n array contains m*n data elements and each element is accessed using two subscripts, i and j, where i<=m and j<=n.

For example, if we want to store the marks obtained by `three` students in `five` different subjects, then we can declare a two-dimensional array as follows:

```
int marks[3][5]
```

A two-dimensional array called marks is declared that has m(3) rows and n(5) columns. The first element of the array is denoted by marks[0][0], the second element as marks[0][1], and so on. Here, marks[0][0] stores the marks obtained by the first student in the first subject, marks[1][0], stores the marks obtained by the second student in the first subject.

The pictorial form of a two dimensional array is given in Fig. 5.22.

Rows or columns	Col 0	Col 1	Col 2	Col 3	Col 4
Row 0	Marks[0][0]	Marks[0][1]	Marks[0][2]	Marks[0][3]	Marks[0][4]
Row 1	Marks[1][0]	Marks[1][1]	Marks[1][2]	Marks[1][3]	Marks[1][4]
Row 2	Marks[2][0]	Marks[2][1]	Marks[2][2]	Marks[2][3]	Marks[2][4]

Figure 5.22 Two-dimensional array

Hence, we see that a 2D array is treated as a collection of 1D array. The elements of the 2D array I turn comprises 1D array (the rows). To understand this, we can also see the representation of a two-dimensional array as shown in Fig. 5.23.

Note Each dimension of the two-dimensional array is indexed from zero to its maximum size minus one. The first index selects the row and the second selects the column.

However, although we have shown a rectangular picture of a two-dimensional array, in memory, these elements will be stored sequentially. Since computer memory is basically one dimensional, a multi-dimensional array cannot be stored in memory as a grid.

Basically, there are two ways of storing a two-dimensional array in memory. The first way is row major order and the second is column major order. Let us see how the elements of a 2D array are

Marks[0]	Marks[0]	Marks[1]	Marks[2]	Marks[3]	Marks[4]
Marks[1]	Marks[0]	Marks[1]	Marks[2]	Marks[3]	Marks[4]
Marks[2]	Marks[0]	Marks[1]	Marks[2]	Marks[3]	Marks[4]

Figure 5.23 Representation of two dimensional array— `Marks[3][5]`

stored in a row major order. Here, the elements of the first row are stored before the elements of the second and third row. That is, the elements of the array are stored row by row where n elements of the first row will occupy the first nth locations. This is illustrated in Fig. 5.24.

(0,0)	(0, 1)	(0, 2)	(0, 3)	(1, 0)	(1, 1)	(1, 2)	(1, 3)	(2, 0)	(2,1)	(2,2)	(2,3)

Figure 5.24 Elements of 2D array in row major order

However, when we store the elements in a column major order, the elements of the first column are stored before the elements of the second and third column. That is, the elements of the array are stored column by column where n elements of the first column will occupy the first nth locations. This is illustrated in Fig. 5.25.

(0, 0)	(1, 0)	(2, 0)	(3, 0)	(0, 1)	(1, 1)	(2, 1)	(3, 1)	(0, 2)	(1, 2)	(2, 2)	(3, 2)

Figure 5.25 Elements of 2D array in column major order

In one-dimensional arrays, we have seen that computer does not keep track of the address of every element in the array. It stores only the address of the first element and calculates the address of other elements from the base address, which is the address of the first element. This is the case with a two-dimensional array as well, wherein the computer stores the base address and the address of the other elements is calculated using the formula as follows:

`Address(A[I][J] = Base_Address + w{M ( J - 1) + (I - 1)}`, if the array elements are stored in column major order.

And, `Address(A[I][J] = Base_Address + w{N ( I - 1) + (J - 1)}`, if the array elements are stored in row major order.

Here, `w` is the number of words stored per memory location

`m`, is the number of columns

`n`, is the number of rows

`I` and `J` are the subscripts of the array element

Example 5.5 Consider a 20 × 5 two-dimensional array `Marks` which has `base address = 1000` and the number of words per memory location of the `array = 2`. Now, compute the address of the element - `Marks[18, 4]` assuming that the elements are stored in row major order.

```
Address(A[I][j] = Base _ Address + w {N(I – 1) + (J – 1)}
Address(Marks[18, 4])  = 1000 + 2{5(18 – 1) + (4 – 1)}
                       = 1000 + 2{5(17) + 3}
                       = 1000 + 2(88)
                       = 1000 + 176 = 1176
```

5.7.2 Initialization of Two-dimensional Arrays

As in other variables, declaring a 2D array only reserves space for the array in the memory. There are no values stored in it. A 2D array is initialized in the same way as a single-dimensional array. For example,

```
int marks[2][3] = {90, 87, 78, 68, 62, 71};
```

The initialization of a 2D array is done in a row-wise manner. The statement given here can also be written as

```
int marks[2][3] = {{90,87,78},{68, 62, 71}};
```

The two-dimensional array has two rows and three columns. Here, the elements in the first row are initialized first and then elements of the second row are initialized.

Therefore, `marks[0][0] = 90` `marks[0][1] = 87` `marks[0][2] = 78` `marks[1][0] = 68` `marks[1][1] = 62` `marks[1][2] = 71`

Therefore, in the example, each row is defined as a one dimensional array of three elements that are enclosed in braces. Note that commas are used to separate the elements in the row as well as to separate the elements of two rows.

In case of one dimensional array, if the array is completely initialized, we may omit the size of the array. The same concept can be applied to a 2D array, except that only the size of the first dimension can be omitted. Therefore, the declaration statement given here is valid.

```
int marks[][3] = {{90,87,78},{68, 62, 71}};
```

In order to initialize the entire 2D `array` to zeros, simply specify the first value as zero. Simply write

```
int marks[2][3] = {0};
```

If some values are missing in the initializer then it is automatically set to zero. For example, the statement given below will initialize the values in the first row but the elements of the second row will be initialized to zero.

```
int marks[2][3] = {{50, 60, 70}};
```

Note An un-initialized array contains unpredictable contents.

5.7.3 Accessing the Elements

The elements in a multi-dimensional array are stored in contiguous memory locations. While accessing the elements, remember that the last subscript varies most rapidly whereas the first varies least rapidly.

In case of one dimensional arrays, we used a single `for` loop to vary the index `i` in every pass, so that all the elements could be scanned. Similarly, since a 2D array contains two subscripts, we will use two `for` loops to scan the elements. The first `for` loop will loop for each row in the `2D` array and the second `for` loop will scan individual columns for every row in the array.

However, individual elements of a two dimensional array can be initialized using the assignment operator as shown here.

```
marks[1][2] = 79; or
marks[1][2] = marks[1][1] + 10;
```

In order to input the values from the keyboard, you must use the following code:

```
for(i = 0;i < 2;i++)
    for(j = 0;j < 2;j++)
        cout<<arr[i][j];
```

Program 5.20 Write a program to print the elements of a 2D array.

```
using namespace std;
#include<iostream>
main()
{   int arr[2][2] = {12, 34, 56,32};
    int i, j;
    for(i = 0;i < 2;i++)
    {   cout<<"\n";
        for(j = 0;j < 2;j++)
            cout<<"\t"<<arr[i][j];
    }
}
```

OUTPUT

```
12   34
56   32
```

Program 5.21 Write a program to generate Pascal's Triangle.

```
using namespace std;
#include<iostream>
main()
{   int arr[7][7]={0};
    int row = 2, col, i, j;
    arr[0][0] = arr[1][0] = arr[1][1] = 1;
    while(row <= 7)
    {   arr[row][0] = 1;
        for(col = 1;col <= row;col++)
            arr[row][col] = arr[row-1][col-1] + arr[row-1][col];
            row++;
    }
    for(i = 0;i < 7;i++)
    {   cout<<"\n";
        for(j = 0;j <= i;j++)
            cout<<"\t"<<arr[i][j];
    }
}
```

OUTPUT

```
1
1   1
1   2   1
1   3   3    1
1   4   6    4    1
1   5   10   10   5   1
1   6   15   20   15  6    1
```

Program 5.22 In a small company, there are five 5 salesmen. Each salesman is supposed

to sell 3 products. Write a program using two- dimensional array to print (i) the total sales by each salesman and (ii) total sales of each item.

```
using namespace std;
#include<iostream>
main()
{   int sales[5][3], i, j, total_sales=0;
    //INPUT DATA
    cout<<"\n ENTER THE DATA";
    for(i = 0;i < 5;i++)
    {   cout<<"\n Enter the sales of 3 items sold by "<<i<<"salesman : ";
        for(j = 0;j < 3;j++)
            cin>>sales[i][j];
    }
    // PRINT TOTAL SALES BY EACH SALESMAN
    for(i = 0;i < 5;i++)
    {   total_sales = 0;
        for(j = 0;j < 3;j++)
            total_sales += sales[i][j];
        cout<<"\n Total Sales By "<<i<<" Salesman = "<<total_sales;
    }
    // TOTAL SALES OF EACH ITEM
    for(i = 0;i < 3;i++)             // for each item
    {   total_sales=0;
        for(j = 0;j < 5;j++)         // for each salesman
            total_sales += sales[j][i];
        cout<<"\n Total sales of "<<i<<" item = "<<total_sales;
    }
}
```

OUTPUT

```
Enter the sales of 3 items sold by 0 salesman = 56 67 78
Enter the sales of 3 items sold by 1 salesman = 78 89 90
Enter the sales of 3 items sold by 2 salesman = 12 23 34
Enter the sales of 3 items sold by 3 salesman = 45 56 67
Total Sales By 0 Salesman = 135
Total Sales By 1 Salesman = 201
Total Sales By 2 Salesman = 257
Total Sales By 3 Salesman = 69
Total Sales By 3 Salesman = 168
Total sales of 0 item = 225
Total sales of 1 item = 280
Total sales of 2 item = 325
```

Program 5.23 In a class, there are 10 students. Each student is supposed to appear in three tests. Write a program using two dimensional array to print the marks obtained by each student in different subjects, total marks and average obtained by each student, and store the average of each student in a separate 1D array so that it can be used to calculate the class average.

```
using namespace std;
#include<iostream>
main()
{   int marks[10][3], i, j;
```

```
    int total_marks[10] = {0};;
    float class_avg = 0.0, total_avg = 0.0;
    float avg[10];
    //INPUT DATA
    cout<<"\n ENTER THE DATA";
    for(i = 0;i < 10;i++)
    {   cout<<"\n Enter the marks of "<<i<<" student in 3 subjects : ";
        for(j = 0;j < 3;j++)
            cin>>marks[i][j];
    }
    // CALCULATE TOTAL MARKS OF EACH STUDENT
    for(i = 0;i < 10;i++)
    {   for(j = 0;j < 3;j++)
            total_marks[i] += marks[i][j];
    }
    // CALCULATE AVERAGE OF EACH STUDENT
    for(i = 0;i < 10;i++)
    {   for(j = 0;j < 3;j++)
        avg[i] = (float)total_marks[i]/3.0;
    }
    // CALCULATE CLASS AVERAGE
    for(i = 0;i < 10;i++)
        total_avg += avg[i];
    class_avg = (float)total_avg/10;
    // DISPLAY RESULTS
    cout<<"\n\n STUD NO. \t MARKS OBTAINED IN THREE SUBJECTS \t TOTAL MARKS \t AVERAGE";
    cout<<"\n\t*******************************************************";
    for(i = 0;i < 10;i++)
    {   cout.width(4);
        cout.precision(2);
        cout<<"\n"<<i;
        for(j = 0;j < 3;j++)
        cout<<"\t\t"<<marks[i][j];
        cout<<"\t\t"<<total_marks[i]<<"\t"<<avg[i];
    }
    cout<<"\n\n CLASS AVERAGE = "<<class_avg;
}
```

OUTPUT

```
ENTER THE DATA
Enter the marks of student 0 in 3 subjects: 78 89 90
Enter the marks of student 1 in 3 subjects: 98 87 76
Enter the marks of student 2 in 3 subjects: 67 78 89
Enter the marks of student 3 in 3 subjects: 90 87 65
Enter the marks of student 4 in 3 subjects: 56 87 97
Enter the marks of student 5 in 3 subjects: 45 67 89
Enter the marks of student 6 in 3 subjects: 66 77 88
Enter the marks of student 7 in 3 subjects: 76 87 98
Enter the marks of student 8 in 3 subjects: 67 88 66
Enter the marks of student 9 in 3 subjects: 66 75 78

 STUD NO        MARKS IN 3  SUBJECTS          TOTAL MARKS     AVERAGE
 0              78    89     90               257             85.67
 1              98    87     76               261             87.00
```

```
STUD NO      MARKS IN 3  SUBJECTS        TOTAL MARKS    AVERAGE
2            67     78     89            234            78.00
3            90     87     65            242            80.67
4            56     87     97            240            80.00
5            45     67     89            201            67.00
6            66     77     88            231            77.00
7            76     87     98            261            87.00
8            67     88     66            221            73.67
9            66     75     78            210            73.00
CLASS AVERAGE = 79
```

Program 5.24 Write a program to read the marks in a two-dimensional array which stores marks of 10 students in five subjects. Write a program to display the highest marks in each subject.

```
using namespace std;
#include<iostream>
main()
{   int marks[10][5], i, j, max_marks;
    for(i = 0;i < 10;i++)
    {   cout<<"\n Enter the marks obtained by "<<i<<"th student";
        for(j = 0;j < 5;j++)
        {   cout<<"\n marks["<<i<<"]["<<j<<"] = ";
                cin>>marks[i][j];
        }
    }
    for(j = 0;j < 5;j++)
    {   max_marks = -999;
        for(i = 0;i < 10;i++)
        {  if(marks[i][j]>max_marks)
                max_marks = marks[i][j];
        }
    cout<<"\n The highest marks obtained in the "<<j<<" subject = "<<marks[i][j];
    }
}
```

SAMPLE OUTPUT

```
The highest marks obtained in the 0 subject = 98
The highest marks obtained in the 1 subject = 94
The highest marks obtained in the 2 subject = 97
The highest marks obtained in the 3 subject = 89
```

5.8 OPERATIONS ON TWO-DIMENSIONAL ARRAYS

We can perform the following operations on a two-dimensional array:

Transpose Transpose of a `m × n` matrix `A` is given as a `n × m matri x B` where,

$$B_{i,j} = A_{j,i}$$

Sum Two matrices that are compatible with each other can be added together, thereby, storing the result in the third matrix. Two matrices are said to be compatible when they have the same number of rows and columns. The elements of the matrices can be added by writing as follows:

$$C_{i,j} = A_{i,j} + B_{i,j}$$

Difference Two matrices that are compatible with each other can be subtracted, thereby, storing the result in the third matrix. The elements of the matrices can be subtracted by writing as follows:

$$C_{i,j} = A_{i,j} - B_{i,j}$$

Product Two matrices can be multiplied with each other if the number of columns in the first matrix is equal to the number of rows of the second matrix. Therefore, $m \times n$ matrix A can be multiplied with a $p \times q$ matrix if $n = q$. The elements of the matrices can be multiplied by writing as follows:

$$C_{i,j} = \sum A_{i},kB_{j},k, \text{ for } k = 1 \text{ to } k<n$$

Program 5.25 Write a program to transpose a 3 × 3 matrix.

```
using namespace std;
#include<iostream>
int main()
{   int i, j, mat[3][3], transposed_mat[3][3];
    cout<<"\n Enter the elements of the matrix ";
    for(i = 0;i < 3;i++)
    {   for(j = 0;j < 3;j++)
        {   cout<<"\n mat["<<i<<"]["<<j<<"] = ";
            cin>>mat[i][j];
        }
    }
    cout<<"\n The elements of the matrix are ";
    for(i = 0;i < 3;i++)
    {   cout<<"\n";
        for(j = 0;j < 3;j++)
            cout<<"\t mat["<<i<<"]["<<j<<"] = "<<mat[i][j];
    }
    for(i = 0;i < 3;i++)
    {   for(j = 0;j < 3;j++)
            transposed_mat[i][j] = mat[j][i];
    }
    cout<<"\n The elements of the transposed matrix are ";
    for(i = 0;i < 3;i++)
    {   cout<<"\n";
        for(j = 0;j < 3;j++)
        cout<<"\t transposed_mat["<<i<<"]["<<j<<"] = "<< transposed_mat[i][j];
    }
}
```

OUTPUT

```
Enter the elements of the matrix
1 2 3 4 5 6 7 8 9
The elements of the matrix are
1 2 3
4 5 6
7 8 9
The elements of the transposed matrix are
1 4 7
2 5 8
7 8 9
```

Program 5.26 Write a program to multiply two m × n matrices.

```
using namespace std;
#include<iostream>
#include<stdlib.h>
int main()
{   int i, j, k;
    int rows1, cols1, rows2, cols2, res_rows, res_cols;
    int mat1[5][5], mat2[5][5], res[5][5];
    cout<<"\n Enter the numbers of rows and columns in the first matrix : ";
    cin>>rows1>>cols1;
    cout<<"\n Enter the numbers of rows and columns in the second
    matrix : ";
    cin>>rows2>>cols2;
    if(cols1 != rows2)
    {   cout<<"\n The number of columns in the first matrix must be equal
        to the number of rows in the second matrix";
        exit(1);
    }
    res_rows = rows1, res_cols = cols2;
    cout<<"\n Enter the elements of the first matrix ";
    for(i = 0;i < rows1;i++)
    {   for(j = 0;j < cols1;j++)
        {   cout<<"\n mat1["<<i<<"]["<<j<<"] = ";
            cin>>mat1[i][j];
        }
    }
    cout<<"\n Enter the elements of the second matrix ";
    for(i = 0;i < rows2;i++)
    {   for(j = 0;j < cols2;j++)
    {   cout<<"\n mat1["<<i<<"]["<<j<<"] = ";
        cin>>mat2[i][j];
        }
    }
    for(i = 0;i < res_rows;i++)
    {   j = 0;
        for(j = 0;j < res_cols;j++)
        {   res[i][j] = 0;
            for(k = 0; k < cols1;k++)
                res[i][j] += mat1[i][k] * mat2[k][j];
        }
    }
    cout<<"\n The elements of the product matrix are ";
    for(i = 0;i < res_rows;i++)
    {   cout<<"\n";
        for(j = 0;j < res_cols;j++)
            cout<<"\t res["<<i<<"]["<<j<<"] = "<<res[i][j];
    }
}
```

OUTPUT

```
Enter the numbers of rows and columns in the first matrix : 2 2
Enter the numbers of rows and columns in the second matrix : 2 2
Enter the elements of the first matrix 1 2 3 4
```

```
Enter the elements of the second matrix 5 6 7 8
The elements of the product matrix are 19 22 43 50
```

5.9 TWO-DIMENSIONAL ARRAYS FOR INTER-FUNCTION COMMUNICATION

There are three ways of passing parts of the two-dimensional array to a function. First, we can pass individual elements of the array. This is done in exactly the same way as we passed the element of a one-dimensional array. Second, we can pass a single row of the two-dimensional array. This is equivalent to passing the entire one-dimensional array to a function that has already been discussed in the previous section. Third, we can pass the entire two- dimensional array to the function. Refer to Fig. 5.26, which shows three ways of using two-dimensional array for inter-function communication.

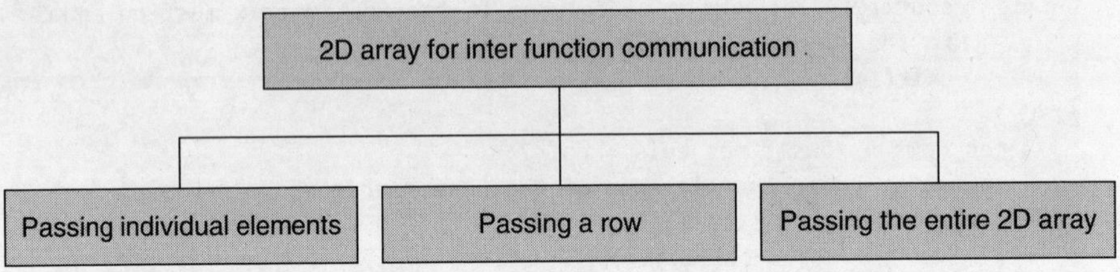

Figure 5.26 Two-dimensional arrays for inter-function communication

5.9.1 Passing a Row

A row of a two-dimensional array can be passed by indexing the array name with the row number. When we send a single row of a two dimensional array, then the called function receives a one dimensional array. Figure 5.27 illustrates how a single row of a two-dimensional array is passed to the called function.

```
        Calling
        Function
main()
{       int arr[2][3]= ({1, 2, 3}, {4, 5, 6} };
        func(arr[1]);
}
            Called Function

void func(int arr[])
{       int i;
        for(i=0;i<5;i++)
            cout<<arr[i] * 10;
}
```

Figure 5.27 Passing two-dimensional arrays for inter function communication

5.9.2 Passing the Entire Two-dimensional Array

To pass a two dimensional array to a function, we use the array name as the actual parameter, as done in the case of a 1D array. However, the parameter in the called function must indicate that the array has two dimensions.

Programming Tip: A compiler error will be generated if you omit the array size in the parameter declaration for any array dimension other than the first.

Program 5.27 Write a menu driven program to read and display an m × n matrix. Find the sum, transpose, and product of two m × n matrices.

```
using namespace std;
#include<iostream>
void read_matrix(int mat[5][5], int, int);
void sum_matrix(int mat1[5][5], int mat2[5][5], int, int);
void mul_matrix(int mat1[5][5], int mat2[5][5], int, int);
void transpose_matrix(int mat2[5][5], int, int);
void display_matrix(int mat[5][5], int r, int c);
int main()
{int option, row, col;
 int mat1[5][5], mat2[5][5];
 do
 {   cout<<"\n ******* MAIN MENU ********";
     cout<<"\n 1. Read the two matrices";
     cout<<"\n 2. Add the matrices";
     cout<<"\n 3. Multiply the matrices";
     cout<<"\n 4. Transpose the matrix";
     cout<<"\n 5. EXIT";
     cout<<"\n\n Enter your option : ";
     cin>>option;
   switch(option)
 {   case 1 : cout<<"\n Enter the number of rows and columns of the matrix : ";
     cin>>row>>col;
     read_matrix(mat1, row, col);
     cout<<"\n Enter the second matrix : ";
     read_matrix(mat2, row, col);
     break;
     case 2 : sum_matrix(mat1, mat2, row, col);
     break;
     case 3 : if(col == row)
         mul_matrix(mat1, mat2, row, col);
     else
         cout<<"\n To multiply two matrices, number of columns in the
         first matrix must be equal to number of rows in the second matrix";
     break;
     case 4:
         transpose_matrix(mat1, row, col);
         transpose_matrix(mat2, row, col);
     break;
   }
 }while(option != 5);
}
void read_matrix(int mat[5][5], int r, int c)
{  int i, j;
   for(i = 0;i < r;i++)
   {  for(j = 0;j < c;j++)
      {  cout<<"\n mat["<<i<<"]["<<j<<"] = ";
         cin>>mat[i][j];
      }
   }
}
void sum_matrix(int mat1[5][5], int mat2[5][5], int r, int c)
```

```
{   int i, j, sum[5][5];
    for(i = 0;i < r;i++)
    {   for(j = 0;j < c;j++)
        sum[i][j] = mat1[i][j] + mat2[i][j];
    }
    display_matrix(sum, r, c);
}
void mul_matrix(int mat1[5][5], int mat2[5][5], int r, int c)
{   int i, j, k, prod[5][5];
    for(i = 0;i < r;i++)
    {   for(j = 0;j < c;j++)
        {   prod[i][j] = 0;
            for(k = 0;k < col;k++)
                prod[i][j] += mat1[i][k] * mat2[k][j];
        }
    }
    display_matrix(prod, r, c);
}
void transpose_matrix(int mat[5][5], int r, int c)
{   int i, j, tp_mat[5][5];
    for(i = 0;i < r;i++)
    {   for(j = 0;j < c;j++)
            tp_mat[i][j] = mat[j][i];
    }
    display_matrix(mat, r, c);
}
void display_matrix(int mat[5][5], int r, int c)
{   int i, j;
    for(i = 0;i < r;i++)
    {   cout<<"\n";
        for(j = 0;j < c;j++)
            cout<<"\t mat["<<i<<"]["<<"j="<<mat[i][j];
    }
}
```

OUTPUT

```
******* MAIN MENU ********
1. Read the two matrices
2. Add the matrices
3. Multiply the matrices
4. Transpose the matrix
5. EXIT
Enter your option: 1
Enter the number of rows and columns of the matrix: 2 2
Enter the first matrix:
mat[0][0] = 1 mat[0][1] = 2
mat[1][0] = 3 mat[1][1] = 4
Enter the second matrix :
mat[0][0] = 2 mat[0][1] = 3
mat[1][0] = 4 mat[1][1] = 5
```

Program 5.28 Write a program to fill a square matrix with value zero on the diagonals, 1 on the upper right triangle and -1 on the lower left triangle.

```
using namespace std;
#include<iostream>
void read_matrix(int mat[5][5], int, int);
void sum_matrix(int mat1[5][5], int mat2[5][5], int, int);
void mul_matrix(int mat1[5][5], int mat2[5][5], int, int);
void transpose_matrix(int mat2[5][5], int, int);
void display_matrix(int mat[5][5], int r, int c);
int main()
{   int option, row, col;
    int mat1[5][5], mat2[5][5];
    do
    {   cout<<"\n ******* MAIN MENU ********";
        cout<<"\n 1. Read the two matrices";
        cout<<"\n 2. Add the matrices";
        cout<<"\n 3. Multiply the matrices";
        cout<<"\n 4. Transpose the matrix";
        cout<<"\n 5. EXIT";
        cout<<"\n\n Enter your option : ";
        cin>>option;
        switch(option)
    {   case 1: cout<<"\n Enter the number of rows and columns of the matrix : ";
                cin>>row>>col;
                read_matrix(mat1, row, col);
                cout<<"\n Enter the second matrix : ";
                read_matrix(mat2, row, col);
                break;
        case 2 : sum_matrix(mat1, mat2, row, col);
                break;
        case3 : if(col == row)
                mul_matrix(mat1, mat2, row, col);
                else
                cout<<"\n To multiply two matrices, number of columns in the
                first matrix must be equal to number of rows in the second matrix";
                break;
        case 4:
                transpose_matrix(mat1, row, col);
                transpose_matrix(mat2, row, col);
                break;
        }
    }while(option != 5);
}
void read_matrix(int mat[5][5], int r, int c)
{   int i, j;
    for(i = 0;i < r;i++)
    {   for(j = 0;j < c;j++)
        {   cout<<"\n mat["<<i<<"]["<<j<<"] = ";
            cin>>mat[i][j];
        }
    }
}
void sum_matrix(int mat1[5][5], int mat2[5][5], int r, int c)
```

```
{   int i, j, sum[5][5];
    for(i = 0;i < r;i++)
    {   for(j = 0;j < c;j++)
            sum[i][j] = mat1[i][j] + mat2[i][j];
    }
    display_matrix(sum, r, c);
}
void mul_matrix(int mat1[5][5], int mat2[5][5], int r, int c)
{   int i, j, k, prod[5][5];
    for(i = 0;i < r;i++)
    {   for(j = 0;j < c;j++)
        {   prod[i][j] = 0;
            for(k = 0;k < c;k++)
                prod[i][j] += mat1[i][k] * mat2[k][j];
        }
    }
    display_matrix(prod, r, c);
}
void transpose_matrix(int mat[5][5], int r, int c)
{   int i, j, tp_mat[5][5];
    for(i = 0;i < r;i++)
    {   for(j = 0;j < c;j++)
            tp_mat[i][j] = mat[j][i];
    }
    display_matrix(mat, r, c);
}
void display_matrix(int mat[5][5], int r, int c)
{   int i, j;
    for(i = 0;i < r;i++)
    {   cout<<"\n";
        for(j = 0;j < c;j++)
            cout<<"\t "<< mat[i][j];
    }
}
```

OUTPUT

```
Enter the number of rows and columns of the matrix : 2 2
1 2 3 4
1 2
3 4
```

5.10 MULTI-DIMENSIONAL ARRAYS

A multi-dimensional array, in simple terms, is an array of arrays. Like we have one index in a single dimensional array and two indices in a two-dimensional array, we have n indices in an n-dimensional array or a multi-dimensional array. Conversely, an n dimensional array is specified using n indices. An n dimensional $m_1 \times m_2 \times m_3 \times \ldots m_n$ array is a collection $m_1 * m_2 * m_3 * \ldots * m_n$ elements. In a multi-dimensional array, a particular element is specified by using n subscripts as `A[I1][I2][I3]'[In]`, where

$$I_1 <= M_1 I_2 <= M_2 \qquad I_3 <= M_3 \qquad \ldots\ldots \qquad I_n <= M_n$$

A multi-dimensional array can contain as many indices as needed and the requirement of the memory increases with the number of indices used. However, practically speaking, we will hardly use more than three indices in any program. Figure 5.28 shows a three-dimensional array. The array has three pages, four rows, and two columns.

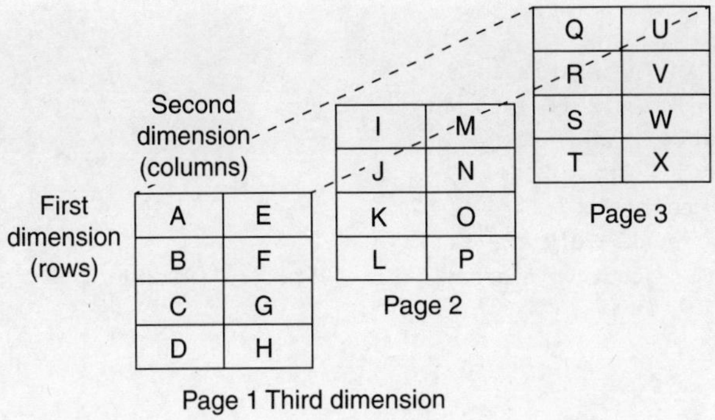

Figure 5.28 Three-dimensional array

A multi-dimensional array is declared and initialized similar to one and two dimensional arrays.

Note A three dimensional array consists of pages. Each page in turn contains m rows and n columns.

Example 5.6 Consider a three-dimensional array defined as int `A[2][3][2]`. Calculate the number of elements in the array. Give the memory representation of the array in row major order and column major order.

(a) Row major order: Write the elements row by row.

In row major order: element of ith row are listed before the elements of row i + 1

(0,0,0) (0,0,1) (0,0,2) (0,1,0) (0,1,1) (0,1,2) (1,0,0) (1,0,1) (1,0,2) (1,1,0) (1,1,1) (1,1,2)

(b) Column major order: Write the elements column by column

Similarly in column major order, elements of column i are listed before the elements of column i + 1

(0,0,0) (0,1,0) (0,0,1) (0,1,1) (0,0,2) (0,1,2) (1,0,0) (1,1,0) (1,0,1) (1,1,1) (1,0,2) (1,1,2)

The three-dimensional array will contain `2*3*2 = 12` elements

Program 5.29 Write a program to read and display a 2 × 2 × 2 array.

```
using namespace std;
#include<iostream>
int main()
{   int array1[3][3][3], i, j, k;
    cout<<"\n Enter the elements of the matrix";
    for(i = 0;i < 2;i++)
    {   for(j = 0;j < 2;j++)
        {   for(k = 0;k < 2;k++)
            {   cout<<"\n array["<<i<<"]["<<j<<"]["<<k<<"] = ";
                cin>>array1[i][j][k];
            }
        }
```

```
    }
    cout<<"\n The matrix is : ";
    for(i = 0;i < 2;i++)
    {  cout<<"\n\n";
        for(j = 0;j < 2;j++)
        {  cout<<"\n";
            for(k = 0;k < 2;k++)
                cout<<"\t array["<<i<<"]["<<j<<"]["<<k<<"] = " <<array1[i][j][k];
        }
    }
}
```

OUTPUT

```
Enter the elements of the matrix
1 2 3 4 5 6 7 8
arr[0][0][0] = 1   arr[0][0][1] = 2
arr[0][1][0] = 3   arr[0][1][1] = 4
arr[1][0][0] = 5   arr[1][0][1] = 6
arr[1][1][0] = 7   arr[1][1][1] = 8
```

Points to Remember

- An array is a collection of similar data elements of the same data type.
- The elements of the array are stored in consecutive memory locations and are referenced by an index (also known as the subscript). Subscript is an ordinal number which is used to identify an element of the array.
- Declaring an array means specifying three things: data type, name, and its size.
- The name of the array is a symbolic reference to the address of the first byte of the array. Therefore, whenever we use the array name, we are actually referring to the first byte of that array. The index specifies an offset from the beginning of the array to the element being referenced.
- A two-dimensional array is specified using two subscripts where first subscript denotes row and the second denotes column. C++ considers the two-dimensional array as an array of one-dimensional arrays.
- A multidimensional array is an array of arrays. Like we have one index in a one-dimensional array, two indices in a two-dimensional array, in the same way we have *n* indices in an *n*-dimensional or multidimensional array.
- Conversely, an n-dimensional array is specified using n indices.

Glossary

Array An array is a collection of similar data elements

Array index Location of an item in an array

Binary search Searches a sorted array by repeatedly dividing the search interval in half. Begin with an interval covering the whole array. If the value of the search key is less than the item in the middle of the interval, narrow the interval to the lower half; else, narrow it to the upper half. Check until the value is found or the interval is empty.

Linear search Searches an array by checking elements one at a time

Lower triangular matrix A matrix A_{ij} forms a lower triangular when $i \geq j$

Matrix A two-dimensional array in which the first index is the row, and the second index is the column

Multi-dimensional or ***n*-dimensional:** An array with exactly *n* dimensions.

One-dimensional array An array with one dimension or one subscript or index

Rectangular matrix An n × m matrix whose size may not be the same in both dimensions

Sparse matrix A matrix that has relatively few non-zero elements

Two-dimensional array An array with two dimensions or two subscripts or indices

Three-dimensional array An array with three dimensions or three subscripts or indices

Upper triangular matrix A matrix A_{ij} forms an upper triangular when $i \leq j$

Exercises

Fill in the Blanks

1. An array is a ______.
2. Every element is accessed using a ______.
3. An expression that evaluates to a ______ value may be used as an index.
4. The elements of an array are stored in ______ memory locations.
5. An 'n' dimensional array contains ______ subscripts.
6. The name of the array acts as a ______.
7. Declaring an array means specifying the ______, ______, and ______.
8. The subscript or the index represents the offset from the beginning of the array to ______.
9. ______ is used to access an element in the array.
10. ______ is the address of the first element in the array.
11. The length of the array is given by the number of ______.
12. ______ means accessing each element of the array for a specific purpose.
13. Performance of the linear search algorithm can be improved by using a ______.
14. An array occupies ______ memory locations.
15. An array name is often known to be a ______ pointer.
16. A multi-dimensional array, in simple terms, is an ______.
17. `arr[3] = 10;` initializes the ______ element of the array with value 10.
18. The ___ search locates the value by starting at the beginning of the array and moving towards its end.

State True or False

1. An array is used to refer to multiple memory locations having the same name.
2. An array need not be declared before being used.
3. An array contains elements of the same data type.
4. A loop is used to access all the elements of the array.
5. All the elements of the array are automatically initialized to zero when the array is defined.
6. An array stores all its data elements in non-consecutive memory location.
7. To copy an array, you must copy the value of every element of the first array into the element of the second array.
8. Lower bound is the index of the last element in the array.
9. A merged array contains contents of the first array followed by the contents of the second array.
10. Binary search is also called sequential search.
11. Linear search is performed on a sorted array.
12. Binary search is the best searching algorithm for all types of arrays.
13. It is possible to pass entire array as a function argument.
14. When an array is passed to a function, the value for each element.
15. When an array is passed to a function, it is always passed by call-by-reference method.
16. Linear search can be used to search a value in any array.
17. Linear search is recommended for small arrays.
18. A two-dimensional array is nothing but an array of one-dimensional arrays.
19. A two-dimensional array contains data of two different types.
20. When an array is declared, its elements are automatically initialized to zero.
21. A char type variable can be used as a subscript in an array.
22. By default, the first subscript of the array is zero.
23. A long int value can be used as an array subscript.
24. An array can have a maximum of four dimensions.

Multiple Choice Questions

1. If an array is declared as `arr[] = {1,3,5,7,9};` what is the value of `sizeof(arr[3 ])`?

   (a) 10 (b) 20
   (c) 30 (d) 40

2. If an array is declared as `arr[] = {1,3,5,7,9};` what is the value of `arr[3]`?

(a) 1 (b) 7
(c) 9 (d) 5

3. If an array is declared as double `arr[50]`, how many bytes will be allocated to it?
(a) 50 (b) 100
(c) 200 (d) 400
4. If an array is declared as int `arr[50]`, how many elements can it hold?
(a) 49 (b) 50
(c) 51 (d) 0
5. If an array is declared as int `arr[5][5]`, how many elements can it store?
(a) 5 (b) 25
(c) 10 (d) 0
6. In linear search, when `VAL` is equal to the first element of the array, which case is it?
(a) Worst case (b) Average Case
(c) Best Case (d) Amortized case

Review Questions

1. Why do we need arrays?
2. What does an array name signify?
3. How is an array represented in memory?
4. How is a two-dimensional array represented in memory?
5. How can arrays be used for inter-function communication?
6. How are multi-dimensional arrays useful?
7. What happens when an array is initialized with fewer initializers as compared to its size?
8. What happens when an array is initialized with more initializers as compared to its size?
9. Why does storing of sparse matrices need extra consideration? How are sparse matrices stored efficiently in the computer's memory?
10. For an array declared as `int arr[50]`, calculate the address of `arr[35]`, if `Base(arr) = 1000` and `w = 2`.
11. Consider a 10 × 5 two dimensional array `Marks` which has base address = 2000 and the number of words per memory location of the array = 2. Compute the address of the element - `Marks[8, 5]`, assuming that the elements are stored in row major order.
12. Given an array, `int arr[] = (9, 18, 27, 36, 45, 54, 63, 72, 81, 90, 99}`; trace the steps of binary search algorithm to find value 90 and 17 from the array.
13. Which technique of searching an element in the array do you prefer to use in specific situations?
14. Explain the concept of array of function pointers with the help of a program.
15. How can a one-dimensional array be used with functions?

Programming Exercises

1. Write a program which deletes all duplicate elements from the array.
2. Write a program that tests the equality of two one-dimensional arrays.
3. Write a program that reads an array of 100 integers. Display all pairs of elements whose sum is 50.
4. Write a program to input an array of 10 numbers and swap the value of the largest and smallest number.
5. Write a program to interchange second element with the second last element.
6. Write a program that calculates the sum of squares of the elements.
7. Write a program to calculate the number of duplicate entries in the array.
8. Write a program to arrange the values of an array in such a way that even numbers preceed the odd numbers.
9. Given a sorted array of integers, write a program to calculate the sum, mean, variance, and standard deviation of the numbers in the array.
10. Write a program to compute the sum and mean of the elements of a two-dimensional array.
11. Write a program that computes the sum of elements that are stored on the main diagonal of a matrix using pointers.
12. Write a program to count the total number of non-zero elements in a two-dimensional array.
13. Write a program to read and display an array of 10 floating point numbers using functions.
14. Write a program to read an array of 10 floating point numbers. Display the mean of these numbers till two decimal places.
15. Write a program to read an array of 10 floating point numbers. Display the smallest number and its position in the array.
16. Write a program to input the elements of a two-dimensional array. Then from this array make two arrays: one that stores all odd elements of the two-dimensional array and the other stores all even elements of the array.

17. Write a program to merge two integer arrays. Also display the merged array in reverse order
18. Write a program to transpose a 3 × 3 × 3 matrix.
19. Write a program to multiply two m × n matrices.
20. Write a menu driven program to add, subtract, and transpose two matrices.
21. Write a program that reads a matrix and displays the sum of its diagonal elements.
22. Write a program that reads a matrix and displays the sum of the elements above the main diagonal. *Hint: Calculate sum of elements of array A, where for an element A_{ij}, $i < j$*
23. Write a program that reads a matrix and displays the sum of the elements below the main diagonal. *Hint: Calculate sum of elementsof array A ,where for an element A_{ij}, $i > j$*
24. Write a program that reads a square matrix of size n × n. Write a function int is Upper Triangular(int a[][], int n) that returns 1 if the matrix is upper triangular. *Hint: Array A is upper triangular if $A_{ij} = 0$ for $i > j$*
25. Write a program that reads a square matrix of size n × n. Write a function int is Lower Triangular(int a[][], int n) that returns 1 if the matrix is lower triangular. *Hint: Array A is lower triangular if $A_{ij} = 0$ for $i < j$*
26. Write a program that reads a square matrix of size n × n. Write a function int is Symmetric (int a[][], int n) that returns 1 if the matrix is upper triangular. *Hint: Array A is symmetric if $A_{ij} = A_{ij}$ for all values of i and j*
27. Write a program to calculate XA + YB where A and B are matrices and X = 2, and Y = 3.
28. Write a program to read an array of 10 floating point numbers. Display the position of the second largest number.
29. Write a program to enter five single digit numbers in an array. Form a number using the array elements.
30. Write a program to find whether number 3 is present in the array arr[] = {1,2,3,4,5,6,7,8}.
31. Write a program to read a sorted floating point array. Update the array to insert a new number.
32. Write a program to read a floating point array. Update the array to delete the number from the specified location.
33. Modify the linear search program so that it operates on a sorted array.
34. Write a program to build an array of 100 random numbers in the range 1 to 100. Perform the following operations on the array.
    (a) Count the number of elements that are completely divisible by 3.
    (b) Display the elements of the array by displaying a maximum of ten elements in one line.
    (c) Display only the even elements of the array by displaying a maximum of ten elements in one line.
    (d) Count the number of odd elements.
    (e) Find the smallest element in the array.
    (f) Find the position of the largest value in the array.
35. Write a program to read two floating point arrays. Merge these arrays and display the resultant array.
36. Write a program to read two sorted floating point arrays. Merge these arrays and display the resultant array.
37. Write a program to read and display a p*q*r array.
38. Write a program to initialize all diagonal elements of a two-dimensional array to zero.
39. Consider a 10 × 10 two-dimensional array which has base address = 1000 and the number of memory locations per element of the array = 2. Now compute the address of the element arr[8][5] assuming that the elements are stored in row major order. Then calculate the same assuming the elements are stored in column major order.
40. Consider an array MARKS[20][5] which stores the marks obtained by 20 students in 5 subjects. Now write a program to
    (a) find the average marks obtained in each subject
    (b) find the average marks obtained by every student
    (c) find the number of students who have scored below 50 in their average
    (d) display the scores obtained by every student

Find the errors (if any) in the following declaration statements

- `int marks(10);`
- `int marks[10, 5];`
- `int marks[10],[5];`
- `int marks[10];`
- `int marks[ ];`
- `int marks[10] [5];`
- `int marks[9+1][6-1];`

Find the errors (if any) in the following initialization statements

- `int marks[ ] = {0,0,0,0};`
- `int marks[2][3] = {10,20,30,40};`
- `int marks[2,3] = {10, 20,30},{40,50,60};`
- `int marks[10] = {0};`

Find the output of the following codes

1.
```
int marks[],n,i,
    for(i = 0; i < n; i++)
    cin>>marks[i];
```
2.
```
int i, mark[];
    for(i = 0; i < 10; i++)
    cin>>marks[i];
```
3.
```
int marks[2][3], i, j;
    for(i = 0; i < 2; i++)
    for(j = 0; j<3;j++)
    cin>>marks[i][j];
```
4.
```
using namespace std;
#include<iostream>
main()
{   int i, arr[10];
    for(i = 0;i < 10;i++)
        arr[i*2] = 1;
    for(i = 0;i < 10;i++)
        arr[i*2+1] = -1;
    for(i = 0;i < 10;i++)
        cout<<"\t "<<arr[i];
}
```
5.
```
using namespace std;
#include<iostream>
main()
{   int arr[] = {0,1,2,0,1,2,0,1,2};
    cout<<"\n"<< arr[3];
    cout<<"\n"<< arr[arr[3]];
    cout<<"\n"<< arr[arr[3] + arr[1]];
    cout<<"\n"<< arr[arr[arr[arr[1]]]];
}
```
6.
```
using namespace std;
#include<iostream>
main()
{  int arr1[] = {0,1,2,0,1,2,0,1,2,0};
   int i, arr2[10];
   for(i = 0;i < 10;i++)
       arr2[i] = arr1[9-i];
   for(i = 0;i < 10;i++)
       cout<<"\t"<< arr2[i];
}
```

Answers

Fill in the Blanks

1. collection of similar data elements; **2.** subscript/index; **3.** integral; **4.** consecutive; **5.** n; **6.** pointer; **7.** data type, name and size; **8.** the element being referenced; **9.** array name; **10.** the number of elements stored in it; **11.** traversing; **12.** sorted array; **13.** array of arrays; **14.** fourth; **15.** linear; **16.** Array of arrays; **17.** Fourth; **18.** Linear

State True or False

1. true	**2.** false	**3.** true	**4.** true	**5.** true	**6.** false	**7.** true	**8.** false
9. true	**10.** false	**11.** false	**12.** false	**13.** true	**14.** true	**15.** false	**16.** true
17. true	**18.** true	**19.** true	**20.** true	**21.** false	**22.** false	**23.** true	**24.** false

Multiple Choice Questions

1. (b); **2.** (b); **3.** (c); **4.** (b); **5.** (b); **6.** (c)

Case Study 2

This case study shows the implementation of concepts discussed in Chapter 4 on Functions and Chapter 5 on Arrays.

C2.1 MERGE SORT

`Merge sort` is a sorting algorithm that uses the divide, conquer, and combine algorithmic paradigm.

`Merge sort` algorithm focuses on two main concepts to improve its performance (running time):

- A smaller list takes few steps and less time to sort than a large list.
- Less steps and less time is needed to create a sorted list from two sorted lists rather than creating it using two unsorted lists.

The basic steps of a `merge sort` algorithm are as follows:

- If the array is of length 0 or 1, then it is already sorted. Otherwise,
- Conceptually divide the unsorted array into two sub-arrays of about half the size.
- Use `merge sort` algorithm recursively to sort each sub-array.
- Merge the two sub-arrays to form a single sorted list.

To understand the merge algorithm, consider the example given here.

Example C2.1 Consider that we have two sub-lists each containing four elements. The same concept can be utilized to merge four sub-lists containing two elements and eight sub-lists having just one element.

9	39	45	81	18	27	72	90
BEG, I		MID	J		END		

Compare `ARR[I]` and `ARR[J]`, the smaller of the two is placed in `TEMP` at the location specified by `INDEX` and subsequently the value I or J is incremented.

TEMP

9							

INDEX

9	39	45	81	18	27	72	90
BEG	I	MID	J END				

TEMP

9	18						
	INDEX						

9	39	45	81	18	27	72	90
BEG	I		MID		J		END

9	18	27					
		INDEX					

9	39	45	81	18	27	72	90
BEG	I	MID			J	END	

9	18	27	39				
			INDEX				

9	39	45	81	18	27	72	90
BEG		I		MID	J	END	

9	18	27	39	45			
				INDEX			

9	39	45	81	18	27	72	90
BEG		I	MID		J	END	

9	18	27	39	45	72		
					INDEX		

When I is greater than MID copy, the remaining elements of the right sub-array in TEMP.

9	39	45	81	18	27	72	90
BEG			MID I			J END	

9	18	27	39	45	72	81	
						INDEX	

9	39	45	81	18	27	72	90
BEG			MID	I	J	END	

9	18	27	39	45	72	81	90
						INDEX	

Program C2.1 Write a program to implement merge sort.

```
using namespace std;
#include<iostream>
void merge(int a[], int, int, int);
void merge_sort(int a[],int, int);
int main()
{
     int arr[10], i, n, j,k;
     cout<<"\n Enter the number of elements
in the array : ";
     cin>>n;
     cout<<"\n Enter the elements
of the array ";
     for(i=0;i<n;i++)
// input array elements
     {
          cin>>arr[i];
     }
     merge_sort(arr, 0, n-1);
// call merge sort function
     cout<<"\n The sorted array is : \n";
     for(i=0;i<n;i++)
          cout<<"\t"<<arr[i];
```

```
}

void merge(int arr[], int beg, int mid,
int end)// merge the arrays
{
    int i=beg, j=mid+1, index=beg,
      temp[10], k;
    while((i<=mid) && (j<=end))
    {
        if(arr[i] < arr[j])
        {
            temp[index] = arr[i];
            i++;
        }
        else
        {
            temp[index] = arr[j];
            j++;
        }
        index++;
    }
    if(i>mid)
    {
        while(j<=end)
        {
            temp[index] = arr[j];
            j++;
            index++;
        }
    }
    else
    {
        while(i<=mid)
        {
            temp[index] = arr[i];
            i++;
            index++;
        }
    }
    for(k=beg;k<index;k++) arr[k] = temp[k];

}
void merge_sort(int arr[], int beg,
int end)// divide the array
{
    int mid;
    if(beg<end)
    {
        mid = (beg+end)/2;
        merge_sort(arr, beg, mid);
        merge_sort(arr, mid+1, end);
        merge(arr, beg, mid, end);
    }
}
```

OUTPUT

```
Enter the number of elements
in the array : 8
Enter the elements of the array
10 7 5 3 1 2 4 6
The sorted array is : 1 2 3 4 5 6 7 10
```

C2.2 QUICK SORT OR PARTITION EXCHANGE SORT

Like `merge sort`, `quick sort` algorithm works by using a divide and conquer strategy to divide a single unsorted array into two smaller sub-arrays.

The `quick sort` algorithm works as follows:

- Select an element pivot from the array elements
- Rearrange the elements in the array in such a way that all elements that are less than the pivot appear before the pivot and all elements greater than the pivot element come after it (equal values can go either way). After such a partitioning, the pivot is placed in its final position. This is called the partition operation.
- Recursively sort the two sub-arrays thus obtained-one with sub-list of lesser value than that of the pivot element and the other having higher value elements).

Like `merge sort`, the base case of the recursion occurs when array has zero or one element because in that case, the array is already sorted. After each iteration of the algorithm, one element (pivot) is always in its final position. Hence, with every iteration, there is one less element to be sorted in the array.

Therefore, the main task in the `quick sort` algorithm is to find the pivot element, which will partition the array into two halves. To understand how we find the pivot element, follow the steps given here. We will take the first element in the array as pivot.

- Set the index of the first element in the array to `loc` and left variables. Set the index of the last element of the array to the right variable.

That is, `loc =0`, `left = 0` and `right = n-1`, where n in the number of elements in the array.

- Start from the element pointed by right and scan the array from right to left, comparing each element on the way with the element pointed by variable `loc`.
  That is, `a[loc]` should be less than `a[right]`.
  (a) If that is the case, then simply continue comparing until *right* becomes equal to `loc`. Because once `right = loc`, then it means the pivot has been placed in its correct position.
  (b) However, if at any point we have `a[loc]>a[right]`, then interchange the two values and jump to step 3.
  (c) Set `loc = right`
- Start from the element pointed by left and scan the array from left to right, comparing each element on the way with the element pointed by variable loc.
  That is, `a[loc]` should be greater than `a[left]`.
  (a) If that is the case, then simply continue comparing until left becomes equal to `loc`. Once `left = loc`, then it means the pivot has been placed in its correct position.
  (a) However, if at any point we have `a[loc]<a[left]`, then interchange the two values and jump to step 2.
  (b) Set `loc = left`.

Example C2.2 Consider the array given here and sort the elements using `quick sort` algorithm.

27	10	36	18	25	45

We choose the first element as the pivot. Set `loc` = 0, `left` = 0, `right` = 5 as,

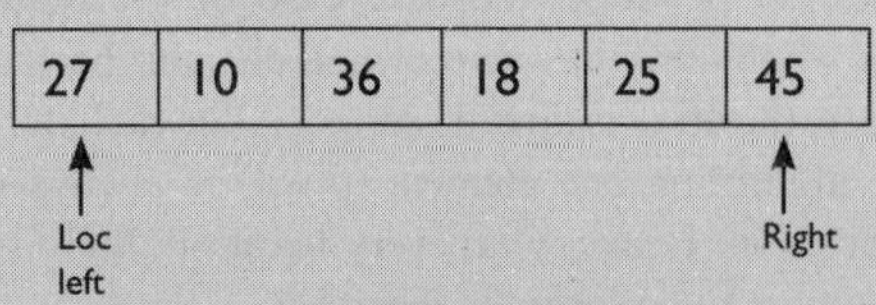

Scan from right to left. Since `a[loc] > a[right]`, decrease the value of right.

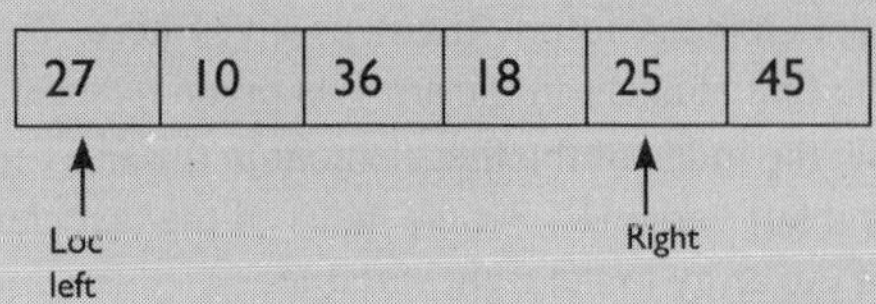

Since, `a[loc] > a[right]`, interchange the two values and set `loc = right`.

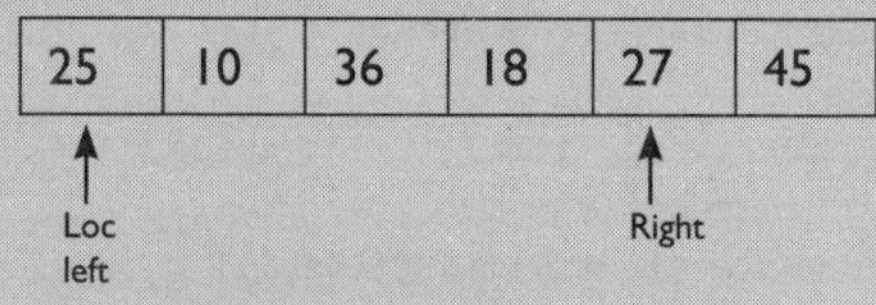

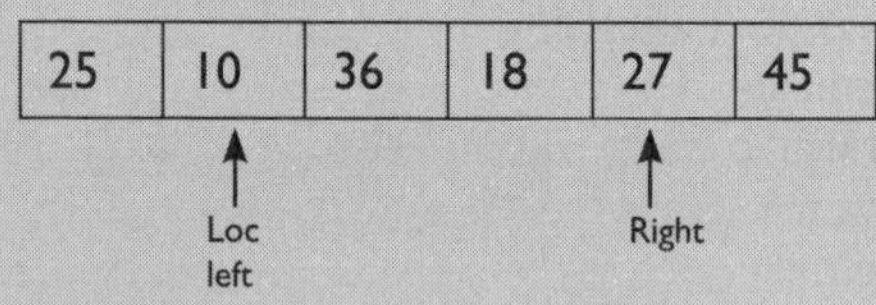

Start scanning from left to right. Since, `a[loc] > a[right]`, increment the value of left.

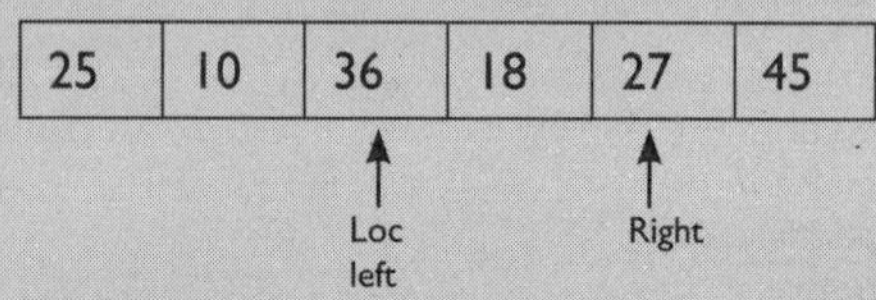

Now since, `a[loc] > a[right]`, interchange the values and set `loc = left`

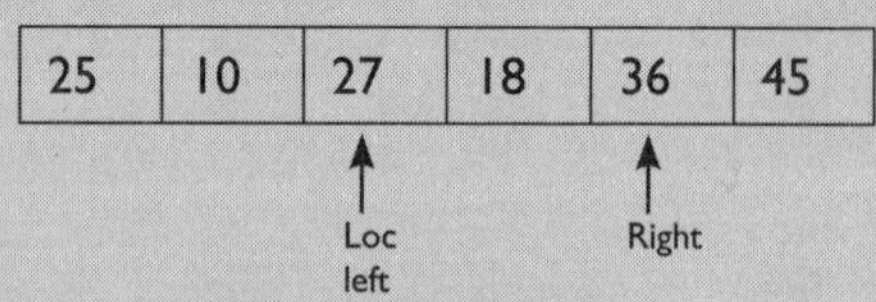

Scan from right to left. Since `a[loc] > a[right]`, decrement the value of right.

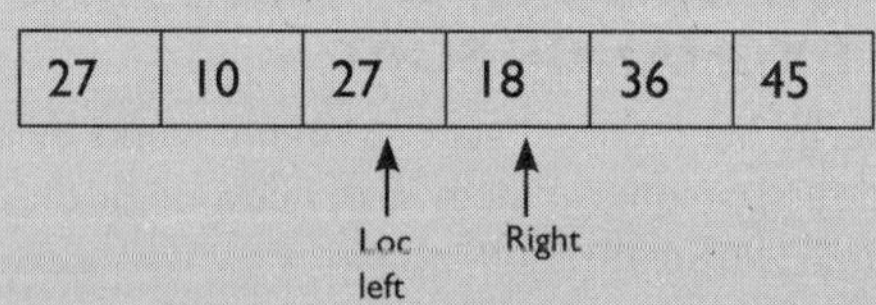

Since, `a[loc] > a[right]`, interchange the two values and set `loc = right`.

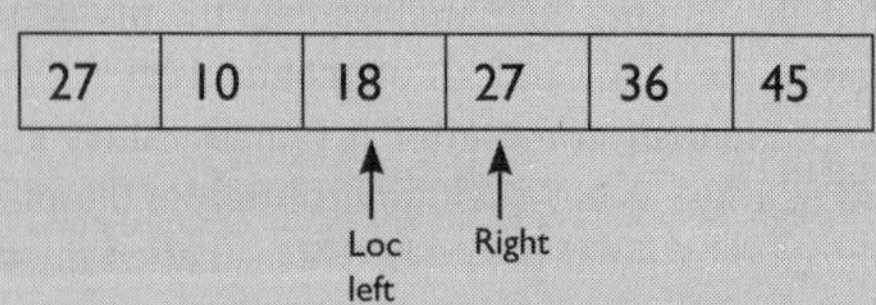

Start scanning from left to right. Since, `a[loc] > a[right]`, increment the value of left.

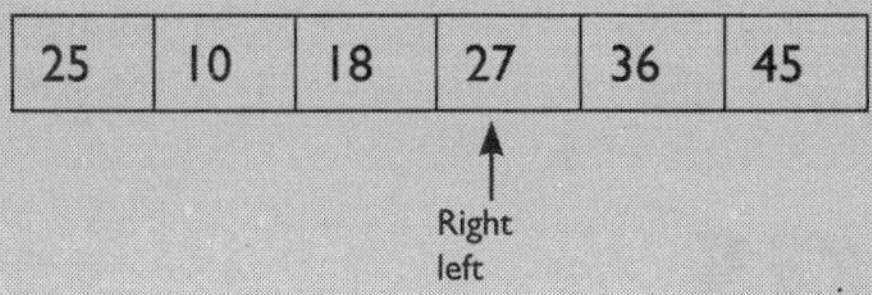

Note, now `left = loc`, so the procedure terminates as the pivot element (the first element of the array, that is, 27) is placed in its correct position. Now, all elements smaller than 25 are placed before it and elements greater than 27 are placed after it.

Now, the left sub-array containing elements 25, 10, 18, and right sub-array containing elements 36 and 45 are sorted in the same manner.

Program C2.2 Write a program to implement `quick sort` algorithm.

```
using namespace std;
#include<iostream>
int partition(int a[], int beg, int end);
//function prototypes
void quick_sort(int a[], int beg, int end);
int main()
{
      int arr[10], i, n, j,k;
      cout<<"\n Enter the number of elements
in the array : ";
      cin>>n;
      cout<<"\n Enter the elements of the
array ";
      for(i=0;i<n;i++)
// enter array elements
      {
            cin>>arr[i];
      }
      quick_sort(arr, 0, n-1);
// call quick sort function
      cout<<"\n The sorted array is : \n";
      for(i=0;i<n;i++)
            cout<<"\t"<< arr[i];
}
int partition(int a[], int beg, int end)
// partition the array
{
      int left, right, temp, loc, flag;
      loc = left = beg;
      right = end;
      flag = 0;
      while(flag != 1)
      {
            while((a[loc] <= a[right])
&& (loc!=right))
                  right--;
            if(loc==right)
                  flag =1;
            else if(a[loc]>a[right])
            {
                  temp = a[loc];
                  a[loc] = a[right];
                  a[right] = temp;
                  loc = right;
            }
            if(flag!=1)
            {
                  while((a[loc] >=
a[left]) && (loc!=left))
                        left++;
                  if(loc==left)
                        flag =1;
                  else if(a[loc]
<a[left])
                  {
                        temp = a[loc];
                        a[loc]
= a[left];
                        a[left] = temp;
                        loc = left;
                  }
            }
      }
      return loc;

}
void quick_sort(int a[], int beg, int end)//
quick sort function
{
      int loc;
      if(beg<end)
      {
            loc = partition(a, beg, end);
            quick_sort(a, beg, loc-1);
            quick_sort(a, loc+1, end);
      }
}
```

OUTPUT

```
Enter the number of elements
in the array : 10
Enter the elements of the
array 10 8 6 4 2 1 3 5 7 9
The sorted array is : 1 2 3
4 5 6 7 8 9 10
```

CHAPTER 6

Strings

KEY Concepts

Reading strings • Writing strings • Operations on strings • Character functions • String functions • Array of strings

INTRODUCTION

In recent times, computers are being widely used for word processing applications such as creating, inserting, updating, and modifying textual data. For example, when you go to a library, names of a book (a string), author (a string), and publisher (string) are stored in the computer. All these details are textual data or string. When you go to bank, your name, account number, and IFSC code are string type data. In your college, your name, address, father's name, course, and other details are stored as strings. Therefore, irrespective of the application, we need to store and manipulate textual data. Some applications also need to search for a particular pattern within a text, delete it, or replace it with another pattern. All these operations require manipulation (reading, displaying, inserting, deleting, modifying, storing, printing, etc) of textual data.

6.1 REPRESENTATION AND DECLARATION OF STRINGS

In C++, a string is nothing but a null-terminated character array. This means that after the last character, a null character (`'\0'`) is stored to signify the end of the character array. For example if we write,

```
char str[] = "HELLO";
```

> **Programming Tip:** Character constants are enclosed in single quotes. String constants are enclosed in double quotes.

We are declaring a character array that has five usable characters namely, `H`, `E`, `L`, `L`, and `O`. Apart from these characters, a null character (`'\0'`) is stored at the end of the string. Therefore, the internal representation of the string becomes `HELLO'\0'`. To store a string of length `5`, we need `5 + 1` locations—one additional location for the null character. The name of the character array or the string is a pointer to the beginning of the string. Figure 6.1 shows the difference between character storage and string storage.

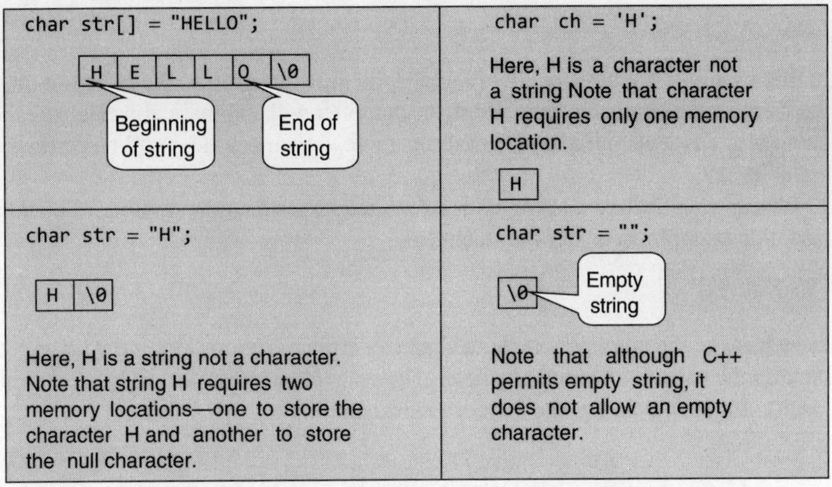

Figure 6.1 Difference between character storage and string storage

If we had declared `str` as

```
char str[5] = "HELLO";
```

then the `null` character will not be appended automatically to the character array. This is because, `str` can hold only `5` characters and the characters in `HELLO` have already filled the space allocated to it.

Note When the compiler assigns a character string to a character array, it automatically appends a null character to the end of the string. Therefore, the size of the string should be equal to maximum number of characters in the string plus one.

str[0]	1000	H
str[1]	1001	E
str[2]	1002	L
str[3]	1003	L
str[4]	1004	O
str[5]	1005	\0

Figure 6.2 Memory representation of a character array

Just as we use subscripts or `index` to access the elements of an array, the same subscripts are also used to access the elements of the character array. The sub script starts with a zero (`0`). All the characters of a string array are stored in successive memory locations. Figure 6.2 shows how `str[]` is stored in memory.

Therefore, in simple terms, a string is a sequence of characters. In Figure 6.2, `1000, 1001, 1002,` etc. are the memory addresses of individual characters. For the sake of simplicity, Figure 6.2 shows that `H` is stored at memory location `1000`; however, in reality, the ASCII codes of characters are stored in memory and not the character itself. Therefore, at address `1000, 72` will be stored as the ASCII code for `H` is `72`.

```
char str[] = "HELLO";
```

Programming Tip: When allocating memory space for a character array, reserve space to hold the null character

This statement declares a constant string as we have assigned value to it while declaring the string. However, the general form of declaring a string is as follows:

```
char str[size];
```

When we declare the string like this, we can store `size - 1` characters in the array because the last character would be the null character. For example, `char mesg[100];` can store maximum 99 usable characters.

Till now, we have seen one way of initializing strings. The other way to initialize a string is to initialize it as an array of characters as follows:

```
char str[] = { 'H', 'E', 'L', 'L', 'O', '\0'};
```

In this example, we have explicitly added the `null character`. We have not mentioned the size of the string or the character array. Here, the compiler will automatically calculate the size based on the number of elements initialized. In this example, 6 memory slots will be reserved to store the string variable, `str`.

We can also declare a string with size much larger than the number of elements that are initialized. For example, consider the statement:

```
char str[10] = "HELLO";
```

In such cases, the compiler creates a character array of size `10`, stores the value `"HELLO"` in it, and terminates the value with a null character. The other elements in the array are automatically initialized to `NULL`. Figure 6.3 shows the memory representation of such a string.

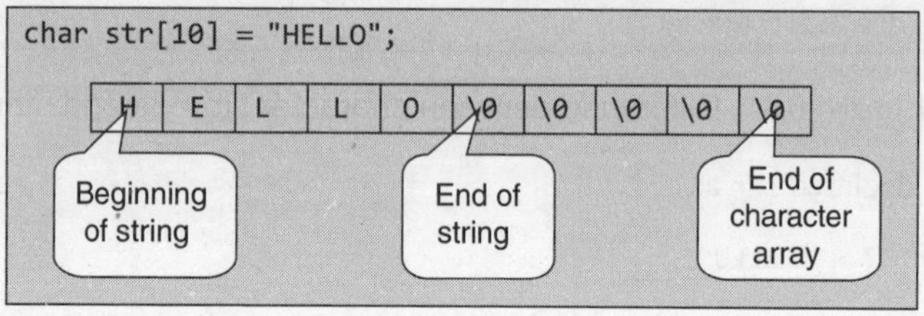

Figure 6.3 Memory representation of a string

However, the following declaration is illegal in C++ and would generate a compile time error because of two reasons. First, the array is initialized with more elements than it can store. Second, initialization cannot be separated from declaration.

```
char str[3];
str = "HELLO";
```

Note An array name cannot be used as the left operand of an assignment operator. Therefore, the following statement is illegal in C++.

```
char str2, str1[]="HI";
str2 = str1;
```

6.1.1 Reading Strings

If we declare a string by writing

```
char str[100];
```

then, `str` can be read in four ways which are explained as follows:

- using `cin`
- using `gets()` function
- using `getchar()`, `getch()`or `getche()` function repeatedly
- using `getline()`

- The string can be read using `cin` by writing

```
cin>>str;
```

Although the syntax of using cin is well-known and easy to use, the main pitfall with this function is that the function terminates as soon as it finds a blank space. For example, if the user enters Hello World,. the str will contain only Hello. This is because the moment a blank space was given, the string was terminated.

- The next method of reading a string is by using gets() function. The string can be read by writing

```
gets(str);
```

gets() is a simple function that overcomes the drawbacks of cin. gets() takes the starting address of the string that will hold the input. The string input using gets() is automatically terminated with a null character.

- String can also be read by calling the getchar(), getch, or getche() repeatedly to read a sequence of single characters, unless a terminating character is entered and simultaneously storing it in a character array as shown here.

Programming Tip: A compile time error will be generated if a string is assigned to a character variable.

```
i = 0;
ch = getchar();                // Get a character
while(ch != '*')
{   str[i] = ch;               // Store the read character in str
    i++;
    ch = getchar();            // Get another character
}
str[i] = '\0';             // terminate str with null character
```

It should be noted that in this method you have to deliberately append the characters with a null character. The other two functions (i.e. cin() and gets()) automatically do so.

Note getch() and getche() work same as getchar(). To use these functions, simply replace getchar() with getch().

- We have already discussed reading strings using getline() in Chapter 2 on Basics of C++ Programming. We had passed two arguments to getline(). The string and the number of characters have to be read. However, you may add another parameter that can act as the terminating character. The string will then be read until the terminate character is entered.

```
cin.getline(str,'*'); // string will be read until * is entered
cin.getline(str,10); // 10 characters will be read
```

Note You must use cin.ignore(); to grab a character off of the input buffer and discard it.

6.1.2 Writing Strings

The string can be displayed on the screen using three ways:

- using cout function
- using puts() function
- using putchar() and putch() function repeatedly

- The string can be displayed using cout by writing

```
cout<<str;
```

- The next method of writing a string is by using `puts()` function. The string can be displayed by writing

```
puts(str);
```

`puts()` is a simple function that overcomes the drawbacks of the `cout.` `puts()` writes a line of output on the screen. It terminates the line with a new line character `('\n')`. `puts()` returns an `EOF` if an error occurs and returns a positive number on success.

- The string can also be written by calling the `putchar()` and `putch()` repeatedly. These functions take a single character of the string and display it on the screen.

```
i = 0;
while(str[i] != '\0')
{
    putchar(str[i]);// Prints the character on the screen one by one
    i++;
}
```

6.2 STRING TAXONOMY

In C++, we can store a string either in fixed-length format or in variable-length format as shown in Fig. 6.4.

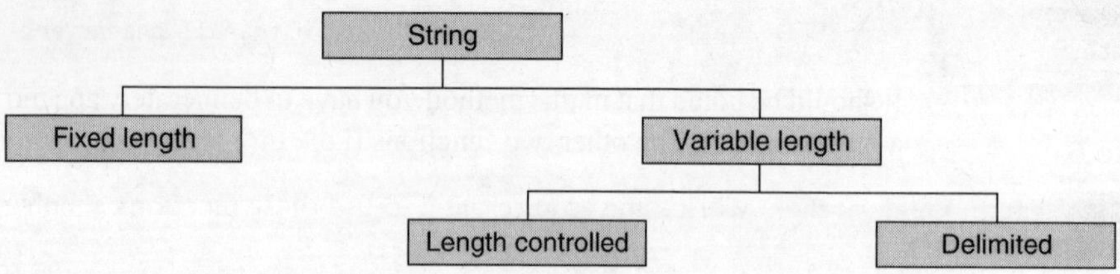

Figure 6.4 String taxonomy

Fixed length string When storing a string in a fixed length format, you need to specify an appropriate size for the string variable. If the size is too small, then you will not be able to store all the elements in the string. On the other hand, if the string size is large, then unnecessarily memory space will be wasted.

Variable length string A better option is to use a variable length format in which the string can be expanded or contracted to accommodate the elements in it. For example, if you declare a string variable to store the name of a student. If a student has a long name of say, 20 characters, then the string can be expanded to accommodate 20 characters. On the other hand, if a student name has only 5 characters, then the string variable can be contracted to store only 5 characters. However, to use a variable length string format, you need a technique to indicate the end of elements that are a part of the string. This can be done either by using length-controlled string or a delimiter.

Length-controlled string In length-controlled string, you need to specify the number of characters in the string. This count is used by string manipulation functions to determine the actual length of the string variable.

There should be a distinction between the usage of string and character array. Basically, a string is stored in an array of characters. If we are using the null character as the string delimiting character, then we treat the part of the array from the beginning to the null character as the string and ignore the rest. Figure 6.5 illustrates this concept.

```
char str[10];
gets(str);
```

If the user enters HELLO, then array of characters can be given as

Although the array has 10 locations, only the first six locations will be treated as a string.

Figure 6.5 Delimited string

> **Note** In C++, a string is a variable length array of characters that is delimited by the null character.

6.3 STRINGS OPERATIONS

In this section, we will read about different string operations. These operations perform their intended task by manipulating every single character that forms the string The name, purpose, and usage of these operations are summarized in Table 6.1.

> **Note** We can apply +, = <, >, and ! on strings by using operator overloading concepts which will discussed later in this book. (Refer to Chapter 11 on Operator Overloading).

Table 6.1 Description and examples for various string operations

Operation	Description	Example
Finding length	The number of characters in the string constitutes the length of the string.	LENGTH("C PROGRAMMING IS FUN") will return 20.
Concatenating two strings	To append second string after the first string	If S1 = "Hello" and S2 = "World", then concatenate(S1, S2) = HelloWorld
Converting characters of a string to upper case	In the memory, the ASCII codes are stored instead of the real value. The ASCII code for A-Z varies from 65 to 91 and the ASCII code for a-z ranges from 97 to 123. If we have to convert a lower case character into upper case, then we just need to subtract 32 from the ASCII value of the character.	Hello when converted into uppercase will display HELLO

(*Contd*)

Table 6.1 (*Contd*)

Operation	Description	Example
Converting characters of a string to lower case	To convert an upper case character into lower case, we just need to add 32 to its ASCII value.	HI when converted into lower case will display hi
Swapping two strings	Exchanging the contents of two strings	If str1 = Hi and str2 = Hello, then swap(str1,str2) will make str1 = Hello and str2 = Hi.
Reverse of a string	To reverse a string, we just need to swap the first character with the last, second character with the second last character, and so on.	If `S1 = "HELLO"`, then reverse of `S1 = "OLLEH"`.
String matching	To find occurrences of a pattern string within another string.	If S1 = "Hello World" and S2 = "ll", then the pattern or string in S2 matches with S1.

Extracting a substring from the middle of a string	To extract a substring from a given string requires information about the following:
	• the main string
	• the position of the first character of the substring in the given string
	• the maximum number of characters or length of the substring
		If we have a string-
		`str[] = "Welcome to the world of programming";`
		`then,`
		`SUBSTRING(str, 15, 5) = world`

Insertion	The insertion operation inserts a string S in the main text, T at the kth position.	`INSERT("XYZXYZ", 3, "AAA") = "XYZAAAXYZ"`
Deletion	The deletion operation deletes a substring from a given text.	DELETE("ABCDXXXABCD", 5, 3) = "ABCDABCD"
Replacement	Replacement operation is used to replace the pattern P_1 by another pattern P_2.	("AAABBBCCC", "BBB", "X") = AAAXCCC("AAABBBCCC", "X", "YYY") = AAABBBCC

Program 6.1 Write a program to find the length of a string.

```
using namespace std;
#include<iostream>
int main()
{   char str[20];
    int i = 0, length;
    cout<<"\n Enter the string: ";
```

```
    cin.getline(str,20);
    while(str[i] != '\0')
        i++;
    length = i;
    cout<<"\n The length of the string is: "<<length;
}
```

OUTPUT

```
Enter the string: HELLO
The length of the string is: 5
```

Program 6.2 Write a program to convert characters of a string in upper case.

```
using namespace std;
#include<iostream>
int main()
{   char str[100], upper_str [100];
    int i = 0;
    cout<<"\n Enter the string:";
    cin.getline(str,100);
    while(str[i] != '\0')
    {   if(str[i]>='a' && str[i]<='z')
            upper_str[i] = str[i] - 32;
        else
            upper_str[i] = str[i];
            i++;
    }
    upper_str[i] = '\0';
    cout<<"\n The string converted into upper case is : ";
    puts(upper_str);
}
```

OUTPUT

```
Enter the string: hello
The string converted into upper case is : HELLO
```

Program 6.3 Write a program to convert characters of a string into lower case.

```
using namespace std;
#include<iostream>
int main()
{   char str[100], lower_str [100];
    int i = 0, j = 0;
    cout<<"\n Enter the string:";
    cin.getline(str, 100);
    while(str[i] != '\0')
    {   if(str[i]>='A' && str[i]<='Z')
                lower_str[j] = str[i] + 32;
        else
                lower_str[i] = str[i];
        i++; j++;
    }
    lower_str[j] = '\0';
    cout<<"\n The string converted into lower case is: ";
    puts(lower_str);
```

```
    return 0;
}
```

OUTPUT

```
Enter the string: HeLLo
The string converted into lower case is:
Hello
```

Program 6.4 Write a program to concatenate two strings.

```
using namespace std;
#include<iostream>
int main()
{   char str1[100], str2[100], str3[100];
    int i=0, j=0;
    cout<<"\n Enter the first string: ";
    cin.getline(str1, 100);
    cout<<"\n Enter the second string: ";
    cin.getline(str2,100);
    while(str1[i] != '\0')
    {   str3[j] = str1[i];
        i++;
        j++;
    }
    i=0;
    while(str2[i] != '\0')
    {   str3[j] = str2[i];
        i++;
        j++;
    }
    str3[j] = '\0';
    cout<<"\n The concatenated string is:";
    puts(str3);
    return 0;
}
```

OUTPUT

```
Enter the first string: Hello,
Enter the second string: How are you?
The concatenated string is: Hello, How are you?
```

Program 6.5 Write a program to append a string to another string.

```
using namespace std;
#include<iostream>
main()
{   char Dest_Str[100], Source_Str[50];
    int i = 0, j = 0;
    cout<<"\n Enter the source string: ";
    cin.getline(Source_Str, 50);
    cout<<"\n Enter the destination string:";
    cin.getline(Dest_Str, 50);
```

```
    while(Dest_Str[i] != '\0')
        i++;
while(Source_Str[j] != '\0')
    {   Dest_Str[i] = Source_Str[j];
        i++;
        j++;
    }
    Dest_Str[i] = '\0';
    cout<<"\n After appending, the destination string is: ";
    puts(Dest_Str);
    return 0;
}
```

OUTPUT

```
Enter the source string: How are you?
Enter the destination string: Hi,
After appending, the destination string is: Hi, How are you?
```

Program 6.6 Write a program to compare two strings.

```
using namespace std;
#include<iostream>
#include<string.h>
main()
{   char str1[50], str2[50];
    int i=0, len1 = 0, len2 = 0, same = 0;
    cout<<"\n Enter the first string: ";
    cin.getline(str1, 50);
    cout<<"\n Enter the second string: ";
    cin.getline(str2, 50);
    len1 = strlen(str1);
    len2 = strlen(str2);
    if(len1 == len2)
    {   while(i<len1)
        {   if(str1[i] == str2[i])
                i++;
            else break;
        }
        if(i==len1)
        {   same=1;
            cout<<"\n The two strings are equal";
        }
    }
    if(len1!=len2)
        cout<<"\n The two strings are not equal";
    if(same == 0)
    {   if(str1[i]>str2[i])
            cout<<"\n String1 is greater than string2";
        else if(str1[i]<str2[i])
            cout<<"\n String2 is greater than string1";
```

```
    }
    return 0;
}
```

OUTPUT

```
Enter the first string: Hello
Enter the second string: Hello
The two strings are equal
```

Program 6.7 Write a program to reverse the given string.

```
using namespace std;
#include<iostream>
#include<string.h>
int main()
{   char str[100], temp;
    int i = 0, j = 0;
    cout<<"\n Enter the string: ";
    cin.getline(str,100);
    j=strlen(str)-1;
    while(i<j)
    {   temp = str[j];
        str[j] = str[i];
        str[i] = temp;
        i++;
        j--;
    }
    cout<<"\n The reversed string is: ";
    puts(str);
    return 0;
}
```

OUTPUT

```
Enter the string: Hi there
The reversed string is: ereht iH
```

Program 6.8 Write a program to swap two strings.

```
using namespace std;
#include<iostream>
#include<string.h>
main()
{   char str1[10], str2[10], temp[10];
    cout<<"\n Enter the first string : ";
    cin.getline(str1,10);
    cout<<"\n Enter the second string : ";
    cin.getline(str2,10);
    strcpy(temp, str1);
    strcpy(str1, str2);
    strcpy(str2, temp);
    cout<<"\n The first string is : "<<str1;
    cout<<"\n The second string is : "<<str2;
}
```

OUTPUT

```
Enter the first string : Hi There
Enter the second string : Hello All
The first string is : Hello All
The second string is : Hi There
```

Program 6.9 Write a program to extract the substring from a given string.

```
using namespace std;
#include<iostream>
int main()
{   char str[100], substr[100];
    int i=0, j=0, n, m;
    cout<<"\n Enter the main string: ";
    cin.getline(str,100);
    cout<<"\n Enter the position from which to start the substring: ";
    cin>>m;
    cout<<"\n Enter the length of the substring: ";
    cin>>n;
    i=m;
    while(str[i] != '\0' && n>=0)
    {   substr[j] = str[i];
        i++;
        j++;
        n--;
    }
    substr[j] = '\0';
    cout<<"\n The substring is : ";
    puts(str);
    return 0;
}
```

OUTPUT

```
Enter the main string : Hi there
Enter the position from which to start the substring: 1
Enter the length of the substring: 7
The substring is : i there
```

Program 6.10 Write a program to insert a string in the main text.

```
using namespace std;
#include<iostream>
main()
{   char text[100], str[20], ins_text[100];
    int i=0, j=0, k=0,pos;
    cout<<"\n Enter the main text: ";
    cin.getline(text,100);
    cout<<"\n Enter the string to be inserted: ";
    cin.getline(str, 20);
    cout<<"\n Enter the position at which the string has to be inserted: ";
    cin>>pos;
    while(text[i]!='\0')
    {   if(i==pos)
        {   while(str[k]!='\0')
```

```
            {   ins_text[j]=str[k];
                j++;
                k++;
            }
        }
        else
        {   ins_text[j]=text[i];
            j++;
        }
        i++;
    }
    ins_text[j]='\0';
    cout<<"\n The new string is: ";
    puts(ins_text);
    return 0;
}
```

OUTPUT

```
Enter the main text: How you?
Enter the string to be inserted: are
Enter the position at which the string has to be inserted: 6
The new string is: How are you?
```

Program 6.11 Write a program to delete a substring from a text.

```
using namespace std;
#include<iostream>
main()
{   char text[200], str[20], new_text[200];
    int i=0, j=0, found=0, k, n=0, copy_loop=0;
    cout<<"\n Enter the main text: ";
    cin.getline(text,200);
    cin.ignore();
    cout<<"\n Enter the string to be deleted: ";
    cin.getline(str, 20);
    cin.ignore();
    while(text[i]!='\0')
    {   j=0, found= 0, k=i;
    while(text[k]==str[j] && str[j]!='\0')
    {   k++;
        j++;
    }
    if(str[j]=='\0')
    copy_loop=k;
    new_text[n] = text[copy_loop];
    i++;
    copy_loop++;
    n++;
    }
    new_text[n]='\0';
    cout<<"\n The new string is: ";
    puts(new_text);
    return 0;
```

```
}
```

OUTPUT

```
Enter the main text: Hello, how are you?
Enter the string to be deleted: , how are you?
The new string is: Hello
```

Program 6.12 Write a program to replace a pattern with another pattern in the text.

```
using namespace std;
#include<iostream>
main()
{   char str[200], pat[20], new_str[200], rep_pat[100];
    int i=0, j=0, k, n=0, copy_loop=0, rep_index=0;
    cout<<"\n Enter the string: ";
    cin.getline(str,200);
    cin.ignore();
    cout<<"\n Enter the pattern: ";
    cin.getline(pat, 20);
    cin.ignore();
    cout<<"\n Enter the replace pattern: ";
    cin.getline(rep_pat, 100);
    while(str[i]!='\0')
    {   j=0,k=i;
    while(str[k]==pat[j] && pat[j]!='\0')
    {   k++;
        j++;
    }
if(pat[j]=='\0')
    {   copy_loop=k;
        while(rep_pat[rep_index] !='\0')
    {   new_str[n] = rep_pat[rep_index];
        rep_index++;
        n++;
        }
    }
    new_str[n] = str[copy_loop];
    i++;
    copy_loop++;
    n++;
    }
    new_str[n]='\0';
    cout<<"\n The new string is: ";
    puts(new_str);
    return 0;
}
```

OUTPUT

```
Enter the string: How ARE you?
Enter the pattern: ARE
Enter the pattern: are
The new string is: How are you?
```

6.4 CHARACTER MANIPULATION FUNCTIONS

Some character manipulation functions contained in header file are called `ctype.h.` and are illustrated in Table 6.2.

Table 6.2 Functions in `ctype.h`

Function	Usage	Example
`isalnum(int c)`	Checks whether character c is an alphanumeric character	`isalnum('A');`
`isalpha(int c)`	Checks whether character c is an alphabetic character	`isalpha('z');`
`iscntrl(int c)`	Checks whether character c is a control character	`cin>>c;iscntrl(c);`
`isdigit(int c);`	Checks whether character c is a digit	`isdigit(3);`
`isgraph()`	Checks whether character c is a graphic or printing character. The function excludes the white space character.	`isgraph('!');`
`isprint(int c);`	Checks whether character c is a printing character. The function includes the white space character.	`isprint('@');`
`islower(int c);`	Checks whether the character c is in lower case	`islower('k');`
`isupper(int c);`	Checks whether the character c is in upper case	`isupper('K');`
`ispunct(int c);`	Checks whether the character c is a punctuation mark	`ispunct('?');`
`isspace(int c);`	Checks whether the character c is a white space character	`isspace(' ');`
`isxdigit(int c);`	Checks whether the character c is a hexadecimal digit	`isxdigit('F');`
`tolower(int c);`	Converts the character c in lower case	`tolower('K') returns k`
`toupper(int c);`	Converts the character c in upper case	`toupper('k') returns K`

Let us use Table 6.2 to see the application of character functions.

Example 6.1 Using character functions

```
using namespace std;
#include<iostream>
#include<ctype.h>
int main()
{   char ch = 'R'; // declare a character
    if(isalpha(ch))   // check if it is an alphabet
    {   cout<<ch<<"is a character.";
        if(isupper(ch))   //check if it is uppercase
        {   cout<<"It is in upper case";
            cout<<"\n In lower case it will be written as : "<<(char) tolower(ch);
            // convert the character in lower case
        }
    }
}
```

OUTPUT

```
R is a character. It is in upper case
In lower case, it will be written as: r
```

6.5 STRING FUNCTIONS DEFINED IN `string.h` HEADER FILE

> **Programming Tip:** Before using string copy and concatenating functions, ensure that the destination string has enough space to store all the elements so that memory overwriting does not take place.

In this section, we will look some commonly used string functions present in the `string.h` header file.

Strcat function The syntax is `char *strcat(char *str1, const char *str2);`

The `strcat` function appends the string pointed to by `str2` to the end of the string pointed to by `str1`. The terminating null character of `str1` is overwritten. The process stops when the terminating null character of `str2` is copied. The argument `str1` is returned. Note that `str1` should be big enough to store the contents of `str2`.

Example 6.2 Concatenating two strings

```
#include<string.h>
using namespace std;
#include<iostream>
int main()
{   char str1[50] = "Programming";
    char str2[] = "In C++";
    strcat(str1, str2); // Concatenating two strings
    puts(str1);
}
```

OUTPUT

```
ProgrammingIn C++
```

Strcat function The syntax is `char *strncat(char *str1, const char *str2, size_t n);`

The function appends the string pointed to by `str2` to the end of the string pointed to by `str1` up to `n` characters long. The terminating null character of `str1` is overwritten. Copying stops when `n` characters are copied or the terminating null character of `str2` is copied. A terminating null character is appended to `str1` before returning to the calling function.

Example 6.3 Appending n characters to a given string

```
#include<string.h>
using namespace std;
#include<iostream>
int main()
{   char str1[50] = "Programming";
    char str2[] = "In C++";
    strncat(str1, str2, 2);// Appending two characters to the string
    puts(str1);
}
OUTPUT
Programming In
```

`strchr` function The syntax is `char *strchr(const char *str, int c);`

This function searches for the first occurrence of the character `c`—an unsigned char—in the string pointed to by the argument `str`. The function returns a pointer pointing to the first matching character, or null if no match was found.

Example 6.4 Searching the first occurrence of the character in the string

```
#include<string.h>
using namespace std;
#include<iostream>
int main()
{   char str[50] = "Programming In C++";
    char *pos;
    pos = strchr(str, 'n');// searching the first occurrence of the character n
    if(pos)
       cout<<"\n n is found in str at position "<<pos-str;
    else
       cout<<"\n n is not present in the string";
}
OUTPUT
n is present in str at position 9
```

`strrchr` function The syntax is `char *strrchr(const char *str, int c);`

This function searches for the first occurrence of the character `c`, an unsigned char, beginning at the rear end and works towards the front in the string pointed to by the argument `str`. The function searches for the last occurrence of the character `c` and returns a pointer pointing to the last matching character or `null` if no match was found.

Example 6.5 Searching the first occurrence from the end of the string

```
using namespace std;
#include<iostream>
#include<string.h>
int main()
{   char str[50] = "Programming In C";
    char *pos;
    pos = strrchr(str, 'n');
    //searching the first occurrence of the character n starting from the end of the given string
    if(pos)
```

```
        cout<<"\n The last position of n is: "<<pos-str;
    else
        cout<<"\n n is not present in the string";
}
```

OUTPUT

```
The last position of n is: 13
```

strcmp function The syntax is `int strcmp(const char *str1, const char *str2);`

It compares the string pointed to by `str1` to the string pointed to by `str2`, returns `zero` if the strings are equal, or else, returns a value less than zero or greater than `zero` if `str1` is less than or greater than `str2` respectively.

Example 6.6 Comparing two strings

```
using namespace std;
#include<iostream>
#include<string.h>
int main()
{   char str1[10] = "HELLO";
    char str2[10] = "HEY";
    if(strcmp(str1,str2)==0) // Comparing the two strings
        cout<<"\n The two strings are identical";
    else
        cout<<"\n The two strings are not identical";
}
```

OUTPUT

```
The two strings are not identical
```

strncmp function The syntax is `int strncmp(const char *str1, const char *str2, size_t n);`

The function compares at most the first `n` bytes of `str1` and `str2`. The process stops comparing after the null character is encountered. The function returns `zero` if the first `n` bytes of the strings are equal. Otherwise, it returns a value less than `zero` or greater than zero if `str1` is less than or greater than `str2` respectively.

Example 6.7 Comparing n characters of a string

```
using namespace std;
#include<iostream>
#include<string.h>
int main()
{   char str1[10] = "HELLO";
    char str2[10] = "HEY";
    if(strncmp(str1,str2,2)==0)// Comparing n characters of a string
        cout<<"\n The two strings are identical";
    else
        cout<<"\n The two strings are not identical";
}
```

OUTPUT

```
The two strings are identical
```

strcpy function The syntax is `char *strcpy(char *str1, const char *str2);`

Copies the string pointed to by `str2` to `str1` including the `null` character of `str2`. Returns the argument `str1`. Note that `str1` should be big enough to store the contents of `str2`.

Example 6.8 Copying a string in another string

```
using namespace std;
#include<iostream>
#include<string.h>
int main()
{   char str1[10], str2[10] = "HELLO";
    strcpy(str1,str2); // Copying a given string in the other string
    puts(str1);
}
```

OUTPUT

```
HELLO
```

`strncpy` function The syntax is `char *strncpy(char *str1, const char *str2, size_t n);`

It copies up to `n` characters from the string pointed to by `str2` to `str1` and stops copying when `n` characters are copied. However, if the null character in `str2` is reached, then the `null` characters are continually copied to `str1` until `n` characters have been copied. Finally, a `null` character must be appended to `str1`. However, if `n` is `zero` or negative, nothing is copied.

Example 6.9 Copying n characters of a string in another string

Programming Tip: Do not use string functions on a character array that is not terminated with a null character.

```
using namespace std;
#include<iostream>
#include<string.h>
int main()
{   char str1[10], str2[10] = "HELLO";
    strncpy(str1,str2, 2);
    //Copying n characters of the given string in another string
    puts(str1);
}
```

OUTPUT

```
HE
```

Note To copy the string `str2` in `str1`, a better way is to write

```
strncpy(str1, str2, sizeof(str1)-1);
```

This would enforce the copying of only that much characters for which `str1` has space to accommodate. We have written size of `str1` minus 1 to store the null character.

`strlen` function The syntax is `size_t strlen(const char *str);`

This function calculates the length of the string `str` up to but not including the `null` character. The function returns the number of characters in the string.

Example 6.10 Calculating length of string

```
using namespace std;
#include<iostream>
#include<string.h>
int main()
{   char str[] = "HELLO";
```

```
    cout<<"\n Length of str is: "<<strlen(str);
    //Calculating and displaying the length of a given string
}
```

OUTPUT

```
Length of str is: 5
```

`Strstr` **function** The syntax is `char *strstr(const char *str1, const char *str2);`

The function is used to find the first occurrence of string `str2` (not including the terminating null character) in the string `str1`. It returns a pointer to the first occurrence of `str2` in `str1`. If no match is found, a `null` pointer is returned.

Example 6.11 Searching the first occurrence of string `str2` in the string `str1`

```
using namespace std;
#include<iostream>
#include<string.h>
int main()
{   char str1[] = "HAPPY BIRTHDAY TO YOU";
    char str2[] = "DAY";
    char *ptr;
    ptr = strstr(str1, str2);// Searching the first occurrence of sunstring in the given string
    if(ptr)
       cout<<"\n Substring Found";
    else
       cout<<"\n Substring Not Found";
}
```

OUTPUT

```
Substring Found
```

`Strspn` **function** The syntax is `size_t strspn( const char *str1, const char *str2 );`

The function returns the index of the first character in `str1` that does not match any character in `str2`.

Example 6.12 Finding the index of the first character in `str1` that does not match any character in `str2`.

```
using namespace std;
#include<iostream>
#include<string.h>
int main()
{   char str1[] = "HAPPY BIRTHDAY TO YOU";
    char str2[] = "HAPPY BIRTHDAY RAM";
    cout<<"\n The position of first character in str2 that does not matches with that in str1 is
"<<strspn(str1,str2);
}
```

OUTPUT

```
The position of first character in str2 that does not matches with that in str1 is 16
```

`Strcspn` **function** The syntax is `size_t strcspn(const char *str1, const char *str2);`

The function returns the index of the first character in `str1` that matches any of the characters in `str2`.

Example 6.13 Finding the index of the first character in `str1` that matches any of the characters in `str2`.

```
using namespace std;
#include<iostream>
#include<string.h>
int main()
{   char str1[] = "PROGRAMMING IN C++";
    char str2[] = "IN";
    cout<<"\n The position of first character in str2 that matches with that in str1 is "<<
strcspn(str1,str2);
}
```

OUTPUT

```
The position of first character in str2 that matches with that in str1 is 8
```

`Strpbrk` function The syntax is `char *strpbrk( const char *str1, const char *str2 );`

The function `strpbrk()` returns a pointer to the first occurrence in `str1` of any character in `str2`, or `NULL` if none are present. The only difference between `strpbrk()` and `strcspn` is that `strcspn()` returns the index of the character and `strpbrk()` returns a pointer to the first occurrence of character in `str2`.

Example 6.14 Finding the first occurrence in `str1` of any character in `str2`.

```
using namespace std;
#include<iostream>
#include<string.h>
int main()
{   char str1[] = "PROGRAMMING IN C++";
    char str2[] = "AB";
    char *ptr = strpbrk(str1,str2);
    if(ptr==NULL)
        cout<<"\n No character matches in the two strings";
    else
        cout<<"\n Character in str2 matches with that in str1";
}
```

OUTPUT

```
No character matches in the two strings
```

`Strtok` function The syntax is `char *strtok( char *str1, const char *delimiter );`

The `strtok` function is used to isolate sequential tokens in a null-terminated string, `str`. These tokens are separated in the string using delimiters. The first time that `strtok` is called, `str` should be specified; subsequent calls, wishing to obtain further tokens from the same string, should pass a null pointer instead. However, the delimiter must be supplied each time, though it may change between calls.

The `strtok` function returns a pointer to the beginning of each subsequent token in the string, after replacing the token itself with a `NULL` character. When all tokens are left, a `null` pointer is returned.

Example 6.15 Removing specified tokens from the string.

```
using namespace std;
#include<iostream>
#include<string.h>
main ()
{   char str[] = "Hello, to, the, world of, programming";
```

```
    char delim[] = ",";
    char *result;
    result = strtok(str, delim);
    while(result!=NULL)
    {   cout<<result;
        result = strtok(NULL, delim);
    }
}
```

OUTPUT

```
Hello to the world of programming
```

`Strtol` function The syntax is `long strtol(const char *str, char **end, int base);`

The `strtol` function converts the string pointed by `str` to a long value. The function skips leading white space characters and stops when it encounters the first non-numeric character. `strtol` stores the address of the first invalid character in `str` in `*end`. If there were no digits at all, then the `strtol` function will store the original value of `str` in `*end`. You may pass `NULL` instead of `*end` if you do not want to store the invalid characters anywhere.

Finally, the third argument base specifies whether the number is in hexa-decimal, octal, binary, or decimal representation.

Example 6.16 Converting a string into its long value

```
using namespace std;
#include<iostream>
#include<stdlib.h>
main ()
{   long num;
    num = strtol("12345 Decimal Value", NULL, 0);
    cout<<"\n"<<num;
    num = strtol("65432 Octal Value", NULL, 8);
    cout<<"\n"<<num;
    num = strtol("10110101 Binary Value", NULL, 2);
    cout<<"\n"<<num;
    num = strtol("A7CB4 Hexadecimal Value", NULL, 16);
    cout<<"\n"<<num;
}
```

OUTPUT

```
12345
27418
181
687284
```

`Strtod` function The syntax is `double strtod(const char *str, char **end);`

The function expects a string `str` that has an optional plus (`"+"`) or minus sign (`"-"`) followed by either

- a decimal number containing a sequence of decimal digits optionally consisting of a decimal-point, or
- a hexadecimal number consisting of a `"0X"` or `"0x"` followed by a sequence of hexadecimal digits optionally containing a decimal-point.

In both cases, the number may be optionally followed by an exponent (`'E'` or `'e'` for decimal constants or a `'P'` or `'p'` for hexadecimal constants), followed by an optional plus or minus sign, followed by a sequence of decimal digits. For decimal constants and hexadecimal constants, the exponent indicates the power of 10 and 2, respectively, by which the number should be scaled.

Example 6.17 Converting a string to decimal or hexadecimal.

```
using namespace std;
#include<iostream>
#include<stdlib.h>
main()
{   double num;
    num = strtod("123.345abcdefg", NULL);
    cout<<"\n"<<num;
}
```

OUTPUT

```
123.345000
```

`atoi()` function Till now, you must have understood that the value 1 is an integer and '1' is a character. Therefore, there is a huge difference when we write the two statements given below

```
int i = 1;      // here i = 1
int i = '1';      // here i = 49, the ASCII value of character 1
```

Similarly, `123` is an integer number but `'123'` is a string of digits. If you want to operate some integer operations on the string `'123'`, `C` provides a function `atoi` that converts a given string into its corresponding integer.

The `atoi()` function converts a given string passed to it as an argument into an integer. The `atoi()` function returns that integer to the calling function. However, the string should start with a number. The `atoi()` will stop reading from the string as soon as it encounters a non-numerical character. The `atoi()` is included in the `stdlib.h` file. Before using this function in your program, you must include this header file. The syntax of `atoi()` can be given as follows:

```
int atoi( const char *str );
```

For example,

```
i = atoi( "123.456" );
RESULT: i = 123
```

`atof()` function The function `atof()` converts the string that it accepts as an argument into a double value and then return that value to the calling function. However, the string must start with a valid number. The string can be terminated with any non-numerical character, other than `"E"` or `"e"`. The syntax of `atof()` can be given as follows:

```
double atof( const char *str );
```

For example,

```
x = atof( "12.39 is the answer" );
RESULT: x = 12.39
```

`atol()` function The function `atol()` converts the string into a long int value. The `atol` function returns the converted long value to the calling function. Like `atoi`, the `atol()` will read from a string until it finds any character that should not be in a long. Its syntax can be given as,

```
long atol( const char *str );
```

For example,

```
x = atol( "12345.6789" );
RESULT: x = 12345L
```

Note atoi(), atof(), and atoll() are a part of stdlib.h header file.

6.6 ARRAY OF STRINGS

Till now, we have seen that a string is an array of characters. For example if we say, `char name[] = "Mohan"`, then name is a string (character array) that has five characters.

Suppose there are 20 students in a class and we need a string that stores names of all the 20 students. We need a string of strings or an array of strings. Such an array of strings would store 20 individual strings. An array of string is declared as follows:

```
char names[20][30];
```

Here, the first index will specify how many strings are needed and the second index specifies the length of every string. We allocate space for 20 names where each name can be maximum 30 characters long. Hence, the general syntax for declaring a two-dimensional array of strings can be given as follows:

```
<data type> <array_name> [<row_size][<column_size>];
```

Let us see the memory representation of an array of strings. If we have an array declared as

```
char name[5][10] = {"Ram", "Mohan", "Shyam", "Hari", "Gopal"};
```

then in memory, the array is stored as shown in Fig. 6.6.

Name[0]	R	A	M	'\0'						
Name[1]	M	O	H	A	N	'\0'				
Name[2]	S	H	Y	A	M	'\0'				
Name[3]	H	A	R	I	'\0'					
Name[4]	G	O	P	A	L	'\0'				

Figure 6.6 Memory representation of a 2D character array

By declaring the array names, we allocate 50 bytes. However, the actual memory occupied is 27 bytes. Therefore, more than half of the memory allocated is wasted.

Program 6.13 Write a program to read and print the names of n students of a class.

```
using namespace std;
#include<iostream>
main()
{   char names[5][10];
    int i, n;
    cout<<"\n Enter the number of students : ";
    cin>>n;
    for(i = 0;i<n;i++)
    {   cout<<"\n Enter the name of "<<i+1<<"th student : ";
```

```
        cin.ignore();
        cin.getline(names[i],10);
    }
    cout<<"\n Names of the students are : \n";
    for(i = 0;i<n;i++)
        puts(names[i]);
}
```

OUTPUT

```
Enter the number of students : 3
Enter the name of 1th student : Aditya
Enter the name of 2th student : Goransh
Enter the name of 3th student : Sarthak
Names of the students are :
Aditya Goransh Sarthak
```

Program 6.14 Write a program to sort names of students.

```
#include<string.h>
using namespace std;
#include<iostream>
main()
{   char names[5][10], temp[10];
    int i, n, j;
    cout<<"\n Enter the number of students : ";
    cin>>n;
    for(i = 0;i<n;i++)
    {   cout<<"\n Enter the name of the "<<i+1<<"th student : ";
        cin.ignore();
            cin.getline(names[i],100);
    }
        for(i = 0;i<n;i++)
        {   for(j = 0;j<n-i-1;j++)
            {   if(strcmp(names[j], names[j+1])>0)
                {   strcpy(temp, names[j]);
                    strcpy(names[j], names[j+1]);
                    strcpy(names[j+1], temp);
                }
            }
        }
    cout<<"\n Names of the students as stored in alphabetical order are : ";
    for(i = 0;i<n;i++)
        puts(names[i]);
}
```

OUTPUT

```
Enter the number of students : 3
Enter the name of 0th student : Sarthak
Enter the name of 1dth student : Goransh
Enter the name of 2dth student : Aditya
Names of the students as sorted in alphabetical order are : Aditya Goransh Sarthak
```

Program 6.15 Write a program to display the following pattern.

H
HE
HEL
HELL
HELLO

Programming Tip: ignore() may take two arguments—number of characters to ignore and the character. For example, cin.ignore(1, '*') will ignore a character when * is found.

```
using namespace std;
#include<iostream>
#include<string.h>
main()
{   char str[10];
 cout<<"\n Enter a string : ";
 cin.getline(str,10);
 for(int i = 0;i<=strlen(str);i++)
 {   cout<<"\n";
     cout.write(str,i);
 }
}
```

Program 6.16 Write a program to display the following pattern.

HELLO
HELL
HEL
HE
H

```
using namespace std;
#include<iostream>
#include<string.h>
main()
{   char str[10];
    cout<<"\n Enter a string : ";
    cin.getline(str,10);
    for(int i = strlen(str);i>=0;i--)
    {   cout<<"\n";
        cout.write(str,i);
    }
}
```

Note peek() does not extract the specified character. For example, cin.peek()=='*' will not process the *.

Program 6.17 Write a program to demonstrate the use of peek() and ignore().

```
using namespace std;
#include<iostream>
#include<string.h>
main()
{   char str[20];
    int i = 0;
    cout<<"\n Enter a string (Press . to stop) : ";
    cin.get(str[i]);
    while(str[i] != '.')
    {   while(cin.peek() == ' ')
                cin.ignore(1,' ');
            i++;
            cin.get(str[i]);
    }
    str[i]='\0';
    cout.write(str,10);
}
```

OUTPUT

```
Enter a string (Press . to stop) : Oxford University Press.
OxfordUniversityPress
```

Program 6.18 Write a program to read and print the text until a * is encountered. Count the number of characters in the text entered.

```
using namespace std;
#include<iostream>
int main()
{   char str[1000];
    int i = 0;
    cout<<"\n Enter * to end";
    cout<<"\n **************";
    cout<<"\n Enter the text : ";
    cin>>str[i];
    while(str[i] != '*')
    {   i++;
        cin>>str[i];
    }
    str[i] = '\0';
    cout<<"\n The text is : ";
    i = 0;
    while(str[i] != '\0')
    {   cout<<str[i];
        i++;
    }
    cout<<"\n The count of characters is : "<<i-1;
}
```

OUTPUT

```
Enter * to end
**************
Enter the sentence: Oxford produces quality books*
The text is: Oxford produces quality books
The count of characters is: 28
```

Program 6.19 Write a program to read multiple lines of text until a * is entered. Then count the number of characters, words, and lines in the text.

```
using namespace std;
#include<iostream>
int main()
{   char str[1000];
    int i = 0, word_count = 1, line_count = 1, char_count = 1;
    cout<<"\n Enter a * to end";
    cout<<"n **************";
    cout<<"\n Enter the text : ";
    str[i] = getchar();
    while(str[i] != '*')
    {   i++;
        str[i] = getchar();
    }
    str[i] = '\0';
    i = 0;
    while(str[i] != '\0')
```

```
    {   if(str[i] == '\n' || i==79)
            line_count++, word_count++;
        if(str[i] == ' ' &&str[i+1] != ' ')
            word_count++;
            char_count++;
        i++;
    }
    cout<<"\n The total count of words is: "<<word_count;
    cout<<"\n The total count of lines is: "<<line_count;
    cout<<"\n The total count of characters is: "<<char_count;
}
```

OUTPUT

```
Enter the text: Hello World
Welcome to the world of C++ programming
Enjoy reading this book
*
The total count of words is: 13
The total count of lines is: 4
The total count of characters is: 63
```

Program 6.20 Write a program to enter a text that has commas. Replace all the commas with semi colons and then display the text.

```
using namespace std;
#include<iostream>
int main()
{   char str[1000], copy_str[1000];
    int i = 0;
    cout<<"\n Enter the text : ";
    cin>>str;
    while(str[i] != '\0')
    {   if(str[i] == ',')
            copy_str[i] = ';';
        else
            copy_str[i] = str[i];
        i++;
    }
    copy_str[i] = '\0';
    cout<< "\n The copied text is : ";
    i = 0;
    while(copy_str[i] != '\0')
    {   cout<<copy_str[i];
        i++;
    }
}
```

OUTPUT

```
Enter the text : Oxford, University, Press,
The copied text is : Oxford; University; Press;
```

Program 6.21 Write a program to enter a text that contains multiple lines. Rewrite this text by printing line numbers before the text of the line starts.

```
using namespace std;
#include<iostream>
int main()
```

```
{   char str[1000];
    int i = 0, linecount = 1;
    cout<< "\n Enter a * to end";
    cout<< "\n **************";
    cout<< "\n Enter the text : ";
    str[i] = getchar();
    while(str[i] != '*')
    {   i++;
        str[i]=getchar();
    }
    str[i] = '\0';
    i=0;
    while(str[i] != '\0')
    {   if(linecount == 1 && i == 0)
            cout<< "\n "<<linecount<<" ";
        if(str[i] == '\n')
        {
            linecount++;
            cout<<"\n "<<linecount<<" ";
        }
        cout.put(str[i]);
        i++;
 }
}
```

OUTPUT

```
Enter a * to end
**************
Enter the text :
Oxford
University
Press
1 Oxford
2 University
3 Press
```

Program 6.22 Write a program to enter a text that contains multiple lines. Display the n lines of text starting from the mth line.

```
using namespace std;
#include<iostream>
int main()
{   char str[1000];
    int i = 0, m, n, j, linecount = 0;
    cout<<"\n Enter a * to end";
    cout<<"\n **************";
    cout<<"\n Enter the text : ";
    str[i] = getchar();
    while(str[i] != '*')
    {   i++;
        str[i] = getchar();
    }
    str[i] = '\0';
    cout<<"\n Enter the line number from which to copy : ";
    cin>>m;
```

```
    cout<<"\n Enter the line number till which to copy : ";
    cin>>n;
    i = 0;
    while(str[i] != '\0')
    {   if(linecount == m )
        {   j = i;
            while(n>0)
            {   cout.put(str[j]);
                j++;
                if(str[j] == '\n')
                {   n--;
                    linecount++;
                    cout<<"linecount<<\t";
                }
            }
        }
        else
        {   i++;
            if(str[i] == '\n')
                linecount++;
        }
    }
}
```

SAMPLE OUTPUT

```
Enter the text: Hello World
Welcome to the world of C++ programming
Enjoy reading this book
Bye*
Enter the line number from which to copy : 1
Enter the line number till which to copy : 3
Welcome to the world of C++ programming
Enjoy reading this book
Bye
```

Program 6.23 Write a program to extract the last N characters of a string.

```
using namespace std;
#include<iostream>
#include<string.h>
int main()
{   char str[100], substr[100];
    int i=0, j=0, n;
    cout<<"\n Enter the string : ";
    cin.getline(str,100);
    cout<<"\n Enter the number of characters to be copied: ";
    cin>>n;
    j = strlen(str) - n+1;
    while(str[j] != '\0')
    {   substr[i] = str[j];
        i++, j++;
    }
    substr[i] = '\0';
    cout<<"\n The substring is : ";
    puts(substr);
```

```
    return 0;
}
```

OUTPUT

```
Enter the string : Hi there
Enter the number of characters to be
copied : 5
The substring is : there
```

Program 6.24 Write a program to enter a text. Then enter a pattern and count the number of times the pattern is repeated in the text.

```
using namespace std;
#include<iostream>
main()
{   char str[200], pat[20];
    int i = 0, j = 0, found = 0, k, count = 0;
    cout<<"\n Enter the string : ";
    cin.getline(str,200);
    cout<<"\n Enter the pattern: ";
    cin.getline(pat,20);
    while(str[i]!='\0')
    {   j = 0, k = i;
        while(str[k]==pat[j] && pat[j]!='\0')
        {   k++;
            j++;
        }
        if(pat[j]=='\0')
        {   found=1;
            count++;
        }
        i++;
    }
    if(found==1)
        cout<<"\n PATTERN FOUND "<<count<<" TIMES";
    else
        cout<<"\n PATTERN NOT FOUND";
}
```

OUTPUT

```
Enter the string : She sells sea shells on the sea shore
Enter the pattern: sea
PATTERN FOUND 2 TIMES
```

Program 6.25 Write a program to find whether a string is palindrome or not.

```
using namespace std;
#include<iostream>
int main()
{   char str[100];
    int i = 0, j, length;
    cout<<"\n Enter the string : ";
    str[i] = getchar();
    while(str[i] != '*')
    {   i++;
        str[i]=getchar();
    }
```

```
    str[i] = '\0';
    length = i;
    i = 0;
    j = length - 1;
    while(i <= length/2)
    {   if(str[i] == str[j])
        {   i++;
            j--;
        }
        else
            break;
    }
    if(i>=j)
        cout<<"\n PALINDROME";
    else
        cout<<"\n NOT A PALINDROME";
}
```

OUTPUT

```
Enter the string : madam
PALINDROME
```

Program 6.26 Write a program to implement a quiz program.

```
using namespace std;
#include<iostream>
#include<string.h>
main()
{   char quest[5][100];
    char option1[3][20],option2[3][20],option3[3][20],option4[3][20], option5[3][20];
    int response[5], correct_ans[5], option, i, marks;
    strcpy(quest[0],"Name the capital of India");
    strcpy(option1[0],"1. Mumbai");
    strcpy(option1[1],"2. New Delhi");
    strcpy(option1[2],"3. Chennai");
    correct_ans[0] = 1;
    strcpy(quest[1],"Name the national bird of India");
    strcpy(option2[0],"1. Peacock");
    strcpy(option2[1],"2. Sparrow");
    strcpy(option2[2],"3. Parrot");
    correct_ans[1]=0;
    strcpy(quest[2],"Name the first prime minister of India");
    strcpy(option3[0],"1. M D Gandhi");
    strcpy(option3[1],"2. S D Sharma");
    strcpy(option3[2],"3. J L Nehru");
    correct_ans[2]=2;
    strcpy(quest[3],"Name the first female president of India");
    strcpy(option4[0],"1. Pratibha Patil");
    strcpy(option4[1],"2. Sonia Gandhi");
    strcpy(option4[2],"3. Indira Gandhi");
    correct_ans[3] = 0;
    strcpy(quest[4],"Name the youngest prime minister of India");
    strcpy(option5[0],"1. Rajiv Gandhi");
    strcpy(option5[1],"2. Sanjay Gandhi");
    strcpy(option5[2],"3. Rahul Gandhi");
    correct_ans[4] = 0;
```

```
do
{   cout<<"\n\n\n\n QUIZ PROGRAM";
    cout<<"\n*******************";
    cout<<"\n 1. Display Questions";
    cout<<"\n 2. Display Correct Answers";
    cout<<"\n 3. Display Result";
    cout<<"\n 4. EXIT";
    cout<<"\n ****************************";
    cout<<"\n\n\n Enter your option : ";
    cin>>option;
    switch(option)
    {   case 1:
            cout<<"\n"<<quest[0]<<"\n";
            for(i=0;i<3;i++)
                cout<<"\n "<<option1[i];
            cout<<"\n\n Enter your answer number : ";
            cin>>response[0];
            cout<<"\n"<<quest[1]<<"\n";
            for(i=0;i<3;i++)
                cout<<"\n"<<option2[i];
            cout<<"\n\n Enter your answer number : ";
            cin>>response[1];
            cout<<"\n"<<quest[2]<<"\n";
            for(i=0;i<3;i++)
                cout<<"\n"<<option3[i];
            cout<<"\n\n Enter your answer number : ";
            cin>>response[2];
            cout<<"\n"<<quest[3]<<"\n";
            for(i=0;i<3;i++)
                cout<<"\n"<<option4[i];
            cout<<"\n\n Enter your answer number : ";
            cin>>response[3];
            cout<<"\n"<<quest[4]<<"\n";
            for(i=0;i<3;i++)
                cout<<"\n"<<option5[i];
            cout<<"\n\n Enter your answer number : ";
            cin>>response[4];
            break;
        case 2:
            cout<<"\n\n CHECK THE CORRECT ANSWERS";
            cout<<"\n ******************************";
            cout<<"\n\n"<<quest[0]<<"\n"<<option1[correct_ans[0]];
            cout<<"\n\n"<<quest[1]<<"\n"<<option2[correct_ans[1]];
            cout<<"\n\n"<<quest[2]<<"\n"<<option3[correct_ans[2]];
            cout<<"\n\n"<<quest[3]<<"\n"<<option4[correct_ans[3]];
            cout<<"\n\n"<<quest[4]<<"\n"<<option5[correct_ans[4]];
            break;
        case 3:
                marks = 0;
                for(i=0;i<=4;i++)
                {   if(correct_ans[i]+1 == response[i])
                        marks++;
                }
                cout<<"\n Out of 5 you score"<<marks;
```

```
                break;
            }
    }while(option!=4);
}
```

OUTPUT

```
QUIZ PROGRAM
******************
1. Display Questions
2. Display Correct Answers
3. Display Result
4. EXIT
****************************
Name the capital of India"
1. Mumbai
2. New Delhi
3. Chennai
Enter your answer number :
```

Note The complete output for the program is very large. Here, we have just given the sample output.

Points to Remember

- A string is nothing but a null-terminated character array.
- A string is terminated with a null character (`'\0'`) to signify the end of the character array.
- A string is a character array from which individual characters can be accessed using a subscript that starts from zero.
- All the characters of a string array are stored in successive memory locations.
- A string can be read from the user by using four ways—using `cin`, `gets()`, `getline()` function or using `getchar()`function repeatedly.
- `cin` terminates as soon as it finds a blank space.
- The `gets()` takes the starting address of the string which will hold the input. The string inputted using `gets()` is automatically terminated with a null character.
- The string can also be read by calling the `getchar()` repeatedly to read a sequence of single characters, unless a terminating character is entered.
- A string can be displayed on the screen using three ways—using `cout`, using `puts()` function, or using `putchar()`function repeatedly.
- The number of characters in the string constitutes the length of the string.
- Appending one string to another string involves copying the contents of the source string at the end of the destination string. There is a library function `strcat(s1, s2)` that concatenates `s2` to `s1`. It is defined in `string.h`.
- Extracting a substring from a given string requires information about three things—the main string, the position of the first character of the substring in the given string, and the maximum number of characters or length of the substring.
- Index operation returns the position in the string where the string pattern first occurs.
- Replacement operation is used to replace the pattern P_1 by another pattern P_2.

Glossary

String An array of characters

String matching The problem of finding occurrences of a pattern string within another string

Substring A string u is a substring of a string v if v = v′uv″ for some prefix v′ and suffix v″

Exercises

Fill in the Blanks

1. Strings are ______.
2. Every string is terminated with a ______.
3. If a string is given as "AB CD", the length of this string is ______.
4. The subscript of a string starts with ______.
5. Characters of a string are stored in ______ memory locations.
6. `char mesg[100];` can store maximum ______ characters.
7. ______ function terminates as soon as it finds a blank space.
8. `LENGTH('')` = ______.
9. The ASCII code for `A-Z` varies from ______.
10. `toupper()` is used to ______.
11. `S1>S2`, means ______.
12. The function to reverse a string is ______.
13. If `S1 = "GOOD MORNING"`, then `Substr_Left(S1, 7) =` .
14. `INDEX("Welcome to the world of programming", "world") =` ______
15. ______ returns the position in the string where the string pattern first occurs.
16. The function `atoi()` is present in ______ header file.
17. `strncat` is used to ______.
18. `strcmp(str1, str2)` returns 1 if ______.
19. ______ function computes the length of a string.
20. Besides `putchar()`, ______ function can be used to print a line of text on the screen.

State True or False

1. A string Hello World can be read using `cin`.
2. Initializing a string as, `char str[] = "HELLO";` is incorrect as a null character has not been explicitly added.
3. The `gets()` takes the starting address of the string which will hold the input.
4. The `gets()` automatically appends a null character at the end of the string read from the keyboard.
5. `tolower()` is define in ctype.h header file.
6. Arithmetic operators can be applied to string variables.
7. String variables can be present either on the left or on the right side of the assignment operator.
8. If S_1 and S_2 are two strings, then concatenation operation produces a string which contains characters of S_2 followed by the characters of S_1.
9. Appending one string to another string involves copying the contents of the source string at the end of the destination string.
10. `S1<S2`, when in dictionary order `S1` precedes `S2`.
11. If `S1 = "GOOD MORNING"`, then `Substr_Right(S1, 5) = MORNING`.
12. Replace (`"AAABBBCCC", "X", "YYY"`) = `AAABBBCC`.
13. When a string is initialized during its declaration, the string must be explicitly terminated with a null character.
14. `strcmp("and","ant")` will return a positive value.
15. Assignment operator can be used to copy the contents of one string into another.

Multiple Choice Questions

1. `LENGTH('0')` =
   (a) –1 (b) 0
   (c) 1 (d) None of these
2. ASCII code for `a-z` ranges from
   (a) 0–26 (b) 35–81
   (c) 97–123 (d) None of these
3. Insert (`"XXXYYYZZZ", 1, "PPP"` =
   (a) `PPPXXXYYYZZZ` (b) `XPPPXXYYYZZZ`
   (c) `XXXYYYZZZPPP`
4. Delete (`"XXXYYYZZZ", 4, 3`) =
   (a) `XXYZ` (b) `XXXYYZZ`
   (c) `XXXYZZ`
5. If `str[] = "Welcome to the world of programming"`, then, `SUBSTRING(str, 15, 5)` =
   (a) world (b) programming
   (c) welcome (d) none of these
6. `strcat()` is defined in which header file?
   (a) `ctype.h` (b) `stdio.h`
   (c) `string.h` (d) `math.h`
7. Using which functions can a string be read?
   (a) `gets()` (b) `scanf()`
   (c) `getchar()` (d) all of these
8. Replace (`"XXXYYYZZZ", "XY", "AB"` =
   (a) `XXABYYZZZ` (b) `XABYYYZZZ`
   (c) `ABXXXYYYZZ`
9. The index of 'U' in Oxford University Press is?
   (a) 5 (b) 6
   (c) 7 (d) 8

10. `s1 = "HI"`, `s2 = "HELLO"`, and `s3 = "BYE"`. How can we concatenate the three strings?
(a) `strcat(s1,s2,s3)`
(b) `strcat(s1(strcat(s2,s3)))`
(c) `strcpy(s1, strcat(s2,s3))`

11. `strlen("Oxford University Press")` is _______?
(a) 22 (b) 23
(c) 24 (d) 25

12. Which function adds a string to the end of another string?
(a) `stradd()` (b) `strcat()`
(c) `strtok()` (d) `strcpy()`

Review Questions

1. What are strings? Discuss some operations that can be performed on strings.
2. Explain how strings are represented in main memory.
3. Explain string operations.
4. How are strings read from the standard input device? Explain the different function used to perform string input operation.
5. Explain how strings can be displayed on the screen.
6. Differentiate between `gets()` and `cin` for entering strings.
7. Explain the drawbacks of `getchar()` and `cin()`. Which function(s) can be used to overcome their shortcomings?
8. How can `putchar()` be used to print a string?
9. Differentiate between a character and a string.
10. Differentiate between a character array and a string.
11. List all the substrings that can be formed from the string "ABCD".
12. Write a short note on array of strings.
13. How is an array of strings represented in the memory?
14. Explain how an array of strings is stored in the main memory with an example.
15. If substring function is given as `SUBSTRING(string, position, length)`, find `S(5,9)` if `S = "Welcome to world of C++ Programming"`
16. If `iIndex` function is given as `INDEX(text, pattern)`, find the `index(T, P)` where `T = "Welcome to world of C++ Programming"` and `P = "of"`.

Programming Exercises

1. Write a program in which a string is passed as an argument to a function.
2. Write a program to concatenate first n characters of a string to another string.
3. Write a program that compares first n characters of one string with first n characters of another string.
4. Write a program that reads your name and displays the ASCII value of each character in your name on a separate line.
5. Write a program that removes leading and trailing spaces from a string.
6. Write a program to read a word and rewrite its characters in alphabetical order.
7. Write a program that accepts an integer value from 0 to 999. Display the value of the number read in words. If the user enters 753, then print seven hundred fifty three.
8. Write a program to insert a word before a given word in the text.
9. Write a program to read a name and then display it in abbreviated form, like Janak Raj Thareja should be displayed as JRT.
10. Write a program to read a name and then display it in abbreviated form, like Janak Raj Thareja should be displayed as J.R. Thareja.
11. Write a program that replaces a given character with another character in the string.
12. Write a program to display the given string array in reverse order.
13. Write a program to count the number of characters, words, and lines in the given text.
14. Write a program to count the number of digits, upper case characters, lower case characters, and special characters in a given string.
15. Write a program to count the total number of occurrences of a given character in the string.
16. Write a program to accept a text. Count and display the number of times the word "the" appears in the text.
17. Write a program to count the total number of occurrences of a word in the text.
18. Write a program to find the last instance of occurrence of a sub-string within a string.
19. Write a program to insert a sub-string in the middle of a given string.
20. Write a program to input an array of strings. Then reverse the string in the format shown below.

"HAPPY BIRTHDAY TO YOU" should be displayed as "YOU TO BIRTHDAY HAPPY"

21. Write a program to append a given string in the following format. "GOOD MORNING MORNING GOOD""

22. Write a program to input a text of at least two paragraphs. Interchange the first and second paragraphs and then re-display the text on screen.

23. Write a program to input a text of at least two paragraphs. Construct an array PAR such that PAR[I] contains the location of the Ith paragraph in TEXT.

24. Write a menu driven program that demonstrates the use of string functions present in the string.h header file.

25. Write a menu-driven program that demonstrates the use of character handling functions present in the ctype.h header file.

26. Write a program to extract the first n characters of a string.

27. Write a program to extract the substring from a given string.

28. Write a program to read a text, delete all the semi-colons it has and finally replace all '.' with a ','.

29. Write a program to copy the last n characters of a character array in another character array. Convert the lower case letters into upper case letters while copying.

30. Write a program to copy n characters of a character array from the mth position in another character array.

31. Write a program to copy a character array in another character array.

32. Write a program to sort names of students.

33. Write a program to read a sentence until a '.' is entered.

34. Write a program to read a sentence. Then count the number of words in the sentence

35. Write a program to read multiple lines of text until a * is entered. Count the number of characters, words, and lines in the text.

36. Write a program to display a list of candidates. Prompt 100 users to cast their vote. Finally display the winner in the elections.

37. Write a program to delete the last character of a string.

38. Write a program to delete the first character of a string.

39. Write a program to count the number of times a given character appears in the string.

Find the errors in the following codes

1.
```
main()
{   char str1[] = "Programming";
    char str2[] = "In C++";
    str1 = str2;
    cout<<str1;
}
```

2.
```
main()
{   char str[] = {'H','e','l','l','o'};
    cout<<str;
}
```

3.
```
main()
{   char str[5] = ""HELLO";
    cout<<str;
}
```

4.
```
main()
{   char str[10];
    strncpy(str, "HELLO", 3);
    cout<<str;
}
```

5.
```
main()
{   char str[10];
    strcpy(str, "Oxford University Press");
    cout<<str;
}
```

6.
```
main()
{   char str[]= "Oxford University Press";
  if(strstr(str, "Uni") == 0)
     cout<<"\n Substring Found";
}
```

7.
```
main()
{ char str1[10], str2[10];
  gets(str1, str2);
  cout<<"\n str1 = <<str1<<" and str2 =
  "<<str2;
}
```

Find the output of the following codes

1.
```
main()
{ char str1[]= {'H', 'I'};
  char str2[] = {'H', 'I', '\0'};
  if(strcmp(str1, str2) == 0)
     cout<<"\n The strings are equal";
  else
     cout<<"\n Strings are not equal";
}
```

2.
```
main()
{ char str[]= "Programming in C";
  int i;
  while(str[i]!='\0')
  {   if(i%2==0)
        cout<<str[i];
```

```
        i++;
    }
}
3. main()
{   char ch = 'k';
    cout<<(char)ch+10;
}
4. main()
{   char str1[] = "Programming";
    char str2[] = "Is Fun";
    strcpy(str1, str2);
    cout<<str1;
}
5. main()
{   char str1[] = "Programming";
    char str2[] = "Is Fun";
    strncpy(str1, str2, 3);
    cout<<str1;
}
6. main()
{   char str1[] = "Programming";
    char str2[] = "Project";
    cout<<strncmp(str1, str2, 3);
}
7. main()
{   char str[] = "Oxford University Press";
    cout<<strstr(str, "Uni");
}
```

Answers

Fill in the Blanks

1. null-terminated character arrays; **2.** null character; **3.** 5; **4.** zero; **5.** consecutive; **6.** 99; **7.** scanf(); **8.** zero; **9.** 65-91; **10.** convert a character into upper case; **11.** when in dictionary order S1 will come after S2; **12.** strrev(); **13.** ORNING; **14.** 15; **15.** index; **16.** stdlib.h; **17.** append the string pointed to by str2 to the end of the string pointed by str 1, **18.** if str1 is greater than str2 respectively; **19.** strlen(); **20.** puts()

State True or False

1. False **2.** False **3.** True **4.** True **5.** True **6.** False **7.** False **8.** False
9. False **10.** True **11.** True **12.** False **13.** True **14.** False **15.** False

Multiple Choice Questions

1. (b); **2.** (c); **3.** (b); **4.** (c); **5.** (a); **6.** (c); **7.** (d); **8.** (a); **9.** (c); **10.** (b); **11.** (b); **12.** (b)

CHAPTER 7

Pointers

KEY Concepts

- Understanding the computer's memory • Pointer declaration • Pointer arithmetic • Null pointers • Generic pointers • Passing arguments to functions using pointers • Pointers and arrays • Pointers and strings • Array of pointers • Pointer to functions • Pointer to pointers • Constant pointer • Pointer to constants • Constant pointer to a constant • Dynamic memory allocation • `New` and `delete` operators

UNDERSTANDING COMPUTER'S MEMORY

Every computer has a primary memory. All our data and programs need to be placed in the primary memory for execution. The primary memory or random access memory (RAM), which is a part of the primary memory is a collection of memory locations (often known as cells) and each location has a specific address. Each memory location is capable of storing one byte of data. Although recent versions of computers are able to store two bytes of data, in this book, we discuss about locations storing one byte of data. Therefore, a `char` type data needs just one memory location and an `int` type data needs two memory locations. Similarly, `float` and `double` type data need four and eight memory locations, respectively.

Generally, a computer has three areas of memory, each of which is used for a specific task. These areas of memory include stack, heap, and global memory.

Stack

A fixed size of stack is allocated by the system and is filled as needed from the bottom to the top, one element at a time. These elements can be removed from the top to the bottom by removing one element at a time. That is, the last element added to the stack is removed first.

When a program has used the variables or data stored in the stack, it can be discarded to enable the stack to be used for other programs to store its data. We have already discussed briefly about the system stack in Functions (Chapter 4) when we discussed the concept of recursion. You will read more about them under Data Structures.

Note Stack is the section of memory that is allocated for automatic variables within functions.

Heap

Heap is a contiguous block of memory that is used by a program when the need arises. A fixed size heap is allocated by the system and is used in a random fashion. Therefore, there is no particular fashion for using the heap.

The addresses of the memory locations in heap that are not currently allocated to the program for use are stored in a free list. When the program requests a block of memory, the dynamic allocation technique (discussed in the end of the chapter) carves out a block from the heap and assigns it to the program.

When the program has finished using that block, it returns that memory block to the heap and the location of the memory in that block is added to the free list.

When compared with heaps, a stack is faster but also smaller and expensive. When a program begins execution with the `main()`, all variables declared within `main()` are allocated space on the stack. Moreover, all the parameters passed to the called function will be stored on the stack.

Global Memory (Data Area)

The block of code that is the `main()` program (along with other functions in the program) is stored in the global memory. The memory in the global area is allocated randomly to store the code of different functions in the program in such a way that one function is not contiguous to another. Besides the function code, all global variables declared in the program are stored in the global memory area.

Other Memory Layouts

C++ provides some more memory areas such as text segment, BSS (the segment that stores uninitialized variables and constants), and shared library segment. These are as follows.

- The text segment is used to store the machine instructions corresponding to the compiled program. This is generally a read-only memory segment. Some books also refer the text segment as the 'code area' as this is the area where the program code is stored.
- BSS is used to store uninitialized global variables.
- Shared libraries segment contains the executable image of shared libraries that are being used by the program.

7.1 DEFINING POINTERS

Every variable has a name and a value associated with it. When a variable is declared, a specific block of memory within the computer is allocated to hold the value of that variable. The size of the allocated block depends on the type of the data. We have already seen a program in Chapter 2 that displays the size of various data types on your system. Note the size of integer may vary from one system to another. For example, on 32-bit systems, the integer variable is allocated four bytes, while on 16-bit systems, it is allocated two bytes.

Consider the following statement.

```
int x = 10;
```

When this statement executes, the compiler sets two bytes of memory aside to hold the value `10`. It also sets up a symbol table in which it adds the symbol `x` and the relative address in memory where those two bytes were set aside.

Therefore, every variable in C++ has a value and a memory location (commonly known as address) associated with it. Some texts use the terms `rvalue` and `lvalue` for the value and the address of the variable, respectively.

The `rvalue` appears on the right side of the assignment statement (i.e. `10` in the statement) and cannot be used on the left side of the assignment statement. Therefore, writing `10 = k;` is illegal.

If we write

```
int x, y;
x = 10;
y = x;
```

Then, in this code, we have two integer variables `x` and `y`. The compiler reserves the memory for integer variable `x` and stores the `rvalue 10` in it. When we say `y=x`, then `x` is interpreted as its `rvalue` (since it is on the right hand side of the assignment operator '='). Therefore, here, `x` refers to the value stored at the memory location set aside for `x`, in this `case 10`. After this statement is executed, the `rvalue` of `y` is also `10`.

Pointers are nothing but memory addresses. A pointer is a variable that contains the memory location of another variable. Therefore, a pointer is a variable that represents the location of a data item, such as a variable or an array element. Hence, we discuss addresses and values in this context. Pointers are used frequently used in C++ as they have a number of useful applications. These applications include the following.

- Pointers are used to pass information back and forth between a function and its reference point.
- Pointers enable programmers to return multiple data items from a function through function arguments.
- Pointers provide an alternate way to access individual elements of the array.
- Pointers are used to pass arrays and strings as function arguments.
- Pointers enable references to functions; therefore, with pointers, the programmer can even pass functions as argument to another function.
- Pointers are used to create complex data structures such as trees, linked lists, linked stacks, linked queues, and graphs.
- Pointers are used for dynamic memory allocation of a variable.

7.2 DECLARING POINTER VARIABLES

A pointer provides access to a variable by using the address of that variable. A pointer variable is, therefore, a variable that stores the address of another variable. The general syntax of declaring pointer variables can be given as follows:

```
data_type *ptr_name;
```

Here, `data_type` is the data type of the value that the pointer will point to. For example,

```
int *pnum;
char *pch;
float *pfnum;
```

Programming Tip: The data type of the pointer varaible and the variable to which it points must be the same.

In each of the statements, a pointer variable is declared to point to a variable of the specified data type. Although all these pointers—`pnum`, `pch`, and `pfnum` point to different data types, they occupy the same amount of space in memory. The extent of space they occupy will depend on the platform wherc the code is going to run. To verify this, execute the following code and observe the result.

Example 7.1 Exploring the size of pointer variables

```
using namespace std;
#include<iostream>
main()
{       int *pnum;
        char *pch;
        float *pfnum;
        double *pdnum;
        long *plnum;
        cout<<"\n Size of integer pointer = "<<sizeof(pnum);
        cout<<"\n Size of character pointer = "<<sizeof(pch);
        cout<<"\n Size of float pointer = "<<sizeof(pfnum);
        cout<<"\n Size of double pointer = "<< sizeof(pdnum);
        cout<<"\n Size of long pointer = "<< sizeof(plnum);
}
```

OUTPUT

```
Size of integer pointer = 2
Size of character pointer = 2
Size of float pointer = 2
Size of double pointer = 2
Size of long pointer = 2
```

Explanation: Hence, we see that all pointer variables irrespective of the type of data they point, occupy exactly the same amount of space in memory.

Now, let us declare an integer pointer variable and start using it in our program code.

```
int x= 10;
int *ptr;
ptr = &x;
```

Programming Tip: A pointer variable can store only address of a variable

In the statement, `ptr` is the name of pointer variable. The `'*'` informs the compiler that `ptr` is a pointer variable and the `int` specifies that it will store the address of an integer variable. An integer pointer variable, therefore, `"points to"` an integer variable and thus stores the address of an integer variable. In the last statement, `ptr` is assigned the address of `x`. The `&` operator retrieves the `lvalue` (address) of `x` and copies that to the contents of the pointer `ptr`.

Consider the memory cells given in Fig. 7.1.

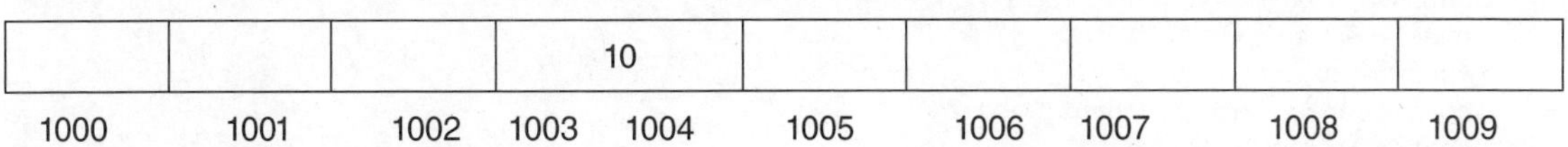

Figure 7.1 Memory representation

Now, since `x` is an integer variable, it will be allocated two bytes. Assuming that the compiler assigns the memory locations `1003` and `1004`, we say the value of `x = 10` and the address of `x` (written as `&x`) is equal to `1003`, that is the starting address of `x` in the memory. When we write, `ptr = &x`, then `ptr = 1003`.

Note Pointers are not allowed to store memory addresses, but they can store only the addresses of variables of a given type. Therefore, writing a statement like int `*ptr = 1000;` is absolutely illegal.

Programming Tip: The address of a memory location is a pointer constant; therefore, it cannot be changed in the program code.

We can dereference a pointer, that is refer to the value of the variable to which it points by using unary `'*'` operator (also known as indirection or the dereference operator) as in `*ptr`. That is, `*ptr = 10`, since `10` is value of `x`. Therefore, * is equivalent to writing `value at address`.

Example 7.2 Illustrating the use of pointer variable

```
using namespace std;
#include<iostream>
int main()
{    int num, *pnum;
     pnum = &num;
     cout<<"\n Enter the number : ";
     cin>>num;
     cout<<"\n The number that was entered is : "<<*pnum;
     cout<<"\n The address of number in memory is : "<< &num;
}
```

OUTPUT

```
Enter the number : 10
The number that was entered is : 10
The address of number in memory is : FFDC
```

Note `%p` control string prints the argument as a memory address in hexadecimal form. `%u` prints the memory address in decimal form.

Programming Tip: A pointer variable cannot be assigned the value of the variable to which it points

Can you tell the value of `*(&num)`? Yes, it is equivalent to writing simply num. The indirection and address operators are the inverse of each other, and when combined in an expression, they cancel each other. For example, if num = 10 and address of num = 1000. Then &num = 1000 and the value stored at 1000 is 10. Therefore, *(&num) = *(1000) = 10, which is equal to num itself.

We can also assign values to variables using pointer variables and modify the value.

Example 7.3 Assigning values to pointer variables

```
using namespace std;
#include<iostream>
int main()
{    int num, *pnum;
     pnum = &num;
     *pnum = 10;
     cout<<"\n *pnum = "<<*pnum;
     cout<<"\n num = "<<num;
     *pnum  = *pnum + 1; // increments the value of num
     cout<<"\n After increment *pnum = "<<*pnum;
     cout<<"\n After increment num = "<<num;
}
```

OUTPUT

```
*pnum = 10
num = 10
After increment *pnum = 11
After increment num = 11
```

Now find the output of the following code.

Example 7.4 Printing the values and addresses of pointer variables

```
using namespace std;
#include<iostream>
int main()
{   int num, *pnum1, *pnum2;
    pnum1 = &num;
    *pnum1 = 10;
    pnum2 = pnum1;
    cout<<"\n Value of num using all three variables (num, *pnum1, *pnum2) = "<< num<<" "<<
    *pnum1<<"  "<< *pnum2;
    cout<<"\n Address of num using all three variables (&num, pnum1, pnum2) = ";
    cout.setf(ios::hex);
    cout<<&num <<"  "<< pnum1<<"  "<< pnum2;
}
```

OUTPUT

```
Value of num using all three variables (num, *pnum1, *pnum2) = 10 10 10
Address of num using all three variables (&num, pnum1, pnum2)
= 0x0012ff50 0x0012ff50 0x0012ff50
```

Programming Tip: It is an error to assign address of a variable to another variable of the same type. The variable to which the adddress is being assigned must be declared as a pointer variable.

Explanation: While the first `cout` statement prints the value of `num`, the second `cout` statement will print the address of `num`. The third cout statement shows the three different ways to refer to the value and address of the same variable. Note that any number of pointers can point to the same address. Hence, the output displays the value and address of `num` using all three variables.

The address of a variable is the address of the first byte occupied by that variable. Basically, the address of the variable is the relative location of the variable with respect to the program's memory space. We cannot change the address of a variable; we can only use them. Although the address of a variable cannot be changed, the variable's address may change during different program runs. That is, if you try to print the address of `num` today, it may print `4010`. When you run the program after a day, it may print the address as `FA12`.

Note that the data type of the pointer variable and the variable whose address it will store must be of the same type. Therefore, the following code is not valid.

```
int x = 10;
float y = 2.0;
int *px;
float *py;
px = &y;          //INVALID
py = &x;          //INVALID
```

Note that it is not necessary that the pointer variable will point to the same variable throughout the program. It can point to any variable as long as the data type of the pointer variable is same as that of the variable it points to. The following code illustrates this concept.

Example 7.5 Pointer variable pointing to different data of the same type

```
using namespace std;
#include<iostream>
main()
{   int a=3, b=5;
    int *pnum;
    pnum = &a;//pnum is pointing to a
    cout<<"\n a = "<<*pnum;
    pnum = &b; //pnum is pointing to b
    cout<<"\n b = "<<*pnum;
}
```

OUTPUT

```
a = 3
b = 5
```

Note Using a uninitialized pointer can cause unpredictable results.

7.3 POINTER EXPRESSIONS AND POINTER ARITHMETIC

Like other variables, pointer variables can also be used in expressions. For example, if `ptr1` and `ptr2` are pointers, the following statements are valid:

```
int num1=2, num2= 3, sum=0, mul=0, div=1;
int *ptr1, *ptr2;
ptr1 = &num1;
ptr2 = &num2;

sum = *ptr1 + *ptr2;
mul = sum * *ptr1;
*ptr2 +=1;
div = 9 + *ptr1/*ptr2 - 30;
```

Programming Tip: A pointer variable that is declared but not initialzed contains garbage value. Hence, such a pointer variable must not be used before it is assigned any variable's address.

The programmer may add integers to or subtract integers from pointers as well as subtract one pointer from the other. We can also use short-hand operators (such as +=, −=, etc.) with the pointers variables as we use with other variables.

C++ also allows comparing pointers by using relational operators in the expressions. For example, `p1 > p2, p1==p2,` and `p1!=p2` are all valid in C++.

When using pointers, unary increment `(++)` and decrement `(--)` operators have greater precedence than the dereference operator `(*)`. However, both these operators have a special behaviour when used as a suffix. In that case, the expression is evaluated with the value it had before being increased. Therefore, the expression

```
*ptr++
```

is equivalent to `*(ptr++)` as `++` has greater operator precedence than `*`. Therefore, the expression will increase the value of `ptr` so that it now points to the next element. This means the statement `*ptr++` does not do the intended task. Therefore, to increment the value of the variable whose address is stored in `ptr`, you should write

```
(*ptr)++
```

Consider another C++ statement:

```
int num1=2, num2=3;
int *p = &num1, *q=&num2;
*p++ = *q++;
```

What will `*p++ = *q++` do? As ++ has a higher precedence than *, both `p` and `q` are increased; however, as the increment operators (++) are used as postfix and not prefix, the value assigned to `*p` is `*q` before both p and q are increased. Then, both values are increased. Therefore, the statement is equivalent to writing:

```
*p = *q;
++p; ++q;
```

Programming Tip: It is an error to subtract two pointer variables.

Let us now summarize the rules for pointer operations:

- A pointer variable can be assigned the address of another variable (of the same type).
- A pointer variable can be assigned the value of another pointer variable (of the same type).
- A pointer variable can be initialized with a `NULL` (or `0`) value.
- Prefix or postfix increment and decrement operators can be applied on a pointer variable.
- An integer value can added to or subtracted from a pointer variable.
- A pointer variable can be compared with another pointer variable of the same type using relational operators.
- A pointer variable cannot be multiplied by a constant.
- A pointer variable cannot be added to another pointer variable.

Program 7.1 Write a program to print Hello world using pointers.

```
using namespace std;
#include<iostream>
int main()
{      char *ch = "Programming in C++ is fun";
       cout<<ch;
}
```

OUTPUT

```
Programming in C++ is fun
```

Program 7.2 Write a program to add two floating point numbers.

```
using namespace std;
#include<iostream>
int main()
{      float num1, num2, sum = 0.0;
       float *pnum1 = &num1, *pnum2 = &num2, *psum = &sum;
       cout<<"\n Enter the two numbers : ";
       cin>>*pnum1>>*pnum2;           // pnum1 = &num1;
       *psum = *pnum1 + *pnum2;
       cout<<"\n "<<*pnum1<<" + "<<*pnum2<<" = "<<*psum;
}
```

OUTPUT

```
Enter the two numbers : 2.5 3.4
2.5 + 3.4 = 5.9
```

Program 7.3 Write a program to find the biggest of three numbers.

```
using namespace std;
#include<iostream>
int main()
{       int num1, num2, num3;
        int *pnum1 = &num1, *pnum2= &num2, *pnum3= &num3;
        cout<<"\n Enter the three numbers : ";
        cin>>*pnum1>>*pnum2>>*pnum3;
        if(*pnum1 > *pnum2  &&  *pnum1 > *pnum3)
            cout<<"\n "<<*pnum1<<" is the largest number";
        if(*pnum2 > *pnum1  &&  *pnum2 > *pnum3)
            cout<<"\n "<<*pnum3<<" is the largest number";
        else
            cout<<"\n "<<*pnum3<<" is the largest number";
}
```

OUTPUT

```
Enter the three numbers : 5  7  3
7 is the largest number
```

7.4 NULL POINTERS

So far, we have studied that pointer variable is a pointer to some other variable of the same data type. However, in some cases we may prefer to have null pointer which is a special pointer value that is known not to point anywhere. This means that a `NULL` pointer does not point to any valid memory address.

To declare a `null` pointer, you may use the predefined constant `NULL`, which is defined in several standard header files, including `<stdio.h>`, `<stdlib.h>`, and `<string.h>`. After including any of these files in your program, just write the following:

```
int *ptr = NULL;
```

You can always check whether a given pointer variable stores address of some variable or contains a null by writing,

```
if ( ptr == NULL)
{       Statement block;
}
```

> **Programming Tip:** It is a logic error to dereference a NULL pointer.

You may also initialize a pointer as a `NULL` pointer by using a constant `0`, like

```
int ptr,
ptr = 0;
```

This is a valid statement in C++, as even `NULL`, which is a preprocessor macro typically has the value or replacement text `0`. However, to avoid ambiguity, it is always better to use `NULL` to declare a null pointer.

> **Programming Tip:** A compiler error will be generated if you assign a pointer of one type to a pointer of another type without a cast.

A function that returns pointer values can return a null pointer when it is unable to perform its task.

Null pointers are used in situations when one or more pointers in the program points to different locations at different times. In such situations, it is always better to set it to a `null` pointer when it does not point anywhere valid, and to test to see if it is a null pointer before using it.

Note A run-time error is generated if you try to dereference a null pointer.

7.5 GENERIC POINTERS

A generic pointer is a pointer variable that has `void` as its data type. The void pointer, or the generic pointer is a special type of pointer that can be pointed at variables of any data type. It is declared like a normal pointer variable but uses the `void` keyword as the pointer's data type. For example,

```
void *ptr;
```

Programming Tip: A pointer variable of type void * cannot be dereferenced.

In C++, since you cannot have a variable of type `void`, the void pointer will, therefore, not point to any data and thus, cannot be dereferenced. You need to cast a void pointer (generic pointer) to another kind of pointer before using it.

Generic pointers are often used when you want a pointer to point to data of different types at different times. For example, look at the code given here.

Example 7.6 Using a `void` pointer.

```
using namespace std;
#include<iostream>
int main()
{       int x=10;
        char ch = 'A';
        void *gp;
        gp = &x;
        cout<<"\n Generic pointer points to the integer value = "<< *(int*)gp;
        gp = &ch;
        cout<<"\n Generic pointer now points to the character "<< *(char*)gp;
}
```

OUTPUT

```
Generic pointer points to the integer value = 10
Generic pointer now points to the character = A
```

Explanation: It is always recommended to avoid using void pointers unless absolutely necessary, as they effectively allow you to avoid type checking.

7.6 PASSING ARGUMENTS TO FUNCTION USING POINTERS

In Chapter 4, we have learnt the call by value method of passing parameters to a function. Using call by value method, it is impossible to modify the actual parameters in the call when you pass them to a function. Furthermore, the incoming arguments to a function are treated as local variables in the function and those local variables get a copy of the values passed from their caller.

Programming Tip: When using pointers to pass arguments to a function, the calling function must pass addresses of the variables as arguments and the called function must dereference the arguments to use them in the function body for processing.

Pointers provide a mechanism to modify data declared in one function using code written in another function. In other words, if data is declared in `func1()` and we want to write code in `func2()` that modifies the data in `func1()`, then we must pass the addresses of the variables we want to change.

The calling function sends the addresses of the variables and the called function must declare those incoming arguments as pointers. In order to modify the variables sent by the caller, the called function must dereference the pointers that were passed to it. Therefore, passing pointers to a function avoids the overhead of copying data from one function to another. Hence, to use pointers for passing arguments to a function, the programmer must do the following:

- Declare the function parameters as pointers.
- Use the dereferenced pointers in the function body.
- Pass the addresses as the actual argument when the function is called.

Note It is an error to return a pointer to a local variable in the called function, because when the function terminates, its memory may be allocated to a different program.

Let us write some programs that pass pointer variables as parameters to functions.

Program 7.4 Write a program to add two integers using functions.

```
using namespace std;
#include<iostream>
void sum( int *a, int *b, int *t);
int main()
{       int num1, num2, total;
        cout<<"\n Enter the two numbers : ";
        cin>>num1>>num2;
        sum(&num1, &num2, &total);
        cout<<"\n Total = "<<total;
}
void sum ( int *a, int *b, int *t)
{       *t = *a + *b;
}
```

OUTPUT

```
Enter the two numbers : 2  3
Total = 5
```

Program 7.5 Write a program to calculate the area of a triangle.

```
using namespace std;
#include<iostream>
void read(float *b, float *h);
void calculate_area(float *b, float *h, float *a);
int main()
{       float base, height, area;
        read(&base, &height);
        calculate_area(&base, &height, &area);
        cout<<"\n Area of the triangle with base "<<base<<" and height "<<height<<" = "
<<area;
}
void read(float *b, float *h)
{       cout<<"\n Enter the base and height of the triangle : ";
        cin>>*b>>*h;
}
void calculate_area( float *b, float *h, float *a)
{       *a = 0.5 * (*b) * (*h);
}
```

OUTPUT

```
Enter the base and height of the triangle : 10  5
Area of the triangle with base 10.0 and height 5.0 = 25.00
```

Hence, we see that functions usually return only one value. Pointers can be used to return more than one value to the calling function. This is done by allowing the arguments to be passed by address which enables the function to alter the values pointed to and therefore, return more than one value.

7.7 POINTERS AND ARRAYS

The concept of array is very much bound to that of pointer. An array occupies consecutive memory locations (refer to Fig. 7.2). For example, if we have an array declared as,

```
int arr[] = {1, 2, 3, 4, 5};
```

then, in memory it would be as represented in Fig. 7.2.

Array notation is a form of pointer notation. The name of the array is the starting address of the array in memory. It is also known as the `base address`. In other words, `base address` is the address

arr[0]	arr[1]	arr[2]	arr[3]	arr[4]
1000	1002	1004	1006	1008

Figure 7.2 Memory representation of `arr[]`

of the first element in the array or the address of `arr[0]`. Now, let us use a pointer variable as given in the statement here.

```
int *ptr;
ptr = &arr[0];
```

Here, `ptr` is made to point to the first element of the array. Execute the code given here and observe the output to clarify the concept.

Example 7.7 Pointer to the first element of the array

```
using namespace std;
#include<iostream>
main()
{       int arr[]={1,2,3,4,5};
        cout<<"\n Address of array = ";
        cout.setf(ios::hex);
        cout<<arr<<"  "<<&arr[0]<<"  "<< &arr;
}
```

OUTPUT

```
Address of array = 0x0012ff40 0x0012ff40 0x0012ff40
```

Programming Tip: The name of the array is actually a pointer that points to the first element of the array.

Similarly, writing `ptr = &arr[2]`, makes `ptr` to point to the third element of the array, that has index `2`. Figure 7.3 shows `ptr` pointing to the third element of the array.

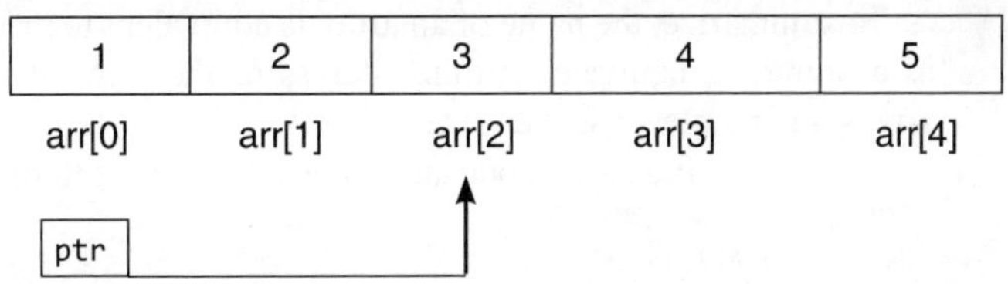

Figure 7.3 `ptr` pointing to the third element of the array

If the pointer variable `ptr` holds the address of the first element in the array, then the address of successive element can be calculated by writing, `ptr++`.

Programming Tip: An error is generated if an attempt is made to change the address of the array.

```
int *ptr = &arr[0];
ptr++;
cout<<"\n The value of the second element of the array is "<<*ptr;
```

The `cout` will print the value `2` because after being incremented, `ptr` points to the next location. One point to note here is that if `x` is an integer variable, then `x++`, adds `1` to the value of x. However, as `ptr` is a pointer variable, when we write `ptr + i`, then adding `i` gives a pointer that points `i` elements further along an array than the original pointer.

Since `++ptr` and `ptr++` are equivalent to `ptr + 1`, incrementing a pointer using the unary ++ operator increments the address it stores by the amount given by `sizeof(type)` where `type` is the data type of the variable it points to (i.e. `2` for an integer).

For example, if `ptr` originally points to `arr[2]`, then `ptr++` will make it to point to the next element, that is, `arr[3]` as shown in Fig. 7.4.

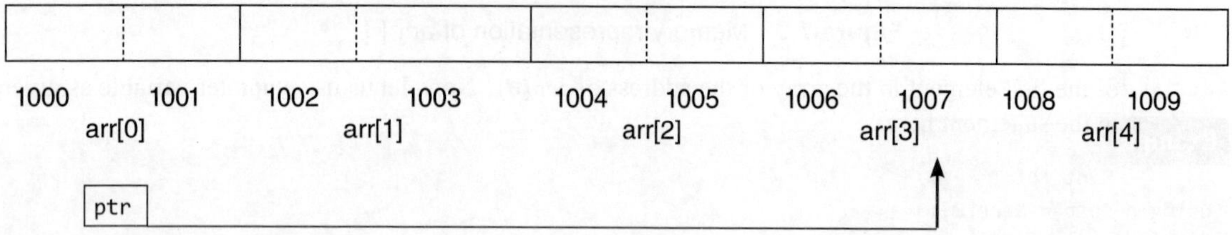

Figure 7.4 `ptr` pointing to the fourth element of the array

It can be noted here that if it had been a character array, every byte in the memory would have been used to store an individual character. `ptr++` would then add only one byte to the address of ptr.

When using pointers, an expression like `arr[i]` is equivalent to writing `*(arr+i)`. If `arr` is the array name, then the compiler implicitly takes `arr = &arr[0]`.

> **Programming Tip:** When an array is passed to a function, we are actually passing a pointer to the function. Therefore, in the function declaration you must declare a pointer to receive the array name.

To print the value of the third element of the array, we can straightaway use the expression `*(arr+2)`. Note that `arr[i] = *(arr + i)`

Many beginners get confused by thinking of array name as a pointer. For example, while we can write

```
ptr = arr;          // that is ptr = &arr[0]
we cannot write
arr = ptr;
```

This is because while `ptr` is a variable, `arr` is a constant. That is, the location at which the first element of `arr` will be stored cannot be changed once `arr[]` has been declared. Therefore, an array name is often known to be a constant pointer.

To summarize, the name of an array is equivalent to the address of its first element, as a pointer is equivalent to the address of the element that it points to. Therefore, arrays and pointers use the same concept.

Look at the following code and understand the result of executing them.

> **Note** Expressions such as `arr[i]`, `i[arr]`, `*(arr+i)` and `*(i+arr)` give the same value.

Example 7.8 To illustrate that array name is same as address of its first element

```
using namespace std;
#include<iostream>
main()
{       int arr[]={1,2,3,4,5};          // array
        int *ptr, i;
        ptr=&arr[2];        // pointer to third element of the array
        *ptr = -1;
        *(ptr+1) = 0;          // modifying value of fourth element of the array using pointer
        *(ptr-1) = 1;          // modifying value of second element of the array using pointer
```

```
        cout<<"\n Array is : ";
        for(i=0;i<5;i++)
                cout<<"    "<<*(arr+i);
}
```

OUTPUT

```
Array is :   1  1  -1  0  5
```

Therefore, in C++, we can add or subtract an integer from a pointer to get a new pointer, pointing somewhere other than the original position. C++ also permits addition and subtraction of two pointer variables. For example, look at the code given here.

Example 7.9 Addition and subtraction of pointer variables

```
using namespace std;
#include<iostream>
main()
{       int arr[]={1,2,3,4,5,6,7,8,9};
        int *ptr1,  *ptr2;
        ptr1 = arr;
        ptr2 = ptr1 + 2;
        cout<<ptr2 -ptr1;
}
```

OUTPUT

```
2
```

Explanation: In the code, `ptr1` and `ptr2` are pointers pointing to the elements of the same array. We may subtract two pointers as long as they point to the same array. Here, the output is `2` because there are two elements between `ptr1` and `ptr2` in the array `arr`.

Note that both pointers must point into the same array or one past the end of the array, otherwise, the behaviour is undefined.

Moreover, C++ also allows pointer variables to be compared with each other. Obviously, if two pointers are equal, then they point to the same location in the array. However, if one pointer is less than the other, it means that the pointer points to some element nearer to the front of the array. As in other variables, relational operators (`>`, `>=`, etc.) can also be applied to pointer variables (refer Table 7.1). This can be understood from the code given here.

Example 7.10 To display an array of given numbers from 1 to 9

```
using namespace std;
#include<iostream>
main()
{       int arr[]={1,2,3,4,5,6,7,8,9};
        int *ptr1, *ptr2;
        ptr1 = arr; // ptr1 pointing to the first element of the array
        ptr2 = &arr[8]; // ptr2 pointing to the last element of the array
        while(ptr1<=ptr2)
        {       cout<<"  "<<*ptr1;
                ptr1++;
        }
}
```

OUTPUT

```
1 2 3 4 5 6 7 8 9
```

Note An object is a named region of storage; an `lvalue` is an expression referring to an object

Table 7.1 Pointer arithmetic

Operation	Condition	Declaration	Description
Assignment	Pointers must be of the same type.	`int *ptr1, *ptr2;`	If we write, `*ptr1=*ptr2`, then both the pointers point to the same location.
Addition of an integer	..	`int i, *ptr;`	If we write, `ptr+i`, then `ptr` will point to ith object after its initial position.
Subtraction of an integer	..	`int i, *ptr;`	If we write, `ptr-i`, then `ptr` will point to ith object before its initial position.
Comparison of pointers	Pointers should point to elements of the same array.	`int *ptr1, *ptr2;`	If we write, `ptr1<ptr2`, then it would return 1 if ptr1 points to an element that is near to the front of the array.
Subtraction of pointers	Pointers should point to elements of the same array.	`int *ptr1, *ptr2;`	If we write `ptr1-ptr2`, then it returns the number of elements between `ptr1` and `ptr2` (provided `ptr1>ptr2`)
NOTE: Addition of pointers is illegal. Therefore, `ptr1+ptr2` is not valid. Moreover, multiplication and division are also not allowed. Therefore, `*ptr1 /= int_a;` or `*ptr1 /= *ptr2; *ptr1 *= int_a;` or `*ptr1 *= *ptr2;` are illegal statements.			

Program 7.6 Write a program to read and display an array of n integers.

```
using namespace std;
#include<iostream>
int main()
{       int i, n;
        int arr[10], *parr = arr;
        cout<<"\n Enter the number of elements : ";
        cin>>n;
        cout<<"\n Enter the elements : ";
        for(i=0; i < n; i++)
                cin>>*(parr+i);
        for(i=0; i < n; i++)
                cout<<"\n arr["<<i<<"] = "<<*(parr+i);
}
```

OUTPUT

```
Enter the number of elements : 3
Enter the elements : 1 2 3
arr[0] = 1
arr[1] = 2
arr[2] = 3
```

Program 7.7 Write a program to find mean of n numbers using arrays.

```
using namespace std;
#include<iostream>
int main()
{       int i, n, arr[20], sum =0;
        int *pn = &n, *parr = arr, *psum = &sum;
        float mean = 0.0, *pmean = &mean;
        cout<<"\n Enter the number of elements in the array : ";
        cin>>*pn;
        cout<<"\n Enter the elements : ";
        for(i=0; i < n; i++)
                cin>>*(parr+i);
        for(i=0; i < *pn; i++)
                *psum += *(arr + i);
        *pmean = *psum / *pn;
        cout<<"\n The sum of these numbers is : "<<*psum;
        cout<<"\n The mean of these numbers is : "<<*pmean;
}
```

OUTPUT

```
Enter the number of elements : 5
1 2 3 4 5
The sum of these numbers is : 15
The mean of these numbers is : 3
```

Difference between reference variable and pointer variable

When we call a function using call-by-address, we are actually creating pointer variables. Though reference and pointer variables may sound similar but they are actually different in many ways, such as,

1. A reference variable means the same variable just with a different name. While a reference variable must refer to some variable (or object) and can never be NULL, a pointer variable on the other hand, may be NULL.
2. A pointer variable can be re-assigned while reference cannot.
3. A pointer variable can be assigned anywhere in the code but a reference variable must be assigned at initialization only.
4. A pointer variable can be assigned NULL directly, whereas reference variable cannot be.
5. Pointer variables can be made to iterate over an array by using the ++ operator (to go to the next item that a pointer is pointing to) but you cannot use a reference variable to do the same.
6. A pointer variable holds a memory address. But, a reference variable has the same memory address as the variable it references.
7. A pointer variable is dereferenced with * to use the value stored at that memory location, but a reference variable can be used directly.

While calling a function, prefer to use call-by-reference. Moreover, if you want to write a code that will work in C as well as C++, then you have no option but to use the call-by-address technique of passing parameters.

7.8 PASSING ARRAY TO FUNCTIONS

An array can be passed to a function using pointers. For this, a function that expects an array can declare that formal parameter in either of the two ways.

```
func(int arr[]);        OR func(int *arr);
```

When we pass the name of the array to a function, the address of the zero element of the array is copied to the local pointer variable in the function. Observe the difference—unlike ordinary variables, the values of the elements are not copied; only the address of the first element is copied.

When a formal parameter is declared in a function header as an array, it is interpreted as a pointer a variable and not an array. With this pointer variable you can access all the elements of the array by using the expression, `array_name + index`. Note to know how many elements are there in the array, you must pass the size of the array as another parameter to the function. So for a function that accepts an array as parameter, the declaration should be as follows.

```
func(int arr[], int n);          OR func(int *arr, int n);
```

Look at the following program which illustrates the use of pointers to pass array to a function.

Program 7.8 Write a program to read and print an array of n numbers, find out the smallest number, and print the position of the smallest number.

```
using namespace std;
#include<iostream>
void read_array(int *arr, int n);
void find_small(int *arr, int n, int *small, int *pos);
int main()
{       int num[10], n, smallest, pos;
        cout<<"\n Enter the size of the array : ";
        cin>>n;
        cout<<"\n Enter the elements of the array : ";
        read_array(num, n);
        find_small(num, n, &smallest, &pos);
        cout<<"\n The smallest number in the array is = "<<smallest<<" at position "<<pos;
}
void read_array( int *arr, int n)
{       for(int i=0;i<n;i++)
                cin>>*(arr+i);
}
void find_small(int *arr, int n, int *small, int *pos)
{       *small = arr[0], *pos=0;
        for(int i=0;i<n;i++)
        {       if( *(arr+i)< *small)
                {       *small = *(arr+i);
                        *pos = i;
                }
        }
}
```

OUTPUT

```
Enter the size of the array : 5
Enter the elements of the array : 1 2 3 4 5
The smallest number in the array is = 1 at position 0
```

Note that it is not necessary that we have to pass the whole array to a function. We can also pass a part of the array also known as a sub-array. A pointer to a sub-array is also an array pointer. For example, if we want to send the array starting from the third element, then we can pass the address of the third element and the size of the sub-array. That is, if there were `10` elements in the array, and we want to pass the array starting from the third element, then only seven elements would be a part of the sub-array. The function call can be written as

```
func(&arr[2], 8);
```

7.9 DIFFERENCES BETWEEN ARRAY NAME AND POINTERS

The first thing to note is that when the memory for an array is allocated, its base address is fixed and it cannot be changed during program execution. In other words, an array name is an address constant. Therefore, its value cannot be changed. To ensure that the address of the array does not get changed even inadvertently, C++ does not allow array names to be used as an `lvalue`. Hence, array names cannot appear on the left side of the assignment operator.

However, you may declare a pointer variable of appropriate type that points to the first element of the array and use it as `lvalue`. Refer to Fig. 7.5. The left side code gives an error as the array name is being used as an `lvalue` for the `++` operator. The code on the right side shows the correct way of doing the same thing.

```
main()
{   int arr[5], i;
    for(i=0i<5;i++)
    {  *arr=0;
       arr++;       //ERROR
    }
    for(i=0;i<5;i++)
    cout<<"   "<< *(arr+i));
}
```

```
main()
{   int arr[5], i, *parr;
    parr = arr;
    for(i=0i<5;i++)
    {
    *parr=0;
    parr++;
    }
    for(i=0;i<5;i++)
    cout<<"   "<<*(arr+i);
}
```

Figure 7.5 Array and pointer

The second thing to remember is that an array cannot be assigned to another array as an array name cannot be used as the `lvalue` (i.e., an array namc cannot be used on the left side of the assignment operator). This is because an array name is a constant pointer and you connot change the position it points to. So writing,

```
int arr1[]={1,2,3,4,5};
int arr2[5];
arr2=arr1;           // will give an error
```

However, one pointer variable can be assigned to another pointer variable of the same type. Therefore, the following statements are valid in C++:

```
int arr1[]={1,2,3,4,5};
int *ptr1, *ptr2;
ptr1=arr1;
ptr2=ptr1;
```

When we write `ptr2=ptr1`, we are not copying the data pointed to. Rather, we are just making two pointers which point to the same location. This is shown in the Fig. 7.6.

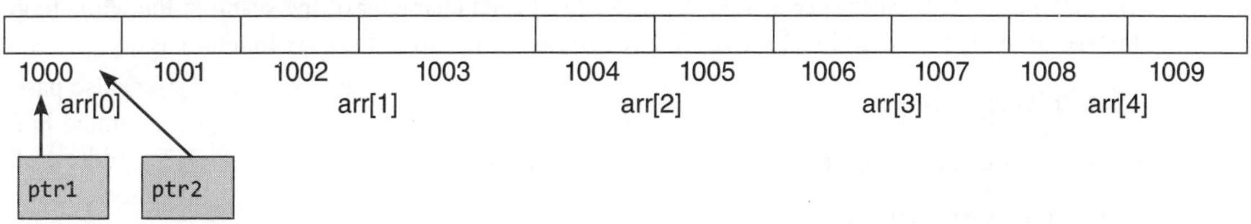

Figure 7.6 Pointers pointing to the same location

The third point of difference lies with the return value of the address operator. The address operator returns the address of the operand. However, when an address operator is applied to an array name, it gives the same value as the array reference without the operator. Therefore, `arr` and `&arr` give the same value. However, this is not true for a pointer variable.

Last but not the least, when the `sizeof` operator is applied to an array name, it returns the number of bytes allocated for the array. However, in case of a pointer variable, the `sizeof` operator returns the number of bytes used for the pointer variable (machine-dependant). Look at the following code which illustrates this concept.

Example 7.11 Finding the size of an array variable and a pointer variable that points to an array

```
using namespace std;
#include<iostream>
main()
{       int arr[]={1,2,3,4,5};          // array
        int *ptr;
        ptr=arr; //pointer to array
        cout<<"\n Size of array = "<<sizeof(arr);
        cout<<"\n Size of pointer variable = "<<sizeof(ptr);
}
```

OUTPUT

```
Size of array = 20
Size of pointer variable = 8
```

7.10 POINTERS AND STRINGS

As discussed in Chapter 6, strings are treated as arrays of characters that are terminated with a binary zero character (written as `'\0'`).

Example 7.12 Printing a text using pointers

```
using namespace std;
#include<iostream>
int main()
{       char str[] = "Oxford";
        char *pstr = str;
        cout<<"\n The string is : ";
        while(*pstr != '\0')
        {       cout<<*pstr;
                 pstr++;
        }
}
```

OUTPUT

```
The string is : Oxford
```

Explanation: In this program, we declare a character pointer `*pstr` to show the string on the screen. We then point the pointer `pstr` at `str`. Next, we print each character of the string in the while loop. Instead of using the `while` loop, we could have straight away used the `puts` function as

```
puts(pstr);
```

Consider here that the function prototype for `puts()` is as follows:

```
int puts(const char *s);
```

Here, the `const` modifier is used to assure the user that the function will not modify the contents pointed to by the source pointer. Note that the address of the string is passed to the function as an argument.

The parameter passed to `puts()` is a pointer which is the address to which it points, or, simply, an address. Therefore, by writing `puts(str);` we pass the address of `str[0]`.

Similarly, when we write `puts(pstr);` we are passing the same address, because we have written `pstr = str;`

Example 7.13 To read a string and then scan each character to count the number of upper and lower case characters entered

```
using namespace std;
#include<iostream>
int main()
{       char str[100], *pstr=str; // pstr is a pointer to string
        int upper = 0, lower = 0;
        cout<<"\n Enter the string : ";
        cin.getline(str,100);
        while(*pstr != '\0')
        // while loop will be executed until the null character is encountered
        {       if(*pstr >= 'A' && *pstr <= 'Z')
                                upper++;
                else if(*pstr >= 'a' && *pstr <= 'z')
                        lower++;
                pstr++;
        }
        cout<<"\n Total number of upper case characters = "<<upper;
        cout<<"\n Total number of lower case characters = "<<lower;
}
```

OUTPUT

```
Enter the string : Oxford University Press
Total number of upper case characters = 3
Total number of lower case characters = 18
```

Program 7.9 Write a program to read and print a text and count the number of characters, words, and lines in the text.

```
using namespace std;
#include<iostream>
int main()
{       char str[100], *pstr=str;
        int chars = 1, lines=1, words=1;
        cout<<"\n Enter the string : ";
        cin.getline(str,100);
        while(*pstr != '\0')
        {       if(*pstr == '\n')
                          lines++;
                if(*pstr == ' ' && *(pstr + 1) != ' ')
                        words++;
                chars++;
                pstr++;
        }
        cout<<"\n Number of characters = "<< chars;
        cout<<"\n Number of lines = "<< lines;
        cout<<"\n Number of words = "<< words;
}
```

OUTPUT
```
Enter the string : Oxford University Press
Number of characters = 24
Number of lines = 1
Number of words = 3
```

Program 7.10 Write a program to copy n characters of a character array from the mth position in another character array.

```
using namespace std;
#include<iostream>
#include<stdio.h>
int main()
{       char str[100], copy_str[100];
        char *pstr=str, *pcopy_str = copy_str;
        int m, n, i=0;
        cout<<"\n Enter the string : ";
        cin.getline(str,100);
        cout<<"\n Enter the position from which to start : ";
        cin>>m;
        cout<<"\n Enter the number of characters to be copied : ";
        cin>>n;
        pstr = pstr + m - 1;
        i=0;
        while(*pstr != '\0' && i <n)
        {       *pcopy_str = *pstr;
                 pcopy_str++;
                 pstr++;
                 i++;
        }
        *pcopy_str = '\0';
        cout<<"\n The copied text is : ";
        puts(copy_str);
}
```

OUTPUT
```
Enter the string : Oxford University Press
Enter the position from which to start : 5
Enter the number of characters to be copied : 5
The copied text is : d Uni
```

7.11 ARRAY OF POINTERS

An array of pointers can be declared as

```
int *ptr[10];
```

This statement declares an array of `10` pointers where each pointer points to an integer variable. For example, look at the code given here.

```
int *ptr[10];
int p=1, q=2, r=3, s=4, t=5;
ptr[0]=&p;
ptr[1]=&q;
ptr[2]=&r;
ptr[3]=&s;
ptr[4]=&t
```

Find out the output of the following statement;

```
cout<<" "<<*ptr[3];
```

The output will be `4` because `ptr[3]` stores the address of integer variables and therefore, `*ptr[3]` will print the value of `s`, that is, `4`. Now look at another code in which we store the address of three individual arrays in the array of pointers.

Example 7.14 Using array of pointers

```
using namespace std;
#include<iostream>
main()
{              int arr1[]={1,2,3,4,5};
               int arr2[]={0,2,4,6,8};
               int arr3[]={1,3,5,7,9};
               int *parr[3] = {arr1, arr2, arr3};
               int i;
               for(i=0;i<3;i++)
                         cout<<" "<< *parr[i];
}
```

OUTPUT

```
1 0 1
```

Explanation: In the `for` loop, `parr[0]` stores the base address of `arr1` (or, `&arr1[0]`). Writing `*parr[0]` will print the value stored at `&arr1[0]`. The same rule applies to `*parr[1]` and `*parr[2]`.

Now, consider an array of character pointers pointed to the strings.

```
char *ptr[3];
```

In the `ptr` array, each element is a character pointer. Therefore, we can assign character pointers to the elements of the array. For example,

```
ptr[0] = str;
```

Another way to initialize an array of characters with three strings can be given as follows:

```
char *ptr[3] = {"Janak","Raj","Paul"};
Here, ptr[0] is Janak, ptr[1] is Raj, and ptr[2] is Paul
```

The memory layout of `ptr` can be given as shown in Fig. 7.7. Note that it requires only `15` bytes to store the three strings.

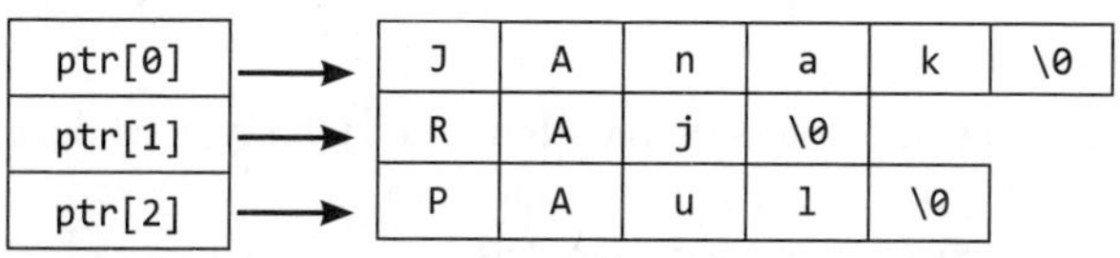

Figure 7.7 Memory layout of `ptr`

However, `char str[3][10]={"Janak", "Raj", "Paul"};` will behave in the same way as that of array of characters. The only difference is the memory layout (Refer to Fig. 7.8). While array of pointers need only `15` bytes of storage, `str` will reserve `30` bytes in memory, despite the fact that some memory locations will be reserved but not utilized.

Here, the grey locations represent the uninitialized memory cells.

J	a	n	a	k	\0		R	a	j	\0		P	a	u	l	\0	

Figure 7.8 Memory layout

Example 7.15 To display the name of the day corresponding to the number using pointers and arrays of characters.

```
using namespace std;
#include<iostream>
char *day_of_week(int);
main()
{       int day_num;
        char *day;
        cout<<"\n Enter the day from 1 to 7 : ";
        cin>>day_num;
        day = day_of_week(day_num);
        if(day)
                cout<<day;
        else
                cout<<"\n Invalid Day";
}
       char *day_of_week(int d)
{       char *week_day[7] = {"SUNDAY", "MONDAY", "TUESDAY", "WEDNESDAY", "THURSDAY", "FRIDAY", "SATURDAY"};
        if(d>=1 || d<=7)
                return week_day[d-1];
        else
                return NULL;
}
OUTPUT
Enter the day from 1 to 7 : 5
THURSDAY
```

An array of pointers whose elements are stored to point to arrays of varying sizes is called a ragged array. Therefore, array of pointers `week_day` and `ptr` in the previous discussion are better known as ragged arrays.

7.12 POINTERS AND 2D ARRAYS

Elements of a two-dimensional array are stored in contiguous memory locations. A two-dimensional array is not the same as an array of pointers to one-dimensional arrays. To declare a pointer to a two-dimensional array, you may write

```
int **ptr;
```

Here int **ptr is an array of pointers (to one-dimensional arrays), while `int mat[5][5]` is a 2D array. They are not the same type and are not interchangeable.

Consider a two-dimensional array declared as

```
int mat[5][5];
```

Individual elements of the array mat can be accessed using either:

```
mat[i][j] or
*(*(mat + i) + j) or
*(mat[i]+j);
```

To understand more fully what is going on, let us replace

```
*(multi + row) with X so the expression
*(*(mat + i) + j) becomes *(X + col)
```

Using pointer arithmetic, we know that the address pointed to by (i.e., value of) X + col + 1 must be greater than the address X + col by an amount equal to sizeof(int).

Since mat is a two-dimensional array, we know that in the expression multi + row as used above, multi + row + 1 must increase in value by an amount equal to that needed to *point to* the next row, which in this case would be an amount equal to COLS * sizeof(int).

Thus, in case of a two-dimensional array, in order to evaluate expression (for a row major 2D array), we must know a total of 4 values:

1. The address of the first element of the array, which is given by the name of the array, i.e., mat in our case
2. The size of the type of the elements of the array, i.e., size of integers in our case
3. The specific index value for the row
4. The specific index value for the column

Note that

```
int (*ptr)[10];
```

declares ptr to be a pointer to an array of 10 integers. This is different from

```
int *ptr[10];
```

which would make ptr the name of an array of 10 pointers to type int. You must be thinking how pointer arithmetic works if you have an array of pointers. For example,

```
int * arr[10];
int ** ptr = arr;
```

In this case, arr has type int **. Since all pointers have the same size, the address of `ptr + i` can be calculated as

```
addr(ptr + i) = addr(ptr) + [sizeof(int *) * i]
= addr(ptr) + [2 * i]
Since arr has type int **,
arr[0] = &arr[0][0],
arr[1] = &arr[1][0], and in general,
arr[i] = &arr[i][0].
```

According to pointer arithmetic, `arr + i = & arr[i]`, yet this skips an entire row of 5 elements, i.e., it skips complete 10 bytes (5 elements each of 2 bytes size). Therefore, if arr is address 1000, then `arr + 2` is address 1010. To summarize, `&arr[0][0]`, `arr[0]`, `arr`, and `&arr[0]` point to the base address.

```
&arr[0][0] + 1 points to arr[0][1]
arr[0] + 1 points to arr[0][1]
arr + 1 points to arr[1][0]
&arr[0] + 1 points to arr[1][0]
```

To conclude, a two-dimensional array is not the same as an array of pointers to 1D arrays. Actually, a two-dimensional array is declared as:

```
int(*ptr)[10];
```

Here, `ptr` is a pointer to an array of `10` elements. The parentheses are not optional. In the absence of these parentheses, `ptr` becomes an array of `10` pointers, not a pointer to an array of `10 ints`.

Note Pointer to a one-dimensional array can be declared as follows:

```
int arr[]={1,2,3,4,5};
int *parr;
parr=arr;
```

Similarly, pointer to a two- dimensional array can be declared as,

```
int arr[2][2]={{1,2},{3,4}};
int (*parr)[2];
parr=arr;
```

Example 7.16 To illustrate the use of a pointer to a 2D array

```
using namespace std;
#include<iostream>
main()
{       int arr[2][2]={{1,2},{3,4}};
        int i, (*parr)[2];
        parr=arr;
        for(i=0;i<2;i++)
        {       for(int j=0;j<2;j++)
                        cout<<"  "<<(*(parr+i))[j];
        }
}
```

OUTPUT

```
1 2 3 4
```

The golden rule to access an element of a two-dimensional array can be given as

```
arr[i][j] = (*(arr+i))[j] = *((*arr+i))+j) = *(arr[i]+j)
```

Therefore,

```
arr[0][0] = *(arr)[0] = *((*arr)+0) = *(arr[0]+0)
arr[1][2] = (*(arr+1))[2] = *((*(arr+1))+2) = *(arr[1]+2)
```

Note

If we declare an array of pointer using	If we declare a pointer to an array using,
`data_type *array_ name[SIZE];`	`data_type (*array_ name)[SIZE];`
Here SIZE represents the number of rows and the space for columns that can be dynamically allocated.	Here SIZE represents the number of columns and the space for rows that may be dynamically allocated

Program 7.11 Write a program to read and display a 3 × 3 matrix.

```
using namespace std;
#include<iostream>
int main()
{       int i, j, mat[3][3];
        cout<<"\n Enter the elements of the matrix ";
        for(i=0;i<3;i++)
        {       for(j=0;j<3;j++)
                        cin>>mat[i][j];
        }
        cout<<"\n The elements of the matrix are ";
        for(i=0;i<3;i++)
        {       cout<<"\n";
                for(j=0;j<3;j++)
                        cout<<"\t"<<*(*(mat + i)+j);
        }
}
```

OR

```
using namespace std;
#include<iostream>
int main()
{
int i, j, mat[3][3];
cout<<"\n Enter elements of the matrix";
for(i=0;i<3;i++)
{ for(j=0;j<3;j++)
cout<<"\n mat["<<i<<"]["<<j<<"] = ";
cin>>((*(mat + i)+j));
}
}
cout<<"\n The elements of the matrix are ";
for(i=0;i<3;i++)
{ cout<<"\n";
for(j=0;j<3;j++)
cout<<"\t mat"<<i<<""<<j<<" ="<< *(*(mat + i)+j);
}
return 0;
}
```

OR

```
using namespace std;
#include<iostream>
void display(int (*)[3]);
int main()
{       int i, j, mat[3][3];
        cout<<"\n Enter the elements of the matrix ";
        for(i=0;i<3;i++)
        {       for(j=0;j<3;j++)
                        cin>>mat[i][j];
        }
      display(mat);
}
void display(int (*mat)[3])
{       int i, j;
        cout<<"\n The elements of the matrix are ";
```

```
        for(i=0;i<3;i++)
        {       cout<<"\n";
                 for(j=0;j<3;j++)
                        cout<<"\t"<<*(*(mat + i)+j);
        }
}
```

OUTPUT

```
Enter the elements of the matrix
1 2 3 4 5 6 7 8 9
The elements of the matrix
1 2 3
4 5 6
7 8 9
```

7.13 POINTERS AND 3D ARRAYS

In this section, we will see how pointers can be used to access a three-dimensional array. We have seen that pointer to a one-dimensional array can be declared as

```
int arr[]={1,2,3,4,5};
int *parr;
parr = arr;
```

Similarly, pointer to a two-dimensional array can be declared as

```
int arr[2][2]={{1,2},{3,4}};
int (*parr)[2];
parr = arr;
```

A pointer to a three-dimensional array can be declared as

```
int arr[2][2][2]={1,2,3,4,5,6,7,8};
int (*parr)[2][2];
parr = arr;
```

We can access an element of a three-dimensional array by writing,

```
arr[i][j][k] = *(*(*(arr+i)+j)+k)
```

Let us look at the example given below.

Example 7.17 To illustrate the use of a pointer to a 3D array

```
using namespace std;
#include<iostream>
main()
{       int i,j,k;
        int arr[2][2][2];
        int (*parr)[2][2]=arr;
        cout<<"\n Enter the elements of a 2 x 2 x 2 array: ";
        for(i=0;i<2;i++)
        {       for(j=0;j<2;j++)
                 {       for(k=0;k<2;k++)
```

```
                        cin>>arr[i][j][k];
                }
        }
        cout<<"\n The elements of the 2 x 2 x 2 array are: ";
        for(i=0;i<2;i++)
        {       for(j=0;j<2;j++)
                {       for(k=0;k<2;k++)
                                cout<< " " <<*(*(*(parr+i)+j)+k);
                }
        }
return 0;
}
```

OUTPUT

```
Enter the elements of a 2 x 2 x 2 array: 1 2 3 4 5 6 7 8
The elements of the 2 x 2 x 2 array are: 1 2 3 4 5 6 7 8
```

Note In the cout statement, you could also have used *(*(*(arr+i)+j)+k) instead of *(*(*(parr+i)+j)+k).

7.14 POINTERS TO FUNCTIONS

C++ allows operations with pointers to functions. We have discussed earlier in this chapter that every function code along with all its variables is allocated some space in the memory. Therefore, every function has an address. Function pointers are pointer variables that point to the address of a function. Like other pointer variables, function pointers can be declared, assigned values, and are used to access the functions they point to.

This is a useful technique for passing a function as an argument to another function. In order to declare a pointer to a function, we have to declare it like the prototype of the function except that the name of the function is enclosed between parentheses `()` and an asterisk `(*)` is inserted before the name. The syntax of declaring a function pointer can be given as follows:

```
return_type(*function_pointer_name)(argument_list);
```

Look at the declaration here in which we declare a pointer to a function that returns an integer value and accepts two arguments—one of integer type and the other of `float` type.

```
int (*func)(int a, float b);
```

Considering the precedence rule, if you do not put the function name within parenthesis, you will end up in declaring a function returning a pointer:

/* function returning pointer to int */

```
int *func(int a, float b);
```

7.14.1 Initializing Function Pointer

As in case of other pointer variables, a function pointer must be initialized prior to use. If we have declared a pointer to the function, then that pointer can be assigned to the address of the right sort of function just by using its name. Like in the case of an array, a function name is turned into an address when it is used in an expression. It is optional to use the address operator (&) in front of the function's name.

For example, if fp is a function pointer and we have a function add() with prototype given as follows:

```
int add(int, int);
```

Then, by writing fp = add; initialize the function pointer fp with the address of add().

7.14.2 Calling a Function using a Function Pointer

When a pointer to a function is declared, it can be called using one of the two forms:

```
(*func)(1,2);
```

or

```
func(1,2);
```

Example 7.18 To illustrate the use of a pointer to a function

```
using namespace std;
#include<iostream>
void print(int n);
void (*fp)(int); // function pointer declaration
main()
{       fp = print;
        (*fp)(10); // initializing function pointer declaration
        fp(20);
}
void print(int value)
{       cout<<"\n"<<value;
}

OUTPUT
10
20
```

Example 7.19 To illustrate how the contents of function pointer (fp) can be changed at run time to point to two different functions

```
using namespace std;
#include<iostream>
float (*func)(float, float);        //Define a function pointer
float add(float, float);
float sub(float, float);
main()
{       func = add;        // function pointer points to add
        cout<<"\n Addition Result = "<<func(9.5, 3.1);
        func = sub;        // function pointer points to sub
        cout<<"\n Subtraction Result = "<<func(9.5, 3.1);
}
```

```
float add(float x, float y)
{       return (x+y);
}
float sub(float x, float y)
{       return (x-y);
}
```

OUTPUT

```
Addition Result = 12.60000
Subtraction Result = 6.40000
```

Let us declare a function pointer and initialize it to `NULL`.

```
int (*fp)(int) = NULL;
```

Now the function pointer does not store address of any function.

7.14.3 Comparing Function Pointers

Comparison operators such as `==` and `!=` can be used in the way they are generally used. Consider the code given here which checks if `fp` actually contains the address of the function `print(int)`.

```
if(fp >0){                              // check if initialized
   if(fp == print)
      cout<<"\n Pointer points to Print";
else
   cout<<"\n Pointer not initialized!";
```

7.14.4 Passing a Function Pointer as an Argument to a Function

A function pointer can be passed as the calling argument of a function. This is in fact necessary if you want to pass a pointer to a callback function. The following code shows how to pass a pointer to a function which returns an int and accepts two int values. Note that in the program below, the function operate calls the functions add and subtract with the following line:

```
result = (*operate_fp) (num1, num2);
```

Example 7.20 Passing a pointer to a function

```
using namespace std;
#include<iostream>
int add(int, int);
int sub(int, int);
int operate(int (*operate_fp) (int, int), int, int);
main()
{
int result;
result = operate(add, 9, 7);
cout <<"\n Addition = "<< result);
result = operate(sub, 9, 7);
cout <<"\n Subtraction = "<< result;
```

```
return 0;
}
int add(int a, int b)
{
return (a + b);
}
int sub(int a, int b)
{
return (a – b);
}
int operate(int (*operate_fp) (int, int), int a, int b)
{
int result;
result = (*operate_fp) (a,b);
return result;
}
```

OUTPUT

```
Addition = 16
Subtraction = 2
```

7.15 ARRAY OF FUNCTION POINTERS

When an array of function pointers is made, the appropriate function is selected using an index. The code given below shows the way to define and use an array of function pointers in C++.

Step 1: Use typedef keyword so that 'fp' can be used as type

typedef int (*fp)(int, int);

Step 2: Define the array and initialize each element to NULL. This can be done in two ways: // with 10 pointers to functions which return an int and take two ints

1. fp funcArr[10] = {NULL};
2. int (*funcArr[10])(int, int) = {NULL};

Step 3: Assign the function's address—'Add' and 'Subtract' funcArr1[0] = funcArr2[1] = Add;

```
funcArr[0] = &Add;
funcArr[1] = &Subtract;
```

Step 4: Call the function using an index to address the function pointer

```
cout<<"\n"<<funcArr[1](2, 3); // short form
cout<<"\n"<<(*funcArr[0])(2, 3); // correct way
```

Program 7.12 Write a program to add, that uses an array of function pointers, subtract, multiply, or divide two given numbers.

```
using namespace std;
#include<iostream>
int sum(int a, int b);
int subtract(int a, int b);
int mul(int a, int b);
```

```
int div1(int a, int b);
int (*fp[4]) (int a, int b);
int main(void)
  {
    int result;
    int num1, num2, op;
    fp[0] = sum;  fp[1] = subtract; fp[2] = mul; fp[3] = div1;
    cout<<"\n Enter the numbers: ";
    cin>>num1>>num2;
    do{
    cout<<"\n 0: Add \n 1: Subtract \n 2: Multiply \n 3: Divide \n 4. EXIT\n";
    cout <<"\n\n Enter the operation: ";
    cin >> op;
    result = (*fp[op]) (num1, num2);
    cout<<"\n Result = "<<result;
    while(op!=4);
    return 0; }

    int sum(int a, int b)
  { return a + b; }
int subtract(int a, int b)
{ return a - b; }
int mul(int a, int b)
{ return a * b; }
int div1(int a, int b)
{ if(b) return a / b; else return 0; }
```

SAMPLE OUTPUT

```
Enter the numbers: 2 3
0: Add
1: Subtract
2: Multiply
3: Divide
4. EXIT
Enter the operation: 0
Result = 5
Enter the operation: 4
```

7.16 POINTERS TO POINTERS

In C++, you are also allowed to use pointers that point to pointers. The pointers, in turn, point to data (or even to other pointers). To declare pointers to pointers, just add an asterisk (`*`) for each level of reference.

For example, if we have a code as follows:

```
int x=10;
int *px;        //pointer to an integer
int **ppx;        // pointer to a pointer to an integer
px=&x;
ppx=&px;
```

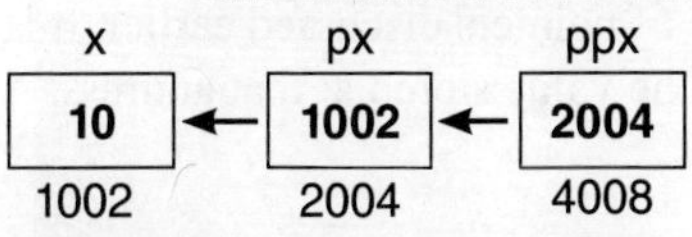

Figure 7.9 Pointer to pointer

Assume the memory location of these variables as shown in Fig. 7.9. Now if we write,

```
cout<<"\n "<< **ppx;
it would print 10, the value of x.
```

7.17 CONSTANT POINTER

A constant pointer is a pointer that cannot change the address it is storing. This means that a constant pointer will point to the same variable irrespective of the situation. Once it is assigned the address of a variable, the constant pointer cannot be made to point to any other variable. However, the value at the address pointed by the constant pointer may be changed. A constant pointer is declared as follows:

```
data_type * const ptr_var = init_address;
```

Like a normal `const` variable, a constant pointer must be initialized during declaration. This initial address cannot be changed later in the program code.

Let us see some valid and invalid use of constant pointers to understand them better as shown in Fig. 7.10.

```
// Valid usage

char c = 'A';
char * const ptr = &c;
*ptr = 'B';
```

```
// Invalid usage

char c = 'A';
char * const ptr;
ptr = &c;
```

Error—uninitialized constant

```
// Invalid usage

char c1 = 'A';
char c2 = 'B';
char * const ptr = &c1;
ptr = &c2;
```

Error—address pointed by ptr cannot be changed

Figure 7.10 Usage of constant pointers

7.18 POINTER TO CONSTANTS

As the name implies, a pointer to a constant is one through which the value of variable it points to cannot be changed. However, the address to which the pointer points to can be changed. A pointer to constant is defined as follows:

```
const data_type * ptr_var;
```

Let us see a valid and an invalid use of pointer to constants to understand them better as shown in Fig. 7.11.

```
// Valid usage

int a = 2, b = 3;
cont int *ptr = &a;
ptr = &b;
```

```
// Invalid usage

int a = 2, b = 3;
cont int *ptr = &a;
*ptr = 5;
```

Error—cannot change the value at the address to which ptr points

Figure 7.11 Usage of pointer to constants

7.19 CONSTANT POINTER TO A CONSTANT

A constant pointer to a constant is a combination of the two types of pointers discussed earlier. It is a pointer that can neither change the address it is pointing to nor the value stored at that address. A constant pointer to constant is declared as follows:

```
const data_type * const ptr_var;
```

Execute the following piece of code and examine the errors.

Example 7.21 Program to illustrate constant pointer to a constant

```
using namespace std;
#include<iostream>
main()
{       int a = 2, b = 3;
        const int *ptr = &a;
        *ptr = 5;       // ERROR
        ptr = &b;       //ERROR
        cout<<*ptr;
}
```

Explanation: Both these statements will result in error as value of a constant pointer is being modified.

7.20 MEMORY ALLOCATION IN C++ PROGRAMS

C++ supports three kinds of memory allocation using different variables—global, static, and automatic. They are explained as follows.

Static allocation When we declare a static or a global variable, static allocation for the variable is done. Each static or global variable is allocated a fixed size of memory space. The number of bytes reserved for the variable cannot change during the execution of the program. Till now, we have been using this technique to define variables, arrays, and pointers.

Automatic allocation When we declare an automatic variable such as a function argument or a local variable, automatic memory allocation is done. The space for an automatic variable is allocated when the compound statement containing the declaration is entered, and is freed when that compound statement is exited.

Dynamic allocation A third important kind of memory allocation is known as dynamic allocation. In the next section, we will read about dynamic memory allocation using pointers.

7.21 MEMORY USAGE

Before studying about dynamic memory allocation, let us first understand how memory is used. Conceptually, memory is divided into two parts—program memory and data memory. Refer to Fig. 7.12.

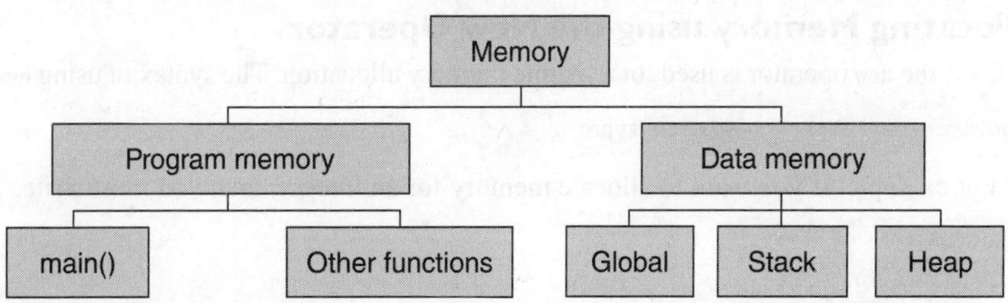

Figure 7.12 Memory usage

While program memory consists of memory used for the `main()` and other called functions in the program, data memory, on the other hand, consists of memory needed for permanent definitions such as global data, local data, constants, and dynamic memory data. The way in which C++ handles memory requirement is a function of the operating system and the compiler.

When a program is being executed, its `main()` and all other functions are always kept in the memory. However, the local variables of the function are available in the memory only when they are active. In Chapter 4, Functions, when we had studied about recursive functions, we had seen that system stack is used to store a single copy of the function and multiple copies of the local variables.

Apart from the stack, we also have a memory allocation known as heap. Heap memory is unused memory allocated to the program and is available to be assigned during its execution. When we allocate memory for variables dynamically, heap acts as a memory pool from which memory is allocated to those variables.

However, this is just a conceptual view of memory and implementation of the memory is entirely in the hands of system designers.

7.22 DYNAMIC MEMORY ALLOCATION

The process of allocating memory to the variables during execution of a program or at run time is known as dynamic memory allocation. Till now, whenever we needed an array, we had declared a static array of fixed size, say `int arr[100];`

When this statement is executed, consecutive space for 100 integers is allocated. It is not uncommon that we may be using only 10 per cent or 20 per cent of the allocated space, thereby, wasting rest of the space. To overcome this problem and to utilize memory efficiently, C++ provides a mechanism of dynamically allocating memory so that only the extent of memory that is actually required is reserved. We reserve space only at run time for variables that are actually required. Dynamic memory allocation gives the best performance in situations when we do not know memory requirements in advance.

Note When we have to dynamically allocate memory for variables in our programs, then pointers are the only way to go forward.

7.22.1 Memory Allocation Process

In computer terminology, free memory region is called the heap. The size of the heap is not constant as it keeps changing when a program is executed. In the course of program execution, some new variables are created and some variables cease to exit when the block in which they were declared is exited. For this reason, it is not uncommon to encounter memory overflow problems (i.e., memory could not be allocated as no more space is available) during dynamic allocation process. When an overflow condition exists, the memory allocation functions mentioned will return a null pointer.

7.22.2 Allocating Memory using the New Operator

In C++, the `new` operator is used for dynamic memory allocation. The syntax of using `new` is as follows:

```
pointer_variable = new data_type
```

For example, if you want to allocate memory for an integer, then you must write,

```
int *ptr;
ptr = new int;
```

However, if you want to allocate memory for more than one element, as in case of an array, then specify the number of elements within brackets `[]`. `new` returns a pointer to the beginning of the new block of memory allocated. Therefore, to dynamically allocate memory for an array of type float you will have to write

```
float *arr = new float[5];
```

Now, arr points to a valid block of memory with space for five elements of type float. Once the memory is allocated, you can access array elements either by writing arr[i] or by writing *(arr+i).

Since memory is allocated from the heap which is a limited resource, there may be a case that when you request memory, it is already exhausted. Therefore, there is no guarantee that all requests to allocate memory using new operator will always be granted by the system. For this reason, you must always check the returned pointer before using it. If new is able to allocate memory, it will return a pointer to the starting address of allocated memory, otherwise, if there is no space in the heap, the program may behave abnormally. Therefore, users must check if the allocation was successful in one of the following ways:

Programming Tip: nothrow is declared in header file <new.h> as an argument for function new.

Handling exceptions In this case, an exception of type bad_alloc is thrown and the program gets terminated if it is not handled. We will read more on exception handling in later chapters of this book.

nothrow method In this case, a bad_alloc exception is not thrown and the program is not terminated. However, a null pointer is returned and the program continues its execution normally. To use the nothrow method, users must write

```
char *arr = new (nothrow) char [5];
```

After writing the statement, users can check for memory allocation failure by checking if arr is a null pointer or a valid address. For this, just write

```
if(arr == NULL)
        cout<<"\n Memory Allocation Failed....";
```

Note The exception handling way is better than the nothrow method since there is no need to explicitly check the value returned after each allocation.

The new operator can also initialize memory during allocation. The syntax for initializing while allocation is as follows:

```
ptr_var = new data_type (init_value);
```

For example, float *ptr = new float (2.8);
will allocate memory for a floating number and initializes it with 2.8

7.22.3 Releasing the Used Space using the delete Operator

When a variable is allocated space during the compile time, the memory used by that variable is automatically released by the system in accordance with its storage class. However, when we dynamically allocate memory, it is our responsibility to release the space when it is not required. This is even more important when the storage space is limited. Therefore, if we no longer need the data stored in a particular block of memory and if we do not intend to use that block for storing any other information, then as a good programming practice, we must release that block of memory for future use. This can be done using the delete operator. The syntax of using the delete operator is

```
delete pointer_variable;
```

This statement releases the memory of a single element using new. To release the memory allocated to a block of consecutive spaces, we must use the following syntax.

```
delete[] pointer_variable;
```

for example, to release the space allocated to `arr`, you must write

```
delete[] arr;
arr = 0;     // reset the pointer to NULL
```

Note After deallocating the space, as a good programming practice, reset the pointer to null.

7.22.4 Alter the Size of Allocated Memory

At times, the memory allocated by using `new` might be insufficient or in excess. In both the situations, we can always change the memory size already allocated. This process is called reallocation of memory. In C++, memory can be reallocated in four simple steps.

- Create a new array of the appropriate type and of the new size.
- Copy the elements from the old array into the new array.
- Delete the old array.
- Rename the new array with the name of the initial array.

Example 7.22 To demonstrate the allocation, reallocation, and deallocation of memory

```
using namespace std;
#include<iostream>
#include<new>
#include<stdlib.h>
main()
{       int *arr = new int[5];
        if(arr == NULL)
        {       cout<<"\n Memory Allocation Failed";
                exit(1);
        }
        cout<<"\n Enter the array elements : ";
        for(int i=0;i<5;i++)
                cin>>arr[i];
        cout<<"\n The array elements are : ";
        for(int i=0;i<5;i++)
                cout<<"  "<<arr[i];
        cout<<"\n\n LETS HAVE A BIGGER ARRAY ...";
        int *temp = new int[10];
        if(temp == NULL)
        {       cout<<"\n\n\n Memory Allocation Failed";
                exit(1);
        }
        cout<<"\n\n\n COPYING THE OLD ARRAY...... ";
        for(int i=0;i<5;i++)
                 temp[i] = arr[i];
        delete [] arr;
        arr = temp;
        cout<<"\n Enter new values : ";
        int j=5;
        for(int i=0;i<5;i++)
                 cin>>arr[j++];
```

```
        cout<<"\n The array elements are : ";
        for(int i=0;i<10;i++)
                cout<<"   "<<arr[i];
        delete [] arr;
}
```

OUTPUT

```
Enter the array elements : 1  2  3  4  5
The array elements are : 1  2  3  4  5
LETS HAVE A BIGGER ARRAY ...
COPYING THE OLD ARRAY......
Enter new values : 6  7  8  9  10
The array elements are : 1  2  3  4  5  6  7  8  9  10
```

7.22.5 Advantages of new/delete Operators over malloc()/free()

While malloc() and free() are extensively used in C to allocate and release memory dynamically, they can be used in C++ as well but are generally not preferred due to the following reasons.

- The new operator calculates the size of the object. For this, it does not require the use of the sizeof() operator.
- New returns a pointer of relevant type. Therefore, it need not be typecasted as in case of malloc().
- The new operator can initialize while allocation. This is not possible in case of malloc().
- The syntax of new and delete is simple.
- New and delete operators can be overloaded (we will discuss this in the chapter on Operator Overloading)
- malloc() simply allocates memory and free() only releases it. However, new constructs objects and allocates memory as well. Similarly, delete not only deallocates memory but also destroys it.

Program 7.13 Write a program to add two vectors (arrays).

```
using namespace std;
#include<iostream>
#include <new>
#define MAX 5
void readVector(float *vector)
{       for(int i=0;i<MAX;i++)
                cin>>vector[i];
}
void addVectors(float *vec1, float *vec2, float *vec3)
{       for(int i=0;i<MAX;i++)
                vec3[i] = vec1[i] + vec2[i];
}
void displayVector(float *vector)
{       for(int i=0;i<MAX;i++)
                cout<<"   "<<vector[i];
}
main()
```

```
{       float *vec1 = new float [MAX];
        cout<<"\n Enter the elements of the first vector : ";
        readVector(vec1);
        float *vec2 = new float [MAX];
        cout<<"\n Enter the elements of the second vector : ";
        readVector(vec2);
        float *vec3 = new float [MAX];
        addVectors(vec1, vec2, vec3);
        cout<<"\n The resultant vector is : ";
        displayVector(vec3);
        delete [] vec1;
        delete [] vec2;
        delete [] vec3;
}
```

OUTPUT

```
Enter the elements of the first vector : 1.1 2.2 3.3 4.4 5.5
Enter the elements of the second vector : 2.3 3.4 4.5 5.1 2.4
The resultant vector is : 3.4 5.6 7.8 9.5 7.9
```

Program 7.14 Write a program to sort an array.

```
using namespace std;
#include<iostream>
#include<new>
void sort(int *arr, int n)
{       for(int i=0;i<n;i++)
        {       for(int j=i+1;j<n;j++)
                {       if(arr[i]>arr[j])
                        {       int temp = arr[i];
                                arr[i] = arr[j];
                                arr[j] = temp;
                        }
                }
        }
}
void display(int *arr, int n)
{       for(int i=0;i<n;i++)
                cout<<"  "<<arr[i];
}
void read(int *arr, int n)
{       for(int i=0;i<n;i++)
                cin>>arr[i];
}
main()
{       int n;
        cout<<"\n Enter the number of elements : ";
        cin>>n;
        int *arr = new int[n];
        if(arr!=NULL)
        {       read(arr, n);
                sort(arr, n);
        }
```

```
        cout<<"\n The sorted array is : ";
        display(arr,n);
}
```

OUTPUT

```
Enter the number of elements : 6
9 2 8 4 7
The sorted array is : 2 4 7 8 9
```

Program 7.15 Write a program to copy a given string into a new string. Memory for the new string must be allocated dynamically.

```
using namespace std;
#include<iostream>
#include<string.h>
void display(char *str)
{       cout<<"\t"<<str;        }
int length(char *str)
{       char *ptr = str;
        while(*ptr != '\0')
                ptr++;
        return ptr-str;
}
void copy_string(char *str1, char *str2)
{    while(*str1 != '\0')
        {               *str2 = *str1;
                str2++, str1++;
        }
        *str2 = '\0';
}
main()
{       char *str = "Oxford";
        int len = length(str);
        char *str1 = new char [len+1];
        copy_string(str, str1);

cout<<"\n The copied String is : ";
        display(str1);
}
```

OUTPUT

```
The copied String is : Oxford
```

7.22.6 Dynamically Allocating 2D Arrays

We have seen how we can allocate a block of memory for an array. Now, we can extend our understanding further to extend the same mode to 2D arrays. A 2D array can be thought of as a collection of *n* number of 1D arrays, where each ID array represents a row. Figure 7.13 shows a 2D array `arr`. `arr` is a `pointer-to-pointer-to-int`: at the first level, it points to a block of pointers, one for each row. We first allocate space for rows in the array. The space allocated to each row is big enough to hold a `pointer-to-int`, or `int *`. If we successfully allocate it, then this space will be filled with pointers to columns (number of `ints`).

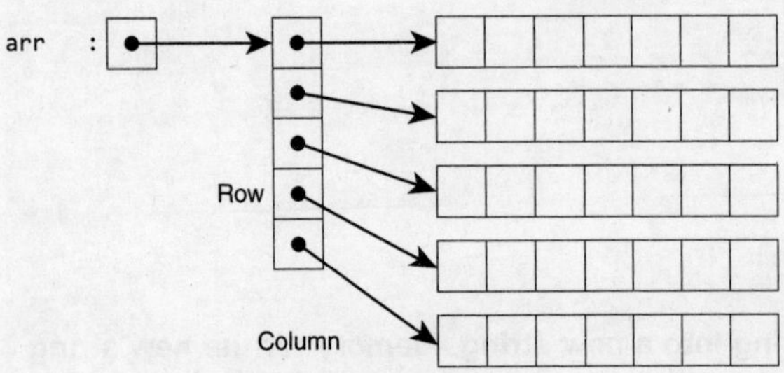

Figure 7.13 Two-dimensional array

A 2D array stored in memory in row major form can be allocated memory dynamically using the following steps:

- Define a pointer to pointer variable. For this, write `int **arr;`
- Allocate memory for storing pointers to rows. Therefore, write

```
arr = new int *[ROWS];
```

- Allocate memory for all columns. For this, write

```
for(int i=0;i<ROWS;i++)
        arr[i] = new int [COLS];
```

Once the memory is allocated for the 2D array, we can use subscripts to access its elements of `arr[i][j]`. When we have to pass such an array to a function, then the prototype of the function will be written as

```
func(int **arr, int ROWS, int COLS);
```

Example 7.23 To illustrate the dynamic allocation of allocate space for a 2D array

```
using namespace std;
#include<iostream>
#include<stdlib.h>
int **AllocateMemory( int **arr, int ROWS, int COLS)
// dynamically allocates memory for the 2D array
{       arr = new int *[ROWS];
        if(arr == NULL) // to check if memory is allocated or not
        {               cout<<"\n Memory could not be allocated";
                exit(-1);
        }
        for(int i=0;i<ROWS;i++) // dynamically allocates memory for each row's columns
                arr[i] =  new int[COLS];
        return arr;
}
void readMat( int **arr, int ROWS, int COLS) // read values in the 2D array
{       for(int i=0;i<ROWS;i++)
        {       for(int j=0;j<COLS;j++)
                        cin>>arr[i][j];
        }
}
void displayMat( int **arr, int ROWS, int COLS) // displays values of 2D array
{       for(int i=0;i<ROWS;i++)
                for(int j=0;j<COLS;j++)
                        cout<<"    "<<arr[i][j];
}
void deleteMat(int **arr, int ROWS) // free memory allocated
{       for(int i=0;i<ROWS;i++)
```

```
            delete arr[i]; // deletes each column and row
        delete [] arr; // deletes the pointer arr
}
main()
{       int **arr, i, j, ROWS, COLS; // arr is a pointer to pointer to int
        cout<<"\n Enter the number of rows and columns in the array : ";
        cin>>ROWS>>COLS;
        arr = AllocateMemory(arr, ROWS, COLS); // function call
        cout<<"\n Enter the values of the array : ";
        readMat(arr, ROWS,COLS); // function call
        cout<<"\n The array is a follows : ";
        displayMat(arr, ROWS, COLS); // function call
        deleteMat(arr, ROWS); // function call
}
```

OUTPUT

```
Enter the number of rows and columns in the array : 2 2
Enter the values of the array : 1 2 3 4
The array is a follows : 1  2  3  4
```

Nowadays, memory debuggers such as `Purify`, `Valgrind`, and `Insure++` are widely used for detecting memory corruption errors.

Points to Remember

- All data and programs need to be placed in the primary memory for execution.
- Pointers are nothing but memory addresses. A pointer is a variable that contains the memory address of another variable.
- The & operator retrieves the `lvalue` (address) of the variable. We can dereference a pointer, that is refer to the value of the variable to which it points by using unary '*' operator.
- The address of a memory location is a pointer constant; therefore, it cannot be changed in the program code.
- Unary increment and decrement operators have greater precedence than the dereference operator (*).
- Null pointer is a special pointer value that is known not to point anywhere. This means that a null pointer does not point to any valid memory address. To declare a null pointer, you may use the predefined constant null and also initialize a pointer as a null pointer by using a `constant 0`.
- A generic pointer is a pointer variable that has `void` as its data type. The generic pointer can be pointed at variables of any data type.
- When the memory for an array is allocated, its base address is fixed and it cannot be changed during program execution.
- When we allocate memory for variables dynamically, a heap acts as a memory pool from which memory is allocated to those variables. The process of allocating memory to the variables during execution of the program or at run time is known as dynamic memory allocation.
- Memory leakage occurs when memory is allocated but not released when it is no longer required.

Glossary

Dereference To look up a value referred to. Usually, the 'value referred to' is the value pointed to by a pointer. Therefore, dereference a pointer means to see what it points to. In C++, a pointer is dereferenced using the unary * operator.

Function pointer A pointer to any function type

Lvalue An expression that appears on the left-hand sign of an assignment operator, hence, something that can perhaps be assigned to. An `lvalue` specifies something that has a location, as opposed to a transient value which is not the address of any object or function. A null pointer points to nothing

Null pointer constant An integral constant expression with value 0 (or such an expression cast to void *), that represents a null pointer

Pointer Variable that stores addresses

Rvalue An expression that appears on the right-hand sign of an assignment operator. Generally, `rvalue` can participate in an expression or be assigned to some other variable.

Exercises

Fill in the Blanks

1. Size of character pointer is _______.
2. Allocating memory at run-time is known as _______.
3. A pointer to a pointer stores _______ of another _______ variable.
4. _______ pointer does not point to any valid memory address.
5. The size of memory allocated for a variable depends on its _______.
6. In 16-bit systems, integer variable is allocated _______ bytes.
7. The _______ appears on the right side of the assignment statement.
8. Pointers are nothing but _______.
9. _______ enable programmers to return multiple values from a function via function arguments.
10. The _______ operator informs the compiler that the variable is a pointer variable.
11. Data and programs need to be placed in the _______ for execution.
12. When compared with heaps, _______ is faster but also smaller and expensive.
13. All variables declared within `main()` are allocated space on the _______.
14. Shared libraries segment contains _______.
15. When memory is de-allocated using delete, it is returned back to the _______.
16. `new` returns _______ if unsuccessful.
17. A two-dimensional integer array is a _______.
18. An un-initialized memory contains _______.
19. Pointer to pointer stores _______.
20. The only integer value that can be assigned to a pointer variable is _______.
21. _______ can be used as parameter declaration to declare an array of integers passed to a function.
22. Dynamically allocated memory can be referred using _______.
23. _______ function returns memory to the heap.
24. A ragged array is implemented using an array of pointers to _______.

State True or False

1. A pointer is a variable.
2. The `&` operator retrieves the `lvalue` of the variable.
3. Array name can be used as a pointer.
4. Unary increment and decrement operators have greater precedence than the dereference operator.
5. The generic pointer can be pointed at variables of any data type.
6. A function pointer cannot be passed as a function's calling argument.
7. In 32-bit systems, integer variable is allocated 4 bytes.
8. `lvalue` cannot be used on the left side of the assignment statement.
9. Pointers provide an alternate way to access individual elements of the array.
10. A pointer is a variable that represents the contents of a data item.
11. A fixed size of stack is allocated by the system and is filled as needed from the top to bottom.
12. All parameters passed to the called function will be stored on the stack.
13. When the memory for an array is allocated, its base address is fixed and it cannot be changed during program execution.
14. An array can be assigned to another array.
15. Memory leakage occurs when memory is allocated but not released when it is no longer required.
16. mat[i][j] is equivalent to *(*(mat + i) + j).
17. It is possible to add two pointer variables.
18. Pointer constants cannot be changed.
19. The value of a pointer is always an address.
20. `*ptr++` will add 1 to the value pointed by `ptr`.
21. Pointers of different types can be assigned to each other without a cast.
22. Adding 1 to a pointer variable will make it point 1 byte ahead of the memory location to which it is currently pointing.
23. Any arithmetic operator can be used to modify the value of a pointer.
24. Ragged arrays consume less memory space.

Multiple Choice Questions

1. The operator * signifies a
   (a) Referencing operator
   (b) Dereferencing operator
   (c) Address operator
   (d) None of these
2. `*(&num)` is equivalent to writing
   (a) `&num` (b) `*num`
   (c) `num` (d) None of these
3. Pointers are used to create complex data structures such as
   (a) Trees (b) Linked list
   (c) Stack (d) Queue
   (e) all of these
4. While declaring pointer variables, which operator do we use?
   (a) Address (b) Arrow
   (c) Indirection (d) Dot
5. Which operator retrieves the `lvalue` of a variable?
   (a) & (b) *
   (c) -> (d) None of these
6. The block code of the `main()` program is stored in
   (a) Stack (b) Heap
   (c) Global (d) BSS
7. For dynamically allocated variables, memory is allocated from which memory area?
   (a) Stack (b) Heap
   (c) Global (d) BSS

Review Questions

1. Write a short note on pointers.
2. Give the advantages of using pointers.
3. Compare pointer and array name.
4. What do you understand by a null pointer?
5. What is a void pointer?
6. Explain the difference between a null pointer and a void pointer.
7. What is an array of pointers? How is it different from a pointer to an array?
8. Write a short note on pointer arithmetic.
9. How are generic pointers different from other pointer variables?
10. What do you understand by the term pointer to a function?
11. Differentiate between `ptr++` and `*ptr++`.
12. How are arrays related to pointers?
13. Can we have an array of function pointers? If yes, illustrate with the help of a suitable example.
14. Explain the term dynamic memory allocation.
15. Differentiate between `malloc()` and `new`.
16. Write a short note on pointers to pointers.
17. Differentiate between a function returning pointer to `int` and a pointer to function returning `int`.
18. Differentiate between pointer to constants and constant to pointers.
19. Explain the call by address technique of passing parameters to function.
20. How are pointers used on two-dimensional arrays?
21. How can you declare a pointer variable?
22. Differentiate between a variable address and a variable's value. How can we access a variable's address and its value using pointers?
23. Explain the different memory areas available to the programmer briefly.
24. What do you understand by dereferencing a pointer variable?
25. Write a short note on pointer expressions and pointer arithmetic.
26. What will `*p++ = *q++` do?
27. Write a short note on pointer and 3D array.
28. How can a pointer be used to access individual elements of an array? Illustrate with an example.
29. Can we assign a pointer variable to another pointer variable? Justify your answer with the help of an example.
30. What will happen if we add or subtract an integer to or from a pointer variable?
31. Is it possible to compare two pointer variables? Illustrate using an example.
32. Can we subtract two pointer variables?
33. With the help of an example, explain how an array can be passed to a function? Is it possible to send just a single element of the array to a function?
34. Can array names appear on the left side of the assignment operator? Why?
35. Differentiate between an array name and an array pointer.
36. How can you have array of function pointers? Illustrate with an example.
37. Briefly discuss memory allocation process in C++ language.
38. With the help of an example, explain how pointers can be used to dynamically allocate space for two-dimensional array.

39. Explain memory corruption with help of suitable examples.
39. Differentiate between `*(arr+i)` and `(arr+i)`.
40. How can we access the value pointed by a pointer to a pointer?

Programming Exercises

1. Explain the result of the following code:
```
int num1=2, num2=3;
int *p = &num1, *q=&num2;
*p++ = *q++;
```
2. Write a program that illustrates passing of character arrays as an argument to a function using pointers.
3. Write a program to print your name using pointers.
4. Write a program to print a character. Print its ASCII value and rewrite the character in upper case.
5. Write a program to find class average. The result should contain only two digits after the decimal.
6. Write a program to calculate area of a circle.
7. Write a program to convert a floating point number into an integer.
8. Write a program to find second largest of three numbers.
9. Write a program to enter a character and then determine whether it a vowel or not.
10. Write a program to test whether a number is positive, negative, or equal to zero.
11. Write a program to take input from the user and then check whether it is a number or a character. If it is a character, determine whether it is in upper case or lower case.
12. Write a program to display the sum and average of numbers from m to n.
13. Write a program to print all even numbers from m–n.
14. Write a program to read numbers until -1 is entered. Display whether the number is prime or composite.
15. Write a program to calculate the area of a triangle.
16. Write a program to add two integers using functions. Use call by address technique of passing parameters.
17. Write a program to take input from the user and then check whether it is a number or a character. If it is a character, determine whether it is in upper case or lower case.
18. Write a program to read a character until * is entered. If the character is in upper case, print it in lower case and vice versa. Count the number of upper and lower case characters entered.
19. Write a program to read and print a text. Count the number of characters, words, and lines in the text.
20. Write a program to copy a character array into another character array.
21. Write a program to copy n characters of a character array from the mth position into another character array.
22. Write a program to copy the last n characters of a character array into another character array. Convert the lower case letters into upper case letters while copying.
23. Write a program to read a text, delete all the semi-colons it has and finally replace all '.' with a ','.
24. Write a program to reverse a string.
25. Write a program to concatenate two strings into a third string.
26. Write a program to read and display values of an integer array. Allocate space dynamically for the array.
27. Write a function to calculate the roots of a quadratic equation. The function must accept arguments and return result using pointers.
28. Write a program using pointers to insert a value in an array.
29. Write a program using pointers to search a value from an array.
30. Write a function that accepts a string using pointers. In the function, delete all the occurrences of a given character and display the modified string on the screen.
31. Write a program to compare two arrays using pointers.

Find the errors (if any) in the following codes

```
1. int ptr, *ptr;
2. int num, *ptr=num;
3. int *ptr=10;
4. int num, **ptr=&num;
5. int *ptr1, *ptr2, *ptr3=*ptr1+*ptr2;
6. int *ptr; cin>>&ptr;
```

Find the errors in the following codes

1.
```
using namespace std;
#include<iostream>
main()
{     int arr[]={1,2,3,4,5};
   int *ptr, i;
   for(i=4;i>=0;i--)
```

```
            cout<<*(ptr-i);
    }
2.  using namespace std;
    #include<iostream>
    main()
    {  char *str1, *str2;
       cout<<"\n Enter the string : ";
       gets(str1);
       while(*str1!='\0')
       {        *str2=*str1;
                 str2++, str1++;
       }
       *str2='\0';
       cout<<"\n String is : ";
       while(*str2!='\0')
       {       cout<<*str2;
                str2++;
       }
    }
3.  using namespace std;
    #include<iostream>
    main()
    {  int a = 2, b = 3;
       const int *ptr = &a;
       *ptr = 5;
       ptr = &b;
       cout<<*ptr;
    }
```

Find the output of the following codes

```
1. main()
   {  int arr[]={1,2,3,4,5};
      int *ptr, i;
      ptr = arr+4;
      for(i=4;i>=0;i--)
              cout<<*(ptr-i);
   }
2. main()
   {  int arr[]={1,2,3,4,5};
      int *ptr, i;
      ptr = arr+4;
      for(i=0;i<5;i++)
              cout<<"\n "<< *(ptr-i);
   }
3. main()
   {  int val=3;
      int *pval=&val;
      cout<<"  "<<++val<<"  "<<*ptr;
   }
4. main()
   {  int val=3;
      int *pval=&val;
      cout<<" "<<val<<"  "<<*ptr++;

   }
```

```
5. main()
   {  int val=3;
      int *pval=&val;
      cout<<"  "<<val<<"  "<<++*ptr;
   }
6. main()
   {     int arr[]={1,2,3,4,5};
         cout<<" "<<*++arr;
   }
7. main()
   {  int arr[]={1,2,3,4,5};
      int *parr - arr+2;
      cout<<"  "<<++*parr-1
     <<"  "<<1+*-parr;
   }
8. main()
   {  int num=5, *ptr=&a, x=*ptr;
      cout<<"  "<<++num<< "
     "<< x+2<< "  "<<*ptr--;
   }
9. main()
   {  int num=5, *ptr=&num;
      cout<< "  "<< *&num;
      cout<<"  "<< *&*&num;
      cout<<"  "<< *&ptr;
      cout<<" "<<**&ptr;
      cout<<"  "<< &**&ptr;
   }
10. main()
   {  int num=5, *ptr=&num;
      cout<<"  "<<num <<"  "
     <<x+2 <<"  "<< (*ptr)--;
   }
11. main()
   {  int arr[]={1,2,3,4,5}, i;
      for(i=0;i<10;i++)
              *(arr+i)=i;
      cout<<"  "<<*(arr[k-1];

   }
12. main()
   {  int arr[]={1,2,3,4,5};
      int i=1,j=2;
      cout<<" "<< *(arr+1+i);
      cout<<" "<< *(arr+*(arr+1));
      cout<<"  "<<*(arr+i)+*(arr+j);
      cout<<"  "<<*(arr+j);
   }
13. main()
   {  char str[]="ABCDEFGH", *pstr=str;
      pstr++;
      while(*pstr!='H')
              cout<< *pstr++;
   }
14. main()
   {      char str[]="ABCDEFGH";
          cout<<(&str[3]-&str[0]);
   }
```

15.
```
main()
{       char *str="ABCDEFGH";
        (*str++);
    cout<<str;
}
```
16.
```
main()
{ char *str="ABCDEFGH";
    str++;
    cout<<str;
}
```
17.
```
main()
{ char *str="AbcDefGh";
    int i=0;
    while(*str)
    {       if(isupper(*str++))
                    i++;
    }
    cout<<i;
}
```
18.
```
main()
{       cout<<"Hello World"+3;
}
```
19.
```
main()
{       int arr[][2]={1,2,3,4,5,6,7,8,9};
       cout<<" "<<sizeof(arr);
}
```
20.
```
main()
{       int arr[2][3]={1,2,3,4,5,6,7,8,9};
       cout<<" "<<sizeof(arr[1]);
}
```
21.
```
main()
{ int arr[5], *parr=arr;
    while(parr < &arr[5])
    {       *parr = parr-arr;
            cout<<" "<<*parr;
            parr++;
    }
}
```
22.
```
main()
{ char *str = "Hello World";
    str[5]='!';
    cout<<str;
}
```
23.
```
main()
{ char *str1 = "Hello World";
    char str2[20] = "Hello World";
    char str3[] = "Hello World";
    cout<<" "<<sizeof(str1)<<"
"<<sizeof(str2)<<" "<<sizeof(str3);
}
```
24.
```
main()
{ register int num=3, *ptr=&num';
    cout<<*ptr;
}
```
25.
```
using namespace std;
#include<iostream>
void func(int (*parr)[3]);
main()
{ int arr[2][3] = {1,2,3,4,5,6};
    func(arr);
    func(arr+1);
}
void func(int (*parr)[3])
{ int i;
    for(i=0i<2;i++)
            cout<<"  "<< (*parr)[i];
}
```

Answers

Fill in the Blanks

1. 1 byte; **2.** dynamic memory allocation; **3.** address, pointer; **4.** null; **5.** data type; **6.** 2; **7.** `rvalue`; **8.** memory addresses; **9.** pointers; **10.** *; **11.** main memory; **12.** stack; **13.** system stack; **14.** executable image of shared libraries that are being used by the program; **15.** heap; **16.** null; **17.** pointer-to-pointer-to-int; **18.** garbage value; **19.** addresses of a pointer variables; **20.** 0; **21.** pointer-to-pointer-to-int; **22.** pointers; **23.** `delete`; **24.** array of varying sizes

State True or False

1. True	**2.** True	**3.** True	**4.** True	**5.** True	**6.** False	**7.** True	**8.** False
9. True	**10.** False	**11.** False	**12.** True	**13.** True	**14.** False	**15.** True	**16.** True
17. True	**18.** True	**19.** True	**20.** True	**21.** False	**22.** False	**23.** False	**24.** True

Multiple Choice Questions

1. (b); **2.** (c); **3.** (e); **4.** (a); **5.** (a); **6.** (a); **7.** (b);

ANNEXURE 2

Deciphering Pointer Declarations

INTRODUCTION

The right-left rule is a widely used rule for creating as well as deciphering C++ declarations. Before starting, let us first understand the meaning of different symbols (Table A2.1) and the way in which they are read.

Table A2.1 Symbols

Symbol	Read as	Location
*	'pointer to'	placed on the left side
[]	'array of'	placed on the right side
()	'function returning'	placed on the right side

A2.1 STEPS TO DECIPHER THE DECLARATION

Step 1 Find the identifier and read as 'identifier is'.

Step 2 Read the symbols on the right of the identifier. For example, if you find '()', then you know that it is a function declaration. So you can now say, 'identifier is function returning'. If you encounter a '[]', then it read it as 'identifier is array of'.

Continue moving right until you either run out of symbols or you encounter a right parenthesis.

Step 3 Now, check the symbols to the left of the identifier. If it is not a symbol given in the table, then just say it. For example, if you encounter int, then just say it as it is. Otherwise, translate it into English using the given table. Continue going left until you either run out of symbols or you encounter a left parenthesis.

```
int *ptr[];
```

Step 4 Repeat steps 2 and 3 until the entire declaration is completely deciphered.

Consider some examples:

Step 1 Find the identifier. Here, the identifier is `ptr`. So, say,

'ptr is'

Step 2 Identify the symbols on the right side of the identifier until you run out of symbols or encounter a left parenthesis. Here, the symbol is[]. So, say
'ptr is array of'

Step 3 Move to left of the identifier until you run out of symbols or encounter a left parenthesis. Here, the symbol is `*`. So, say,
'ptr is array of pointer to'

```
int *(*func())();
```

Step 4 Continue moving left. Here, you find `int`. So, say,
'ptr is array of pointer to int'.

Now decipher the following declaration:

Step 1 Find the identifier. Here, the identifier is `func`. So, say,
'func is'

Step 2 Identify the symbols on the right side of the identifier until you run out of symbols or encounter a left parenthesis. Here, the symbol is `()`. So, say
'func is function returning'

Step 3 Move to left of the identifier until you run out of symbols or encounter a left parenthesis. Here, the symbol is *. So, say,
'func is function returning pointer to'

Step 4 Can't move left anymore because of the left parenthesis, so now move to right. Here, you will find a symbol `()`. So, say,
'func is function returning pointer to function returning'

Step 5 Can't move right anymore as all symbols have exhausted so move to left. Here, you will encounter a '*'. So, say,
'func is function returning pointer to function returning pointer to'

Step 6 Continue moving left. Here, you will find `int`. So, say,
'func is function returning pointer to function returning pointer to int'.

Some declarations also contain array size and function parameters. If you encounter a symbol as '`[10]`', then read it as 'array (size 10)'. If you encounter something like '`(int *,char)`', then read it as 'function expecting (int *,char) and returning...'.

Now, consider such an example and decipher the following declaration:

```
int (*(*func)(int*, char))[3][5];
```

Use the steps illustrated here and check your answer. It is

```
  "func  is pointer to function expecting (int *,char) and
returning pointer to array (size 3) of array (size 5) of int."
```

A2.2 SOME ILLEGAL DECLARATIONS IN C++

It is quite possible that you end up with some illegal declarations using this rule. Therefore, you must be very clear about what is legal in C++ and what is not allowed in the language. For example, consider a declaration givenhere.

```
int *((*func)())[][];
```

This can be deciphered as, 'func is pointer to function returning array of pointer to int'. However,a function cannot return an array;only a pointer can return an array . Therefore, this declaration is illegal.

Let us look at some more illegal combinations in C++ language:

```
[]() - C++ does not permit an array of functions
()() - A function cannot return a function
()[] - A function cannot return an array
```

Table A2.2 gives the declaration, meaning, and its remarks as valid or invalid.

Table A2.2 Declarations

Declaration	Meaning	Remarks
float num;	num is a float	Valid
char *ch;	ch is a pointer to char	Valid
int arr[];	arr is an array ofint	Valid
float func();	func is a function returningfloat	Valid
int **ptr;	ptr is a pointer to pointer toint	Valid
char (*ptr)[];	ptr is a pointer to array of char	Valid
char (*ptr)();	ptr is a pointer to function returning char	Valid
float *ptr[];	ptr is an array of pointers tofloat	Valid
int mat[][];	mat is an array of array ofint	Valid
int func[]()	func is an array of function returningint	Invalid
float *func();	func is a function returning pointer tofloat	Valid
float func()[];	func is a function returning array offloat	Invalid
float func()();	func is a function returning function returningfloat	Invalid
int ***ptr;	ptr is a pointer to pointer to pointer toint	Valid
int (**ptr)[];	ptr is a pointer to pointer to array ofint	Valid
float (**func)();	func is a pointer to pointer to a function returningfloat	Valid
char *(*ptr)[];	ptr is a pointer to array of pointer to char	Valid
float (*ptr)[][];	ptr is a pointer to array of array offloat	Valid
float (*ptr)[]();	ptr is a pointer to array of function returningfloat	Invalid
char *(*(ptr)();	ptr is a pointer to function returning a pointer to char	Valid
char (*ptr)()[];	ptr is a pointer to function returning an array of char	Invalid

(*Contd*)

Table A2.2 (*Contd*)

Declaration	Meaning	Remarks
int (*ptr)()();	ptr is a pointer to function returning function returningint	Invalid
float **ptr[];	ptr is an array of pointer to pointer toint	Valid
char (*ptr[])[];	ptr is an array of pointer to array of char	Valid
char (*ptr[])();	ptr is an array of pointer to function returning char	Valid
float *ptr[][];	ptr is an array of array of pointer tofloat	Valid
int arr[][][];	arr is an array of array of array ofint	Valid
int arr[][]();	arr is an array of array of function returningint	Invalid
float *arr[]();	arr is an array of function returning pointer to float	Invalid
int arr[]()[];	arr is an array of function returning array ofint	Invalid
float **func();	func is a function returning pointer to float pointer (orpointer tofloat)	Valid
char *func()[];	func is a function returning array of char pointer	Invalid
float (*func())[];	func is a function returning pointer to array of float	Valid
float (*func())();	func is a function returning pointer to function returningfloat	Valid
char func()[][];	func is a function returning array of array of char	Invalid
char func()[]();	func is a function returning array of array of function returning char	Invalid
char *func()();	func is a function returning function returning char pointer	Invalid

CHAPTER 8

Structure, Union, and Enumerated Data Types

KEY Concepts

Structure • Operations on structures • Nested structures • Array of structures • Typedef • Self-referential structures • Union • Operations on unions • Enumerated data types

INTRODUCTION

A structure is similar to records. It stores related information about an entity. A structure is basically a user-defined data type that can store related information, even of different data types, together. The major difference between a structure and an array is that an array contains related information but the information has the same data type.

A structure is, therefore, a collection of variables under a single name. The variables within a structure are of different data types and each type has a name that is used to select it from the structure.

8.1 STRUCTURE DECLARATION

A structure is declared using the keyword `struct`, followed by a structure name. All the variables of a structure are declared within the structure. A structure type is generally declared by using the following syntax:

```
struct struct-name
{   data_type var-name;
    data_type var-name;
    ...
};
```

> **Programming Tip:** Do not forget to place a semicolon after the definition of structures and unions.

For example, we have to define a structure for a student. The related information can be `roll_number`, `name`, `course`, and `fees`. This structure can be declared as follows:

```
struct student
{   int r_no;
    char name[20];
    char course[20];
    float fees;
};
```

Here, structure has become a user-defined data type. Each var-name declared within a structure is called a member of the structure. The structure declaration, however, does not allocate any memory or consume storage space. It just gives a template that conveys to the compiler how the structure is laid out in memory and gives details of member names. Like any other data type, memory is allocated for the structure when we declare a variable of the structure. For example, we can define a variable of student by writing

```
student stud1;
```

Here, student is a data type and stud1 is a variable. There is another way of declaring variables. In the following syntax, the variable is declared at the time of structure declaration.

Programming Tip: The variable of a structure or a union can be declared at the time of structure/union definition by placing the variable name after the closing brace and before the semicolon.

```
struct student
{   int r_no;
    char name[20];
    char course[20];
    float fees;
}stud1, stud2;
```

In the declaration, we declare two variables—stud1 and stud2 of structure student. Therefore, when you want to declare more than one variable of the structure, separate the variables using a comma. When we declare variables of the structure, a separate memory is allocated for each variable.

Note Structure type and variable declaration of a structure can be either local or global, depending on their placement in the code.

Finally, member names and names of the structure follow the same rules as laid down for the names of ordinary variables. However, care should be taken to ensure that the name of structure and the name of a structure member should not be the same. Moreover, the structure name and its variable name should be different.

8.2 TYPEDEF DECLARATIONS

The typedef, derived from type definition, is a keyword that enables the programmer to create a new data type name for an existing data type. By using typedef, no new data is created; rather, an alternate name is given to a known data type.

The general syntax of using the typedef keyword is given as follows:

```
typedef existing data type new_data_type
```

Note that typedef statement does not occupy any memory; it simply defines a new type. For example, if we write

```
typedef int INTEGER;
```

Programming Tip: C++ does not allow declaration of variables at the time of creating a typedef definition. Therefore, variables must be declared in an independent statement.

Then, `INTEGER` is the new name of data type `int` to declare variables using the new data type name, precede the variable name with the data type name (new). Therefore, to define an integer variable, we may now write

```
INTEGER num=5;
```

When we precede a `struct` name with `typedef` keyword, then `struct` becomes a new type. It is used to make the construct shorter with more meaningful names for types already defined by C++ or for types that have been declared. With a `typedef` declaration, `new_data_type` becomes a synonym for the `type`.

For example,

```
typedef struct student
{   int r_no;
    char name[20];
    char course[20];
    float fees;
};
```

Now that you have preceded the structure's name with the keyword `typedef`, the student becomes a new data type. Therefore, you can directly declare variables of this new data type as you declare variables of type `int`, `float`, `char`, `double`, etc. To declare a variable of structure `student`, you will write,

```
student stud1;
```

Note that we have not written `struct student stud1`. Consider the following statements:

```
typedef char name[10];
name name1, name2;
```

After these statements, the type name becomes a new data type which is a `10` element array of characters. Therefore, we write

- `name1[3]`, to access the fourth element of name1
- `name1` or `& name1[0]`, to access the staring address of name1

However, `typedef` is frequently used to create reference type or alias as follows:

```
typedef float & FLOATREF;
FLOATREF a = b;          is same as writing,
float &a = b;
```

Note All structure declarations in C++ are typedef by default; therefore, explicit use of the struct keyword during structure-variable definition is optional. They are used when creating structure's pointer or reference type.

8.3 INITIALIZATION OF STRUCTURES

A structure can be initialized in the same way as other data types. Initializing a structure means assigning some constants to the members of the structure. When the user does not explicitly initialize the structure, C++ automatically initializes the structure. For `int` and `float` members, the values initialized to zero and `char` and string members are initialized to the `'\0'` by default.

The initializers are enclosed in braces and are separated by commas. However, care must be taken to see that the initializers match their corresponding types in the structure definition.

The general syntax to initialize a structure variable is given as follows:

```
struct struct_name
{   data_type member_name1;
    data_type member_name2;
    data_type member_name3;
    .......................................
}struct_var = {constant1, constant2, constant 3,...};
OR
struct struct_name
{   data_type member_name1;
    data_type member_name2;
    data_type member_name3;
    .......................................
};
struct_name struct_var = {constant1, constant2, constant 3,...};
```

For example, we can initialize a student `structure` by writing

Programming Tip: It is an error to assign a structure of one type to a structure of another type.

```
struct student
{   int r_no;
    char name[20];
    char course[20];
    float fees;
}stud1 = {01, "Rahul", "BCA", 45000};
```

or by writing

```
struct student stud1 = {01, "Rahul", "BCA", 45000};
```

If all members of a structure are not initialized, it is called partial initialization. In case of partial initialization, the first few members of the structure are initialized and the rest that are un-initialized are assigned default values.

Note CPU (or computer) stores structures using the concept of word boundary which will be discussed in Annexure 3 along with slack byte.

8.4 ACCESSING THE MEMBERS OF A STRUCTURE

Each member of a structure can be used like a normal variable, but its name will be a bit longer. A structure member variable is generally accessed using a `'.'` or a dot operator. The syntax of accessing a structure a member of a structure is as follows:

Programming Tip: A member of the structure cannot be accessed directly using its name. Rather, you must use the structure name followed by dot operator before specifying the member name.

```
struct_var.member_name
```

The dot operator is used to select a particular member of the structure. For example, to assign value to the individual data members of the structure variable `stud1`, we may write

```
stud1.r_no = 01;
stud1.name = "Rahul";
stud1.course = "BCA";
stud1.fees = 45000;
```

To input values for data members of the structure variable `stud1`, we may write

```
cin>>stud1.r_no;
cin.getline(stud1.name, 20);
```

Similarly, to print the values of structure variable stud1, we may write

```
cout<<stud1.course;
cout<<stud1.fees;
```

Memory is allocated only when we declare variables of or instantiate the structure. In the absence of any variable, structure definition is just a template that will be used to reserve memory when a variable of type `struct` will be declared.

Once the variables of a structure are defined, we can perform a few operations on them. For example, we can use the assignment operator '=' to assign the values of one variable to another.

Note →,.,() and [] have highest priority of all the operators. This is evident from the following statement `stud1.fees++` will be interpreted as `(stud1.fees)++`.

8.5 COPYING AND COMPARING STRUCTURES

Programming Tip: An error will be generated if you try to compare two structure variables.

We can assign a structure to another structure of the same type. For example, if we have two structure variables `stud1` and `stud2` of type `struct` student given as

```
struct student stud1 = {01, "Rahul", "BCA", 45000};
struct student stud2;
```

To assign one structure variable to another, we will write

```
stud2 = stud1;
```

This statement initializes the members of `stud2` with the values of members of `stud1`.

C++ does not permit comparison of one structure variable with another structure variable. However, individual members of one structure can be compared with individual members of another structure. When we compare one structure member with another, the comparison will behave like any other ordinary variable's comparison. For example, to compare the fees of two students, we will write

```
if(stud1.fees > stud2.fees)
    Do something
```

Program 8.1 Write a program using structures to read and display the information about a student.

```
using namespace std;
#include<iostream>
int main()
{   struct student
    {   int roll_no;
        char name[20];
        float fees;
    };
    struct student stud1;
    cout<<"\n Enter the roll number : ";
    cin>>stud1.roll_no;
    cout<<"\n Enter the name : ";
    cin.ignore();
    cin.getline(stud1.name, 20);
    cout<<"\n Enter the fees : ";
    cin>>stud1.fees;
```

```
    cout<<"\n ********STUDENT'S DETAILS *******";
    cout<<"\n ROLL No. = "<<stud1.roll_no;
    cout<<"\n NAME. = "<<stud1.name;
    cout<<"\n FEES = "<<stud1.fees;
}
```

OUTPUT

```
Enter the roll number : 01
Enter the name : Rahul
Enter the fees : 45000
********STUDENT'S DETAILS *******
ROLL No. = 01
NAME. = Rahul
FEES = 45000.00
```

Program 8.2 Write a program to read, display, add, and subtract two complex numbers.

```
using namespace std;
#include<iostream>
int main()
{   struct complex
    {   int real;
        int imag;
    };
    complex c1, c2, sum_c, sub_c;
    int option;
    do
    {   cout<<"\n ******** MAIN MENU *********";
        cout<<"\n 1. Read the complex numbers ";
        cout<<"\n 2. Display the complex numbers";
        cout<<"\n 3. Add the complex numbers";
        cout<<"\n 4. Subtract the complex numbers";
        cout<<"\n 5. EXIT";
        cout<<"\n Enter your option : ";
        cin>>option;
        switch(option)
        {   case 1:
                cout<<"\n Enter the real and imaginary parts of the first complex
                number : ";
                cin>>c1.real>>c1.imag;
                cout<<"\n Enter the real and imaginary parts of the second complex
                number : ";
                cin>>c2.real>>c2.imag;
                break;
            case 2:
                cout<<"\n The first complex number is : "<<c1.real<<" + "
                <<c1.imag<<"i";
                cout<<"\n The second complex number is : "<< c2.real<<" + "
                <<c2.imag<<"i";
                break;
            case 3 :
                sum_c.real = c1.real + c2.real;
                sum_c.imag = c1.real + c2.imag;
                cout<<"\n The sum of two complex numbers is : "<<sum_c.real
                <<" + "<< sum_c.imag<<"i";
```

```
                break;
            case 4 :
                sub_c.real = c1.real - c2.real;
                sub_c.imag = c1.real - c2.imag;
                cout<<"\n The difference between two complex numbers is : "
                <<sub_c.real <<" + "<< sub_c.imag<< "i";
                break;
        }
    }while(option != 5);
}
```

SAMPLE OUTPUT

```
Enter the real and imaginary parts of the first complex number : 5 2
n Enter the real and imaginary parts of the second complex number : 3 4
The sum of two complex numbers is : 8 + 6i
```

Program 8.3 Write a program to enter two points and then calculate the distance between them.

```
using namespace std;
#include<iostream>
#include<math.h>
int main()
{   struct point
    {   int x, y;
    };
    point p1, p2;
    float distance;
    cout<<"\n Enter the coordinates of the first point : ";
    cin>>p1.x>>p1.y;
    cout<<"\n Enter the coordinates of the second point : ";
    cin>>p2.x>>p2.y;
    distance = sqrt(pow((p1.x - p2.x), 2) - (pow((p1.y - p2.y), 2)));
    cout<<"\n The coordinates of the first point are : "<<p1.x<< " "<<p1.y;
    cout<<"\n The coordinates of the second point are : "<<p2.x<<" " <<p2.y;
    cout<<"\n Distance between p1 and p2 = "<<distance;
}
```

OUTPUT

```
Enter the coordinates of the first point : 2 3
Enter the coordinates of the second point : 9 9
The coordinates of the first point are : 2x 3y
The coordinates of the second point are : 9x 9y
Distance between p1 and p2 = 3.60551
```

8.6 NESTED STRUCTURES

A structure can be placed within another structure and may contain another structure as its member. This kind of structure is called a nested structure.

Let us now see how we declare nested structures or structures that contain structures. Although it is possible to declare a nested structure with one declaration, declaring it in this way is not recommended. An easier and clearer way is to declare the structures separately and then group them in the high-level structure. When this is done, care must be taken to check that nesting must be done from inside out (from the lowest level to the most inclusive level). Declare the inner-most structure, followed by the next level structure, working towards the outer and the most inclusive structure.

```
using namespace std;
#include<iostream>
struct
{   char first_name[20];
    char mid_name[20];
    char last_name[20];
}NAME;
struct
{   int dd;
   int mm;
   int yy;
}DATE;
struct student
{   int r_no;
    NAME name;
    char course[20];
    Date DOB;
    float fees;
};
```

In this example, the structure student contains two other structures—`NAME` and `DATE`. Both these structures have their own fields. Just as structure `NAME` has three fields—`first_name, mid_name, and last_name,` the structure `DATE` also has three fields—`dd, mm, and yy,` which specify the day, month, and year of the date. To assign value to the structure fields, we will write

```
student stud1;
stud1.name.first_name = "Janak";
stud1.name.mid_name = "Raj";
stud1.name.last_name = "Thareja";
stud1.course = "BCA";
stud1.DOB.dd = 15;
stud1.DOB.mm = 09;
stud1.DOB.yy = 1990;
stud1.fees = 45000;
```

Note that in case of nested structures we use the dot operator in conjunction with the structure variables to access the members of the innermost as well as the outermost structures. The use of nested structures is illustrated in the program given here.

Program 8.4 Write a program to read and display information of a student using structure within a structure.

```
using namespace std;
#include<iostream>
int main()
{   struct DOB
    {   int day;
        int month;
        int year;
    };
    struct student
    {   int roll_no;
        char name[20];
        float fees;
        struct DOB date;
```

```
    };
    student stud1;
    cout<<"\n Enter the roll number : ";
    cin>>stud1.roll_no;
    cout<<"\n Enter the name : ";
        cin.ignore();
    cin.getline(stud1.name, 20);
    cout<<"\n Enter the fees : ";
    cin>>stud1.fees;
    cout<<"\n Enter the DOB : ";
    cin>>stud1.date.day>>stud1.date.month>>stud1.date.year;
    cout<<"\n ********STUDENT'S DETAILS*******";
    cout<<"\n ROLL No. = "<< stud1.roll_no;
    cout<<"\n NAME. = "<<stud1.name;
    cout<<"\n FEES. = "<< stud1.fees;
    cout<<"\n DOB = "<<stud1.date.day<<" - "<<stud1.date.month<<" - "<<stud1.date.year;
}
```

OUTPUT

```
Enter the roll number : 01
Enter the name : Rahul
Enter the fees : 45000
Enter the DOB : 25 09 1991
********STUDENT'S DETAILS*******
ROLL No. = 01
NAME. = Rahul
FEES. = 45000.00
DOB = 25-09-1991
```

8.7 ARRAYS OF STRUCTURES

In the above sections, we have seen how to declare a structure and assign values to its data members. Now, we will look at how we declare the array of a structure. For this purpose, let us first analyse where we would need the array of structures.

Programming Tip: It is an error to omit array subscripts when referring to individual structures of an array of structures.

In a class, we have, at least, 30 students. Therefore, the same definition of the structure can be used for all 30 students. This would be possible when we make an array of the structure. An array of a structure is declared in the same way as we had declared an array of a built-in data type.

The general syntax for declaring an array of structure can be given as follows:

```
struct student
{   int r_no;
    char name[20];
    char course[20];
    float fees;
};
```

Consider the following example for given structure definition.

```
struct student
{   int r_no;
    char name[20];
    char course[20];
    float fees;
};
```

A student array can be declared simply by writing,

```
student stud[30];
```

Now, to assign values to the ith student of the class, we will write,

```
stud[i].r_no = 09;
stud[i].name = "RASHI";
stud[i].course = "MCA";
stud[i].fees = 60000;
```

In order to initialize the array of structure variables at the time of declaration, you should write as follows:

```
student stud[3] = {{01, "Aman", "BCA", 45000},{02, "Aryan", "MCA", 60000},
{03, "John", "BCA", 45000}};
```

The use of array of structures is illustrated in the programs given here.

Program 8.5 Write a program to read and display information of all the students in the class.

```
using namespace std;
#include<iostream>
int main()
{   struct student
    {   int roll_no;
        char name[20];
        float fees;
        char DOB[80];
    };
    struct student stud[50];
    int n, i;
    cout<<"\n Enter the number of students : ";
    cin>>n;
    for(i=0;i<n;i++)
    {   cout<<"\n Enter the roll number : ";
        cin>>stud[i].roll_no;
        cout<<"\n Enter the name : ";
        cin.ignore();
        cin.getline(stud[i].name, 20);
        cout<<"\n Enter the fees : ";
        cin>>stud[i].fees;
        cout<<"\n Enter the DOB : ";
        cin>>stud[i].DOB;
    }
    for(i=0;i<n;i++)
    {   cout<<"\n ********DETAILS OF "<<i+1<<"STUDENT*******";
        cout<<"\n ROLL No. = "<< stud[i].roll_no;
        cout<<"\n NAME. = "<<stud[i].name;
        cout<<"\n FEES = "<< stud[i].fees;
        cout<<"\n DOB = "<<stud[i].DOB;
    }
}
```

SAMPLE OUTPUT

```
********DETAILS OF 1 STUDENT*******
```

```
ROLL No. = 1
NAME. = Dev Malhotra
FEES = 12345
DOB = 30-08-10
```

Program 8.6 Write a program to read and display the information of all the students in the class. Edit the details of the ith student and redisplay the entire information.

```
using namespace std;
#include<iostream>
#include<string.h>
int main()
{   struct student
    {   int roll_no;
        char name[20];
        float fees;
        char DOB[80];
    };
    student stud[50];
    int n, i, rolno, new_rolno;
    float new_fees;
    char new_DOB[80], new_name[80];
    cout<<"\n Enter the number of students : ";
    cin>>n;
    for(i=0;i<n;i++)
    {   cout<<"\n Enter the roll number : ";
        cin>>stud[i].roll_no;
        cout<<"\n Enter the name : ";
        cin.ignore();
        cin.getline(stud[i].name,20);
        cout<<"\n Enter the fees : ";
        cin>>stud[i].fees;
        cout<<"\n Enter the DOB : ";
        cin>>stud[i].DOB;
    }
    cout<<"\n Enter the record number of the rolno of the student
            whose record has to be edited : ";
    cin>>rolno;
    cout<<"\n Enter the new roll number : ";
    cin>>new_rolno;
    cout<<"\n Enter the new name : ";
    cin>>new_name;
    cout<<"\n Enter the new fees : ";
    cin>>new_fees;
    cout<<"\n Enter the new date of birth : ";
    cin>>new_DOB;
    stud[rolno].roll_no = new_rolno;
    strcpy(stud[rolno].name, new_name);
    stud[rolno].fees = new_fees;
    strcpy(stud[rolno].DOB, new_DOB);
    for(i=0;i<n;i++)
    {   cout<<"\n ********DETAILS OF "<<i+1<<" STUDENT*******";
        cout<<"\n ROLL No. = "<< stud[i].roll_no;
        cout<<"\n NAME. = "<<stud[i].name;
        cout<<"\n FEES. = "<<stud[i].fees;
```

```
        cout<<"\n DATE OF BIRTH = "<<stud[i].DOB;
    }
}
```

OUTPUT

```
********DETAILS OF 1 STUDENT*******
ROLL No. = 1
NAME. = Dev Malhotra
FEES = 12345
DOB = 30-08-10
```

8.8 STRUCTURES AND FUNCTIONS

To make structures completely useful, we must have a mechanism to pass them to functions and return them. A function may access the members of a structure in three ways as shown in Fig. 8.1.

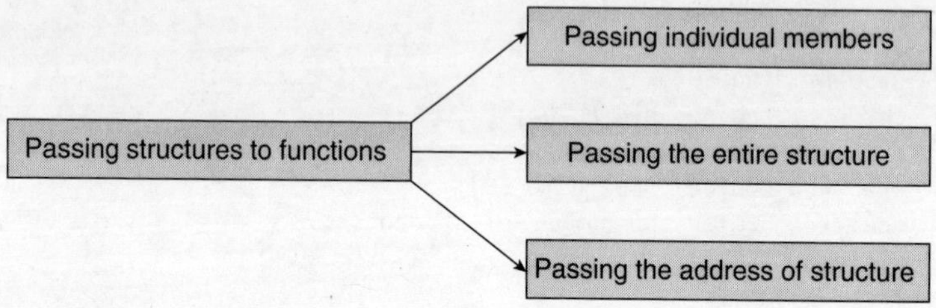

Figure 8.1 Passing structures to a function

8.8.1 Passing Individual Members

To pass any individual member of the structure to a function, we must use the direct selection operator to refer to the individual members for the actual parameters. The called program does not know if the two variables are ordinary variables or structure members. Look at the code given here which illustrates this concept.

Example 8.1 Program that passes individual structure elements to a function

```
using namespace std;
#include<iostream>
typedef struct
{   int x;
    int y;
}POINT;
void display(int, int);
main()
{   POINT p1 = {2, 3};
    display(p1.x, p1.y);
}
void display( int a, int b)
{   cout<<"\n The coordinates of the point are : "<<a<<"  "<<b;
}
```

OUTPUT

```
The coordinates of the point are : 2 3
```

Explanation: In the above program, x and y are individual members of the structure.

8.8.2 Passing the Entire Structure

Programming Tip: An array of structure can also be passed to a function

Just like any other variable, we can pass an entire structure as function argument. When a structure is passed as an argument, it is passed using call by value method. A copy of each member of the structure is made. No doubt, this is a very inefficient method especially when the structure is very big or the function is called frequently. Therefore, in such a situation passing and working with pointers may be more efficient.

The general syntax for passing a structure to a function and returning a structure can be given as:

```
struct_name func_name(struct_name struct_var);
```

This syntax can vary as per the need. For example, in some situations, we may want a function to receive a structure but return a void or value of some other data type.

Example 8.2 Write a program that passes array of structures to a function

```
using namespace std;
#include<iostream>
struct Employee
{   int emp_Id;
    char name[10];
    float salary;
};
void read_data(Employee e[])
{   for(int i=0;i<3;i++)
    {   cout<<"\n\n  Enter the EMP ID : ";
        cin>>e[i].emp_Id;
        cout<<"\n Enter the name : ";
        cin.ignore();
        cin.getline(e[i].name, 10);
        cout<<"\n Enter the salary : ";
        cin>>e[i].salary;
    }
}
void display(Employee e[])
{   for(int i=0;i<3;i++)
    {   cout<<"\n\n  EMP ID : "<<e[i].emp_Id;
        cout<<"\n NAME : "<<e[i].name;
        cout<<"\n SALARY : "<<e[i].salary;
    }
}
int main()
{
    Employee e[3];
    read_data(e);
    display(e);
}
```

Example 8.3 Program to show how a structure is passed to the function using call-by-value method

```
using namespace std;
#include<iostream>
typedef struct
{   int x;
    int y;
```

```
}POINT;
void display(POINT);
int main()
{   POINT p1 = {2, 3};
    display(p1);
}
void display( POINT p)
{   cout<<p.x <<" "<< p.y;
}
```

OUTPUT

```
2 3
```

Explanation: In the program, note that structure variable p1 is passed to the function display().

8.8.3 Returning Structures

Functions can return a structure either by making a copy of the structure variable of by returning its reference. For example, continuing with Example 8.3, if we had a function get_Point() that returns a POINT variable, then any of the two techniques could have been used

a. By copying the structure variable.

```
POINT get_Point()
{   POINT P1;
    P1.x = 4;
    P1.y = 5;
return P1;
    }
```

b. By returning a reference to the structure variable

```
POINT & get_Point(Point &P)
{   P.x = 4;
    P.y = 5;
return &P;
}
```

Therefore, the syntax of returning a structure is

```
struct_name func_name(parameters if any);
```

Program 8.7 Write a program to read, display, add, and subtract two distances. Distance must be defined using kilometres and metres.

```
using namespace std;
#include<iostream>
struct DISTANCE
{   int kms;
    int meters;
};
DISTANCE d1, d2, d3, d4;
DISTANCE add_distance(DISTANCE d1, DISTANCE d2)
{   DISTANCE sum;
    sum.meters = d1.meters + d2. meters;
    sum.kms = d1.kms + d2.kms;
```

```
    if(sum.meters >=1000)
    {   sum.meters = sum.meters%1000;
    sum.kms += 1;
    }
    return sum;
}
DISTANCE subtract_distance(DISTANCE d1, DISTANCE d2)
{   DISTANCE sub;
    if(d1.kms > d2.kms)
    {   sub.meters = d1.meters - d2. meters;
        sub.kms = d1.kms - d2.kms;
    }
    else
    {   sub.meters = d2.meters - d1. meters;
        sub.kms = d2.kms - d1.kms;
    }
    if(sub.meters < 0)
    {   sub.kms = sub.kms - 1;
        sub.meters = sub.meters + 1000;
    }
    return sub;
}
main()
{   int option;
    do
    {   cout<<"\n ******** MAIN MENU *********";
        cout<<"\n 1. Read the distances ";
        cout<<"\n 2. Display the distances";
        cout<<"\n 3. Add the distances";
        cout<<"\n 4. Subtract the distances";
        cout<<"\n 5. EXIT";
        cout<<"\n Enter your option : ";
        cin>>option;
        switch(option)
        {   case 1:
                cout<<"\n Enter the kms and metres in the first distance : ";
                cin>>d1.kms>>d1.meters;
                cout<<"\n Enter the kms and metres in the second distance : ";
                cin>>d2.kms>>d2.meters;
                break;
            case 2:
                cout<<"\n The first distance is : "<<d1.kms<<" kms "<<d1.
                        meters<< " metres";
                cout<<"\n The second distance is : "<<d2.kms<<" kms"<<d2.
                        meters<<" metres";
                break;
            case 3 :
                d3 = add_distance(d1, d2);
                cout<<"\n The sum of two distances is : "<<d3.kms<<" kms"
                        <<d3.meters<<" metres";
                break;
            case 4 :
                d4 = subtract_distance(d1, d2);
```

```
            cout<<"\n The difference between two distances is : "<<d4.
                        kms<<" kms "<<d4.meters<<" metres";
            break;
        }
    }while(option != 5);
}
```

SAMPLE OUTPUT

```
The sum of two distances is : 10 kms 400 metres
```

Let us summarize some points that must be considered while passing a structure to the called function.

- If the called function is returning a copy of the entire structure then it must be declared as `struct` followed by structure name.
- The structure variable used as parameter in the function declaration must be same as that of actual argument in the called function (and that should be the name of the `struct` type)
- When a function returns a structure then in the calling function the returned structure must be assigned to a structure variable of the same type

8.8.4 Passing Structures Through Pointers

Programming Tip: Using pointers to pass a structure to a function much more efficient than sending a structure using call-by-value method,

Passing large structures to function using call-by-value method is very inefficient. Therefore, it is better to pass structures through pointers. It is possible to create a pointer to almost any type in C++, including user-defined types. It is extremely common to create pointers to structures. Like in other cases, a pointer to a structure is never a structure in itself, but is merely a variable that holds the address of a structure. The syntax to declare a pointer to a structure can be given as follows:

```
struct struct_name
{   data_type member_name1;
    data_type member_name2;
    data_type member_name3;
    ...................................
}*ptr;
OR
struct struct_name *ptr;
```

For our student structure, we can declare a pointer variable by writing

```
struct student *ptr_stud, stud;
```

Next, we assign the address of stud to the pointer using the address operator (`&`) as we would do in case of any other pointer. To assign the address, we will write

```
ptr_stud = &stud;
```

To access the members of the structure, we may write

```
/* get the structure, then select a member */
(*ptr_stud).roll_no;
```

Programming Tip: The selection operator (->) is a single token, so do not place any white space between them.

Since parenthesis have a higher precedence than *, writing this statement would work well. However, this statement is not easy for a beginner to work with. So users can use another operator known as 'pointing-to' operator (->). Here, it is being used as follows:

```
/* the roll_no in the structure ptr_stud points to */
ptr_stud->roll_no = 01;
```

Thus, this statement is far easier than its alternative.

Program 8.8 Write a program using pointer to structure to initialize the members in the structure.

```
using namespace std;
#include<iostream>
#include<string.h>
struct student
{   int r_no;
    char name[20];
    char course[20];
    float fees;
};
main()
{   struct student stud1, stud2, *ptr_stud1, *ptr_stud2;
    ptr_stud1 = &stud1;
    ptr_stud2 = &stud2;
    ptr_stud1->r_no = 01;
    strcpy(ptr_stud1->name, "Rahul");
    strcpy(ptr_stud1->course, "BCA");
    ptr_stud1->fees = 45000;
    cout<<"\n Enter the details of the second student :";
    cout<<"\n Enter the Roll Number =";
    cin>>ptr_stud2->r_no;
    cout<<"\n Enter the Name = ";
    cin.ignore();
    cin.getline(ptr_stud2->name, 20);
    cout<<"\n Enter the Course = ";
    cin>>ptr_stud2->course;
    cout<<"\n Enter the Fees = ";
    cin>>ptr_stud2->fees;
    cout<<"\n DETAILS OF FIRST STUDENT";
    cout<<"\n ---------------------------------------------";
    cout<<"\n ROLL NUMBER = "<< ptr_stud1->r_no;
    cout<<"\n NAME = "<<ptr_stud1->name;
    cout<<"\n COURSE = "<<ptr_stud1->course;
    cout<<"\n FEES = "<<ptr_stud1->fees;
    cout<<"\n\n\n\n DETAILS OF SECOND STUDENT";
    cout<<"\n ---------------------------------------------";
    cout<<"\n ROLL NUMBER = "<<ptr_stud2->r_no;
    cout<<"\n NAME = "<<ptr_stud2->name;
    cout<<"\n COURSE = "<<ptr_stud2->course;
    cout<<"\n FEES = "<< ptr_stud2->fees;
}
```

OUTPUT

```
Enter the details of the second student :
Enter the Roll Number = 02
Enter the Name = Aditya
Enter the Course = MCA
Enter the Fees = 60000
DETAILS OF FIRST STUDENT
----------------------------------------------
ROLL NUMBER = 01
NAME = Rahul
COURSE = BCA
FEES = 45000.00
DETAILS OF SECONDFIRST STUDENT
----------------------------------------------
ROLL NUMBER = 02
NAME = Aditya
COURSE = MCA
FEES = 60000.00
```

Program 8.9 Write a program using pointer to structure to initialize the members in the structure using an alternative technique.

```
using namespace std;
#include<iostream>
struct student
{   int r_no;
    char name[20];
    char course[20];
    float fees;
};
main()
{   struct student *ptr_stud1;
    struct student stud1 = {01, "Rahul", "BCA", 45000};
    ptr_stud1 = &stud1;
    cout<<"\n DETAILS OF STUDENT";
    cout<<"\n ---------------------------------------------";
    cout<<"\n ROLL NUMBER = "<< ptr_stud1->r_no;
    cout<<"\n NAME = "<< ptr_stud1->name;
    cout<<"\n COURSE = "<<ptr_stud1->course;
    cout<<"\n FEES = "<< ptr_stud1->fees;
}
```

OUTPUT

```
DETAILS OF STUDENT
----------------------------------------------
ROLL NUMBER = 01
NAME = Rahul
COURSE = BCA
FEES = 45000.00
```

Program 8.10 Write a program using array of pointer to structure to read and display data of a student.

```
using namespace std;
#include<iostream>
struct student
```

```
{   int r_no;
    char name[20];
    char course[20];
    int fees;
};
student *ptr[3];
main()
{   int i;
    for(i=0;i<3;i++)
    {   ptr[i] = new student;
        cout<<"\n Enter the data for the "<<i+1<<"th student ";
        cout<<"\n \t ROLL NO. : ";
        cin>>ptr[i]->r_no;
        cout<<"\n \t NAME : ";
        cin.ignore();
        cin.getline(ptr[i]->name,20);
        cout<<"\n \t COURSE : ";
        cin.getline(ptr[i]->course,20);
        cout<<"\n \t FEES : ";
        cin>>ptr[i]->fees;
    }
    cout<<"\n DETAILS OF STUDENT";
    cout<<"\n ---------------------------------------------";
    for(i=0;i<3;i++)
    {   cout<<"\n ROLL NUMBER = "<< ptr[i]->r_no;
        cout<<"\n NAME = "<<ptr[i]->name;
        cout<<"\n COURSE = "<<ptr[i]->course;
        cout<<"\n FEES = "<<ptr[i]->fees;
    }
}
```

OUTPUT

```
DETAILS OF STUDENT
---------------------------------------------
ROLL NUMBER = 01
NAME = Rahul
COURSE = BCA
FEES = 45000.00
```

Program 8.11 Write a program to read, display, add, and subtract two heights. Height must be defined using feet and inches.

```
using namespace std;
#include<iostream>
typedef struct
{   int ft;
    int inch;
}HEIGHT;
HEIGHT h1, h2, h3;
HEIGHT add_height(HEIGHT *, HEIGHT *);
HEIGHT subtract_height(HEIGHT *, HEIGHT *);
main()
{   int option;
    do
    {   cout<<"\n ******** MAIN MENU *********";
        cout<<"\n 1. Read height ";
        cout<<"\n 2. Display height";
```

```
        cout<<"\n 3. Add two heights";
        cout<<"\n 4. Subtract two heights";
        cout<<" 5. EXIT";
        cout<<"\n Enter your option : ";
        cin>>option;
        switch(option)
        {   case 1:
                cout<<"\n Enter the feet and inches of the first height : ";
                cin>>h1.ft>>h1.inch;
                cout<<"\n Enter the feet and inches of the second height : ";
                cin>>h2.ft>>h2.inch;
                break;
            case 2:
                cout<<"\n The first height is : "<<h1.ft<<" ft "<<h1.inch<<" inches";
                cout<<"\n The second height is : "<<h2.ft<<" ft "<<h2.inch<<" inches";
                break;
            case 3 :
                h3 = add_height(&h1, &h2);
                cout<<"\n The sum of two heights is : "<<h3.ft<<" ft "<<h3.
                            inch<<" inches";
                break;
            case 4 :
                h3 = subtract_height(&h1, &h2);
                cout<<"\n The difference of two heights is : "<<h3.ft<<" ft "<<h3.
                            inch<<" inches";
                break;
        }
    }while(option != 5);
}
HEIGHT add_height(HEIGHT *h1, HEIGHT *h2)
{   HEIGHT sum;
    sum.ft=0;
    sum.inch = h1->inch + h2->inch;
    while(sum.inch >= 12)
    {   sum.inch -= 12;
        sum.ft++;
    }
    sum.ft += h1->ft + h2->ft;
    return sum;
}
HEIGHT subtract_height(HEIGHT *h1, HEIGHT *h2)
{   HEIGHT sub;
    if( h1->ft > h2->ft)
    {   if(h1->inch < h2->inch)
        {   h1->inch += 12;
            h1->ft--;
        }
        sub.inch = h1->inch - h2->inch;
        sub.ft = h1->ft - h2->ft;
    }
    else
    {   if(h2->inch < h1->inch)
        {   h2->inch += 12;
            h2->ft--;
        }
```

```
        sub.inch = h2->inch - h1->inch;
        sub.ft = h2->ft - h1->ft;
    }
    return sub;
}
```

SAMPLE OUTPUT

```
The difference of two heights is : 7ft 3 inches
```

Program 8.12 Write a program to illustrate the use of arrays within structure.

```
using namespace std;
#include<iostream>
struct student
{   char name[20];
    int roll_no;
    int marks[3];
};
void display(struct student* s)
{   int i;
    cout<<"\n\n\n NAME : "<<s->name <<" \n ROLL NO = "<<s->roll_no<<"\n";
    for(i=0;i<3;i++)
        cout<<" "<<s->marks[i];
}
main()
{   struct student *s[5];
    int i,j;
    for(i=0;i<3;i++)
    {   s[i]= new student;
        cout<<"\n\n Enter the name of "<<i+1<<" student : ";
        cin.getline(s[i]->name,20);
        cin.ignore();
        cout<<"\n Enter the roll number of "<<i+1<<"th student : ";
        cin>>s[i]->roll_no;
        cout<<"\n Enter the marks obtained in three subjects by the
                "<<i+1<<"th student : ";
        for(j=0;j<3;j++)
            cin>>s[i]->marks[j];
        cin.ignore();
    }
    cout<<"\n \n\n ******DETAILS*****";
    for(i=0;i<5;i++)
        display(s[i]);
}
```

OUTPUT

```
NAME : Rahul
ROLL NO = 01
78 89 91
```

8.9 SELF-REFERENTIAL STRUCTURES

Self-referential structures are those structures that contain a reference to data of its same type. In addition to other data, a self-referential structure contains a pointer to a data that is of the same type as that of the structure. For example, consider the structure node given here.

Programming Tip: It is an error to use a structure/ or union variable as a member of its own struct type structure or union type union respectively.

```
struct node
{   int val;
    struct node *next;
};
```

Here, the structure node will contain two types of data—an integer `val` and a pointer to a node. There is a need for such a structure as a self-referential structure is the foundation of other data structures. We will be using them throughout this book and their purpose will be clearer when we discuss linked lists, trees, and graphs.

8.10 C++ EXTENSION TO STRUCTURES

All the points that we have learnt so far are supported both by C as well as C++. However, C++ goes a step further to extend the concept of structures to support OOP philosophy. In C++, a structure can have data as well as functions as its members. Functions defined within a structure can operate on any data defined within that structure.

A structure can also specify its data and functions as private, so that they cannot be accessed by functions defined outside the structure. Note that in the program given in the following section, the structure data members and member functions are accessed using the dot operator.

Program 8.13 Write a program to read, display, add, and subtract two times. Time must be defined using hour, minutes, and seconds.

```
using namespace std;
#include<iostream>
typedef struct TIME
{   int hr;
    int min;
    int sec;
    TIME add_time(TIME t1, TIME t2)
    {   TIME sum;
        sum.min=0, sum.hr=0;
        sum.sec = t1.sec + t2.sec;
        while(sum.sec>=60)
        {   sum.sec -=60;
            sum.min++;
        }
        sum.min += t1.min + t2.min;
        while(sum.min>=60)
        {   sum.min -=60;
            sum.hr++;
        }
        sum.hr += t1.hr + t2.hr;
    return sum;
}
TIME subtract_time(TIME t1, TIME t2)
{   TIME sub;
    if( t1.hr > t2.hr)
    {   if(t1.sec <t2.sec)
        {   t1.sec+=60;
            t1.min--;
        }
        sub.sec = t1.sec - t2.sec;
        if(t1.min < t2.min)
        {   t1.min+=60;
```

```
            t1.hr--;
        }
        sub.min = t1.min - t2.min;
        sub.hr = t1.hr - t2.hr;
        }
        else
        {   if(t2.sec <t1.sec)
            {   t2.sec+=60;
                t2.min--;
            }
            sub.sec = t2.sec - t1.sec;
            if(t2.min < t1.min)
            {   t2.min+=60;
                t2.hr--;
            }
            sub.min = t2.min - t1.min;
            sub.hr = t2.hr - t1.hr;
        }
        return sub;
    }
};
TIME t1, t2, t3;
int main()
{   cout<<"\n Enter the hrs, mins, and secs of the first time : ";
    cin>>t1.hr>>t1.min>>t1.sec;
    cout<<"\n Enter the hrs, mins, and secs of the second time : ";
    cin>>t2.hr>>t2.min>>t2.sec;
    t3 = t1.add_time(t1, t2);
    cout<<"\n The sum of two times is : "<<t3.hr<<" hrs "<<t3.min<<" mins "<<t3.
sec<<" secs";
    t3 = t1.subtract_time(t1, t2);
    cout<<"\n The difference of two times is : "<<t3.hr<<" hrs "<<t3.min<<" mins "<<t3.
sec<<" secs";
}
```

OUTPUT

```
Enter the hrs, mins, and secs of the first time : 5 39 46
Enter the hrs, mins, and secs of the second time : 2 52 33
The sum of two times is :8 32 19
```

8.11 UNION

Like structure, a union is a collection of variables of different data types. The only difference between a structure and a union is that in case of unions, you can only store information in one field at any one time.

To better understand union, think of it as a chunk of memory that is used to store variables of different types. When a new value is assigned to a field, the existing data is replaced with the new data.

Therefore, unions are used to save memory. They are useful for applications that involve multiple members, where values need not be assigned to all the members at any one time.

8.11.1 Declaring a Union

The syntax for declaring a union is same as that of declaring a structure. The only difference is that instead of using the keyword `struct`, the keyword `union` would be used. The syntax for union declaration can be given as follows:

```
union union-name
{   data_type var-name;
    data_type var-name;
    ...
};
```

Again, the `typedef` keyword can be used to simplify the declaration of `union` variables.

The most important thing to remember about a union is that the size of a union is the size of its largest field. This is because a sufficient number of bytes must be reserved to store the largest sized field.

8.11.2 Accessing a Member of a Union

A member of a union can be accessed using the same syntax as that of a structure. To access the fields of a union, use the dot operator(`.`). The union variable name is followed by the dot operator and by the member name. The syntax for accessing a member of a union is given as,

```
union_variable_name.field_name
```

> **Programming Tip:** It is an error to initialize any other union member except the first member.

8.11.3 Initializing Unions

A striking difference between a structure and a union is that in case of a union, the fields share the same memory space, and fresh data replaces any existing data. However, a union variable is initialized in the same way as we initialize a structure variable. The syntax for initializing a union variable is given as,

```
union_variable_name.field_name = value;
```

8.12 UNIONS INSIDE STRUCTURES

A union can be very useful when declared inside a structure. In this section, we will see some programs that make use of union imbibed in a structure to understand how it can be used to write efficient programs that makes effective use of memory space.

Example 8.4 Consider an example in which you want a field of a structure to contain a string or an integer, depending on what the user specifies. The following code illustrates such a scenario.

```
using namespace std;
#include<iostream>
struct student
{   union
    {   char name[20];
        int roll_no;
    };
    int marks;
};
main()
{   struct student stud;
    char choice;
    cout<<"\n You can enter the name or roll number of the student";
    cout<<"\n Do you want to enter the name? (Yes or No) : ";
    cin>>choice;
    if(choice=='y' || choice=='Y')
    { cout<<"\n Enter the name : ";
      cin.getline(stud.name, 20);
```

```
    }
    else
    { cout<<"\n Enter the roll number : ";
      cin>>stud.roll_no;
    }
    cout<<"\n Enter the marks : ";
    cin>>stud.marks;
    if(choice=='y' || choice=='Y')
    cout<<"\n Name : "<<stud.name;
    else
    cout<<"\n Roll Number : "<<stud.roll_no;
    cout<<"\n Marks : "<<stud.marks;
}
```

OUTPUT

```
You can enter the name or roll number of the student
Do you want to enter the name? (Yes or No) Y
Enter the name : Saisha
Enter the marks : 85
Name : Saisha
Marks : 85
```

Note This code is Microsoft-specific code.

Explanation: In the code, we have a union embedded within a structure. As we know, the fields of a union will share memory, in the main program, we ask the user which data he would like to store and depending on his choice the appropriate field is used.

Note Pointing to unions, passing unions to functions, and passing pointers to unions to function are all done in the same way as that of structs.

8.13 ENUMERATED DATA TYPES

The enumerated data type is a user-defined type based on the standard integer type. An enumeration consists of a set of named integer constants. In other words, in an enumerated type, each integer value is assigned an identifier. This identifier, also known as an enumeration constant, can be used as symbolic names to make the program more readable.

To define enumerated data types, we use the keyword `enum`, which is the abbreviation for `ENUMERATE`. Enumerations create new data types to contain values that are not limited to the values fundamental data types may take. The syntax of creating an enumerated data type can be given as follows.

```
enum enumeration_name { identifier1, identifier2, ……., identifiern };
```

The `enum` keyword is basically used to declare and initialize a sequence of integer constants. Here, `enumeration_name` is optional. Consider the example given here which creates a new type of variable called `COLORS` to store colours constants.

```
enum COLORS {RED, BLUE, BLACK, GREEN, YELLOW, PURPLE, WHITE};
```

Note that no fundamental data type is used in the declaration of `COLORS`. After this statement, `COLORS` has become a new data type. Here, `COLORS` is the name given to the set of constants. In case you do not assign any value to a constant, the default value for the first one in the list—`RED` (in our case), has the value of 0. The rest of the undefined constants have a value 1 more than its previous one. That is, if you do not initialize the constants, then each one would have a unique value. The first would be zero and the rest would count upwards. In our example,

```
RED = 0, BLUE = 1, BLACK = 2, GREEN = 3, YELLOW = 4, PURPLE = 5, WHITE = 6
```

If you want to explicitly assign values to these integer constants, then you should specifically mention those values as shown here.

```
enum COLORS {RED = 2, BLUE, BLACK = 5, GREEN = 7, YELLOW, PURPLE, WHITE = 15};
```

As a result of the above statement, now

```
RED = 2, BLUE = 3, BLACK = 5, GREEN = 7, YELLOW = 8, PURPLE = 9, WHITE = 15
```

Example 8.5 To illustrate the declaration and access of enumerated data types

```
using namespace std;
#include<iostream>
main()
{   enum {RED=2, BLUE, BLACK=5, GREEN=7, YELLOW, PURPLE, WHITE=15};
    cout<<"\n RED = "<<RED;
    cout<<"\n BLUE = "<<BLUE;
    cout<<"\n BLACK = "<<BLACK;
    cout<<"\n GREEN = "<<GREEN;
    cout<<"\n YELLOW = "<<YELLOW;
    cout<<"\n PURPLE = "<<PURPLE;
    cout<<"\n WHITE = "<<WHITE;
}
```

OUTPUT

```
RED = 2
BLUE = 3
BLACK = 5
GREEN = 7
YELLOW = 8
PURPLE = 9
WHITE = 15
```

Note The value of an enumerator constant is always of `int` type. Therefore, the storage associated with an enumeration variable is the storage required for a single int value. The enumeration constant or a value of enumerated type can be used anywhere in the program where the C++ language permits an integer expression.

The following rules apply to the members of an enumeration list:

- An enumeration list may contain duplicate constant values. Therefore, two different identifiers may be assigned the same value, say 3.
- The identifiers in the enumeration list must be different from other identifiers in the same scope with the same visibility including ordinary variable names and identifiers in other enumeration lists.

- Enumeration names follow the normal scoping rules. Every enumeration name must be different from other enumeration, structure, and union names with the same visibility.

Note If we create an enumerated type without `enumeration_name`, it is known as an anonymous enumerated type. For example, `enum {OFF, ON};` declares an enumerated type that has two constants `OFF` with a value 0 and `ON` with a value 1.

8.13.1 Enum Variables

We have seen that enumerated constants are basically integers; therefore, programs with statements such as `int fore_color = RED;` are considered to be a legal statement in C++.

In extension to this, C++ also permits to declare variables of an enumerated data type in the same way as we create variables of other basic data type. The syntax for declaring a variable of an enumerated data type can be given as follows:

```
enumeration_name variable_name;
```

To create a variable of `COLORS`, we may write

```
COLORS bg_color;
```

This declares a variable called `bg_color`, which is of the enumerated data type, `COLORS`. Another way to declare a variable can be as illustrated in the statement.

```
enum COLORS {RED, BLUE, BLACK, GREEN, YELLOW, PURPLE, WHITE} bg_color,fore_color;
```

8.13.2 Assigning Values to Enumerated Variables

Once the enumerated variable has been declared, values can be stored in it. However, an enumerated variable can hold only declared values for the type. For example, to assign the colour black to the background colour, we will write

```
bg_color = BLACK;
```

Note that once an enumerated variable has been assigned a value, we can store its value in another variable of the same type. The following statements illustrate this concept.

```
enum COLORS bg_color, border_color;
bg_color = BLACK;
border_color = bg_color;
```

8.13.3 Enumeration Type Conversion

Enumerated types can be implicitly or explicitly cast. For example, the compiler can implicitly cast an enumerated type to an integer when required. However, when we implicitly cast an integer to an enumerated type, the compiler will either generate an error or warning message.

To understand this, answer one question. If we write:

```
enum COLORS {RED, BLUE, BLACK, GREEN, YELLOW, PURPLE, WHITE};
COLORS c;
c = BLACK + WHITE;
```

Here, `c` is an enumerated data type variable. If we write `c = BLACK + WHITE`, then logically, it should be `2 + 6 = 8`; which is basically a value of type `int`. However, the left hand side of the assignment operator is of the type `enum COLORS`. So, the statement would complain an error. To remove the error, you can do either of two things. First, declare `c` to be an `int`. Second, cast the right hand side in the following manner:

```
c = COLORS(BLACK + WHITE);
```

We summarize the ways of assigning values to enumerated data type variable as

```
enum COLORS (RED, BLUE, BLACK, GREEN, YELLOW, PURPLE, WHITE};
enum COLORS c;
c = BLACK; // valid in C++
c = 2;     // illegal in C++
c = COLORS(2); // Right way
c = (COLORS)2; // Also correct
```

8.13.4 Comparing Enumerated Types

C++ also allows using comparison operators on enumerated data type. The following statements illustrate this concept:

```
bg_color = COLORS(6);
if(bg_color == WHITE)
    fore_color = BLUE;
fore_color = BLUE;
if(bg_color == fore_color)
    cout<<"\n NOT VISIBLE";
```

Since enumerated types are derived from integer type, they can be used in a `switch case` statement. For example, consider the following code demonstrates the use of enumerated type in a `switch case` statement.

```
enum {RED, BLUE, BLACK, GREEN, YELLOW, PURPLE, WHITE} bg_color;
switch(bg_color)
{   case RED:
    case BLUE:
    case GREEN:
            cout<<"\n It is a primary color";
            break;
    case default:
            cout<<"\n It is not a primary color";
            break;
}
```

8.13.5 Input or Output Operations on Enumerated Types

Since enumerated types are derived types, they cannot be read or written using formatted input or output functions available in C++. When we read or write an enumerated type, we read or write it as an integer. The compiler would implicitly do the type conversion as discussed earlier. The following statements illustrate this concept.

```
COLORS {RED, BLUE, BLACK, GREEN, YELLOW, PURPLE, WHITE};
COLORS c;
cin>>c;
cout<<"\n Color = "<<c;
```

Program 8.14 Write a program to display the name of the colours using enumerated type.

```
using namespace std;
#include<iostream>
enum COLORS {RED, BLUE, BLACK, GREEN, YELLOW, PURPLE, WHITE};
main()
{   COLORS c;
    string color_name[] = {"RED", "BLUE", "BLACK", "GREEN", "YELLOW","PURPLE", "WHITE"};
    for(int i = RED; i! = WHITE; i++)
        cout<<"\t "<<color_name[i];
}
```

OUTPUT

```
RED BLUE BLACK GREEN YELLOW PURPLE
```

Points to Remember

- A structure stores related information about an entity. It is a user-defined data type that can store related information, even of different data types, together. The major difference between a structure and an array is that an array contains related information but all that information has the same data type.
- A structure is declared using the keyword `struct` followed by a structure name.
- The structure definition does not allocate any memory. Like any other data type, memory is allocated for the structure when we declare a variable of the structure
- When the user does not explicitly initializes the structure then C++ automatically does that.
- In addition to other data, a self referential structure contains a pointer to a data that is of the same type as that of the structure.
- The only difference between a structure and a union is that in case of unions, you can only store information in one field at any one time.
- C++ automatically initialize the structure if the user does not initialize the same. For `int` and `float` members, the values are initialized to zero and char and string members are initialized to the `'\0'` by default
- A structure member variable is generally accessed using a `'.'` or a dot operator.
- Unions are used to save memory. They are useful for applications that involve multiple members, where values need not be assigned to all the members at any one time

Glossary

Copying structures Assigning a structure to another structure of the same type

Enumerated data type A user-defined type that consists of a set of named integer constants.

Nested structure A structure placed within another structure. That is, a structure that contains another structure as its member.

Self referential structures Structures that contain a reference to data of its same type.

Structure initialization Assigning constants to structure members

Structure A user defined data type that can store related information of different data types together.

Typedef declaration A keyword that makes that creates synonym for the type.

Union A collection of variables of different data types

Exercises

Fill in the Blanks

1. Structure is a _____ data type.
2. A structure is same as that of _____.
3. _____ contains related information of the same data type.
4. _____ contains related information of the same or different data type(s).
5. Memory is allocated for a structure when _____ is done.
6. _____ is just a template that will be used to reserve memory when a variable of type `struct` will be declared.
7. A _____ is a collection of variables under a single name.
8. A structure is declared using the keyword `struct` followed by a _____.
9. When we precede a `struct` name with _____, then the `struct` becomes a new type.
10. For `int` and `float` structure members, the values are initialized to _____.
11. Char and string structure members are initialized to the _____ by default.
12. A structure member variable is generally accessed using a _____.
13. A structure can be placed within another structure is called a _____.
14. _____ structures contain a reference to data of the same type.
15. Keyword `typedef` is used to _____.
16. _____ is a collection of data under one name in which memory is shared between the members.
17. The selection operator is used to _____.
18. _____ permits sharing of memory among different types of data.

State True or False

1. Structure contains related information but all that information has the same data type.
2. A `struct` type is a primitive data type.
3. Structure declaration reserves memory for the structure.
4. Initializing a structure means assigning some constants to the members of the structure.
5. When the user does not explicitly initialize the structure, then C++ automatically does the same.
6. The dereference operator is used to select a particular member of the structure.
7. New variables can be created using the `typedef` keyword.
8. Memory is allocated for a structure only when we declare variables of the structure.
9. A nested structure contains another structure as its member.
10. C++ permits to copying of one structure variable to another.
11. Union and structure are initialized in the same way.
12. A structure cannot have a union as its member.
13. C++ permits nested unions.
14. In an enumerated type, integer value can be assigned to only one enumeration constant.
15. Declaring an enumerated type automatically creates a variable.
16. The identifiers in an enumerated type are automatically assigned values.
17. A field in a structure can itself be a structure.
18. No two members of a union should have the same name.
19. No two identifiers in an enumerated type must have the same value.
20. A union can have another union as its member.
21. A union can be a member of a structure.

Multiple Choice Questions

1. Data structure that can store related information together is
   (a) Array (b) String
   (c) Structure (d) All of these
2. Data structure that can store related information of different data types together is called
   (a) Array (b) String
   (c) Structure (d) All of these
3. Memory for a structure is allocated at the time of

(a) Structure definition
(b) Structure variable declaration
(c) Structure declaration

4. A structure member variable is generally accessed using
(a) Address operator
(b) Dot operator
(c) Comma operator
(d) Ternary operator

5. A structure can be placed within another structure is known as
(a) Self-referential structure
(b) Nested structure
(c) Parallel structure

6. A union member variable is generally accessed using
(a) Address operator
(b) Dot operator
(c) Comma operator
(d) Ternary operator

7. `Typedef` can be used with which of the following types?
(a) `struct` (b) `union`
(c) Enumerated (d) All of these

8. The enumerated type is derived from which of the following types?
(a) `int` (b) `float`
(c) `double` (d) `char`

Review Questions

1. What is a structure? What is the advantage of using structures?
2. How is a structure name different from a structure variable?
3. Structure declaration reserves memory for the structure. Comment on this statement with valid justification.
4. Differentiate between a structure and an array.
5. Write a short note on structures and functions
6. Explain the utility of `typedef` keyword in structures.
7. Explain with an example how structures are initialized.
8. Is it possible to create an array of structure? Explain with the help of an example.
9. What do you understand by a union?
10. Differentiate between a union and a structure.
11. Explain how members of a union are accessed using a program code.
12. In which applications do we use union?
13. Write a short note on nested structures.

Programming Exercises

1. Declare a structure(s) that represents the following hierarchical information:
(a) Student
(b) Roll Number
(c) Name
  (i) First name
  (ii) Middle name
  (iii) Last name
(d) Sex
(e) Date of birth
  (i) Day
  (ii) Month
  (iii) Year
(f) Marks
  (i) English
  (ii) Mathematics
  (iii) Computer science
2. Define a structure to store the name, an array `marks[]` that stores marks of five different subjects, and a character grade. Write a program to display the details of the student whose name is entered by the user. Use the structure definition of first question to make an array of student. Display the name of the students who have secured less than 40 per cent of aggregate.
3. Modify question 2 to print each student's average marks, class average (that includes average of all the student's marks).
4. Make an array of student as illustrated in question 1 and write a program to display the details of the student with the given DOB.
5. Make an array of student as illustrated in question 1 and write a program to delete the record of the student with the given last name.
6. Write a program using structures to read and display the information about a student.
7. Write a program to find biggest of three numbers using structures.
8. Write a program to enter two points and calculate the distance between them.
9. Write a program to read, display, add, and subtract two complex numbers.
10. Write a program to read and display information of a student using structure within a structure.

11. Write a program to read and display the information of all the students in the class. Then edit the details of the ith student and redisplay the entire information.
12. Write a program to read, display, add and subtract two distances. The distance must be defined using kilometres and metres.
13. Write a program to read, display, add, and subtract two heights. Height must be defined using feet and inches.
14. Write a program to read, display, add, and subtract two times. Time must be defined using hours, minutes, and seconds.
15. Write a program that uses a structure called *date* that is passed to a function *Leap Year* to determine if the year is a leap year.
16. Write a program using pointer to structure to initialize the members in the structure. Use functions to print the student's information.
17. Write a program using pointer to structure to initialize the members in the structure.
18. Write a program using pointer to structure to initialize the members in the structure using an alternative technique.
19. Define a structure date containing three integers—day, month, and year. Write a program using functions to read data, to validate the date entered by the user and then print the date on the screen. For example, if you enter 29, 2, and 2010, then that is an invalid date as 2010 is not a leap year. Similarly, 31, 6, and 2007 is invalid as June does not have 31 days.
20. Using the structure definition of the previous program, write a function to increment that. Make sure that the incremented date is a valid date.
21. Modify the above program to add a specific number of days to the given date.
22. Using the structure definition of 28th question, write a function to compare two date variables.
23. Write a program to define a structure vector. Then write functions to read data, print data, add two vectors and scale the members of a vector by a factor of 10.
24. Write a program to define a structure for a hotel that has members- name, address, grade, number of rooms, and room charges. Write a function to print the names of a hotel in a particular grade. Write a function to print names of a hotel that has room charges less than the specified valuc.
25. Write a program to define a union and a structure both having exactly the same members. Using the `sizeof` operator, print the size of structure variable as well as union variable and comment on the result.
26. Declare a structure time that has three fields—hour, minutes, and seconds. Create two variables start_time and end_time. Input their values from the user. If start_time does not reach the end_time, display GOOD DAY on the screen.
27. Declare a structure fraction that has two fields—numerator and denominator. Create two variables and compare them using function. Return 0 if the two fractions are equal, -1 if the first fraction is less than the second, and 1 otherwise. You may convert a fraction into a floating point number for your convenience.
28. Declare a structure `POINT`. Input the co-ordinates of a point variable and determine the quadrant in which it lies. The following table can be used to determine the quadrant.

Quadrant	X	Y
1	Positive	Positive
2	Negative	Positive
3	Negative	Negative
4	Positive	Negative

29. Write a program to calculate the area of a geometric figure—circle, rectangle, or triangle. Write a function to calculate the area. The function must receive one parameter which is a structure that contains the type of figure and the size of the components needed to calculate the area must be a part of a union. Note that a circle requires just one component, rectangle requires two components, and a triangle requires the size of three components to calculate the area.
30. Write a program to create a structure with information given here. Then read and print the data.

`Employee[10]`
(a) Emp_Id
(b) Name
 (i) First Name
 (ii) Middle Name
 (iii) Last Name
(c) Address
 (i) Area
 (ii) City
 (iii) State

(d) Age
(e) Salary
(f) Designation

31. Write a program that has a structure Student. Besides all other details, the structure must have a union that either stores the age of the student or his date of birth
32. Write a program that has a structure with a union.
33. Write a program that uses enumerated data type for months of the year.
34. Write a program that calculates the result of a student and has an enumerated type variable GRADE. Assign 10 to grade Excellent, 9 to A+, so and so forth.
35. Write a program to print your name using pointers.

Find the errors in the following codes

1.
```
struct
{ int item_code;
float price;
}
```
2.
```
struct product
{
char prod_name[20];
float price;
}product p[10];
```
3.
```
struct student
{   char name[20];
  int id;
}name = "Ram", 9;
```
4.
```
union student
{   char name[20];
  int id;
}s = {"Ram",01};
```
5.
```
union student
{   char name[20];
  int id;
  struct DOB
  { int dd, mm, yy;
  };
}s = {"Ram",1, 2, 3,5};
```

Find the output of the following codes

1.
```
main()
{  struct values
   {  int i;
      float f;
   }v;
   v.i=2;
   v.f=2.3;
   cout<<"\n"<<v.i<<" "<<v.f;
}
```
2.
```
struct values
{     int i;
      float f;
}v;
main()
{     i=2;
      f=2.3;
      cout<<"\n"<<i<<" "<<f;
}
```
3.
```
struct values
{     int i;
      float f;
}v;
main()
{     static values v = {5, 2.3};
      cout<<"\n"<<v.i<<" "<<v.f;
}
```
4.
```
struct values
{     int i=2;
      float f=3.4;
}v;
main()
{     static values v;
      cout<<"\n"<<v.i<<" "<<v.f;
}
```
5.
```
struct values
{     int i;
      float f;
}v={2, 3.4};

main()
{     cout<<"\n"<<v.i<<" "<<v.f;
}
```
```
struct first
{     int i;
      float f;
};
```
6.
```
struct second
{     int i;
      float f;
};
main()
{     struct first f = {7,4.5};
      struct second s = {4,3.4};
      int diff;
      diff = f.i - s.i;
      cout<<"\n "<<diff;
}
```
7.
```
struct values
{     int i;
      int val[10];
}v={1,2,3,4,5,6,7,8,9}, *ptr=&v;
main()
{     cout<<"\n"<<v.i<<" "<<ptr->i;
```

```
        cout<<"\n"<<v.val[3]<<" "<<ptr-
        >val[3]<<" "<<*(v.val+3);
    }
8.  struct values
    {   int i;
        float f;
    };
    void change(values *v, int a, float b)
    {   v->i=a;
        v->f=b;
    }
    main()
    {   values val = {2, 3.4};
        cout<<"\n"<<val.i<<" "<<val.f;
        change(&val, 5, 7.9);
        cout<<"\n"<<val.i<<" "<<val.f;
    }
```

Answers

Fill in the Blanks

1. user defined; **2.** records; **3.** array; **4.** structure; **5.** strucure variable declaration; **6.** structure definition; **7.** structure declaration; **8.** structure name; **9.** typedef; **10.** 0; **11.** \0; **12.** dot operator; **13.** nested structure; **14.** self referential; **15.** create a new data type name for an existing data type; **16.** union; **17.** refer to the individual members for the actual parameters; **18.** union

State True or False

1. false **2.** false **3.** false **4.** true **5.** true **6.** false **7.** false **8.** true
9. true **10.** true **11.** false **12.** false **13.** true **14.** false **15.** false **16.** true
17. false **18.** true **19.** false **20.** true **21.** true

Multiple Choice Questions

1. (d); **2.** (c); **3.** (b); **4.** (b); **5.** (b); **6.** (b); **7.** (d); **8.** (a)

ANNEXURE 3

Bit-Fields and Slack Bytes in Structures

INTRODUCTION TO BIT FIELDS

Like C, C++ facilitates users to store integer members into memory spaces smaller than the compiler would ordinarily allow. These space-saving structure members are called bit fields. In addition to this, it also permits the users to explicitly declare the width in bits. Bit fields are generally used in developing application programs that must force a data structure to correspond to a fixed hardware representation and are unlikely to be portable.

Therefore, besides having declarators for members of a structure or union, a structure declarator can also be a specified number of bits, generally known as a bit field. A bit field is interpreted as an integral type. The syntax for specifying a bit field can be given as

```
type-specifier declarator: constant-expression
```

In the syntax, the constant-expression is used to specify the width of the field in bits. The type-specifier for the declarator must be unsigned int, signed int, or int, and the constant-expression must be a non-negative integer value. If the value of the constant expression is zero, the declaration has no declarator.

A3.1 KEY POINTS ABOUT BIT FIELDS

- C++ does not permit arrays of bit fields, pointers to bit fields, and functions returning bit fields.
- C++ permits ordinary member variables along with bit fields as structure members.
- The declaratoris optional and is used to name the bit field.
- Bit fields can only be declared as part of a structure.
- The address-of operator (`&`) cannot be applied to bit-field components. This means you cannot use `scanf` to read values into a bit field. To read a value, you may use a temporary variable and then assign its value to the bit field.
- Bit fields that are not named cannot be referenced and their contents at run time are unpredictable. However, they can be used as dummy fields, for alignment purposes.
- Bit fields must be long enough to contain the bit pattern.
- When a value that is out of range is assigned to a bit field, the low-order bit pattern is preserved and the appropriate bits are assigned.

- Although the maximum bit field length is 64 bits,for portability reasons, do not use bit fields greater than 32 bits in size.
- Bit fields with a length of 0 must be unnamed.

```
short num: 15
```

Let us look at a structure that has bit fields

```
struct
{
    unsigned short a: 2;
    unsigned short b: 1;
    int c: 7;
    unsigned short d: 4;
};
```

In the structure, the size of the structure is two bytes. Bit fields have the same semantics as the integer type. This means a bit field is used in expressions in exactly the same way as a variable of the same base type would be used, regardless of how many bits are in the bit field.

Note When `char, short, int,` and `long bit` fields are not explicitly signed or unsigned, these can be treated as signed or unsigned both. Therefore, `int num : 3`, may have the range of values from 0 – 7 or –4 – 3.

A3.2 WORD BOUNDARY AND SLACK BYTE IN A STRUCTURE

A *word boundary* is the size of word (in bytes) in which CPU processes (reads or writes) data at a time. The size of word boundary is machine dependent and is usually 2 bytes or 4 bytes. Let us assume that CPU supports a word boundary of 4 bytes word boundary. Therefore, the members of structure will be stored after left aligning with the word boundary.

Slack Byte (Padding byte) To further understand the concept of word boundary in a structure, let now consider a structure which takes a `char` and an `int` value as input. In the output, the character data takes one byte and an integer variable takes 4 bytes. So, the size of the structure should have been 5. But the output says that the size of the structure is 8. This is because that 3 bytes are added for padding (to make it of complete word boundary). Hence, these 3 bytes which are actually unoccupied is known as the *slack byte*.

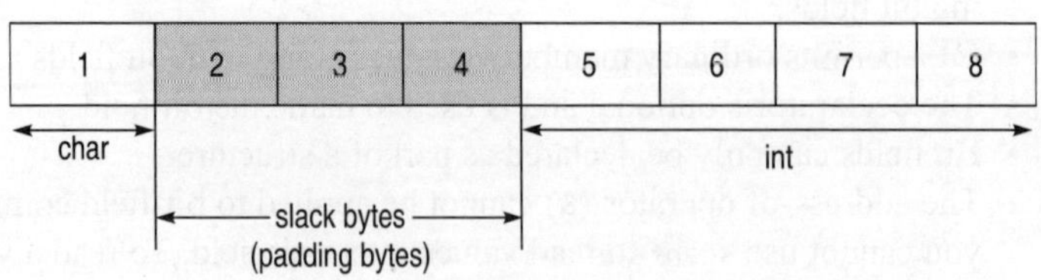

Structure Padding or Slack bytes

Though, slack byte wastes memory space but they are inserted for speed optimization. CPU aligns bytes on word boundary so that it can read/write them from structure faster and in a much efficient manner. When we declare structure variables, each one of them may contain the slack bytes. Note that the slack byte contains undefined (garbage) values.

Case Study 3

This case study shows the implementation of concepts discussed in Chapter 6 on Strings.

C3.1 JOSEPHUS PROBLEM

In Josephus problem, n people stand in a circle waiting to be executed. The counting starts at some point in the circle and proceeds in a specific direction around the circle. In each step, a certain number of people are skipped and the next person is executed or eliminated. The elimination of people makes the circle smaller and smaller. In the last step, only one person remains and is declared the 'winner.'

Therefore, if there are n number of people and a number k which indicates that $k - 1$ people are skipped and the kth person in the circle is eliminated, then the problem is to choose a position in the initial circle so that the given person becomes the winner.

Example

If there are five (n) people and every second (k) person is eliminated, then first the person at position two is eliminated followed by the person at position four, followed by person at position one, and finally, the person at position five is eliminated. Therefore, the person at position three becomes the winner (refer to Fig. C3.1).

Try the same process with $n = 7$ and $k = 3$. You will find that person at position four is the winner. The elimination goes in the sequence of 3, 6, 2, 7, 5, and 1.

Figure C3.1 Josephus problem

Program C3.1 Given here is a code of Josephus problem that finds solution using a circular linked list.

```
using namespace std;
#include<iostream>
struct node
{
      int player_id;
      struct node *next;
};
struct node *start, *ptr, *new_node;
int main()
{
      int n, k, i, count;
      cout<<"\n Enter the number of players : ";
      cin>>n;
      cout<<"\n Enter the value of k
(every kth player gets eliminated): ";
      cin>>k;

      // Create circular linked list
containing all the players
      start = new node;

      start->player_id = 1;
      ptr = start;

      for(i = 2; i<= n; i++)
      {
            new_node = new node;
            ptr->next = new_node;
            new_node->player_id = i;
            new_node->next=start;
            ptr=new_node;
      }

      for(count = n; count > 1; count--)
      {
            for(i = 0; i< k - 1; ++i)
                  ptr = ptr->next;

            ptr->next = ptr->next->next;
// Remove the eliminated player from the
circular linked list.
      }

      cout<<"\n The WINNER is Player
"<<ptr->player_id;

      return 0;
}
```

OUTPUT

```
Enter the number of players : 5
Enter the value of k (every kth
player gets eliminated): 2
The WINNER is Player 3
```

CHAPTER 9

Classes and Objects

KEY Concepts

Class declaration and definition • Objects • Nested member functions • Inline member functions • Memory allocation for objects • Array of objects • Passing and returning objects • Classes and pointers • Friend functions and classes • Local, empty, and nested classes

INTRODUCTION

The object-oriented programming paradigm centres on modelling real world problems. It makes a clear-cut boundary between data and functions. However, it stores them together in a single entity known as class.

Classes form the building blocks of the object-oriented programming paradigm. They simplify the development of large and complex projects and help produce software which is easy to understand, modular, re-usable, and easily expandable.

Syntactically, classes are similar to structures, as seen in Chapter 8 on Structure, Union, and Enumerated Data Types. However, the only difference between a structure and a class is that by default, members of a class are private, while members of a structure are public. If you can recollect, both data members and member functions of the structure could be accessed from the `main()` using the dot operator. This means that both data as well as functions were public that could be used by any function in the program. Although there is no general rule as when to use a structure and when to use a class, generally, C++ programmers use structures for holding data and classes to hold data and functions.

9.1 SPECIFYING A CLASS

A class is the basic mechanism to provide data encapsulation. Data encapsulation is an important feature of object-oriented programming paradigm. It binds data and member functions in a single entity in such a way that data can be manipulated only through the functions defined in that class. When defining a class, we are actually creating a new user-defined data type which will be treated in the same way as other built-in data types.

The process of specifying a class consists of two steps—class declaration and function definitions (Fig. 9.1). While class declaration specifies the type and scope of its

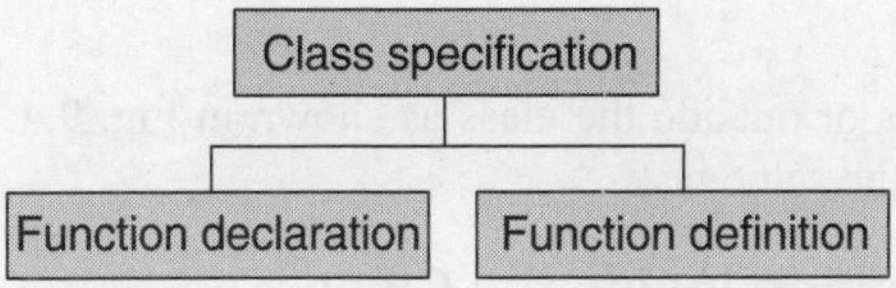

Figure 9.1 Class specification

members—private, public, or protected, function definition specifies how functions perform their intended task.

9.1.1 Class Declaration

The syntax for class declaration is given in Fig. 9.2(a) and a sample class declaration is shown in Fig. 9.2(b).

Programming Tip: Missing semicolon at the end of class definition will result in a compilation error.

```
class class_name
{ private:
    data declarations;
    function declarations;
  public:
    data declarations;
    function declarations;
};
```

(a)

```
class Rectangle
{ private:
    float length;
    float breadth;
  public:
    void get_data();
    void show_data();
    float area();
};
```

(b)

Figure 9.2 (a) Syntax of class declaration (b) Sample class

The keyword `class` denotes that the `class_name` that follows is user-defined data type. The body of the class is enclosed within curly braces and terminated with a semicolon, as in structures. Data members and functions are declared within the body of the class. These data and functions form the members of the class.

Data and functions are grouped under two sections—`private and public`. They are also called visibility labels or access specifiers. Although there is one more visibility label, i.e., `protected`, we will discuss only private and public labels in this chapter. Protected label will be discussed in Chapter 12 on Inheritance.

Private All data members and member functions declared private can be accessed only from within the class. They are strictly not accessible by any entity—function or class—outside the class in which they have been declared. In C++, data hiding is implemented through the private visibility label.

Public Data and functions that are public can be accessed from outside the class.

By default, members of the class, both data and function, are private. If any visibility label is missing, they are automatically treated as private members.

Note A class having all its members as private is completely hidden from the outside world and does not serve any purpose.

Figure 9.3 shows that private members of a class can be accessed from outside the class only through the public member functions. Moreover, public data and public member functions can be accessed from outside the class.

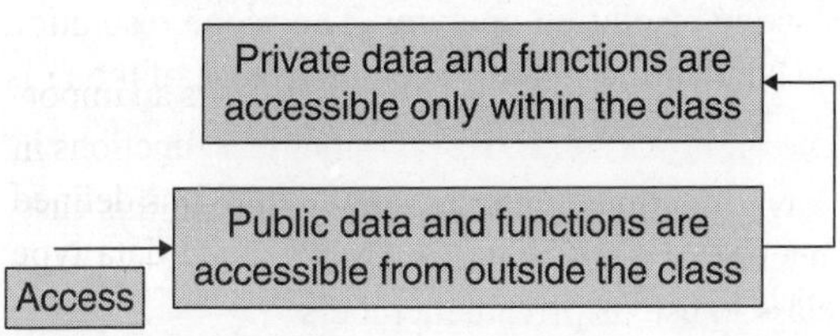

Figure 9.3 Accessing members of a class

In the sample class 'Rectangle', there are two private data members that include length and breadth of float type, and three public member functions. In the class declaration, we have specified the prototypes of the member functions. We could have also specified any function in the private section, but we place data in private section and functions in the public section.

9.1.2 Function Definition

Member functions can be defined either inside the class or outside the class as shown in Fig. 9.4. However, wherever they may be defined, they perform the same task.

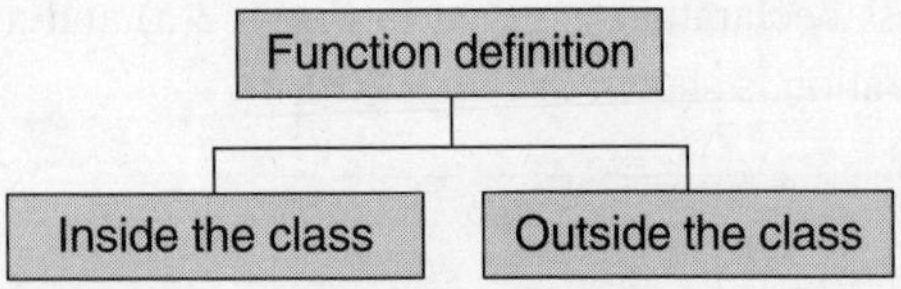

Figure 9.4 Function definition

Defining a Function Inside the Class

In this method, function declaration or prototype is replaced with function definition inside the class. Though it increases the execution speed of the program, it consumes more space. A function defined inside the class is treated as an inline function by default, provided they do not fall into the restricted category of inline functions.

Note Functions that cannot be inline include functions having loop, switch, or go to statements, static variables, or recursive code.

As a good practice, you must define only small functions inside the class. Let us try to define the `get_data()` inside the class.

Programming Tip: Initializing data variables when defined in a class declaration will result in a compilation error.

```
class rectangle
{   private:
        float length;
        float breadth;
    public:
        void get_data()
        {   cout<<"\n Enter the length and breadth of the rectangle: ";
            cin>>length>>breadth;
        }
        void show_data();
        float area();
};
```

In the code, `get_data()` is an `inline` member function of the class `rectangle`. This function is used to read the values of private data members of the class from the users.

Defining a Function Outside the Class

Member functions defined outside the class are defined in the same way as other normal functions. However, the only difference between a member function and a normal function is that a member function is specified using a membership identity label in the function header. The identity label informs the compiler about the class to which the function belongs to. Figure 9.5 shows the general form of a normal function and that of a class member function defined outside the class.

`class_name::` and `function_name` tell the compiler that scope of the function is restricted to the `class_name`. Hence, the name of the `::` operator is scope resolution operator. The scope resolution operator identifies and specifies the context to which an identifier refers. The importance of the `::` is even more prominent in the following cases:

- When different classes in the same program have functions with the same name. In this case, the `::` operator will tell the compiler which function belongs to which class.
- To restrict the non-member functions of the class to use its private members.
- Allows a member function of the class to call another member function directly without using the dot operator.

```
return_type function_name(list of arguments)
{
FUNCTION BODY
}
```

(a)

Scope resolution operator

```
return_type class_name :: function_name(list of arguments)
{
FUNCTION BODY
}
```

(b)

Figure 9.5 (a) Normal function definition (b) Member function definition outside the class

Following is an example for defining the function (`area()`) outside the class:

```
float Rectangle :: area(void)
{   return length * breadth;
}
```

Defining a member function outside the class reduces the execution speed but takes more space.

9.2 CREATING OBJECTS

We have studied that a class just gives a blueprint or a template that specifies what type of data can be operated by which function. To use a class, we must create variables of the class also known as objects. The process of creating objects of the class is called class instantiation. Memory is allocated only when we create object(s) of the class.

Since C++ treats all user-defined data types as its built-in type, the technique of creating variables of a class is exactly the same as that used for creating variables of basic data types. Therefore, the syntax of defining an object (variable) of a class is as follows:

```
class_name object_name;
```

To create object of our `class Rectangle`, we must write

```
Rectangle rect;
```

> **Programming Tip:** Declaring data members as public goes against the concept of data hiding.

Here, `Rectangle` is the `class_name` and `rect` is the name of the object. We can also define objects by placing their names immediately after the closing brace. For example, consider the code given here.

```
class Rectangle
{   private:
        float length;
        float breadth;
    public:
        void get_data();
        void show_data();
        float area();
}rect1, rect2, rect3;
```

The code creates three objects of type `Rectangle`. However, creating objects in this manner must be avoided; a good programming practice is to declare objects close to the place where they are used and not at the time of class definition.

9.3 ACCESSING OBJECT MEMBERS

There are two types of class members—private and public. While private members can be only accessed through public members, public members, on the other hand, can be called from `main()` or any function outside the class. The syntax of calling an object member is as follows:

```
object_name.function_name(arguments);
```

Therefore, to call a function of our class Rectangle, we will have to write

```
rect1.get_data();
```

Note Object members cannot be accessed without the dot operator. They can be accessed only with the name of the object, followed by the dot operator and the member.

Let us take an example of a class and see the right and wrong ways of accessing its members.

```
class Sample
{   private:
        int a;
void func1()
        {SOME CODE}
    public:
        int b;
void func2();
        {SOME CODE}
};
main()
{   Sample s;
    s.a = 1;                //Wrong, a is private, cannot be accessed in main()
    s.func1();              //Wrong, func1() is a private function
    s.b = 2;                //Right, b is a public data
    s.func2();              //Right, func2() is a public function
    a = 3;                  //Wrong, a is private data
    b = 4;                  //Wrong b cannot be accessed without object name
    func2();                //Wrong can't be accessed without object name and '.'
}
```

Note Usually, functions that are not meant to be called from outside the class or that are meant to perform some processing for public member functions can be declared as private member functions.

9.4 NESTED MEMBER FUNCTIONS

We have learnt that only an object of a class can call any member function of that class using the dot operator. However, when we use nested functions—a function inside another function—we do not need the object name. A member function can directly call another function of that class. For example,

```
class Rectangle
{   private:
    float length;
    float breadth;
    public:
    void get_data()      {      cin>>length>>breadth;      }
    void show_data()
    {   cout<<"Length = "<<length<<" Breadth = "<<breadth<<" and Area = "<<area();
    }
        int area()     {      return length * breadth;      }
};
```

In this example, data members of the class are directly accessible by the member functions. Member functions do not need the dot operator to use the data members. Similarly, when we call a member function from within another member function, we do not need the name of the object or the dot operator. The member function can be directly called by using its name along with arguments, if any.

9.5 MAKING A MEMBER FUNCTION INLINE

We have seen that member functions can be either defined inside the class or outside the class. While defining a function inside the class makes the code shorter, as a good programming practice, member functions must be defined outside the class. This will not only enhance clarity but will also result in separating the details of implementation from the class definition which is a basic objective concept of object-oriented programming.

However, programmers do not want to compromise speed for code clarity. We have seen that all functions defined inside the class are treated as inline by default. Therefore, the overhead of function call is completely avoided and the code executes faster. However, to gain the same benefits while separating the implementation details, C++ enables programmers to make a member function defined outside the class an inline. This can be done by using the keyword `inline` in the header line of function definition. For example, consider the code given here which makes `show_data()`, a function defined outside the class as an inline function.

```
class Rectangle
{   private:
    float length;
    float breadth;
    public:
        void get_data()      {      cin>>length>>breadth;      }
        void show_data();
};
inline void Rectangle :: show_data(void)
{       cout<<"Length = "<<length<<" Breadth = "<<breadth;
}
```

Program 9.1 Write a program to calculate area of a rectangle.

```
using namespace std;
#include<iostream>
class Rectangle
{   private:
        float length;
        float breadth;
    public:
```

```
        void get_data()
        {   cout<<"\n Enter the length and breadth of the rectangle: ";
            cin>>length>>breadth;
        }
        void show_data()
        {   cout<<"\n Length = "<<length<<" \t Breadth = "<<breadth;
        }
        float area()
        {cout<<"\n AREA = "<<length * breadth;      }
};
main()
{   Rectangle rect; // rect is an object of class Rectangle
    rect.get_data(); //get_data(), show_data() and area() are public member functions
    rect.show_data();
    rect.area();
}
```

OUTPUT

```
Enter the length and breadth of the rectangle: 5 2
Length = 5 Breadth = 2
AREA = 10
```

Program 9.2 Write a program to implement student's class. The program must demonstrate the use of nested member function, arrays within the class, and making a function defined outside the class an inline function.

```
using namespace std;
#include<iostream>
#include<string.h>
class Student
{   private:
        int roll_no;
        char name[20];
        int marks[3];
        int total(void);
    public:
        void set_data(int r, char *n, int m1, int m2, int m3);
        void display_data()
        {   cout<<"\n STUDENT'S DETAILS ";
            cout<<"\n ROLL NUMBER : "<<roll_no;
            cout<<"\n NAME : "<<name;
            cout<<"\n MARKS : "<<total();
    }
};
inline void Student :: set_data(int r, char *n, int m1, int m2, int m3)
{   roll_no = r;
    strcpy(name,n);
    marks[0] = m1, marks[1] = m2, marks[2] = m3;
}
int Student :: total()
{   int sum = 0;
    for(int i=0;i<3;i++)
    sum += marks[i];
    return sum;
}
```

```
main()
{   Student s1;
    int r, m1,m2,m3;
    char n[20];
    cout<<"\n Enter the roll number : ";
    cin>>r;
    cout<<"\n Enter the name : ";
    cin.ignore();
    cin.getline(n,20);
    cout<<"\n Enter the marks in 3 subjects : ";
    cin>>m1>>m2>>m3;
    s1.set_data(r, n, m1, m2, m3);
    s1.display_data();
}
```

OUTPUT

```
Enter the roll number : 01
Enter the name : Aditya
Enter the marks in 3 subjects : 85 90 95
STUDENT'S DETAILS
ROLL NUMBER : 01
NAME : Aditya
MARKS : 270
```

Program 9.3 Write a program to enter the code and price of items. The user must feed the quantity in which he wants a product. The program must calculate and display the final bill.

```
using namespace std;
#include<iostream>
#include<iomanip>
class Store
{   private:
        int item_code[10];
        float price[10];
    public:
        void get_data();
        void display_data();
        void calculate_bill(int quant[]);
};
void Store :: get_data()
{   for(int i=0;i<10;i++)
    {   cout<<"\n Enter the code of "<<i+1<<"th item : ";
        cin>>item_code[i];
        cout<<"\n Enter the price of "<<i+1<<"th item : ";
        cin>>price[i];
    }
}
void Store :: display_data()
{   cout<<"\n ITEM CODE \t PRICE ";
    for(int i=0;i<10;i++)
    cout<<"\n \t"<<item_code[i]<<setw(12)<<price[i];
}
void Store :: calculate_bill(int quant[])
{   float total_amt = 0;
    for(int i; i=0;i<10;i++)
```

```
        total_amt += quant[i] * price[i];
        cout<<"\n *************BILL**************";
        cout<<"\nITEM \t PRICE \t Quantity \t SUB TOT \n\n";
        for(i=0;i<10;i++)
        cout<<setw(3)<<item_code[i]<<setw(12)<<price[i]<<setw(10)<<quant[i]
        <<setw(15)<<quant[i] * price[i]<<"\n";
        cout<<"\n **********************************";
        cout<<"\n TOTAL = "<<setw(28)<<total_amt;
}
main()
{   Store s;
    int q[10] = {0};
    s.get_data();
    s.display_data();
    cout<<"\n Enter the quantity of each product you want to buy : ";
    for(int i=0;i<10;i++)
    cin>>q[i];
    s.calculate_bill(q);
}
```

OUTPUT

```
*************BILL**************";
ITEM    PRICE  Quantity   SUB TOT
  1      100       3         300
  2      200       2400
  3      300       1         300
  4      400       00
  5      500       00
  6      600       00
  7      700       1700
  8      800       2         1600
  9      900       32700
  10     1000      00
**********************************
TOTAL = 6000
```

Program 9.4 Write a program to enter a rational number, simplify, and display it.

```
using namespace std;
#include<iostream>
#include<stdlib.h>
class Fraction
{   private:
        int num;
        int deno;
        void simplify();
        int GCD(int a, int b);
    public:
        void get_data()
        {   cout<<"\n Enter the numerator :";
            cin>>num;
            cout<<"\n Enter the denominator : ";
            cin>>deno;
            if(deno == 0)
            {   cout<<"\n Fraction Not Possible";
```

```
                exit(1);
            }
        }
        void display_data()
        {   simplify();
            cout<<num<<" / "<<deno;
        }
};
void Fraction :: simplify(void)
{   cout<<"\n The Simplified fraction is : ";
    int common_divisor = GCD(num, deno);
    num = num/common_divisor;
    deno = deno/common_divisor;
}
int Fraction :: GCD(int a, int b)
{   if(b == 0)
        return a;
    else
        return GCD(b, a%b);
}
main()
{   Fraction f;
    f.get_data();
    f.display_data();
}
```

OUTPUT

```
Enter the numerator : 12
Enter the denominator : 56
The Simplified fraction is : 3 / 14
```

Program 9.5 Write a program to demonstrate the concept of function overloading in the member functions of a class.

```
using namespace std;
#include<iostream>
#include<string.h>
class Person
{   private:
        int age;
        char name[20];
        float salary;
    public:
        void set_data();
        void set_data(int a);
        void set_data(int a, char n[]);
        void set_data(int a, char n[], float s);
        void show_data();
};
void Person :: set_data()
{   cout<<"\n Enter the age : ";
    cin>>age;
    cout<<"\n Enter the name : ";
    cin.ignore();
    cin>>name;
```

```
    cout<<"\n Enter the salary : ";
    cin>>salary;
}
void Person :: set_data(int a)
{   age = a;
    cout<<"\n Enter the name : ";
    cin.ignore();
    cin.getline(name,20);
    cout<<"\n Enter the salary : ";
    cin>>salary;
}
void Person :: set_data(int a, char n[])
{   age = a;
    strcpy(name, n);
    cout<<"\n Enter the salary : ";
    cin>>salary;
}
void Person :: set_data(int a, char n[], float s)
{   age = a;
    strcpy(name, n);
    salary = s;
}
void Person :: show_data()
{   cout<<"\n NAME : "<<name;
    cout<<"\n AGE : "<<age;
    cout<<"\n SALARY : "<<salary;
}
main()
{   Person p;
    p.set_data(25);
    p.show_data();
}
```

OUTPUT

```
Enter the name : Laxmi
Enter the salary : 99999
NAME : Laxmi
AGE : 25
SALARY : 99999
```

9.6 MEMORY ALLOCATION FOR CLASS AND OBJECTS

Before learning how memory is allocated to objects, let us recapitulate some important points about objects.

- An object is an instance of a class.
- Every object is identifiable.
- Objects communicate with classes through passing messages known as function calls.
- Every object is defined by a state or value of variables.
- The state of the object can be changed by one or more operation performed by member function(s) of that class.
- Memory for a class is allocated only when one or more objcets of that class is created.

The last point is only partly true because when a class is specified, memory for member functions of class is allocated. When one or more objects are created, separate chunks of memory for storing data members are allocated to each object as shown in Fig. 9.6. This type of memory allocation is quite justified because while each object has a different set of values for its data members, they execute the same piece of function code. Hence, it is better to store function code in one place and let all the objects of that class share the function code.

Note Memory for member functions is allocated only once—when the class is defined. Therefore, a single copy of member function is shared among all objects.

```
class Rectangle
{  private:
     float length;
     float breadth;
   public:
     void get_data()
   {
     cin>>length>>breadth;
   }
     void show_data()
   {
   cout<<length<<breadth;
   }
}R1, R2, R3;
```

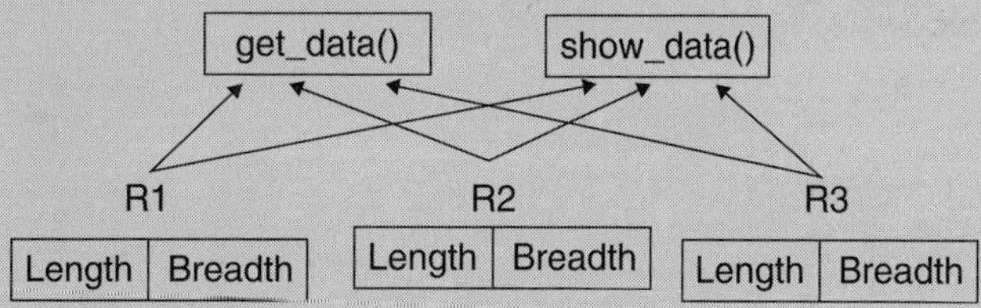

Figure 9.6 Objects sharing functions but having their own data

9.6.1 Memory Allocation for Static Data Members

C++ permits programmers to define static data members within a class using the `static` keyword. When a data member is declared as static, the following must be noted:

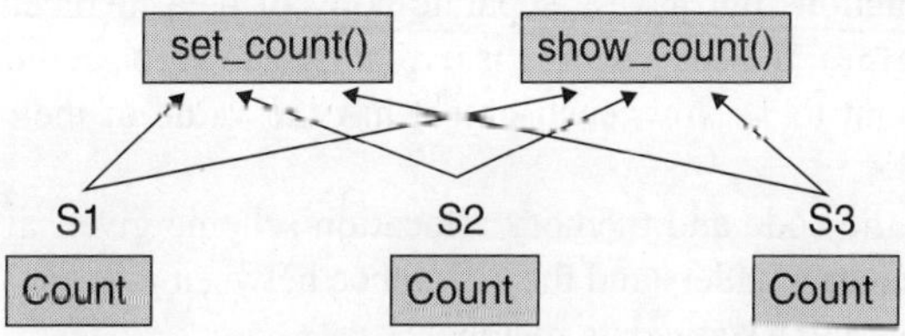

Figure 9.7 Memory allocation for the class sample having non-static data members

- Irrespective of the number of objects created, only a single copy of the static member is created in memory as shown in Fig. 9.8.
- All objects of a class share the static member.
- All static data members are initialized to zero when the first object of that class is created.
- Static data members are visible only within the class but their lifetime is the entire program.

Relevance

Static data members are usually used to maintain values that are common for the entire class. For example, to keep a track of how many objects of a particular class has been created.

Place of Storage

Although static data members are declared inside a class, they are not considered to be a part of the objects. Consequently, their declaration in the class is not considered as their definition. A static data member is defined outside the class. This means that even though the static data member is declared in class scope, their definition persist in the entire file. A static member has a file scope.

However, since a static data member is declared inside the class, they can be accessed only by using the class name and the scope resolution operator.

Example 9.1 Write a program to create multiple objects of a class that has non-static data members.

```
using namespace std;
#include<iostream>
class Sample
{   private:
    int count;
    public:
    void set_count()
    {   count = 1;      }
    void show_count()
    {   cout<<"\n COUNT = "<<count++;      }
};
main()
{   Sample s1, s2, s3;
    s1.set_count();
    s2.set_count();
    s3.set_count();
    s1.show_count();
    s2.show_count();
    s3.show_count();
}
```

OUTPUT

```
COUNT = 1
COUNT = 1
COUNT = 1
```

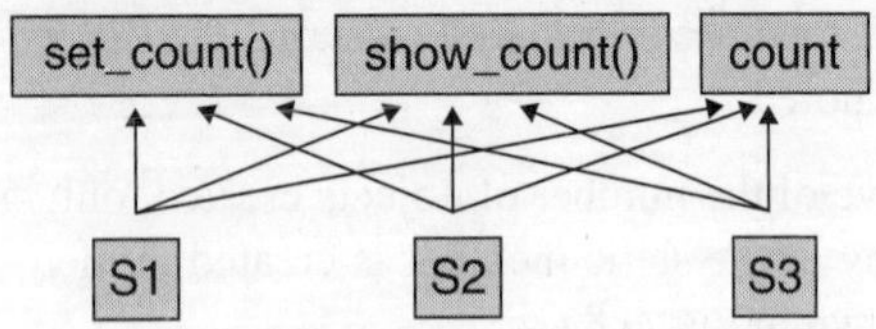

Figure 9.8 Memory allocation for the class Sample having static data member

Explanation: All three objects—S1, S2, and S3—share the member functions but have a separate copy of data member count. In `main()`, the `set_count()` is explicitly called to set the value of count to 1. Now, each object has the value of their `count = 1`.

Look at the code and memory allocation scheme given in Fig. 9.8 to clearly understand the difference between a normal data member and a static data member.

Example 9.2 Class having a `static` data member

```
using namespace std;
#include<iostream>
class Sample
{   private:
    static int count;
    public:
    void show_count()
    {   cout<<"\n COUNT = "<<count++;      }
};
int Sample :: count = 1;
main()
{   Sample s1, s2, s3;
    s1.show_count();
    s2.show_count();
       s3.show_count();
    }
```

Programming Tip: An uninitialized static data member is initialized with zero by the compiler.

```
OUTPUT
COUNT = 1
COUNT = 2
COUNT = 3
```

Explanation: All three objects—S1, S2, and S3—share the member functions as well as the static data member. Only one copy of the static data member exists in the memory. There is no need for a function to explicitly set the value of count because the value of static data member has been initialized to 1 outside the class definition. Now, each object increments the value of count and hence the output.

Note Memory for member functions and static data members is allocated per class and not per object. The class sample has no data member (except static count), but this does not means no memory space will be allocated to the objects of Sample. In such cases, a minimum memory is set aside for object. Therefore, size of S1, S2, and S3 is 1 byte.

9.6.2 Static Member Functions

C++ not only allows data members of a class to be static but also supports static member functions. Any static member—whether data or function—is allocated to memory only once and is not a part of any object but is shared by all the objects of that class. Additionally, a static member function has the following features:

- It can access only the static members—data and/or functions—declared in the same class.
- It cannot access non-static members because they belong to an object but static functions have no object to work with.
- Since it is not a part of any object, it is called using the class name and the scope resolution operator.
- As static member functions are not attached to an object, the `this` pointer does not work on them.
- A static member function cannot be declared as virtual function.
- A static member function cannot be declared with `const`, volatile type qualifiers.

Don't worry if last three points are not clear. You will understand these concepts when we will deal with them in detail later in this book. In this chapter, we take a small example that makes use of static member function and is usually implemented in solutions designed for real-world problems. The function is used to automatically generate the next ID.

Note Static and non-static member functions in the same class with same names and same number and types of arguments are not allowed in C++. Therefore, `static void print(float);` and `void print(float)` is illegal.

Example 9.3 Static member function

```
using namespace std;
#include<iostream>
class ID_Generator
{   private:
        static int next_ID;          // next_ID is a static data member
    public:
```

```
        static int GenNextID()        // GenNextID is a static member function
    {     cout<<"\n NEXT ID = "<<next_ID++;      }
};
int ID_Generator :: next_ID = 1;
main()
{   for(int i=0;i<5;i++)
    ID_Generator :: GenNextID();
}
```

OUTPUT

```
NEXT ID = 1
NEXT ID = 2
NEXT ID = 3
NEXT ID = 4
NEXT ID = 5
```

Explanation: The program is used to automatically generate the next, unique identification number. Every time the static function is called, it increments the value of static variable by 1. In this program, we have not made any object of the class. This is because our class has only one member function and that is `static`. Static member functions are not invoked in conjunction with objects. They are called using the class name and the scope resolution operator.

9.6.3 Static Object

In Chapter 4, we have seen that a variable declared as static is automatically initialized to zero. Now, an object is a combination of variables. Therefore, to initialize all the variables of an object to zero, we have two techniques:

- Make a constructor and explicitly set each variable to 0. We will read about it in the next chapter.
- To declare the object as static, when an object of a class is declared static, all its members are automatically initialized to zero.

Consider the program given here which demonstrates this concept.

Example 9.4 Static object

```
using namespace std;
#include<iostream>
#include<iomanip>
class Sample
{   private:
        int a;
        int b;
    public:
    void show_data()
    {     cout<<"\n a = "<<a<<" and b = "<<b;
    }
    void add()
    {   a += 10;
        b += 20;
    }
};
main()
{   static Sample s;      // Creating static object
```

```
    s.show_data();     // invoking member function using static object
    s.add();
    s.show_data();
}
```

OUTPUT

```
a = 0       b = 0
a = 10      b = 20
```

Explanation: In the program, since `s` is a static object, its data members are automatically initialized to zero. In `add()`, the value of a is incremented by 10 and value of b is incremented by 20. When `show_data()` is called again, the modified values are displayed.

9.7 ARRAY OF OBJECTS

Just as we have arrays of basic data types, C++ allows programmers to create arrays of user-defined data types as well. Therefore, it is possible to make an array of class data type or array of objects. They are usually defined to handle a group of objects that reside in a contiguous memory location. For example, there is not one student in a class, rather a class has `n` number of students. Therefore, we can declare an array of class student by simple writing

```
student s[20]; // assuming there are 20 students in a class
```

When this statement gets executed, the compiler will set aside memory for storing details of `20` students. This means that in addition to the space required by member functions, `20 * sizeof(student)` bytes of consecutive memory locations will be reserved for objects at the compile time.

An array of objects uses the same concepts as that of arrays of other data types. An individual object of the array of objects is referenced by using an index, and the particular member is accessed using the dot operator. Therefore, if we write,

```
s[i].get_data()
```

then the statement when executed will take the details of the *i*th student.

9.8 DYNAMIC MEMORY ALLOCATION FOR ARRAY OF OBJECTS

In the previous section, we have seen how to create static array of objects. We call it static, because memory was allocated for the objects at the compile time. Moreover, the allocated memory had to be contiguous. Therefore, a better idea is to use pointers to objects. This approach is far more flexible as it allows objects to be dynamically allocated during execution or run time, as and when required. We can declare an array of pointers of objects in the same way as we did for creating structure variables. For example, the statement

```
student *s[20];
```

will create an array of pointers to 20 student objects. Note that instead of reserving space for 20 student objects we are reserving space for 20 pointers to student objects which is far less than the former one. Figure 9.9 shows array of pointers to objects points to objects in memory.

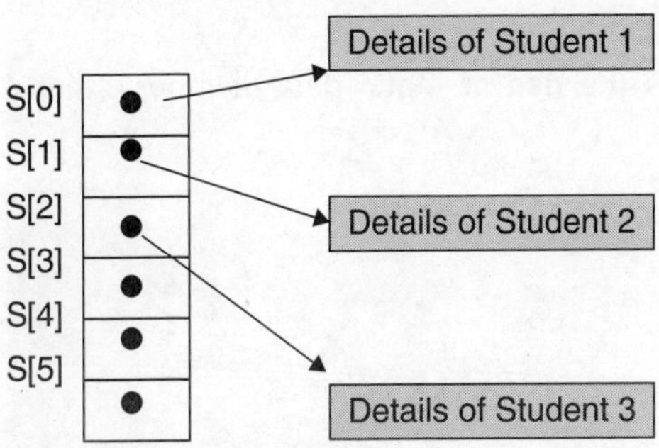

Figure 9.9 Array of pointers to objects

However, to access a member of the object you must write

```
s[i]->get_data(); and not s[i].get_data();
```

Note Pointers to objects is usually used to create and manipulate data structures such as linked lists, stacks, queues, trees, graphs, and so on.

Program 9.6 Write a program that demonstrates the use of array of objects.

```
using namespace std;
#include<iostream>
#include<iomanip>
class Faculty
{   private:
        char name[20];
        char deptt[20];
    public:
        void get_data() // get details of a single object
        {   cout<<"\n Enter the name : ";
            cin.getline(name, 20);
            cout<<"\n Enter the department : ";
            cin.ignore();
            cin.getline(deptt, 20);
        }
        void show_data()
        {     cout<<name<<setw(20)<<deptt<<"\n";     }
};
main()
{   Faculty f[5]; // array of objects
    int i;
    for(i=0;i<5;i++)
    f[i].get_data(); // invoking function with a single object
    cout<<"\n NAME "<<setw(20)<<"Department \n\n";
    for(i=0;i<5;i++)
    f[i].show_data();
}
```

OUTPUT

```
NAME                 DEPARTMENT
Mansi Sood           Computer Science
Akanksha Bansal      Chemistry
Jaya Gera            Psychology
Namita Aggarwal      English
Shweta Tyagi         Mathematics
```

Program 9.7 Write a program that demonstrates the use of static data member, static member function, and array of objects.

```
using namespace std;
#include<iostream>
#include<iomanip>
class student
{   private:
        static int next_ID; // static data member
        int roll_no;
        char name[20];
    public:
        static int GenNextID() // static member function
```

```
        {   return next_ID++;     }
        void get_data()
        {   roll_no = student :: GenNextID(); // invoking static function
            cout<<"\n Enter the name : ";
            cin.getline(name,20);
        }
        void display_data()
        {   cout<<setw(12)<<roll_no<<setw(20)<<name<<"\n";     }
};
int student :: next_ID = 1101;
main()
{   student s[5]; // array of objects
    int i;
    for(i=0;i<5;i++)
        s[i].get_data();
        cout<<"\n\n\tROLL NO."<<setw(20)<<"NAME\n";
    for(i=0;i<5;i++)
        s[i].display_data();
}
```

OUTPUT

```
ROLL NO.                NAME
1101                    Aman
1102                    Chaitanya
1103                    Dev
1104                    Gornash
1105                    Kartik
```

Program 9.8 Write a program to display information about the faculty members. Allocate memory for the objects dynamically.

```
using namespace std;
#include<iostream>
#include<iomanip>
class Faculty
{   private:
        char name[20];
        char deptt[20];
    public:
        void get_data()
        {   cout<<"\n Enter the name : ";
            cin.getline(name, 20);
            cout<<"\n Enter the department : ";
            cin.getline(deptt, 20);
        }
        void show_data()
        {     cout<<name<<setw(20)<<deptt<<"\n";     }
};
main()
{   Faculty *f[10]; // f is an array of pointer to Faculty
    char ch = 'Y';
    int n=0;
    while(n<10)
    {   f[n] = new Faculty; // dynamically allocate memory for object
        f[n]->get_data(); //invoke member function of object
        cout<<"\n Continue (Y/N): ";
        cin>>ch;
```

```
        cin.ignore();
        if(ch == 'N')
        break;
        n++;
    }
    cout<<"\n NAME "<<setw(20)<<"Department \n\n";
    for(int i=0;i<=n;i++)
    f[i]->show_data();
    delete[] f;
}
```

SAMPLE OUTPUT

```
NAME                DEPARTMENT
Mansi Sood          Computer Science
Akanksha Bansal     Chemistry
Jaya Gera           Psychology
Namita Aggarwal     English
Shweta Tyagi        Mathematics
```

9.9 OBJECTS AS FUNCTION ARGUMENTS

Similar to variables, objects can also be passed as arguments to functions. Similar to basic data type arguments, objects can also be passed to functions in the following three ways:

Pass-by-value In this technique, a copy of the actual object is created and passed to the called function. Therefore, the actual (object) and the formal (copy of object) arguments are stored at different memory locations. This means that any changes made in formal object will not be reflected in the actual object.

Pass-by-reference In this method, the address of the object is implicitly passed to the called function.

Pass-by-address In this technique, the address of the object is explicitly passed to the called function.

Since both pass by reference and pass-by-address techniques send the address of the actual object to the called function, any changes made in the object are reflected to actual object. Moreover, these two techniques must be preferred as they prevent duplication of object and hence, reduce memory space requirements of a program. Example 9.5 demonstrates how an object is passed as an argument using the three techniques discussed.

Example 9.5 Passing object as an argument

```
using namespace std;
#include<iostream>
class myClass
{   private:
        int num;
    public:
        void get_data()
        {   cout<<"\n Enter a number : ";
            cin>>num;
        }
        void set_data(myClass o2)     // function accepts object
```

```
        {   num = o2.num;
        }
        // function accepts address of object
        void set_data(int a, myClass &o2)
        {   num = o2.num;
        }
        void set_data(myClass *o2) // function accepts pointer
        {   num = o2->num;
        }
        void show_data()
        {   cout<<"\n Num = "<<num;
        }
};
main ()
{   myClass o1, o2, o3, o4;
    int a=0;
    o2.get_data();
    o1.set_data(o2);            //call by value
    o3.set_data(&o2);       //call by pointer
    o4.set_data(a, o2);         //call by reference
    o1.show_data();
    o2.show_data();
    o3.show_data();
}
```

OUTPUT

```
Enter a number: 7
NUM = 7
NUM = 7
NUM = 7
```

Explanation: In this program, only the value of object o2 has been entered by the user. Values of other objects—o1, o3, and o4—have been set through the o2 object using call-by-value, call-by-pointer, and call-by-reference techniques, respectively. When we called the function through call-by-reference, we had sent an extra argument that was absolutely not required. However, the argument was just passed to have some small difference in the function header so that the compiler does not generate any error. As per the rules of function overloading, reference variables are not overloaded. In simple terms, `void set_data(myClass obj);` is exactly same as `void set_data( myClass &obj)`.

Note that as two functions with the same header are not allowed, just a small difference was made in the function header to avoid any error.

9.10 RETURNING OBJECTS

C++ not only allows users to pass objects to functions as arguments but also allows functions to return objects. The syntax is the same as that for a normal variable. You can return an object using the following three methods:

- Returning by value which makes a duplicate copy of the local object.
- Returning by using a reference to the object. In this way, the address of the object is passed implicitly to the calling function.
- Returning by using the '`this` pointer' which explicitly sends the address of the object to the calling function.

Consider the code given here.

```
Complex Complex :: add(Complex &c2)
{   Complex c3;
    c3.real = real + c2.real;
    c3.imag = imag + c2.imag;
    return c3;
}
```

In the code, the function accepts an object using reference, performs addition of two complex numbers, and returns a local object c3 by making its duplicate copy.

```
Complex &Complex :: compare(Complex &c2)
{   if(real < c2.real)
        return c2;
    else if(real == c2.real)
    {   if(imag < c2.imag)
            return c2;
        else
        return *this;
    }
}
```

The function compares two complex numbers. In this code, there are two points to be noted:

- `if(real < c2.real)`, then `c2` is returned using reference. Check the function header; the function returns an object using an address either implicitly or explicitly. Since we are writing return `c2`, it means that object `c2` is being returned using a reference.
- If object `c2` is greater than `c1` (the object that invoked the compare function), then `c2` is returned to the caller using reference in which the address of the object was implicitly passed. However, if `c1` is greater, then it is being returned using a special pointer called `this` pointer.

9.11 this POINTER

C++ uses the `this` keyword to represent the object that invoked the member function of the class. `this` pointer is an implicit parameter to all member functions and can, therefore, be used inside a member function to refer to the invoking object. To understand this, consider the program code given here.

Example 9.6 Use `this` pointer to represent the invoking object

```
using namespace std;
#include<iostream>
class Sample
{   private:
        int a;
    public:
    void set_data(int num)
    {   a = num;    }
    void show_data()
    {      cout<<a; }
};
main()
{
    int num = 10;
    Sample s;
```

```
    s.set_data(num);
    s.show_data();
}
```

OUTPUT

```
10
```

Explanation: In `main()`, when the function `set_data()` is called, the invoking object is `s`. Therefore, the pointer `this` will be automatically set to the address of `s` and is implicitly passed as an argument to the member function. This means that while we are calling the function as

```
s.set_data(num);
```

the compiler on the other hand, is calling it as

```
s.set_data(&s, num);
```

Now, inside the member function, while we write `a = num`, however, it is actually being referred to as

```
this->a = num; or as  (*this).a = num;
```

Therefore, right from the first program, we have been using the `this` pointer. Since C++ permits the use of shorthand form like `a = num`, we need not complicate our code and explicitly mention the `this` pointer by writing `this->a = num`.

Let us consider another example; when we write

```
Complex C1, C2, C3;
C3 = C1.compare(c2);
```

Programming Tip: `this` pointer is a constant pointer so any attempt to change it will result in a compilation error.

In the statements given here, we are calling the function that compares two complex numbers. Here, `c1` is invoking the member function `compare()` and `c2` is being passed as an argument. Actually, we are passing two objects and not just one object. The invoking object `c1` is implicitly passed. Hence, the above statement is equivalent to writing,

```
C3 = C1.compare(&C1, C2);
```

An important point to note here is that the `this` pointer is a pointer accessible only within the non-static member functions of a `class`, `struct`, or `union` type. Why not static members? Recall that static members are accessed using the class name. They cannot be associated with any object of the class and the `this` pointer refers to the invoking object of the member. Hence, the `this` pointer is not applicable in case of static members.

Note `this` pointer is a constant pointer that holds the address of the current object. It is a hidden pointer inside every class member function that is internally created at the time of function call.

In addition, an object's `this` pointer is not a part of the object itself. This can be concluded by applying the `sizeof` statement on the object.

The `*this` is commonly used to return the current object from a member function. This can be done by writing,

```
return *this;
```

Note that in the compare function of complex class, when we write `real< c2.real`, means that real part of the invoking object (`c1`) is being compared with that of `c2`.

Program 9.9 Write a program to add and subtract two fractions. Let the add() accept the objects using call-by-value technique, subtract() using call-by-reference, and multiply() accept using the call-by-address technique.

```
using namespace std;
#include<iostream>
class Fraction
{   private:
        int num;
        int deno;
        void simplify();
        int GCD(int a, int b);
    public:
        void get_data()
        {   cout<<"\n Enter the numerator :";
            cin>>num;
            cout<<"\n Enter the denominator : ";
            cin>>deno;
            if(deno == 0)
            {   cout<<"\n Fraction Not Possible";
                exit(1);
            }
        }
        void display_data()
        {   simplify();
            cout<<num<<" / "<<deno;
        }
        void add(Fraction f1, Fraction f2);
        void subtract(Fraction &f1, Fraction &f2);
        void multiply(Fraction *f1, Fraction *f2);
};
void Fraction :: simplify(void)
{   int common_divisor = GCD(num, deno);
    num /= common_divisor;
    deno /= common_divisor;
}
int Fraction :: GCD(int a, int b)
{   if(b == 0)
        return a;
    else
        return GCD(b, a%b);
}
void Fraction :: add(Fraction f1, Fraction f2)
{
    num = (f1.num * f2.deno) + (f2.num * f1.deno);
    deno = f1.deno * f2.deno;
    display_data();
}
void Fraction :: subtract(Fraction &f1, Fraction &f2)
{
    num = (f1.num * f2.deno) - (f2.num * f1.deno);
    deno = f1.deno * f2.deno;
    display_data();
}
void Fraction :: multiply(Fraction *f1, Fraction *f2)
{
```

```
    num = f1->num * f2->num;
    deno = f1->deno * f2->deno;
    display_data();
}
main()
{   Fraction f1, f2,f3;
    f1.get_data();
    f2.get_data();
    cout<<"\n Result of Addition = ";
    f3.add(f1,f2);
    cout<<"\n Result of Subtraction = ";
    f3.subtract(f1,f2);
    cout<<"\n Result of Multiplication = ";
    f3.multiply(&f1,&f2);
}
```

OUTPUT

```
Enter the numerator : 3
Enter the denominator : 5
Enter the numerator : 4
Enter the denominator : 9
Result of Addition = 47 / 45
Result of Subtraction = 7 / 45
Result of Multiplication = 4 / 15
```

Program 9.10 Write a program that adds two complex numbers. The object must be passed through reference and the result must be returned by value.

```
using namespace std;
#include<iostream>
class Complex
{   private:
        int real;
        int imag;
    public:
        void get_data()
        {  cin>>real>>imag;  }
        void display_data()
        {  cout<<real<<" + "<<imag<<" i";  }
        Complex add(Complex &);
};
Complex Complex :: add(Complex &c2)
{   Complex c3;
    c3.real = real + c2.real;
    c3.imag = imag + c2.imag;
    return c3;
}
main()
{   Complex c1, c2, c3;
    cout<<"\n Enter the real and imaginary parts of first complex number : ";
    c1.get_data();
    cout<<"\n Enter the real and imaginary parts of second complex number : ";
    c2.get_data();
    c3 = c1.add(c2);
    cout<<"\n Result of addition = ";
    c3.display_data();
}
```

OUTPUT

```
Enter the real and imaginary parts of first complex number : 2 3
Enter the real and imaginary parts of second complex number : 4 5
Result of addition = 6 + 8 i
```

Program 9.11 Write a program that compares and subtracts two complex numbers. The object must be passed through reference and the result must be returned using this pointer.

```
using namespace std;
#include<iostream>
#include<math.h>
class Complex
{   private:
        int real;
        int imag;
    public:
            void get_data()
            {  cin>>real>>imag;  }
            void display_data()
            {  cout<<real<<" + "<<imag<<" i";  }
            Complex &compare(Complex &);
            Complex &subtract(Complex &);
};
Complex &Complex :: compare(Complex &c2)
{   if(real < c2.real)
        return c2;
    else if(real == c2.real)
    {   if(imag < c2.imag)
            return c2;
        else
            return *this;
    }
}
Complex &Complex :: subtract(Complex &c2)
{   real -= c2.real;
    imag -= c2.imag;
    return *this;
}
main()
{   Complex c1, c2, c3;
    cout<<"\n Enter the real and imaginary parts of first complex number : ";
    c1.get_data();
    cout<<"\n Enter the real and imaginary parts of second complex number : ";
    c2.get_data();
    c3 = c1.compare(c2);
    cout<<"\n The largest complex number = ";
    c3.display_data();
    cout<<"\n The result of subtraction = ";
    c3 = c1.subtract(c2);
    c3.display_data();
}
```

OUTPUT

```
Enter the real and imaginary parts of first complex number : 7 6
```

```
Enter the real and imaginary parts of second complex number : 2 4
The largest complex number = 7 + 6 i
The result of subtraction = 5 + 2 i
```

Program 9.12 Write a program to find the sum of numbers explicitly using `this` pointer (on right side of assignment operator).

```
using namespace std;
#include<iostream>
class Numbers
{   private:
        int a;
    public:
        void set_data(int x)
        {   a = x;     }
            void add(Numbers &n)
        {   int sum = n.a += this->a;
            cout<<"\n SUM = "<<sum;
        }
};
main()
{   Numbers n1, n2;
    n1.set_data(10);
    n2.set_data(20);
    n1.add(n2);
}
```

OUTPUT

```
SUM = 30
```

Program 9.13 Write a program that displays the name of topper in a class.

```
using namespace std;
#include<iostream>
#include<string.h>
class Student
{   private:
        char name[20];
        int marks;
    public:
        void get_data()
        {   cout<<"\n Enter the name : ";
    cin.ignore();
            cin.getline(name, 20);
            cout<<"\n Enter the marks : ";
            cin>>marks;
        }
        void show_data()
        {   cout<<"\n NAME : "<<name;
            cout<<"\n MARKS : "<<marks;
        }
        friend void find_Topper(Student S[], int n);
};
void find_Topper(Student S[], int n)
{   int highest_marks = S[0].marks;
```

```
    char topper_name[20];
    strcpy(topper_name, S[0].name);
    for(int i=1;i<n;i++)
    {   if(highest_marks<S[i].marks)
        strcpy(topper_name, S[i].name);
    }
    cout<<"\n The Topper of the class is : "<<topper_name;
}
main()
{   Student s[5];
    int n;
    cout<<"\n Enter the number of students : ";
    cin>>n;
    for(int i=0;i<n;i++)
        s[i].get_data();
    for(int i=0;i<n;i++)
        s[i].show_data();
    find_Topper(s, n);
}
```

SAMPLE OUTPUT

```
Enter the number of students : 3
Enter the name : Sarthak
Enter the marks : 90
Enter the name : Aditya
Enter the marks : 80
Enter the name : Goransh
Enter the marks : 100
The Topper of the class is : Goransh
```

Program 9.14 Write a program to display the list of students according to their ranks.

```
using namespace std;
#include<iostream>
#include<string.h>
class Student
{   private:
        char
    name[20];
        int marks;
    public:
        void get_data()
        {   cout<<"\n Enter the name : ";
    cin.ignore();
            cin.getline(name, 20);
            cout<<"\n Enter the marks : ";
            cin>>marks;
        }
        void show_data()
        {   cout<<"\n NAME : "<<name;
            cout<<"\n MARKS : "<<marks;
        }
        friend void Sort_Rankwise(Student S[], int n);
};
```

```
void Sort_Rankwise(Student S[], int n)
{
    for(int i=0;i<n;i++)
    {   for(int j=0;j<n-1;j++)
        {   if(S[j].marks<S[j+1].marks)
        {   int temp_marks = S[j].marks;
        S[j].marks = S[j+1].marks;
                S[j+1].marks = temp_marks;
                char temp_name[20];
                strcpy(temp_name, S[j].name);
                strcpy(S[j].name, S[j+1].name);
                strcpy(S[j+1].name, temp_name);
            }
        }
    }
    for(int i=0;i<n;i++)
    {   cout<<"\n NAME : "<<S[i].name;
        cout<<"\n MARKS : "<<S[i].marks;
        cout<<"\n --------------------";
    }
}
main()
{   Student s[5];
    int n;
    cout<<"\n Enter the number of students : ";
    cin>>n;
    for(int i=0;i<n;i++)
        s[i].get_data();
    for(int i=0;i<n;i++)
        s[i].show_data();
    cout<<"\n ***** RANK WISE SORTED DETAILS ******";
    Sort_Rankwise(s, n);
}
```

OUTPUT

```
Enter the number of students : 3
Enter the name : Sarthak
Enter the marks : 90
Enter the name : Aditya
Enter the marks : 80
Enter the name : Goransh
Enter the marks : 100
***** RANK WISE SORTED DETAILS ******
Goransh 100
Sarthak 90
Aditya     80
```

9.12 CONSTANT PARAMETERS AND MEMBERS

To prevent inadvertent changes to any of the member of the class, C++ has two mechanisms to control changes:

- constant member functions
- constant objects as parameters

Constant member functions are used when a particular member function should strictly not attempt to change the value of any of the class's data member. For example, `display_data()` has nothing to do with changing the values. Therefore, it is advisable to declare such member functions as const. The syntax for declaring a `const` member function is

> **Programming Tip:** Any attempt to change the value of a constant parameter will result in a compilation error.

```
return_type function_name(arguments) const;
```

Therefore, `display_data()` can be declared as `const` by writing,

```
void display_data() const;
```

Note that the keyword `const` should be suffixed in function header during declaration and definition. Once a member function is declared as `const`, any attempt to alter a data member will result in a compiler error.

Example 9.7 Constant member functions

```
using namespace std;
#include<iostream>
class Employee
{   private:
        int emp_no;
        float sal;
    public:
        void set_data(int e, float s);
        void show_data() const; // constant member function, cannot modify data values
};
void Employee :: set_data(int e, float s)
{   emp_no = e;
    sal = s;
}
void Employee :: show_data() const
{   cout<<"\n EMP NO. = "<<emp_no<<" \n Salary = "<<sal;
}
main()
{   Employee e;
    e.set_data(1, 10000);
    e.show_data();
}
```

OUTPUT

```
EMP NO. = 1
Salary = 10000
```

When we pass constant objects as parameters, then members of the object—whether private or public—cannot be changed. This is even more important when we are passing an object to a non-member function. For example, if we have non-member function increment that accepts the object of a class and an amount by which the salary has to be incremented, then the code can be given as follows:

```
void increment(Employee e, float amt)
{   e.sal += amt;
}
```

However, such an act is not recommended as the prime concern of an object-oriented programming language is data hiding. Data members of a class should be modified only through the member functions of the class. Hence, to prevent any changes by non-member of the class, we must pass the object as a constant object. The function will then receive a read-only copy of the object and will not be allowed to make any changes to it. To pass a const object to the increment function, we must write

```
void increment(Employee const e, float amt);
```

To pass a const object through reference, you must write

```
void increment(Employee const &e, float amt);
```

Now, the function can access and use the members of employee but cannot modify it.

9.13 POINTERS WITHIN A CLASS

Now that we have studied pointers in detail and are quite comfortable with programming with pointers, let us try to use them inside a class to dynamically allocate memory for arrays and strings. The benefit of using pointers is same as what we had studied earlier. Pointers help us to execute the following functions:

- Pointers help us to allocate memory at run time. For normal variables, memory is allocated at compile time. Therefore, users must specify the length of the array or string in advance. However, with pointers, we can use the new operator for dynamic allocation of memory. Users may input any size and that size may vary from one execution of the program to the other.
- The size of the memory allocated cannot be changed during compile time in case of an array. However, using pointers, the size of the array or string may be increased or decreased.

Consider the program given here for understanding the concept.

Example 9.8 Using pointers within a class

```
using namespace std;
#include<iostream>
class Array
{   private:
        int *arr; // arr is a pointer to integer
        int size;
    public:
        void get_data(int n);
        int get_sum();
        void display_data();
};
void Array :: get_data(int n)
{   size = n;
    arr = new int[size];      //dynamically allocate memory for array
    for(int i=0;i<size;i++)
        cin>>arr[i];
}
void Array :: display_data()
{   for(int i=0;i<size;i++)
        cout<<"\t"<<arr[i];
    cout<<"\n Sum of elements = "<<get_sum();
    cout<<"\n Average of numbers = "<<float(get_sum()/size);
}
```

```
int Array :: get_sum()
{   int sum = 0;
    for(int i=0;i<size;i++)
        sum += arr[i];
      return sum;
}
main()
{      Array a; //a is an object of class Array
      int n;
      cout<<"\n Enter the number of elements : ";
      cin>>n;
      a.get_data(n);
      a.display_data();
}
```

OUTPUT

```
Enter the number of elements : 9
1    2    3    4    5    6    7    8    9
Sum of elements = 45
Average of numbers = 5
```

Explanation: In the program, an object of class array is created in `main()`. The class has two data member—an integer pointer variable and an integer size. When the `get_data()` is called with a parameter specifying the size of the array, memory is dynamically allocated for the array, and its elements are entered.

Program 9.15 Write a program that uses a class movie to display the name of movie as well as the name of actor and actress who worked in it. Demonstrate the use of constant objects, member functions, and pointers within classes.

```
using namespace std;
#include<iostream>
#include<string.h>
class Movie
{   private:
        char *name;
        char *actor;
        char *actress;
    public:
        void set_data(char const *n, char const *a, char const *b);
        char const *show_name(void)      const;
        char const *show_actor(void)      const;
        char const *show_actress(void)      const;
};
void Movie :: set_data(char const *n, char const *a, char const *b)
{   name = new char[strlen(n) + 1];
    strcpy(name, n);
    actor = new char[strlen(a) + 1];
    strcpy(actor, a);
    actress = new char[strlen(b) + 1];
    strcpy(actress, b);
}
char const * Movie :: show_name(void)      const
{   return name;          }
char const * Movie :: show_actor(void)      const
```

```
{   return actor;           }
char const * Movie :: show_actress(void)     const
{   return actress;           }
void display(Movie const &m)
{   cout<<"\n Movie : "<<m.show_name();
    cout<<"\n Actor : "<<m.show_actor();
    cout<<"\n Actress : "<<m.show_actress();
}
main()
{   Movie m1, m2;
    m1.set_data("Three Idiots", "Aamir Khan", "Kareena Kapoor");
    cout<<"\n Movie : "<<m1.show_name();
    cout<<"\n Actor : "<<m1.show_actor();
    cout<<"\n Actress : "<<m1.show_actress();
    m2.set_data("Namastey London", "Akshay Kumar", "Katrina Kaif");
    display(m2);
}
```

OUTPUT

```
Movie : Three Idiots
Actor : Aamir Khan
Actress : Kareena Kapoor
Movie : Namastey London
Actor : Akshay Kumar
Actress : Katrina Kaif
```

9.14 LOCAL CLASSES

A local class is the class which is defined inside a function. Till now, we were creating global classes since these were defined above all the functions, including `main()`. However, as the name implies, a local class is local to the function in which it is defined and therefore is known or accessible only in that function. However, there are certain guidelines that must be followed while using local classes, which are as follows.

- Local classes can use any global variable but along with the scope resolution operator.
- Local classes can use static variables declared inside the function.
- Local classes cannot use automatic variables.
- Local classes cannot have static data members.
- Member functions must be defined inside the class.
- Private members of the class cannot be accessed by the enclosing function (until and unless it is declared as FRIEND, we will read about it in next section).

Note A local class is defined within the scope of a function and thus, nested within a function.

Example 9.9 Local class

```
using namespace std;
#include<iostream>
int NUM;
main()
{   class Sample
    {   private:
        int a;
```

> **Programming Tip:** Making an object of a local class outside the function in which it is defined will result in a compilation error.

```
            public:
            void get_data()
            {       cout<<"\n Enter the value of a : ";
                    cin>>a;
                    cout<<"\n Enter the value of global variable : ";
                    cin>>::NUM;
            }
            void show_data()
            {       cout<<"\n Class Private Data Member = "<<a;
                    cout<<"\n Global Variable = "<<::NUM;
            }
            };
    Sample s;
            s.get_data();
            s.show_data();
            }
```

OUTPUT

```
Enter the value of a : 10
Enter the value of global variable : 20
Class Private Data Member = 10
Global Variable = 20
```

Explanation: In the program, we see that a global variable is accessed as a local variable but with a difference of the prefixed scope resolution operator.

Note that it is not necessary that local classes must be defined in `main()`. You can define them in any function. For example, you could have defined it in `func()` and called `func()` from `main()`, as shown here.

```
using namespace std;
#include<iostream>
int NUM; // global variable
void func();
main()
{  func();
}
void func()
{  class Sample
   {  -----
      ----
   };
   Sample s;
   s.get_data();
   s.show_data();
}
```

9.15 NESTED CLASSES IN C++

C++ allows programmers to create a class inside another class. This is called nesting of classes. When a `class B` is nested inside another `class A`, `class B` is not allowed to access `class A`'s members. Although in the current version, there is no major advantage in making nested classes, it is said that the next C++ standard will allow a nested class to have access to the members of the nesting `class A`.

The following points must be noted about nested classes.

- A nested class is declared and defined inside another class.
- The scope of the inner class is restricted by the outer class.

- While declaring an object of inner class, the name of the inner class must be preceded with the name of the outer class.

Example 9.10 Nested classes

```
using namespace std;
#include<iostream>
class A
{  public:
          class B
          {  private:
                int num;
             public:
                void large(int x, int y)
                {  num = x;
                   if(num<y)
                      num = y;
                }
                void show_data()
                {  cout<<"\n Large = "<<num;    }
                };
};
main()
{  A::B b;
   b.large(100, 200);
   b.show_data();
}
```

OUTPUT

```
Large = 200
```

Explanation: In this program, `class B` is declared and defined within the scope of `class A`. there are no data members or member functions in `class A`. However, a `class B` is declared in the public section of `class A`. `Class B` has a private member `num` and public member functions `large()` which finds larger of two numbers to assign it to `num` and `show()` which displays the larger number. In `main()`, note how an object of `class B` is created. It is specified in conjunction with class a (the outer class).

9.16 COMPLEX OBJECTS (OBJECT COMPOSITION)

Complex objects are objects that are built from smaller or simpler objects. For example, a car is built using a metal frame, an engine, some tyres, a transmission, a steering wheel, and several other parts. Similarly, a computer system is made up of several parts such as CPU, motherboard, memory, and so on. This process of building complex objects from simpler ones is called composition or containership.

In object-oriented programming languages, object composition is used for objects that have a has-a relationship to each other. For example, a car has-a metal frame, has-an engine, etc. A personal computer has-a CPU, a motherboard, and other components.

Until now, we have been using classes that have data members of built-in type. While this worked well for simple classes, for designing classes that simulate real world applications, programmers often need data members that belong to other simpler classes.

Note In composition, complex classes have data members belonging to other simpler classes.

Benefits

- Each individual class can be simple and straightforward.
- A class can focus on performing one specific task.
- The class is easier to write, debug, understand, and usable by other programmers.
- While simpler classes can perform all the operations, the complex class can be designed to coordinate the data flow between simpler classes.
- It lowers the overall complexity of the complex object because the main task of the complex object would then be to delegate tasks to the sub-objects, who already know how to do them.

Scope of Use

Although there is no well-defined rule to state when a programmer must use composition, as a rule of thumb, each class should be built to accomplish a single task. The task should be to either perform some part of manipulation or be responsible for coordinating other classes but cannot perform both tasks. For example,

```
class Point

{   private:
        int x;
        int y;
    // code
};
class Location
{   Private:
        Point Source;
        Point Destination
    //code;
};
```

In the classes given here, `Location` uses objects of class `Point` as its data members. Hence, `Location` is a complex class which uses a simple class `Point`. Let us have a look at the program that makes use of composition or containership.

Example 9.11 Using composition or containership

```
using namespace std;
#include<iostream>
class One
{   private:
        int num;
    public:
        void set(int i)
        {   num = i;
        }
        int get()
        {   return num;
        }
};
class Two
{   public:
```

```
        One O;
        void show()
        {   cout<<"\n Number = "<<O.get();
        }
};
int main()
{   Two T;
    T.O.set(100);
    T.show();
}
```

OUTPUT

```
Number = 100
```

Explanation: Note that in the program, `class Two` has an object of `class One`. To access a member of `One`, we must use the object of `Two` as in `T.O.set(100)`; moreover, since `num` is a private member of `One`, we must use a public function to access its value.

9.17 EMPTY CLASSES

An empty class is one in which there are no data members and no member functions. These type of classes are not frequently used. However, at times, they may be used for exception handling, discussed in a later chapter. The syntax of defining an empty class is as follows:

```
class class_name{};
```

Example 9.12 Empty class

```
using namespace std;
#include<iostream>
class Empty{};
main()
{   Empty e;
    cout<<"\n Size of empty class = "<<sizeof(Empty);
    cout<<"\n Size of empty class's object = "<<sizeof(e);
    cout<<"\n Address of empty class's object = "<<hex<<&e;
}
```

OUTPUT

```
Size of empty class = 1
Size of empty class's object = 1
Address of empty class's object = 0x844ffee4c
```

Explanation: From the output of this program, it is clear that minimum memory, i.e., `1 byte`, is reserved for an empty class.

Program 9.16 Write a program to demonstrate the use of structure with a class.

```
using namespace std;
#include<iostream>
#include<string.h>
struct Date
{   int dd;
```

```
    int mm;
    int yy;
};
class Student
{   private:
        int roll_no;
        char *name;
        Date DOB;
    public:
        void get_data(int r,char *str, Date &d);
        void show_data();
};
void Student :: get_data(int r, char *str, Date &d)
{   roll_no = r;
    name = new char[strlen(str)+1];
    strcpy(name, str);
    DOB = d;
}
void Student :: show_data()
{   cout<<"\n Roll No = "<<roll_no;
    cout<<"\n Name = "<<name;
    cout<<"\n DOB = "<<DOB.dd<<" - "<<DOB.mm<<" - "<<DOB.yy;
}
main()
{   Student s;
    Date d = {18, 06, 14};
    s.get_data(1, "Aditya",d);
    s.show_data();
}
```

OUTPUT

```
Roll No = 1
Name = Aditya
DOB = 18-06-14
```

Program 9.17 Write a program to demonstrate the use of union inside a class.

```
using namespace std;

#include<iostream>
union info
{   int roll_no;
    char name[20];
};
class Student
{   private:
        info i;
        int marks;
        char find_grade();
    public:
        void get_data(char ch);
        void show_data(char ch);
};
void Student :: get_data(char ch)
{       if(ch == 'N')
```

```
    {   cout<<"\n Enter the name of the student : ";
        cin.ignore();
        cin.getline(i.name, 20);
    }
    else
    {   cout<<"\n Enter the roll number : ";
        cin>>i.roll_no;
    }
        cout<<"\n Enter the marks : ";
        cin>>marks;
}
void Student :: show_data(char ch)
{   if(ch == 'N')
        cout<<"\n NAME : "<<i.name;
    else
        cout<<"\n RollNumber : "<<i.roll_no;
        cout<<"\n MARKS : "<<marks;
        cout<<"\n GRADE : "<<find_grade();
}
char Student :: find_grade()
{   if(marks>=75)
        return 'O';
    if(marks>=60 && marks<75)
        return 'A';
    if(marks>=50 && marks<60)
        return 'B';
    if(marks>=40 && marks<50)
        return 'C';
    else
        return 'F';
}
main()
{
    Student s;
    char ch;
    cout<<"\n Do you want to enter name or roll number of the student (N/R) : ";
    cin>>ch;
    s.get_data(ch);
    s.show_data(ch);
}
```

OUTPUT

```
Do you want to enter name or roll number of the student (N/R) : N
Enter the name of the student : Goransh
Enter the marks : 100
NAME : Goransh
MARKS : 100
GRADE : O
```

Program 9.18 Write a program that displays information about a book using a local class.

```
using namespace std;
#include<iostream>
#include<string.h>
void display();
```

```
main()
{   display();
}
void display()
{   class Book
    {   private:
            char *title;
            long int isbn;
        public:
            void set_data(char *t, double v)
            {   title = new char [strlen (t) + 1];
                strcpy(title, t);
                isbn = v;
            }
            void show_data()
            {   cout<<"\n TITLE : "<<title;
                cout<<"\n ISBN : "<<isbn;
            }
    };
    Book b;
    b.set_data("Programming in C++", 98712568);
    b.show_data();
}
```

OUTPUT

```
TITLE : Programming in C++
ISBN : 98712568
```

Program 9.19 Write a program to add two numbers using nested classes.

```
using namespace std;
#include<iostream>
class A
{   public:
        int x;
        void get_data()
        {   cout<<"\n Enter the value of x : ";
            cin>>x;
        }
        class B
        {   private:
                int y;
            public:
                void get_data()
                {   cout<<"\n Enter the value of y : ";
                    cin>>y;
                }
                void sum()
                {   A a;
                    a.get_data();
                    cout<<a.x<<" "<<y;
                    cout<<"\n SUM = "<<a.x + y;
                }
        };
};
```

```
main()
{   A::B b;
    b.get_data();
    b.sum();
}
```

OUTPUT

```
Enter the value of y : 10
Enter the value of x : 20
SUM = 30
```

Program 9.20 Write a program to demonstrate use of three classes that are nested one inside another.

```
using namespace std;
#include<iostream>
class A
{   public:
        int x;
            void get_data()
        {   cout<<"\n Enter the value of x : ";
            cin>>x;
        }
        class B
        {   public:
                int y;
                void get_data()
                {   cout<<"\n Enter the value of y : ";
                    cin>>y;
                }
        class C
        {   public:
                int z;
                void get_data(A &a, A::B &b)
                {   a.get_data();
                    b.get_data();
                    cout<<"\n Enter the value of z : ";
                    cin>>z;
                }
                void show_data(A &a, A::B &b)
                {   cout<<"\n A's x = "<<a.x;
                    cout<<"\n B's y = "<<b.y;
                    cout<<"\n c's z = "<<z;
                }
            };
        };
};
main()
{   A a;
    A::B b;
    A::B::C c;
    c.get_data(a, b);
    c.show_data(a, b);
}
```

OUTPUT

```
Enter the value of x : 100
Enter the value of y : 200
Enter the value of z : 300
A's x = 100
B's y = 200
c's z = 300
```

Program 9.21 Write a program to display student's details using nested class.

```
using namespace std;
#include<iostream>
class Student
{   private:
        int roll_no;
        int marks;
    public:
        class date
        {   private:
                int dd, mm, yy;
            public:
                void read_date()
                {   cout<<"\n Enter the DOB : ";
                    cin>>dd>>mm>>yy;
                }
                void show_date()
                {   cout<<"\n DOB : "<<dd<<" - "<<mm<<" - "<<yy;
                }
    }DOB;
    void read_details()
    {   cout<<"\n Enter the roll no : ";
        cin>>roll_no;
        cout<<"\n Enter the marks : ";
        cin>>marks;
        DOB.read_date();
    }
    void show_details()
    {   cout<<"\n Roll Number : "<<roll_no;
        cout<<"\n Marks : "<<marks;
        DOB.show_date();
    }
};
main()
{   Student s;
    s.read_details();
    s.show_details();
}
```

OUTPUT

```
Enter the roll no : 17
Enter the marks : 99
Enter the DOB : 17 02 2007
Roll Number : 17
Marks : 99
DOB : 17 - 02 - 2007
```

9.18 FRIEND FUNCTION

Till now, we have studied that since data hiding is a fundamental concept of object-oriented programming, a non-member function cannot access an object's private or protected data. However, at times, this restriction makes the code too long and complex. So, to overcome this problem, C++ supports the use of friend functions and friend classes.

A friend function of a class is a non-member function of the class that can access its private and protected members (keyword protected will be discussed in Chapter 12 on Inheritance). Just as we allow our friends to use our personal belongings, a friend function of a class is allowed to access the members of that class. Friend functions help implement data encapsulation in C++. They keep data of a class private from all external functions and classes except from those that are explicitly declared as friend and thus permitted to access.

To declare an external function as a friend of the class, you must include function prototype in the class definition. The prototype must be preceded with keyword `friend`.

The template to use a `friend` function can be given as follows:

```
class class_name
{   --------
    --------
    friend return_type function_name(list of arguments);
    --------
    --------
};
return_type function_name(list of arguments)
{   --------
    --------
}
```

Following are some important points related to friend function:

- `Friend` function is a normal external function that is given special access privileges.
- A `friend` function is defined outside that class' scope. Therefore, they cannot be called using the '.' or '->' operator. These operators are used only when they belong to some class.
- While the prototype for `friend` function is included in the class definition, it is not considered to be a member function of that class.
- The `friend` declaration can be placed either in the private or in the public section.
- A `friend` function of the class can be member and `friend` of some other class.
- A function `friend` of one class can be `friend` of another class.
- Since `friend` functions are non-members of the class, they do not require `this` pointer.
- The keyword `friend` is placed only in the function declaration and not in the function definition.
- A function can be declared as `friend` in any number of classes.
- A `friend` function can access the class's members directly using the object name and dot operator followed by the specific member.

Programming Tip: Accessing a `friend function` the object name will result in a compilation error.

`Friend` functions are frequently used to perform operations that are conducted on two different classes and thus require access to private or protected members of both classes. This type of usage will be clear when we will use them for Operator Overloading in Chapter 11.

Note While any non-member function of a class can access its public members, only the `friend` functions can access its private and protected members.

Consider the following program.

Example 9.13 `friend` function

```
using namespace std;
#include<iostream>
class Distance
{   private:
        int meters;
        int kms;
        friend float convert_meters(Distance &d);
        public:
            void get_data()
        {   cout<<"\n Enter kms and metres : ";
            cin>>kms>>meters;
        }
};
float convert_meters(Distance &d)
{   return ((d.kms * 1000) + d.meters);
}
main()
{   Distance d;
    d.get_data();
    cout<<"\n Distance in meters = "<<convert_meters(d);
}
```

OUTPUT

```
Enter kms and metres : 5 800
Distance in meters = 5800
```

Explanation: In the program, the function `convert_meters()` is an external function `friend` to class `Distance`. Now, consider another program in which a function is `friend` to two different classes. The program accepts objects of two classes and finds which one of them is larger.

Example 9.14 Accepting objects of two different classes

```
using namespace std;
#include<iostream>
class B;
class A
{   private:
        int x;
    public:
        friend void large(A &, B &);
        void get_data()
        {   cout<<"\n Enter x : ";
            cin>>x;
        }
};
class B
{   private:
        int y;
    public:
```

```
        friend void large(A &, B &);
        void get_data()
        {   cout<<"\n Enter y : ";
            cin>>y;
        }
};
void large(A &a, B &b)
{   if(a.x > b.y)
        cout<<a.x<<" (class A) is grater";
    else
        cout<<b.y<<" (class B) is grater";
}
main()
{   A a;
    a.get_data();
    B b;
    b.get_data();
    large(a,b);
}
```

OUTPUT

```
Enter x : 89
Enter y : 98
98 (class B) is grater
```

Explanation: In the program, note that we have written `class B;` and then defined `class B` later in the program. The statement `class B;` is called forward declaration and is used to tell the compiler that such a class will be defined later in the program. This is important because in `class A`, we have a `friend` function which accepts objects of another class that has not yet been defined. For the compiler to know `B`, we have to instruct the compiler that `B` is a class and declare it before it is defined.

9.19 FRIEND CLASS

Similar to friend function, a `friend` class is one which can access the private and/or protected members of another class. To declare all members of `class A` as friends of `class B`, write the following declaration in `class A`.

```
friend class B;
```

Now A says B: you are my friend and can, therefore, use my private members.

The template for making a `friend` class is as follows:

```
class B;
class A
{   friend class B;
    data members
    member functions
};
class B
{   data members
    member functions
};
```

Note `Friend` function or friend class should be created with caution as they contradict the concept of data hiding.

Points to be Noted

- Similar to `friend` function, a class can be a friend to any number of classes.
- When we declare a class as friend, then all its members also become the friend of the other class.
- You must first declare the friend becoming class (forward declaration).
- A friendship must always be explicitly specified. If `class A` is a friend of `class B`, then `class B` can access private and protected members of `class B`. Since `class B` is not declared a friend of `class A`, `class A` cannot access private and protected members of `class B`.
- A friendship is not transitive. This means that friend of a friend is not considered a friend unless explicitly specified. For example, if `class A` is a friend of `class B` and `class B` is a friend of `class C`, then it does not imply—unless explicitly specified—that `class A` is a friend of `class C`.

Consider Example 9.15 given here and note that `class A` has said that `class B` is its friend and can use its private members. `Class B` takes full advantage of friendship and swaps its contents with `class A`'s contents.

Example 9.15 Swapping numbers using `friend` classes

```
using namespace std;
#include<iostream>
class B; // forward declaration of class B
class A
{   friend class B; // class B is a friend of class A
    private:
        int x;
    public:
        void get_data()
        {   cout<<"\n Enter x : ";
            cin>>x;
        }
        void show_data()
        {   cout<<"\n A's x = "<<x;     }
};
class B
{   private:
        int y;
    public:
        void get_data()
        {   cout<<"\n Enter y : ";
            cin>>y;
        }
        void show_data()
        {   cout<<"\n B's y = "<<y;     }
        void swap(A &a)
        {   int temp = a.x;
            a.x = y;
            y = temp;
        }
};
```

```
main()
{   A a;
    B b;
    a.get_data();
    b.get_data();
    a.show_data();
    b.show_data();
    b.swap(a);
    cout<<"\n After Swapping";
    a.show_data();
    b.show_data();
}
```

OUTPUT

```
Enter x : 3
Enter y : 5
A's x = 3
B's y = 5
After Swapping
A's x = 5
B's y = 3
```

Explanation: In the program, `x` is a member of `class A` and `y` is a member of `class B`. Since `class B` is a friend of `class A`, it is using the private member of A in the `swap()`.

Program 9.22 Write a program to find mean of two numbers belonging to two different classes using `friend` function.

```
using namespace std;
#include<iostream>
#include<iomanip>
class B;
class A
{   private:
        int x;
    public:
        friend float mean(A &, B&);
        void get_data()
        {   cout<<"\n Enter x : ";
            cin>>x;
        }
};
class B
{   private:
        int y;
    public:
        friend float mean(A &, B &);
        void get_data()
        {   cout<<"\n Enter y : ";
            cin>>y;
        }
};
float mean(A &a, B &b)
{   return (float)((a.x + b.y)/2.0);
}
```

```
main()
{   A a;
    a.get_data();
    B b;
    b.get_data();
    cout<<"\n MEAN = "<<mean(a, b);
}
```

OUTPUT

```
Enter x : 5
Enter y : 10
MEAN = 7.5
```

Program 9.23 Write a program that adds two numbers belonging to different classes. Demonstrate the use of `friend` function in one class that is a member function of the second class.

```
using namespace std;
#include<iostream>
class A;
class B
{   private:
        int y;
    public:
        void get_data(A &);
        void show_data(A &);
};
class A
{   private:
        int x;
        friend void B :: get_data(A &);
        friend void B :: show_data(A &);
};
void B :: get_data(A &a)
{       cout<<"\n Enter class A's x : ";
        cin>>a.x;
        cout<<"\n Enter class B's y : ";
        cin>>y;
}
void B :: show_data(A &a)
{       cout<<"\n A's x = "<<a.x;
        cout<<"\n B's y = "<<y;
        cout<<"\n SUM = "<<a.x + y;
}
main()
{       A a;
        B b;
        b.get_data(a);
        b.show_data(a);
}
```

OUTPUT

```
Enter class A's x : 8
Enter class B's y : 7
A's x = 8
B's y = 7
SUM = 15
```

Program 9.24 Write a program to increment the salary of employee using `friend` class.

```
using namespace std;
#include<iostream>
class Increment;
class Employee
{   private:
        int deptt_id;
        float sal;
    public:
        friend class Increment;
        void get_data();
        void show_data();
};
void Employee :: get_data()
{   cout<<"\n Enter the Department Id (0/1) : ";
    cin>>deptt_id;
    cout<<"\n Enter salary : ";
    cin>>sal;
}
void Employee :: show_data()
{   cout<<"\n Department Id : "<<deptt_id;
    cout<<"\n Salary : "<<sal;
}
class Increment
{   public:
        void inc(Employee &e)
        {   if(e.deptt_id == 0)
                e.sal += 10000;
            else
                e.sal += 20000;
        };
};
main()
{   Employee e;
    Increment i;
    e.get_data();
    e.show_data();
    i.inc(e);
    cout<<"\n AFter incrementing salary";
    e.show_data();
}
```

OUTPUT

```
Enter the Department Id (0/1) : 0
Enter salary : 20000
After incrementing salary
Department Id : 0
Salary : 30000
```

Program 9.25 Write a program to calculate area of a cuboid. Convert the cuboid into a cube using a `friend` class.

```
using namespace std;
#include<iostream>
class Cube;
class Cuboid
```

```
{   private:
        int length;
        int breadth;
        int height;
    public:
        void set_data(Cube &);
        void get_data()
        {   cout<<"\n Enter the length, breadth and height : ";
            cin>>length>>breadth>>height;
    }
        int calculate_area()
        {   return length * breadth * height;
        }
};
class Cube
{   private:
        int side;
        friend class Cuboid;
    public:
        void get_data()
        {   cout<<"\n Enter the side : ";
            cin>>side;
        }
};
    void Cuboid :: set_data( Cube &c)
    {   length = breadth = height = c.side;
    }
main()
{   Cuboid cuboid1;
    cuboid1.get_data();
    cout<<"\n AREA = "<<cuboid1.calculate_area();
    Cube cube1;
    cube1.get_data();
    cuboid1.set_data(cube1);
    cout<<"\n AREA = "<<cuboid1.calculate_area();
}
```

OUTPUT

```
Enter the length, breadth and height : 2 3 4
AREA = 24
Enter the side : 5
AREA = 125
```

9.20 BIT-FIELDS IN CLASSES

Bit field is a wonderful feature of C++ that allows users to reserve the exact amount of bits required for storage of values. For example, the minimum number of bits reserved when we declare a variable is eight bits or one byte in case of `char`. If our variable can take only one of two values—1 or 0, we need just one bit. Similarly, if the variable can take any value from 0–3, then we need only two bits. Eight bits will be required only when we need values to vary from 0–7.

In order to save space, C++ facilitates users to store integer members into memory spaces smaller than the compiler would ordinarily allow. These space-saving members are called bit fields. In addition to this, C++ permits users to explicitly declare width in bits. Bit fields are generally used in developing application programs that must force a data structure to correspond to a fixed hardware representation and are unlikely to be portable.

The syntax for specifying a bit field can be given as follows:

```
type-specifier declarator: constant-expression
```

In the syntax, the constant-expression specifies the width of the field in bits. The declarator has a type-specifier which can be unsigned int, signed int, or int.

constant-expression must be a non-negative integer value. In case its value is zero, the declaration has no *declarator*.

Following are the key points about bit fields:

- C++ does not permit arrays of bit fields, pointers to bit fields, and functions returning bit fields.
- C++ permits ordinary member variables along with bit fields as class members.
- The declarator is optional and is used to name the bit field.
- Bit fields can only be declared as part of the class.
- The `address-of` operator (&) cannot be applied to bit-field components.
- Bit fields that are not named cannot be referenced, and their contents at run time are unpredictable. However, they can be used as 'dummy' fields for alignment purposes.
- Bit fields must be long enough to contain the bit pattern.
- When a value that is out of range is assigned to a bit field, the low-order bit pattern is preserved and the appropriate bits are assigned.
- Although the maximum bit field length is 64 bits, for portability reasons, do not use bit fields greater than 32 bits in size.
- Bit fields with a length of `0` must be unnamed.
- Arrays of bit field are not permitted.

Let us look at a class that has bit fields.

```
class Test
{   unsigned short a: 2;
    unsigned short b: 1;
    int c: 7;
    unsigned short d: 4;
};
```

In this structure, the size of the structure is two bytes. Bit fields have the same semantics as the integer type. Therefore, a bit field can also be used in an expression as a variable of basic data type.

The C++ standard requires the allowable data types for a bit field to include qualified and unqualified signed `int`, and unsigned `int` in addition to the following types:

- int
- short, signed short, unsigned short
- char, signed char, unsigned char
- long, signed long, unsigned long
- long long, signed long long, unsigned long long

Bit fields are basically used to represent single bit flags, with each flag stored in a separate bit.

Note In all implementations, the default integer type for a bit field is unsigned.

Consider the program given here that makes use of bit fields within C++ classes.

Example 9.16 Using bit fields within classes

```
using namespace std;
#include<iostream>
#define MATHS 0
#define COMPUTER 1
#define ENGLISH 2
#define IP 1
#define DU 2
#define JNU 3
#define DTU 4
#define AU 5
class Choice
{   private:
        unsigned course : 2;
        unsigned university : 3;
    public:
        void set_data()
        {   course = COMPUTER;
            university = DTU;
        }
        void show_data()
        {   cout<<"\n COURSE = "<<course;
            cout<<"\n UNIVERSITY = "<<university;
        }
};
main()
{   Choice c;
    cout<<"\n Size of Choice's object = "<<sizeof(c);
    c.set_data();
    c.show_data();
}
```

OUTPUT

```
Size of Choice's object = 2
COURSE = 1
UNIVERSITY = 4
```

Explanation: In the program, only two bits of storage is reserved for course and three bits is reserved for university. Note that the size of the class is far less than what it had been if data members were normal integer variables.

9.21 POINTERS AND CLASS MEMBERS

Just as we have pointers to normal variables and functions, we can also have pointers to class data members and class's member functions.

9.21.1 Declaring and Assigning Pointer to Data Members of a Class

Recollect that the syntax for declaring a pointer to normal variable is as follows:

```
data_type *ptr_var;
```

The syntax for declaring a pointer to a class data member is as follows:

```
data_type class_name :: *ptr_var;
```

The difference in the syntax arises because while a normal variable and a pointer to a normal variable can be used directly, a class's variable and a pointer to a class's variable have to be used along with class name and the scope resolution operator.

The syntax for assigning an address to a normal pointer variable is

```
ptr_var = &variable;
```

Similarly, the syntax for assigning the address of a class's data member to a pointer pointing to it is

```
ptr_var = &class_name :: data_member_name;
```

We can declare and assign pointer variables in the same line by writing

```
data_type *ptr_var = &variable;
```

Similarly, we can declare and assign a pointer to a class data member by writing

```
data_type class_name :: *ptr_var = &class_name :: data_member_name;
```

Accessing Data Members Using Pointers

To access a normal variable of a class we write

```
obj.data_member_name; or obj_ptr->data_member_name, if we have a pointer to object.
```

Similarly, to access the same data member using a pointer to the data member, we have to dereference the pointer and write

```
obj.*ptr_var; or obj_ptr->*ptr_var;
```

Consider the program given here and see how a pointer to data member is created and accessed with an object (t) and then using a pointer to object (*tp).

Example 9.17 Program to demonstrate pointer to data member

```
using namespace std;
#include<iostream>
class Test
{   public:
        int x;
        void show_data();
};
void Test :: show_data()
{   cout<<"\n x = "<<x;     }
main()
{   Test t; // create object
    int Test :: *ptr = &Test :: x; //create pointer to member
    t.*ptr = 20;     // access member through pointer
    t.show_data();
    Test *tp = new Test; // dynamically allocate memory for object
    tp->*ptr = 80; //using pointer to member
    tp->show_data();
}
```

OUTPUT

```
x = 20
x = 80
```

Note The .* operator also called the member dereferencing operator is used to access class members using a pointer to member. It is used with object of the class.

9.21.2 Pointer to Member Functions

Pointers can also be used to point to member functions of a class. The syntax for declaring and assigning a pointer to member function can be given as follows:

```
return_type(class_name :: *ptr_name)(arg_type) :: & clas_name :: function_name;
```

We can also separate declaration and assignment by writing,

```
return_type(class_name :: *ptr_name)(arg_type);
ptr_name = & clas_name :: function_name;
```

The general format to call a function using a pointer to member function is

```
(object_name.*ptr_name)(args);
```

Consider the program given here which uses a pointer to a member function.

Example 9.18 Pointer to a member function

```
using namespace std;
#include<iostream>
class Test
{   public:
        void show_msg();
};
void Test :: show_msg()
{       cout<<"\n Hello World !!!";      }
main()
{       void (Test :: *fp)(void);
        fp = &Test :: show_msg;
        Test t;
        (t.*fp)();
}
```

OUTPUT

```
Hello World !!!
```

Note To have a pointer to data member and member function, you must declare them in the public section of the class.

Program 9.26 Write a program that adds two integer members of a class. Use `friend` function, pointer to data member, and pointer to member function.

```
using namespace std;
#include<iostream>
class Numbers
{   private:
        int a;
        int b;
    public:
```

```
        void set_data()
        {   a=10, b=20;     }
        friend int add(Numbers &);
};
int add(Numbers &N)
{   int Numbers :: *ptr1 = &Numbers :: a;
    int Numbers :: *ptr2 = &Numbers :: b;
    return N.*ptr1 + N.*ptr2;
}
main()
{   Numbers N;
    void (Numbers :: *ptr_set_data)(void) = &Numbers :: set_data;
    (N.*ptr_set_data)();
    cout<<"\n SUM = "<<add(N);
}
```

OUTPUT

```
SUM = 30
```

Program 9.27 Write a program to compare two numbers of a class. Use `friend` function, pointer to data members, pointer to member function, and pointer to the object.

```
using namespace std;
#include<iostream>
class Numbers
{   private:
        int a;
        int b;
    public:
        void set_data()
        {   a=10, b=20;     }
        friend int compare(Numbers *);
};
int compare(Numbers *N)
{   int Numbers :: *ptr1 = &Numbers :: a;// accessing data number a
    int Numbers :: *ptr2 = &Numbers :: b;// accessing data number b
    if (N->*ptr1 > N->*ptr2)// comparing data members
        return 1;
    else if (N->*ptr1 < N->*ptr2)
        return -1;
    else return 0;
}
main()
{   Numbers *N = new Numbers;
    void (Numbers :: *ptr_set_data)(void) = &Numbers :: set_data;
    (N->*ptr_set_data)();//pointer to member functions
    int res = compare(N);
    if(res == 0)
        cout<<"\n EQUAL";
    else if(res == 1)
        cout<<"\n First Number is greater";
    else
        cout<<"\n Second Number is greater";
}
```

OUTPUT

```
Second Number is greater
```

Points to Remember

- The difference between a structure and a class is that, by default, members of a class are private, while by default members of a structure are public.
- When we define a class, we are actually creating a new user-defined data type which will be treated in the same way as other built in data types are treated.
- Memory is allocated only when we create object(s) of the class.
- `class_name :: function_name` tell the compiler that the scope of the function is restricted within the `class_name`.
- Member functions can be either defined inside or outside the class.
- When a class is specified, the memory for class's member functions is allocated. When one or more objects are created, separate chunks of memory for storing data members are allocated to each object.
- Static data members are usually used to maintain values that are common for the entire class. For example, to keep a track of how many objects of a particular class has been created.
- Static member functions are not invoked in conjunction with objects. They are called using the class name and the scope resolution operator.
- Since both techniques—pass by reference and pass by address—send the address of the actual object to the called function, any changes made in the object are reflected to actual object.
- Constant member functions are used when a particular member function should strictly not attempt to change the value of any of the class's data member.
- Friend functions are frequently used to perform operations that are conducted on two different classes and thus require access to private or protected members of both.
- Bit field allows users to reserve the exact amount of bits required for storage of values.

Glossary

Class An entity in object-oriented programming that stores data and functions together

Class instantiation The process of creating objects of the class

Empty class A class with no data members and no member functions

Friend class A class which can access the private and/ or protected members of another class

Friend function A non-member function of the class that can access its private and protected members

Local class Class which is defined inside a function

Nested class Class inside another class

Object Variable of a class

Private members Members that can be accessed from within the class in which they are declared

Public members Members that can be accessed from outside the class

`this` **keyword** Represents the object that invoked the member function of the class

Exercises

Fill in the Blanks

1. A class provides _______.
2. Class ______ specifies the type and scope of its members.
3. Data hiding is implemented through the ______ visibility label.
4. A function defined inside the class is treated as an ______ function.
5. Variables of a class are called ______.
6. Member functions can be accessed with ______ and ______.
7. An object is an _____ of a class.
8. Memory for member functions is allocated when ________.
9. Static data members are automatically initialized to ____.
10. In ______ technique, a copy of the actual object is created and passed to the called function.

11. Local classes can use any global variable but with ________.
12. While declaring an object of inner class, name of the inner class must be preceded with ______.
13. ______ function and ______ classes breaks the rules of data hiding in C++.
14. Keyword `friend` is used in function ________ but not in function ________.
15. Friendships are ________.
16. ______ allows users to reserve the exact amount of bits required for storage of values.
17. ______ operator cannot be applied to bit-field components.
18. The default integer type for a bit field is ______.
19. Keywords `private` and `public` are called ______ specifiers.

State True or False

1. By default, members of a structure are private.
2. Members of the structure can be accessed from the `main()` using the dot operator.
3. All members declared public can be accessed only from within the class.
4. We can have a class with all private members.
5. We cannot have private member functions.
6. Memory is allocated only when we declare the class.
7. All member functions defined outside the class are inline.
8. All objects of the class share its member functions.
9. Only one copy of the static member is created in memory.
10. Static data members are a part of the object.
11. Static and non-static member functions in the same class with same names and same number and types of arguments is possible.
12. `this` pointer is passed explicitly to the member function.
13. `this` pointer is not a part of the object itself.
14. Local classes can have static data members.
15. Member functions of a local class can be defined inside or outside the class.
16. Friend functions are external functions with special access privileges.
17. Friend functions can access `this` pointer.
18. Friendship is implicitly specified.
19. You can have arrays of bit fields.
20. Unnamed bit fields can be referenced.
21. A programmer can change the value of `this` pointer.

Multiple Choice Questions

1. Which of the following is the lifetime of a static variable?
   (a) Function (b) Class
   (c) Entire program (d) All files
2. An object with no data members is allocated ____ bytes of memory.
   (a) 0 (b) 1
   (c) 2 (d) 4
3. In which method, address of object is implicitly passed to the called function?
   (a) Pass-by-value
   (b) Pass-by-reference
   (c) Pass-by-address
   (d) Both (b) and (c)
4. `const` should be suffixed in function header at which places?
   (a) Function declaration
   (b) Function definition
   (c) Both of these
   (d) None of these
5. A local class is defined inside a ____.
   (a) Class (b) Function
   (c) Program (d) File
6. Friend functions are called using the following operator.
   (a) . (b) ->
   (c) ,* (d) None of these
7. With which function can a friend function be declared?
   (a) Public (b) Private
   (c) Protected (d) Any of these
8. A class can be a friend to ____ number of classes.
   (a) N (b) n-1
   (c) 2 (d) 1
9. You should not use bit fields of size greater than how many bits?
   (a) 64 (b) 32
   (c) 16 (d) 8
10. Which operator is called member dereferencing operator?
    (a) . (b) ->
    (c) ,* (d) None of these
11. To have a pointer to class member you must declare it in which section?

(a) Public (b) Private
(c) Protected (d) Any of these

12. Which members of a class can friend functions access?
(a) Public (b) Private
(c) Protected (d) Any of these
13. Which members can the object of a class access?
(a) Public (b) Private
(c) Protected (d) Any of these
14. Which concept of object-oriented programming does a class support?
(a) Data encapsulation (b) Data hiding
(c) Data abstraction (d) All of these
15. Where should you initialize a static data member?
(a) In main()
(b) Inside class
(c) In member function
(d) After class definition
16. A static member function can access only ____.
(a) Private data members
(b) Public data members
(c) Static data members
(d) Other static member functions
17. In declaration `class Test{ int x; };`, `x` is which type of member?
(a) Public (b) Private
(c) Protected (d) Any of these

Review Questions

1. What is a class? Explain its significance in OOP.
2. Differentiate between a structure and a class in C++.
3. What do you understand by visibility labels?
4. Explain the significance of the scope resolution operator
5. What is class instantiation?
6. What are nested member functions? Explain with the help of an example.
7. Illustrate with an example how a function defined outside the class can be made inline.
8. When memory is allocated for class data members and member functions?
9. What are static data members? Why are they needed?
10. Write a short note on static member functions.
11. What are static objects? Write a short code to explain their concept.
12. Explain the concept of dynamic memory allocation for array of objects with an example.
13. Explain the techniques by which an object can be passed as an argument to a function.
14. Why is call by address and call by reference preferred over call by value technique of passing object as argument to the function?
15. How can we return an object from a function?
16. Write a short note on `this` pointer.
17. Why should we not use `this` pointer with static members of the class?
18. Which functions should be declared as constant member functions?
19. When do we pass constant objects as parameters?
20. What is a nested class? Explain its features with help of an example.
21. Define empty class.
22. What is a local class? Give a program that uses a local class.
23. What are friend functions? Are they a threat to data hiding? How do they help in data encapsulation?
24. What is a friend class?
25. Illustrate the significance of bit fields with an example.
26. List the rules for defining static members in a class
27. Does C++ allow users to have two functions with same name—while one function is a class member and another an external function? Justify your answer.
28. Is there any way to access class private members without its object? Justify your answer.

Programming Exercises

1. Make a class `triangle`. Enter its three sides and calculate its area.
2. Write a program that has a class triangle with an overloaded function `Area()`. If two sides are entered, then calculate area as ½ `* side1 * side2`. However, if three sides are given, then calculate the area using Heron's formula.
3. Write a program `Employee` with members `name, emp_no, deptt, and salary`. Demonstrate the use of inline functions and overloaded functions.
4. Write a program to enter the `code` and `price` of items. The user must feed the quantity in which he wants a product. The program must calculate and display the final bill.
5. Write a menu driven program to `read, display, simplify, add, and subtract` two rational numbers.

6. Write a menu driven program to read, display, add, and subtract two complex numbers.
7. Write a menu driven program to read, display, add, and subtract two distances.
8. Write a menu driven program to read, display, add, and subtract two time objects.
9. Write a menu driven program to read, display, add, and subtract two height objects.
10. Write a program to read two points and calculate the distance between them.
11. Write a class that has an array of integers as data members and `read()`, `display()`, `find_largest()`, `find_smallest()`, `sum()`, and `find_mean()` as its member functions
12. Write a program that demonstrates the use of static data member, static member function, and array of objects.
13. Make a class book with members `title, author, publisher, and ISBN number`. Memory for all these members should be allocated dynamically. The functions of the class should read and display the data.
14. Write a program that uses a structure within a class.
15. Write a program that uses union within a class.
16. Write a program that uses bit-fields within a class.
17. Write a program that uses a class within a class.
18. Write a program that uses a friend function to swap members of a class.
19. Write a program to find the mean of two numbers belonging to two different classes using `friend` function.
20. Write a program to change the course of a student using `friend class`.
21. Write a program to calculate area of a rectangle. Convert this rectangle into a square using a `friend class`.
22. Write a program that exchanges two integer members of a class. Use friend function, pointer to data member, and pointer to member function.
23. Write a program to add two numbers of a class. Use `friend` function, pointer to data members, pointer to member function, and pointer to the object.
24. Write a program that has a class student with data members—`roll_no and marks` in three subjects. Allocate memory for students dynamically. There must be a member function to edit the details of students.
25. Add another member function in the previous program that displays marks of a particular student only when asked for.
26. Write a program to dynamically allocate two arrays and add them in a third array.
27. Write a program that has a class account with data members as `name of holder, account_no, acc_type`, and balance. Design functions for the class to assign initial values, deposit amount, withdraw amount, and display the information.
28. Write a program that has a class `Temperature` with two data members—`centigrade` and `Fahrenheit`. Use overloaded functions to `set_data` in such a way that if `Fahrenheit` is 0, convert Celsius into Fahrenheit and vice versa.
29. Write a program that reads records of n students and sorts them in descending order of their marks.
30. Write a program that uses `friend` function to add two matrices.
31. Write a program with private data members and one public member function. Data should be read in using a private member function.
32. Write a program that concatenates two strings defined as private members in a class using friend function. The strings to be concatenated must belong to objects `S1` and `S2` of class string.
33. Write a menu-driven program to add, subtract, multiply, divide, and check for equality of two fractions.
34. Write a program to add two polynomials.

Find the errors in the following codes

1.
```
using namespace std;
#include<iostream>
class Numbers
{   private:
        int a;
        int b;
    public:
        void set_data(int x, int y)
        {   a = x, b = y;  }
};
main()
{   set_data(10, 20);
}
```

2.
```
using namespace std;
#include<iostream>
class Numbers
{   private:
        int a;
        int b;
    public:
        void set_data(int x, int y)
        {   a = x, b = y;  }
```

```
    };
    main()
    {   Numbers n;
        n.set_data(10, 20, 30);
    }
3.  using namespace std;
    #include<iostream>
    class Numbers
    {   private:
            int a;
            int b;
        public:
            void set_data(int x, int y)
            {   a = x, b = y;  }
    };
    main()
    {   Numbers *n;
        n.set_data(10, 20);
    }
4.  using namespace std;
    #include<iostream>
    class Numbers
    {   private:
            int a;
            int b;
        public:
            void set_data(int x, int y)
            {   a = x, b = y;  }
    };
    main()
    {   Numbers n;
        n.a = 10, n.b=20;
    }
5.  using namespace std;
    #include<iostream>
    class Test
    {   private:
            static int count;
        public:
            static void show_data()
            {   cout<count++;  }
    };
    int Test :: count = 1;
    main()
    {   Test t;
        t.show_data();
    }
6.  using namespace std;
    #include<iostream>
    class Numbers;
    void Display()
    {   int a, b;
        class Numbers
        {   int a, b;
            public:
            void set_data(int x, int y)
            {   a = x, b = y;  }
            void show_data()
            {   cout<<"a  =  "<<(float) a <<"  b =
            "<<(float)b;    }
        };
        Numbers n1;
        n1.set_data(20, 30);
        n1.show_data();
    }
    main()
    {   Display();
        Numbers n2;
    }
7.  using namespace std;
    #include<iostream>
    class Sample
    {   public
            void set_data(char c)
            {ch = c;    }
            void show_data()
            {   cout<<a<<" "<<ch; }
        private:
            int a = 10;
            char ch;
    };
    main()
    {   Sample s;
        s.set_data('A');
        s.show_data();
    }
8.  using namespace std;
    #include<iostream>
    class Sample
    {   public:
            void set_data(char c);
            void show_data();
        private:
            int a = 10;
            char ch;
    };
    void set_data(char c)
    {ch = c;    }
    void show_data()
    {   cout<<a<<" "<<ch; }
    main()
    {   Sample s;
        s.set_data('A');
        s.show_data();
    }
```

Find the output of the following codes

```
1.  using namespace std;
    #include<iostream>
    class Test
    {   private:
            static int count;
```

```
    public:
        static void show_data()
        {   cout<count++; }
};
main()
{   Test t;
    t.show_data();
}
```

2.
```
using namespace std;
#include<iostream>
void Display()
{   int a, b;
    class Numbers
    {   int a, b;
        public:
        void set_data(int x, int y)
        {   a = x, b = y; }
        void show_data()
        {   cout<<"a = "<<(float) a <<" b =
        "<<(float)b;    }
    };
    Numbers n1;
    n1.set_data(20, 30);
    n1.show_data();
}
main()
{   Display();
    Numbers n2;
}
```

3.
```
using namespace std;
#include<iostream>
class Sample
{   int a = 10;
    char ch;
void set_data(char c)
    {ch = c;   }
    void show_data()
    {   cout<<a<<" "<<ch; }
};
main()
{   Sample s;
    s.set_data('A');
    s.show_data();
}
```

4.
```
using namespace std;
#include<iostream>
class Sample
{   public:
        void set_data(char c);
        void show_data();
    private:
        int a = 10;
        char ch;
};
void set_data(char c)
{ch = c;   }
void show_data()
{   cout<<a<<" "<<ch; }
main()
{   Sample s;
    s.set_data('A');
    s.show_data();
}
```

Answers

Fill in the Blanks

1. Data encapsulation and abstraction; **2.** Declaration; **3.** Private; **4.** Inline; **5.** Objects; **6.** Object and dot operator; **7.** Instance; **8.** Class is declared; **9.** 0; **10.** Pass-by-value; **11.** Scope resolution operator; **12.** Name of outer class; **13.** Friend, friend; **14.** Declaration, definition; **15.** Non-transitive; **16.** Bit fields; **17.** Address; **18.** Unsigned; **19.** Access;

True or False

1. False	**2.** True	**3.** False	**4.** True	**5.** False	**6.** False	**7.** False	**8.** True
9. True	**10.** False	**11.** False	**12.** False	**13.** True	**14.** False	**15.** False	**16.** True
17. False	**18.** False	**19.** False	**20.** False	**21.** False			

Multiple Choice Questions

1. (c); **2.** (c); **3.** (b); **4.** (c); **5.** (b); **6.** (d); **7.** (d); **8.** (a); **9.** (b); **10.** (c); **11.** (a); **12.** (d); **13.** (a); **14.** (d); **15.** (d); **16.** (c); **17.** (b)

CHAPTER 10

Constructors and Destructors

KEY Concepts

Different types of constructors • Constructor overloading • Destructors • Constant objects • Anonymous objects • Object copy • Anonymous classes

INTRODUCTION

In Chapter 9 on Classes and Objects, we have learnt that to initialize the private members of a class, we used a function known an `set_data()`. The values for private members were passed as arguments to the function as shown in the code given here.

Example 10.1 Initializing private members of class

```
using namespace std;
#include<iostream>
class Sample
{   private:
        int x;
    public:
        void set_data(int i)
        {    x = i;   }
        void show_data()
        {   cout<<"\n x = "<<x;   }
};
main()
{   Sample s;
    s.set_data(10);
    s.show_data();
}
```

OUTPUT

```
x=10
```

Explanation: In the program, observe carefully that we are first creating an object of the class. We are explicitly calling a class member function to initialize its data members. Though there is no problem in this code, a basic concept of object-oriented is not followed here. We know that C++ treats all its user-defined data types at par with its built-in data types. Therefore, when we write, `int x = 10;` to initialize an integer variable at the time of its declaration, then it is normal to question as to why cannot write a code that initializes the object's data members while it is being created or declared.

Therefore, to resolve this dissimilar behaviour, C++ provides a member function called the constructor which enables an object to initialize itself when it is created. Like constructor, there is another member function called the destructor which de-initializes an object. We will read more about this function in the following sections.

10.1 CONSTRUCTOR

A constructor is a special member function of a class which is automatically invoked at the time of creation of an object to initialize or construct the values of data members of the object. However, some special points to note about a constructor function are as follows.

- The name of the constructor is the same as that of the class to which it belongs.
- A constructor must be declared in the public section.
- It should not be explicitly called because a constructor is automatically invoked when an object of a class is created.
- A constructor can never return any value; therefore, unlike a normal function, a constructor does not have any return value (not even `void`).
- A constructor cannot be inherited and virtual. We will read about this aspect in Chapter 12 on Inheritance.
- The address of a constructor cannot be referred to in programs. Therefore, pointers and references do not work with constructors.
- A constructor cannot be declared as static, volatile, or `const`.
- Like a normal function, a constructor function can also be overloaded.
- Like a normal function, a constructor function can also have default arguments.

Note The C++ run time mechanism ensures that constructor is the first member function to be executed when an object of that class is created.

Like a normal class member function, a constructor can be either defined inside the class or outside the class. The syntax for declaring and defining a constructor inside the class can be given as shown in Fig. 10.1(a). Similarly, the syntax for declaring and defining a constructor outside the class can be given as shown in Fig. 10.1(b).

```
class  class_name
{      private:
            ......
       public:
            class_name()
            {
              ........
            }
 .....
};
```

(a)

```
class class_name
{       private:
            ......
        public:
          class_name(); // constructor declared
 ......
};
class_name :: class_name() // constructor defined
{
 ........
}
```

(b)

Figure 10.1 (a) Declaring and defining a constructor within a class, (b) Defining a constructor outside the class

10.2 TYPES OF CONSTRUCTORS

A constructor function can be classified as follows:

- Dummy constructor
- Default constructor
- Parameterized constructor
- Copy constructor
- Dynamic constructor

Figure 10.2 gives the classification of constructors.

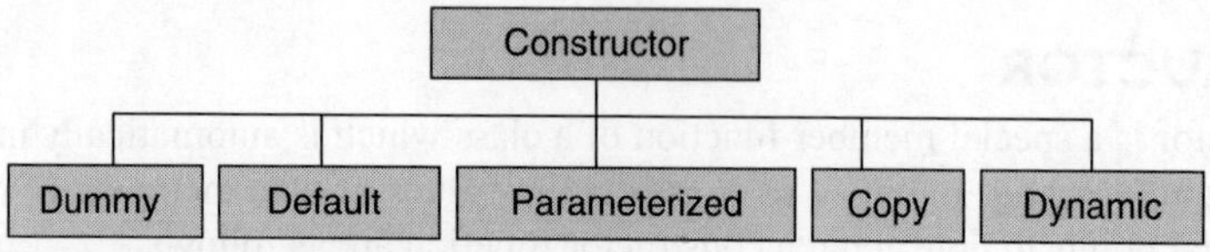

Figure 10.2 Types of constructors

10.2.1 Dummy Constructor (Do Nothing Constructor)

In Chapter 9, we had been writing programs without any constructor. In such cases, the C++ run time mechanism calls a dummy constructor which does not perform any action. Here, action means does not initialize any data member and thus, the variables acquire a garbage (irrelevant) value. Consider the program given here that makes use of a dummy constructor.

Example 10.2 Dummy constructor

```
using namespace std;
#include<iostream>
class Numbers
{  private:
       int x;
   public:
       void show_data()
       {  cout<<"\n x = "<<x;   }
};
main()
{  Numbers N; // Dummy constructor is called
   N.show_data();
}

OUTPUT
x = 3983 (garbage value)
```

10.2.2 Default Constructor

A constructor that does not take any argument is called a default constructor. The default constructor simply allocates storage for the data members of the object. It may even initialize the values of those data members. Let us rewrite the same program given earlier but with a default constructor.

Example 10.3 Default constructor

```
using namespace std;
#include<iostream>
class Numbers
{  private:
```

```
        int x;
    public:
        Numbers()       // Default Constructor
        {  x = 0;   }
        void show_data()
        {   cout<<"\n x = "<<x;    }
};
main()
{   Numbers N;     // Default constructor is called
    N.show_data();
}
```

OUTPUT

```
x = 0
```

10.2.3 Parameterized Constructor

A constructor that accepts one or more parameters is called a parameterized constructor. The program code given here uses a parameterized constructor to initialize the data member of the class.

Example 10.4 Initialize data member of the class through parameterized constructor

```
using namespace std;
#include<iostream>
class Numbers
{   private:
        int x;
    public:
        Numbers(int i)     // Parameterized Constructor
        {  x = i;   }      // equivalent to writing this->x = i;
        void show_data()
        {   cout<<"\n x = "<<x;    }
};
main()
{   Numbers N(10);         // Parameterized constructor is called
    N.show_data();
}
```

OUTPUT

```
x = 10
```

10.2.4 Copy Constructor

A copy constructor takes an object of the class as an argument and copies data values of members of one object into the values of members of another object. Since it takes only one argument, it is also known as a one argument constructor. The primary use of a copy constructor is to create a new object from an existing one by initialization. For this, the copy constructor takes a reference to an object of the same class as an argument.

Example 10.5 Copy constructor

```
using namespace std;
#include<iostream>
```

```
class Numbers
{   private:
        int x;
    public:
        Numbers(Numbers & N)        // Copy Constructor
        {   x = N.x;   }
        Numbers(int i)
        {   x = i;   }
        void show_data()
        {   cout<<"\n x = "<<x;   }
};
main()
{   Numbers N1(20);         // Parameterized Constructor called
    Numbers N2(N1);         // Copy constructor is called
    N2.show_data();
    Numbers N3 = N1;        // Copy constructor called
    N3.show_data();
}
```

OUTPUT

```
x = 20
x = 20
```

Explanation: In the program, the first object `N1` invokes the parameterized constructor to initialize its data members. The objects `N2` and `N3` invoke the copy constructor. There are two ways of invoking the copy constructor. The first is invoked by writing `Numbers N2(N1);` and the second way is writing `Numbers N3 = N1;`. Both the statements perform the same task of initializing the data member of `N2` and `N3` with the value of data member of `N1`.

Besides these explicit calls to the copy constructor, the copy constructor is implicitly called when a function accepts an object as an argument using the call-by-value technique or returns an object by value. In both the cases, a copy of the object is made and passed to the destination function.

Note A copy constructor is called for at the time of invocation. If an assignment is made after the object has been created, then the assignment operator, and not the copy constructor, would work. In the program, if we write

```
Numbers N1(20), N2;
N1 = N2; // here the assignment operator would work.
```

Why Do Copy Constructors Take Objects by Reference and Not by Value?

Copy constructors take objects by reference and not by value. As mentioned earlier, when an object is passed by value, the copy constructor is implicitly called to create a copy of the original argument. If the copy constructor had been designed to accept the object by value, then it would have resulted in an infinite recursion; the copy constructor would have called another copy constructor, which in turn, would have called another copy constructor, and so on, thereby consuming more time and space. To avoid such a situation, C++ mandates the copy constructor's parameter to be passed by reference.

Note The parameter to the copy constructor can be declared as `const` if you want the original object's data members values should not be altered.

10.2.5 Dynamic Constructor

Dynamic constructors, as the name suggests, are those constructors in which memory for data members is allocated dynamically. Dynamic constructor enables the program to allocate the right amount of memory to data members of the object during execution. This is even more beneficial when the size of data members is not the same each time the program is executed. The memory allocated to the data members is released when the object is no longer required and when the object goes out of scope.

Example 10.6 Dynamic constructor

```
using namespace std;
#include<iostream>
class Array
{   private:
        int *arr;
        int n;
    public:
        Array()
        {   n = 0;      }
        Array(int);
        void show_data();
};
Array :: Array(int num)
{   n = num;
    arr = new int [n];   // memory allocated for array dynamically
    cout<<"\n Enter the elements : ";
    for(int i=0;i<n;i++)
        cin>>arr[i];
}
void Array :: show_data()
{   for(int i=0;i<n;i++)
        cout<<" "<<arr[i];
}
main()
{   int size;
    cout<<"\n Enter the size of the array : ";
    cin>>size;
    Array Arr(size);   //calls constructor and allocates memory
    Arr.show_data();
}
```

OUTPUT

```
Enter the size of the array : 5
Enter the elements : 1 2 3 4 5
1 2 3 4 5
```

10.3 CONSTRUCTOR WITH DEFAULT ARGUMENTS

Like other functions, constructors can also have default arguments. When an object of a class is created, the C++ compiler calls the suitable constructor for initializing that object. Consider the program given here which makes use of a constructor with default arguments.

Example 10.7 Constructor with default arguments

> **Programming Tip:** A compiler error will be generated if you try to return any value from a constructor or a destructor. You can call a constructor from a destructor.

```
using namespace std;
#include<iostream>
class Student
{private:
        int roll_no;
        int marks;
  public:
        Student()
        {   roll_no = 0;
            marks = 0;
        }
        Student(int r, int m = 0)
        {   roll_no = r;
            marks = m;
        }
        void show_data()
        {   cout<<"\n ROLL NO. = "<<roll_no;
            cout<<"\t MARKS = "<<marks;
        }
};
main()
{   Student S1;         // default constructor called
    S1.show_data();
    Student S2(3);
    S2.show_data();
    Student S3(05, 98);
    S3.show_data();
}
```

OUTPUT

```
ROLL NO. = 0    MARKS = 0
ROLL NO. = 3    MARKS = 0
ROLL NO. = 5    MARKS = 98
```

Explanation: In the program, when the first object is created without any arguments, the default constructor would be called and data members will be initialized with zero. While creating the second object, one parameter is explicitly passed and the second argument is missing. Therefore, the default value will be used to initialize the missing data member. However, during the third object, both parameters are explicitly passed. Therefore, the default value will be overridden and the parameter's value will be used to initialize the data member.

Note The missing argument(s) must always be the trailing ones.

Now consider the same code again with a slight modification.

```
using namespace std;
#include<iostream>
class Student
{   private:
        int roll_no;
        int marks;
```

Programming Tip: C++ allows users to place default arguments in the definition of a constructor rather than in the declaration.

```
        public:
            Student()           //constructor 1
            {   roll_no = 0;
                marks = 0;
            }
            Student(int r = 0, int m = 0)    // constructor 2
            {   roll_no = r;
                marks = m;
            }
            void show_data()
            {   cout<<"\n ROLL NO. = "<<roll_no;
        cout<<"\t MARKS = "<<marks;
    }
};
main()
{   Student S1;    // which constructor to call? ERROR
    S1.show_data();
    Student S2(03);
    S2.show_data();
    Student S3(05, 98);
    S3.show_data();
}
```

Explanation: If you compile this program, you will get an error. In the program, there are two constructors: one is the default constructor and the second is with both default arguments. When this program is compiled, the compiler gets confused which one of the two constructors to call as both of them satisfy the condition to be called during creation of object `S1`. Hence, an error will be shown. The moment you remove any one of the constructor the program will compile successfully.

Note A constructor that has all default arguments is similar to a default (no – argument) constructor.

10.4 CONSTRUCTOR OVERLOADING

Programming Tip: You can call a constructor from main() since a constructor is like a member function declared in the public section.

Like normal functions, constructors can also be overloaded. When a class has multiple constructors, they are called overloaded constructors. Some important features of over loaded constructors are as follows:

- They have the same name; the names of all the constructors is the name of the class.
- Overloaded constructors differ in their signature with respect to the number and sequence of arguments passed.

When an object of the class is created, the specific constructor is called. Consider the program code given here which uses the concept of overloaded constructors.

Example 10.8 Multiple constructors in a program

```
using namespace std;
#include<iostream>
#include<string.h>
class Person
{   private:
        int age;
        char first_name[10];
```

```
        char middle_name[10];
        char last_name[10];
    public:
        Person()              //Constructor 1 - default constructor
        {   age = -1;
            strcpy(first_name, "\0");
            strcpy(middle_name, "\0");
            strcpy(last_name, "\0");
        }
        Person(int a)      //Constructor 2 - constructor with one argument
        {   age = a;
            strcpy(first_name, "\0");
            strcpy(middle_name, "\0");
            strcpy(last_name, "\0");
        }
        Person(int a, char *fn)      //Constructor 3 - constructor with two arguments
        {   age = a;
            strcpy(first_name, fn);
            strcpy(middle_name, "\0");
            strcpy(last_name, "\0");
        }
        Person(int a, char *fn, char mn[])
//Constructor 4 - constructor with three arguments
        {   age = a;
            strcpy(first_name, fn);
            strcpy(middle_name, mn);
            strcpy(last_name, "\0");
        }
        Person(int a, char *fn, char mn[], char * ln)
// Constructor 5 - constructor with four arguments
        {   age = a;
            strcpy(first_name, fn);
            strcpy(middle_name, mn);
            strcpy(last_name, ln);
        }
        void show_data()
        {   cout<<"\n NAME : "<<first_name<<" "<<middle_name<<" "<<last_name;
            cout<<"\t\t AGE : "<<age;
        }
};
main()
{
    Person P1;                                   //Constructor 1 called
    P1.show_data();
    Person P2(18);                               //Constructor 2 called
    P2.show_data();
    Person P3(21,"Goransh");                     //Constructor 3 called
    P3.show_data();
    Person P4(25,"Aditi","Raj");                 //Constructor 4 called
    P4.show_data();
    Person P5(32,"Pallav", "Raj", "Thareja");    //Constructor 5 called
    P5.show_data();
}
```

OUTPUT

```
NAME :          AGE = -1
NAME :          AGE = 18
NAME :Goransh       AGE = 21
NAME :Aditi Raj       AGE = 25
NAME :Pallav Raj Thareja       AGE = 32
```

Note When an array of objects is created, the constructor is called for each object. Therefore, if we say class student s[5], then the constructor will be called five times not once.

Program 10.1 Write a program that uses an overloaded constructor to dynamically allocate memory to an array and thus find the largest of its elements.

```
using namespace std;
#include<iostream>
class Array
{   private:
        int *arr;
        int n;
    public:
        Array()
        {   n = 0;      }
        Array(int);
        void show_data();
        int largest();
};
Array :: Array(int num)
{   n = num;
    arr = new int [n];
    cout<<"\n Enter the elements : ";
    for(int i=0;i<n;i++)
        cin>>arr[i];
}
void Array :: show_data()
{   for(int i=0;i<n;i++)
        cout<<" "<<arr[i];
}
int Array :: largest()
{   int largest = arr[0];
        for(int i=1;i<=n;i++)
        {   if(arr[i]>largest)
            largest = arr[i];
        }
        return largest;
}
main()
{   int size;
    cout<<"\n Enter the size of the array : ";
    cin>>size;
    Array Arr(size);
    Arr.show_data();
    cout<<"\n Largest = "<<Arr.largest();
}
```

Programming Tip: You can call a constructor from a destructor and vice versa.

OUTPUT
```
Enter the size of the array : 5
Enter the elements : 1 0 3 6 4
1 0 3 6 4
Largest = 6
```

Program 10.2 Write a program that uses dynamic constructor to allocate memory to an array. Count the number of even and odd elements.

```
using namespace std;
#include<iostream>
class Array
{   private:
        int *arr;
        int n;
        int num_even;
        int num_odd;
    public:
        Array(int);
        void show_data();
};
Array :: Array(int num)
{   n = num;
    num_even = 0;
    num_odd = 0;
    arr = new int[n];
    cout<<"\n ENter the elements : ";
    for(int i=0;i<n;i++)
        cin>>arr[i];
}
void Array :: show_data()
{   int i;
    cout<<"\n Array is ";
    for(i=0;i<n;i++)
        cout<<" "<<arr[i];
    for(i=0;i<n;i++)
    {   if(arr[i]%2 == 0)
            num_even++;
        else
            num_odd++;
    }
    cout<<"\n Number of evens = "<<num_even;
    cout<<"\n Number of odds = "<<num_odd;
}
main()
{   int size;
    cout<<"\n Enter the size of the array : ";
    cin>>size;
    Array Arr(size);
    Arr.show_data();
}
```

OUTPUT
```
Enter the size of the array : 7
ENter the elements : 1 2 3 4 5 6 7
```

```
Array is 1 2 3 4 5 6 7
Number of evens = 3
Number of odds = 4
```

Program 10.3 Write a program that uses overloaded constructors and dynamically allocates memory to a string. Demonstrate the use of copy constructor.

```
using namespace std;
#include<iostream>
#include<string.h>
class String
{   private:
        int length;
        char *str;
    public:
        String()
        {   length = 0;   }
        String(char *s)
        {   length = strlen(s);
            str = new char[length + 1];
            strcpy(str, s);
        }
        String(String &s)
        {   length = s.length;
            str = new char[length + 1];
            strcpy(str, s.str);
        }
        void show_str()
        {   cout.write(str, length); }
};
main()
{   String s1("Welcome to the world of programming");
    String s2 = s1;
    cout<<"\n String (s2) = ";
    s2.show_str();
}
```

OUTPUT

```
String (s2) = Welcome to the world of programming
```

Program 10.4 Write a class that stores a string and all its status details such as number of upper case characters, vowels, and so on.

```
using namespace std;
#include<iostream>
#include<string.h>
class String
{   private:
        int length;
        int num_vowels;
        int num_uppers;
        int num_words;
        int num_characters;
        char *str;
    public:
```

```
        String()
        {   length = 0;
            num_vowels = 0;
            num_uppers = 0;
            num_words = 1;
            num_characters = 0;
        }
        String(char *s)
        {   length = strlen(s);
            num_vowels = 0;
            num_uppers = 0;
            num_words = 1;
            num_characters = 0;
            str = new char [length + 1];
            strcpy(str, s);
        }
        void show_str()
        {   cout.write(str, length);   }
        void show_details();
};
void String :: show_details()
{   int i = 0;
    while(str[i] != '\0')
    {   switch(str[i])
        {   case 'A':
            case 'a':
            case 'E':
            case 'e':
            case 'I':
            case 'i':
            case 'O':
            case 'o':
            case 'U':
            case 'u':  num_vowels ++;
                       break;
        }
        if(str[i]>='A' && str[i]<='Z')
            num_uppers++;
        if(str[i] == ' ' && str[i+1] != ' ')
            num_words++;
        num_characters++;
        i++;
    }
    cout<<"\n Number of vowels = "<<num_vowels;
    cout<<"\n Number of upper case characters = "<<num_uppers;
    cout<<"\n Number of characters = "<<num_characters;
    cout<<"\n Number of words = "<<num_words;
}
main()
{   String s1("Welcome To The World Of Programming");
    s1.show_str();
    s1.show_details();
}
```

OUTPUT

```
Welcome To The World Of Programming
Number of vowels = 10
Number of upper case characters = 6
Number of characters = 35
Number of words = 6
```

Program 10.5 Write a program to add two polynomials.

```
using namespace std;
#include<iostream>
class Polynomial
{   private:
        int coeff[10];
        int exponent[10];
        int num_terms;
    public:
        Polynomial();
        void get_data();
        Polynomial & add(Polynomial &, Polynomial &);
        void show_data();
};
Polynomial :: Polynomial()
{   num_terms = 0;
    for(int i=0;i<10;i++)
        coeff[i] = exponent[i] = 0;
}
void Polynomial :: get_data()
{   cout<<"\n Enter the terms";
    int i;
    for(i=0;;i++)
    {   cin>>coeff[i]>>exponent[i];
        if(coeff[i] == 0)
            break;
    }
    num_terms = i;
}
void Polynomial :: show_data()
{   int i;
    for(i=0;i<num_terms;i++)
    {   cout<<coeff[i]<<"x"<<exponent[i];
        if(i<num_terms-1)
            cout<<" + ";
    }
}
Polynomial & Polynomial :: add(Polynomial &P1, Polynomial &P2)
{   int i=0, j=0, k = 0;
    while(i != P1.num_terms || P2.num_terms != j)
    {   if(P1.exponent[i] == P2.exponent[j])
        {   coeff[k] = P1.coeff[i] + P2.coeff[j];
            exponent[k] = P1.exponent[i];
            i++, j++, k++;
        }
        else if(P1.exponent[i] > P2.exponent[j])
        {   coeff[k] = P1.coeff[i];
```

```
            exponent[k] = P1.exponent[i];
            k++, i++;
        }
        else
        {   coeff[k] = P2.coeff[j];
            exponent[k] = P2.exponent[j];
            k++, j++;
        }
    }
    num_terms = k;
}
main()
{   Polynomial P1;
    P1.get_data();
    cout<<"\n The first polynomial is : ";
    P1.show_data();
    Polynomial P2;
    P2.get_data();
    cout<<"\n The second polynomial is : ";
    P2.show_data();
    Polynomial P3;
    cout<<"\n The resultant polynomial is : ";
    P3.add(P1, P2);
    P3.show_data();
}
```

OUTPUT

```
Enter the terms : 1 5 2 4 3 3 4 2 5 1 0 0
The first polynomial is : 1x5 + 2x4 + 3x3 + 4x2 + 5x1
Enter the terms : 2 5 5 3 4 1 0 0
The second polynomial is : 2x5 + 5x3 + 4x1
The resultant polynomial is : 3x5 + 2x4 + 8x3 + 4x2 + 9x1
```

Program 10.6 Write a program that uses a date structure within a class. Enter the manufacturing date and expiry date of the product. The program must display the years, months, and days that are left for expiry.

```
using namespace std;
#include<iostream>
typedef struct Date
{   int dd;
    int mm;
    int yy;
};
class Product
{   private:
        Date mfg_date;
        Date exp_date;
    public:
        Product()
        {   mfg_date.dd = 0, mfg_date.mm = 0, mfg_date.yy = 0;
            exp_date.dd = 0, exp_date.mm = 0, exp_date.yy = 0;
        }
        Product(Date &D1, Date &D2)
        {   mfg_date = D1;
```

```
            exp_date = D2;
        }
        void chk_expiry();
};
void Product :: chk_expiry()
{   int days = exp_date.dd - mfg_date.dd;
    if(days<0)
    {   days += 30;
        exp_date.mm -= 1;
    }
    int months = exp_date.mm - mfg_date.mm;
    if(months <0)
    {   months += 12;
        exp_date.yy -= 1;
    }
    int years = exp_date.yy - mfg_date.yy;
    if(years>=0)
        cout<<"\n "<<years<<" Yrs "<<months<<" Months "<<days<<" Days
        left for expiry";
        cout<<"\n PRODUCT EXPIRED";
}
main()
{
    Date M_Date = {28, 6, 14};
    Date E_Date = {29, 9, 16};
    Product P(M_Date, E_Date);
    P.chk_expiry();
}
```

OUTPUT

```
2 Yrs 3 Months 1 Days left for expiry
```

Program 10.7 Write a program to deposit or withdraw money in a bank account.

```
using namespace std;
#include<iostream>
#include<string.h>
class Account
{   private:
        int acc_no;
        char name[20];
        float balance;
    public:
        void get_data()
        {   cout<<"\n Enter the account number : ";
            cin>>acc_no;
            cout<<"\n Enter the initial balance : ";
            cin>>balance;
            cout<<"\n Enter the name of the account holder : ";
            cin.ignore();
            cin.getline(name, 20);
        }
        void show_data()
        {   cout<<"\n Name : ";
            cout<<name;
```

```
            cout<<"\n Account Number : "<<acc_no;
            cout<<"\n Balance : "<<balance;
        }
        void withdraw()
        {   int amt;
                cout<<"\n Enter the amount to withdraw : ";
                cin>>amt;
        if((balance-amt)<500)
        cout<<"\n You must maintain minimum balance in the account so your
        transaction could not be completed";
    else
        balance -= amt;
    }
        void deposit()
        {   int amt;
            cout<<"\n Enter the amount to deposit : ";
            cin>>amt;
            balance += amt;
        }
};
main()
{   Account Acc;
    Acc.get_data();
    Acc.show_data();
    char choice;
    cout<<"\n Do you want to withdraw or deposit amount (W/D) : ";
    cin>>choice;
    if(choice == 'W')
        Acc.withdraw();
    else
        Acc.deposit();
    Acc.show_data();
}
```

OUTPUT

```
Enter the account number : 1101
Enter the initial balance : 10000
Enter the name of the account holder : Dev
Name : Dev
Account Number : 1101
Balance : 10000
Do you want to withdraw or deposit amount (W/D) :D
Enter the amount to deposit : 20000
Name : Dev
Account Number : 1101
Balance : 30000
```

Program 10.8 Write a program to display the cheapest book available on a subject.

```
using namespace std;
#include<iostream>
#include<string.h>
typedef class Book
{   private:
        char author[20];
```

```
        char title[30];
        int price;
    public:
        Book()
        {   strcpy(author,"\0");
            strcpy(title,"\0");
            price = 0;
        }
        Book(char *a, char *t, int p)
        {   strcpy(author,a);
            strcpy(title, t);
            price = p;
        }
        void show_data()
        {   cout<<"\n AUTHOR : "<<author;
            cout<<"\n TITLE : "<<title;
            cout<<"\n PRICE : "<<price;
        }
        friend void chk_cheapest(Book **B, int n);
};
void chk_cheapest(Book **B, int n)
{   int cheapest = B[0]->price;
    char cheapest_title[30];
    strcpy(cheapest_title,B[0]->title);
    for(int i=1;i<n;i++)
    {   if(B[i]->price<cheapest)
            strcpy(cheapest_title, B[i]->title);
    }
        cout<<"\n CHEAPEST TITLE = "<<cheapest_title;
}
main()
{   Book *b[10], B1;
    int n, p, i;
    char a[20], t[30];
    cout<<"\n How many books C++ books are there?";
    cin>>n;
    for(i=0;i<n;i++)
    {   cout<<"\n Enter the author's name : ";
        cin.ignore();
        cin.getline(a, 20);
        cout<<"\n Enter the title : ";
        cin.getline(t, 30);
        cout<<"\n Enter the price : ";
        cin>>p;
        b[i] = new Book(a, t, p);
    }
    for(i=0;i<n;i++)
        b[i]->show_data();
    chk_cheapest(b, n);
}
```

OUTPUT

```
How many books C++ books are there? 3
Enter the author's name : Balaguruswamy
```

```
Enter the title : OOP with C++
Enter the price : 350
Enter the author's name : Kanetkar
Enter the title : Let us C++
Enter the price : 295
Enter the author's name : Thareja
Enter the title : Programming in C++
Enter the price : 395
CHEAPEST TITLE = Let us C++
```

Program 10.9 Write a menu-driven program that keeps a record of books and journals available in the library.

```
using namespace std;
#include<iostream>
class Lib_Records
{   private:
        int num_books;
        int num_journals;
        int num_poor_cond_journals;
        int num_poor_cond_books;
        int num_reading_material;
    public:
        Lib_Records()
        {   num_books = num_journals = num_poor_cond_books = num_poor_cond_journals
        =  num_reading_material = 0;
        }
        void show_data()
        {   cout<<"\n Number of Books = "<<num_books;
            cout<<"\n Number of Journals = "<<num_journals;
            cout<<"\n Number of Books in Poor Condition = "<<num_poor_cond_books;
            cout<<"\n Number of Journals in Poor Condition = "<<num_poor_cond_journals;
            cout<<"\n Total Reading Material = "<<num_reading_material;
        }
        void add_book()
        {   num_books++; num_reading_material++;    }
        void add_journal()
        {   num_journals++;    num_reading_material++;    }
        void show_books()
        {   cout<<"\n There are "<<num_books<<" books in the Library";    }
        void show_journals()
        {   cout<<"\n There are "<<num_journals<<" journals in the Library"; }
        void set_poor_cond()
        {   char ch;
            cout<<"\n Which reading material is in poor condition - B/J ? ";
            cin>>ch;
            if(ch=='B')
            {   num_books--;
                num_poor_cond_books++;
            }
            else
            {
                num_journals--;
                num_poor_cond_journals++;
```

```
            }
            num_reading_material--;
        }
};
main()
{   int option;
    Lib_Records LR;
    do
    {   cout<<"\n ****** MENU ********\n";
        cout<<"\n 1. ADD A BOOK";
        cout<<"\n 2. ADD A JOURNAL";
        cout<<"\n 3. DISPLAY TOTAL NUMBER OF BOOK";
        cout<<"\n 4. DISPLAY TOTAL NUMBER OF JOURNALS";
        cout<<"\n 5. SET A MATERIAL IN POOR CONDITION";
        cout<<"\n 6. DISPLAY DETAILS";
        cout<<"\n 7. EXIT";
        cout<<"\n ***********************";
        cout<<"\n Enter your option : ";
        cin>>option;
        switch(option)
        {   case 1:LR.add_book();
                    break;
            case 2:LR.add_journal();
                    break;
            case 3:LR.show_books();
                    break;
            case 4:LR.show_journals();
                    break;
            case 5:LR.set_poor_cond();
                    break;
            case 6:LR.show_data();
                break;
        }
    }while(option!=7);
}
```

SAMPLE OUTPUT

```
// Enter the data yourself, the O/P will be somewhat like what is given below
Number of Books = 25
Number of Journals = 18
Number of Books in Poor Condition = 3
Number of Journals in Poor Condition = 5
Total Reading Material = 33
```

Program 10.10 Write a program to add two binary numbers of four digits.

```
using namespace std;
#include<iostream>
class Binary
{   private:
        int num[5];
    public:
        Binary();
        void get_data();
```

```
        void show_data();
        Binary & add(Binary &, Binary &);
};
Binary :: Binary()
{   for(int i=0;i<4;i++)
        num[i] = 0;
}
void Binary :: get_data()
{   cout<<"\n Enter a four digit binary number : ";
    for(int i=0;i<4;i++)
    cin>>num[i];
}
void Binary :: show_data()
{   for(int i=0;i<4;i++)
        cout<<num[i];
}
Binary & Binary :: add(Binary &B1, Binary &B2)
{   int carry[5] = {0};
    for(int i=0;i<4;i++)
    {   if(B1.num[i] == 0 && B2.num[i] == 0)
            num[i] = 0;
        else if(B1.num[i] == 0 && B2.num[i] == 1)
            num[i] = 1;
        else if(B1.num[i] == 1 && B2.num[i] == 0)
            num[i] = 1;
        else if(B1.num[i] == 1 && B2.num[i] == 1)
        {   num[i] = 0;
            carry[i+1] = 1;
        }
        num[i] +=carry[i];
        if(num[i]==2)
        {   num[i] = 0;
            carry[i+1] = 1;
        }
    }
        return *this;
}
main()
{   Binary B1;
    B1.get_data();
    Binary B2;
    B2.get_data();
    Binary B3;
    B3.add(B1, B2);
    cout<<"\n SUM OF TWO BINARY NUMBERS = ";
    B3.show_data();
}
```

OUTPUT

```
A four digit binary number : 1011
A four digit binary number : 0011
SUM OF TWO BINARY NUMBERS = 1001
(Note the program accepts digits in reverse)
```

Program 10.11 Write a program that randomly displays the details of a class period (subject and teacher).

```
using namespace std;
#include<iostream>
#include<string.h>
#include<stdlib.h>
#include<time.h>
time_t t;
char *subject[] = {"C++","Data Structures","C","DataWarehousing","Fundamentals"};
char *teacher[] = {"Mansi Sood","Jaya Gera","Namita Aggarwal","Shweta Tyagi","Akanksha
Bansal"};
class Period
{   private:
        char *sub_name;
        char *teacher_name;
    public:
        Period()
        {   sub_name = NULL;
            teacher_name = NULL;
        }
        Period( char *s, char *n);
        void show_details();
};
Period :: Period( char *s, char *n)
{   sub_name = new char [strlen(s) + 1];
    strcpy(sub_name, s);
    teacher_name = new char[strlen(n) + 1];
    strcpy(teacher_name, n);
}
void Period :: show_details()
{   cout<<"\n SUBJECT : ";
    cout<<sub_name;
    cout<<"\n TEACHER : "<<teacher_name;
}
main()
{   srand((unsigned)time(&t));
    int n = rand()%5;
    Period P(subject[n], teacher[n]);
    P.show_details();
}
```

OUTPUT

```
SUBJECT : Data Structures
TEACHER : Jaya Gera
```

10.5 DESTRUCTORS

Like a constructor, a destructor is also a member function that is automatically invoked. However, unlike the constructor which constructs the object, the job of destructor is to destroy the object. For this, it deallocates the memory dynamically allocated to the variable(s) or perform other clean up operations.

10.5.1 Important Features

- The name of the destructor is also the same as that of the class. However, the destructor's name is preceded by the tilde symbol '~'.
- A destructor is called when an object goes out of scope.
- A destructor is also called when the programmer explicitly deletes an object using the delete operator.
- Like a constructor, a destructor is also declared in the public section.
- The order of invoking a destructor is the reverse of invoking a constructor.
- Destructors do not take any argument and hence cannot be overloaded.
- A destructor does not return any value.
- A destructor must be specifically defined to free (de-allocate) the resources such as memory and files opened that have been dynamically allocated in the program.
- The address of a destructor cannot be accessed in the program.
- An object with a constructor or a destructor cannot be used as a member of a union.
    - Constructors and destructors cannot be inherited. We will discuss this topic in Chapter 12 on Inheritance.
    - Unlike constructors, destructors can be virtual. We will read more on this in Chapter 12 on Inheritance.

Note A class can have only one destructor.

Consider the program code and its output which makes it clear that the invocation timing of a destructor is just the reverse of a constructor.

Example 10.9 Calling a constructor, destructor

Programming Tip: Deleting an object more than once is a serious error.

```
using namespace std;
#include<iostream>
class Sample
{   private:
        int x;
    public:
        Sample(int n)
        {   x = n;
            cout<<"\n Constructor Called for object with value : "<<x;
    }
    ~Sample()
    {   cout<<"\n Destructor Called for object with value : "<<x;
    }
};
main()
{   Sample S1(1);
    Sample S2(2);
    Sample S3(3);
}
```

OUTPUT

```
Constructor Called for object with value : 1
Constructor Called for object with value : 2
Constructor Called for object with value : 3
Destructor Called for object with value : 3
Destructor Called for object with value : 2
Destructor Called for object with value : 1
```

Note If the programmer has not defined any destructor, then the C++ compiler automatically declare a destructor as an inline public member function of its class.

Program 10.12 Write a program that uses static variables to keep a track of number of objects created, number of objects destroyed, and number of active objects in a program.

```
using namespace std;
#include<iostream>
class Sample
{   private:
        static int num_objects;
        static int num_objects_destroyed;
    public:
        Sample()
        {   num_objects++;   }
        ~Sample()
        {   num_objects_destroyed++;   }
        void show_data()
        {   cout<<"\n\n\n Number of objects created : "<<num_objects;
            cout<<"\n Number of objects destroyed : "<<num_objects_destroyed;
            cout<<"\n Number of objects active : "<<num_objects - num_objects_destroyed;
        }
};
int Sample :: num_objects = 0;
int Sample :: num_objects_destroyed = 0;
void my_func()
{   Sample s8, s9;
    s9.show_data();
}
main()
{   Sample s1, s2, s3;
    {   s1.show_data();
        Sample s4;
        {   Sample s5;
            s5.show_data();
        }
    }
    s3.show_data();
    my_func();
    s2.show_data();
}
```

OUTPUT

```
Number of objects created : 3
Number of objects destroyed : 0
Number of objects active : 3
Number of objects created : 5
Number of objects destroyed : 0
Number of objects active : 5
Number of objects created : 5
Number of objects destroyed : 2
Number of objects active : 3
```

```
Number of objects created : 7
Number of objects destroyed : 2
Number of objects active : 5
Number of objects created : 7
Number of objects destroyed : 4
Number of objects active : 3
```

Program 10.13 Write a program that dynamically allocates memory to a matrix. Add two matrices, display the resultant matrix, and finally free the memory space.

```
#include<iostream.h>
class Matrix
{   private:
        int **parr;
        int rows;
        int cols;
    public:
        Matrix()
        {   rows = cols = 0;
            parr = NULL;
        }
        ~Matrix();
        Matrix(int r, int c);
        void get_data();
        void show_data();
        Matrix &add(Matrix &A1, Matrix &A2);
};
Matrix :: Matrix(int r, int c)
{   rows = r;
    cols = c;
    parr = new int *[rows];
    for(int i=0;i<rows;i++)
        parr[i] = new int [cols];
}
Matrix :: ~Matrix()
{   for(int i=0;i<rows;i++)
        delete parr[i];
    delete parr;
    cout<<"\n DESTROYED";
}
void Matrix :: get_data()
{   for(int i=0;i<rows;i++)
    {   for(int j=0;j<cols;j++)
        cin>>parr[i][j];
    }
}
void Matrix :: show_data()
{   for(int i=0;i<rows;i++)
    {   cout<<"\n";
            for(int j=0;j<cols;j++)
            cout<<" "<<parr[i][j];
    }
}
Matrix & Matrix :: add(Matrix &A1, Matrix &A2)
```

```
{   for(int i=0;i<rows;i++)
    {   for(int j=0;j<cols;j++)
            parr[i][j] = A1.parr[i][j] + A2.parr[i][j];
    }
    return *this;
}
main()
{   int r, c;
    cout<<"\n Enter the number of rows and columns of 2D Arrays : ";
    cin>>r>>c;
    Matrix Arr1(r,c), Arr2(r,c), Arr3(r,c);
    cout<<"\n Enter the first matrix : ";
    Arr1.get_data();
    cout<<"\n Enter the second matrix : ";
    Arr2.get_data();
    Arr3.add(Arr1,Arr2);
    cout<<"\n Array 1 is :\n";
    Arr1.show_data();
    cout<<"\n Array 2 is :\n";
    Arr2.show_data();
    cout<<"\n Resultant Array is :\n";
    Arr3.show_data();
}
```

OUTPUT

```
Enter the number of rows and columns of 2D Arrays : 2 2
Enter the first matrix : 1 2 3 4
Enter the second matrix : 5 6 7 8
Resultant Array is :
6 8
10 12
Destroyed
Destroyed
Destroyed
```

Program 10.14 Write a program that dynamically allocates memory to a string. Encrypt this string and de-allocate the memory.

```
using namespace std;
#include<iostream>
#include<string.h>
class String
{   private:
        int len;
        char *str;
    public:
        String(char *s)
        {   len = strlen(s);
            str = new char[len+1];
            strcpy(str, s);
        }
        ~String()
        {   len = 0;
            delete []str;
        }
```

```
        void show_string()
        {   cout<<str;
        }
        char * encrypt();
};
char * String :: encrypt()
{   int i = 0;
    while(i<len)
    {   str[i] += 3;
        i++;
    }
    show_string();
}
main()
{   String S1("ABCDE");
    cout<<"\n Original String : ";
    S1.show_string();
    cout<<"\n Encrypted String : ";
    S1.encrypt();
}
```

OUTPUT

```
Original String : ABCDE
Encrypted String : DEFGH
```

Program 10.15 Write a program to sort an array that has been allocated memory dynamically.

```
using namespace std;
#include<iostream>
class Array
{   private:
        int size;
        int *arr;
    public:
        Array()
        {   size = 0;
            arr = NULL;
        }
        Array(int n)
        {   size = n;
            arr = new int [size];
        }
        ~Array()
        {   cout<<"\n Destroyed ";
            delete [] arr;
            size = 0;
        }
        void get_data();
        void show_data();
        void sort();
};
void Array :: get_data()
{   for(int i=0;i<size;i++)
        cin>>arr[i];
}
```

```
void Array :: show_data()
{   for(int i=0;i<size;i++)
        cout<<" "<<arr[i];
}
void Array :: sort()
{   for(int i=0;i<size;i++)
    {   for(int j=0;j<size-i;j++)
        {   if(arr[j]>arr[j+1])
            {   int temp = arr[j];
                arr[j] = arr[j+1];
                arr[j+1] = temp;
            }
        }
    }
}
main()
{   Array arr(7);
    cout<<"\n Enter the array elements : ";
    arr.get_data();
    cout<<"\n Original Array : ";
    arr.show_data();
    arr.sort();
    cout<<"\n Sorted Array : ";
    arr.show_data();
}
```

OUTPUT

```
Enter the array elements : 9 1 8 3 6 4 5
Original Array : 9 1 8 3 6 4 5
Sorted Array : 1 3 4 5 6 8 9
Destroyed
```

Note Unlike local objects, static objects are constructed only the first time they are defined. These objects are destroyed at the end of the program.

10.5.2 Interesting Points about Constructors and Destructors

- You can call a constructor from `main()` by writing

```
object_name.constructor name
```

However, to call a destructor from `main()`, you must specify the object name as well as the class name. For example, if we have a class `Sample`, and `s` as the object of `Sample`, then to call its constructor we must write,

```
s.Sample();
```

To call the destructor, you need to write

```
s.Sample :: ~Sample();
```

- You can call a constructor from a destructor. You can also call a destructor from a constructor as shown in Fig. 10.3

<table>
<tr>
<td>

```
class Sample
{     -------
      -------
      Sample()
      {     --------
      Sample :: ~ Sample();
      }
      -------
};
```

Note: The destructor is being called using the class name.

</td>
<td>

```
class Sample
{     --------
      --------
      ~Sample()
      {      Sample();
             --------
      }
};
```

Note: The constructor is being called without using the class name. However, it may result in recursive call of constructor-destructor till stack overflows and abnormal program termination occurs.

</td>
</tr>
<tr>
<td>

```
class Sample
{     -------
      -------
      Sample()
      {     ---- ----

      Sample :: ~ Sample();

      }
      -------
};
```

Note: The destructor is being called using the class name.

</td>
<td>

```
class Sample
{     --------
      --------
      ~Sample()
      { Sample();

      ----- ---
      }

};
```

Note: The constructor is being called without using the class name.

</td>
</tr>
<tr>
<td>

```
class Sample
{     -------
      -------
      Sample()
      {     --------
       Sample :: ~ Sample();
      }
      -------
};
```

Note: The destructor is being called using the class name.

</td>
<td>

```
class Sample
{     --------
      --------
      ~Sample()
      {      Sample();
             --------
      }
};
```

Note: The constructor is being called without using the class name.

</td>
</tr>
</table>

Figure 10.3 Calling destructor

- If calling a constructor or a destructor is based on some decision, then it is called a conditional constructor or a conditional destructor, as shown in Fig. 10.4.
- C++ allows constructors and destructors to be defined in the `private` section. However, it is a good programming habit to declare them in the `public` section. When a constructor or a destructor is declared as `private`, it cannot be called implicitly. They have to be called explicitly through a public member function as shown here.

<pre>class Sample
{   -------
      ------- 	
      Sample()
      {   if(cond)
       Sample :: ~ Sample();
      }
       ------- 	
};</pre>
	<pre>class Sample
	{ --------
	      -------- 	
	      ~Sample()
	      { if(cond)
	  Sample();
	              -------- 	
	      }
	};</pre>

Figure 10.4 Conditional destructor

```
using namespace std;
#include<iostream>
class Sample
{
    int val; //Stores the Data
    Sample()   //Private Constructor
    {
            val = 10;
    }
    public:
            static Sample Initialize()
//Static Member Function generally called the Factory Method.
    {
            return Sample(); //Return the Object.
    }
    void Display() //Used to display the result.
    {
            cout<<"Value of Data is "<<val<<endl;
    }
};
main()
{
    Sample Obj = Sample::Initialize();
//Static Member function called to return the object.
    Obj.Display();
}
```

OUTPUT

```
Value of Data is 10
```

- C++ allows programmers to have a class named `main`. However, when there is a class named `main`, the use of keyword `class` before `main` (the `class_name`) is mandatory. This is shown in the code given below.

```
class main
{  private:
      int x;
   public:
```

```
        main()
        {   x = 10;
            cout<<"\n x = "<<x;
        }
~main()
        {   cout<<"\n Destroyed";
        }
    };
main()
{   class main M;
}
```

OUTPUT

```
 x = 10
 Destroyed
```

- You may call a constructor recursively.
- We know that program execution starts with `main()`. However, when the program has a global object (one defined before `main()`), the constructor of the global objects gets called before the `main()`. However, the destructor of the global object is executed after the execution of `main()`. Execute the code given here to understand this concept.

Example 10.10 Global object

```
using namespace std;
#include<iostream>
class Sample
{   public:
        Sample()
        {   cout<<"\n IN CONSTRUCTOR";   }
        ~Sample()
       {   cout<<"\n IN DESTRUCTOR";   }
};
Sample s;
main()
{   cout<<"\n IN MAIN";
}
```

OUTPUT

```
IN CONSTRUCTOR
IN MAIN
IN DESTRUCTOR
```

10.6 OBJECT COPY

In our programs, we frequently copy object to reuse all or part of its data in a new context. There are different strategies for copying an object `A` into another object `B`.

Shallow copy In this method, all the members of `A` will be copied into members of `B`. If the member holds a memory address, it copies the memory address, and if the member holds a value of primitive type it copies the value of the primitive type. The disadvantage of this method is that if the memory address of a B's data member is modified, then the memory address that A's member point also gets modified. Moreover, it just copies the address, it neither allocates memory nor copies value.

Note that the default copy constructor and default assignment operators use the shallow copy, which is also known as a member-wise copy. In a shallow copy, C++ copies each member of the class individually using the assignment operator. It is the best method for simple classes that do not contain any dynamically allocated memory.

Deep copy In this method, the data is actually copied. Therefore, gives different result from shallow copy. The main advantage is that A and B do not depend on each other. However, it is a slow method.

Lazy copy This method has advantages of both the previous methods. During initial copying, it uses shallow copy and also uses a counter to track how many objects share the data. When an attempt is made to modify the object, it can determine if the data is shared and can then go for deep copy, if necessary.

Consider the `String` class given here.

```
class String
{   private:
        char *name;
        int len;
    public:
        String(char *n)
        {   len = strlen(n);
            name = new char[len+1];
            strcpy(name, n);
        }
        ~String()
        {   delete[] name;
            len=0;
        }
};
Now, if we write,
String S1("Hello");
String S2 = S1;
```

The statement will invoke the default copy constructor which will do a shallow copy. Therefore, the address stored in `S1.name` will be copied in `S2.name`. As a result, both the object will be pointing to the same memory location and any change done by one object will be reflected in both. When any one of the object goes out of scope, the destructor will free the allocated memory to which both objects were pointing. If you try to print `S1.name` after `S2` has gone out scope, you will see that the program does not display the string.

The solution to this problem could be to do a deep copy. A deep copy will assign the duplicate object to its own local copy, so that any changes made by the duplicate object will not affect the original object. However, doing a deep copy requires programmers to write their own copy constructors and overloaded assignment operators.

10.7 CONSTANT OBJECTS

Since C++, treats user defined variables same as built in data type variables, it permits users to declare constant objects as we have `const int`, `const float`, etc. The syntax for defining a constant object is as follows:

```
class_name const object_name(parameter);
```

10.7.1 Key Features of Constant Object

- Constant object can be initialized only by a constructor. This means that a constant object is initialized during its creation.
- Data members of the constant object cannot be modified by any member function. This means that member function can only read the values of data members and not modify them.
- Constant objects behave as read only object. Their data members are read only members.

Let us consider a small program which declares a constant object.

Example 10.11 Constant object

```
using namespace std;
#include<iostream>
#include<string.h>
class Quotation
{   private:
        char *quote;
        char *author;
    public:
        Quotation(char *q, char *a)
        {   quote = new char[strlen(q) + 1];
            strcpy(quote, q);
            author = new char[strlen(a) + 1];
            strcpy(author, a);
        }
        void show_details()const
        {   cout<<"\n"<<quote<<" - "<<author;
        }
};
main()
{   Quotation const QT("Jai Hind", "NetajiSubhash Chandra Bose");
    QT.show_details();
}
```

OUTPUT

```
Jai Hind - NetajiSubhash Chandra Bose
```

Explanation: In the program, `QT` is a constant object and `show_details()` is a constant member function. Now, if you make a member function that tries to change the quote or its author, will result in an error.

Note Constant objects should be accessed only by constant member functions.

10.8 ANONYMOUS OBJECTS

In all our programs until now, we have used named objects. C++ also allows users to create anonymous or nameless objects. A nameless object is created by using the following syntax.

```
class_name(arguments if any);
```

For example, consider the code given below.

Example 10.12 Anonymous or nameless object

```
using namespace std;
#include<iostream>
class Number
{   private:
        int x;
    public:
    Number()
    { x = 0;   }
        Number(int n)
        {   x = n;
        }
        int return_data()
        {   return x;
        }
    friend Number add(Number &, Number &);
};
Number add(Number &N1, Number &N2)
{   return Number(N1.x + N2.x);
}
main()
{   Number N1(2);
    Number N2(5);
    cout<<"\n x = "<<add(N1, N2).return_data();
}
```

OUTPUT

```
X = 7
```

Explanation: In the code, observe carefully the `add()` in which we have returned a nameless object. In the `return` statement, we have not created a named object. Rather, an anonymous object has been created that is initialized to value `7` because `N1.x + N2.x = 7`. The unnamed object is destroyed immediately after this statement.

Even in `main()`, note how we have called `add()`. No named object has been used to invoke the member function of the class. The `add()` returns an object, and we use that unnamed object to invoke the member function.

10.8.1 Scope of Anonymous Objects

Anonymous objects are primarily used to pass or return objects to/from functions without having to create temporary objects unnecessarily. However, an important point to note here is that anonymous objects can only be passed or returned by value. Therefore, in case a reference has to be passed to a function or a reference has to be returned from a function, then you must create a named object.

10.8.2 Advantages of Anonymous Objects

- It results in shorter, cleaner, and efficient code.
- There is no need to think about meaningful names for objects that are going to exist temporarily.
- When a named object is used, it has to be declared and then used. With unnamed objects, no separate declaration statements are required.

- Unnamed object uses memory more efficiently. Many a time, named objects exists even after they have been used and are now no longer required. However, with named objects, the objects are destroyed soon after their usage is over, that is, when the statement in which they are used is terminated.

Note It is not possible to create more than one anonymous object at a time.

10.9 ANONYMOUS CLASSES

Anonymous class also called a nameless class is a class that is defined without any name. A class can be defined as anonymous when

- the class has a very short body
- only one instance of the class is needed

However, there are some constraints that must be kept in mind while using anonymous classes. These restrictions are as follows.

- Anonymous classes cannot have a constructor.
- Anonymous classes cannot have a destructor.
- Anonymous classes cannot be passed as arguments to functions.
- Anonymous classes cannot be used to return values from functions.

Consider the program code given here.

Example 10.13 Anonymous class

```
using namespace std;
#include<iostream>
typedef class                         // class name missing
{  private:
      int x;                          //data member
   public:
      void get_data()                 //member function
      {  cout<<"\n Enter the value of x : ";
         cin>>x;
      }
      void show_data()
      {  cout<<"\n x = "<<x;
      }
}Number;
main()
{  Number N1;   // object of a nameless class. Number is used as an alternate name
                for nameless class as we have used typedef
   N1.get_data();
   N1.show_data();
}
```

OUTPUT

```
Enter the value of x : 7
x = 7
```

Explanation: In the code, observe the following points:

- Keyword `class` is preceded with keyword `typedef`.
- There is no `class_name`.
- Right after the class definition, the class is instantiated, that is, an object of the class is created.
- The object name is used to create one or more instances of the class.

Points to Remember

- The name of the constructor is the same as that of the class to which it belongs.
- A constructor must be declared in the public section.
- A constructor is automatically invoked when an object of a class is created.
- The copy constructor is implicitly called when a function accepts an object as an argument using the call-by-value technique or returns an object by value. In both cases, a copy of the object is made and passed to the destination function.
- When an object of a class is created, the C++ compiler calls the suitable constructor for initializing that object.
- When a class has multiple constructors, it is called overloaded constructors.
- Like constructor, destructor is also a member function that is automatically invoked.
- A destructor must be specifically defined to free or de-allocate resources like memory or files opened that have been dynamically allocated in the program.
- Anonymous objects are primarily used to pass or return objects to or from functions without having to create temporary objects unnecessarily.

Glossary

Anonymous class A class that is defined without any name

Conditional constructor or conditional destructor A constructor or a destructor which is called based on some decision

Constructor A special member function of a class which is automatically invoked at the time of creation of an object to initialize or construct the values of data members of the object

Copy constructor A constructor that takes an object of the class as an argument and copies data values of one object's members into the values of another object's members

Default constructor A constructor that does not take any argument

Dynamic constructor A constructor in which memory for data members are allocated dynamically

Parameterized constructor A constructor that accepts one or more parameters

Exercises

Fill in the Blanks

1. ______ can be used to initialize data members at the time of object creation.
2. Name of the constructor of class `main` will be _____.
3. ______ is the first member function to be executed when an object of that class is created.
4. Copy constructor takes a _____ to an object of the same class as an argument.
5. The missing argument(s) must always be the ______ ones.
6. Overloaded constructors differ in their ________.
7. Name of the destructor is preceded by the ______ symbol.
8. In the absence of a destructor, C++ compiler declares a destructor as an ______.
9. The constructor of the global objects gets called ______.
10. Constant object can be initialized only by a______.

State True or False

1. A constructor is automatically invoked when an object goes of scope.
2. A constructor can be declared only in the public section.
3. A constructor can be called explicitly.
4. A function can be overloaded.
5. Constructors and destructors must be defined inside the class.
6. Copy constructor allocates memory for data members dynamically.
7. Constructors can also have default arguments.
8. It is compulsory to place default arguments in the definition of a constructor.
9. It is possible to overload constructors.
10. A destructor is called every time an object is created.
11. The order of invoking a destructor is the same as that of invoking a constructor.
12. The address of constructors and destructors can be accessed in programs.
13. An object with a constructor or a destructor cannot be used as a member of a union.
14. Constructors and destructors can be inherited.
15. Constructors can be virtual but destructor cannot be virtual.
16. Anonymous objects can only be passed or returned by reference.
17. An unnamed object uses memory more efficiently.
18. Anonymous classes can also have constructors and destructors.
19. Destructors can be overloaded.
20. Constructors and destructors can return values.

Multiple Choice Questions

1. A constructor can be
   (a) Virtual (b) Static
   (c) Volatile (d) None of these
2. Which constructor does not initialize any data member?
   (a) Dummy (b) Default
   (c) Copy (d) Parameterized
3. Which constructor does not take any argument?
   (a) Dummy (b) Default
   (c) Copy (d) Parameterized
4. Which constructor creates a new object from an existing one?
   (a) Dummy (b) Default
   (c) Copy (d) Parameterized
5. Which type of constructor is similar to a constructor that has all default arguments?
   (a) Dummy (b) Default
   (c) Copy (d) Parameterized
6. If you write `Student s[30];` where `Student` is the name of the class, how many times will the constructor function be invoked?
   (a) 29 (b) 1
   (c) 30 (d) 31
7. Ideally, in which section must constructors and destructors be declared?
   (a) Private (b) Public
   (c) Protected (d) Any of these
8. If you write `Student s[30];` where `Student` is the name of the class, how many times will the destructor function be invoked?
   (a) 29 (b) 1
   (c) 30 (d) 31
9. How many destructors can a class have?
   (a) 0 (b) 1
   (c) 2 (d) N
10. Constant object can be initialized only by______.
    (a) Constructor (b) Member function
    (c) `Main()` (d) destructor
11. How many anonymous objects can a class have at a particular time?
    (a) 0 (b) 1
    (c) 2 (d) N
12. Constructors and destructors are automatically invoked by________.
    (a) Operating system (b) Compiler
    (c) Main() (d) object
13. `Sample S1 = S2;` will invoke ________ type of constructor?
    (a) Dummy (b) Default
    (c) Copy (d) Parameterized
14. At the maximum, how many parameters can a destructor accept?
    (a) 0 (b) 1
    (c) 2 (d) N

Review Questions

1. What is the significance of a constructor?
2. Is it mandatory to define a constructor for every class?
3. Can a C++ program that has a class execute without a constructor?
4. Why a constructor is called a special member function?
5. Outline the similarities and dissimilarities between a constructor and a member function.
6. Explain some key features of a constructor.
7. Discuss the different types of constructors.
8. What are the techniques of invoking a copy constructor?
9. Why does copy constructor accept the objects by reference and not by value?
10. Can you have a constructor with all default arguments? Justify your answer.
11. Explain the concept of overloaded constructors with the help of an example.
12. Differentiate between a constructor and a destructor.
13. Explain the features of a destructor function.
14. Highlight the similarities in a constructor and a destructor.
15. Can you explicitly call a constructor and a destructor from `main()`? If yes, how?
16. How can a destructor be called from a constructor?
17. How will you invoke a private constructor?
18. Explain the significance of nameless objects.
19. Write a short note on anonymous classes.
20. Differentiate between a local and a global object.

Programming Exercises

1. Write a program that demonstrates the use of a dummy constructor.
2. Write a program that demonstrates the use of a default constructor.
3. Write a program that demonstrates the use of a parameterized constructor.
4. Write a program that demonstrates the use of a copy constructor.
5. Write a program that demonstrates the use of a dynamic constructor.
6. Write a program that demonstrates the use of default arguments in a constructor.
7. Write a program that uses an overloaded constructor to dynamically allocate memory to an array and find the smallest of its elements.
8. Write a program that uses dynamic constructor to allocate memory to an array. Count the number of prime and composite elements.
9. Write a program to dynamically allocate memory to string objects. Use copy constructor to copy one string into another.
10. Write a class that stores a string and its status details such as number of lower case characters, consonants, and so on.
11. Write a program that performs all string functions.
12. Write a menu-driven program to read, add, and subtract two polynomials.
13. Write a program that uses a date structure within a class. Enter any date and your birth date. The program must display your exact age in years, months, and days.
14. Write a program that uses a time structure within a class. Enter any time and your favourite show's time. The program must display how much time is left for it to start.
15. Write a menu-driven program to add or delete items from your inventory of stationary items.
16. Write a program to display the cheapest mobile available in the specified range.
17. Write a menu-driven program that keeps a record of video DVDs available in the shop.
18. Write a menu program to read, add, subtract, and divide two binary numbers of four digits.
19. Write a program that displays the details of books in the library at random.
20. Write a program to keep a track of number of objects created, number of objects destroyed, and number of active objects in a program.
21. Write a menu-driven program to read, add, subtract, multiply, divide, and transpose two matrices.
22. Write a program to display the details of a student. The details should be given according to sorted names of the students.
23. Write a program that demonstrates the use of constant objects.
24. Write a program that demonstrates the use of nameless objects.
25. Write a program that demonstrates the use of nameless classes.
26. Write a menu-driven program that reads title of the book from the user. Check if the book is

available and display the details about the book such as author, price, and number of copies available. If the user wants three copies, calculate the bill. Delete the count of books wanted from available copies. The program must also have functions to update the number of copies available and the price of the book.

27. Write a program that calculates commission of 10 salesmen. For every salesman, a target is defined. If he sells products less than the target assigned, he gets no commission. If he completes the target, he gets a 10 per cent commission on the extra sales made; if he sells beyond the target, he gets a 25 per cent commission on extra sales. The program must record the sales of each month made by the salesman. The commission is calculated at the end of the year.
28. Write a program that displays the details of a cricket player. The details must include his name, matched played, run rate, wickets taken, maiden overs, overs played, number of centuries, half centuries, etc.

Find the errors in the following codes

1.
```
using namespace std;
#include<iostream>
class Sample
{  Sample()
     {  cout<<"\n IN CONSTRUCTOR";   }
   ~Sample()
     {  cout<<"\n IN DESTRUCTOR";  }
};
main()
{  Sample s;
}
```
2.
```
using namespace std;
#include<iostream>
class Sample
{  private:
      int x;
   public:
      Sample(int n)
      {  x = n;
         cout<<"\n IN CONSTRUCTOR";
      }
      ~Sample()
      {  cout<<"\n IN DESTRUCTOR";   }
};
main()
{  Sample s;
}
```
3.
```
using namespace std;
#include<iostream>
class Sample
{  private:
      int x;
   public:
      Sample(n)
      {  x = n;
      cout<<"\n IN CONSTRUCTOR";
      }
      ~Sample()
      {  cout<<"\n IN DESTRUCTOR";  }
};
main()
{  Sample s;
}
```
4.
```
using namespace std;
#include<iostream>
class Sample
{  private:
      int x;
   public:
      void Sample(int n)
      {  x = n;
      }
      void show_data()
      {  cout<<"\n x = "<<x;  }
};
main()
{  Sample s;
   s.show_data();
}
```
5.
```
using namespace std;
#include<iostream>
class Sample
{  private:
      int x;
   public:
      Sample(int n)
      {  x = n;
      }
      void show_data()
      {  cout<<"\n x = "<<x;   }
      ~Sample(int n)
      {  cout<<"\n Destroyed";
      }
};
main()
{  Sample s;
   s.show_data();
}
```
6.
```
using namespace std;
#include<iostream>
class Sample
{  private:
      int x;
   public:
```

```
        Sample(int n)
        {   x = n;
        }
        voidshow_data()
        {   cout<<"\n x = "<<x;   }
        void ~Sample()
        {   cout<<"\n Destroyed";
        }
    };
    main()
    {   Sample s;
        s.show_data();
    }
```

7.
```
using namespace std;
#include<iostream>
    class Sample
    {   private:
            int x;
        public:
            Sample(int n)
            {   x = n;   }
            Sample(Sample S)
            {   x = S.x;
            }
        void show_data()
        {   cout<<"\n x = "<<x;   }
};
main()
{   Sample s1(3);
    Sample s2 = s3;
    S2.show_data();
}
```

8.
```
using namespace std;
#include<iostream>
class item
{   static int count;
    public:
        item()
    {   count++;   }
    int getcount()
    {   return count;   }
    int *getcadd()
    {   return count;  }
};
int item::count = 0;
main()
{   item ob1;
    item ob2;
    cout<<ob1.getcount()<<' ';
    cout<<ob2.getcount()<<' ';
    cout<<ob1.getcadd()<<' ';
    cout<<ob2.getcadd()<<' ';
}
```

Find the output of the following codes

1.
```
using namespace std;
#include<iostream>
class Sample
{   private:
        int x;
    public:
        Sample()
       { cout<<"\n IN CONSTRUCTOR";   }
        ~Sample()
       { cout<<"\n IN DESTRUCTOR";   }
};
main()
{   Sample s;
    cout<<(unsigned)s.Sample::Sample();
}
```

2.
```
using namespace std;
#include<iostream>
class Sample
{   private:
        int x;
    public:
        Sample()
       { cout<<"\n IN CONSTRUCTOR";   }
        ~Sample()
       { cout<<"\n IN DESTRUCTOR";   }
        void display()
       { cout<<(&Sample());   }
};
main()
{   Sample s;
    s.display();
}
```

3.
```
using namespace std;
#include<iostream>
class Sample
{   private:
        int x;
    public:
        Sample(int n)
        {   x = n;
        }
void show_data()
    {   cout<<"\n x = "<<x;   }
};
main()
{   Sample s(3);
    Sample *ptr = &s;
    cout<<ptr;
}
class Sample
{   public:
    Sample()
```

```
{  initialize();
   cout<<"\n CONSTRUCTOR";
}
void initialize()
{  show_str();
   cout<<"\n Function - initialize";
void show_str()
{  cout<<"\n HI";  }
};
main()
{  Sample s;
}
```

Answers

Fill in the Blanks

1. Constructor; **2.** Main **3.** Constructor; **4.** Reference; **5.** Trailing; **6.** Signature; **7.** Tilde; **8.** Inline public member function of its class; **9.** Before `main()`; **10.** Constructor

State True or False

1. True	**2.** False	**3.** True	**4.** True	**5.** False	**6.** False	**7.** True	**8.** False
9. True	**10.** False	**11.** False	**12.** False	**13.** True	**14.** False	**15.** False	**16.** False
17. True	**18.** False	**19.** False	**20.** False				

Multiple Choice Questions

1. (d); **2.** (a); **3.** (b); **4.** (c); **5.** (b); **6.** (c); **7.** (b); **8.** (c); **9.** (b); **10.** (a); **11.** (b);**12.** (b); **13.** (c); **14.** (a)

Case Study 4

This case study shows the implementation of concepts discussed in Chapters 9 and 10 on Classes and Objects and Constructors and Destructors.

C4.1 INTERPOLATION SEARCH

Interpolation search,sometimes known as extrapolation search, is asearching technique that finds a specified value in a sorted array. The concept of interpolation search is similar to how we search for names in a telephone book or for keys by which the book's entries are ordered. For example, when looking for a name 'Bharat' in the telephone directory, we know that it will be near the extreme left, so applying a binary search technique by dividing the list in two halves each time is not at all a good idea. We must start scanning the extreme left in the first pass itself.

In the interpolation search, in each step, the remaining search space for the item to be found is calculated. The calculation is done based on the values at the bounds of the search space and the value of the item to be searched. The value found at this estimated position is then compared with the value being searched for. If the two values are equal, the search is complete.

However, if the values are not equal, then depending on the comparison, the remaining search space is reduced to the part before or after the estimated position. Therefore, we see that interpolation search is similar to the binary search technique. However, the important difference in the two techniques is that binary search always selects the middle value of the remaining search space. It discards half of the values based on the comparison between the value found at the estimated position and the value to be searched. However, in interpolation search, interpolation is used to find an item near the one being searched for and then linear search is used to find the exact item.

Figures C4.1 and C4.2 will help you visualize how the search space is divided in case of binary search and the interpolation search.

When the n elements in the list to be sorted are uniformly distributed (average case), the interpolation search makes about $\log(\log(n))$ comparisons. However, in the worst case, that is when the elements increase exponentially, the algorithm can make up to $O(n)$ comparisons.

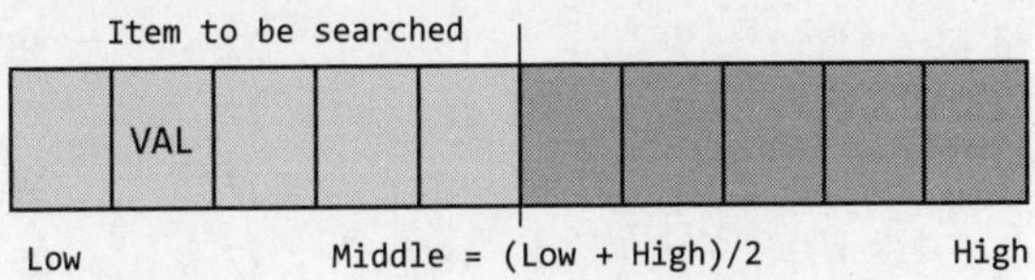

Figure C4.1 Binary search divides the list into two equal halves

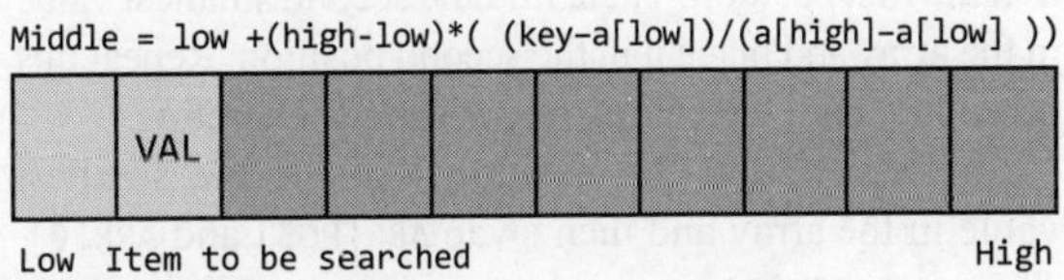

Figure C4.2 Binary search divides the list into two equal halves

Example C4.1 Given a list of numbers a[] = {1, 3,5,7,9,11,13,15, 17, 19, 21}. Search for value 19 using interpolation search technique.

```
Low = 0, High = 10, VAL = 19, a[Low] = 1,
a[High] = 21
Middle = Low + (High – Low)*((VAL-a[Low]) /
(a[High] – a[Low] ))
Middle = 0 +(10 – 0)* ((19 – 1) / (21 – 1) )
= 0 +10* 0.9 = 9
a[middle] = 19 which is equal to value to be
searched.
```

C4.2 SELECTION SORT

Selection sort is a sorting algorithm that has quadratic running time complexity given as $O(n^2)$, thereby, making it inefficient to be used on large lists. Although selection sort performs worse than insertion sort algorithm, it is noted for its simplicity and also has performance advantages over more complicated algorithms in certain situations. Selection sort is the generally used choice for sorting files with very large objects or records and small keys.

Technique

Consider an array `ARR` with N elements. The selection sort takes $N-1$ passes to sort the entire array and works as

Example C4.2 Sort the array using selection sort.

PASS	LOC	ARR[0]	ARR[1]	ARR[2]	ARR[3]	ARR[4]	ARR[5]	ARR[6]	ARR[7]
1	1	9	39	81	45	90	27	72	18
2	7	9	18	81	45	90	27	72	39
3	5	9	18	27	45	90	81	72	39
4	7	9	18	27	39	90	81	72	45
5	7	9	18	27	39	45	81	72	90
6	6	9	18	27	39	45	72	81	90

follows. First, find the smallest value in the array and place it in the first position. Then, find the second smallest value in the array and place it in the second position. Repeat this procedure until the entire array is sorted. Therefore,

In Pass 1, find the position POS of the smallest value in the array and then swap `ARR[POS]` and `ARR[0]`. Therefore, `ARR[0]` is sorted.

In Pass 2, find the position POS of the smallest value in sub-array of $N - 1$ elements. Swap `ARR[POS]` with `ARR[1]`. Now, `A[0]` and `A[1]` is sorted.

In Pass 3, find the position POS of the smallest value in sub-array of $N - 2$ elements. Swap `ARR[POS]` with `ARR[2]`. Now, `ARR[0]`, `ARR[1]`, and `ARR[2]` are sorted.

In Pass $N - 1$, find the position POS of the smaller of the elements `ARR[N-2]` and `ARR[N-1}`. Swap `ARR[POS]` and `ARR[N-2]` so that `ARR[0], ARR[1], …, ARR[N-1]` is sorted.

Program C4.1 Selection Sort

```
using namespace std;
#include<iostream>
class Array // define class
{    private:
          int *arr;
          int size;
          int smallest(int k);
     public:
          Array(int n)
// allocate space for array
          {    size = n;
               arr = new int[size];
          }
          void read()
          {    for(int i=0; i<size;i++)
                    cin>>arr[i];
          }
          void display()
          {    for(int i=0; i<size;i++)
                    cout<<"\t"<<arr[i];
          }
          void selection_sort();
          int interpolation_search(int val);
};
int Array :: smallest(int k)
// find smallest element
{    int pos = k, small=arr[k], i;
     for(i=k+1;i<size;i++)
     {    if(arr[i]< small)
          {    small = arr[i];
               pos = i;
          }
     }
     return pos;
}
void Array :: selection_sort()
// perform sorting
{    int k, pos, temp;
     for(k=0;k<size;k++)
     {    pos = smallest(k);
// initially first element is considered
to be the smallest element
          temp = arr[k];
          arr[k] = arr[pos];
          arr[pos] = temp;
     }
}
int Array :: interpolation_search(int val)
// search an element
{
     int mid, low=0, high=size;
     while(arr[low] <= val&&arr[high] >= val)
     {
          mid = low + (high - low)*
((val - arr[low]) / (arr[high] - arr[low]));
          if(val == arr[mid])
```

```
	return mid;
		if(val<arr[mid])
	high = mid - 1;
		else
			low = mid + 1;
	}
	return -1;
}
int main()
{	int n, val float pos;
	cout<<"\n Enter the number of
	elements in the array : ";
	cin>>n;
	Array Arr(n);
	cout<<"\n Enter the elements of the
	array ";
	Arr.read();
	Arr.selection_sort();
	cout<<"\n The sorted array is : ";
	Arr.display();
	cout<<"\n Enter the value to be
	searched : ";
	cin>>val;
	pos = Arr.interpolation_search(val);
	if(pos == -1)
		cout<<"\n"<<val<<" is not found
		in the array";
	else
		cout<<"\n"<<val<<" is found
		at position "<<pos;
}
```

OUTPUT

```
Enter the number of elements
in the array : 7
Enter the elements : 7 6 5 4 3 2 1
The sorted array is : 1 2 3 4 5 6 7
Enter the value to be searched : 6
6 is found at position 5
```

CHAPTER 11

Operator Overloading and Type Conversions

KEY Concepts

Syntax of operator overloading • Overloading unary operators • Overloading binary operators • Overloading special operators • Type conversions

INTRODUCTION

The utility of operators such as `+, =, *, /, >, <`, and so on is predefined in any programming language. Programmers can use them directly on built-in data types to write their programs. However, these operators do not work for user-defined types such as objects. Therefore, C++ allows programmers to redefine the meaning of operators when they operate on class objects. This feature is called *operator overloading*. With this feature, the overloading principle is not only applied to functions but also on operators.

Operator overloading allows programmers to extend the meaning of existing operators so that in addition to the basic data types, they can be also applied to user-defined data types.

11.1 SCOPE OF OPERATOR OVERLOADING

With operator overloading, a programmer is allowed to provide his own definition for an operator to a class by overloading the built-in operator. This enables the programmer to perform specific computation when the operator is applied on class objects and apply a standard definition when the same operator is applied on a built-in data type.

Therefore, while evaluating an expression with operators, C++ looks at the operands around the operator. If the operands are of built-in types, C++ calls a built-in routine. If the operator is being applied on user-defined operand(s), the C++ compiler checks if the programmer has an overloaded operator function that it can call. If such a function whose parameters match the type(s) and number of the operands exists in the program, the function is called; otherwise, a compiler error is generated.

Another Form of Polymorphism

Like function overloading, operator overloading is also a form of compile time polymorphism. Operator overloading is, therefore, less commonly known as operator adhoc polymorphism since different operators have different implementations depending on their arguments. Operator overloading is generally defined by the language, the programmer, or both.

Advantages of Operator Overloading

We can easily write C++ programs without the knowledge of operator overloading; however, the knowledge and use of this feature can help us in many ways. Some of them are as follows:

- Operator overloading enables programmers to use notation closer to the target domain. For example, to add two matrices, we can simply write `M1 + M2`, rather than writing `M1.add(M2)`.
- With operator overloading, a similar level of syntactic support is provided to user-defined types as provided to the built-in types.
- In scientific computing where computational representation of mathematical objects is required, operator overloading provides great ease to understand the concept.
- Operator overloading makes the program clear. For example, the statement

  `div(mul(M1, M2), add(M1,M2));` can be better written as `M1 * M2 / M1+M2`

Programming Tip: Only existing operators can be overloaded.

11.2 SYNTAX FOR OPERATOR OVERLOADING

When an operator has to be overloaded, it is declared in the public section. The syntax for an operator overloading function can be given as

```
class class_name
{--------
    public:
        return_type operator op(arguments if any)
        {   ---------
            //Function Body
            ----------
        }
        ----------
};
```

Here, `op` is the operator that has to be overloaded and `operator` is the keyword. For example, if you want to add two objects of class `Complex`, then `op` stands for `+`. The entire function can be written as

```
Complex operator +(Complex &c2)
{       Complex Temp;
        Temp.real = real + c2.real;
        Temp.imag = imag + c2.imag;
        return Temp;
}
```

Although C++ does not restrict as to what should be the `return type`, ideally, overloaded operators should return an object of the class either by value or by reference (preferred) so that the returned value can be used in the calling function. Moreover, this will help to make the objects behave in the same way as built-in types behave when an operation is performed on them. Therefore, after writing the function, we can add two complex objects by writing, `c3 = c1 + c2;` same way as we write `c = a + b;` for two integer variables.

11.3 OPERATORS THAT CAN AND CANNOT BE OVERLOADED

In C++, barring a few operators, programmers can overload almost any operator. The operators that can be overloaded are given in Table 11.1.

Table 11.1 Operators that can be overloaded

Unary	Binary	Others
! ++ -- ~	+ - * / % ^ = == += != -= & | && || *= /= %= ^= &= <<= >>= <<>>	[] () => ->* `new` `delete`

However, the exceptional operators that cannot be overloaded are as follows:

- Scope resolution operator (`::`)
- Member selection operator (`.`)
- Member selection through a pointer to a function (`.*`)
- Ternary operator (`?:`)
- Size of operator (`sizeof`)

Important Points about Operator Overloading

- Operator overloading should not change the operation performed by an operator. You cannot redefine the meaning of an operator. Therefore, when the + operator will be overloaded, it will always perform addition and not subtraction, multiplication, or any other operation.
- The two operators—the assignment operator(`=`) and the address operator(`&`)—need not be overloaded. This is because these two operators are already overloaded in the C++ library. For example, when you write `Complex1 = Complex2`, then the contents of object `Complex2` will be copied into the contents of object `Complex1` automatically. Similarly, the address operator returns the address of every object in memory.
- Operator overloading cannot alter the precedence and the associativity of operators. However, you may use parenthesis to change the order of evaluation.
- New operators such as `like **, <>, |&`, and so on cannot be created. Only existing operators can be overloaded.
- When operators such as `&&, ||`, and, are overloaded, they lose their special properties of short-circuit evaluation and sequencing. This means that after overloading, say `&&` operator, you cannot expect `&&=` to perform the `logical AND` as well as assignment. To perform both the operations, you must specifically overload `&&=` operator and not just `&&` operator.
- Overloaded operators cannot have default arguments.
- All overloaded operators except the assignment operator are inherited by derived classes. This will be clear in Chapter 12 on Inheritance.
- Arity or the number of operands cannot be changed. Therefore, a unary operator such as `++`, `--`, `!`, and so on will always be applied on one operand and binary operator such as `+`, `-`, `*`, and so on will be applied on two operands.
- Overloading an operator that is not associated with the scope of a class is not permissible. This means that the overloaded operator must have access to at least one object of the class in which it is being overloaded. This object may be accessed implicitly (using member function) or explicitly (using the friend function).

Note Operator overloading extends the semantics of an operator without changing its syntax.

11.4 IMPLEMENTING OPERATOR OVERLOADING

Operator overloading is usually implemented in two ways as follows:

Programming Tip: Operator overloading cannot be used to define new operators.

- Through member function
- Through friend function

Although operators can be easily overloaded using any of these techniques, the choice of technique is just a matter of programmer's convenience. However, you must consider the major difference when overloading using a member and/or a friend function as shown in Table 11.2.

Table 11.2 Differences between operator overloading using member function and friend function

Member function	Friend function
• Number of explicit parameters is reduced by one, as the calling object is implicitly supplied as an operand. • Unary operators take no explicit parameters. • Binary operators take one explicit parameter. • Left-hand operand has to be the calling object. • `obj2 = obj1 + 10;` is permissible but `obj2 = 10 + obj1;` is not permissible.	• Number of explicit parameters is more. • Unary operators take only one parameter. • Binary operators take two parameters. • Left-hand operand need not be an object of the class. • `obj2 = obj1 + 10;` as well as `obj2 = 10 + obj1;` is permissible.

11.5 OVERLOADING UNARY OPERATORS

Unary operators work only on a single operand. Some examples of unary operators are as follows:

- Increment operator (`++`)
- Decrement operator (`--`)
- Unary minus operator (`-`)
- Logical not operator (`!`)

As stated earlier, unary operators can be overloaded using a friend function or a member function. In both the cases, the unary operator operates on the object for which it was called. Usually, the operator is specified on the left side of the object, as in `++obj`, `-obj`, and `!obj`. However, the operator may appear on the right side of the object when it is a post-fix increment or a post-fix decrement such as `obj++` or `obj--`.

11.5.1 Using a Member Function to Overload a Unary Operator

The syntax for operator overloading using a member function can be given as

```
return_type operator op()
```

where `return_type` is the return type and *op* is the operator to be overloaded. Let us consider a small program that overloads the unary operator using member function. We know that if we have a number say, `7`, then the `unary` operator when applied to it will make it negative, which is `-7`. However, if we apply the same operator to a number say `-10`, then the result would be `10` (positive).

Example 11.1 Overloading `unary` operator with member function

```
using namespace std;
#include<iostream>
```

```
class Number
{   private:
        int x;
    public:
        Number()
        {   x = 0;     };
        Number(int n) //parameterized constructor
        {   x = n;     }
        void operator-()  // operator overloaded function
        {   x = -x;}
        void show_data()
        {   cout<<"\n x = "<<x;       }
};
main()
{   Number N(7);   // create object
    N.show_data();
    -N;            // invoke operator overloaded function
    N.show_data();
}
```

OUTPUT

```
x = 7
x = -7
```

11.5.2 Returning Object

The operator overloading function in Example 11.1 does not return any value. However, if we want to have a statement like `N2 = -N1;` then the above code must return a value (an object). Therefore, the function code can be modified to return a value as shown in Example 11.2 given here.

Example 11.2 Returning Object

```
using namespace std;
#include<iostream>
class Number
{   private:
        int x;
    public:
        Number()
        {   x = 0;     };
        Number(int n)
        {   x = n;     }
        Number operator-()    // operator overloading function returns an object
        {       Number temp;
            temp.x = -x;
            return temp;       //object returned
        }
        void show_data()
        {   cout<<"\n x = "<<x;       }
};
main()
{       Number N1(-10), N2;
        N2 = -N1;      // return value assigned to another object
        N2.show_data();
}
```

OUTPUT
```
x = 10
```

11.5.3 Returning a Nameless Object

The function code operator overloading could be made simpler and shorter by returning a nameless object. This could be done by writing

Programming Tip: Binary operator will be applied on two operands.

```
Number operator -()
{       x = -x;
    return Number(x);
}
```

Note There is no restriction on the return types of the unary operators.

11.5.4 Using a Friend Function to Overload a Unary Operator

When a unary operator is overloaded using a friend function, then you must ensure the following:

- The function will take one operand as an argument.
- This operand will be an object of the class.
- The function will use the private members of the class only with the object name.
- The function may take the object by using value or by reference. However, if the object is passed using value, then any changes made to the data members of the object in the function will not be reflected back in the calling function. Therefore, if you want the changes to persist, pass the object by reference.
- The function may or may not return any value. It depends on the usage. Since we had to assign the value to another object we have returned.
- The friend function does not have access to the `this` pointer.

The syntax for operator overloading using a member function can be given as

```
friend return_type operator op (class_name object)
```

where `return_type` is the return type, and `op` the operator to be overloaded and object is an instance of the class on which the operator has to be applied. The program given here performs the same operation but using a friend function.

Example 11.3 Friend function for operator overloading

```
using namespace std;
#include<iostream>
class Number
{   private:
        int x;
    public:
        Number()
        {     x = 0;      };
        Number(int n)
        {     x = n;      }
        void show_data()
        {     cout<<"\n x = "<<x;      }
        friend Number & operator-(Number &);      //friend function declared
```

```
};
Number & operator -(Number &N)
{   N.x = -N.x;             //use objectname with data member
    return N;           //return object
}
main()
{   Number N1(100), N2;
    N2 = -N1;      // overloaded operator function called
    N2.show_data();
}
```

OUTPUT

```
x = -100
```

Note Operator overloaded functions return values so that a cascaded assignment expression can be formed.

11.5.5 Overloading the Prefix Increment and Decrement Operators

The syntax for overloading prefix increment and decrement operators is

```
operator ++()
{      // code
}
```

In Example 11.4, we have overloaded the ++ and - operators. While ++ operator has been overloaded using a member function, the - operator on the other hand has been overloaded using a friend function. Although operators can be overloaded in any of the two ways, we have used both the techniques for better clarity. Note that the function code for both the operators first changes the original value and then returns the object with the modified value.

Example 11.4 Overloading ++ and - operators

Programming Tip: ,?:, :: and sizeof operators cannot be overloaded.

```
using namespace std;
#include<iostream>
class Number
{   private:
        int x;
    public:
        Number()
        {   x = 0;      }
        Number(int n)
        {      x = n;      }
        void show_data()
        {      cout<<"\n x = "<<x;      }
        Number operator++()       // overloaded increment operator using member function
        {   x++;
            return Number(x);
        }
        friend Number & operator--(Number &);
};
Number & operator--(Number &N)          // overloaded decrement operator using friend function
{   N.x = N.x - 1;
```

```
    return N;
}
main()
{   Number N1(10), N2, N3(20), N4;
    N2 = ++N1;            //overloaded increment operator called
    N2.show_data();
    N4 = --N3;            //overloaded decrement operator called
    N4.show_data();
}
```

OUTPUT

```
x = 11
x = 19
```

11.5.6 Overloading the Post-fix Increment and Post-fix Decrement Operators

Although the prefix and post-fix increment operators both have the same symbol ++, they have different tasks to perform. Here, the question arises as to how the compiler knows which version to call for. To distinguish between the overloaded prefix and the post-fix operator function, there is a slight change in the signature of post-fix operation. Instead of writing `Number operator ++()`, we write `Number operator ++(int)`.

Here, `int` is a dummy argument. Therefore, we have used function overloading for the operator overloaded functions. Always remember that in overloaded post-fix operators, `int` is just a dummy argument to give a signal to the compiler to create the post-fix notation of the operator. Observe carefully that `int` is not followed by a variable name just because its value will never be used. Look at the program given here which overloads both the prefix and post-fix increment as well as decrement operators.

Note When the compiler sees `++obj` (pre-increment), it generates a call to `operator++()`; but when it sees `obj++`, it generates a call to `operator++(int)`.

Example 11.5 Overloading postfix ++ and - operators

```
using namespace std;
#include<iostream>
class Number
{   private:
        int x;
    public:
        Number()
        {   x = 0;      }
        Number(int n)
        {   x = n;      }
        void show_data()
        {   cout<<"\n x = "<<x;      }
        Number operator++()      // Prefix increment operator
        {   x++;
        return Number(x);
        }
        Number operator--()      // Prefix decrement operator
        {   x--;
```

```
        return Number(x);
        }
        Number operator++(int)          // Postfix increment operator
        {   return Number(x++);
        }
        Number operator --(int)          // Postfix decrement operator
        {     return Number(x--);
        }
};
main()
{   Number N1(10), N2, N3(20), N4, N5(30), N6, N7;
    N2 = ++N1;
    cout<<"\n Prefix Increment";
    N2.show_data();
    cout<<"\n Prefix Decrement";
    N4 = --N3;
    N4.show_data();
    cout<<"\n Postfix Increment";
    N6 = N5++;
    N6.show_data();
    cout<<"\n Postfix Decrement";
    N7 = N5--;
    N7.show_data();
}
```

OUTPUT

```
Prefix Increment
x = 11
Prefix Decrement
x = 19
Postfix Increment
x = 30
Postfix Decrement
x = 31
```

Programming Tip: Unary operator will be applied only on a single operand.

Note In case of friend function, the signature for an overloaded post-fix operator would have been `friend Number & operator ++ (Number &, int);` and the function call would have been same as before - `N++;` where `N` is an object of the class.

Program 11.1 Write a program to apply unary operators ++, ——, —, and & on a point.

```
using namespace std;
#include<iostream>
class Point
{     private:
           int x, y;
      public:
           Point()
           {     x=y=0;     }
           Point(int a, int b)
           {     x= a, y = b;      }
           void get_data()
```

```
        {     cout<<"\n Enter the x and y co=ordnates : ";
              cin>>x>>y;
        }
        void show_data()
        {     cout<<"\n The x and y co=ordnates of the point are : ";
              cout<<x<<"x "<<y<<"y";
        }
        void operator++()
        {     ++x, ++y;     }
        void operator--()
        {     --x, --y;     }
        friend Point & operator-(Point &);
        Point * operator&()
        {     return this;     }
};
Point & operator-(Point &P)
{     P.x = -P.x;
      P.y =  P.y;
      return P;
}
main()
{     Point P1;
      P1.get_data();
      P1.show_data();
      ++P1;
      cout<<"\n After Incrementing";
      P1.show_data();
      --P1;
      cout<<"\n After Decrementing";
      P1.show_data();
      -P1;
      cout<<"\n After Unary Minus Operator";
      P1.show_data();
      cout<<"\n Address of P1 = "<<&P1;
}
```

OUTPUT

```
Enter the x and y co=ordnates : 4 5
The x and y co=ordnates of the point are : 4x 5y
After Incrementing
The x and y co=ordnates of the point are : 5x 6y
After Decrementing
The x and y co=ordnates of the point are : 4x 5y
After Unary Minus Operator
The x and y co=ordnates of the point are : -4x -5y
Address of P1 = 0x8fc1fff2
```

Program 11.2 Write a program to apply unary operators ++ and — — on a distance.

```
using namespace std;
#include<iostream>
class Distance
{     private:
            int kms, m;
      public:
            Distance()
```

```
        {     kms = 0, m=0;     }
        void get_data()
        {     cout<<"\n Enter the distance : ";
              cin>>kms>>m;
        }
        void show_data()
        {     cout<<kms<<"kms "<<m<<"mts";     }
        void operator++()
        {     kms++;     }
        void operator--()
        {     kms--;     }
};
main()
{     Distance D;
      D.get_data();
      D.show_data();
      ++D;
      cout<<"\n After Incrementing";
      D.show_data();
      --D;
      cout<<"\n After Decrementing";
      D.show_data();
}
```

OUTPUT

```
ENter the distance : 5 200
5 kms 200 mts
After Incrementing
6 kms 200 mts
After Decrementing
5 kms 200 mts
```

> **Assignment** Write the same program to increment meters. Check if meters is >1000, then increment kilometres.

Program 11.3 Write a program to increment and decrement time (in seconds).

```
using namespace std;
#include<iostream>
class Time
{     private:
          int h,m,s;
      public:
          Time()
          {     h=m=s;     }
          void get_data()
          {     cout<<"\n Enter the time :      ";
               cin>>h>>m>>s;
          }
          void show_data()
          {     cout<<"\n Time : "<<h<<":"<<m<<":"<<s;
          }
          friend Time & operator++(Time &);
          Time & operator--();
};
Time & operator++(Time &T)
{     T.s++;
      if(T.s==60)
```

```
      {     T.s = 0;
            T.m++;
      }
      if(T.m==60)
      {     T.m = 0;
            T.h++;
      }
      return T;
}
Time & Time :: operator--()
{     s--;
      if(s<0)
      {     s+=60;
          m--;
      }
      if(m<0)
      {     m+=60;
            h--;
      }
      return *this;
}
main()
{     Time T;
      T.get_data();
      T.show_data();
      ++T;
      cout<<"\n After Incrementing";
      T.show_data();
      --T;
      cout<<"\n After Decrementing";
      T.show_data();
}
```

OUTPUT

```
Enter the time :  6 59 59
Time : 6:59:59
After Incrementing
Time : 7:0:0
After Decrementing
Time : 6:59:59
```

Program 11.4 Write a program to overload the increment and decrement operators on the array class.

```
using namespace std;
#include<iostream>
class Array
{     private:
          int arr[10];
          int size;
      public:
          Array();
          Array(int);
          void show_data();
          void operator++();
          void operator--();
```

```
};
Array :: Array()
{     for(int i=0;i<10;i++)
            arr[i] = 0;
            size = 0;
}
Array :: Array(int n)
{   size = n;
    cout<<"\n Enter the array elements : ";
    for(int i=0;i<size;i++)
            cin>>arr[i];
}
void Array :: show_data()
{     for(int i=0;i<size;i++)
            cout<<" "<<arr[i];
}
void Array :: operator++()
{     for(int i=0;i<size;i++)
            arr[i]++;
}
void Array :: operator--()
{     for(int i=0;i<size;i++)
            arr[i]--;
}
main()
{     int n;
      cout<<"\n ENter the size of the array : ";
      cin>>n;
      Array A(n);
      cout<<"\n The original array is :;
      A.show_data();
      ++A;
      cout<<"\n After incrementing the array is : ";
      A.show_data();
      --A;
      cout<<"\n After decrementing the array is: ";
      A.show_data();
}
```

OUTPUT

```
ENter the size of the array : 5
Enter the array elements : 1 2 3 4 5
The original array is : 1 2 3 4 5
Array after incrementing is : 2 3 4 5 6
Array after decrementing is : 1 2 3 4 5
```

Program 11.5 Write a program to overload the unary increment, decrement, and negation operator on a binary number.

```
using namespace std;
#include<iostream>
class Binary
{     private:
            int bin[4];
      public:
```

```
            Binary();
            void get_data();
            void show_data();
            Binary & operator++();
            Binary & operator--();
            Binary & operator~();
};
Binary :: Binary()
{     for(int i=0;i<4;i++)
            bin[i] = 0;
}
void Binary :: get_data()
{     for(int i=0;i<4;i++)
            cin>>bin[i];
}
void Binary :: show_data()
{     for(int i=0;i<4;i++)
            cout<<bin[i];
}
Binary & Binary :: operator++()
{     int i, carry[4];
      for(i=0;i<4;i++)
            carry[i] = 0;
      bin[0]++;
      i=0;
      while(1)
      {     if(bin[i]>=2)
            {     bin[i] = 0;
                  carry[i+1] = 1;
            }
            i++;
            bin[i] += carry[i];
            if(bin[i]<2)
                  break;
      }
      return *this;
}
Binary & Binary :: operator~()
{     for(int i=0;i<4;i++)
      {     if(bin[i]==0)
                  bin[i] = 1;
            else bin[i] = 0;
      }
      return *this;
}
Binary & Binary :: operator--()
{     int i, borrow[4];
      for(i=0;i<4;i++)
            borrow[i] = 0;
      bin[0]--;
      i=0;
      while(1)
      {     if(bin[i]<0)
            {     bin[i] = 1;
                  borrow[i+1] = 1;
            }
```

```
            i++;
            bin[i] -= borrow[i];
            if(bin[i]>0)
                break;
        }
        return *this;
}
main()
{       Binary B;
        cout<<"\n Enter the Binary Number : ";
        B.get_data();
        cout<<"\n Binary Number is : ";
        B.show_data();
        ++B;
        cout<<"\n After Incrementing : ";
        B.show_data();
        ~B;
        cout<<"\n After Negation : ";
        B.show_data();
        --B;
        cout<<"\n After Decrementing : ";
        B.show_data();
}
```

Programming Tip: Overloading does not change the precedence of the operator.

OUTPUT

```
Enter the Binary Number : 1101
Binary Number is : 1101
After Incrementing : 0011
After Negation : 1100
After Decrementing : 0100
```

Assignment Write the same program using the negate operator.

Program 11.6 Write a program to increment and decrement a fraction.

```
using namespace std;
#include<iostream>
#include<stdlib.h>
class Fraction
{       private:
            int num;
            int deno;
            void simplify();
            int GCD(int a, int b);
        public:
            void get_data()
            {   cout<<"\n Enter the numerator :";
                cin>>num;
                cout<<"\n Enter the denominator : ";
                cin>>deno;
                if(deno == 0)
                {     cout<<"\n Fraction Not Possible";
                      exit(1);
                }
            }
            void display_data()
            {    simplify();
```

```
                cout<<num<<" / "<<deno;
            }
            Fraction & operator++();
            Fraction & operator--();
};
void Fraction :: simplify(void)
{     cout<<"\n The Simplified fraction is : ";
      int common_divisor = GCD(num, deno);
      num /= common_divisor;
      deno /= common_divisor;
}
int Fraction :: GCD(int a, int b)
{     if(b == 0)
            return a;
      else
            return GCD(b, a%b);
}
Fraction & Fraction :: operator++()
{     num += deno;
      return *this;
}
Fraction & Fraction :: operator--()
{     num -= deno;
      return *this;
}
main()
{     Fraction f;
      f.get_data();
      cout<<"\n FRACTION IS : ";
      f.display_data();
      ++f;
      cout<<"\n AFTER INCREMENTING : ";
      f.display_data();
      --f;
      cout<<"\n AFTER DECREMENTING : ";
      f.display_data();
}
```

OUTPUT

```
Enter the numerator 3
Enter the denominator 5
FRACTION IS : 3 / 5
AFTER INCREMENTING : 8 / 5
AFTER DECREMENTING 3 / 5
```

Program 11.7 Write a program to find the next date using unary increment operator.

```
using namespace std;
#include<iostream>
class Date
{     private:
            int d,m,y;
      public:
```

```
		void get_data()
		{	cout<<"\n Enter the day, month and year : ";
			cin>>d>>m>>y;
		}
		void show_data()
		{	 cout<<d<<" - "<<m<<" - "<<y;		}
		Date & operator++();
};
Date & Date :: operator++()
{	d++;
	if(m==1 || m==3 || m==5 || m==7 || m==8 || m==10 || m==12)
	{	if(d>31)
		{	d=1;
			m++;
			if(m>12)
				m = 1, y++;
		}
	}
	else if(m==4 || m==6 || m==9 || m==11)
	{	if(d>30)
		{	d = 1;
			m++;
			if(m>12)
				m=1, y++;
		}
	}
	else
	{	if((y % 4 == 0 && y % 100 != 0) || (y % 400 == 0))
		{	if(d>29)
				d=1, m++;
		}
		else
		{	if(d>28)
				d=1, m++;
		}
	}
	return *this;
}
main()
{	Date D;
	D.get_data();
	cout<<"\n DATE IS : ";
		D.show_data();
		cout<<"\n THE NEXT DATE WILL BE : ";
		++D;
		D.show_data();
	}
```

Programming Tip: Write and debug a function and then change it to an operator overloaded. function.

OUTPUT

```
Enter the day, month and year : 8 7 2014
DATE IS : 8 - 7 - 2014
THE NEXT DATE WILL BE : 9 - 7 - 2014
```

11.6 OVERLOADING BINARY OPERATORS

Binary means two and binary operators mean operators that work with two opearnds. Like unary operators, binary operators such as `+`, `-`, `*`, `/`, `=`, `<`. `>`, `!`, `%`, `^`, `&&`, `||`, `<<`, and `>>` can also be overloaded. Binary operators are also overloaded either using member functions or friend functions. While the member function will be invoked using an object of the class and will accept one argument, the friend function, on the other hand, will accept two arguments.

The syntax of overloading a binary operator using a member function can be given as

```
return_type operator op(arg)
```

Here, `operator` is the keyword, `op` is the operator to be overloaded, and `arg` is the argument of any type that will be used in the function. While the first operand or the object which invokes the function, is taken implicitly, the other operand on the other hand, is passed explicitly. Therefore, the first operand's data members can be accessed directly without using the dot operator but the second object's data members must be accessed using the dot operator. For example, if `c1` and `c2` are objects of complex type, then overloaded `+` operator can be called `c3 = c1 + c2;` this is equivalent to `c3 = c1.operator+(c2);`

Note Binary operators must explicitly return a value. They might not attempt to change the original values of the arguments.

Similarly, the syntax to overload a binary operator using a friend function is

```
friendreturn_type operator op(arg1, arg2)
```

Here, `arg1` and `arg2` are arguments of any type. However, one of them must compulsorily be of the class type. When the binary `+` operator is overloaded in class complex using friend function, then it will be invoked as `c3 = c1 + c2;` which is equivalent to writing `c3 = operator+(c1, c2);`

Note There is no restriction on the return type of a binary operator overloaded function.

Operators such as `=`, `()`, `[]`, and `->` cannot be overloaded using friend functions.

Program 11.8 Write a program to add two arrays using classes and operator overloading.

Programming Tip: Operator overloaded function can be invoked only by an object of the class.

```
using namespace std;
#include<iostream>
class Array
{       private:
                int arr[10];
                int size;
        public:
                Array();
                Array(int);
        void show_data();
        Array operator+(Array &);
};
Array :: Array()
{       for(int i=0;i<10;i++)
                arr[i] = 0;
        size = 0;
}
Array :: Array(int n)
{       size = n;
```

```
        cout<<"\n Enter the array elements ";
        for(int i=0;i<size;i++)
            cin>>arr[i];
}
void Array :: show_data()
{       for(int i=0;i<size;i++)
            cout<<" "<<arr[i];
}
Array Array :: operator+(Array &A)
{       Array Temp;
        Temp.size = size;
        for(int i=0;i<size;i++)
            Temp.arr[i] = arr[i] + A.arr[i];
        return Temp;
}
main()
{       int n;
        cout<<"\n Enter the size of the arrays : ";
        cin>>n;
        Array A1(n), A2(n), A3;
            A3 = A1 + A2;
            cout<<"\n The resultant array is ";
            A3.show_data();
        }
```

Programming Tip: new and delete operators are overloaded using static member functions.

OUTPUT

```
Enter the size of the arrays : 5
Enter the array elements 1 2 3 4 5
Enter the array elements 6 7 8 9 10
The resultant array is 7 9 11 13 15
```

Program 11.9 Write a program to add two arrays using `friend` function and operator overloading.

```
using namespace std;
#include<iostream>
class Array
{   private:
        int arr[10];
        int size;
    public:
        Array();
        Array(int);
        void show_data();
        friend Array operator+(Array, Array);
};
Array :: Array()
{   for(int i=0;i<10;i++)
        arr[i] = 0;
    size = 0;
}
Array :: Array(int n)
{       size = n;
    cout<<"\n Enter the array elements ";
    for(int i=0;i<size;i++)
```

```
        cin>>arr[i];
}
void Array :: show_data()
{   for(int i=0;i<size;i++)
        cout<<"  "<<arr[i];
}
Array operator+(Array A1, Array A2)
{   Array Temp;
    Temp.size = A1.size;
    for(int i=0;i<Temp.size;i++)
        Temp.arr[i] = A1.arr[i] + A2.arr[i];
    return Temp;
}
main()
{   int n;
    cout<<"\n Enter the size of the arrays : ";
    cin>>n;
    Array A1(n), A2(n), A3;
    A3 = A1 + A2;
    cout<<"\n The resultant array is ";
    A3.show_data();
}
```

OUTPUT

```
Enter the size of the arrays : 5
Enter the array elements 1 2 3 4 5
Enter the array elements 6 7 8 9 10
The resultant array is 7 9 11 13 15
```

Program 11.10 Write a program to subtract two matrices.

```
using namespace std;
#include<iostream>
class Matrix
{     private:
           int r, c;
           int mat[3][3];
      public:
           Matrix();
           Matrix(int rows, int cols);
           void show_data();
           void get_data();
           Matrix operator-(Matrix &);
};
Matrix :: Matrix()
{     r = c = 0;
}
Matrix :: Matrix(int rows, int cols)
{     r = rows, c = cols;
}
void Matrix :: get_data()
{     cout<<"\n Enter the matrix : ";
      for(int i=0;i<r;i++)
      {     for(int j=0;j<c;j++)
```

Programming Tip: A member function takes one argument less than the friend function.

```
                cin>>mat[i][j];
            }
        }
        void Matrix :: show_data()
        {     for(int i=0;i<r;i++)
              {     cout<<"\n";
                   for(int j=0;j<c;j++)
                        cout<<" "<<mat[i][j];
              }
}
Matrix Matrix :: operator-(Matrix &M)
{     Matrix Temp(r, c);
      for(int i=0;i<r;i++)
      {     for(int j=0;j<c;j++)
                 Temp.mat[i][j] = mat[i][j] - M.mat[i][j];
      }
      return Temp;
}
main()
{     Matrix M1(2,2), M2(2,2), M3;
      M1.get_data();
      M2.get_data();
      M3 = M1 - M2;
      cout<<"\n The resultant Matrix is : ";
      M3.show_data();
}
```

OUTPUT

```
Enter the matrix : 9 7 5 3
Enter the matrix : 7 5 1 2
The resultant Matrix is :
2 2
4 1
```

Assignment Write the same program to check if the size of matrix is same before performing any operation.

Program 11.11 Write a program to add and subtract two distances.

```
using namespace std;
#include<iostream>
class Distance
{     private:
           int kms, m;
      public:
           Distance()
           {     kms = m = 0;     }
           void get_data()
           {     cin>>kms>>m;     }
           void show_data()
           {     cout<<kms<<"kms "<<m<<" mtrs";     }
           Distance operator+(Distance &D)
           {     Distance Temp;
                Temp.m = m + D.m;
                if(Temp.m>=1000)
                {     Temp.kms++;
                     Temp.m -= 1000;
                }
```

```
                Temp.kms += kms + D.kms;
                return Temp;
            }
            Distance operator-(Distance &D)
            {      Distance Temp;
                   Temp.m = m - D.m;
                   Temp.kms = kms - D.kms;
                   if(Temp.m<0)
                   {     Temp.m+=1000;
                         Temp.kms-=1;
                   }
                   return Temp;
            }
};
main()
{      Distance D1, D2, D3, D4;
       cout<<"\n ENter the first distance : ";
       D1.get_data();
       cout<<"\n ENter the second distance : ";
       D2.get_data();
       cout<<"\n ENter the third distance : ";
       D3.get_data();
       D4 = D1 + D3 - D2;
       cout<<"\n D1 + D3 - D2 = ";
       D4.show_data();
}
```

Programming Tip: Binary operators must return an object of the class.

OUTPUT

```
ENter the first distance : 6 700
ENter the second distance : 4 900
ENter the third distance : 8 200
D1 + D3 - D2 = 10 kms
```

Program 11.12 Write a program to add, subtract, and check for equality of two fractions.

```
using namespace std;
#include<iostream>
class Fraction
{      private:
            int num, deno;
            void simplify();
            int GCD(int a, int b);
       public:
            Fraction()
            {      num = deno = 0;      }
            void get_data()
            {      cin>>num>>deno;
            }
            void show_data()
            {      simplify();
                   cout<<num<<" / "<<deno;
            }
            Fraction operator+(Fraction &);
            Fraction operator-(Fraction &);
```

```
          Fraction operator*(Fraction &);
          Fraction operator/(Fraction &);
          int operator==(Fraction &F);
          int operator>(Fraction &F);
};
void Fraction :: simplify(void)
{     int common_divisor = GCD(num, deno);
      num /= common_divisor;
      deno /= common_divisor;
}
int Fraction :: GCD(int a, int b)
{     if(b == 0)
          return a;
      else
          return GCD(b, a%b);
}
Fraction Fraction :: operator+(Fraction &F)
{     Fraction Temp;
      Temp.num = num * F.deno + F.num * deno;
      Temp.deno = deno * F.deno;
      return Temp;
}
Fraction Fraction :: operator-(Fraction &F)
{     Fraction Temp;
      Temp.num = num * F.deno - F.num * deno;
      Temp.deno = deno * F.deno;
      return Temp;
}
Fraction Fraction :: operator*(Fraction &F)
{     Fraction Temp;
      Temp.num = num * F.num;
      Temp.deno = deno * F.deno;
      return Temp;
}
Fraction Fraction :: operator/(Fraction &F)
{     Fraction Temp;
      Temp.num = num * F.deno;
      Temp.deno = deno * F.num;
      return Temp;
}
int Fraction :: operator==(Fraction &F)
{     int n = num * F.deno;
              int d = F.num * deno;
              if (n==d)
                  return 1;
              else
                  return 0;
          }
          int Fraction :: operator>(Fraction &F)
          {     int n = num * F.deno;
                int d = F.num * deno;
                if (n>d)
                    return 1;
                else
```

Programming Tip: Binary operator overloaded function must not change the data of the objects invoking that function.

```
        return 0;
}
main()
{     Fraction F1, F2, F3;
      cout<<"\n Enter the first fraction : ";
      F1.get_data();
      cout<<"\n Enter the second fraction : ";
      F2.get_data();
      F3 = F1 + F2;
      cout<<"\n ADDITION = ";
      F3.show_data();
      F3 = F1 - F2;
      cout<<"\n SUBTRACTION = ";
      F3.show_data();
      F3 = F1 * F2;
      cout<<"\n MULTIPLICATION = ";
      F3.show_data();
      F3 = F1 / F2;
      cout<<"\n DIVISION = ";
      F3.show_data();
      if(F1 == F2)
           cout<<"\n EQUAL FRACTIONS";
      else if (F1>F2)
           cout<<"\n F1 is greater than F2";
      else cout<<"F1 is less than F2";
}
```

OUTPUT

```
Enter the first fraction : 3 5
Enter the second fraction : 4 7
ADDITION = 41 / 45
SUBTRACTION = 1 / 35
MULTIPLICATION = 12 / 35
DIVISION = 21 / 20
F1 is greater than F2
```

Program 11.13 Write a program to add, subtract, multiply, and divide two complex numbers.

```
using namespace std;
#include<iostream>
class Complex
{     private:
           int real,imag;
      public:
           Complex()
           {     real = imag = 0;        }
           void get_data()
           {      cin>>real>>imag;     }
           void show_data()
           {     if(imag<0)
                  cout<<real<<" "<<imag<<" i";
                  else
                  cout<<real<<" + "<<imag<<"i";     }
           Complex operator+(Complex &);
```

```
            Complex operator-(Complex &);
            Complex operator*(Complex &);
            Complex operator/(Complex &);
};
Complex Complex :: operator+(Complex &C)
{      Complex Temp;
       Temp.real = real + C.real;
       Temp.imag = imag + C.imag;
       return Temp;
}
Complex Complex :: operator-(Complex &C)
{      Complex Temp;
       Temp.real = real - C.real;
       Temp.imag = imag - C.imag;
       return Temp;
}
Complex Complex :: operator*(Complex &C)
{      Complex Temp;
       Temp.real = real * C.real - imag * C.imag;
       Temp.imag = real * C.imag + imag * C.real;
       return Temp;
}
Complex Complex :: operator/(Complex &C)
{      Complex Temp;
       float deno;
       deno = C.real * C.real + C.imag *C.imag;
       Temp.real = (real * C.real + imag * C.imag)/deno;
       Temp.imag = (imag*C.real - real * C.imag)/deno;
       return Temp;
}
int main()
{      Complex C1, C2, C3, C4;
       cout<<"\n Enter the first complex number : ";
       C1.get_data();
       cout<<"\n Enter the second complex number : ";
       C2.get_data();
       cout<<"\n Enter the third complex number : ";
       C3.get_data();
       C4 = (C1 * C3);
       C4 = C4 + C2;
       C4 = C4/C1;
       cout<<"\n RESULT : ";
       C4.show_data();
}
```

OUTPUT

```
Enter the first complex number : 8 4
Enter the second complex number : 7 9
Enter the third complex number : 8 3
RESULT 9 + 3i
```

Program 11.14 Write a program to overload binary +, −, =, and > operators for binary numbers.

```
using namespace std;
#include<iostream>
class Binary
{      private:
```

```
        int num[5];
    public:
        Binary();
        void get_data();
        void show_data();
        Binary operator+(Binary &);
        Binary operator-(Binary &);
        int operator!=(Binary &);
};
Binary :: Binary()
{   for(int i=0;i<4;i++)
        num[i] = 0;
}
void Binary :: get_data()
{   cout<<"\n Enter a four digit binary number : ";
    for(int i=0;i<4;i++)
        cin>>num[i];
}
void Binary :: show_data()
{   for(int i=0;i<4;i++)
        cout<<num[i];
}
Binary Binary :: operator+(Binary &B)
{   Binary Temp;
    int carry[5] = {0};
    for(int i=0;i<4;i++)
    {   if(num[i] == 0 && B.num[i] == 0)
            Temp.num[i] = 0;
        else if(num[i] == 0 && B.num[i] == 1)
            Temp.num[i] = 1;
        else if(num[i] == 1 && B.num[i] == 0)
            Temp.num[i] = 1;
        else if(num[i] == 1 && B.num[i] == 1)
        {   Temp.num[i] = 0;
            carry[i+1] = 1;
        }
        Temp.num[i] +=carry[i];
        if(Temp.num[i]==2)
        {   Temp.num[i] = 0;
            carry[i+1] = 1;
        }
    }
    return Temp;
}
Binary Binary :: operator-(Binary &B)
{   Binary Temp;
    int borrow[5] = {0};
    for(int i=0;i<4;i++)
    {   Temp.num[i] = num[i] - B.num[i] - borrow[i];
        while(Temp.num[i]<0)
        {   Temp.num[i] += 2;
            Temp.num[i] -= borrow[i];
            borrow[i+1] = 1;
        }
    }
    return Temp;
```

```
}
int Binary :: operator!=(Binary &B)
{     int i;
      for(i=0;i<4;i++)
      {     if(num[i]!=B.num[i])
                  break;
      }
      if(i==4)
            return 0;
      else
            return 1;
}
main()
{     Binary B1;
      B1.get_data();
      Binary B2;
      B2.get_data();
      Binary B3;
      B3 = B1 + B2;
      cout<<"\n SUM OF TWO BINARY NUMBERS = ";
      B3.show_data();
      B3 = B1 - B2;
      cout<<"\n DIFFERENCE BETWEEN TWO BINARY NUMBERS = ";
      B3.show_data();
      if(B1 != B2)
            cout<<"\n The Binary Numbers ARe Not Equal";
      else
            cout<<"\n The Binary Numbers ARe Equal";
}
```

OUTPUT

```
Enter a four digit binary number : 0 0 1 0
Enter a four digit binary number : 1 1 0 0
SUM OF TWO BINARY NUMVERS = 1 1 0 1
DIFFERENCE BETWEEN TWO BINARY NUMVERS = 1 0 0 0
The Binary Numbers Are Equal
```

Program 11.15 Write a program to overload +=, ==, and > operators on Strings.

```
using namespace std;
#include<iostream>
#include<string.h>
class String
{     private:
            char * str;
            int len;
      public:
            String()
            {     len = 0;
                  str = NULL;
            }
            String(char *s)
            {     len = strlen(s);
                  str = new char[len+1];
                  strcpy(str, s);
            }
            void show_data()
```

```
        {     cout<<str;     }
        String & operator+=(String &s);
        int operator==(String &s);
        int operator>(String &s);
};
String & String :: operator+=(String &S)
{     len += strlen(S.str) + 1;
      strcat(str, S.str);
      return *this;
}
int String :: operator==(String &S)
{     if(strcmp(str, S.str)==0)
          return 1;
      else return 0;
}
int String :: operator>(String &S)
{     if(strcmp(str, S.str)>0)
          return 1;
      else return 0;
}
main()
{     char s[10];
      String S1("Hello");
      cout<<"\n Enter a string : ";
      cin>>s;
      String S2(s);
      if(S1==S2)
          cout<<"\n EQUAL STRINGS";
      if(S1>S2)
          cout<<"\n FIRST STRING IS GREATER THAN SECOND";
      else
          cout<<"\n SECOND STRING IS GREATER THAN FIRST";
      S1 += S2;
      cout<<"\n AFTER CONCATENATION : ";
      S1.show_data();
}
```

OUTPUT

```
Enter a string : World
SECOND STRING IS GREATER THAN FIRST
AFTER CONCATENATION: HelloWorld
```

11.7 OVERLOADING SPECIAL OPERATORS

In this section, we will discuss about overloading some special operators such as `<<`, `>>`, `[]`, `()`, `->`, `new`, and `delete`. Before we discuss overloading of these operators, let us quickly revise their functions.

`new`—to dynamically allocate memory

`delete`—to free the memory allocated dynamically

`<<`—to display a message

`>>`—to accept input from users

`[]` and `()`—are subscript operators

`->`—to access a class member

11.7.1 Overloading New and Delete Operators

C++ allows programmers to overload the `new` and `delete` operators because of the following reasons:

- To allow users to allocate memory in a customized way.
- To allow users to debug the program and keep track of memory allocation and deallocation in their programs.
- To allow users to perform additional operations while allocating or deallocating memory.

The syntax for overloading the `new` operator can be given as follows:

```
void* operator new(size_t size);
```

The overloaded new operator receives a parameter `size` of type `size_t`, which specifies the number of bytes of memory to be allocated.

The return type of the overloaded new must be `void*`. The overloaded function returns a pointer to the beginning of the block of memory allocated.

Similarly, the syntax for the overloaded `delete` operator can be given as

```
void operator delete(void*);
```

The function receives a parameter `ptr` of type `void*` which has to be deleted. Note that the function should not return anything.

Note that both of these overloaded `new` and `delete` operator functions are `static` members by default. Therefore, they do not have access to the `this` pointer.

Note To delete an array of objects, the operator `delete[]` must be overloaded.

The program code given here demonstrates the use of overloaded `new` and `delete` operators.

Example 11.6 Overloading `new` and `delete` operators

```
using namespace std;
#include<iostream>
class Array
{   private:
        int *arr;
    public:
        void * operator new(size_t size)
        {    void *parr = ::new int[size];  // dynamicallyallocatingspaceusingoverloadednewoperator
             return parr;
             }
             void operator delete(void *parr)
             {     ::delete parr;   } // dynamicallyde-allocatingspaceusingoverloadeddeleteoperator
                void get_data();
                void show_data();
};
void Array :: get_data()
{   cout<<"\n Enter the elements : ";
   for(int i=0;i<5;i++)
         cin>>arr[i];
}
void Array :: show_data()
{   cout<<"\n The array is : ";
```

```
    for(int i=0;i<5;i++)
            cout<<" "<<arr[i];
}
main()
{      Array *A = new Array;    // calls the overloaded new operator
      A->get_data();
      A->show_data();
      delete A;             // calls the overloaded delete operator
}
```

OUTPUT

```
Enter the elements : 1 2 3 4 5
The array is : 1 2 3 4 5
```

In the program, `::new` and `::delete` refer to the global `new and delete operators provided` by the C++ library.

Advantages of Overloading

- The overloaded new operator function can accept arguments; therefore, a class can have multiple overloaded new operator functions. This gives the programmer more flexibility in customizing memory allocation for objects. For example,

```
void * operator new(size_t size, char c)
{      void *ptr;
       ptr = malloc(size);
       if(ptr != NULL)
              *ptr = c;
       return ptr;
}
main()
{      char *ch = new('#') char;
}
```

Programming Tip: The return type of the overloaded new must be void*.

This code will not only allocate memory for a single character but will also initialize the allocated memory with the #character.

- The overloaded new operator also enables programmers to squeeze some extra performance out of their programs. For example, in a class, to speed up the allocation of new nodes, a list of deleted nodes is maintained so that their memory can be reused when new nodes are allocated. In this case, the overloaded `delete` operator will add nodes to the list of deleted nodes and the overloaded new operator will allocate memory from this list rather than from the heap to speedup memory allocation. The global `new` operator can be used only when the list of deleted nodes is empty.
- Overloaded `new` or `delete` operators also provide garbage collection for class's objects.
- Programmers can add exception handling routine in the overloaded `new` operator function.
- Programmers can use C++ memory allocation functions such as `malloc()` and `realloc()` to allocate and re-allocate memory dynamically. For example, the function codes given here allocate, re-allocate, and free memory dynamically.

```
void * operator new(size_t size)
{      void *ptr = malloc(size);
       if(ptr == NULL)
```

```
        {     cout<<"\n Memory could not be allocated";
                exit(1);
        }
        else return *ptr;
}
void * realloc(void * ptr, size_t size);
void operator delete(void * ptr)
{       free(ptr);
}
```

The `realloc()` is used to change the size of the allocated block at address `ptr` with the size. The address pointed to by `ptr` may change if the block is shifted to another location in memory. This can happen when size bytes are not available in the previous allocated space. For example, if `10` bytes were allocated and now the user has called `realloc()` to allocate `20` bytes, then the address pointed by `ptr` may change to point at the address where `20` bytes are available contiguously. The `realloc()` returns the new value of `ptr`. However, if `realloc()` fails, it returns `NULL` and does not free the original memory. Therefore, when using `realloc()`, you must save the previous pointer value.

Note While a user can have any number of overloaded new operators, there can be only one overloaded `delete` operator. `delete` is different from `delete[]`.

11.7.2 Overloading Subscript Operators [ ] and ( )

The subscript operator—`[]`—is used to access array elements and can be overloaded to enhance its functionality with classes. The syntax of overloading the subscript operator can be given as follows:

```
Identifier[expression]
```

where `identifier` is the object of the class. The syntax is interpreted as

```
identifier.operator[](expression)
```

From the syntax, it is clear that the subscript operator is a binary operator in which the first operator is an object of the class and the second operand is an integer index.

Note The overloaded operator [ ] ( ) must be defined as a non-static member function of a class.

Example 11.7 Overloading `[]` operator

```
using namespace std;
#include<iostream>
class Array
{     private:
            int arr[10];
      public:
            Array();
            void get_data();
            void show_data();
            int & operator[](int i);
};
Array :: Array()
{     for(int i=0;i<10;i++)
```

```
            arr[i] = 0;
}
void Array :: get_data()
{       cout<<"\n Enter the array elements : ";
        for(int i=0;i<10;i++)
                cin>>arr[i];
}
void Array :: show_data()
{       cout<<"\n The Array is : ";
       for(int i=0;i<10;i++)
            cout<<" "<<arr[i];
}
int& Array :: operator[](int i)
{       return arr[i];      //returns value at specified index
}
main()
{       Array A;    //create object
        A.get_data();    //invokes member function
        A.show_data();
        cout<<"\n Modified Array Elements Are : ";
        for(int i=0;i<10;i++)
            cout<<" "<<A[i] * 2; //invokes overloaded [] operator
}
```

Programming Tip: Overloaded new operators speed up the memory allocation process.

OUTPUT

```
Enter the array elements : 1 2 3 4 5 6 7 8 9 10
The Array is : 1 2 3 4 5 6 7 8 9 10
Modified Array Elements Are : 2 4 6 8 10 12 14 16 18 20
```

The overloaded subscript operator given here is a very simple one that returns the element at the specified index. You can enhance the function code to check for array bounds by writing,

```
int & Array :: operator[](int i)
{       if(i<0 || i>9)    //checking for valid indexes
     {      cout<<"\n Array index out of bounds";
            exit(1);
    }
     else
            return arr[i];
}
```

You can have another version of the overloaded subscript operator function as,

```
const int & Array :: operator[](int i) const
{       return arr[i];
}
```

The `const` version of the subscript operator is called when its object itself is `const`.

Note The overloaded subscript operator function must return a value by reference.

Overloading Subscript Operator () rather than []

When there are multiple subscripts, it is better to overload the `operator()` rather than `operator[]`. This is because the `operator[]` always takes exactly one parameter, but `operator()` can take any number of parameters. Let us consider a small piece of code to learn how `operator()` is overloaded for a two-dimensional matrix.

Example 11.8 Overloading`()` for a two-dimensional matrix

```
using namespace std;
#include<iostream>
#include<stdlib.h>
class Matrix
{     private:
          int arr[2][2];
      public:
          Matrix();
          void get_data();
          void show_data();
          int& operator()(int i, int j); //()operator overloaded function declaration
};
Matrix :: Matrix()
{     for(int i=0;i<2;i++)
          for(int j=0;j<2;j++)
              arr[i][j] = 0;
}
void Matrix :: get_data()
{     cout<<"\n Enter the Matrix elements : ";
      for(int i=0;i<2;i++)
          for(int j=0;j<2;j++)
              cin>>arr[i][j];
}
void Matrix :: show_data()
{     cout<<"\n The Matrix is : ";
      for(int i=0;i<2;i++)
      {    cout<<"\n";
           for(int j=0;j<2;j++)
            cout<<" "<<arr[i][j];
      }
}
int & Matrix :: operator()(int i, int j) // overloaded () operator
{    if(i<0 || i>9 || j<0 || j>9)
     {          cout<<"\n Matrix index out of bounds";
                exit(1);
     }
          else
          return arr[i][j];
}
main()
{     Matrix M;
      M.get_data();
```

```
        M.show_data();
        cout<<"\n Modified Matrix Elements Are : ";
        for(int i=0;i<2;i++)
        {     for(int j=0; j<2;j++)
                 cout<<" "<<M(i,j)*2;    //invoking overloaded operator function
        }
}
```

OUTPUT

```
Enter the Matrix elements : 1 2 3 4
The Matrix is :
1 2
3 4
Modified Matrix Elements Are : 2 4 6 8
```

11.7.3 Overloading Class Member Access Operator (->)

C++ allows programmers to control class member access by overloading the member access operator (`->`). The -> operator is a unary operator as it takes only one operand, that is the object of the class. The syntax for overloading the -> operator can be given as,

```
class_ptr *operator->()
```

where `class_ptr` is a pointer of class type. Before overloading the class member access operator, the overloaded -> operator function must be a non-static member function of the class. The program given here demonstrates the functionality of overloaded member access operator.

Example 11.9 Overloading -> operator

```
using namespace std;
#include<iostream>
class Sample
{     public:
          int num;
          Sample(int n)
          {   num = n;   }
          Sample * operator->(void)    //overloaded operator ->function
          {   return this;    }
};
main()
{     Sample *ptr = new Sample(10);
      cout<<"\n Number = "<<ptr->num;    // using normal object pointer
      Sample S(20);
      cout<<"\n Number = "<<S->num;    //using overloaded -> operator
}
```

OUTPUT

```
Number = 10
Number = 20
```

Explanation: In the program, `ptr` is an object pointer and S is an object of class sample. The class member access operator has been overloaded to return a pointer to the invoking object. Therefore, the statement, `s->num` is equivalent to writing `this->num`.

11.7.4 Overloading Input and Output Operators

C++ allows input and output of built-in data types using the stream extraction operator `>>` and the stream insertion operator `<<`. The capabilities of these operators can be extended to perform input and output for user-defined types. However, before overloading the extraction and insertion operators, you must know the following aspects:

- `cin` and `cout` are defined in class `iostream`.
- While `cin` is an object of `istream` class, `cout` is an object of the `ostream` class. We will read more on the relationship between `istream, ostream, iostream, cin,` and `cout` later in chapter File Handling.
- The insertion and extraction of operators will be overloaded by using a friend function because we need to call these functions without any object.
- The insertion and extraction operators must return the value of the left operand—the `ostream` or `istream` object—so that multiple `<<` or `>>` operators may be used in the same statement. The syntax for overloading the `>>` function can be given as

Programming Tip: () operator is overloaded when there are multiple subscript values.

```
friend ostream & operator << (ostream & output , My_class&obj)
{   // code
}
```

Example 11.10 Overloading << and >> operators

```
using namespace std;
#include<iostream>
class Date
{     private:
            int dd, mm, yy;
    public:
        friend istream & operator >> (istream & input , Date &D)
        {     input>>D.dd>>D.mm>>D.yy;
              return input;
        }
        friend ostream & operator << (ostream & output , Date &D)
        {     cout<<D.dd<<" - "<<D.mm<<" - "<<D.yy;
              return output;
        }
};
main()
{     Date D;
      cout<<"\n Enter the Date : ";
      cin>>D;     //overloaded >> is invoked
      cout<<"\n DATE : ";
      cout<<D;    //overloaded << is invoked
}
```

OUTPUT

```
Enter the Date : 17 2 2007
DATE : 17 - 2 - 2007
```

Explanation: The input and output of the program shows that a class object can be input and output in the same way as is done for a variable of basic data type.

11.8 TYPE CONVERSIONS

In Chapter 2, we have seen that when constants and variables of different basic data types are mixed together in a single expression, automatic type conversions takes place. Since C++ treats user-defined data types same as built-in types, it should also allow expressions consisting of mixed user-defined and basic data types. However, the main problem in user-defined types is that the compiler has no idea about the user-defined data types and about their conversion to other data types.

Therefore, to overcome this problem, programmers must specifically design routines that convert basic data types to user-defined data types or vice versa. With regard to data conversion, there can be three possibilities as given in Fig. 11.1. These are as follows:

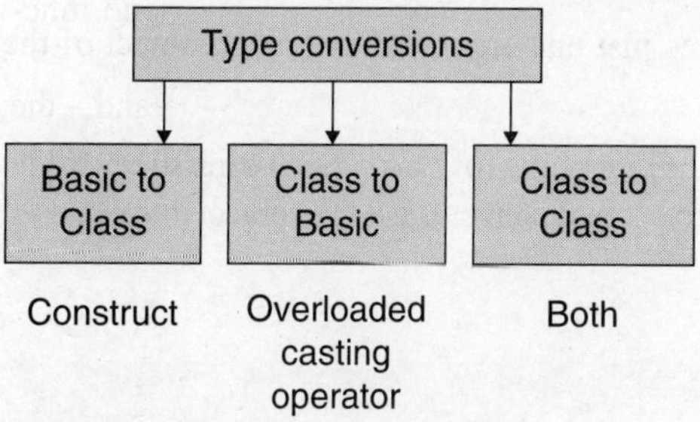

Figure 11.1 Type conversions

- Conversion from basic data type to class type
- Conversion from class type to basic data type
- Conversion from one class type to another class type

11.8.1 Conversion from Basic to Class Type

A variable of basic data type is converted into a data member of a user-defined class with the help of a constructor function defined in the class as had been the practice so far. This is given in Fig. 11.2. For example, when we used to write

```
String(char *s)
{     strcpy(str, s);
}
```

> **Programming Tip:** Overloaded -> operator function must be a non-static member function of the class.

We are building the string object from the basic data type of char.

Figure 11.2 Conversion from basic to class type

From the `main()`, we invoke the constructor by writing,

```
String S1 = name; or
String S1(name);
```

In both the cases, the object of the class must appear on the left.

For example, String S1 = “Hello”;

Or, String S1(“Hello”);

11.8.2 Conversion from Class to Basic Data Type

A user-defined class type can be converted into a basic type using the overloaded casting operator as shown in Fig. 11.3.

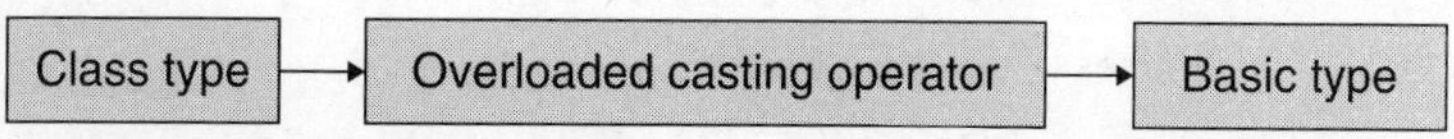

Figure 11.3 Conversion from Class type to basic data type

The syntax of an overloaded casting operator can be given as follows:

```
operator type_name()
{     -----
```

```
    FUNCTION BODY
    ------
}
```

While defining the overloaded casting operator, the following aspects must be adhered to:

- The function can be declared and/or defined within the class.
- The function converts the class type into the `type_name`. For example, operator `int()` will convert a class type to `int`.
- The function does not have any return type.
- The function does not take any argument.
- The casting operator is a unary operator that takes just one argument that is the object of the class that invokes this function.

Let us consider a small program that converts minutes `(int)` into time (of `class Type`) consisting of data members in `hrs` and `mins`. The program also does the reverse job of converting a `Time` object into `minutes`.

Example 11.11 Converting basic data type to class type

```
using namespace std;
#include<iostream>
class Time
{     private:
             int h, m;
   public:
         Time()
         {   h = m = 0;    }
         Time(int t)   // converting int to class
         {   h = t / 60;
             m = t % 60;
         }
         void get_data()
         {   cin>>h>>m;  }
         void show_data()
         {   cout<<h<<" hrs"<<m<<" mins";    }
         operator int()     //converting class to int
         {   int t = h*60 + m;
             return t;
         }
};
main()
{    int min;
     cout<<"\n Enter the minutes : ";
     cin>>min;
     Time T1;
     T1 = min;             //constructor called
     T1.show_data();
     cout<<"\n Enter the number of hrs and mins : ";
     T1.get_data();
     min = T1;      //casting operator called
```

```
    cout<<"\n Total Minutes = "<<min;
}
```

OUTPUT

```
Enter the minutes : 135
2 hrs 15 mins
Enter the number of hrs and mins : 3 40
Total Minutes = 400
```

Explanation:

- The constructor is invoked when we had written `T1 = min;` in the constructor function `min` is used to construct the class object. The same constructor function could have also been invoked by writing Time `T1(min);`
- The casting operator is invoked by writing `min = T1`. The same function could have also been invoked by writing `min = int(T1);`

Program 11.16 Write a program to demonstrate the use of type conversions with distance class.

```
using namespace std;
#include<iostream>
class Distance
{     private:
              int kms, m;
    public:
         Distance()
         {     kms = m = 0;     }
         Distance(int D)
         {     kms = D / 1000;
               m = D % 1000;
         }
         void get_data()
         {   cin>>kms>>m;   }
         void show_data()
         {   cout<<kms<<" kms"<<m<<" mts";   }
         operator int()
         {   int D = kms*1000 + m;
             return D;
         }
         operator float()
         {   float Distance_kms = kms + (float)m/1000;
             return Distance_kms;
         }
};
main()
{     int dist;
     cout<<"\n Enter the distance in metres : ";
     cin>>dist;
     Distance D1;
     D1 = dist;
     D1.show_data();
     cout<<"\n Enter the number of kms and metres : ";
     D1.get_data();
```

```
    dist = D1;
    cout<<"\n Total Metres = "<<dist;
    float k = D1;
    cout<<"\n Total KiloMetres = "<<k;
}
```

OUTPUT

```
Enter the distance in metres : 1234
1 kms 234 mts
Enter the number of kms and metres : 5 678
Total Metres = 5678
Total KiloMetres = 5.678
```

Program 11.17 Write a program to perform type conversions on the array class.

```
using namespace std;
#include<iostream>
class Array
{     private:
              int arr[10];
      public:
          Array();
          Array(int *a);
          void show_data();
          operator int();
          operator float();
};
Array :: Array()
{     for(int i=0;i<10;i++)
              arr[i] = 0;
}
Array :: Array(int *a)
{     for(int i=0;i<10;i++)
              arr[i] = a[i];
}
void Array :: show_data()
{     for(int i=0;i<10;i++)
          cout<<" "<<arr[i];
}
Array :: operator int()
{     int tot = 0;
      for(int i=0;i<10;i++)
            tot += arr[i];
      return tot;
}
Array :: operator float()
{     int tot = 0;
      for(int i=0;i<10;i++)
            tot += arr[i];
      return (float)(tot/10);
}
main()
{     int a[10];
      cout<<"\n Enter the 10 numbers : ";
      for(int i=0;i<10;i++)
            cin>>a[i];
```

```
    Array Arr(a);
    cout<<"\n Array Elements Are : ";
    Arr.show_data();
    int sum = Arr;
    cout<<"\n SUM of 10 numbers = "<<sum;
    float avg = Arr;
    cout<<"\n AVERAGE of 10 numbers = "<<avg;
}
```

OUTPUT

```
Enter the 10 numbers : 2 4 6 8 10 12 14 16 18 20
Array Elements Are : 2 4 6 8 10 12 14 16 18 20
SUM of 10 numbers = 110
AVERAGE of 10 numbers = 11
```

Program 11.18 Write a program to convert temperature from Celsius to Fahrenheit and vice versa using classes and type conversions concept.

```
using namespace std;
#include<iostream>
class Temperature
{     private:
            float temp_Far;
      public:
          Temperature()
          {   temp_Far = 0;   }
          void get_data()
          {   cout<<"\n Enter the Temperature in FAHRENHEIT : ";
              cin>>temp_Far;
          }
          Temperature(int c)
          {   temp_Far = (1.8 * c) + 32;   }
          void show_data()
          {   cout<<"\n TEMPERATURE IN FAHRENHEIT = "<<temp_Far;
          }
          operator float()
          {   return (float)((temp_Far - 32) / 1.8);   }
};
main()
{     Temperature T1;
      int Temp_Cel;
      cout<<"\n Enter the Temperature in Celsius : ";
      cin>>Temp_Cel;
      T1 = Temp_Cel;
      T1.show_data();
      Temperature T2;
      T2.get_data();
      float temp = T2;
      cout<<"\n T2 = "<<temp;
}
```

OUTPUT

```
Enter the Temperature in Celsius : 0
TEMPERATURE IN FAHRENHEIT = 32
```

```
Enter the Temperature in FAHRENHEIT : 273
T2 = 133.88
```

Program 11.19 Write a program to convert char* to string class and vice versa.

> **Programming Tip:** When performing conversion in the source class, a typecast operator is used.

```
using namespace std;
#include<iostream>
#include<string.h>
class String
{     private:
          char *str;
          int len;
      public:
          String()
          {   len = 0;
          }
          String(char *s)
{   len = strlen(s);
    str = new char[len+1];
    strcpy(str, s);
}
void get_data()
{   char s[20];
    cin.getline(s, 20);
    len = strlen(s);
    str = new char[len+1];
    strcpy(str, s);
}
void show_data()
{   cout<<str;   }
operator char*()
{   return str;   }
};
main()
{     String S1;
      char name[20];
      cout<<"\n Enter your name : ";
      cin.getline(name, 20);
      S1 = name;
      cout<<"\n NAME : ";
      S1.show_data();
      String S2;
      cout<<"\n Enter your designation : ";
      S2.get_data();
      char *desig;
      desig = S2;
      cout<<"\n DESIGNATION : "<<desig;
}
```

OUTPUT

```
Enter your name : DR. Shubha PARMAR
NAME : DR. Shubha PARMAR
Enter your designation : ASSOCIATE PROFESSOR
DESIGNATION : ASSOCIATE PROFESSOR
```

11.8.3 Conversion from Class to Class Type

Often, in real word modelling, there is a need to convert an object of one class into that of another. To perform this type of conversion, we write,

```
Obj_Dest = Obj_Source;
```

Here, `Obj_Source` is an object of the source class and `Obj_Dest` is an object of the destination class. The conversion can be implemented in two ways—either by using a constructor or a casting operator function. The choice of choosing one of the ways depends on where the conversion is being done, in the source class or in the destination class.

Conversion in the Source Class

When performing conversion in the source class, a `typecast` operator is used. The syntax of such an operator function can be given as

```
operator typename()
```

where `operator` is the keyword and `typename` may be a built-in or user-defined type. `Typename` usually refers to the destination type, and therefore, in this context, `typename` refers to the destination class. This means that in case of casting operator function, the conversion is done in the source class and the result is passed to the object of destination class.

Conversion in Destination Class

When performing conversion in the destination class, a single argument constructor is used. The argument is an object of the source class which is passed to the destination class for conversion.

The syntax for such a constructor function can be given as

```
Class1(Class2 Obj2)
{    ---------
     // Conversion Steps
     --------
};
```

Program 11.20 Write a program to convert a square into a rectangle. Perform the conversion in the destination class.

```
using namespace std;
#include<iostream>
class Rectangle;
class Square
{     private:
            int side;
      public:
            Square(int s)
          {   side = s;   }
            int get_side()
            {   return side;    }
};
class Rectangle
{     private:
            int length, breadth;
     public:
            Rectangle(int l, int b)
```

```
            {     length = l;
                  breadth = b;
            }
            Rectangle(Square S)
            {   int sqr_side = S.get_side();
                length = breadth = sqr_side;
            }
            void show_data()
            {   cout<<"\n Length = "<<length<<" and Breadth = "<<breadth;
            }
};
main()
{     Rectangle R(10, 20);
      R.show_data();
      Square S(50);
      R = S;
      R.show_data();
}
```

OUTPUT

```
Length = 10 and Breadth = 20
Length = 50 and Breadth = 50
```

Program 11.21 Write a program to convert a rectangle into a square. Perform the conversion in the source class.

> **Programming Tip:** When performing conversion in the destination class, a single argument constructor is used.

```
            using namespace std;
            #include<iostream>
            class Square;
            class Rectangle
            {     private:
                        int length, breadth;
                  public:
                        Rectangle()
                        {   length = breadth = 0;   }
                        Rectangle(int l, int b)
                        {   length = l;
                            breadth = b;
            }
            void show_data()
            {   cout<<"\n Length = "<<length<<" and Breadth = "<<breadth;
            }
};
class Square
{     private:
            int side;
      public:
            Square(int s)
            {   side = s;   }
            operator Rectangle()
            {   Rectangle R(side, side);;
                return R;
             }
};
```

```
main()
{     Rectangle R(10, 20);
          R.show_data();
          Square S(50);
          R = S;
          R.show_data();
}
```

OUTPUT

```
Length = 10 and Breadth = 20
Length = 50 and Breadth = 50
```

Program 11.22 Write a program to convert a distance specified in which distance is divided in two parts—m and kms. Convert the distance in metres. Note that metres is specified as a member of another class. Perform conversion in the source class.

```
using namespace std;
#include<iostream>
class Dist_m_kms;
class Dist_m
{    private:
            int metres;
     public:
         Dist_m()
         {  metres = 0;   }
            Dist_m(int m)
         {  metres = m;
         }
         void show_data()
         {   cout<<"\n Distance Covered = "<<metres<<"mts";
         }
};
class Dist_m_kms
{    private:
             int mts, kms;
     public:
          Dist_m_kms(int k, int m)
          {  kms = k;
             mts = m;   }
             operator Dist_m()
          {  int dist = kms * 1000 + mts;
             Dist_m DM(dist);
             return DM;
          }
          void show_Dist_kms_m()
          {   cout<<"\n Distance Travelled = "<<kms<<" and "<<mts;}
};
main()
{     Dist_m_kms Source_D(12, 200);
      Source_D.show_Dist_kms_m();
      Dist_m Dest_D;
      Dest_D = Source_D;
      Dest_D.show_data();
}
```

OUTPUT

```
Distance Travelled = 12 kms and 200mts
Distance Covered = 12200 mts
```

Program 11.23 Write a program to convert data of class student having members' roll number and marks in three subjects to another class student that stores just the roll number and the average. Perform conversion in the destination class.

```
using namespace std;
#include<iostream>
class Student_1;
class Student_2
{     private:
          int roll_no;
          int marks[3];
      public:
          void get_data();
          int get_rno(){   return roll_no;   }
          float get_avg();
};
void Student_2 :: get_data()
{     cout<<"\n Enter Roll Number : ";
      cin>>roll_no;
      cout<<"\n Enter marks in three subjects : ";
      for(int i=0;i<3;i++)
          cin>>marks[i];
}
float Student_2 :: get_avg()
{     int total = 0;
      for(int i=0;i<3;i++)
            total += marks[i];
     return (float)total/3;
}
class Student_1
{     private:
            int rno;
            float avg;
            char grade;
     public:
          Student_1()
          { rno = 0, avg = 0,   grade = ' ';   }
          Student_1(Student_2 S)
          {  rno = S.get_rno();
             avg = S.get_avg();
             if(avg>=60)
                    grade = 'A';
             else if(avg>=50 && avg<60)
                    grade = 'B';
             else if(avg>=40 && avg<30)
                    grade = 'C';
             else grade = 'D';
          }
          void show_data()
          {  cout<<"\n ROLL NUMBER : "<<rno;
             cout<<"\n AVERAGE : "<<avg;
```

```
            cout<<"\n GRADE : "<<grade;
        }
};
main()
{     Student_2 Source_Stud;
      Source_Stud.get_data();
      Student_1 Dest_Stud;
      Dest_Stud = Source_Stud;
      Dest_Stud.show_data();
}
```

OUTPUT

```
Enter Roll Number : 1234
Enter marks in three subjects : 56 67 78
ROLL NUMBER : 1234
AVERAGE : 67
GRADE : A
```

Program 11.24 Write a program to convert polar co-ordinates specified in one class into rectangular co-ordinates. Perform conversion in the source class.

```
using namespace std;
#include<iostream>
#include<math.h>
class Polar;
class Rectangular
{     private:
          double x;
          double y;
      public:
          Rectangular()
          {    x = y = 0;         }
          Rectangular(double xco, double yco)
          {    x = xco;
               y = yco;
          }
          void show_data()
          {    cout<<"\n X-coordinate = "<<x;
               cout<<"\n Y-coordinate = "<<y;
          }
};
class Polar
{     private:
          int radius;
          int angle;
      public:
          Polar(int r, int a)
          {    radius = r;
               angle = a;
          }
          operator Rectangular()
          {    double xco = radius * cos(angle);
               double yco = radius * sin(angle);
               return Rectangular(xco, yco);
```

```
        }
};
main()
{    Polar P(27, 1.567);
     Rectangular R;
     R = P;
     R.show_data();
}
```

OUTPUT

```
X-coordinate = 14.58
Y-coordinate = 22.71
```

Program 11.25 Assign int to `circle` object, assign `circle` object to `int`, and convert `circle` object into `line` object. Operator casting is done in source class `circle`.

```
using namespace std;
#include<iostream>
class Circle;
class Line{
private:
float length;
public:
Line() {length=0; }                //Default Constructor
Line(float l) { length=l; }        //Parameterized Constructor
void show() {cout<<"\nLength="<<length; }
};
class Circle{
private:
int radius;
public:
Circle() { radius=0; }                //Default Constructor
Circle(int r) { radius=r; }
//Parameterized Constructor - For Built-in type to class
void operator=(int r);             //declaration
operator int();             //For Class to Built-in type
operator Line();            //For class to class Conversion
void show() { cout<<"\nRadius="<<radius; }
};
void Circle::operator=(int r) {radius=r; }        // (I) primitive to class Conversion
  Circle::operator int() { return radius; }       // (II)class to primitive Conversion
  Circle::operator Line()          //(III) class to class Conversion
   {
   float l=2*3.14*radius; //Find Circumference
   Line temp(l);          //Create temporary line with length=c
   return temp;
   }
int main()
{
   Circle c;
   c=5;          //c.operator=(5);          I fn Called
   int a=c; // operator int()          II fn Called
   Line l=c; //operator Line()          III fn Called
   c.show(); l.show(); cout<<"\na="<<a;
}
```

```
OUTPUT
Radius=5
Length=31.5
a=5
```

Points to Remember

- Operator overloading is also a form of compile-time polymorphism.
- Operator overloading is syntactic sugar, as it enables the programmers to use notation closer to the target domain.
- Although C++ puts no restrictions on what should be the return type, ideally, overloaded operators should return an object of the class either by value or by reference.
- Operator overloading cannot change the operation performed by an operator.
- Unary operator will always be applied on one operand and binary operator will be applied on two operands.
- The subscript operator is a binary operator in which the first operator is an object of the class and the second operand is an integer index.
- The overloaded subscript operator function must return a value by reference.
- The casting operator is a unary operator that takes just one argument—object of the class that invokes this function.
- C++ allows programmers to control class member access by overloading the member access operator (->).
- The insertion and extraction operators will be overloaded by using a friend function because we need to call these functions without any object.
- A variable of basic data type is converted into a data member of a user-defined class with the help of a constructor function defined in the class
- A user-defined class type can be converted into a basic type using the overloaded casting operator

Glossary

Operator overloading The feature that enables C++ programmers to redefine the meaning of operators when they operate on class objects

Exercises

Fill in the Blanks

1. Operators can be redefined using ______ concepts.
2. Operator overloading is also a form of ______ polymorphism.
3. When the + operator is overloaded using member function, `obj1 + obj2` is equivalent to writing ______.
4. When the + operator is overloaded using a friend function, `obj1 + obj2` is equivalent to writing ______.
5. ______ and ______ operators are already overloaded in C++.
6. `obj2 = 10 + obj1;` is permissible only when implemented with ______ function.
7. When ~ operator is overloaded using a member function, then the function is invoked by ______.
8. Overloaded `new` and `delete` operators must be ______ members of the class.
9. `::new` is called ______.
10. Subscript operator is a ______ operator .
11. The overloaded subscript operator function must return a value by ______.
12. ______ is an object of `istream` class.
13. `cout` is defined in ______ class.
14. The casting operator is a ______ operator.
15. When type conversions is done in the source class ______ is used.

State True or False

1. Operator overloading extends the functionality of predefined operators.
2. Operator overloading implements the concept of polymorphism.

3. When operators are overloaded, we cannot have more than one operator in an expression.
4. It is mandatory for an operator-overloaded function to return an object.
5. Member selection operator can be overloaded.
6. You cannot change the order of evaluation of operators in an expression.
7. We can create new operators using the concepts of operator overloading.
8. Overloaded operators can have default arguments.
9. The friend function does not have access to the `this` pointer.
10. It is mandatory for binary operator overloaded function to return an object.
11. Programmers can use the C memory allocation functions in the overloaded new operator function.
12. ->operator is a binary operator.
13. The << and >> operators can be overloaded only by using a friend function.
14. The type casting function does not have any return type.
15. A member function is used to convert data from one class to another.
16. With operator overloading, class data can be converted into basic data type.

Multiple Choice Questions

1. Choose the operator which can be overloaded.
   (a) `::` (b) `.`
   (c) `.*` (d) None of these
2. Can operator overloading change the operation performed by an operator?
   (a) Yes
   (b) No
   (c) Conditionally
   (d) With restrictions
3. Which operator is not inherited by derived classes?
   (a) `=` (b) `.`
   (c) `.*` (d) `<<`
4. With member function implementation, unary operator takes how many explicit parameters?
   (a) 0 (b) 1
   (c) 2 (d) 3
5. With friend function implementation, binary operator takes how many explicit parameters?
   (a) 0 (b) 1
   (c) 2 (d) 3
6. Choose the binary operators which cannot be overloaded.
   (a) `->` (b) `>>=`
   (c) `[]` (d) None of these
7. Choose the binary operators which cannot be overloaded using friend function.
   (a) `=` (b) `()`
   (c) `[]` (d) All of these
8. The return type of the overloaded new must be
   (a) `int` (b) `int*`
   (c) `void*` (d) `void`
9. The return type of the overloaded delete must be
   (a) `Int` (b) `int*`
   (c) `void*` (d) `void`
10. A user can have how many overloaded new operator functions?
    (a) 0 (b) 1
    (c) 2 (d) n
11. A user can have how many overloaded delete operator functions?
    (a) 0 (b) 1
    (c) 2 (d) n
12. The second operand of the overloaded subscript operator function is
    (a) `Int` (b) `int*`
    (c) `void*` (d) `void`
13. In case of multiple subscripts, which operator is overloaded?
    (a) `{}` (b) `()`
    (c) `[]` (d) `<>`
14. How many arguments does a type casting operator function accept?
    (a) 0 (b) 1
    (c) 2 (d) N
15. When type conversions is performed in destination class, which among the following is used?
    (a) Typecast operator
    (b) Member function
    (c) Constructor
    (d) Data members

Review Questions

1. Define the term 'operator overloading' and explain its significance.
2. How does operator overloading support the concept of polymorphism?
3. Can we perform function overloading on operator overloaded operators? If yes, how?
4. What are the advantages of overloading the operators?
5. Explain the syntax of overloaded operator function defined as a class member function.

6. Give the syntax of overloaded operator function defined as a friend function.
7. List at least five operators that can be overloaded. Give the implementation of any one of them in detail.
8. List the operators that cannot be overloaded.
9. What advantage do we get when operator overloaded function returns an object?
10. What are the two techniques in which an operator can be overloaded?
11. Explain the syntax for unary operator overloading using a member function.
12. Give the syntax for unary operator overloading using a friend function.
13. Explain the syntax for overloading a binary operator using a member function.
14. Give the syntax for overloading a binary operator using a member function using a friend function.
15. Why do we need a different notation for overloading post-fix increment or decrement operators?
16. In an overloaded binary operator function, why does friend function take two objects and member function take just one object?
17. When is it necessary to use a friend function for operator overloading?
18. Give a few reasons to overload the new and delete operators.
19. Explain the syntax for overloading the new operator.
20. Explain the syntax and significance of overloading -> operator.
21. Can we overload << and >>operators by using a member function of the class? Justify your answer.
22. How can we convert a variable of basic data type into a class type and vice versa?
23. Explain the syntax of type casting operator.
24. How do we convert data from one class to another?

Programming Exercises

1. Write a program to demonstrate unary operator using a member function.
2. Write a program to demonstrate unary operator using a friend function.
3. Write a program to demonstrate binary operator using a member function.
4. Write a program to demonstrate binary operator using a friend function.
5. Write a menu-driven program to overload at least five unary operators on a point class using class member functions.
6. Write a menu-driven program to overload at least five unary operators on a distance class using class friend functions.
7. Write a menu-driven program to overload at least five unary operators on a time class.
8. Write a menu-driven program to overload at least five unary operators on a height class.
9. Write a menu-driven program to overload at least five unary operators on an array class.
10. Write a menu-driven program to overload at least five unary operators on a binary class.
11. Write a menu-driven program to overload at least five unary operators on a fraction class.
12. Write a menu-driven program to overload at least five unary operators on a date class.
13. Write a menu-driven program to overload +=, -=, *=, %= operators on the array class.
14. Write a menu-driven program to overload +=, -=, *=, /= operators on the matrix class.
15. Write a menu-driven program to overload +=, -=, ==, >=,<= operators on the distance class.
16. Write a menu-driven program to overload +=, -=, ==, >=, <= operators on the time class.
17. Write a menu-driven program to overload +=, -=, ==, >=, <= operators on the height class.
18. Write a menu-driven program to overload +=, -=, *=, /=, ==, >=, <= operators on the binary class.
19. Write a menu-driven program to overload +=, -=, *=, /=, ==, >=, <= operators on the complex class.
20. Write a menu-driven program to overload +=, -=, *=, /=, ==, >=, <= operators on the polynomial class.
21. Write a menu-driven program to overload +=, -=, *=, /=, ==, >=, <= operators on the fraction class.
22. Write a menu-driven program to overload +=, -=, *=, /=, ==, >=, <= operators on the complex class.
23. Write a menu-driven program to overload +=, -=, ==, >=, <= operators on the string class.
24. Write a program to demonstrate the use of overloaded [] operator.
25. Write a program to demonstrate the use of overloaded () operator.
26. Write a program to demonstrate the use of overloaded ->operator.
27. Write a program to demonstrate the use of overloaded <<and >>operators.

28. Write a program to convert minutes into class time with data members as hrs and mins.
29. Write a program to convert class time with data members in hrs and mins into minutes.
30. Write a menu-driven program that performs conversions to and from distance class to distance covered.
31. Write a menu-driven program that performs conversions to and from array class.
32. Write a menu-driven program that performs conversions to and from string class.
33. Write a menu-driven program that performs conversions from a square to rectangle class. Perform conversions in both sources as well as destination class.
34. Write a menu-driven program to convert distance specified using metres and kilometres in one class into distance specified in metres in another class. Perform conversion in both source as well destination class.
35. Write a program to convert polar co-ordinates specified in one class into rectangular co-ordinates. Perform conversion in the destination class.
36. Write a program to convert currency specified in Rupees in one class into dollars in another class.
37. Write a program to convert temperature specified in Celsius in one class into Fahrenheit in another class.
38. Write a program to implement a timer using increment operator overloading.
39. Write a program to convert miles into a class distance with data in kilometres.
40. Write a program to convert metres miles into a class distance with data in kilometres.

Find the errors in the following codes

1.
```
using namespace std;
#include<iostream>
class Count
{  int counter;
   public:
     Count()
     {  counter = 0;  }
     Count operator++()
     {  counter++;
        return Count(counter);
     }
};
main()
{  Count C;
   C++;
}
```

2.
```
using namespace std;
#include<iostream>
class Count
{  int counter;
   public:
     Count(int c)
     {  counter = c;  }
     int operator+(Count C1)
     {  Count temp(0);
        temp.counter = counter
        C1.counter;
        return counter;
     }
};
main()
{  Count C1(10), C2(5), C3(0);
   C3 = C1 + C2;
}
```

3.
```
using namespace std;
#include<iostream>
class Count
{  int counter;
   public:
     Count(int c)
     {  counter = c;  }
     void operator++()
     {  ++counter; }
};
int main()
{  Count C(10);
   C++;
   cout<<C.counter;
}
```

Find the output of the following codes

1.
```
using namespace std;
#include<iostream>
{
      int i;
      public:
        Integer(int ii)
        {       i = ii;
        }
        const Integer operator+(const
Integer &rv)const
        {
           cout<<"operator+";
           return Integer(i + rv.i);
        }
        Integer& operator+=(const Integer&
rv)
        {
           cout<<"operator+=";
```

```
            i += rv.i;
            return*this;
        }
    };
int main()
{
    int i =1, j =2, k =3;
    k += i + j;
    Integer ii(1), jj(2), kk(3);
    kk += ii + jj;
}
```

2.
```
using namespace std;
#include<iostream>
class Numbers
{
    private:
      int arr[10];
    public:
      int& operator[](const int n)
      {
        return arr[n];
      }
};
int main()
{
    Numbers N;
    N[5]=4;
    cout<< N[5];
}
```

3.
```
using namespace std;
#include<iostream>
const int MAX =4;
class safearray
{
    private:
        int arr[MAX];
    public:
    int & operator[](int n)
    {
        if(n == MAX - 1)
        {
          int temp;
          for(int i =0; i < MAX; i++)
           {
             if(arr[n +1]> arr[n])
              {
                temp = arr[n];
                arr[n]= arr[n +1];
                arr[n +1]= temp;
              }
           }
        }
        return arr[n];
    }
};
int main()
{
    safearray SArr;
    for(int j =0; j < MAX; j++)
    SArr[j]= j*10;
    for(int j =0; j < MAX; j++)
    {
      int temp = SArr[j];
      cout<<"Element "<< j <<" is "<< temp;
    }
}
```

4.
```
using namespace std;
#include<iostream>
class A
{
    public:
        int x;
        A(int n =0)
        {   x = n;   }
        int & operator[](int n)
        {
          cout<<"0";
          return x;
        }
        int operator[](int n)const
        {
          cout<<"1";
          return x;
        }
};
void foo(const A& a)
{
    int z = a[2];
}
int main()
{
    A a(7);
    a[3]=8;
    int z = a[2];
    foo(a);
}
```

5.
```
using namespace std;
#include<iostream>
const int MAX =10;
class safeArr
```

```
{
    private:
        int arr[MAX];
    public:
        safeArr()
        {
          register int i;
          for(i =0; i < MAX; i++)
          arr[i]= i;
        }
        int & operator[](int i)
        {
          if(i > SIZE)
          {
              cout<<"Index out of bounds";
              return arr[0];
          }
          return arr[i];
        }
};
int main()
{
safeArr A;
cout<< A[5];
cout<< A[12];
}
```

Answers

Fill in the Blanks

1. Operator overloading; **2.** Compile time; **3.** `obj1.add(oj2)`; **4.** `add(obj1, obj2)`; **5.** = and &; **6.** Friend; **7.** Object of the class; **8.** Non-static; **9.** Global new operator; **10.** Binary; **11.** Reference; **12.** `Cin`; **13.** `Ostream`; **14.** Unary; **15.** Typecast operator

State True or False

1. True	**2.** True	**3.** False	**4.** False	**5.** False	**6.** False	**7.** False	**8.** False
9. True	**10.** False	**11.** True	**12.** False	**13.** True	**14.** True	**15.** False	**16.** False

Multiple Choice Questions

1. (d); **2.** (b); **3.** (a); **4.** (a); **5.** (c); **6.** (d); **7.** (d); **8.** (c); **9.** (d); **10.** (d); **11.** (b); **12.** (a); **13.** (b); **14.** (a); **15.** (c)

Case Study 5

This case study shows the implementation of concepts discussed in Chapters 12 and 13 on Inheritance and File Handling.

Program C5.1 Using concepts of inheritance discussed in Chapter 12 and file handling discussed in Chapter 13, simulate the process of adding records of Books and Magazines in a library.

```
using namespace std;
#include<iostream>
#include<string.h>
class Library
{
	private:
		char *title;
		char *pub;
		int acc_no;
	public:
		Library(char t[],
char p[], int ano)
		{	int len = strlen(t);
			title = new char[len+1];
			strcpy(title, t);
			len = strlen(p);
			pub = new char[len+1];
			strcpy(pub, p);
			acc_no = ano;
		}
		void show_details()
		{ cout<<"\n Title : "<<title;
		  cout<<"\n Publisher : "<<pub;
		  cout<<"\n Accession No.:"<<acc_
		  no;
		}
};
class Book :  public Library
{	private:
		char *author;
		int edition;
	public:
		Book(char t[], char p[],
int ano, char a[], int e) :
Library(t, p, ano)
		{	int len = strlen(a);
			author =
new char[len+1];
			strcpy(author, a);
			edition = e;
		}
	void show_details()
	{	Library::show_details();
		cout<<"\n Author : "<<author;
		cout<<"\n Edition : "<<edition;
	}
};
class Magazine :  public Library
{	private:
		char *editor;
		int issue;
	public:
		Magazine(char t[], char p[],
int ano, char e[], int i) :
Library(t, p, ano)
		{	int len = strlen(e);
			editor = new
char[len+1];
			strcpy(editor, e);
			issue = i;
	}
	void show_details()
	{	Library::show_details();
		cout<<"\n Editor :"<<editor;
		cout<<"\n Issue : "<<issue;
	}
};
int main()
{
	int issue,n, e, ano,count_books=0,
count_magazines = 0;
	char ch, t[20], p[20], a[20], ed[20];
	Book *Bptr[10];
	Magazine *Mptr[10];
	cout<<"\n Enter the details. ";
	cout<<"\n ***********
**************************";
	cout<<"\n Book (b), Magazine (m),
 Exit(*) : ";
	cin>>ch;
	while(ch!='*')
	{	cout<<"\n Enter
the title : ";
		cin.ignore();
		cin.getline(t,20);
		cout<<"\n Enter
the publisher name : ";
```

```
            cin.ignore();
            cin.getline(p,20);
            cout<<"Enter
the accession number : ";
            cin>>ano;
            if(ch == 'b')
            {     cout<<"\n Enter
the author's name : ";
                  cin.ignore();
                  cin.getline(a,20);
                  cout<<"\n Enter
the Edition : ";
                  cin>>e;
                  Bptr[count_
books++] = new Book(t,p,ano,a,e);
            }
            if(ch == 'm')
            {
                  cout<<"\n Enter
the editor's name: ";
                  cin.ignore();
                  cin.getline(ed,20);
                  cout<<"\n Enter
the Issue No. : ";
                  cin>>issue;
                  Mptr[count_
magazines++] = new Magazine
(t,p,ano,ed, issue);
            }
            cout<<"\n Book(b),
Magazine(m), Exit(*) : ";
            cin>>ch;
      }
      cout<<"\n LIBRARY DETAILS ";
      cout<<"\n
*********************";
      int i=0;
      while(i<count_books)
      {     cout<<"\n\t BOOK ";
            Bptr[i++]->show_details();
            cout<<"\n
*********************";
      }
      for(i=0;i<count_magazines;i++)
      {    cout<<"\n\t MAGAZINE";
            Mptr[i]->show_details();
            cout<<"\n
*********************";
      }
}
```

OUTPUT

```
Enter the details.
*************************************
Book (b), Magazine (m), Exit(*) : b
Enter the title : C++
Enter the publisher name : OUP
Enter the accession number : 9712
Enter the author's name : Thareja
Enter the Edition : 1
Book (b), Magazine (m), Exit(*) : m
Enter the title : Chip
Enter the publisher name : XYZ
Enter the accession number : 1234
Enter the editor's name: David
Enter the Issue No. : 4
Book (b), Magazine (m), Exit(*) : b
Enter the title :DBMS
Enter the publisher name :McGraw Hill
Enter the accession number :3490
Enter the author's name :Rama Krishnan
Enter the Edition :2
Book (b), Magazine (m), Exit(*) : *
LIBRARY DETAILS
*********************
BOOK
Title :C++
Publisher :OUP
Accession No. : 9712
Author :Thareja
Edition :1
*********************
MAGAZINE
Title :Chip
Accession No. : 1234
Publisher :XYZ
Editor :David
Issue :4
*********************
BOOK
Title :DBMS
Publisher :McGraw Hill
Accession No. : 3490
Author :Rama Krishnan
Edition :2
*********************
```

Assignment Enhance this program C5.1 to edit and delete records.

CHAPTER 12

Inheritance and Run-Time Polymorphism

KEY Concepts

Defining derived classes • Access specifiers • Types of inheritance • Ambiguities • Constructors • Virtual base classes • Abstract classes • Pure virtual functions • Object slicing • Run-time polymorphism • Virtual constructors and virtual destructors

INTRODUCTION

Reusability is an important feature of object oriented programming (OOP). Reusing an existing piece of code offers manifold benefits. It not only saves the effort and cost required to build a software product but also enhances its reliability. Therefore, programmers need not re-write, re-debug, and re-test the code that has already been tested and being used in existing software.

To support reusability, C++ supports the concept of reusing existing classes as it allows programmers to create new classes that reuse prewritten and tested classes. The existing classes are adapted as per user's requirements so that the newly formed classes can be incorporated in the current software application being developed.

The technique of creating a new class from an existing class is called inheritance. The old or existing class is called the base class and the new class is known as the derived class or sub-class. The derived classes are created by first inheriting the data and methods of the base class and then adding new specialized data and functions in it. During the process of inheritance, the base class remains unchanged. The concept of inheritance is, therefore, frequently used to implement the `is-a` relationship.

For example, teacher `is-a` person, student `is-a` person; while both teacher and student are a person in the first place, both also have some distinguishing features. Therefore, all the common traits of teacher and student are specified in the `Person` class and specialized features are incorporated in two separate classes of `Teacher` and `Student`.

Similarly, a dentist or a surgeon is a doctor and doctor is a person. Fig. 12.1 illustrates the concept of inheritance which follows a top-down approach to problem solving. In top-down design approach, generalized classes are designed first and specialized classes are derived by inheriting or extending generalized classes.

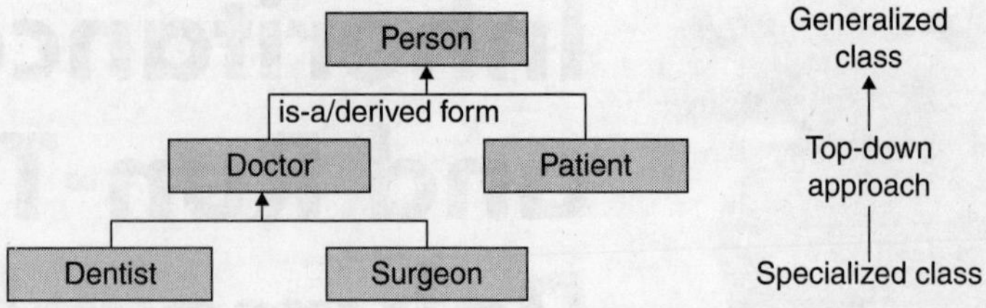

Figure 12.1 Is-a relationship between classes

Note The derived class inherits all the capabilities of the base class and adds refinements and extensions of its own.

12.1 DEFINING DERIVED CLASSES

A class can be derived from one or more base classes using the following syntax:

```
class derived_class_name : [access-specifier] base_class_name
{   ------
    ------
    ------
};
```

According to the syntax, the `derived_class_name` is derived from the `base_class_name`, thereby inheriting some or all of its members. The `access-specifier`, also known as the `visibility-mode`, is optional and if present, can be either `public`, `private`, or `protected`. If no `access-specifier` is written, then by default, the class will be derived in `private` mode.

12.2 ACCESS SPECIFIERS

As stated in the above section, there are three types of access specifiers, private, public and protected. In this section we will have a look at all three of them in detail.

Private Private is the highest level of data hiding. When a base class is privately inherited by a derived class, then `public` members of the base class become `private` members of the derived class. The access to `private` members cannot be inherited but the derived class can access them using `public` member functions of the base class. This means that the object of a privately inherited class cannot access the inherited members.

Note Private members of the base class can never become members of the derived class.

Public Public is the lowest and the most open level of data hiding. When a base class is publicly inherited by a derived class, then `public` members of the base class become `public` members of the derived class. The access to `private` members cannot be inherited but the derived class can access them using public member functions of the base class. This means that the object of the derived class can access the `public` member functions of the derived class but cannot access its `private` members.

Note A derived class can access all the non-private members of the base class.

Protected Until now, we have used only two access specifiers—`private` and `public`. However, there is a third access specifier called the `protected` specifier. A `protected` specifier lies between private and public. While this specifier is less restricted than private, it is more restricted than the public specifier. A data member or a member function declared as protected can be accessed by the class in which it is defined—as in private—and the class which is immediately derived from it. No other class except these two can access the protected members of a class.

Table 12.1 specifies the accessibility of the three visibility modes in the same class, derived class, and outside class.

Table 12.1 Visibility modes

Specifier or class	Same class	Derived class	Any other class	Friend function	Friend class
Private	Yes	No	No	Yes	Yes
Protected	Yes	Yes	No	Yes	Yes
Public	Yes	Yes	Yes	Yes	Yes

Note The keywords private, protected, and public may appear in any order and any number of times in class declaration.

12.2.1 Inheriting Protected Members

When a protected member is inherited in private mode, the protected member of the base class becomes private member of the derived class. Although these members can be accessed in the derived class, these are not available for further inheritance (in case of multi-level inheritance) because private members cannot be inherited as shown in Fig. 12.2.

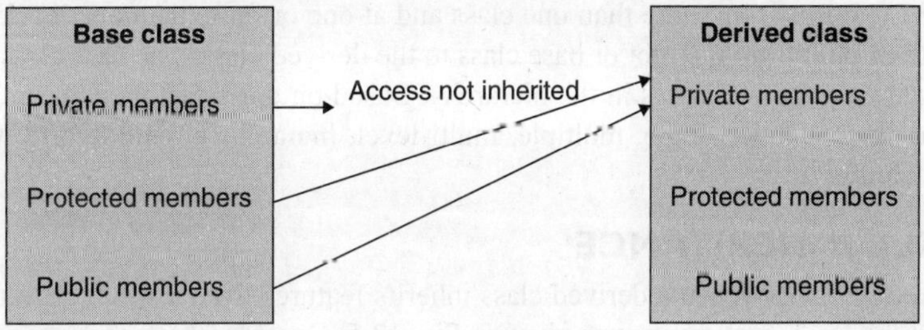

Figure 12.2 A class derived in private mode

However, when a protected member is inherited in public mode, it becomes a protected member of the derived class. Therefore, it can be easily accessed in the derived class and can be used for further inheritance as shown in Fig. 12.3.

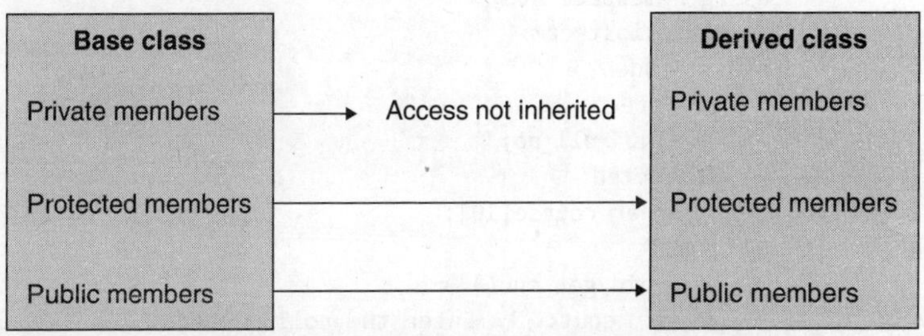

Figure 12.3 A class derived in public mode

12.2.2 Inheriting the Class in Protected Mode

A base class can be inherited in `protected` mode. This type of derivation is known as `protected` derivation. When a class is inherited in `protected` mode, the `public` and `protected` members of the class becomes `protected` members of the derived class as shown in Fig. 12.4.

> **Programming Tip:** Avoid the protected label whenever you can attain the same result with the private label.

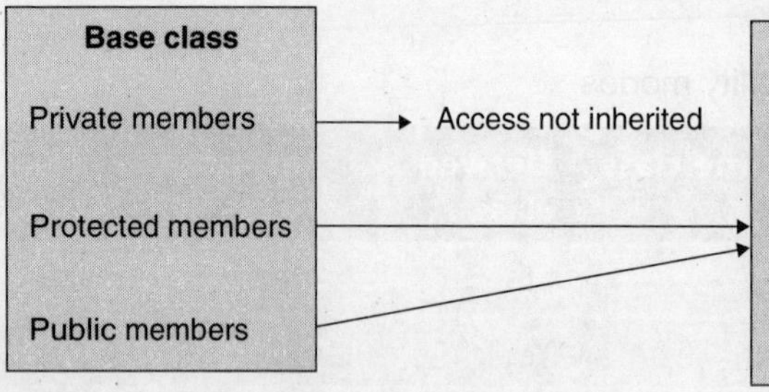

Figure 12.4 A class derived in protected mode

Things to Remember

A derived class cannot inherit the following base class functions:

- Constructors, destructors, and copy constructors
- Overloaded operators of the base class (except overloaded assignment operator)
- Friend functions of the base class
- Access to private members of the base class

12.3 TYPES OF INHERITANCE

The derived class can inherit some or all of the features of the base class. Moreover, a class can inherit features from more than one class and at one or more than one level. Here, level means the length of path from the root or base class to the derived class. The base class itself might have been derived from other classes in the hierarchy. Based on these factors, we can have different types of inheritance such as single, multiple, multi-level, hierarchical, and hybrid which are illustrated in this chapter.

12.4 SINGLE INHERITANCE

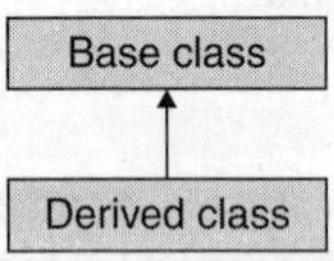

Figure 12.5 Single inheritance

When a derived class inherits features from a single base class, it is called single inheritance as given in Fig. 12.5. Consider the program given here that uses single inheritance to display the details of a student.

Example 12.1 Single inheritance

```
using namespace std;
#include<iostream>
class Student
{   private:
        int roll_no;
    protected:
        char course[10];
    public:
        void get_rno()
        {   cout<<"\n Enter the roll number : ";
            cin>>roll_no;
```

```
        }
        void show_rno()
        {   cout<<"\n ROLL NO : "<<roll_no;
        }
};
class Result : public Student
{   private:
        int marks[3];
    public:
        void get_data();
        int total();
        void display()
        {   show_rno();
            cout<<"\n COURSE : "<<course;
            cout<<"\n TOTAL MARKS : "<<total();
        }
};
void Result :: get_data()
{   get_rno();
    cout<<"\n Enter the course : ";
    cin.ignore();
    cin.getline(course,10);
    cout<<"\n Enter marks in three subjects : ";
    for(int i=0;i<3;i++)
        cin>>marks[i];
}
int Result :: total()
{       int tot_marks = 0;
    for(int i=0;i<3;i++)
        tot_marks += marks[i];
    return tot_marks;
}
main()
{   Result R;
    R.get_data();
    R.display();
    //R.get_rno();                    //Ok
    //R.roll_no = 12;                 // not allowed
    //strcpy(R.course, "BCA") ;       // not allowed
}
```

Programming Tip: A derived class inherits the entire base class but it does not inherit access to use base class's private members.

OUTPUT

```
Enter the roll number : 1234
Enter the course : BCA
Enter marks in three subjects :   67 78 89
ROLL NO : 1234
COURSE : BCA
TOTAL MARKS : 234
```

Explanation: In the program, there are two classes—`Student` and `Result`. The class `Student` hold information about student (`roll number, course`) and has functions to read and display the roll number. The class `Result` stores the marks of the student in three subjects, calculates the total marks, and displays all the information.

Note that `Result` is derived in `public` from class `Student`. Therefore, `private` member of `roll_no` cannot be accessed, protected member of `course` becomes protected member of `Result`, and the two `public` member functions becomes `public` members of the derived class. This means that all the members of the base class except the `roll_no` are accessible by the derived class.

In the `get_data()`, from `Result` class you can directly access course and `get_rno()` but not the `roll_no`. To access the `roll_no` you have to access the `private` member indirectly through a `public` member function of the class. In `main()`,the object of the derived class can access the `public` member function of the base class but not the `private` or the `protected` members.

Program 12.1 Write a program in which class `Result` inherits `Student` in private mode.

```
using namespace std;
#include<iostream>
class Student
{   private:
        int roll_no;
    protected:
        char course[10];
    public:
        void get_rno()
        {   cout<<"\n Enter the roll number : ";
            cin>>roll_no;
        }
        void show_rno()
        {   cout<<"\n ROLL NO : "<<roll_no;
        }
};
class Result : private Student
{   private:
        int marks[3];
    public:
        void get_data();
        int total();
        void display()
        {   show_rno();
            cout<<"\n COURSE : "<<course;
            cout<<"\n TOTAL MARKS : "<<total();
        }
};
void Result :: get_data()
{   get_rno();
    cout<<"\n Enter the course : ";
    cin.ignore();
    cin.getline(course,10);
    cout<<"\n Enter marks in three subjects : ";
    for(int i=0;i<3;i++)
        cin>>marks[i];
}
int Result :: total()
{        int tot_marks = 0;
    for(int i=0;i<3;i++)
        tot_marks += marks[i];
    return tot_marks;
}
```

```
main()
{   Result R;
    R.get_data();
    R.display();
    //R.get_rno();          //not allowed
    //R.roll_no = 12;       // not allowed
    //strcpy(R.course, "BCA") ;           // not allowed
}
```

OUTPUT

```
Enter the roll number : 1
Enter the course : BTECH
Enter marks in three subjects : 97 98 99
COURSE : BTECH
ROLL NO : 1
TOTAL MARKS : 294
```

Program 12.2 Write a program in which class `Result` inherits `Student` in protected mode.

```
using namespace std;
#include<iostream>
class Student
{   private:
        int roll_no;
    protected:
        char course[10];
    public:
        void get_rno()
        {   cout<<"\n Enter the roll number : ";
            cin>>roll_no;
        }
        void show_rno()
        {   cout<<"\n ROLL NO : "<<roll_no;
        }
};
class Result : protected Student
{   private:
        int marks[3];
    public:
        void get_data();
        int total();
        void display()
        {   show_rno();
            cout<<"\n COURSE : "<<course;
            cout<<"\n TOTAL MARKS : "<<total();
        }
};
void Result :: get_data()
{   get_rno();
    cout<<"\n Enter the course : ";
    cin.ignore();
    cin.getline(course,10);
    cout<<"\n Enter marks in three subjects : ";
    for(int i=0;i<3;i++)
        cin>>marks[i];
}
```

```
int Result :: total()
{ int tot_marks = 0;
    for(int i=0;i<3;i++)
        tot_marks += marks[i];
    return tot_marks;
}
main()
{   Result R;
    R.get_data();
    R.display();
    //R.get_rno();              //not allowed
    //R.roll_no = 12;           // not allowed
    //strcpy(R.course, "BCA") ; // not allowed
}
```

OUTPUT

```
Enter the roll number : 1
Enter the course : BTECH
Enter marks in three subjects : 97 98 99
COURSE : BTECH
ROLL NO : 1
TOTAL MARKS : 294
```

12.5 CONSTRUCTORS AND DESTRUCTORS IN DERIVED CLASSES

We have seen that constructors play an important role in initializing an object during creation and allocating the required resources like memory. Similarly, destructors are important for deallocating the resources from the object when it goes out of scope. While having these manager functions in base and/or derived classes, the programmer must keep the following in mind:

- If the base class constructor does not take any argument, the derived class may not have a constructor.
- If the base class has a constructor with one or more arguments, then the derived class must have a constructor function to pass the arguments to the base class constructor.
- It is the derived class's responsibility to pass arguments to the base class because in the `main()`, we will create objects only of the derived class and not of the base class.
- If both the derived class and base class has constructors, the base class constructor is executed first and then the constructor in the derived class is executed.
- The order of execution of destructors is just the reverse of constructor. First, the destructor of derived class is called and then the destructor of base class is called. The program given here illustrates this concept.

Example 12.2 Using destructors and constructors

```
using namespace std;
#include<iostream>
class Student
{   private:
        int roll_no;
    protected:
        char course[10];
    public:
        Student()
```

```
        {   cout<<"\n In Student's Constructor";
            roll_no = 0, course[0] = '\0';
        }
        ~Student()
        {   cout<<"\n In Student's Destructor";
        }
        void get_rno()
        {   cout<<"\n Enter the roll number : ";
            cin>>roll_no;
        }
        void show_rno()
        {   cout<<"\n ROLL NO : "<<roll_no;
        }
};
class Result : protected Student
{   private:
        int marks[3];
    public:
        Result()
        {   cout<<"\n In Result's Constructor";
            marks[0] = marks[1] = marks[2] = 0;
        }
        ~Result()
        {   cout<<"\n In Result's Destructor";
        }
        void get_data();
        int total();
        void display()
        {   show_rno();
            cout<<"\n COURSE : "<<course;
            cout<<"\n TOTAL MARKS : "<<total();
        }
};
void Result :: get_data()
{   get_rno();
    cout<<"\n Enter the course : ";
    cin.ignore();
    cin.getline(course,10);
    cout<<"\n Enter marks in three subjects : ";
    for(int i=0;i<3;i++)
        cin>>marks[i];
}
int Result :: total()
{       int tot_marks = 0;
    for(int i=0;i<3;i++)
        tot_marks += marks[i];
    return tot_marks;
}
main()
{   Result R;
    R.get_data();
    R.display();
}
```

```
OUTPUT
In Student's Constructor
Result's Constructor
Enter the roll number : 1234
Enter the course : BCA
Enter marks in three subjects :   67 78 89
ROLL NO : 1234
COURSE : BCA
TOTAL MARKS : 234
In Result's Destructor
In Student's Destructor
```

Explanation: Here, we see that the base class constructor is called and executed before executing the statements in the body of the derived class. The advantages of invoking the base class constructor before the derived class are as follows:

- If base class constructor has to be changed in future, then the base class as well as all the inherited classes can use the changes. This eases the job of code enhancement and maintenance.
- Logically, a child cannot exist without parent(s).
- Practically, a child often uses variables and functions of the `parent class`. Therefore, instantiating the `parent class` before the child class ensures that those variables are initialized and ready to use by the time a derived class is created.

Note The order of execution of destructors is just the reverse of constructor since compile time objects get memory from stack memory in the LIFO or last in first out order. Since the derived class object came after the base class, it is destructed before the object of the base class.

12.5.1 Invoking Constructors with Arguments

As discussed earlier, if the base class accepts arguments, then it is the responsibility of the derived class to supply initial values to the base class. When the object of the derived class is created in `main()`, all the initial values required are supplied together. Then the constructor of the derived class receives the entire list of values and passes them on to the base constructors.

Note Base constructors are called and executed before executing the statements in the derived constructor.

In such a case, the syntax for defining a derived constructor is as follows:

```
derived_class_name(arg_list1, arg_list2):base(arg_list1)
{  -------
   // initialize derived class members with arg_list2
   -------
}
```

According to the syntax, the header line of the derived class's constructor has two parts separated by a colon (`:`). The first part provides the list of the arguments passed to the derived class constructor and the second part contains a call to the base class constructor.

Example 12.3 Invoking constructors with arguments

```
using namespace std;
#include<iostream>
```

```
#include<string.h>
class Student
{   private:
        int roll_no;
    protected:
        char course[10];
    public:
        Student(int rno, char *c)
        {   roll_no = rno;
            strcpy(course, c);
        }
        void show_rno()
        {   cout<<"\n ROLL NO : "<<roll_no;
        }
};
class Result : protected Student
{   private:
        int marks[3];
    public:
        Result(int rno, char *c, int m1, int m2, int m3) : Student(rno, c)
        {   marks[0] = m1;
            marks[1] = m2;
            marks[2] = m3;
        }
        void get_data();
        int total();
        void display()
        {   show_rno();
            cout<<"\n COURSE : "<<course;
            cout<<"\n TOTAL MARKS : "<<total();
        }
};
int Result :: total()
{        int tot_marks = 0;
    for(int i=0;i<3;i++)
        tot_marks += marks[i];
    return tot_marks;
}
main()
{   int rno, m1, m2, m3;
    char course[10];
    cout<<"\n Enter the roll number : ";
    cin>>rno;
    cout<<"\n Enter the course : ";
    cin.ignore();
    cin.getline(course, 10);;
    cout<<"\n Enter marks in three subjects : ";
    cin>>m1>>m2>>m3;
    Result R(rno, course, m1, m2, m3);
    R.display();
}
```

OUTPUT

```
Enter the roll number :1
```

```
Enter the course :BTECH
Enter marks in three subjects :97 98 99
COURSE :BTECH
ROLL NO :1
TOTAL MARKS :294
```

Explanation: In the program, class `Result` has been derived from `Student` in protected mode. Therefore, `Result` can use all protected as well as public members of `Student`. The private members are being used only through public member function `total()`.

12.6 MULTI-LEVEL INHERITANCE

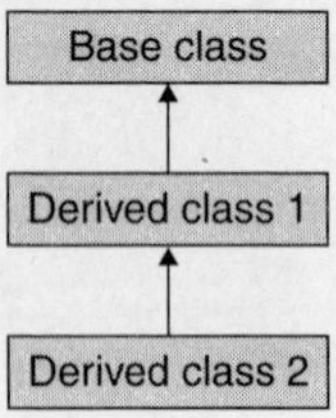

Figure 12.6 Multi-level inheritance

The technique of deriving a class from an already derived class is called multi-level inheritance. In Fig. 12.6, `base class` acts as the base for derived `class 1`, which in turn, acts as a base for `derived class 2`. Therefore, `derived class 1` is known as the intermediate base class as this class provides a link for inheritance between the `base class` and the `derived class 2`. The chain of classes from `base class ->derived class 1 ->derived class 2` is known as the inheritance path. In multi-level inheritance, the number of levels can go up to any number based on the requirement. Consider the same program with multi-level inheritance.

Example 12.4 Multi-level inheritance

```
using namespace std;
#include<iostream>
#include<string.h>
class Student
{  protected:
       int roll_no;
       char name[20];
       char course[10];
   public:
       void get_data()
       {  cout<<"\n Enter roll number : ";
          cin>>roll_no;
          cout<<"\n Enter name : ";
          cin.ignore();
          cin.getline(name, 20);
          cout<<"\n Enter course : ";
          cin.getline(course, 10);
       }
       int get_rno()
       {  return roll_no;
       }
       char * get_name()
       {  return name;
       }
       char * get_course()
       {  return course;
       }
};
class Marks : public Student
{  protected:
       int marks[3];
```

```
    public:
        void get_marks()
        {   cout<<"\n Enter marks in three subjects : ";
            cin>>marks[0]>>marks[1]>>marks[2];
        }
        int total()
        {   return (marks[0] + marks[1] + marks[2]);
        }
};
class Result : public Marks
{   public:
        void display()
        {   cout<<"\n ROLL NUMBER : "<<get_rno();
            cout<<"\n NAME : "<<get_name();
            cout<<"\n COURSE : "<<get_course();
            cout<<"\n TOTAL MARKS : "<<total();
        }
};
main()
{   Result R;
    R.get_data();
    R.get_marks();
    R.display();
}
```

OUTPUT

```
Enter roll number : 1234
Enter name : Aditi Raj
Enter course : MCA
Enter marks in three subjects : 99 98 100
ROLL NUMBER : 1234
NAME : Aditi Raj
COURSE : MCA
TOTAL MARKS : 297
```

Explanation: In the program, `class Result` is derived from `Student` in public mode. It can use all the members of the class, except private members. However, these `private` members are being used through the `public` member function `total()`.

12.7 CONSTRUCTOR IN MULTI-LEVEL INHERITANCE

In multi-level inheritance, the constructor is executed in the order of inheritance. Whatever be the type of inheritance, it is always the responsibility of the derived class to supply the initial values to its base class. Therefore, the object of the derived class accepts the entire list of values, passes them as arguments to its constructor from where they are finally passed to the base constructor in the order in which they are declared in the derived class. Moreover, the sequence of calling destructors would just be the opposite of that of constructors. Note the output of the following program.

Example 12.5 Constructor and destructor in multi-level inheritance

```
using namespace std;
#include<iostream>
```

```
#include<string.h>
class Student
{   protected:
        int roll_no;
        char name[20];
        char course[10];
    public:
        Student(int r, char *n, char *c)
        {   roll_no = r;
            strcpy(name, n);
            strcpy(course, c);
            cout<<"\n In STUDENT's constructor - Base Class";
        }
        ~Student()
        {   cout<<"\n In STUDENT's Destructor - Base Class";   }
        int get_rno()
        {   return roll_no;
        }
        char * get_name()
        {   return name;
        }
        char * get_course()
        {   return course;
        }
};
class Marks : public Student
{   protected:
        int marks[3];
    public:
        Marks(int r, char *n, char *c, int m1, int m2, int m3):Student(r,n,c)
        {   marks[0] = m1;
            marks[1] = m2;
            marks[2] = m3;
            cout<<"\n In MARK's Constructor - Intermediate Class";
        }
        ~Marks()
        {   cout<<"\n In MARK's Destructor - Intermediate Class";   }
        int total()
        {   return (marks[0] + marks[1] + marks[2]);
        }
};
class Result : public Marks
{   public:
        Result(int r, char *n, char *c, int m1, int m2, int m3) : Marks(r, n, c, m1, m2, m3)
        {   cout<<"\n In RESULT's Constructor - Derived Class";   }
        ~Result()
        {   cout<<"\n In RESULT's Destructor - Derived Class";   }
        void display()
        {   cout<<"\n ROLL NUMBER : "<<get_rno();
            cout<<"\n NAME : "<<get_name();
            cout<<"\n COURSE : "<<get_course();
            cout<<"\n TOTAL MARKS : "<<total();
        }
};
```

```
main()
{   int rno, m1,m2,m3;
    char n[20], c[10];
    cout<<"\n Enter roll number : ";
    cin>>rno;
    cout<<"\n Enter name : ";
    cin.ignore();
    cin.getline(n, 20);
    cout<<"\n Enter course : ";
    cin.getline(c, 10);
    cout<<"\n Enter marks in three subjects : ";
    cin>>m1>>m2>>m3;
    Result R(rno, n, c, m1, m2, m3);
    R.display();
}
```

OUTPUT

```
In STUDENT's constructor - Base Class
In MARK's Constructor - Intermediate Class
In RESULT's Constructor - Derived Class
Enter roll number : 1234
Enter name : Aditi Raj
Enter course : MCA
Enter marks in three subjects : 99 98 100
ROLL NUMBER : 1234
NAME : Aditi Raj
COURSE : MCA
TOTAL MARKS : 297
In RESULT's Destructor - Derived Class
In MARK's Constructor - Intermediate Class
In STUDENT's Destructor - Base Class
```

Note Constructors can only call constructors from their immediate base class.

Program 12.3 Write a program in which `class` Batsman inherits `class` Person. Use single inheritance.

```
using namespace std;
#include<iostream>
class Person
{   protected:
        char name[20];
        int age;
    public:
        void get_Person_data()
        {   cout<<"\n Enter the name : ";
            cin.getline(name,20);
            cout<<"\n Enter age : ";
            cin>>age;
        }
        void show_data()
        {   cout<<"\n NAME : "<<name;
            cout<<"\n AGE : "<<age;
        }
```

```
};
class Batsman : public Person
{   protected:
        int runs_taken;
        float batting_average;
        int ODIs_played;
        int no_half_centuries;
        int no_centuries;
        float strike_rate;
    public:
        void get_Details()
        {   get_Person_data();
            cout<<"\n Enter No. of ODI's Played : ";
            cin>>ODIs_played;
            cout<<"\n Enter the batting average : ";
            cin>>batting_average;
            cout<<"\n Enter the Strike Rate : ";
            cin>>strike_rate;
            cout<<"\n Enter the number of half centuries and centuries made : ";
            cin>>no_half_centuries>>no_centuries;
            cout<<"\n Enter Number of runs made : ";
            cin>>runs_taken;
        }
        void show_Details()
        {   show_data();
            cout<<"\n ODI's PLAYED : "<<ODIs_played;
            cout<<"\n No. Of Half Centuries : "<<no_half_centuries;
            cout<<"\n No. Of Centuries : "<<no_centuries;
            cout<<"\n BATTING AVERAGE : "<<batting_average;
            cout<<"\n STRIKE RATE : "<<strike_rate;
        }
};
main()
{   Batsman B;
    B.get_Details();
    B.show_Details();
}
```

OUTPUT

```
Enter the name :
Sachin Tendulkar
Enter age : 45
Enter No. of ODI's Played : 463
Enter the batting average : 44.83
Enter the Strike Rate : 86.23
Enter the number of half centuries and centuries made : 96 49
Enter Number of runs made : 18426
NAME : Sachin Tendulkar
AGE : 45
ODI's PLAYED : 463
No. Of Half Centuries : 96
No. Of Centuries : 49
BATTING AVERAGE : 44.83
STRIKE RATE : 86.23
```

Program 12.4 Write a program that uses multi-level inheritance to implement `classes–Node`, `Server`, and `Device`.

```
using namespace std;
#include<iostream>
class Node
{   protected:
        char brand_name[20];
        int mfg_yr;
        int no_warranty_years;
    public:
        void get_Node_data()
        {   cout<<"\n Enter the Brand Name : ";
            cin.ignore();
            cin.getline(brand_name, 20);
            cout<<"\n Enter the Year of Manufacturing : ";
            cin>>mfg_yr;
            cout<<"\n Enter the number of warranty years : ";
            cin>>no_warranty_years;
        }
        void show_Node_data()
        {   cout<<"\n BRAND NAME : "<<brand_name;
            cout<<"\n YEAR OF MANUFACTURING : "<<mfg_yr;
            cout<<"\n NO. OF WARRANTY YEARS : "<<no_warranty_years;
        }
};
class Server : public Node
{   protected:
            int MTTF;
            int MTTR;
            int TPS;
    public:
        void get_Server_data()
        {   get_Node_data();
            cout<<"\n Enter the Mean Time To Failure : ";
            cin>>MTTF;
            cout<<"\n Enter the Mean Time To Recover : ";
            cin>>MTTR;
            cout<<"\n Enter the Transactions Per Second : ";
            cin>>TPS;
        }
        void show_Server_data()
        {   show_Node_data();
            cout<<"\n MTTF : "<<MTTF;
            cout<<"\n MTTR : "<<MTTR;
            cout<<"\n TPS : "<<TPS;
        }
};
class Device : public Server
{   protected:
        int num_nodes;
    public:
        void get_data();
        void show_data();
```

```
};
void Device :: get_data()
{   cout<<"\n Enter the number of Server Nodes : ";
    cin>>num_nodes;
    for(int i=0;i<num_nodes;i++)
        get_Server_data();
}
void Device :: show_data()
{   for(int i=0;i<num_nodes;i++)
        show_Server_data();
}
main()
{   Device D;
    D.get_data();
    D.show_data();
}
```

OUTPUT

```
Enter the number of Server Nodes : 2
Enter the Brand Name : Asus
Enter the Year of Manufacturing : 2010
Enter the number of warranty years : 3
Enter the Mean Time To Failure : 250
Enter the Mean Time To Recover : 2
Enter the Transactions Per Second : 20
Enter the Brand Name : Samsung
Enter the Year of Manufacturing : 2011
Enter the number of warranty years : 4
Enter the Mean Time To Failure : 360
Enter the Mean Time To Recover : 3
Enter the Transactions Per Second : 45
BRAND NAME : Asus
YEAR OF MANUFACTURING : 2010
NO. OF WARRANTY YEARS : 3
 F : 250
  20

        Samsung
        TURING : 2011
         RS : 4
```

ved class inherits features from more than one base class in Fig. 12.7, it is called multiple inheritance. The syntax iple inheritance can be given as follows:

```
lass derived_class_name : visibility mode base1_
class_name, visibility mode base1_class_
```

```
name, ...... visibility mode basen_class_name
{
    --------
}
```

12.9 CONSTRUCTORS AND DESTRUCTORS IN MULTIPLE INHERITANCE

In case of multiple inheritance, the base class is constructed in the same order in which they appear in the declaration of the derived class. Similar to previous cases of inheritance, the destructor would be invoked in just the reverse sequence.

Continuing with our same program (Example 12.1), let us rewrite the program code using multiple inheritance technique. In the program given here, class `Marks` and `Student` are inherited by a single class `Result`.

Example 12.6 Multiple inheritance

```
using namespace std;
#include<iostream>
#include<string.h>
class Marks
{   protected:
        int marks[3];
    public:
        Marks(int m1, int m2, int m3)
        {   marks[0] = m1;
            marks[1] = m2;
            marks[2] = m3;
            cout<<"\n In MARK's Constructor - Second Base Class";
        }
        ~Marks()
        {   cout<<"\n In MARK's Destructor - Second Base Class";    }
        int total()
        {   return (marks[0] + marks[1] + marks[2]);
        }
};
class Student
{   protected:
        int roll_no;
        char name[20];
        char course[10];
    public:
        Student(int r, char *n, char *c)
        {   roll_no = r;
            strcpy(name, n);
            strcpy(course, c);
            cout<<"\n In STUDENT's constructor - First Base Class";
        }
        ~Student()
        {   cout<<"\n In STUDENT's Destructor - First Base Class ";    }
        int get_rno()
        {   return roll_no;
```

```
        }
        char * get_name()
        {   return name;
        }
        char * get_course()
        {   return course;
        }
};
class Result : public Student, public Marks
{   public:
        Result(int r, char *n, char *c, int m1, int m2, int m3) : Student(r, n, c),
Marks(m1, m2, m3)
        {   cout<<"\n In RESULT's Constructor - Derived Class";   }
        ~Result()
        {   cout<<"\n In RESULT's Destructor - Derived Class";   }
        void display()
        {   cout<<"\n ROLL NUMBER : "<<get_rno();
            cout<<"\n NAME : "<<get_name();
            cout<<"\n COURSE : "<<get_course();
            cout<<"\n TOTAL MARKS : "<<total();
        }
};
main()
{   int rno, m1,m2,m3;
    char n[20], c[10];
    cout<<"\n Enter roll number : ";
    cin>>rno;
    cout<<"\n Enter name : ";
    cin.ignore();
    cin.getline(n, 20);
    cout<<"\n Enter course : ";
    cin.getline(c, 10);
    cout<<"\n Enter marks in three subjects : ";
    cin>>m1>>m2>>m3;
    Result R(rno, n, c, m1, m2, m3);
    R.display();
}
```

OUTPUT

```
In STUDENT's constructor - First Base Class
In MARK's Constructor - Second Base Class
In RESULT's Constructor - Derived Class
Enter roll number : 1234
Enter name : Aditi Raj
Enter course : MCA
Enter marks in three subjects : 99 98 100
ROLL NUMBER : 1234
NAME : Aditi Raj
COURSE : MCA
TOTAL MARKS : 297
In RESULT's Destructor - Derived Class
In MARK's Constructor - Second Base Class
In STUDENT's Destructor - First Base Class
```

Explanation: From the output, it is clear that even though the class `Marks` has been defined before `Student`, the constructor for `Student` is called before that of `Marks`. This is because the constructors are invoked in the sequence of inheritance. In our derived class declaration statement, the order of inheritance is `Student` and then `Marks`.

12.10 AMBIGUITY IN MULTIPLE INHERITANCE

In multiple inheritance, when a class inherits features from more than one base class, there may be a case when two or more classes have a function with the same name. In such cases, if the object of the derived class tries to access that function, then it will result in ambiguity as it will not be clear to the compiler which base's class member function or member variable should be invoked. The ambiguity simply means the state when the compiler is confused. Consider the program given here which illustrates this situation.

```
#include<iostream.h>
class B1
{   public:
        void show_data()
        {   cout<<"\n In Base Class 1";
        }
};
class B2
{   public:
        void show_data()
        {   cout<<"\n In Base Class 2";
        }
};
class D : public B1, public B2
{   public:
        D()
        {   cout<<"\n In Derived Class Constructor";
        }
};
main()
{   D derived_obj;
    derived_obj.show_data();    // which one to call?
}
```

12.10.1 Solution for the Ambiguity Problem

The ambiguity can be resolved by using the scope resolution operator to specify the class whose member function has to be invoked. For example, in `main()`, we should write

```
derived_obj.B1::show_data(); or derived_obj.B2::show_data();
```

We can also define a function in the derived class as `void display()` which would call its base class `show_data()` function by writing

```
classD
{   public:
        void display()
        {   B1::show_data();
            B2::show_data();
        }
};
```

12.10.2 No Ambiguity in Single Inheritance

In single inheritance, if the derived class and the base class both have a function with the same name, then the function in the derived class overrides the function of the base class. Consider the code given here.

Example 12.7 Single inheritance with no ambiguity problem

```
using namespace std;
#include<iostream>
class Base_class
{  public:
        void show_data()
        {   cout<<"\n In Base Class ";
        }
};
class Derived_class : public Base_class
{  public:
        void show_data()
        {   cout<<"\n In Derived Class";
        }
};
main()
{  Derived_class derived_obj;
   derived_obj.show_data();
}
```

OUTPUT

```
In Derived Class
```

Explanation: In this program, when the object of the derived class invokes the `show_data()`, then the function in the derived class would be invoked. To invoke the base class version of the function, we must use the scope resolution operator given as follows:

```
derived_obj.Base_class::show_data();
```

12.11 HIERARCHICAL INHERITANCE

When a class is inherited by more than one class, it is called hierarchical inheritance as shown in Fig. 12.8. This type of inheritance is usually implemented when certain features at one level are to be shared by many features at the next level. Some examples are as follows.

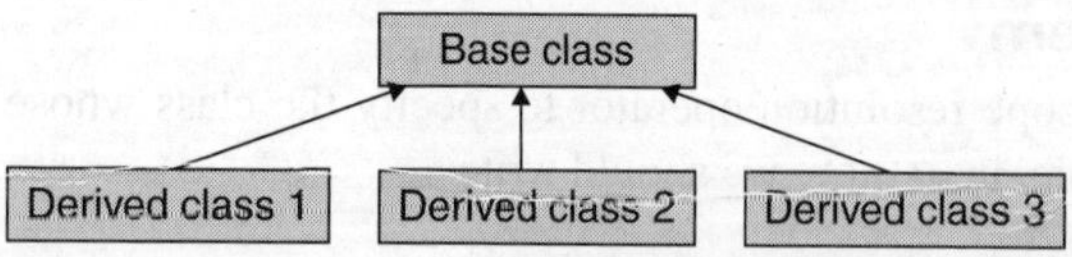

Figure 12.8 Hierarchical inheritance

- Base class account can be inherited by three classes such as savings account, fixed deposit account, and current account.
- Student class can be inherited by three separate classes such as science, commerce, and humanities
- Faculty class can be inherited by *n* number of departments such as commerce, mathematics, computer science, electronics, and so on.

In all these examples, a class hierarchy is formed in which the base class will include all the features that are common to the derived classes. The derived class can inherit the features of the base class and extend its features to better suit the requirements of the problem at hand. Consider the program given here in which the class `Student` acts as the base class for two classes—`academic details` and `accounts details`.

Example 12.8 Hierarchical inheritance

```
using namespace std;
#include<iostream>
#include<string.h>
class Student
{   protected:
        int roll_no;
        char name[20];
    public:
        void get_Stud_Details()
        {   cout<<"\n Enter the roll number : ";
            cin>>roll_no;
            cout<<"\n Enter the name : ";
            cin.ignore();
            cin.getline(name, 20);
        }
};
class Academic : public Student
{   protected:
        int marks;
        char grade;
    public:
        void get_Acad_Details()
        {   get_Stud_Details();
            cout<<"\n Enter the marks : ";
            cin>>marks;
            cout<<"\n Enter the grade : ";
            cin>>grade;
        }
        void show_Acad_Details()
        {   cout<<"\n ROLL NUMBER : "<<roll_no;
            cout<<"\n NAME : "<<name;
            cout<<"\n MARKS : "<<marks;
            cout<<"\n GRADE : "<<grade;
        }
};
class Accounts : public Student
{   protected:
        float fees;
        char DUES;
    public:
        void get_Accounts_Details()
        {       get_Stud_Details();
            cout<<"\n Enter the fees : ";
            cin>>fees;
            cout<<"\n Is there any dues lest (Y/N) : ";
            cin>>DUES;
        }
        void show_Accounts_Details()
        {   cout<<"\n ROLL NUMBER : "<<roll_no;
```

```
            cout<<"\n NAME : "<<name;
            cout<<"\n FEES : "<<fees;
            cout<<"\n DUES : "<<DUES;
        }
};
main()
{   Accounts AD;
    AD.get_Accounts_Details();
    AD.show_Accounts_Details();
    Academic AcD;
    AcD.get_Acad_Details();
    AcD.show_Acad_Details();
}
```

OUTPUT

```
Enter the roll number : 1239
Enter the name : Saisha
Enter the fees :45920
Is there any dues lest (Y/N) : N
ROLL NUMBER : 1239
NAME : Saisha
FEES : 45920
DUES : N
Enter the roll number : 809
Enter the name : Dev
Enter the marks : 91
Enter the grade : O
ROLL NUMBER : 809
NAME : Dev
MARKS : 91
GRADE : O
```

Explanation: The program shows that academic details are stored in a separate class and the accounts details are stored in a separate class. The program uses inheritance to display all the information about a student. Such type programs increases re-usability of codes.

12.12 CONSTRUCTORS AND DESTRUCTORS IN HIERARCHICAL INHERITANCE

Conceptually, hierarchical inheritance is similar to single inheritance; hence, the order of execution of constructors and destructors will be same as specified in case of single inheritance. First, the constructor of the base class would be invoked followed by that of `derived class`. Since we have more than one derived classes from the same base class, the constructor of the base class would be invoked multiple times—once for each derived object.

Example 12.9 Hierarchical inheritance containing constructors and destructors

```
using namespace std;
#include<iostream>
#include<string.h>
class Student
{  protected:
       int roll_no;
```

```
        char name[20];
    public:
        Student(int rno, char *n)
        {   roll_no = rno;
            strcpy(name, n);
        }
        ~Student()
        {   cout<<"\n In Student Destructor";
        }
};
class Academic : public Student
{   protected:
        int marks;
        char grade;
    public:
        Academic(int rno, char *n, int m, char g):Student(rno, n)
        {   marks = m;
            grade = g;
        }
        ~Academic()
        {   cout<<"\n In Academics Destructor";
        }
        void show_Acad_Details()
        {   cout<<"\n ROLL NUMBER : "<<roll_no;
            cout<<"\n NAME : "<<name;
            cout<<"\n MARKS : "<<marks;
            cout<<"\n GRADE : "<<grade;
        }
};
class Accounts : public Student
{   protected:
        float fees;
        char DUES;
    public:
        Accounts(int rno, char *n, float f, char d):Student(rno, n)
        {   fees = f;
            DUES = d;
        }
        ~Accounts()
        {   cout<<"\n In Accounts Destructor";
        }
        void show_Accounts_Details()
        {   cout<<"\n ROLL NUMBER : "<<roll_no;
            cout<<"\n NAME : "<<name;
            cout<<"\n FEES : "<<fees;
            cout<<"\n DUES : "<<DUES;
        }
};
main()
{   int rno, m;
    char n[20], g, d;
    float f;
    cout<<"\n Enter the roll number : ";
    cin>>rno;
```

```
    cout<<"\n Enter the name : ";
    cin.ignore();
    cin.getline(n, 20);
    cout<<"\n Enter the fees : ";
    cin>>f;
    cout<<"\n Is there any dues left (Y/N) : ";
    cin>>d;
    Accounts AD(rno,n, f, d);
    AD.show_Accounts_Details();
    cout<<"\n Enter the marks : ";
    cin>>m;
    cout<<"\n Enter the grade : ";
    cin>>g;
    Academic AcD(rno,n, m, g);
    AcD.show_Acad_Details();
}
```

OUTPUT

```
Enter the roll number : 1239
Enter the name : Saisha
Enter the fees :45920
Is there any dues lest (Y/N) : N
ROLL NUMBER : 1239
NAME : Saisha
FEES : 45920
DUES : N
Enter the marks : 91
Enter the grade : O
ROLL NUMBER : 809
NAME : Dev
MARKS : 91
GRADE : O
In Academics Destructor
In Student Destructor
In Accounts Destructor
In Student Destructor
```

12.13 HYBRID INHERITANCE

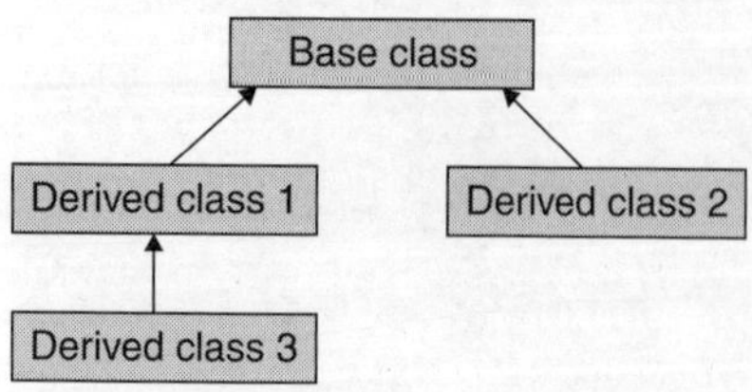

Figure 12.9 Hybrid inheritance

Deriving a class that involves more than one form of inheritance is called hybrid inheritance. For example, in Fig. 12.9, `derived class 3` is derived from base class using multi-level as well as hierarchical inheritance. Let us rewrite the program on `student's result` to implement hybrid inheritance. In the program, there are two classes—`Marks` and `Activities`. The class `result` will inherit both these classes and generate result. Finally, the `result` class would act as the base class for `student` which will display the entire information about a particular user.

Example 12.10 Hybrid inheritance

```
using namespace std;
#include<iostream>
```

```
class Marks
{   protected:
        int marks[3];
    public:
        void get_test_marks()
        {   cout<<"\n Enter the marks in three subjects : ";
            cin>>marks[0]>>marks[1]>>marks[2];
        }
        int total_test_marks()
        {   return (marks[0] + marks[1] + marks[2]);
        }
};
class Activities
{   protected:
        int acts[2];
    public:
        void get_act_marks()
        {   cout<<"\n Enter marks in two activities : ";
            cin>>acts[0]>>acts[1];
        }
        int total_act_marks()
        {   return (acts[0] + acts[1]);
        }
};
class Student : public Marks, public Activities
{   protected:
        int roll_no;
        char name[20];
    public:
        void get_details()
        {   cout<<"\n Enter the roll number : ";
            cin>>roll_no;
            cout<<"\n Enter the name : ";
            cin.ignore();
            cin.getline(name, 20);
            get_test_marks();
            get_act_marks();
        }
};
class Result : public Student
{   public:
        void get_data()
        {   get_details();   }
        void show_data()
        {   cout<<"\n ROLL NUMBER : "<<roll_no;
            cout<<"\n NAME : "<<name;
            cout<<"\n TOTAL MARKS : "<<total_test_marks() + total_act_marks();
        }
};
main()
{   Result R;
    R.get_data();
    R.show_data();
}
```

OUTPUT

```
Enter the roll number : 1234
Enter the name : Anushka Lamba
Enter the marks in three subjects : 98 97 87
Enter marks in two activities : 92 85
ROLL NUMBER : 1234
NAME : Anushka Lamba
TOTAL MARKS : 459
```

Program 12.5 Write a program using multiple inheritance that allows class `LCD_TV` to inherit two classes—`product` and `manufacturer`.

```
using namespace std;
#include<iostream>
class Product
{   protected:
        char model[10];
        int mfg_yr;
        int no_warranty_yr;
    public:
        void get_Product_data()
        {   cout<<"\n Enter the Model Number : ";
            cin.getline(model, 10);
            cout<<"\n Enter the Year of Manufacturing : ";
            cin>>mfg_yr;
            cout<<"\n Enter the number of Warranty Years : ";
            cin>>no_warranty_yr;
        }
        void show_Product_data()
        {   cout<<"\n Model : "<<model;
            cout<<"\n Manufacturing Year : "<<mfg_yr;
            cout<<"\n Number of Warranty Years : "<<no_warranty_yr;
        }
};
class Manufacturer
{   protected:
            char brand[20];
            char country[20];
    public:
            void get_Mfg_Details()
            {   cout<<"\n Enter the Brand Name : ";
                cin.getline(brand, 20);
                cout<<"\n Enter the Country Name : ";
                cin.getline(country, 20);
            }
            void show_Mfg_Details()
            {   cout<<"\n BRAND : "<<brand;
                cout<<"\n COUNTRY : "<<country;
            }
};
class LCD_TV : public Manufacturer, public Product
{   protected:
        int inches;
        float price;
```

```
    public:
        void get_data()
        {   get_Mfg_Details();
            get_Product_data();
            cout<<"\n Enter the Size : ";
            cin>>inches;
            cout<<"\n Enter the Price : ";
            cin>>price;
        }
        void show_data()
        {   show_Mfg_Details();
            show_Product_data();
            cout<<"\n SIZE : "<<inches;
            cout<<"\n PRICE : "<<price;
        }
};
main()
{   LCD_TV TV;
    TV.get_data();
    TV.show_data();
}
```

OUTPUT

```
Enter the Brand Name : Samsung
Enter the Country Name : Japan
Enter the Model Number : S102
Fnter the Year of Manufacturing : 2014
Enter the number of Warranty Years : 3
Enter the Size : 32
Enter the Price : 35000
BRAND : Samsung
COUNTRY : Japan
Model : S102
Manufacturing Year : 2014
Number of Warranty Years : 3
SIZE : 32
PRICE : 35000
```

Program 12.6 Write a program that has a class `employee` inherited by two classes— `contract` and `permanent`.

```
using namespace std;
#include<iostream>
class Employee
{   protected:
        int id;
        char name[20];
        char desig[20];
    public:
        void get_Emp_data()
        {   cout<<"\n Enter Employee ID : ";
            cin>>id;
            cout<<"\n Enter the Name : ";
            cin.ignore();
            cin.getline(name, 20);
```

```
            cout<<"\n Enter the Designation : ";
            cin.getline(desig, 20);
        }
        void show_Emp_data()
        {   cout<<"\n EMP ID : "<<id;
            cout<<"\n NAME : "<<name;
            cout<<"\n DESIGNATION : "<<desig;
        }
};
class Contract : public Employee
{   protected:
        int num_hrs;
        float wages_perhr;
    public:
        void get_Cont_data()
        {   get_Emp_data();
            cout<<"\n Enter the number of hours : ";
            cin>>num_hrs;
            cout<<"\n Enter the wages per hour : ";
            cin>>wages_perhr;
        }
        void show_Cont_data()
        {   show_Emp_data();
            cout<<"\n NUMBER OF HOURS WORKED : "<<num_hrs;
            cout<<"\n WAGES PER HOUR : "<<wages_perhr;
            cout<<"\n SALARY : "<<num_hrs * wages_perhr;
        }
};
class Permanent : public Employee
{   protected:
        float basic;
        float DA;
        float TA;
        float HRA;
    public:
        void get_Per_data()
        {   get_Emp_data();
            cout<<"\n Enter the Basic Pay : ";
            cin>>basic;
            cout<<"\n Enter the HRA : ";
            cin>>HRA;
            cout<<"\n Enter the TA : ";
            cin>>TA;
            DA = basic + 0.10 * basic;
        }
        float cal_salary()
        {   return (basic + HRA + TA + DA);
        }
        void show_Per_data()
        {   show_Emp_data();
            cout<<"\n SALARY (BASIC + HRA + DA + TA) = "<<cal_salary();
        }
};
```

```
main()
{   Contract C;
    C.get_Cont_data();
    C.show_Cont_data();
    Permanent P;
    P.get_Per_data();
    P.show_Per_data();
}
```

OUTPUT

```
Enter Employee ID : 1234
Enter the Name : Anjani Kumar
Enter the Designation : Assistant Professor
Enter the number of hours : 30
Enter the wages per hour : 1000
EMP ID : 1234
NAME : Anjani Kumar
DESIGNATION : Assistant Professor
NUMBER OF HOURS WORKED : 30
WAGES PER HOUR : 1000
SALARY : 30000
Enter Employee ID : 5678
Enter the Name : Kamesh Bathla
Enter the Designation : Senior Manager
Enter the Basic Pay : 12000
Enter the HRA : 30000
Enter the TA : 40000
EMP ID : 5678
NAME : Kamesh Bathla
DESIGNATION : Senior Manager
SALARY (BASIC + HRA + DA + TA) = 95200
```

Program 12.7 Write a program that implements hybrid inheritance. Classes `Student` **and** `Faculty` **inherit the class** `Person`. **Class** `Faculty` **must be inherited by the class** `Publications`.

```
using namespace std;
#include<iostream>
class Person
{   protected:
        char name[20];
        int age;
        char sex;
    public:
        void get_Person_data()
        {   cout<<"\n Enter the name : ";
            cin.getline(name, 20);
            cout<<"\n Enter the age : ";
            cin>>age;
            cout<<"\n Enter the sex : ";
            cin>>sex;
        }
        void show_Person_data()
        {   cout<<"\n NAME : "<<name;
            cout<<"\n AGE : "<<age;
            cout<<"\n Sex : "<<sex;
```

```
    }
};
class Student : public Person
{   protected:
        int roll_no;
        char course[10];
    public:
        void get_Student_data()
        {   get_Person_data();
            cout<<"\n Enter the Roll Number : ";
            cin>>roll_no;
            cout<<"\n Enter the Course : ";
            cin.ignore();
            cin.getline(course, 10);
        }
        void show_Student_data()
        {   show_Person_data();
            cout<<"\n ROLL NUMBER : "<<roll_no;
            cout<<"\n COURSE : "<<course;
        }
};
class Faculty : public Person
{   protected:
        char desig[20];
        char deptt[20];
    public:
        void get_Faculty_data()
        {   cout<<"\n Enter the Designation : ";
            cin.ignore();
            cin.getline(desig, 20);
            cout<<"\n Enter the Department : ";
            cin.getline(deptt, 20);
        }
        void show_Faculty_data()
        {   cout<<"\n DESIGNATION : "<<desig;
            cout<<"\n DEPARTMENT : "<<deptt;
        }
};
class Publications : public Faculty
{   protected:
        int no_RP;
        int no_Books;
        int no_Art;
    public:
        void get_Pub_data()
        {   get_Person_data();
            get_Faculty_data();
            cout<<"\n Enter the number of Research Papers Published : ";
            cin>>no_RP;
            cout<<"\n Enter the number of Books published : ";
            cin>>no_Books;
            cout<<"\n Enter the number of Articles Published : ";
            cin>>no_Art;
        }
```

```
        void show_Pub_data()
        {   show_Person_data();
            show_Faculty_data();
            cout<<"\n NO. OF RESEARCH PAPERS : "<<no_RP;
    cout<<"\n NO. OF BOOKS PUBLISHED : "<<no_Books;
            cout<<"\n No. of Articles Written : "<<no_Art;
        }
};
int main()
{   Student S;
    S.get_Student_data();
    S.show_Student_data();
    Publications P;
    P.get_Pub_data();
    P.show_Pub_data();
}
```

OUTPUT

```
Enter the name : Srishti Aneja
Enter the age : 20
Enter the sex : F
Enter the Roll Number : 1234
Enter the Course : BCA
NAME : Srishti Aneja
AGE : 20
Sex : F
ROLL NUMBER : 1234
COURSE : BCA
Enter the name : Shubha Rai
Enter the age : 61
Enter the sex : F
Enter the Designation : Associate Professor
Enter the Department : Computer Science
Enter the number of Research Papers Published : 15
Enter the number of Books published : 8
Enter the number of Articles Published : 10
NAME : Shubha Rai
AGE : 61
Sex : F
DESIGNATION : Associate Professor
DEPARTMENT : Computer Science
NO. OF RESEARCH PAPERS : 15
NO. OF BOOKS PUBLISHED : 8
No. of Articles Written : 10
```

Program 12.8 Write a program with class `Bill`. The users have the option to pay the bill either by cheque or by cash. Use the inheritance to model this situation.

```
using namespace std;
#include<iostream>
#include<string.h>
class Bill
{   private:
        int item_code[5];
        float price[5];
```

```
        float total;
    public:
        Bill(int items[], float p[])
        {   total = 0;
            for(int i=0;i<5;i++)
            {   item_code[i] = items[i];
                price[i] = p[i];
                total += p[i];
            }
        }
        void show_Bill_Details()
        {   cout<<"\n ITEM \t\t PRICE";
            for(int i=0;i<5;i++)
            {   cout<<"\n"<<item_code[i]<<"\t\t"<<price[i];
            }
            cout<<"\n **********************";
            cout<<"\n TOTAL = "<<total;
        }
};
class Cash_Payment : public Bill
{   private:
        int *denomination;
        int *value;
        int num;
    public:
        Cash_Payment(int items[], float p[], int deno[], int v[], int n) :
Bill(items, p)
        {   num = n;
            denomination = new int[num];
            value = new int[num];
            for(int i=0;i<num;i++)
            {   denomination[i] = deno[i];
                value[i] = v[i];
            }
        }
        void show_Cash_Payment_Details()
        {   show_Bill_Details();
            cout<<"\n Customer has entered "<<num<<" notes";
            for(int i=0;i<num;i++)
            {   cout<<"\n"<<denomination[i]<<"\t"<<value[i];
            }
        }
};
class Cheque_Payment : public Bill
{   private:
        long int chec_no;
        char bank_name[30];
    public:
        Cheque_Payment(int items[], float p[], long int cno, char name[]) :
Bill(items, p)
        {   chec_no = cno;
            strcpy(bank_name, name);
        }
        void show_Check_Payment_Details()
```

```
        {   show_Bill_Details();
            cout<<"\n CHEQUE NUMBER : "<<chec_no;
            cout<<"\n BANK NAME : "<<bank_name;
        }
};
int main()
{   int n, c[10], option i;
    float p[10];
    cout<<"\n Enter the number of items : ";
    cin>>n;
    for(i=0;i<n;i++)
    {   cout<<"\n Enter the item code : ";
        cin>>c[i];
        cout<<"\n Enter the price : ";
        cin>>p[i];
    }
    cout<<"\n Would you like to pay by cheque or cash (1/2): ";
    cin>>option;
    if(option==1)
    {   char name[30];
        long int c_num;
        cout<<"\n Enter the name of the bank : ";
        cin.ignore();
        cin.getline(name, 30);
        cout<<"\n Enter the cheque number : ";
        cin>>c_num;
        Cheque_Payment Chek(c,p,c_num,name);
        Chek.show_Check_Payment_Details();
    }
    else
    {   int num, d[10], v[10];
        cout<<"\n Enter the number of notes with different denominations : ";
        cin>>num;
        for(i=0;i<num;i++)
        {   cout<<"\n Enter the denomination of note : ";
            cin>>d[i];
            cout<<"\n Enter the number of notes with denomination "<<d[i]<<" : ";
            cin>>v[i];
        }
        Cash_Payment CP(c, p, d, v, num);
        CP.show_Cash_Payment_Details();
    }
}
```

OUTPUT

```
Enter the number of items : 5
Enter the item code : 1
Enter the price : 1000
Enter the item code : 2
Enter the price : 2000
Enter the item code : 3
Enter the price : 3000
Enter the item code : 4
```

```
Enter the price : 4000
Enter the item code : 5
Enter the price : 5000
Would you like to pay by cheque or cash (1/2): 2
Enter the number of notes with different denominations : 3
Enter the denomination of note : 1000
Enter the number of notes with denomination 1000: 8
Enter the denomination of note : 500
Enter the number of notes with denomination 1000: 10
Enter the denomination of note : 100
Enter the number of notes with denomination 1000: 20
ITEM       PRICE
 1         1000
 2         2000
 3         3000
 4         4000
 5         5000
*******************
 TOTAL = 15000
Customer has entered 3 notes
1000        8
500         10
100         20
```

12.14 MULTI-PATH INHERITANCE

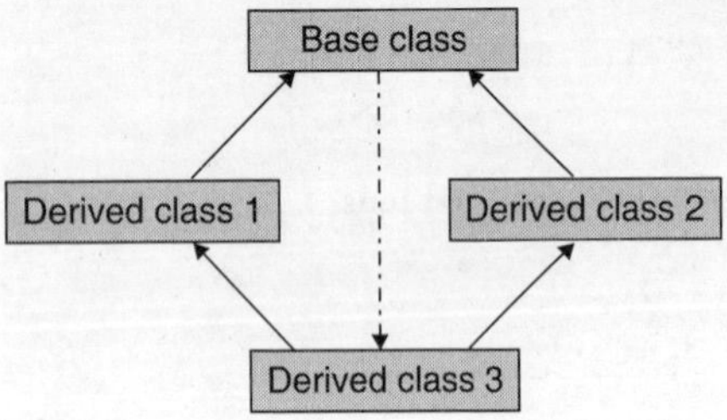

Figure 12.10 Multi-path inheritance

Deriving a class from other derived classes that are, in turn, derived from the same base class is called multi-path inheritance as given in Fig. 12.10. If you observe carefully, you will find that this type of inheritance is actually a combination of three different kinds of inheritance—hierarchical, multiple, and multi-level. As seen from Fig. 2.10, the `derived class` has two immediate base classes—`Derived_Class1` and `Derived_Class2`. Both these base classes are themselves derived from the `Base_Class`, thereby forming a grandparent, parent, and child in a relationship. The `derived class` inherits the features of the `Base_class` (grandparent) through two separate paths. Therefore, the `Base_class` is also known as the indirect base class.

12.14.1 Problem in Multi-path Inheritance or Diamond Problem

The derived class inherits the members of the base class (grandparent) twice, through `parent1` (`Derived_Class1`) and `parent 2`(`Derived_Class2`). This results in ambiguity because a duplicate set of members is created. This ambiguous situation must be avoided.

12.15 VIRTUAL BASE CLASSES

The solution to the problem of ambiguity in multi-path inheritance is by making the common `base class or grandparent class` into a `virtual base class`. This is done by using the keyword `virtual` while declaring the direct or intermediate base classes or parent classes. The syntax for defining a virtual base class while being inherited by immediate base class can be given as follows:

```
class derived_class : virtual access-specifier base class
{   ------
    ------
};
OR
class derived_class : access-specifier virtual base class
{   ------
    ------
};
```

The keyword `virtual` ensures that only one copy of the base class (grandparent) is inherited, irrespective of the number of inheritance paths that exist between the virtual base class and the derived class.

Note Keywords `virtual` and `access-specifier` can be used in any order.

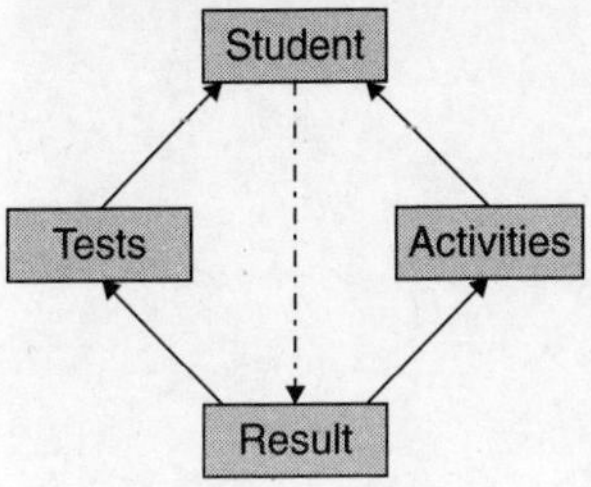

Figure 12.11 Multi-path inheritance

The program given here calculates the result of a student using multiple as well as multi-level inheritance in conjunction with the keyword `virtual`. Classes `Tests` and `activities` inherit class `student` (multiple inheritance), class `result` inherits `Tests` and `Activities` to calculate the final result as shown in Fig. 12.11.

Example 12.11 Multi-path inheritance using keyword `virtual`

```
using namespace std;
#include<iostream>
class Student
{   protected:
        int roll_no;
        char name[20];
    public:
        void get_Stud_data()
        {   cout<<"\n Enter the roll number : ";
            cin>>roll_no;
            cout<<"\n Enter the name : ";
            cin.ignore();
            cin.getline(name, 20);
        }
        void show_Stud_data()
        {   cout<<"\n ROLL NUMBER : "<<roll_no;
            cout<<"\n NAME : "<<name;
        }
};
class Tests : virtual public Student
{   protected:
        int marks[3];
    public:
        void get_Marks()
        {   cout<<"\n Enter the marks in three subjects : ";
            cin>>marks[0]>>marks[1]>>marks[2];
        }
        int total_marks()
        {   return (marks[0] + marks[1] + marks[2]);   }
};
class Activities : virtual public Student
{   protected:
```

```
        int acts[2];
    public:
        void get_Acts_Score()
        {   cout<<"\n Enter the score in two Activities : ";
            cin>>acts[0]>>acts[1];
        }
        int total_score()
        {   return (acts[0] + acts[1]);   }
};
class Result : public Tests, public Activities
{   public:
        void show_total()
        {
            cout<<"\n TOTAL : "<<total_marks() + total_score();
        }
};
main()
{   Result R;
    R.get_Stud_data();
    R.get_Marks();
    R.get_Acts_Score();
    R.show_Stud_data();
    R.show_total();
}
```

OUTPUT

```
Enter the roll number :1234
Enter the name :Saisha Bajaj
Enter the marks in three subjects :100 100 100
Enter the score in two Activities :100 100
ROLL NUMBER :1234
NAME :Saisha Bajaj
TOTAL :500
```

Explanation: In the program, after using the keyword `virtual`, only a single copy of the `base class` will exist. Therefore, the `result` will have just a single copy of `members with roll_no, name, get_Stud_data(), and show_Stud_data()`.

Note The constructor for a virtual `base class` is invoked before any non-virtual `base class`. If there are multiple virtual `base classes`, then they are invoked in the order in which they are declared.

12.16 OBJECT SLICING

We have seen that the object of a derived class can be assigned to an object of its base class; however, the same rule does not apply for the object of a base class. This process is called object slicing. Object slicing occurs because when the derived class object is assigned to an object of the base class, and the additional features of the derived class are sliced off from the objects of base class.

Example 12.12 Object slicing

```
using namespace std;
#include<iostream>
class Base
```

```
{   protected:
        int a;
    public:
        Base(int x)
        {   a = x;   }
        virtual void show()
        {   cout<<"\n In Base : a = "<<a;
        }
};
class Derived : public Base
{   private:
        int b;
    public:
        Derived(int x, int y) : Base(x)
        {   b = y;    }
        virtual void show()
        {   cout<<"\n In Derived : a = "<<a<<" and b = "<<b;
        }
};
main()
{   Base B(5);
    Derived D(2,3);
    B = D;          // derived object is assigned to base class object
    B.show();       //additional features cannot be accessed
}
```

OUTPUT

```
In Base : a = 2
```

From the output of the program, it is clear that the additional member of derived object (`j`) is sliced off when it is assigned to the object of the base class. To avoid the problems associated with object slicing, the programmer can take the following steps:

- Use pointers or references to the objects of the derived class.
- Make the base class an abstract class so that no object of the base class can be created. Declare the virtual function as pure virtual function.

We will discuss both these techniques in this chapter.

12.17 POINTERS TO DERIVED CLASS

Until now, we have seen that irrespective of the type of inheritance, it provides a hierarchical organization of classes. The objects of these classes share certain common features in addition to their specific features.

We can declare pointers to direct to either the base class or to the derived classes. Pointers to object of base class are compatible with pointers to object of derived class. Therefore, a single base class pointer can point to objects of the base as well as to the objects of the derived classes. However, this statement does not hold true for the reverse as a pointer to derived class

Object cannot point to objects of base class object as shown in Fig. 12.12.

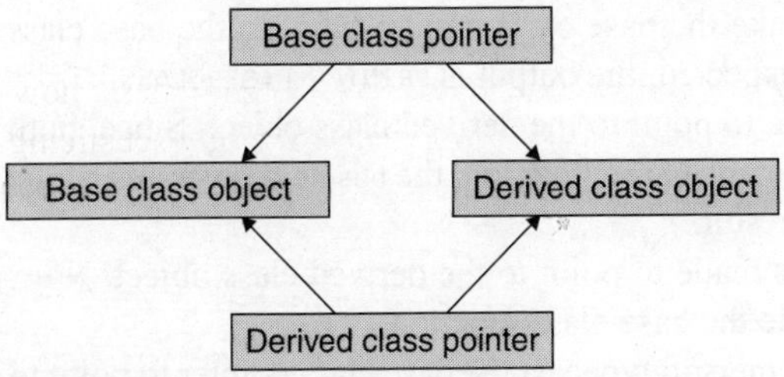

Figure 12.12 Type compatibility of base and derived class pointers

According to Fig. 12.12, it is clear that the base class pointer can point to either the base class object or the derived class object. However, the pointer can access only those public members of the derived class that have been inherited from the base class. In no way, it can access the members of the derived class that are unique to it.

If the derived class has a member with the same name as that of the base class, then any reference to that member will access the member of the base class.

Note To access all the members of the derived class, you must use a pointer to the derived class.

Look at the program code given here and observe the output.

Example 12.13 Pointer to derived class

```
using namespace std;
#include<iostream>
class Base
{   public:
        void print()
        {   cout<<"\n PRINT - BASE CLASS";
        }
};
class Derived : public Base
{   public:
        void print()
        {   cout<<"\n PRINT - DERIVED CLASS";
        }
};
main()
{   Base B, *bptr;
    Derived D, *dptr;
    bptr = &B;     // Base class ptr points to base class object
    bptr->print();
    bptr = &D;     // Base class ptr points to derived class object
    bptr->print();
    dptr = &D;     // Derived class ptr points to derived class object
    dptr->print();
}
```

OUTPUT

```
PRINT - BASE CLASS
PRINT - BASE CLASS
PRINT - DERIVED CLASS
```

Programming Tip: Only class member functions can be declared as virtual. Regular functions or friend functions cannot be declared as virtual.

Explanation: In the program, we make the base class pointer point to the base class object and then call the `print()`. As expected, the output is `PRINT - BASE CLASS`.

Then the base class pointer is made to point to the derived class object. Since, both the `base` and `derived` classes have the same name function, the `base` class version of the function will be invoked. Hence, the result.

Finally, the derived class pointer is made to point to the derived class object. Now, the derived class function will override the base class function.

Note that C++ also allows programmers to typecast the base class pointer to point to the derived class. In the program, this could have been written by writing,

```
((Derived *)bptr)->print();
```

The statement will generate an output as `PRINT - DERIVED CLASS`

Note Pointer to a class at a particular level can point to that class as well as to the classes that are below that level in the class hierarchy.

12.17.1 Upcasting, Downcasting, and Cross-casting

Upcasting means converting a derived-class pointer to a base-class pointer. Downcasting, on the other hand, refers to casting a base class pointer to a derived class pointer.

Cross-casting refers to casting a derived class pointer to a proper base class pointer when there are multiple base classes in the case of multiple inheritance. It involves casting from one base class pointer into another base class pointer. The syntax of cross casting is as follows:

```
Base_class_ptr = dynamic_cast< Base_class_ptr>Derived_class_pointer.
```

We will study about `dynamic_cast` given in the syntax in Chapter STL and new features in C++.

12.18 RUN-TIME POLYMORPHISM

From the beginning, we have been emphasizing that polymorphism is an important concept of OOP. Till now, we have also seen how static polymorphism is implemented in C++ using function overloading and operator overloading techniques. In this section, we will learn how virtual functions are used to implement run-time or dynamic polymorphism.

Note Binding means the process used for converting variables and functions into machine language addresses.

Run-time polymorphism, also known as late binding or dynamic polymorphism, allows objects of different classes to respond to the same message but in different forms. However, the binding between the function call and the appropriate virtual function to be called is postponed until the runtime or execution of the program. Therefore, the appropriate member function to be called is decided at the run time. Such functions are called virtual functions and the corresponding classes are called polymorphic classes. This is in striking contrast with function overloading and operator overloading due to the following reasons.

- In function overloading, the compiler calls the appropriate function by matching the signature of the function with the arguments specified in function call.
- In operator overloading, the compiler calls operator functions to operate on user defined data types with the same interface as that of standard data types.

In both the cases, the compiler has all the information about the type and number of operands, and can easily invoke the appropriate function. However, with virtual functions, the compiler does not know which function to call in advance; therefore, this decision is postponed till the execution of the program. Figure 12.13 highlights the difference between static and dynamic polymorphism.

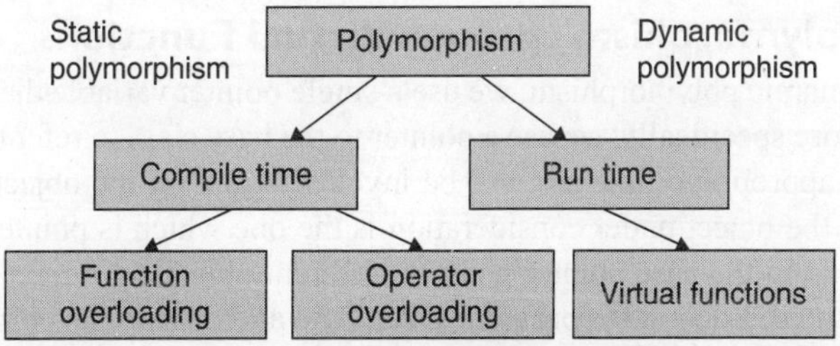

Figure 12.13 Static vs Dynamic Polymorphism

Note Compile time polymorphism is also known as static binding, early binding, or static linking.

12.19 VIRTUAL FUNCTIONS

Consider the following code:

```
class Base
{  -----
   public:
      void show()
      {  -----  }
};
class Derived : public Base
{-----
   public:
      void show()
      {  -----  }
};
```

Programming Tip: Virtual functions should be declared in the public section of a class to realize their complete benefits.

In the code, the function `show()` has the same prototype in both the classes; therefore, to print values of objects of both the classes, we may use the class resolution operator that specifies the class while invoking the function. However, this does not involve run-time polymorphism. Therefore, in C++, we have virtual functions to implement dynamic polymorphism.

When we have the same function name in the base as well as the derived class, the function in the base class is declared as `virtual`. To declare a virtual function, precede the function prototype with the keyword `virtual`. The syntax for defining a virtual function is as follows:

```
virtual return_type function_name (arguments)
{  --------
}
```

For example,

```
virtual void show();
```

This statement declares the function `show()` as a virtual function. The `virtual` function provides a means by which functions of the base class can be overridden by the functions of the derived class.

Note A class that declares or inherits a virtual function is called a polymorphic class.

12.19.1 Run-time Polymorphism through Virtual Functions

To implement dynamic polymorphism, we use a single pointer variable that points to objects of different classes. More specifically, we use a pointer to the base class to refer to all the derived objects. At run time, the appropriate function will be invoked based on the object is currently under consideration. Here, the object under consideration is the one which is pointed to by the base pointer. Therefore, by making the base pointer point to different objects, different versions of virtual functions can be executed. Look at the program given here and observe its output.

Example 12.14 Virtual function

```
using namespace std;
#include<iostream>
class Base
{   public:
        void print()
        {   cout<<"\n PRINT - BASE CLASS";
        }
        virtual void show()
        {   cout<<"\n SHOW – BASE CLASS";
        }
};
class Derived : public Base
{   public:
        void print()
        {   cout<<"\n PRINT - DERIVED CLASS";
        }
        void show()
        {   cout<<"\n SHOW - DERIVED CLASS";
        }
};
main()
{   Base B, *bptr;
    Derived D;
    bptr = &B;     // Base class ptr points to base class object
    bptr->print();
    bptr->show();
    bptr = &D;     // Base class ptr points to derived class object
    bptr->print();
    bptr->show();
}
```

OUTPUT

```
PRINT - BASE CLASS
SHOW - BASE CLASS
PRINT - BASE CLASS
SHOW - DERIVED CLASS
```

Programming Tip: Only class member functions can be declared as virtual. Regular functions or friend functions cannot be declared as virtual.

Explanation: In the program, `print()` and `show()` are functions with the same name and prototype in both the base and the derived class. In `main()`, when we invoke the `print()` through a base class pointer, the base class definition is invoked, irrespective of whether the base class pointer holds the address of the base class object or the derived class's object. However, since `show()` is a virtual function, C++ dynamically calls the appropriate function depending on the object pointed by the base class pointer. The type of pointer has no role to play in deciding which function to call.

We could have also written, `Base *bptr = new Base();` or `Base *bptr = new Derived();`

Note Dynamic polymorphism is achieved only through a pointer to the base class.

Refer to Fig. 12.14, which graphically illustrates the accessibility of members using pointers to the base class and derived classes.

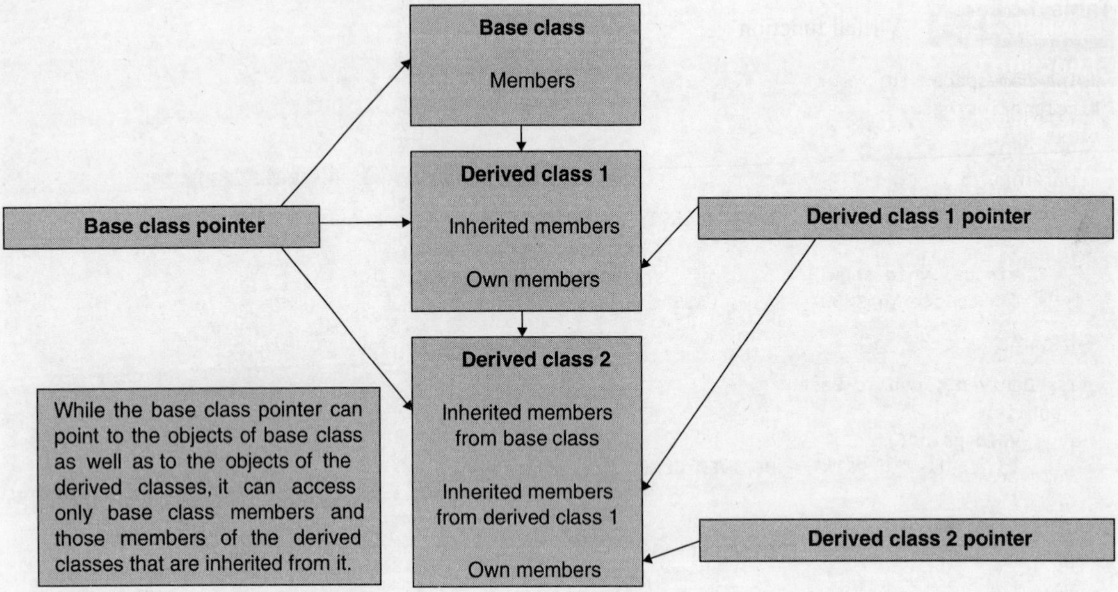

Figure 12.14 Base class pointers and derived class pointers

> **Note** C++ also allows programmers to create an array of base pointers to point to the base class and derived classes objects.

12.19.2 Rules for Virtual Functions

When incorporating virtual function(s) in a class, the programmers must keep the following points in mind:

- Virtual functions must be members of a class.
- Virtual functions must be declared in the public section so that the object can invoke that function.
- If the virtual function is declared in the class but defined outside the class, then the virtual keyword is used in function declaration but not in definition.
- Virtual functions cannot be static members.
- Virtual functions must be accessed using a pointer to the object.
- A virtual function cannot be declared as a friend of another class.
- Virtual functions must be defined in the base class even if their definition has no significance.
- The prototype of virtual functions in the base class and in the derived class must be the same. This is because if the functions of the base and derived class have the same name but have a different prototype, then it becomes function overloading and not function overriding. Refer to Table 12.2 for differences between function overloading and function overriding.
- It is not mandatory for derived classes to redefine virtual functions. If the derived class has given a specific definition for the virtual function, then the derived class version of the function is invoked; otherwise, the base class version of the function is called.
- A class may have a virtual destructor but it cannot have a virtual constructor.

Table 12.2 Differences between overloading and overriding

Function overloading	Function overriding
• Providing multiple definition of the function by changingsignature, means change number of parameters change datatype of parameters return type does not play any role	• Redefinition of parent class function inside its child class with same signature, that is return type and parameters must be same.
• It can be done in parent class and inside its child class.	• It can only be done inside child class.
• It comes under compile time polymorphism.	• It is used to achieve run-time polymorphism.
• It is also known as universal polymorphism.	• It is also known as adhoc polymorphism.

• For example
`void area(int l);`
`void area(float r); //Rule II`
 	
`or`
`void area(int r); //Rule I`
`void area(int l, int b);`
	• For example:
	`class Circle`
	`{ public: void area() {`
	`cout<<"pi*r*r";} }`
	
	`class Sphere:public Circle`
	`{public: void area() {cout<<`
	`"4*pi*r*r"; } }`

Note Function overriding is the mechanism by which function definition in the derived class overrides or replaces the function definition in the base class. Note that the two functions have the same name and prototype.

Guiding Principle

Never use virtual functions in constructors or destructors. This is because if a base class makes a virtual function call implemented by the derived class, that function may be using variables that have not yet been initialized, since the derived class has not been initialized. Therefore, in such cases, C++ invokes the virtual function with the base class object, thereby defeating the purpose of calling a virtual function.

12.20 PURE VIRTUAL FUNCTIONS

As a good programming habit, we must redefine the virtual functions in the derived classes because function in the base class just gives a template for the derived classes and therefore has not much functionality to implement. Therefore, it is recommended to declare such virtual functions as empty, or without any definition. These do-nothing functions that have no definition are called pure virtual functions.

To declare a virtual function, the prototype of the function is preceded with the keyword `virtual` and followed by a `= 0;`. For example, to declare a pure virtual function `show();` we need to write

```
virtual void show() = 0;
```

where = 0 informs that only declaration is provided in the class without definition. Otherwise, the compiler will assume it as a virtual function whose definition is specified outside the class.

When a class has a pure virtual function, it is the responsibility of each derived class to define that function. If the derived class does not define the virtual function, it must also declare that function as a pure virtual function. A class that has a pure virtual function is called an abstract class. C++ does not allow programmers to create an object of the abstract class.

Look at the program given here which uses a pure virtual function `show()`.

Example 12.15 Using pure virtual function `show()`

```
using namespace std;
#include<iostream>
class Base
{   public:
        void print()
        {   cout<<"\n PRINT - BASE CLASS";
        }
        virtual void show() = 0;
};
class Derived : public Base
{   public:
        void print()
        {   cout<<"\n PRINT - DERIVED CLASS";
        }
        void show()
        {   cout<<"\n SHOW - DERIVED CLASS";
        }
};
main()
{   Base *bptr;
    Derived D;
    bptr = &D;      // Base class ptr points to derived class object
    bptr->print();
    bptr->show();
}
```

OUTPUT

```
PRINT - BASE CLASS
SHOW - DERIVED CLASS
```

Explanation: In the program, class `Base` has a pure virtual function `show()`. To implement the definition of this function is the responsibility of the class inheriting `Base`.

Note Classes that are derived from the base class and provide the implementation of the pure virtual functions are called concrete classes.

12.21 ABSTRACT BASE CLASSES

An abstract class corresponds to an abstract concept. For example, a polygon may refer to a rectangle, triangle, or any other closed figure. Therefore, an abstract class is a class that is specifically defined to lay a foundation for other classes that exhibits a common behaviour or similar characteristics. It is primarily used only as a base class for inheritance.

> **Programming Tip:**
> Instantiating an object of an abstract class causes a compilation error.

Since an abstract class is an incomplete class, users are not allowed to create its object. To use such a class, programmers must derive it, keeping in mind that they must implement all pure virtual functions specified in that class.

Features

- Abstract base classes have at least one pure virtual function
- Classes inheriting abstract classes must either define all pure virtual functions or must themselves become an abstract class.
- There can be no object of an abstract class.
- Pointers or references to abstract classes can be created.
- An abstract class can have other data members and member functions in addition to the pure virtual functions.

Uses

- Abstract classes provide a common and standardized interface to the sub-classes so that all derived classes operate in a similar fashion.
- Abstract class enables new applications to be easily added to a pre-defined system.

Example 12.16 Program to print Ubuntu is awesome using an abstract class

```
using namespace std;
#include<iostream>
class sample
{
    public:
        virtual void example()=0;
};
class Ex1:public sample
{
    public:
        void example()
        {
            cout<<"Ubuntu";
        }
};
class Ex2:public sample
{
    public:
        void example()
        {
            cout<<" is awesome";
        }
};
int main()
{
    sample *ptr[2];
    Ex1 e1;
    Ex2 e2;
    ptr[0]= &e1;
    ptr[1]= &e2;
    ptr[0]->example();
    ptr[1]->example();
}
```

OUTPUT

```
Ubuntu is awesome
```

Example 12.17 Implementing `mango` and `orange` class from abstract base `fruit`

```
using namespace std;
#include<iostream>
class Fruit{      //Abstract Class
public:
virtual void taste()=0;      //PVF
void show()
{ cout<<"\n I am a Fruit"; } //Abstract class can also have Normal Function
};
class Mango:public Fruit     //Concrete Class
{
public:
void taste()      //fn overriding
    {
        cout<<"\n Mango is Sweet";
    }
};
class Orange:public Fruit
{
public:
void taste()      //fn overriding
    {
        cout<<"\n Orange is Sour";
    }
void color()      //additional fn
    {
        cout<<"\n Orange is Orangish";
    }
};
class Alfanso: public Mango
{
            //Not Compulsory to implement taste() as it definition from Mango
};
int main()
{
// Fruit f; //Error -Can't create object of abstract class
    Fruit *g; //Ok-Pointers can be create
    Mango m; //Ok - Concrete class object
    Orange o;
    Alfanso a;
    g=&m;      //Pointer points to mango object
    g->taste();       //Output: Mango is Sweet
    g=&o;      //Pointer points to Orange object
    g->taste();       //Output: Orange is sour
    Alfanso al;
    g=&al;     //Pointer points to Alfanso object
    g->taste();       //Output: Mango is Sweet
}
```

```
OUTPUT
Mango is sweet
Orange is sour
Mango is Sweet
```

Let us see some more examples as given in Table 12.3 where we can apply the concept of abstract classes in real-world examples.

Table 12.3 Abstract class versus concrete class

Abstract parent class	Concrete child class	Pure virtual function in parent
Shape	Circle, rectangle, triangle	virtual void area()=0;
Animal	Dog, cat, horse	virtual void sound()=0;
Fruit	Mango, orange, apple	virtual void taste()=0;

12.22 CONCEPT OF VTABLES

When a class has a virtual function, the compiler creates a VTABLE, in which the address of the virtual function is inserted. When the object of that class is created, the compiler inserts a hidden pointer called VPTR or virtual pointer to point to the VTABLE for that object.

Note Each row of the VTABLE is a function pointer that points to a virtual function.

When the function is called using the base class, the compiler secretly inserts a code to fetch the VPTR to look up for the function stored in the VTABLE. This allows the compiler to call the right function at the run time. Figure 12.15 provides a clear understanding of the concept.

```
class Polygon
{    public:
          virtual void area();
          virtual void
perimeter();
};
```

```
Polygon.vptr = address of
Polygon.vtable

Polygon.vtable[0] = &Polygon::area()

Polygon.vtable[1]   =
&Polygon::perimeter()
```

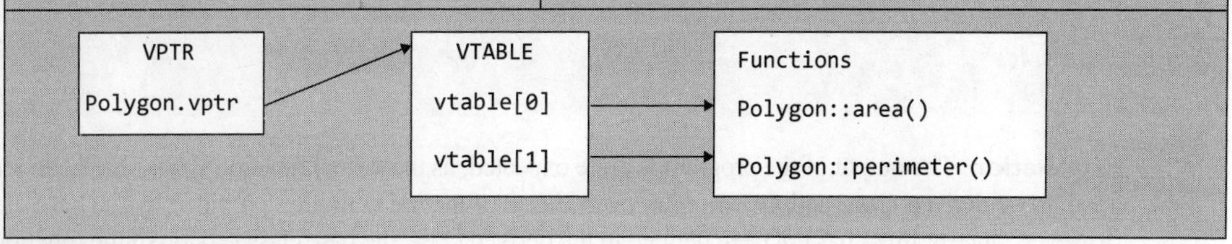

Figure 12.15 Virtual pointer and virtual table

Important pointers

- The VTABLE is created for each class that has a virtual function and for the classes derived from it.
- Dynamic binding is accomplished with the help of VTABLE and VPTR.
- VTABLE is an array of pointers to virtual functions.

Programming Tip: By default, VPTR is added as the first member of the object.

- VTABLE is created by the compiler at the compile time.
- During run time, the appropriate virtual function is called by fetching the address of the virtual function from the VTABLE
- A VTABLE is shared amongst all the objects belonging to the same class.
- The compiler secretly inserts a hidden code in the constructor of each class having a virtual function that initializes the VPTR of its objects with the address of the VTABLE.
- For pure virtual functions, a null pointer is stored in the VTABLE of the abstract class.
- The VPTR is inherited to all the derived classes

Note The address of virtual function is placed in the VTABLE and the VPTR is used to point to the virtual function.

Example 12.18 Creating VTABLEs and VPTRs

```
using namespace std;
#include<iostream>
class Base
{   public:
      virtual void print()
      {   cout<<"\n Base :: print()";
      }
      virtual void show()
      {   cout<<"\n Base :: show()";
      }
};
class Derived : public Base
{   public:
      void show()
      {   cout<<"\n Derived :: show()";
      }
};
main()
{   Base *b = new Derived();    //*b is assigned Derived class's VPTR
    b->show();
    b->print();
}
```

OUTPUT

```
Derived :: show()
Base :: print()
```

Explanation: The output of the program is quite expected, as the virtual function show() has been redefined in the derived class, and the compiler overrides the function definition provided by the base class. However, since print() has not been defined in the derived class, the base class version of the function is invoked. Let us now see the VTABLE and VPTR for both these classes.

From Fig. 12.16, we can conclude the following points:

- When a derived class is constructed, its base class is constructed first which creates the VTABLE.
- If the derived class overrides any of the base classes virtual functions, the entries in the VTABLE are overwritten by the derived class constructor.

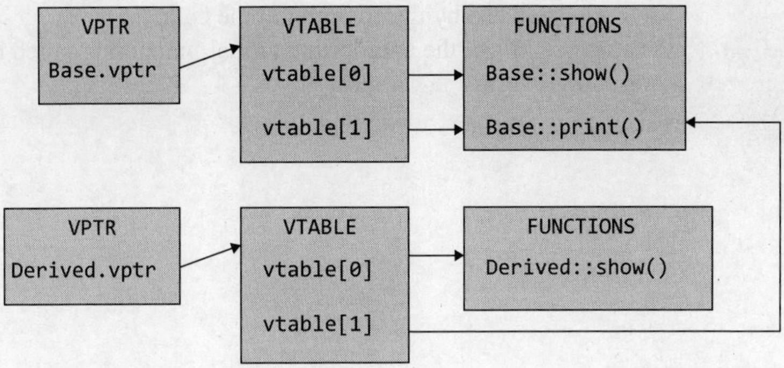

Figure 12.16 Virtual table

12.23 VIRTUAL CONSTRUCTOR AND DESTRUCTORS

While C++ allows programmers to define virtual destructors, it strictly disallows making virtual constructors. The reasons behind not having virtual constructors are as follows.

> **Programming Tip:** Apart from inline, no other keyword is allowed in the declaration of constructor.

- C++ is a static-typed language which means that the C++ compiler must be aware of the class type to create the object during the compile time of the program.
- While calling a constructor, if the VTABLE had not been created, there is an answer as to how will the call to virtual constructor be resolved.
- Moreover, in C++, object creation and object type are tightly coupled but a virtual constructor decouples object creation from its type. The choice of object to be created is decided dynamically by the compiler, based on the name of constructor used along with the new keyword. Hence, there is no need of virtual constructor.

12.23.1 Virtual Destructor

We have seen that a destructor is defined to deallocate memory and perform certain clean-up operations for a class object when the object goes out of scope or is explicitly destroyed. In inheritance, the sequence in which destructors is called just the reverse of the sequence of calling the constructors. However, the need for a virtual destructor will be clear only when we see an example code that does not uses a virtual destructor. Consider the code given as follows.

Example 12.19 Virtual destructor

```
using namespace std;
#include<iostream>
class Base
{   public:
        Base()
        {   cout<<"\n In Base Class Constructor";
        }
        ~Base()
        {   cout<<"\n In Base Class Destructor";
        }
};
class Derived : public Base
{   public:
        Derived()
        {   cout<<"\n In Derived Class Constructor";
```

```
        }
        ~Derived()
        {   cout<<"\n In Derived Class Destructor";
        }
};
main()
{   Base *bptr = new Derived();
    delete bptr;
}
```

OUTPUT

```
In Base Class Constructor
In Derived Class Constructor
In Base Class Destructor
```

Programming Tip: C++ also allows you to have pure virtual destructors. But then it makes the class an abstract class.

Explanation: From the output of the program, we see that while constructors are called in the right order, the destructor of the derived class does not get called. Ideally, program termination occurs with destruction of the derived class object which did not take place here. To solve this problem, we must declare the base class destructor as virtual.

A virtual destructor ensures that the destructor for any class that is derived from the base class will be called. Consider the output of the same program with the destructor declared as

```
virtual ~Base()
{   cout<<"\n In Base Class Destructor";
}
```

OUTPUT

```
In Base Class Constructor
In Derived Class Constructor
In Derived Class Destructor
In Base Class Destructor
```

According to the output, both constructors and destructors are called in the right sequence. To conclude, the guiding principle is that if a class has one or more virtual functions, then that class should also have a virtual destructor.

Note To define a virtual destructor, use the keyword `virtual` before the ~ symbol.

12.24 PROS AND CONS OF INHERITANCE

To conclude our discussion on inheritance, let us examine some major advantages and disadvantages of inheritance. The advantages are as follows.

- When a class is derived from another class, the code of the base class can be directly used by the derived class. The derived class need not rewrite the code that has already been written. This leads to code reusability.
- Reusability of code, in turn, enhances the reliability of a code as users know they are using a pre-written, debugged, and a tested code.

- Programmers can share their codes at several levels. This not only reduces development cost but also decreases the effort and time spent on code maintenance.
- When multiple classes inherit the same base class, it ensures that all derived classes follow the same structure.
- Inheritance helps in rapid prototyping and generation of complete code in less time as the programmers need to focus only on the new or additional portion of the system, forgetting about other details.
- Inheritance helps programmers avoid code redundancy and supports code extensibility by permitting base class functionality to be overridden by derived classfunctionality.
- Inheritance facilitates creation of class libraries.

However, the downside of inheritance is as follows.

- Inherited functions often work slower than specialized codes.
- A program requires more memory space to store its own code and the code of other classes that it is using.
- Overuse or improper use of inheritance may lead to poorly designed or even wrong solutions.
- Often, data members defined in the base class are not used in the derived class. This affects the program's performance as unnecessarily memory is allocated to them. A solution to this problem may be specialized inheritance, which is even more complex to implement.
- In inheritance, base and derived classes are tightly coupled. Therefore, if you change the code of the base class, it would affect all the derived classes.

Containership

Containership is the ability of a class to contain objects of one or more classes as member data. For example, `class One` can have an object of `class Two` as its data member. This would allow the object of `class One` to call the public functions of `class Two`. Here, `class One` becomes the container, while `class Two` becomes the contained class.

Containership is also called composition because, as in our example, `class One` is composed of `class Two`. In OOP, containership represents a has-a relationship. It is important to note that, even though the container has access to execute all the public methods of the contained class, it is not able to alter or provide additional functionality.

Composition is generally used when the features of an existing class is needed inside the new class, but not its interface. For this, existing class's object is embedded in the new class. The programmer will use the interface of the new class but implementation details of the original class.

Differences between Inheritance and Containership

Inheritance	Containership
• Enables a class to inherit data and functions from a base class by extending it	• Enables a class to contain objects of different classes as its data member.
• The derived class may override the functionality of base class.	• The container class cannot alter or override the functionality of the contained class.
• The derived class may add data or functions to the base class.	• The container class cannot add anything to the contained class.
• Inheritance represents a is-a relationship.	• Containership represents a has-a relationship.
• For example, a student is a person.	• For example, `class One` has a `class Two`.

Points To Remember

- The derived classes are created by first inheriting the data and methods of the base class and then adding new specialized data and functions in it.
- Therefore, base class members that should not be accessible to the member functions of derived classes should be declared private in the base class.
- When a base class is publicly inherited by a derived class, public members of the base class become public members of the derived class.
- A data member or a member function declared as protected can be accessed by the class in which it is defined (as in private) and the class which is immediately derived from it.
- If the derived and base class have constructors, the base class constructor is executed first. The order of execution of destructors is just the reverse of constructor.
- Pointers to object of base class are type compatible with pointers to object of derived class.
- Run-time binding is implemented using virtual functions.
- When a class has a pure virtual function, then it is the responsibility of each derived class to define that function. If the derived class does not define the virtual function, it must also declare that function as a pure virtual function.
- Abstract classes provide a common and standardized interface to the sub classes so that all derived classes operate in a similar fashion.
- When a class has a virtual function, the compiler creates a VTABLE, in which the address of the virtual function is inserted. When the object of that class is created, the compiler inserts a hidden pointer called VPTR or virtual pointer to point to the VTABLE for that object.
- While C++ allows programmers to define virtual destructors, it strictly disallows making virtual constructors.

Glossary

Base class A class that is created with the intention of deriving other classes from it

Binding The process used for converting variables and functions into machine language addresses

Concrete classes Classes that are derived from the base class and provide the implementation of the pure virtual functions

Cross casting Casting from derived class to proper base class when there are multiple base classes in the case of multiple-inheritance

Derivation Creating a new class using the inheritance property

Derived class A class that inherits some other class(s)

Down casing Casing from base class pointer to derived class pointer

Function overriding Mechanism by which function definition in the derived class overrides or replaces the function definition in the base class

Hierarchical inheritance When a class is inherited by more than one class

Inheritance Linking two or more classes with each other in a hierarchical manner so that their properties and functions can be shared

Multi-level inheritance The technique of deriving a class from an already derived class

Multi-path inheritance Deriving a class from other derived classes that are in turn derived from the same base class

Multiple inheritance When a derived class inherits features from more than one base class

Polymorphic class A class that declares or inherits a virtual function

Protected derivation When a base class can be inherited in protected mode, it is called protected derivation

Single inheritance When a derived class inherits features from a single base class

Upcasting Converting a derived-class reference or pointer to a base-class

Exercises

Fill in the Blanks

1. The technique of creating a new class from an existing class is called ________.
2. Inheritance is frequently used to implement the ________ relationship.
3. The visibility-mode can be ________, ________, or ________.
4. When a protected member is inherited in public mode, it becomes a ________ member of the derived class.
5. In multi-level inheritance, the constructor is executed in the order of ________.
6. Ambiguity problem is solved by using the ________ keyword.
7. To access all the members of a derived class, you must declare a pointer to the ________ class.
8. Compile time polymorphism is a variant of ________ binding.
9. ________ functions are used to implement dynamic binding.
10. A function is declared as virtual in the ________ class.
11. Virtual functions cannot be ________ members of the class.
12. ________ are do-nothing functions.
13. ________ classes have at least one pure virtual function.
14. The address of the virtual function is inserted in ________.
15. Each row of the VTABLE is a ________ that points to a ________.

State True or False

1. The visibility mode is optional.
2. Private is the lowest level of data hiding.
3. Private members are never inherited.
4. In public inheritance, the object of the derived class can access the public member functions of the derived class.
5. A protected member cannot be accessed by a friend function or a friend class.
6. A derived class inherits the constructors as well as destructors.
7. If both the derived and base class has constructors, the base class constructor is executed first.
8. Constructors can only call constructors from their immediate base class.
9. Constructor for a virtual base class is invoked before any non-virtual base class.
10. The object of a derived class cannot be assigned to an object of its base class.
11. Base class pointers point to either the base class or to the derived classes.
12. A base class pointer can point to all the members of the derived class.
13. Only class member functions can be declared `virtual`.
14. Typecasting the base class pointer to point to the derived class is not permissible in C++.
15. It is mandatory to declare virtual functions in the public section.
16. A virtual function can be declared as a friend of another class.
17. A class may have a virtual constructor but it cannot have a virtual destructor.
18. It is not mandatory for the derived classes to redefine virtual functions.
19. Users can create its objects of an abstract class. An abstract class can have only pure virtual functions.
20. The VTABLE is created for each class that has a virtual function and for the classes derived from it.
21. A VTABLE is shared amongst all the objects belonging to the same class.
22. The VPTR is inherited to all the derived classes.
23. Pure virtual destructors are allowed in C++.
24. Inheritance helps in data hiding.
25. While defining a derived class, some changes may have to be done in the base class.
26. We can prevent inheritance of all members of the base class by making the base class virtual.
27. When an object of the derived class is created, memory is allocated to all data members of both base and the derived class.
28. A class with a virtual function can be instantiated.

Multiple Choice Questions

1. If class A uses features of class B, then A is called the ________ class and B is called the ________ class.
   (a) Base, derived (b) Derived, base
   (c) Base, base (d) Derived, derived

2. If no access specifier is written, by default, the class will be derived in which mode?
(a) Public (b) Private
(c) Protected (d) None of these
3. In private inheritance, public members of the base class become _______ members of the derived class.
(a) Public (b) Private
(c) Protected (d) None of these
4. A private member can be accessed in?
(a) Same class (b) Friend class
(c) Friend function (d) All of these
5. A class cannot inherit _______
(a) Overloaded operators
(b) Private members
(c) Friend function of the base class
(d) All of these
6. Ambiguity problems occur in which type of inheritance?
(a) Multi-level (b) Multiple
(c) Multi-path (d) Hierarchical
7. Object slicing can be resolved using
(a) Pointers (b) References
(c) Abstract class (d) All of these
8. Objects of which class cannot be created?
(a) Base class (b) Derived class
(c) Abstract class (d) All of these
9. Virtual table is created by
(a) Base class (b) Derived class
(c) Compiler (d) Linker
10. The only keyword allowed in the declaration of constructor is
(a) Inline (b) Virtual
(c) Protected (d) static
11. If a class has one or more virtual functions, then that class should also have a _______.
(a) Constructor (b) Pure Virtual function
(c) Virtual destructor (d) destructor
12. A private data member can be accessed through
(a) Private member function
(b) Public member function
(c) Protected member function
(d) All of these
13. In multi-level inheritance, the middle class acts as
(a) Base class (b) Derived class
(c) Both of these (d) None of these
14. In protected inheritance, protected members of the base class become _______ members of the derived class.
(a) Public (b) Private
(c) Protected (d) Inaccessible

Review Questions

1. Explain the need for inheritance.
2. Differentiate between a base class and a derived class.
3. Give the syntax of defining a derived class.
4. Explain the significance of different access specifiers used in inheritance.
5. Is there any way by which a derived class can access private members of the base class? If yes, how?
6. What happens when a protected member is inherited in private mode and public mode?
7. Explain the different types of inheritance.
8. Explain the concept of single inheritance with the help of a program code.
9. Differentiate between public, private, and protected inheritance using suitable examples.
10. Is it mandatory for the derived class to have a constructor?
11. What are the advantages of calling a base class constructor before a constructor of the derived class?
12. Explain the syntax of defining a derived class constructor.
13. Explain the concept of multi-level inheritance with the help of a suitable program code.
14. Explain the concept of multiple inheritance with the help of a program.
15. In multiple inheritance, what is the order of calling the constructors? Explain with a sample code.
16. What is a diamond problem?
17. Explain the concept of hierarchical inheritance with the help of a suitable program code.
18. What do you understand by a virtual base class?
19. When does object slicing occur?
20. Differentiate between compile time binding and run-time binding.
21. Differentiate between run-time and compile time polymorphism.
22. How is run-time polymorphism achieved in C++?
23. What do you mean by the term 'function overriding'?
24. Why must the prototype of virtual functions in the base class and in the derived class must be the same?
25. Why should we not use virtual functions within a constructor or a destructor?
26. Differentiate between virtual functions and pure virtual functions.

27. What is an abstract class? When are they needed?
28. What is virtual table? How is it related to virtual pointer?
29. Why cannot we have virtual constructors?
30. What are the advantages and disadvantages of inheritance?
31. Differentiate between containership and inheritance.

Programming Exercises

1. Define a class `Employee`. Display the personal and salary details of five employees using single inheritance.
2. Define a class `Student` with data members as `rollno` and `name`. Derive a class `Fees` from `Student` that has a data member fees and functions to submit fees and generate receipt. Derive another class `Result` from `Student` that displays the marks and grade obtained by the student.
3. Define a class `Employee` with data members as `empno, name,` and `designation`. Derive a class `Qualification` from `Employee` that has data members `UG, PG,` and `experience`. Create another class `Salary` which is derived from both these classes to display the details of the employee and compute their increments based on their experience and educational qualification.
4. Write a program that has a class `Student` to store the details of students in a class. Derive another class `Toppers from` the `Student` that stores records of only top three students of the class.
5. Write a program that has a class `Person`. Derive a class `Baseball_Player` from `Person` and display all the details of a famous baseball player.
6. Write a program that extends the class `Shape` to calculate the area of a circle and a cone. (***Hint:*** *To calculate area of a circle only one variable is required so when creating object, pass the other variable with value 1*).
7. Write a program that extends the class `Result` so that the final result of the `Student` is evaluated based on the marks obtained in tests, activities, and sports.
8. Write a program that extends the `Employee` class so that it stores two more data members—`DOB` and `Date of Hiring`. The `Date` must be defined as a separate class.
9. Write a program that has a class `Train` with data members—`no_of_seats_1st`, `no_of_seats_2Tier`, and `no_of_seats_3Tier`—and member functions to set and display data. Derive a class `Reservation` that has data members—`seats_booked_1st`, `seats_booked_2Tier`, and `seats_booked_3Tier`—and functions to book and cancel tickets, and display status.
10. Write a program that has a class `Distance` with members—`kms` and `metres`. Derive classes `School` and `Office` which store the distance from your house to school and office along with other details.
11. Write a program that extends the class `Employee`. Derive a class `Manager` from `Employee` so that it lists all the details of the manager as well as the details of employees working under that manager.
12. Write a program for a publishing company that markets both printed books and audio-visual lectures stored on CDs. Write a class `Publication` that stores `title` and `price`. Derive a class `book` which has an additional member as `no_pages` and a class `Lecture` with member `play_time`.

Find the errors in the following codes

1.
```
using namespace std;
#include<iostream>
class Student
{   char name[10];
  public:
    void getName()
    {   cout<<"\n Enter Name : ";
        cin.getline(name, 10);
    }
};
class Course: public Info
{   char name[10];
  public:
    void getName()
    {   cout<<"\n Enter Course : ";
        cin.getline(name, 10);
    }
    void show()
    {   cout<<name<<" studies "<<name;   }
};
main()
{   Course C;
    C.getName();
    C.show();
}
```

2.
```
using namespace std;
#include<iostream>
```

```
class Student
{ public:
char name[10];
  Student(){ }
    virtual ~Student()
    { cout<<"\n In Student Destructor";
    }
    void getName()
    { cout<<"\n Enter Name : ";
        cin.getline(name, 10);
    }
};
class Course: public Student
{ int rollno;
  char course[10];
  public:
    Course(){ }
    ~Course()         {   cout<<"\n    In
Destructor - Course";  }
    void getNO()
    {   cin>>rollno;
        cin>>course;
    }
    void show()
    {   cout<<"\n DETAILS : "<<name<
<" studies "<<course;   }
};

main()
{ Student *s = new Course();
  s.getName();
  s->getNo();
  (*s).show();
  delete s;
}
```

3.
```
using namespace std;
#include<iostream>
class One
{ protected:
    int a;
  public:
    One(int x)
    {   a =   x ;   }
    virtual void print() = 0;
};
class Two : public One
{ private:
    float b;
  public:
    Two(int x, float y)
    {   b = y;  }
    void print()
    {   cout<<"\n a = "<<a<<" and b = "<<
b;  }
};
main()
{   One O;
    O.print();
    Two T(2, 4.5);
    One *optr = &T;
    T->print();
}
```

4.
```
using namespace std;
#include<iostream>
class One
{ protected:
    int a;
  public:
    One(int x)
    {   a =    x ;   }
    virtual void print() = 0;
};
class Two : public One
{ private:
    float b;
  public:
    Two(int x, float y) : One (x,y)
    {   }
    void print()
    {   cout<<"\n a = "<<a<<" and b = "<<
b;  }
};
main()
{ One O;
  O.print();
  Two T(2, 4.5);
  One *optr = &T;
  T->print();
}
```

5.
```
using namespace std;
#include<iostream>
class One
{   public:
    One()
    {   cout<<"\n 1";  }
};
class Two : public One, Three
{   public:
    Two()
    {   cout<<"\n 2";  }
```

```
};
class Three
{  public:
      Three()
      {   cout<<"\n 3";   }
};
main()
{  Three T;
}
```

6.
```
using namespace std;
#include<iostream>
class One
{  private:
      int x;
   protected:
      int y;
   public:
      int z;
};
class Two : public One
{  public:
      void Func1()
      {   x=2, y=3, z=4;   }
};
main()
{   Two two;
    two.x=5;
    two.y=10;
    two.z=15;
}
```

7.
```
using namespace std;
#include<iostream>
class One
{  private:
      int x;
   public:
      void show()
      {   cout<<"\n x";   }
};
class Two
{  private:
      int y;
   public:
      void show()
      {   cout<<"\n y";   }
};
class Three : public One, public Two
{
};
main()
{   Three three;
    three.show();
}
```

Find the output of the following codes

1.
```
using namespace std;
#include<iostream>
class One
{  int x;
   public:
      void setX(int i) {x = i;}
      void print() { cout << x; }
};
class Two: public One
{   public:
      Two() {setX(10); }
};
class Three: public One
{   public:
      Three() {setX(20); }
};
class Four: public Two, public Three
{};
int main()
{   Four f;
    f.print();
}
```

2.
```
using namespace std;
#include<iostream>
class One
{  int x;
   public:
      One(int i) { x = i; }
      void print() { cout << x; }
};
class Two: virtual public One
{   public:
      Two():One(10) { }
};
class Three: virtual public One
{   public:
      Three():One(10) { }
};
class Four: public Two, public Three
{   };
int main()
{   Four f;
    f.print();
}
```

3.
```
using namespace std;
#include<iostream>
class One
{   public:
    ~One()
        {     cout<<"\n In one's destruc-
tor";   }
    virtual void show(){  cout<<"\n In O
ne :: show()";   }
};
class Two: public One
{   public:
    ~Two()
    {   One *o = this;
        o->show();
    }
    void show()
    {  cout<<"\n In Two :: show()";
    }
};
main()
{ Two T;
}
```

4.
```
using namespace std;
#include<iostream>
class One
{   public:
    One()
    {    cout<<"\n 1";   }
};
class Two : Public One
{   public:
    Two()
    {    cout<<"\n 2";   }
};
class Three
{   public:
    Three()
    {    cout<<"\n 3";   }
};
class Four
{   public:
    Four()
    {    cout<<"\n 4";   }
};
class Five : public Three, public Four
{   public:
    Five()
    {    cout<<"\n 5";   }
};
class Six : Two, virtual Five
{   public:
    Six()
    {   cout<<"\n 6";   }
};
main()
{   Six S;
}
```

5.
```
using namespace std;
#include<iostream>
class One
{   private:
    int x;
    public:
    virtual void show() = 0;
};
class Two : public One
{   private:
    int y;
    public:
    virtual void show()
    {   }
};
class Three : public Two
{
};
main()
{   Three three;
    three.show();
}
```

6.
```
using namespace std;
#include<iostream>
class One
{   private:
    int x;
    public:
    virtual void show() = 0;
};
class Two : public One
{   private:
    int y;
  public:
    void show()
    {   cout<<"\n y";   }
};
main()
{   One x;
    Two.y;
    x = y;
}
```

7.
```
using namespace std;
#include<iostream>
class One
{   private:
      int x;
   public:
      virtual void show() = 0;
};
class Two : public One
{   public:
      int y;
      void show()
      {   cout<<"\n y";   }
};
main()
{   One O;
   Two T;
   O = T;
   T.y = 20;
}
```

8.
```
using namespace std;
#include<iostream>
class One
{   public:
      One()
         {     cout<<"\n In One's construc-
tor";   }
      virtual ~One() = 0;
};
class Two: public One
{   public:
      Two()
         {    cout<<"\n In Two's construc-
tor";   }
      ~Two()
         {     cout<<"\n In Two's destruc-
tor";   }
};
main()
{   One *O = new Two();
delete O;
}
```

9.
```
using namespace std;
#include<iostream>
class One
{   private:
      int x;
};
class Two:   One
{   public:
      void show()
      {   cout<<"\n In Two";
      }
};
main()
{   One one;
    Two two;
    two - one;
    two.show();
}
```

10.
```
using namespace std;
#include<iostream>
class One
{   protected:
      int x;
};
class Two:   One
{   public:
      void set_data()
      {   x=20;
      }
};
main()
{   Two two;
    two.set_data();
}
```

11.
```
using namespace std;
#include<iostream>
class One
{   protected:
      int x;
};
class Two:   One
{   public:
      void set_data()
      {   x=20;
      }
};
main()
{   One *o;
    Two *t;
    t = o;
    o = t;
}
```

12.
```
using namespace std;
#include<iostream>
class One
{   protected:
      int x;
};
```

```
class Two: One
{   public:
      void set_data()
      {   x=20;
      }
};
main()
{   One *o = new Two();
    Two *t = o;
}
```

13.
```
using namespace std;
#include<iostream>
class three_d
{
   int x, y, z;
   public:
      three_d()
      { x = y = z =0;}
      three_d(int i, int j, int k)
      { x = i; y = j; z =k;}
      three_d operator()(three_d obj);
       three_d operator()(int a, int b,
 int c);
            friend  ostream  &operator<<(os-
tream & out, three_d obj);
};
three_d three_d::operator()(three_dobj)
{
   three_d temp;
   temp.x=(x + obj.x)/2;
   temp.y=(y + obj.y)/2;
   temp.z=(z + obj.z)/2;
   return temp;
}
three_d       three_d       ::       operator()
(int a, int b, int c)
{
      three_d temp;
      temp.x= x + a;
      temp.y= y + b;
      temp.z= z + c;
      return temp;
}
ostream &operator<<(ostream &out, three_d
obj)
{
  out<< obj.x<<", "<< obj.y<<",
  "<<obj.z;
      return out;
}
int main()
{
   three_d  objA(1,  2,  3),  objB(10,  10,
   10), objC;
   objC = objA(objB(100, 200, 300));
   cout<< objC;
}
```

14.
```
using namespace std;
#include<iostream>
class Base
{
   int i;
   public:
      void setI(int n)
      {   i = n;
      }
      int getI()
      {   return i;
      }
};
class Derived : public Base
{
   int j;
   public:
      void setJ(int n)
      {   j = n;
      }
      int mul();
};
int Derived::mul()
{
   return j * get();
}
int main()
{
   DerivedClass ob;
   ob.setI(10);
   ob.setJ(4);
   cout<< ob.mul();
}
```

15.
```
using namespace std;
#include<iostream>
class Base
{
   public:
      virtual void myFunction()
      {
         cout<<"1";
      }
};
```

```
class Derived1 :public Base
{
   public:
      void myFunction()
      {
         cout<<"2";
      }
};
class Derived2 :public Derived1
{
   public:
      void myFunction()
      {
         cout<<"3";
      }
};
int main()
{
   Base *bp;
   Base bob;
   Derived1 DO1;
   Derived2 DO2;
   bp =&bob;
   bp->myFunction();
   bp = &DO1;
   bp -> myFunction();
   bp =&derivedObject2;
   bp -> myFunction();
}
```

16.
```
using namespace std;
#include<iostream>
class One
{
   public:
   One(int n)
      {
         cout<< n;
      }
};
class Two : public One
{
   public:
      Two(int n, double d) : One(n)
      {
         cout<< d;
      }
};
class Three : public Two
{
   public:
   Three(int  n,  double  d,  char  ch)  :
   Two(n, d)
      {
         cout<<ch;
      }
};
int main()
{
   Three three(5, 4.3, 'R');
}
```

Answers

Fill in the Blanks

1. Inheritance; **2.** Is-a; **3.** Public, private, or protected; **4.** Protected; **5.** Inheritance; **6.** Virtual; **7.** Derived; **8.** Static; **9.** Virtual; **10.** Base; **11.** Static; **12.** Pure virtual functions; **13.** Abstract; **14.** VTABLE; **15.** Function pointer, virtual function;

State True or False

1. True	**2.** False	**3.** True	**4.** True	**5.** False	**6.** False	**7.** True	**8.** True
9. True	**10.** False	**11.** True	**12.** False	**13.** True	**14.** False	**15.** False	**16.** False
17. False	**18.** True	**19.** False	**20.** False	**21.** True	**22.** True	**23.** True	**24.** True
25. True	**26.** False	**27.** False	**28.** True				

Multiple Choice Questions

1. (b); **2.** (b); **3.** (b); **4.** (d); **5.** (c); **6.** (d); **7.** (c); **8.** (c); **9.** (a); **10.** (c); **11.** (b); **12.** (c); **13.** (c); **14.** (c)

CHAPTER 13

File Handling

KEY Concepts

• Streams • Classes for file stream operations • Opening and closing Files • Detecting EOF • File modes • File pointers Types of files • Sequential I/O functions • Error handling • Accepting command line arguments

INTRODUCTION

A file is a collection of data stored on a secondary storage device like hard disk. Until now, we had been processing data that was entered through the keyboard. However, this task can become very tedious, especially when there is a huge amount of data to be processed. A better solution, therefore, is to combine all the input data into a file and then design a C++ program to read this data from the file whenever required.

Broadly speaking, a file is basically used because real-life applications involve large amounts of data, and in such situations, the console-oriented input and output (I/O)operations pose two major problems as follows:

- First, it becomes cumbersome and time consuming to handle huge amount of data through terminals.
- Second, when doing I/O using terminal, the entire data is lost when either the program is terminated or computer is turned off. Therefore, it becomes necessary to store data on a permanent storage or the disks and read whenever necessary, without destroying the data.

In order to use files, we have to learn file I/O operations—how data is read or written to a file. Although file I/O operations are almost same as terminal I/O, the only difference is that when doing file I/O, the user must specify the name of the file from which data should be read or written. In this chapter, we will read about reading and writing data in files.

13.1 STREAMS IN C++

A stream is a logical interface to the devices that are connected to the computer.

It is widely used as a logical interface to a file where a file can refer to a disk file, the computer screen, keyboard, etc. Although files may differ in the form and capabilities, all streams are the same.

In C++, the standard streams are termed as pre-connected input and output channels between a text terminal and the program (when it begins execution).

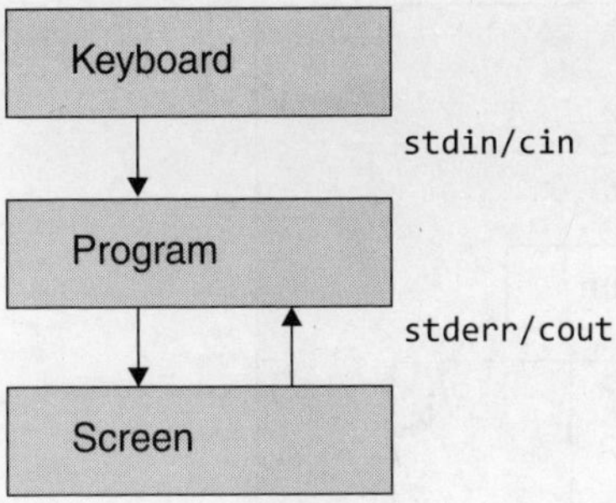

Figure 13.1 Standard streams

The three standard streams in C++ language are console input (`cin`), console output (`cout`), and console error (`cerr`) (refer to Fig. 13.1).

Console input (cin) or standard input (stdin) Standard input is the stream from which the program receives its data. The program requests transfer of data using the `read` operation. However, not all programs require input. Generally, unless redirected, input for a program is expected from the keyboard.

Console output (cout) or standard output (stdout) Standard output is the stream where a program writes its output data. The program requests data transfer using the `write` operation. However, not all programs generate output.

Console error (cerr) or standard error (stderr) Standard error is basically an output stream used by programs to report error messages or diagnostics. It is a stream, independent of standard output and can be redirected separately. No doubt, the standard output and standard error can also be directed to the same destination.

Console log (`clog`) It is a fully buffered version of `cerr`.clog which is mainly used to report problems.

Note A stream is linked to a file using an open operation and disassociated from a file using a close operation.

Programming Tip cerr and clog are always redirected to console.

In C++, the standard streams `cin`, `cout`, `cerr`, and `clog` defined in the `iostream.h` header file are automatically opened before `main()` and closed after the `main()` is executed. The standard input and output devices such as keyboard and monitor are connected with these stream objects. However, these streams may be redirected to any other device or file. For example, users can write as follows:

```
shell: first>File1
```

to redirect the output of the example program `first.cpp` to `File1`.

Consider the program given here that redirects the output of `first.cpp` to `File1`. We will, therefore, get only two messages on console output.

Example 13.1 Redirect the output of one program to file

```
using namespace std;
#include<iostream>
int main()
{   cout<<"\n Hello- cout";
    cerr<<"\n Hello World- cerr";
    clog<<"\n Hello C++ - clog";
}

OUTPUT
Hello World- cerr
Hello C++ - clog
```

13.2 CLASSES FOR FILE STREAM OPERATIONS

C++ supports a set of classes that defines file handling functions. Figure 13.2 shows the hierarchy of C++ classes that have been specifically written for handling file operations. From Fig. 13.2, it

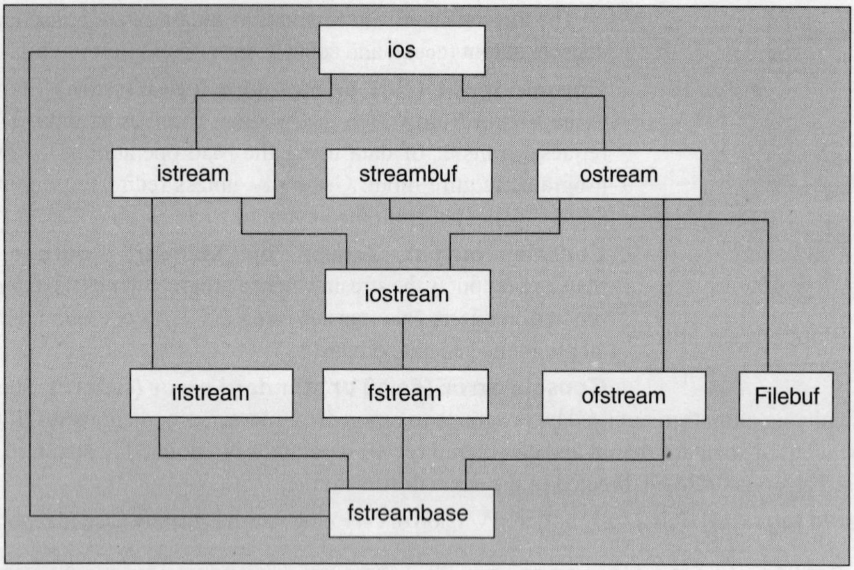

Figure 13.2 Classes for file stream operations

is clear that `ifstream`, `ofstream`, and `fstream` are derived from `fstream base` and from `iostream.h`. Classes that manage the disk files are declared in `fstream.h`. Therefore, `fstream.h` must be included in any program that uses files.

`filebuf` It is used to set the file buffer for read and write operations. It contains `open()` and `close()` as its member.

`fstreambase` It provides functions common to the file streams. This file is the base class for `ifstream`, `ofstream`, and `fstream`, and contains `open()` and `close()` as its members.

`ifstream` It provides functions for data input. Therefore, the `open()` defined as its member opens a stream in the input mode by default. Moreover, `ifstream` inherits functions such as `get()`, `getline()`, `read()`, `seekg()`, and `tellg()` functions from the `istream` class.

`ofstream` It provides functions for data output. Therefore, the `open()` defined as its member, opens a stream in the output mode by default. Moreover, `ofstream` inherits functions like `put()`, `write()`, `seekp()`, and `tellp()` functions from the `ostream` class.

`fstream` It provides functions for both input and output operations. For this, it inherits all the functions from `istream` and `ostream` through the `iostream` class. The `open()` defined as its member opens the stream in input mode by default.

13.3 OPENING AND CLOSING OF FILES

Before we perform I/O operations on a file, the file must be first opened to get a handle. The file handle serves as a pointer to the file. However, to obtain this handle, the user must specify the name of the file, data type, purpose, and the opening method. The file name may or may not contain an extension. If the extension is specified, then it must be separated from the file name using a `dot` or `period` as in `file_name.extension`, for example, `MyFile.txt`.

Note To get a file pointer, the file must be created and be linked to the filename.

> **Programming Tip:** The number and type of characters in the file name depends on the operating system.

The data type and the structure of the file stream is defined using stream classes, `ifstream`, `ofstream`, or `fstream`, depending on the purpose of its usage, depending on whether the file is being opened for reading data or writing. For example, if we know that we are opening the file only to read data, the data type of the file can be `ifstream`, and if we are opening for writing data, the file must be opened using `ostream` class. If the file is being opened for simultaneous read and write operations, then it must be opened using `fstream` class.

In C++, a file can be opened either by using the constructor function of the class or by using the member function `open()` of the class as shown in Fig. 13.3.

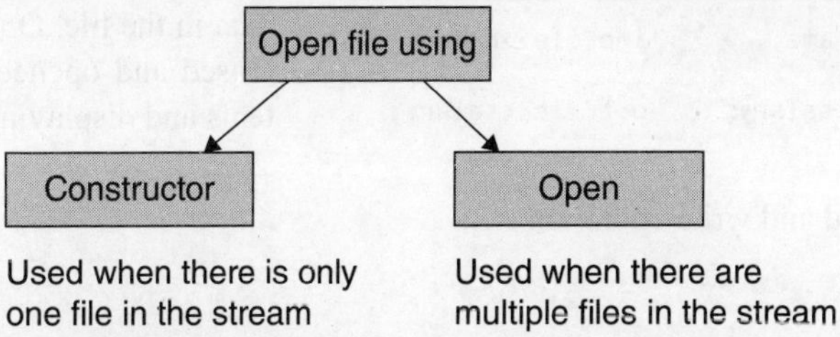

Figure 13.3 Opening files

While the constructor function is preferred when there is a single file to be opened in the stream, the `open()`, on the other hand, is used when there are multiple files to be used.

When a file is used, it must be closed as well. A file can be closed either by explicitly using the `close()` member function of the class or automatically by the destructor of the class, when the file stream object goes out of scope.

13.3.1 Opening Files using Constructors

Until now, we have read that a constructor function is used to initialize an object while it is being created. When we open a file using the constructor function, the filename is used to initialize the file stream object. Therefore, to access a file for reading, writing, or appending, follow the two simple steps given as follows:

Step 1 Create a file stream object. For example, ofstream is used to create the output stream and ifstream is used to create the input stream.

Step 2 Initialize the file stream object by specifying the file name.

The syntax for opening a file using a constructor function is as follows:

```
streamclass_name file_objectname ("filename");
```

If the file is in the current directory, then only the filename needs to be specified; if the file is not in the current directory, then the complete pathname must be given. For example, to open a file `student.txt` for reading data, we write as

```
ifstream inpFile("student.txt");
```

Now, `inpFile` is an object of class `ifstream` that will be used to manage the input stream. Name of the object can be any valid identifier in C++.To open the `employee.txt` file with output stream, you must write,

```
ofstream outFile("exployee.txt");
```

Once the file is opened, read and write operations are performed in exactly the same way as is done for console input and output as shown in Table 13.1.

Let us examine the difference between- `cout<<"HELLO";` and `outFile<<"HELLO";` The first statement writes `HELLO` on screen and the second statement writes it in `outFile`.

Note In MS-DOS, the file name can have eight characters, followed by a dot and an extension of three characters. In Unix, file name can have 255 characters and any number of extensions separated by dots.

Table 13.1 Read and write operations on files

Operation	Console	File stream
READ	`cin>>name;`	`inpFile>>name;`
WRITE	`cout<<salary;`	`outFile<<salary;`

Consider the example program given here. It opens the file, `Employee` twice. First, the user enters data through console and writes that data in the file. Once data is written, the file is closed and opened again for reading its contents and displaying it on console.

Example 13.2 Read and write operation

```
using namespace std;
#include<iostream>
#include<fstream>
int main()
{   int i;
    char name[10];
    float sal;
    ofstream outFile("Employee");   // create an object and open the file using constructor
    for(i=0;i<3;i++)
    {   cout<<"\n Enter the name and salary of Employee "<<i+1<<" : ";
        cin>>name>>sal;
        outFile<<"\n"<<name<<"\t"<<sal;   // write to file
    }
    outFile.close();   // close the file after writing data
    ifstream inpFile("Employee");   // open the file for reading data
    for(i=0;i<3;i++)
    {   inpFile>>name;      // read from file
        inpFile>>sal;
        cout<<"\n EMPLOYEE "<<i+1<<" : ";
        cout<<name<<"\t"<<sal;
    }
    inpFile.close();
}
```

OUTPUT

```
Enter the name and salary of Employee 1: Dev 1234
Enter the name and salary of Employee 2: Aditya 4321
Enter the name and salary of Employee 3: Sarthak 3456
Employee 1: Dev 1234
Employee 2: Aditya 4321
Employee 3: Sarthak 3456
```

Explanation: Note that in the program, we have created two file stream objects—`outFile` and `inpFile` to put and get data from the file respectively. The statement `outFile.close();` disconnects the file `Employee` from the output stream `outFile`. However, even after executing this statement, the `ofstream` object as well as the file `Employee` still exists. They are only disconnected from each other. At a later point in the program, the file may be re-connected with `outFile` for writing some other data.

Note
- When a file is opened for writing, the file may or may not exist.
- If the file already exists, its entire contents are deleted and an empty file is presented for writing.
- If the file did not exist, then a new file is created and contents are written into it.

13.3.2 Opening Files using Member function

A file can also be opened explicitly by using `open()`, defined as member function of the class, instead of using the constructor function. As stated earlier, the main advantage of opening files using `open()` is that it can be used to associate multiple files with the same object at different times.

This is especially more essential when the application is required to process a set of files sequentially. In such cases, a single stream object can be created and be used to open each file in turn. The syntax for opening a file using the `open()` can be given as follows:

```
file_stream_class stream_object ("file_name"); or
file_stream_class stream_object;
stream_object.open("file_name")
```

13.3.3 Test for errors

Untilnow, we have been assuming that a file operation is always successful. Every time we had attempted to open a file, it could be opened successfully. However, this may not always be true. For example, if the user tries to open a non-existent file in read-mode or tries to open a read-only file in write mode, then the file operation definitely fails.

Therefore, it is always recommended to test for errors by using the operator `!` with an instance of the `ifstream`, `ofstream`, or `fstream`. The operator `!` is overloaded and returns a non-zero value if an error(s) is encountered and a zero otherwise. The statements given here open a file using the `open()` and check if the file was opened successfully.

```
ifstream inpFile("employee.txt");
if(!inpFile)
{     cerr<<"\n File could not be opened";
      exit(1);
}
```

If the file could not be opened, a message is displayed on the screen and the program terminates. In case the file opened successfully, the instructions specified after the `if` block are executed. Let us write the same program that performs the same function but uses `open()` to open the file.

Example 13.3 Use of `open()`

```
using namespace std;
#include<iostream>
#include<fstream>
#include<stdlib.h>
int main()
{   int i;
    char name[10];
    float sal;
```

```
    ofstream outFile;
    outFile.open("Employee");
    if(!outFile)
    {   cout<<"\n File Could Not Be Opened";
        exit(1);
    }
    for(i=0;i<3;i++)
    {   cout<<"\n Enter the name and salary of Employee "<<i+1<<" : ";
        cin>>name>>sal;
        outFile<<"\n"<<name<<"\t"<<sal;
    }
    outFile.close();
    ifstream inpFile("Employee");    //open file for reading
    if(!inpFile)    // check if file was opened successfully
    {   cout<<"\n File Could Not Be Opened";
        exit(1);
    }
    for(i=0;i<3;i++)
    {   inpFile>>name;
        inpFile>>sal;
        cout<<"\n EMPLOYEE "<<i+1<<" : ";
        cout<<name<<"\t"<<sal;
    }
    inpFile.close();    // close file
}
```

OUTPUT

```
Enter the name and salary of Employee 1: Dev 1234
Enter the name and salary of Employee 2: Aditya 4321
Enter the name and salary of Employee 3: Sarthak 3456
Employee 1: Dev 1234
Employee 2: Aditya 4321
Employee 3: Sarthak 3456
```

Note Only a limited number of files can be opened at a time. This constraint is specified by the operating system. For example, in MS DOS, the entry `FILES = 20` in CONFIG.SYS means that maximum 20 files can be opened at a time. Any attempt to open more than 20 files will result in a failure.

13.4 DETECTING THE END-OF-FILE

In Example 13.3, we have specified that the program will read names and salaries of three employees. However, in real-world programs, we may not know the number of records stored in the file. We need to analyse whether we have reached the end of the file or not. Therefore, in our file handling programs, we need to continuously check for `end-of-file` condition to prevent reading data further from the file.

There are two ways to detect the end-of-file condition. First, to use `while(inpFile)` which returns a zero if any error occurs in the file operation,including `end-of-file`. The second approach is to use the `eof()` member function of the `ios` class. The `eof()` returns a non-zero value if the `end-of-file (eof)` condition is encountered and a zero, otherwise. Table 13.2 summarizes the differences between the two approaches.

Table 13.2 Differences between approaches to detect EOF

While(ifstream_object_name)	While(ifstream_object_name.eof()!=0)

• Will return 0 if any error occurs and stop reading.
• Can stop reading even if any other error (except EOF) occurs.
• USAGE
`while(inpFile)`
`{ getline(name, 20);`
`cout<<name;}`
	• Will return 1 if EOF is encountered and stop reading.
	• Will read till EOF is not reached.
	• USAGE
	`while(inpFile.eof()!=0)`
	`{ getline(name, 20);`
	`cout<<name;}`
	OR the while statement can be also written as
	`while(!inpFile.eof())`

Program 13.1 Write a program that reads Questions from one file and their corresponding answers from another file.

```
using namespace std;
#include<iostream>
#include<fstream>
#include<stdlib.h>
int main()
{   ofstream outFile;
    outFile.open("Questions");
    outFile<<"\n Who is the Prime Minister of India ?";
    outFile<<"\n Which virus spread recently in Africa ?";
    outFile<<"\n Who won the FIFA World Cup 2014 ? ";
    outFile.close();

    outFile.open("Answers");
    outFile<<"\n Narendra Modi";
    outFile<<"\n Ebola";
    outFile<<"\n Germany";
    outFile.close();
    char quest[80], ans[30];
    ifstream inpFile;
    inpFile.open("Questions");
    cout<<"\n ************** SAMPLE QUESTIONS FOR QUIZ CONTEST ************";
    while(inpFile.eof() == 0)
    {   inpFile.getline(quest, 80);
        cout<<"\n"<<quest;
    }
    inpFile.close();
    inpFile.open("Answers");
    cout<"\n\n\n ************ ANSWERS FOR SAMPLE QUESTION ************\n";
    while(inpFile.eof()==0)
    {   inpFile.getline(ans, 20);
        cout<<"\n"<<ans;
    }
    inpFile.close();
}
```

OUTPUT

```
************** SAMPLE QUESTIONS FOR QUIZ CONTEST ************
Who is the Prime Minister of India ?
Which virus spread recently in Africa ?
Who won the FIFA World Cup 2014 ?
************ ANSWERS FOR SAMPLE QUESTION ************
Narendra Modi
Ebola
Germany
```

Program 13.2 Write a program that reads the two files created in the previous question simultaneously

```
using namespace std;
#include<iostream>
#include<fstream.h>
#include<stdlib.h>
int main()
{   char quest[80], ans[30];
    cout<<"\n ************** SAMPLE QUESTIONS FOR QUIZ CONTEST ************";
    ifstream inpFile1, inpFile2;
    inpFile1.open("Questions");
    inpFile2.open("Answers");

    while(inpFile1.eof() == 0 || inpFile2.eof() == 0)
    {   inpFile1.getline(quest, 80);
        cout<<"\n"<<quest;
        inpFile2.getline(ans, 20);
        cout<<"\t"<<ans;
    }
    inpFile1.close();
    inpFile2.close();
}
```

OUTPUT

```
************** SAMPLE QUESTIONS FOR QUIZ CONTEST ************
Who is the Prime Minister of India ?    Narendra Modi
Which virus spread recently in Africa ?  Ebola
Who won the FIFA World Cup 2014 ?    Germany
```

13.5 FILE MODES

Until now, we had been opening files in the default mode. Basically, the constructor function and the `open()` used to open a file needs two parameters such as filename and the file mode. However, we had provided only the first parameter, which is the filename. For the second parameter, the default values were used.

The file mode is used to specify the purpose for which the file is being opened. Table 13.3 specifies the default opening file modes for an `ifstream` and `ofstream` object. The other file modes are given in Table 13.4. A file can be opened using one or a more than one constants defined in `ios` for the file mode parameter. The syntax for opening a particular file using a specific file mode(s) can be given as follows:

Table 13.3 File modes

Class	Mode	Meaning
ifstream	ios::in	Read only
ofstream	ios::out	Write only

```
stream_object_name.open("filename",
file_mode);
```

Table 13.4 Additional file modes

File mode	Purpose	Class
ios::app	Append mode. Writes all the output at the end of the file.	ofstream
ios::ate	Moves the file pointer to the end-of-file when the file is opened. However, I/O operations can be performed anywhere within the file.	ofstream / ifstream
ios::trunc	If the file already exists, its contents will be truncated before opening the file. It is also the default action for ios::out, if ios::ate, ios::app, or ios::in are not specified.	ofstream
ios::binary	Opens the file in binary mode	ofstream / ifstream
ios::nocreate	Fails the open() function if the file does not exist	ofstream
ios::noreplace	Fails the open() function if the file already exist	ofstream

Important pointers

- When a file is opened in `ios::out` mode, it is automatically opened using the `ios::trunc` mode
- `ios::app` as well as `ios::ate` moves the file pointer to the end of the file when it is opened. If the file does not exist, it creates the file.
- `ios::app` allows new data to be written only at the end of the file.
- `ios::ate` allows data to be added or modified anywhere in the file.
- The `fstream` class does not provide a default mode, so it must be explicitly specified while opening files with `fstream` object.
- For `ifstream` or `ofstream` class objects, the file mode need not be specified as default values can be used.
- Programmers can combine two modes using the bitwise `OR` operator. For example, `outFile("Employee", ios::ate | ios::nocreate)` would open the Employee file for adding or modifying existing data. If the file does not exist, the `open()` will fail but will not create the file named Employee.

For example, assume that a file contains `HELLO`.
Then opening file using `ios::out`, and writing `Hi` would result in `Hi` stored in the file.
Opening the file in `ios::out` and `ios::app`, would result in `HELLO Hi`.

Note While creating files, we can even supply a third argument that specifies the access permissions. By default, a file is created for both read and write. However, programmers can also set the permissions as O_RDWR, O_CREAT, O_APPEND, O_WRONLY, O_SYNC, S_IRUSR, S_IWUSR, S_IRGRP.

Programming Tip: File permission is not used in ios::nocreate mode.

13.6 FILE POINTERS AND THEIR MANIPULATORS

With every file, the file management system associates two pointers often known as file pointers that facilitate the movement across the file for reading and/or writing data.

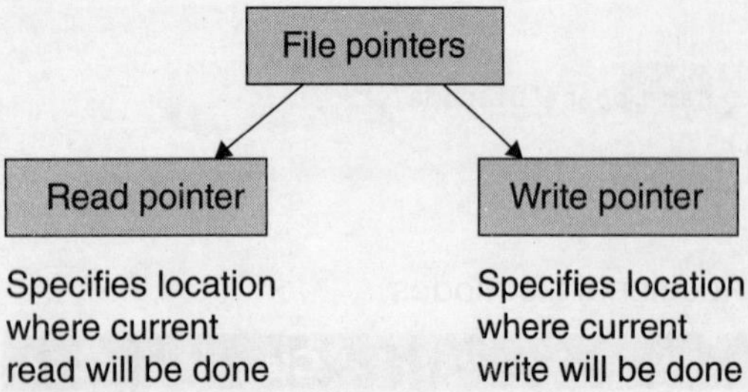

Figure 13.4 Types of file pointers

The two types of file pointers are read pointer and the write pointer as shown in Fig. 13.4. While the read pointer is called, the get pointer specifies a location from where the current read operation is initiated. The write or the put pointer specifies a location from where the current write operation is initiated. Once the read or write operation is completed, the appropriate pointer is automatically advanced.

The position of these file pointers is very much dependent on the mode-read, write, or append-in which the file is opened. For example,

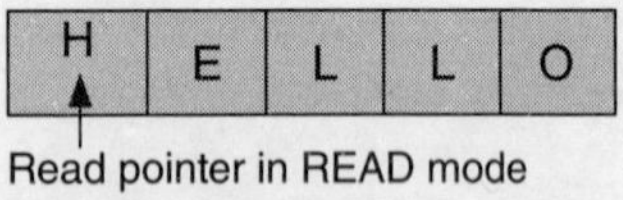

Figure 13.5 5ios::in mode

Figure 13.6 ios::out mode

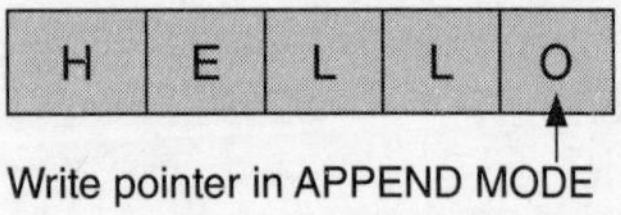

Figure 13.7 ios::app mode

- when we open a file in `ios::in` mode, then the read pointer is automatically set at the beginning of the file. This allows users to start reading data from the beginning as shown in Fig. 13.5.
- when the file is opened in `ios::out` mode, then the existing contents of the file are deleted and the write pointer is set at the beginning of the file so that data can be written from the start as shown in Fig. 13.6.
- when the file is opened in `ios::app` mode, the existing contents remains intact and the write pointer is set to the end of the file so that the data can be written at the end (after the existing contents) as shown in Fig. 13.7.

13.6.1 Manipulating File Pointers

The file stream classes of C++ provide functions for setting a file pointer to any desired position in the file and to retrieve the current position of the file pointers. These functions give the programmer control over the positions in the file from which read and/or write operations can be performed. Table 13.5 summarizes the file manipulation functions supported by the C++ I/O system.

Table 13.5 Manipulation functions

Function	Member of	Utility	Example	Effect
`seekg()`	`ifstream`	Moves the get pointer to the specified position	`inpFile. seekg(10);`	Moves the get pointer to byte 10.
`seekp()`	`ofstream`	Moves the put pointer to the specified position	`outFile. seekp(10);`	Moves the put pointer to byte 10.
`tellg()`	`ifstream`	Gives the current position of the get pointer	`inpFile. tellg();`	Returns 10 if the get pointer is at byte 10 in the file
`tellp()`	`ofstream`	Gives the current position of the put pointer	`outFile. tellp();`	Returns 10 if the put pointer is at byte 10 in the file

> **Note** In all the file manipulating functions, the bytes are specified from the beginning of the file.

13.6.2 Specifying the Offset

We have seen that `seekg()` and `seekp()`move the get pointer and the put pointer to a specific location in the file. The variant that we have used for these functions in the previous section takes a single argument, the absolute position in the file.

However, there is another variant of `seekg()` and `seekp()` functions. It can also accept two arguments—the `offset` and the `reference position`. The syntax for a two argument `seekg()` or `seekp()` is

```
seekg(offset, reference_postion);
seekp(offset, reference_postion);
```

Table 13.6 Reference position

Reference_position	Location in file
`ios::beg`	Beginning of the file
`ios::cur`	Current location of the pointer
`ios::end`	End of the file

Here, the parameter offset specifies the number of bytes through which the file pointer has to be moved and `reference_position` is any constant of the three mentioned in Table 13.6. These constants are defined in the `ios` class. Using Table 13.6, let us conclude the action of the following function calls:

- `inpFile.seekg(10, ios::beg)`—moves to `10` bytes starting from the beginning of the file
- `inpFile.seekg(10, ios::cur)`—moves to `10` bytes starting from the current position of the file pointer
- `inpFile.seekg(0, ios::end)`—moves to the end of the file
- `inpFile.seekg(0, ios::beg)`—moves to the beginning of the file
- `inpFile.seekg(0, ios::cur)`—stays at the current location of the file pointer
- `inpFile.seekg(-10, ios::cur)`—moves `10` bytes backward starting from the current position of the file pointer
- `inpFile.seekg(-10, ios::end)`—moves `10` bytes backward from the end of the file

Example 13.4 Using file manipulating functions

```
using namespace std;
#include<iostream>
#include<fstream>
int main()
{   int pos;
   fstream outFile;   //create object
   outFile.open("Message",ios::out);   // open file for writing
   outFile<<"WELCOME TO THE WORLD OF C++ PROGRAMMING";
   cout<<"\n The current position of Write pointer is : ";
   cout<<outFile.tellp();   //display current position
```

```
    cout<<"\n Enter the position to move : ";
    cin>>pos;
    outFile.seekg(pos,ios::beg);    //move pointer to specified position

    cout<<"\n The position of Get Pointer is : ";
    cout<<outFile.tellg();        // position of get pointer
    cout<<"\n Enter the position to move from current position : ";
    cin>>pos;

    outFile.seekg(pos,ios::cur);

    cout<<"\n The position of Get pointer is : ";
    cout<<outFile.tellg();
    cout<<"\n Enter the position to move from end : ";
    cin>>pos;

    outFile.seekg(pos,ios::end);        //relocate get pointer

    cout<<"\n The position of Get pointer is : ";
    cout<<outFile.tellg();        //current position of get pointer
}
```

OUTPUT

```
The current position of Write pointer is : 39
Enter the position to move : 4
The position of Get Pointer is : 4
Enter the position to move from current position : 7
The position of Get pointer is : 11
Enter the position to move from end :  10
The position of Get pointer is : 29
```

13.7 TYPES OF FILES

Like C, C++ supports two types of files—text files and binary files.

13.7.1 ASCII Text Files

A text file is a stream of characters that can be sequentially processed by a computer in forward direction. Hence, a text file is usually opened for only one kind of operation such as reading, writing, or appending at any given time. As text files only process characters, they can only read or write data one character at a time. In C++, a text stream is treated as a special kind of file.

Depending on the requirements of the operating system and on the operation that has to be performed—read/write operation—on the file, newline characters may be converted to or from carriage-return (enter key) or linefeed combinations. Besides this, other character conversions may also be done to satisfy the storage requirements of the operating system. However, these conversions occur transparently to process a text file.

In a text file, each line contains zero or more characters and ends with one or more characters that specify the end of line. Each line in a text file can have a maximum of 255 characters. Note that a line in a text file is not a C++ string, and is not terminated by a null character. When data is written to a text file, each newline character is converted to a carriage return/line feed character. Similarly, when data is read from a text file, each carriage return or line feed character is converted in to newline character.

When a text file is used, there are actually two representations of data—internal or external. For example, an int value will be represented as two or four bytes of memory internally but externally, the intvalue will be represented as a string of characters representing its decimal or hexadecimal value.

> **Note** In a text file, each line of data ends with a new line character. Each file ends with a special character called the end-of-file (eof) marker.

> **Programming Tip:** The contents of a binary file are not human readable. If you want that data stored in the file must be human-readable, then store the data in a text file.

13.7.2 Binary Files

A binary file is a file which may contain any type of data, encoded in binary form for computer storage and processing purposes. Like a text file, a binary file is a collection of bytes. Note that in C++, a byte and a character are equivalent. Therefore, a binary file is also referred to as a character stream with following two essential differences:

- A binary file does not require any special processing of the data and each byte of data is transferred to or from the disk unprocessed.
- C++ places no constructs on the file and it may be read from, or written to, in any manner the programmer wants.

While text files can be processed sequentially, binary files, on the other hand, can be either processed sequentially or randomly depending on the needs of the application. In C++, to process a file randomly, the programmer must move the current file position to an appropriate place in the file before reading or writing data. For example, if a file is used to store records (using structures) of students, then to update a particular record, the programmer must first locate the appropriate record, read the record into memory, update it, and finally write the record back to disk at its appropriate location in the file.

> **Note** Binary files store data in the internal representation format. Therefore, an int value will be stored in binary form as 2 or 4 byte value. The same format is used to store data in memory as well as in file. Like text file, binary file also ends with an EOF marker.

In a text file, an integer value 123 will be stored as a sequence of three characters as 1, 2, and 3. Each character will take one byte, and therefore, to store the integer value 123, we need three bytes as shown in Fig. 13.8. However, in a binary file, the int value 123 will be stored in two bytes in the binary form. This clearly indicates that binary files take less space to store the same piece of data and eliminates conversion between internal and external representations and are, thus, more efficient than the text files.

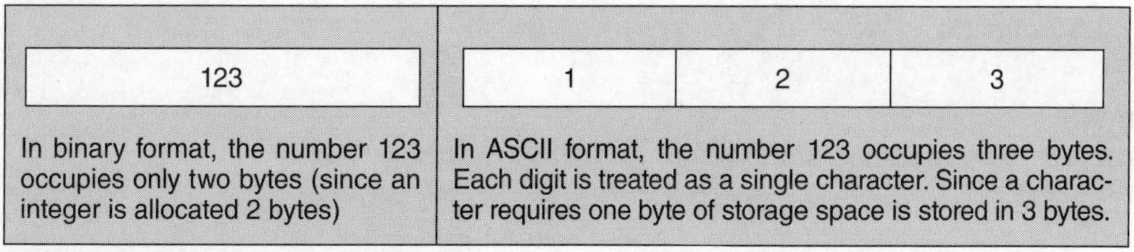

Figure 13.8 Binary and ASCII format

13.8 SEQUENTIAL INPUT AND OUTPUT FUNCTIONS

The file stream classes support functions such as `get()`, `put()`, `read()`, and `write()` for performing sequential or random input and output operations. While sequential read or write refers to process all preceding data items before a particular data item, the term 'random,' on the other hand,refers to manipulating a data item in any order.

For example, in sequential access,the record of the tenth employee can be accessed by sequentially traversing through the records of first nine employees. However, in random access, the file system can directly process the record of the tenth employee without going through the records of prior nine employees. While `get()` and `put()` can handle a single character at a time, `read()` and `write()` on the other hand, are used for reading and writing blocks of binary data.

13.8.1 get() and put()

The `get()` reads a single character from the associated stream and the `put()` is used to write a single character to the associated stream.

Note `get()` and `put()` are member functions defined in the `fstream` class.

Example 13.5 Using `get()` and `put()`

```
using namespace std;
#include<iostream>
#include<fstream>
#include<string.h>
int main()
{   int i;
    char comment[80];
    char ch;
    cout<<"\n Enter your feedback about this college : ";
    cin.getline(comment,80);
    int len = strlen(comment);
    fstream FILE;
    FILE.open("Feedback", ios::in | ios::out);
    for(int i=0;i<len;i++)
       FILE.put(comment[i]);
    FILE.seekg(0);
    cout<<"\n USER'S FEEDBACK : ";
    for(i = 0;i<len;i++)
    {   FILE.get(ch);
        cout<<ch;
    }
    FILE.close();
}
```

OUTPUT

```
Enter your feedback about this college : It's a very good college
USER'S FEEDBACK : It's a very good college
```

Explanation: In the program,we have first written the comment in the file, character by character. After writing the contents, the file pointer is pointing to the last character of the file. For setting back to the start of the file, we have used the seekg().

Note The `fstream` object can handle both input and output simultaneously.

Program 13.3 Write a program to count the number of characters and number of lines in a file.

```
using namespace std;
#include<iostream>
#include<fstream>
#include<string.h>
#include<stdlib.h>
int main()
{   fstream FILE;
    int ch, no_of_characters=0, no_of_lines=0;
    char filename[20];
    cout<<"\n Enter the filename : ";
    cin.getline(filename,20);
    FILE.open(filename, ios::in);
    if(!FILE)
    {   cout<<"\n Error Opening The File";
        exit(1);
    }
    while(FILE.eof()==0)
    {   ch = FILE.get();
        if(ch=='\n')
           no_of_lines++;
           no_of_characters++;
    }
    if(no_of_characters > 0 )
        cout<<"\n In the file "<<filename<<" there are " <<no_of_lines<<" lines and
"<<no_of_characters<<" characters";
    else
        cout<<"\n File is empty";
    FILE.close();
}
```

OUTPUT

```
Enter the filename : exercise.cpp
In the file exercise.cpp there are 29 lines and 322 characters
```

Program 13.4 Write a program to compare two files.

```
using namespace std;
#include<iostream>
#include<fstream>
int main()
{   fstream FILE1, FILE2;
    int ch1, ch2;
    char filename1[20], filename2[20];
    cout<<"\n Enter the name of the first filename : ";
    cin.getline(filename1,20);
    cin.ignore();
    cout<<"\n Enter the name of the second filename : ";
    cin.getline(filename2, 20);
    FILE1.open(filename1, ios::in);
    FILE2.open(filename2, ios::in);
```

```
    while(FILE1.eof()==0 && FILE2.eof()==0)
    {   ch1 = FILE1.get();
        ch2 = FILE2.get();
    }
    if(ch1==ch2)
        cout<<"\n Files are identical";
    else
        cout<<"\n Files are not identical";
    FILE1.close();
    FILE2.close();
    return 0;
}
```

OUTPUT

```
Enter the name of the first filename : exercise.cpp
Enter the name of the second filename : try.cpp
Files are not identical
```

Program 13.5 Write a program to copy one file into another. Copy one character at a time.

```
using namespace std;
#include<iostream>
#include<fstream>
#include<stdlib.h>
int main()
{   fstream FILE1, FILE2;
   int ch;
   char filename1[20], filename2[20];
   cout<<"\n Enter the name of the first filename : ";
   cin.getline(filename1,20);
   cin.ignore();
   cout<<"\n Enter the name of the second filename : ";
   cin.getline(filename2,20);
   FILE1.open(filename1, ios::in);
   FILE2.open(filename2, ios::out);
   if(!FILE1 || !FILE2)
   {   cout<<"\n Error opening the file";
      exit(1);
   }
   while(FILE1.eof()==0)
   {      ch = FILE1.get();
          FILE2.put(ch);
   }
   cout<<"\n FILES COPIED";
   FILE1.close();
   FILE2.close();
   return 0;
}
```

OUTPUT

```
Enter the name of the first filename : comments.txt
Enter the name of the second filename : dup_file.txt
FILES COPIED
```

13.8.2 read() and write() Functions

Until now, we have been dealing with text files in which data is written using ASCII values but practically speaking binary files are more efficient to handle. In this section, we will be using `read()` and `write()` to handle data with binary files. Automatically, this implies that data on the disk will be stored in the same format in which they are stored in the computer's memory.

`read()` and `write()` functions take two arguments—the address of the variable that has to be written and the size of that variable in bytes.

The address of the variable during a write operation specifies the memory location from which data will be read and then written to the file. Similarly, during the read operation, the address denotes the memory location at which data read from the file will be stored. The size of the variable is used to determine the number of bytes to be transferred.

The syntax of `read()` and `write()` is as follows:

```
ifstream_object_namen.read((char *)&var, sizeof(var));
ofstream_object_namen.write((char *)&var, sizeof(var));
```

Note The address of the variable is casted to type `char *`.

Example 13.6 Program to demonstrate the use of storing an integer array in a binary file

```
using namespace std;
#include<iostream>
#include<fstream>
int main()
{   int marks[]={98, 67, 89, 100, 45,65, 51, 78, 12, 43};
    int arr[10]={0};
    fstream FILE;   //create object
    FILE.open("temp", ios::out|ios::binary);    //open file for writing
    FILE.write((char *)marks, sizeof(marks));   //write data
    FILE.close();   //close file
    FILE.open("temp",ios::in|ios::binary);    //open for reading
    FILE.read((char *)arr, sizeof(marks));    //read data
    cout<<"\n MARKS OBTAINED : ";
    for(int i = 0;i<10;i++)
      cout<<"\t"<<arr[i];           //display data
    FILE.close();          //close file
}
```

OUTPUT

```
MARKS OBTAINED : 98, 67, 89, 100, 45,65, 51, 78, 12, 43
```

The real power of `read()` and `write()` functions lies in their ability to handle class objects directly as a single unit. While the `read()` reads the data members of the class from the file byte by byte with no conversion, the `write()`, on the other hand, copies the class's data members from memory byte by byte with no conversion.

Note Only data members of the class object are written to the file and not the member functions.

Consider the program given here that uses the `read()` and `write()` functions to store and retrieve the details about employees to and from a file called `employee.txt`. The information about an employee is stored in terms of an object of the class. Note that only the object's data members are stored in the file. Once retrieved, the value of data members is displayed using class member function.

Example 13.7 Use of `read()` and `write()` functions to store and retrieve the details about employees to and from a file

```
using namespace std;
#include<iostream>
#include<fstream>
class Employee
{   private:
        int emp_code;
        char name[20];
        int hra;
        int da;
        int ta;
    public:
        void read_data()
        {   cout<<"\n\n Enter the employee code : ";
            cin>>emp_code;
            cin.ignore();
            cout<<"\n\n Enter the name of the employee : ";
            cin>>name;
            cout<<"\n\n Enter the HRA, DA and TA : ";
            cin>>hra>>da>>ta;
        }
        void show_data()
        {   cout<<"\n\n EMP CODE   : "<<emp_code;
            cout<<"\n\n NAME : "<<name;
            cout<<"\n\n HRA, DA and TA : "<<hra<<"\t"<<da<<"\t"<<ta;
        }
};
main()
{
   fstream FILE;
   Employee e[5];
   int i;
   FILE.open("employee.txt", ios::out | ios::binary); //opening file for writing
   cout<<"\n Enter the details of five employees";
   cout<<"\n ---------------------------------------------------";
   for(i=0;i<5;i++)
   {   e[i].read_data();   // reading employee details from user
       FILE.write((char*)&e[i], sizeof(e[i])); //writing employee data to file
   }
   FILE.close();
   FILE.open("employee.txt", ios::in | ios::binary); //opening file for reading
   for(i=0;i<5;i++)
   {   FILE.read((char*)&e[i], sizeof(e[i])); //reading employee data from file
       e[i].show_data();   // displaying details of employee
   }
```

```
    return 0;
}
```

OUTPUT

```
Enter the details of five employees
----------------------------------------------------
Enter the employee code : 1
Enter the name of the employee : Geeta
Enter the HRA, DA and TA : 10000 7000 4000
Enter the employee code : 2
Enter the name of the employee : Reeta
Enter the HRA, DA and TA : 9000 8700 5700
Enter the employee code : 3
Enter the name of the employee : Babita
Enter the HRA, DA and TA : 5670 5300 1010
Enter the employee code : 4
Enter the name of the employee : Nandita
Enter the HRA, DA and TA : 8097 7095 9907
Enter the employee code : 5
Enter the name of the employee : Anshita
Enter the HRA, DA and TA : 8900 9700 7080
EMP CODE  : 1
NAME : Geeta
HRA, DA and TA : 10000 7000 4000
EMP CODE  : 2
NAME : Reeta
HRA, DA and TA : 9000 8700 5700
.............
EMP CODE  : 5
NAME : Anshita
HRA, DA and TA : 8900 9700 7080
```

Important Points

Detecting end of file In the program given earlier, we knew that we had record of five employees. If we do not know how many records we have to read, then we can use the `eof()`.

Finding the number of objects We can use the `tellg()` function to calculate the number of objects. This can be done by dividing the size of the file by the size of each object. For example, if the size of the file is 100 bytes and the size of one object is 20 bytes, obviously, there are five records or objects in the file,as obtained by calculating 100/20.

Finding the location of a particular object In a file that stores objects of equal size, the location of a particular object (`m`) can be calculated as `(m - 1) * object_length`.

Moving the file pointer to a particular object Once the location of the *m*th object is known, the `get` and `put` `file` pointers can be set to that location using `seekg()` or `seekp()` functions.

Note Binary files are more accurate and provide faster access to file because no conversion is required for performing read or write.

Program 13.6 Write a program to store records of an employee in `employee.txt` file using binary mode.

```
using namespace std;
#include<iostream>
#include<fstream>
class Employee
{   private:
      int emp_code;
      char name[20];
      int hra;
      int da;
      int ta;
    public:
      void read_data()
      {   cout<<"\n\n Enter the employee code : ";
          cin>>emp_code;
          cin.ignore();
          cout<<"\n\n Enter the name of the employee : ";
          cin>>name;
          cout<<"\n\n Enter the HRA, DA and TA : ";
          cin>>hra>>da>>ta;
      }
      void show_data()
      {   cout<<"\n\n EMP CODE  : "<<emp_code;
          cout<<"\n\n NAME : "<<name;
          cout<<"\n\n HRA, DA and TA : "<<hra<<"\t"<<da<<"\t"<<ta;
      }
};
int main()
{
   fstream FILE;
   Employee e;
   int i;
   FILE.open("employee.txt", ios::app | ios::binary);
   cout<<"\n Enter the details of the new employee";
   cout<<"\n ---------------------------------------------------";
   e.read_data();
   FILE.write((char*)&e, sizeof(e));
   FILE.close();
   FILE.open("employee.txt", ios::in | ios::binary);
   for(i=0;i<6;i++)
   {   FILE.read((char*)&e, sizeof(e));
       e.show_data();
   }
   return 0;
}
```

OUTPUT

```
Enter the details of the new employee
---------------------------------------------------
```

```
Enter the employee code : 10
Enter the name of the employee : Meeta
Enter the HRA, DA and TA : 3450 6789 8306
EMP CODE  : 1
NAME : Geeta
HRA, DA and TA : 10000 7000 4000
EMP CODE  : 2
NAME : Reeta
HRA, DA and TA : 9000 8700 5700
............
EMP CODE  : 5
NAME : Anshita
HRA, DA and TA : 8900 9700 7080
EMP CODE  : 10
NAME : Meeta
HRA, DA and TA : 3450 6789 8306
```

Program 13.7 Write a program to count the number of records stored in `employee.txt` file.

```
using namespace std;
#include<iostream>
#include<fstream>
class Employee
{   private:
      int emp_code;
      char name[20];
      int hra;
      int da;
      int ta;
    public:
      void read_data()
      {   cout<<"\n\n Enter the employee code : ";
          cin>>emp_code;
          cout<<"\n\n Enter the name of the employee : ";
          cin>>name;
          cout<<"\n\n Enter the HRA, DA and TA : ";
          cin>>hra>>da>>ta;
      }
      void show_data()
      {   cout<<"\n\n EMP CODE  : "<<emp_code;
          cout<<"\n\n NAME : "<<name;
          cout<<"\n\n HRA, DA and TA : "<<hra<<"\t"<<da<<"\t"<<ta;
      }
};
int main()
{
   fstream FILE;
   Employee e;
   FILE.open("employee.txt", ios::ate | ios::in | ios::binary);
   int location = FILE.tellp();
   cout<<"\n Number of bytes written in file = "<<location;
   int num_objects = location / (sizeof(e));
```

```
    cout<<"\n Size of each object = "<<sizeof(e);
    cout<<"\n Number of objects in file = "<<num_objects;
    return 0;
}
```

OUTPUT

```
Number of bytes written in file = 168
Size of each object = 28
Number of objects in file = 6
```

Program 13.8 Write a program to edit a record stored in `employee.txt` file.

```
using namespace std;
#include<iostream>
#include<fstream>
class Employee
{   private:
      int emp_code;
      char name[20];
      int hra;
      int da;
      int ta;
    public:
      void read_data()
      {   cout<<"\n\n Enter the employee code : ";
          cin>>emp_code;
          cout<<"\n\n Enter the name of the employee : ";
          cin>>name;
          cout<<"\n\n Enter the HRA, DA and TA : ";
          cin>>hra>>da>>ta;
      }
      void show_data()
      {   cout<<"\n\n EMP CODE  : "<<emp_code;
          cout<<"\n\n NAME : "<<name;
          cout<<"\n\n HRA, DA and TA : "<<hra<<"\t"<<da<<"\t"<<ta;
      }
};
int main()
{
   fstream FILE;
   Employee e;
   int no;

   FILE.open("employee.txt", ios::ate | ios::in | ios::out | ios::binary);
   cout<<"\n Enter the object number whose record has to be updated : ";
   cin>>no;
   int location = (no-1)*sizeof(e);
   FILE.seekp(location);
   cout<<"\n Enter the new details - ";
   e.read_data();
   FILE.write((char*)&e, sizeof(e));
   FILE.seekg(0);
```

```
    cout<<"\n\n FILE UPDATED .......";
    while(FILE.eof()==0)
    {   FILE.read((char*)&e, sizeof(e));
        e.show_data();
    }
}
```

OUTPUT

```
Enter the object number whose record has to be updated : 2
Enter the new details -
Enter the employee code : 100
Enter the name of the employee : Geetika
Enter the HRA, DA and TA : 9012 8765 4321
FILE UPDATED ……";
EMP CODE  : 1
NAME : Geeta
HRA, DA and TA : 10000 7000 4000
EMP CODE  : 100
NAME : Geetika
HRA, DA and TA : 9012 8765 4321
.............
EMP CODE  : 5
NAME : Anshita
HRA, DA and TA : 8900 9700 7080
EMP CODE  : 10
NAME : Meeta
HRA, DA and TA : 3450 6789 8306
```

AN ALTERNATE WAY TO DISPLAY RECORDS

```
int num_objects = FILE.tellp()/sizeof(e);
for(int i=0;i<num_objects;i++)
{   FILE.read((char*)&e, sizeof(e));
    e.show_data();
    getche();
}
```

Program 13.9 Write a program to randomly read the record of a particular employee stored in `employee.txt` file.

```
using namespace std;
#include<iostream>
#include<fstream>
class Employee
{   private:
      int emp_code;
      char name[20];
      int hra;
      int da;
      int ta;
    public:
      void read_data()
      {   cout<<"\n\n Enter the employee code : ";
```

```
            cin>>emp_code;
            cout<<"\n\n Enter the name of the employee : ";
            cin>>name;
            cout<<"\n\n Enter the HRA, DA and TA : ";
            cin>>hra>>da>>ta;
        }
        void show_data()
        {   cout<<"\n\n EMP CODE  : "<<emp_code;
            cout<<"\n\n NAME : "<<name;
            cout<<"\n\n HRA, DA and TA : "<<hra<<"\t"<<da<<"\t"<<ta;
        }
};
int main()
{
   fstream FILE;
   Employee e;
   int no;

   FILE.open("employee.txt", ios::ate | ios::in | ios::binary);
   cout<<"\n Enter the object number whose record has to be read : ";
   cin>>no;
   int location = (no-1)*sizeof(e);
   FILE.seekp(location);
   FILE.read((char*)&e, sizeof(e));
   e.show_data();
}
```

OUTPUT

```
Enter the object number whose record has to be read : 5
EMP CODE  : 5
NAME : Anshita
HRA, DA and TA : 8900 9700 7080
```

Program 13.10 Write a program to print the records of employees stored in `employee.txt` file in reverse order.

```
using namespace std;
#include<iostream>
#include<fstream>
class Employee
{   private:
      int emp_code;
      char name[20];
      int hra;
      int da;
      int ta;
    public:
      void read_data()
      {   cout<<"\n\n Enter the employee code : ";
          cin>>emp_code;
          cout<<"\n\n Enter the name of the employee : ";
```

```
        cin>>name;
        cout<<"\n\n Enter the HRA, DA and TA : ";
        cin>>hra>>da>>ta;
    }
    void show_data()
    {   cout<<"\n\n EMP CODE  : "<<emp_code;
        cout<<"\n\n NAME : "<<name;
        cout<<"\n\n HRA, DA and TA : "<<hra<<"\t"<<da<<"\t"<<ta;
    }
};
int main()
{
   fstream FILE;
   Employee e;

   FILE.open("employee.txt", ios::ate | ios::in | ios::binary);
   int num_objects = FILE.tellp()/sizeof(e);
   for(int i=num_objects;i>0;i--)
   {   int location = (i-1)*sizeof(e);
       FILE.seekg(location);
       FILE.read((char*)&e, sizeof(e));
       e.show_data();
   }
}
```

OUTPUT

```
EMP CODE  : 10
NAME : Meeta
HRA, DA and TA : 3450 6789 8306
EMP CODE  : 5
NAME : Anshita
HRA, DA and TA : 8900 9700 7080
............
EMP CODE  : 100
NAME : Geetika
HRA, DA and TA : 9012 8765 4321
EMP CODE  : 1
NAME : Geeta
HRA, DA and TA : 10000 7000 4000
```

13.9 ERROR HANDLING DURING FILE OPERATIONS

Until now, we have dealt only with one type of error that occurs during opening files. We had assumed that rest everything works absolutely fine; however, in real time, users may access files without any pre-defined access pattern. In such a scenario, our assumptions may lead to big problems especially when users try to do the following:

- Open a non-existent file in read-mode.
- Open a read-only in `ios::out` mode.
- Open a file with invalid name.
- Read beyond the end-of-file.

- Write more data in a file stored on disk when no sufficient disk space is available.
- Manipulate data stored in an unopened file.
- No file is connected with the stream object.
- Media errors which may occur while reading or writing data

Stream-State Flag

Class `ios` has a member function called stream-state as given in Fig. 13.9 that records information on the status of a file that is currently being used.

Unused	Unused	Unused	Unused	Hard error	Invalid operation	R/w fail	End-of-file

Figure 13.9 Stream state flag

The `ios` class has several member functions to access the status of a file stream. These functions are summarized in Table 13.7. With the help of these functions, programmers can check the status and immediately take corrective measures if the need arises.

Table 13.7 Functions for accessing status of file stream

Function	Utility	Usage
`eof()`	Returns a non-zero value (true) if end-of-file is encountered; otherwise, returns 0.	`while(FILE.eof()==0)` `{ // Process }`
`fail()`	Returns true if read/write operation has failed; otherwise, returns false.	`if(FILE.fail())` `{ // File not opened }`
`bad()`	Returns true if either in an invalid operation is attempted or any unrecoverable error has occurred. Returns false if it is possible to recover from error and continue operation.	`if(FILE.bad())` `{ // Error }`
`good()`	Returns true if no error has occurred. In other words, if all the above functions are false. Therefore, when FILE. good() returns true, it means that everything is fine and further operations can be carried out.	`if(FILE.good())` `{ // Process }`
`clear()`	Clears the error states and proceeds further processing with file.	`FILE.clear();`
`rdstate()`	Reads the status state data member defined in class ios.	`FILE.rdstate();`

13.10 ACCEPTING COMMAND LINE ARGUMENTS

C++ facilitates programmers to pass command line arguments. Command-line arguments are given after the name of a program in command-line operating systems such as DOS or Linux, and are passed in to the program from the operating system.

Note Command-line arguments facilitate supply of arguments to `main()` at the time of invoking the program.

Until now, no arguments were passed to the `main()`. However, now, in order to understand command line arguments, you must first understand the full declaration of the main function.

The `main()` can accept two arguments,

- The first argument is an integer value that specifies number of command line arguments.
- The second argument is a full list of all of the command line arguments.

The full declaration of `main()` can be given as follows:

```
int main (int argc, char *argv[])
```

The integer, `argc` specifies the number of arguments passed into the program from the command line, including the name of the program.

The array of character pointers, `argv` contains the list of all the arguments. `argv[0]` is the name of the program, or an empty string if the name is not available. `argv[1]` to `argv[argc - 1]` specifies the command line argument. In the C++ program, every element in the `argv` can be used as a string. Moreover, elements of `argv` can also be accessed as a two dimensional array. Note that `argv[argc]` is a null pointer.

Programming Tip: Command line arguments are separated by a space.

In other words, each element of the array `argv` is a pointer where each pointer points to a string. Therefore, `argv[0]` points to a string that contains the first parameter on the command line which is the program's name, `argv[1]` points to the next parameter, and so on. Look at the program given here which illustrates the use of command line arguments.

Example 13.8 Using command line arguments

```
using namespace std;
#include<iostream>
#include<fstream>
int main(int argc, char *argv[])
{
int i;
cout<<"\n Number of arguments passed = "<<argc;
for (i=0; i<argc; i++)
cout<<"\n argv[i] ="<<argv[i];
return 0;
}
```

OUTPUT

```
Number of arguments passed = 3
argv[0] = exercise
argv[1] = first
argv[2] = second
```

Explanation: In the program, the `main()` accepts command line arguments through `argc` and `argv`. In the `main()` function, the value of `argc` is printed which gives the number of arguments passed. Then, each argument passed is printed in the `for` loop using the array of pointers, `argv`. To execute this program, we need to write

```
C:\TC\BIN> myprog WELCOME TO THE WORLD OF C++ PROGRAMMING
```

Here, `myprog` is the name of the file containing the program that has to be executed and rest all are additional arguments. In the program, `argc = 8`, including file name and arguments, and the contents of `argv` are as follows:

```
argv[0] = myprog    argv[1] = WECLCOME    argv[2] = TO         argv[3] = THE
argv[4] = WORLD    argv[5] = OF    argv[6] = C++    argv[7] = PROGRAMMING
```

Program 13.11 Write a program to print the text of a file on screen by printing the text line by line and displaying the line numbers before the text in each line. The filename should be supplied as command line argument.

```
using namespace std;
#include<iostream>
#include<fstream>
int main(int argc, char *argv[])
{
   fstream FILE;
   char text[100], ch;
   int line = 1;
   int i = 0;

   if(argc != 2)
   {   cout<<"\n Full information is not provided";
       return 0;
   }
   FILE.open(argv[1], ios::in);
   if(!FILE)
   {   cout<<"\n File Opening Error";
       return 0;
   }
   i = 0;
   while( FILE.eof() == 0)
   {   FILE.get(ch);
       if (ch == '\n')
       {   line++;
         text[i] = '\0';
         cout<<line<<"  "<< text;
         i = 0;
      }
      text[i] = ch;
      i++;
   }
   text[i] = '\0';

   cout<<text;
   FILE.close();
   return 0;
}
```

OUTPUT

```
In the DOS SHELL type,
c:\tc\bin>exercise comments.txt
excellent book
```

Program 13.12 Write a program to read a file that contains characters. Encrypt the data in this file while writing it into another file.

```
using namespace std;
#include<iostream>
#include<fstream>
int main(int argc, char *argv[])
{   fstream FILE1, FILE2;
    char ch;

    if(argc != 3)
    {   cout<<"\n Full information is not provided";
        return 0;
    }
    FILE1.open(argv[1], ios::in);
    if(!FILE1)
    {   cout<<"\n File Opening Error";
        return 0;
    }
    FILE2.open(argv[2], ios::out);
    if(!FILE2)
    {   cout<<"\n File Opening Error";
        return 0;
    }
    while ( FILE1.eof() == 0)
   {   FILE1.get(ch);
       FILE2.put(ch + 4);
   }
   FILE1.close();
   FILE2.close();
   cout<<"\n FILE ENCRYPTED";
   return 0;
}
```

OUTPUT

```
c:\tc\bin>exercise comments.txt newcom.txt
FILE ENCRYPTED
```

Program 13.13 Write a program to read a file that contains small case characters. Then write these characters into another file with all lower case characters converted into upper case.

```
using namespace std;
#include<iostream>
#include<fstream>
int main(int argc, char *argv[])
{   fstream FILE1, FILE2;
    char ch;
    if(argc != 3)
    {   cout<<"\n Full information is not provided";
        return 0;
    }
    FILE1.open(argv[1], ios::in);
    if(!FILE1)
```

```
    {   cout<<"\n File Opening Error";
        return 0;
    }
    FILE2.open(argv[2], ios::out);
    if(!FILE2)
    {   cout<<"\n File Opening Error";
        return 0;
    }
   while ( FILE1.eof() == 0)
   {   ch = FILE1.get();
       if(ch == ' ')
         FILE2.put(ch);
       else
         FILE2.put(ch - 32);
   }
   FILE1.close();
   FILE2.close();
   cout<<"\n File copied with upper case characters";
   return 0;
}
```

OUTPUT

```
c:\tc\bin>exercise comments.txt ncom.txt
File copied with upper case characters
```

Program 13.14 Write a program to merge two files into a third file. The names of the files must be entered using command line arguments.

```
using namespace std;
#include<iostream>
#include<fstream>
int main(int argc, char *argv[])
{   fstream FILE1, FILE2, FILE3;
    char ch;
    if(argc != 4)
    {   cout<<"\n Full information is not provided";
        return 0;
    }
    FILE1.open(argv[1], ios::in);
    if(!FILE1)
    {   cout<<"\n File Opening Error";
        return 0;
    }
    FILE2.open(argv[2], ios::in);
    if(!FILE2)
    {   cout<<"\n File Opening Error";
        return 0;
    }
    FILE3.open(argv[3], ios::out);
    if(!FILE3)
    {   cout<<"\n File Opening Error";
        return 0;
    }
```

```
    while(FILE1.eof()==0)
    {   FILE1.get(ch);
        FILE3.put(ch);
    }
    while(FILE2.eof()==0)
    {   FILE2.get(ch);
        FILE3.put(ch);
    }
    FILE1.close();
    FILE2.close();
    FILE3.close();
    cout<<"\n Files Merged";
    return 0;
}
```

OUTPUT

```
c:\tc\bin>exercise comments.txt ncom.txt newcom.txt
Files Merged
```

Program 13.15 Write a program to count the number of lower case, upper case, numbers, and special characters present in the contents of a file.

```
using namespace std;
#include<iostream>
#include<fstream>
int main(int argc, char *argv[])
{   fstream FILE1;
    int ch, upper_case = 0, lower_case = 0, numbers = 0, special_chars = 0;
  if(argc != 2)
  {   cout<<"\n Full information is not provided";
      return 0;
  }
  FILE1.open(argv[1], ios::in);
  if(!FILE1)
  {   cout<<"\n File Opening Error";
      return 0;
  }
  int i = 0;
  while(FILE1.eof() == 0)
  {   ch = FILE1.get();
      if (ch >= 'A' && ch <= 'Z')
         upper_case++;
      if (ch >= 'a' && ch <= 'z')
         lower_case++;
      if (ch >= '0' && ch <= '9')
         numbers++;
    else
       special_chars++;
  }
  FILE1.close();
  cout<<"\n Number of upper case characters = "<< upper_case;
  cout<<"\n Number of lower case characters = "<< lower_case;
```

```
    cout<<"\n Number of digits  = "<<numbers;
    cout<<"\n Number of special characters = "<< special_chars;
    return 0;
}
```

OUTPUT

```
c:\tc\bin>exercise newcom.txt
Number of upper case characters = 13
Number of lower case characters = 13
Number of digits  = 0
Number of special characters = 32
```

Points to Remember

- A file is basically used because real-life applications involve large amounts of data.
- Standard streams such as `cin, cout, cerr, and clog` are termed as pre-connected input and output channels between a text terminal and the program,when it begins execution.
- Standard error is an output stream used by programs to report error messages or diagnostics.
- A stream is linked to a file using an open operation and disassociated from a file using a `close`.
- A file can be opened either by using the constructor function of the class or by using the member function `open()` of the class. While the constructor function is preferred when there is a single file to be opened in the stream, the `open()`, on the other hand, is used when there are multiple files to be used.
- There are two ways to detect the `end-of-file` condition. First, to use `while(inpFile)` which returns a zero if any error(s) occurs in the file operation (including `end-of-file`). The second approach is to use the `eof()` member function of the `ios` class.
- The file mode is used to specify the purpose for which the file is being opened.
- When the file is opened in `ios::out` mode, the existing contents of the file are deleted and the write pointer is set at the beginning of the file so that data can be written from the start.
- The file stream classes support functions like `get()`, `put()`, `read()`, and `write()` for performing sequential or random input and output operations.
- Class `ios` has a member function called stream-state flag (refer to Fig. 13.9) that records information on the status of a file that is currently being used.
- A binary file is a file which may contain any type of data, encoded in binary form for computer storage and processing purposes.

Glossary

Binary file A file which may contain any type of data, encoded in binary form for computer storage and processing purposes

File A collection of data stored on a secondary storage device like hard disk

Stream A logical interface to the devices that are connected to the computer

Exercises

Fill in the Blanks

1. ______ are termed as pre-connected input and output channels between a text terminal and the program.
2. _______, _______, and _______ are standard streams in C++.
3. _____ and _____ are always redirected to `console`.
4. _______ is a fully buffered version of `cerr`.
5. The standard streams are defined in the _________ header file.
6. _________ provides functions common to the file streams.

7. The _____ operator is overloaded and returns a non-zero value if an error(s) is encountered and a zero otherwise.
8. The `eof()` returns a _____ if the end-of-file condition is encountered.
9. The _____ is used to specify the purpose for which the file is being opened.
10. The contents of a _____ file are not human readable.
11. When we open a file in `ios::in` mode, the read pointer is automatically set at the _____ of the file.
12. The _____ records information on the status of a file that is currently being used.
13. _____ reads the status state data member defined in class `ios`.
14. _____ facilitate supply of arguments to `main()` at the time of invoking the program.

State True or False

1. Standard error is an input stream.
2. The standard output and standard error cannot be directed to the same destination.
3. `filebuf` is used to set the file buffer for read and write operations.
4. `get()`, `getline()`, `read()`, `seekg()`, and `tellg()` are members of both `istream` and `ifstream` classes.
5. `ostream` inherits functions from the `ofstream` class.
6. Every filename must have an extension.
7. In MS-DOS, the file name can have eight characters followed by a dot and an extension of three characters.
8. We can open as many files as we want at a given time.
9. `Ios::app` allows data to be added or modified anywhere in the file.
10. The `fstream` class does not provide a default mode.
11. Binary files can be either processed sequentially or at random.
12. Text files can be processed only sequentially.
13. `get()` and `put()` can be used to read and `write()` multiple characters from the associated stream.
14. File pointer contains the address of the file.
15. `tellg()` and `tellp()` functions can be used interchangeably.

Multiple Choice Questions

1. From which stream does the program receive data?
   (a) `cin` (b) `cout`
   (c) `cerr` (d) All of these
2. In which stream does the program writes its output data?
   (a) `cin` (b) `cout`
   (c) `cerr` (d) All of these
3. Which function links a stream to a file?
   (a) `Connect()` (b) `Link()`
   (c) `Open()` (d) All of these
4. Which class inherits all the functions from istream and ostream through the iostream class?
   (a) `ifstream` (b) `ofstream`
   (c) `fstreambase` (d) `fstream`
5. The number and type of characters in the file name depends on _____.
   (a) Compiler
   (b) Programming language
   (c) Operating system
   (d) All of these
6. The filename in Unix can have how many characters?
   (a) 8 (b) 30
   (c) 31 (d) 33
7. `Open()` fails if the file already exists in which file mode?
   (a) `ios::trunc`
   (b) `ios::nocreate`
   (c) `ios::write`
   (d) `ios::noreplace`
8. `Open()` fails if the file does not exist in which file mode?
   (a) `ios::trunc` (b) `ios::nocreate`
   (c) `ios::write` (d) `ios::noreplace`
9. When a file is opened in `ios::out` mode, it is automatically opened using which mode?
   (a) `ios::trunc` (b) `ios::nocreate`
   (c) `ios::write` (d) `ios::noreplace`
10. File permission are not used in which mode?
    (a) `ios::trunc` (b) `ios::nocreate`
    (c) `ios::write` (d) `ios::noreplace`
11. Which function returns true if either in an invalid operation is attempted or any unrecoverable error has occurred?
    (a) `Bad()` (b) `Good()`
    (c) `Fail()` (d) `Rdstate()`

Review Questions

1. Why do we need files?
2. What are streams?
3. Explain the standard streams in C++.
4. How is a stream linked to a file?
5. Write a short note on hierarchy of classes for file operations.
6. Explain the process of opening a file.
7. How can an opened file be closed?
8. When will you prefer to open a file using a constructor?
9. What happens when a file opened for writing does not exist?
10. Why do we need to check for errors while performing operations on files?
11. What are the two ways of detecting `end-of-file`?
12. What do you understand by file mode?
13. What are file pointers? Categorize them and explain their significance.
14. Explain the syntax of seek functions with the help of relevant examples.
15. Differentiate between a text file and a binary file.
16. Explain the syntax of `read()` and `write()`.
17. What kind of errors can occur during file operations?
18. What are command line arguments?
19. Explain the function declaration of `main()`.
20. Write statements using `seekg()` to perform the following tasks:
    (a) To move the pointer 25 positions backward from the end of the file
    (b) To go to the beginning of the file
    (c) To move 30 bytes backward from the current position
    (d) To go the 40th byte in the file

Programming Exercises

1. Write a program that writes students details in a file.
2. Write a program that reads students details from the file created in Question 1.
3. Repeat questions 1 and 2 with a file created in binary mode.
4. Write a menu-driven program that reads details of a faculty. Provide options to add a new record, delete a record, update an existing record and display all or a particular record.
   Hint To delete a record, make a temporary file. Copy all the records except the one to be deleted. Then, rename the temporary file as the main file.
5. Write a menu-driven program that reads, stores, appends, adds, displays, and edits all information about a book.
6. Write a program that reads a letter stored in a file.
7. Write a program that reads numbers as command line arguments. Add these numbers and display the average.
8. Write a program that reads a file that contains integers. Read the integers and categorize them as even or odd. Store all the even integers in a file called `EVEN.TXT` and all odd numbers in `ODD.TXT`.
9. Write a program that deals with multiple files at a time, like one file can store the name of the countries (5) and the other stores the names of their prime ministers. Read the contents from these two files and display the contents of the two files simultaneously. For example, India Narendra Modi.
10. Write a menu-driven program that when executed in `DOS` prompt using the following sample format, performs the required operation:
    (a) Copyfile `first.txt second.txt`
    (b) `Comparefile first.txt second.txt`
    (c) `Encryptfile first.txt second.txt`
    (d) `Decryptfile first.txt second.txt`
    (e) `Sortfile first.txt second.txt`
11. Write a program that reads a file character by character.
12. Write a program that demonstrates the use of error handling conditions in files.
13. Write a program that reads a file and counts the number of even and odd integers stored in it.
14. Write a program that demonstrates the use of command line arguments.
15. Write a program that reads lines from a file. Display those lines on screen with line numbers, numbers of characters in the line displayed at the end of the line.
16. Write a menu-driven program that maintains a file `DIRECTORY` that stores the name and telephone number of a person. The program must allow users to add new contacts, search a contact based on name, search a contact based on phone number, update the number, update the name, and delete a contact.
17. Write a program that reads a file and copies its contents in another file. While copying, replace all full stops with commas.

18. Write a program that exchanges the contents of two files.
19. Write a menu-driven program file that maintains information about products sold. Add functions to add, delete, and update records.
20. Write a program that writes data to a file in such a way that each character after a full stop is capitalized and all numbers are written in brackets.

Find the errors in the following codes

1.
```
using namespace std;
#include<iostream>
#include<fstream>
int main()
{   char buffer[100];
ifstream inFile("exercise.c");
ofstream outFile("try.c");
while(inFile.get(buffer))
{   inFile.get();
    outFile<<buffer;
}
inFile.close();
outFile.close();
}
```
2.
```
using namespace std;
#include<iostream>
#include<fstream>
int main()
{   char buffer[100];
ifstream inFile("comments.
txt", ios::nocreate);
while(!inFile)
{   inFile.getline(buffer,100);
    cout<<buffer;
}
inFile.close();
}
```
3.
```
using namespace std;
#include<iostream>
#include<fstream>
int main()
{   char buffer[100];
ifstream inFile("comments.
txt", ios::nocreate);
while(inFile!=0)
{   inFile.getline(buffer,100);
    cout<<buffer;
}
inFile.close();
}
```
4.
```
using namespace std;
#include<iostream>
#include<fstream>
int main()
{   char buffer[100];
ifstream inFile("comments.
txt", ios::nocreate);
while(!inFile)
{   inFile.getline(buffer,100);
    cout<<buffer;
}
inFile.close();
}
```
5.
```
using namespace std;
#include<iostream>
#include<fstream>
int main()
{   char buffer[100];
ifstream inFile("comments.
txt", ios::nocreate);
while(!inFile.getline(buffer,100))
     cout<<buffer;
inFile.close();
}
```
6.
```
using namespace std;
#include<iostream>
#include<fstream>
void show()
{   char ch;
while(inFile)
{   inFile.get(ch);
   cout<<ch;
}
}
int main()
{   ifstream inFile;
inFile.open("Text.txt");
if(inFile!=0)
   show();
else
   cout<<"\n No Output";
inFile.close();
}
```
7.
```
using namespace std;
#include<iostream>
#include<fstream>
int main()
{   ofstream outFile;
outFile.open("Text.txt");
char str[20];
cin>>str;
outFile<<str;

ifstream inFile;
inFile.open("Text.txt");
inFile>>str;
cout<<str;
```

```
   inFile.close();
   }
8. using namespace std;
   #include<iostream>
   #include<fstream>
   int main()
   {    fstream inFile;
   inFile.open("Text.txt");
   while(inFIle.eof()==0)
      cout<<(char)inFile.get();
   inFile.close();
   }
```

Find the output of the following codes

```
1. using namespace std;
   #include<iostream>
   #include<fstream>
   int main()
   {    char *buffer = "Hello World !!!";
   fstream File;
   File.open("Text.txt", ios::in | ios::out);
   for(int i=0;i<strlen(buffer);i++)
      File.put(buffer[i]);
   File.seekg(0);
   char ch;
   cout<<"\n Contents of the File are : ";
   while(File)
   {    File.get(ch);
        cout<<ch;
   }
   File.close();
   }
2. using namespace std;
   #include<iostream>
   #include<fstream>
   int main()
   {    ofstream outFile;
        ifstream inFile;
        cout<<"\n Size of inFile =
   "<<sizeof(inFile);
        cout<<"\n Size of outFile =
   "<<sizeof(outFile);
   }
3. using namespace std;
   #include<iostream>
   #include<fstream>
   int main()
   {    ofstream File;
        File.open("Text.txt");
        char ch;
        while(cin)
        {    cin.get(ch);
             File<<ch;
        }
        File.close();
   }
4. using namespace std;
   #include<iostream>
   #include<fstream>
   int main()
   {    char buffer[100];
   fstream File("Text.
   txt", ios::binary | ios::in | ios::out);
   for(int i=0;i<50;i++)
      File<<i;
   File.seekp(2);
   File<<"Programming in C++ is Fun";
   File.seekp(4);
   File.read(buffer, 100);
   buffer[50]= 0;
   cout<<"\n"<<buffer;
   }
```

Answers

Fill in the Blanks

1. Streams; **2.** `cin, cout, cerr`; **3.** `cerr, clog`; **4.** `clog`; **5.** `iostream.h`; **6.** `fstream base`; **7.** !; **8.** non-zero value; **9.** file mode; **10.** binary; **11.** beginning; **12.** stream-state; **13.** `rdstate()`; **14.** Command line arguments

State True or False

1. False	**2.** False	**3.** True	**4.** True	**5.** False	**6.** False	**7.** True	**8.** False
9. False	**10.** True	**11.** True	**12.** True	**13.** False	**14.** False	**15.** False	

Multiple Choice Questions

1. (a); **2.** (b); **3.** (c); **4.** (d); **5.** (c); **6.** (c); **7.** (d); **8.** (b); **9.** (a); **10.** (b); **11.** (a)

Case Study 6

This case study shows the implementation of concepts discussed in Chapter 11 on Operator Overloading and Type Conversions.

Program C6.1 Create a class that imitates the functionality of the basic data type.

```
using namespace std;
#include<iostream>
class Int
{     private:
            int value;
      public:
            Int()
            {     value = 0;
            }
            Int(int num)
            {     value  = num;
            }
            int operator+(Int &B)
            {     return (value + B.value);
            }
            int operator-(Int &B)
            {     return (value - B.value);
            }
            int operator*(Int &B)
            {     return (value * B.value);
            }
            float operator/(Int &B)
            {     return (float)(value / B.
value);
            }
            int operator%(Int &B)
            {     return (value % B.value);
            }
            void operator &()
            {     cout<<this;
            }
            void operator *()
            {     cout<<value;
            }
            friend istream & operator >>
(istream & input, Int &A)
            {     input>>A.value;
                  return input;
            }
            friend ostream & operator
 << (ostream & output, Int &A)
            {     cout<<A.value;
                  return output;
            }
};
int main()
{
      clrscr();
      Int a = 12;
      Int b, c;
      cout<<"\n Enter the second value : ";
      cin>>b;
      char option;
      do
      {     cout<<"\
n\n ********* MAIN MENU **********";
            cout<<"\n a. Addition";
            cout<<"\n b. Subtraction";
           cout<<"\n c. Multiplication";
            cout<<"\n d. Division";
            cout<<"\n e. Modulus";
            cout<<"\n f. Use Address
Operator (&)";
            cout<<"\n g. Use Dereference
Operator (*)";
            cout<<"\n h. Exit";
            cout<<"\n
*******************************";
            cout<<"\
n\n Enter your option : ";
            cin>>option;
            switch(option)
            {     case 'a':
                        c = a + b;
                        cout<<"\n"<<a<< " + "
<<b<<" = "<<c;
                        break;
                  case 'b':
                        c = a - b;
```

```
                    cout<<"\n"<<a<< " - "
<<b<<" = "<<c;
                    break;
               case 'c':
                    c = a * b;
                    cout<<"\n"<<a<< " * "
<<b<<" = "<<c;
                    break;
               case 'd':
                    c = a / b;
                    cout<<"\n"<<a<< " / "
<<b<<" = "<<c;
                    break;
               case 'e':
                    c = a % b;
                    cout<<"\n"<<a<< " + "
<<b<<" = "<<c;
                    break;
               case 'f':
          cout<<"\n Address of a (&a) = ";
                    &a;
          cout<<"\n Address of b (&b) = ";
                    &b;
                    break;
               case 'g':
          cout<<"\n Value of a (*a) = ";
                    *a;
          cout<<"\n Value of b (*b) = ";
                    *b;
                    break;
          }
     }while(option!='h');
}
```

OUTPUT

```
Enter the second value : 6

********* MAIN MENU **********
a. Addition
b. Subtraction
c. Multiplication
d. Division
e. Modulus
f. Use Address Operator (&)";
g. Use Dereference Operator (*)";
h. Exit
********************************
Enter your option : a
12 + 6 = 6
```

CHAPTER 14

Templates

KEY Concepts

• Use of templates • Function templates • Class templates • Templates versus macros • Class templates with inheritance • Class templates with operator overloading • Pros and cons of templates

INTRODUCTION

To reduce code duplication and generate short and simpler code, C++ supports the use of templates to define the same code for multiple data types. This means that a C++ function or a class that performs similar operations on different data types such as integers, float, and double can be unified with a single template function or class with functions that are flexible enough to deal with all three data types.

Templates fall under the category of meta-programming and auto code generation, although the generated code is never visible to the users.

> **Note** With templates, programmers can define a family of functions or classes that can operate on different types of data.

Templates allow programmers to write functions and classes to be defined with any type or of a general type. Until now, we have been writing non-template functions in which the function parameters are declared to be of a particular type. While calling the function, the arguments passed to the function must strictly match the data types of the parameters. However, with a template function, that function can be called with any compatible type. Templates act as a model of function or a class that can be used to generate functions or classes. During compilation of a program that has templates, the C++ compiler generates one or more functions or classes based on the specified template. Figure 14.1 clarifies this concept.

Therefore, through templates, C++ supports the concept of generic programming. Generic programming is a technique of programming in which a general code is written first. The code is instantiated only when the need arises for specific types that are provided as parameters.

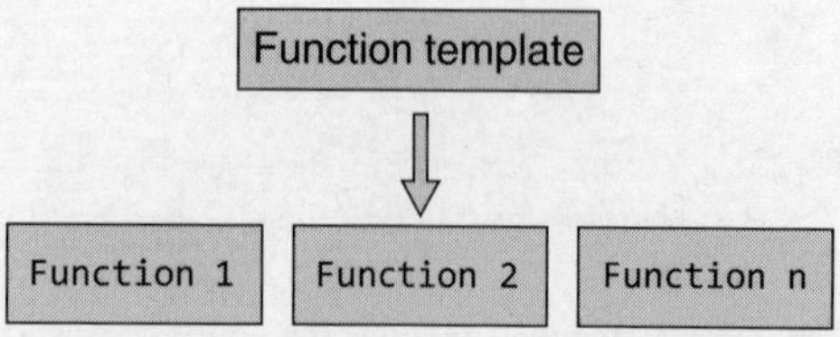

Figure 14.1(a) Generated functions

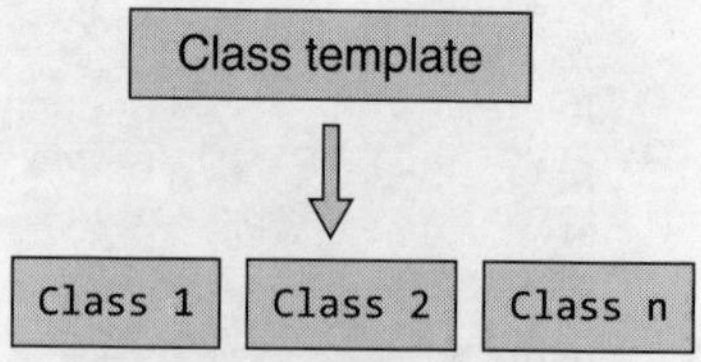

Figure 14.1(b) Generated classes

Note Entities such as class or function created using generic programming are called generics.

14.1 USE OF TEMPLATES

- Templates are widely used to implement the standard template library (STL) to define containers, iterators, and algorithms. For example, containers include vectors, queues, sets, maps, hash tables, and functions to sort their objects specified as a template.
- Templates are used to create abstract data types and classify algorithms and data structures. This means that templates allow programmers to define the behaviour of the class without specifying the datatype of variables that will be handled by the operations of the class. For example, the template array class can store data for any and every different datatype.
- Class templates are generally used to implement containers which we will be discussing later in this book.

14.2 FUNCTION TEMPLATES

Several important functions that we use frequently have to operate on different data types. However, to make the same code operate on every other data type, we need to repeat the code with a particular type. For example, if we need to find the square of an integer, long integer, and double and floating point value, we must write separate functions for all of these data types.

A better alternative is to write a function template, also known as a generic function or function templates. Function templates are functions that serve as a pattern for creating other similar functions. This enables programmers to write functions without having to specify the exact type(s) of some or all of the variables. Instead, we define the function using placeholder types (i.e. for which no data type is specified), called template type parameters.

Syntax The syntax for defining a function template can be given as shown in Fig. 14.2.

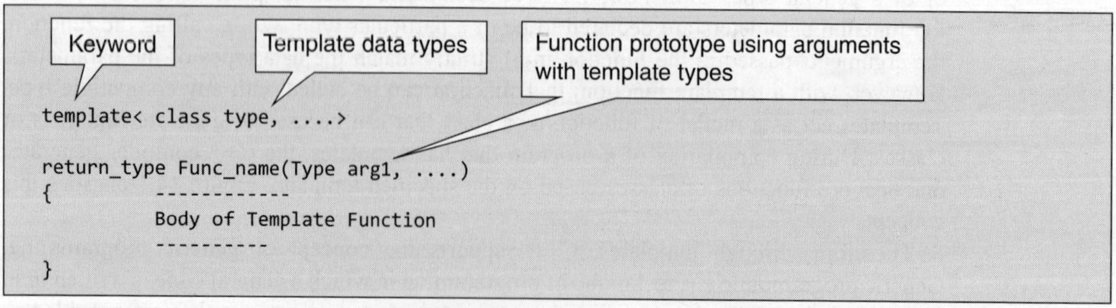

Figure 14.2 Syntax of a function template

As seen in Fig. 14.2, the syntax for defining a function template begins with the keyword template followed by a list of template type arguments also called generic data types. The template function will use generic data types (or general data types) since the exact data types of arguments will be known only at the time of function call. In the syntax, the template keyword informs the compiler that what follows is a template. Here, `class` is a keyword and `type` is the name of the generic parameter that will be replaced with a concrete parameter during function call.

Programming Tip: The template declaration and definition must be in the same file.

The template declaration is followed by the function prototype, which is almost the same as that of a normal function except that it uses data of template types, since exact data types are not known at the time of function declaration and/or definition.

When the template function is called, the compiler identifies the data type of the parameters and creates a function internally and finally makes a call to it. The programmers are completely unaware of the code generation done by the compiler. Let us see a simple function template that finds the square of a number.

Example 14.1 Finding square of a number using function template

```
using namespace std;
#include<iostream>
template<class Type>
Type square(Type num)
{   return num*num;
}
main()
{   int num1 = 3;
    cout<<"\n Square of "<<num1<<" = "<<square(num1);//int is replaced with Type
    float num2 = 5.6;
    cout<<"\n Square of "<<num2<<" = "<<square(num2);//float is replaced with Type
    double num3 = 123.456;
    cout<<"\n Square of "<<num3<<" = "<<square(num3);//double is replaced with Type
}
```

OUTPUT

```
Square of 3 = 9
Square of 5.6 = 31.59999299
Square of 123.456 = 15241.383936
```

- In the program, compilers generate n copies of the code under the template function, where n is the number of calls to the function `square()`.
- The first copy is invoked with an integer data, second with a floating point data, and third with a double type data.
- Once an internal function is generated for a particular data type, all future invocation to the template function with the same data type will refer to it.
- The template function can be invoked using either the explicit or implicit template expression. For example, `square()` can be invoked either by writing `square<int>(value)` or by writing `square(value)`.

Table 14.1 Differences between templates and macros

Templates	Macros
• Code is simpler and easier to write and understand	• More chances of mistakes
• Easy to debug	• Difficult to find errors as they are handled by pre-processor
• Being a function call, they are less efficient than macros	• More efficient as they are compiled inline
• Templates perform type checking during compile time and are considered to be type safe	• Macros do not perform any type checking

14.2.1 Templates versus Macros

When function templates and macros perform the same job, then we need to analyse why we need to use templates. Table 14.1 gives a comparison between the two types.

14.2.2 Guidelines for Using Template Functions

While using template functions, programmers must keep the following points in mind.

Generic Data Types

- Every template data type must be used in the function declaration and/or definition. Failing to do so results in an error and will be treated as an invalid template. For example, a template definition like the one given here is an error.

```
template<class Type1>
int square(int num) // Error: Type 1 is not used as an argument
{   return num*num;
}
```

- Using only some and not all generic types as function arguments also results in an error. Therefore, the following definition will also generate an error.

```
template<class Type1, class Type2>
int square(Type1 num) //Error: Type 2 is not used as an argument
{  Type2 res = num * num;
   return res;
}
```

Programming Tip: It is an error to define a function template without the template prefix.

Overloaded Function Templates

- Like normal functions, template functions can also be overloaded. In such cases, the template function has the same name but different number or type of arguments. Consider the overloaded function `display()` in the program given here.

Example 14.2 Template function overloading

```
using namespace std;
#include<iostream>
template<class Type>
void display(Type num)
{   cout<<"\n"<<num;
}
template<class Type1, class Type2>
void display(Type1 mes, Type2 num)
{   cout<<"\n"<<mes<<num;
}
main()
{   int num = 5;
   char *m =  "The number is :  ";

   display(num);
   display(m, num);
}
```

OUTPUT

```
5
The number is : 5
```

When the compiler encounters an overloaded template function, it uses the following rules to select a suitable template.

- If an exact match is found using an ordinary function, the compiler calls it.
- If an exact match is not found, it looks for a function template from which an exact match can be generated. If found, it calls for the same.
- If no match can be found, ordinary overloading resolution for the function is tried.
- If no match is still found, an error is generated.
- In case more than one match is found, then an ambiguity error is generated.

Recursive Template Functions

- C++ also allows programmers to call nested or recursive template functions. For example, consider the program code given here that finds factorial of a number.

Example 14.3 Nested or recursive template functions

```
using namespace std;
#include<iostream>
template<class Type>
Type fact(Type num)
{   if(num==1)
      return 1;
   else
      return (num*fact(num-1));
```

```
}
main()
{   int num1 = 5;
    cout<<"\n Factorial of  "<<num1<<" = "<<fact(num1);
    long int num2 = 10;
    cout<<"\n Factorial of  "<<num2<<" = "<<fact(num2);
}
```

OUTPUT

```
Factorial of 5 = 120
Factorial of 10 = 3628800
```

Function Templates with User-defined Types

- C++ allows programmers to use user-defined types in function template. For example, you can use the `display()` to print an integer, char, string, a structure, etc., to show its contents. For example, `display()` prints the contents of all its individual data members on screen.

```
template<class Type1>
void display(Type1 &stud)
{   cout<<"\n Roll Number :  "<<stud.rno;
    cout<<"\n Name :  "<<stud.name;
    cout<<"\n MARKS :  "<<stud.marks;
}
```

Note Template is a model that serves as a pattern for creating similar objects.

Program 14.1 Write a program to find greater of two given values.

```
using namespace std;
#include<iostream>
template<class Type>
Type find_greater(Type a, Type b)
{   if(a>b)
       return a;
    else return b;
}
main()
{   int inum1 = 4, inum2 = 5;
    float fnum1 = 4.8, fnum2 = -5.3;
    char c1 = 'A', c2 = 'Z';
    cout<<"\n Greater of two integers is :  "<<find_greater(inum1, inum2);
    cout<<"\n Greater of two floating point numbers is :  "<<find_greater(fnum1, fnum2);
    cout<<"\n Greater of two characters is :  "<<find_greater(c1, c2);
}
```

OUTPUT

```
Greater of two integers is : 5
Greater of two floating point numbers is : 4.8
Greater of two characters is : Z
```

Program 14.2 Write a program to swap two variables of any type.

```
using namespace std;
#include<iostream>
template<class Type>
void swap_it(Type &a, Type &b)
{   Type temp = a;
    a = b;
    b = temp;
}
main()
{   int inum1 = 4, inum2 = 5;
    float fnum1 = 4.8, fnum2 = -5.3;
    char c1 = 'A', c2 = 'a';

    cout<<"\n inum1 = "<<inum1<<" and inum2 = "<<inum2;
    cout<<"\n fnum1 = "<<fnum1<<" and fnum2 = "<<fnum2;
    cout<<"\n c1 =  "<<c1<<" and c2 =  "<<c2;

    swap_it(inum1, inum2);
    swap_it(fnum1, fnum2);
    swap_it(c1,c2);
    cout<<"\n\n After Swapping ";
    cout<<"\n\n inum1 =  "<<inum1<<" and inum2 =  "<<inum2;
    cout<<"\n fnum1 =  "<<fnum1<<" and fnum2 =  "<<fnum2;
    cout<<"\n c1 =  "<<c1<<" and c2 =  "<<c2;
}
```

OUTPUT

```
inum1 = 4 and inum2 = 5
fnum1 = 4.8 and fnum2 = -5.3
c1 = A and c2 = a
After Swapping
inum1 = 5 and inum2 = 4
fnum1 = -5.3 and fnum2 = 4.8
c1 = a and c2 = A
```

Program 14.3 Write a program to sum the elements of an array.

```
using namespace std;
#include<iostream>
#define MAX 10
template<class Type>
Type sum(Type Array[])
{   Type Total = 0;
    for(int i=0;i<MAX;i++)
       Total += Array[i];
    return Total;
}
template<class Type>
void read(Type Array[])
{   for(int i=0;i<MAX;i++)
       cin>>Array[i];
}
main()
```

```
{   int Array[MAX];
    cout<<"\n Enter the array elements :  ";
    read(Array);
    cout<<"\n Sum of elements =  "<<sum(Array);
}
```

OUTPUT

```
Enter the array elements : 1 2 3 4 5 6 7 8 9 10
Sum of elements = 55
```

Program 14.4 Write a program using template function to return the element stored at a particular index.

```
using namespace std;
#include<iostream>
#define MAX 10
template<class Type>
Type value(Type Array[], int pos)
{   Type val;
    val = Array[pos-1];
    return val;
}
template<class Type>
void read(Type Array[])
{   for(int i=0;i<MAX;i++)
        cin>>Array[i];
}
main()
{   float Array[MAX];
    int position;
    cout<<"\n Enter the array elements :  ";
    read(Array);
    cout<<"\n Enter the position :  ";
    cin>>position;
    cout<<"\n Value stored at Array[ "<<position<<"] = "<<value(Array, position);
}
```

OUTPUT

```
Enter the array elements : 1 2 3 4 5 6 7
Enter the position : 4
Value stored at Array[4] = 5
```

Program 14.5 Write a program to search an element in the array using linear search.

```
using namespace std;
#include<iostream>
#define MAX 10
template<class Type>
int search(Type Array[], Type val)
{
   for(int i=0;i<MAX;i++)
   {   if(Array[i]== val)
          return i;
   }
   return -1;
```

```
}
template<class Type>
void read(Type Array[])
{   for(int i=0;i<MAX;i++)
      cin>>Array[i];
}
main()
{   char Array[MAX];
   char  val;
   cout<<"\n Enter the array elements :  ";
   read(Array);
   cout<<"\n Enter the value to be searched :  ";
   cin>>val;
   int pos = search(Array, val);
   if(pos==-1)
      cout<<"\n "<<val<<" is not present in the array ";
   else
      cout<<"\n "<<val<<" is stored at position  "<<pos<<" in the Array";
}
```

OUTPUT

```
Enter the array elements : G H J K E P N O D B
Enter the value to be searched : K
K is stored at position 3 in the Array
```

Program 14.6 Write a program to sort an array.

```
using namespace std;
#include<iostream>
#define MAX 10
template<class Type>
void swap_it(Type &a, Type &b)
{   Type temp = a;
    a = b;
    b = temp;
}
template<class Type>
void read(Type Array[])
{   for(int i=0;i<MAX;i++)
      cin>>Array[i];
}
template<class Type>
void print(Type Array[])
{   for(int i=0;i<MAX;i++)
      cout<<"\t "<<Array[i];
}
template<class Type>
void sort(Type Array[])
{   for(int i=0;i<MAX;i++)
    {   for(int j= 0;j<MAX-i;j++)
        {   if(Array[j] > Array[j+1])
              swap_it(Array[j], Array[j+1]);
        }
```

```
    }
}
main()
{   char Array[MAX];
    cout<<"\n Enter the array elements :  ";
    read(Array);
    cout<<"\n The sorted array is :  ";
    sort(Array);
    print(Array);
    float Array1[MAX];
    cout<<"\n Enter the array elements :  ";
    read(Array1);
    cout<<"\n The sorted array is :  ";
    sort(Array1);
    print(Array1);
}
```

OUTPUT

```
Enter the array elements : Q W E R T Y U I O P
The sorted array is : E I O P Q R T U W Y
Enter the array elements : 6.4 7.9 9.7 4.6 2.3 3.2 4.8 8.4 4.5 9.1
The sorted array is : 2.3 3.2 4.5 4.6 4.8 6.4 7.9 8.4 9.1 9.7
```

Program 14.7 Write a program that uses more than one generic argument.

```
using namespace std;
#include<iostream>
template<class Type1, class Type2, class Type3>
void display(Type1 Rollno, Type2 Name, Type3 Avg)
{   cout<<"\n ROLL NO :  "<<Rollno;
    cout<<"\n NAME :  "<<Name;
    cout<<"\n AVERAGE :  "<<Avg;
}
main()
{   int rno;
    char name[10];
    float avg;
    cout<<"\n Enter the roll number :  ";
    cin>>rno;
    cout<<"\n Enter the name :  ";
    cin.ignore();
    cin.getline(name,10);
    cout<<"\n Enter the average :  ";
    cin>>avg;
    display(rno, name, avg);
}
```

OUTPUT

```
Enter the roll number : 01
Enter the name : Keshav
Enter the average : 99.9
ROLL NO : 01
NAME : Keshav
AVERAGE : 99.9
```

Program 14.8 Write an overloaded template function area that calculates area of different shapes.

```
using namespace std;
#include<iostream>
template <class Type>
float area(Type l, Type b)
{   return l*b;
}
template <class Type>
float area(Type side)
{   return side * side;
}
template <class Type>
float area(Type l, Type b, Type h)
{   return l*b*h;
}
template <class Type1, class Type2, class Type3>
void area(Type1 PI, Type2 r, Type3 h, Type3 &area)
{   area =  PI*r*r*h;
}
main()
{   float area_rect;

    float length = 3.4, breadth = 4.5;
    area_rect = area(length, breadth);
    cout<<"\n Area of the Rectangle with Length  "<<length<<" and Breadth  "<<breadth<<"
=  "<<area_rect;

    int l = 2, b= 3, h = 5;
    int area_box = area(l,b,h);
    cout<<"\n Area of the Box with Length  "<<l<<" and Breadth "<<b<<" and height
"<<h<<" =  "<<area_box;

    int s = 10;
    int area_square = area(s);
    cout<<"\n Area of the square with Side  "<<s<<" =  "<<area_square;

    int radius = 7;
    float PI = 3.14;
    double height = 3.5;
    double a;
    cout<<"\n Area of a Circle with Radius  "<<radius<<" and Height"<<height<<" =  ";
    area(PI,radius, height, a);
    cout<<a;
}
```

OUTPUT

```
Area of the Rectangle with Length 3.4 and Breadth 4.5 = 15.3
Area of the Box with Length 2 and Breadth 3 and height 5 = 30
Area of the square with Side 10 = 100
Area of a Circle with Radius 7 and Height 3.5 = 76.93
```

Program 14.9 Write a program that uses recursive template function for binary search.

```
using namespace std;
#include<iostream>
#include<string.h>
template <class Type>
int Bsearch(Type *Array, Type val, int beg, int end)
{   if(beg>end)
      return -1;
    int mid = (beg + end)/2;

    if(Array[mid]<val)
       return Bsearch(Array, val, mid+1, end);
    else if(Array[mid]>val)
       return Bsearch(Array, val, beg, mid-1);
    return mid;
}
main()
{   char Arr[] =  "ABCDEFG ";
    char ch;
    cout<<"\n Enter the value to be searched :  ";
    cin>>ch;
    int pos;
    int len = strlen(Arr);
    pos = Bsearch(Arr, ch, 0, len);
    if(pos!=-1)
       cout<<"\n "<<ch<<" found at position  "<<pos;
    else
       cout<<"\n "<<ch<<" not found in the array ";
}
```

OUTPUT

```
Enter the value to be searched : D
D found at position 3
```

Program 14.10 Write an overloaded function `display()` to print the details of a student on screen.

```
using namespace std;
#include<iostream>
struct Student
{   int rno;
    char name[10];
    float marks;
};
template <class Type1, class Type2, class Type3>
void display(Type1 rno, Type2 name, Type3 marks)
{   cout<<"\n Roll Number :  "<<rno;
    cout<<"\n Name :  "<<name;
    cout<<"\n MARKS :  "<<marks;
}
template <class Type1>
void display(Type1 &stud)
{   cout<<"\n Roll Number :  "<<stud.rno;
    cout<<"\n Name :  "<<stud.name;
    cout<<"\n MARKS :  "<<stud.marks;
```

```
}
int main()
{   int rn = 1;
    char name[] =  "Arjun ";
    float marks = 98.7;

    display(rn, name, marks);

    Student S = {2, "Karan ", 97.8};
    display(S);
}
```

OUTPUT

```
Roll Number : 1
Name : Arjun
MARKS : 98.7
Roll Number : 2
Name : Karan
MARKS : 97.8
```

14.3 CLASS TEMPLATE

Like functions, we can also declare classes to operate on different data types. Such classes are called class templates. Class templates specify how individual classes can be constructed so that every individual class supports similar operations on different data types. Therefore, templates enable programmers to create abstract classes that define the behaviour of the class without actually knowing what data type will be handled by the class operations.

Defining a class template is similar to defining an ordinary class except the two differences:

- The template class is prefixed with `template<class Type>` that tells the compiler that a template is being declared.
- The use of `Type` in declaring members of the class.

The syntax for declaring a class template is as follows:

```
template<class Type1, class Type2, ....>
class class_name
{   ...........
    // Body of the class
    ................
};
```

Note C++ allows programmers to use more than one generic data type in a class template.

For example, a template class `Array` that can handle arrays of any data type can be written as,

Programming Tip: Function templates cannot be partially specialized.

```
template<class Type>
class Array
{   private:
      Type *arr;
      int size;
    public:
      Array(int n)
```

```
    {   arr = new Type [n];
        size = n;
    }
    void read();
    void print();
};
```

A class created from a template is called a template class. The syntax for creating an object of the template class is as follows:

```
class_name <Type> object_name(arguments…);
```

Therefore, to declare objects of the template class `Array`, we may write

```
Array <int> A(5);
Array <char> B(7);
```

The process of creating an object of a class or in other words, the process of creating a specific class from a template is called instantiation. An instantiated object of a template class is called a specialization. If a class template is specialized by some but not all parameters it is called partial template specialization and if all the parameters are specialized, it is a full specialization.

Note Class template provides a specification for generating classes based on template parameters.

The compiler looks for any errors only when the class is instantiated. Therefore, as a good programming habit, you must first write and debug an ordinary class and then convert it into a template class. This means that it is always recommended to go from a concrete class to an abstract class.

Key Points to Know About Class Templates

- C++ allows programmers to specify default types for the template class data types. The syntax for specifying default data types can be given as follows:

```
template<class Type1, class Type2 = int>
class class_name
{   ....................
// Body of the class
....................
};
```

Programming Tip: Every member function in a class template is a function template.

- To define a member function of a template class outside the class, it must be treated as a function template and the following syntax must be used.

```
template<class Type>
return_type class_name<Type> :: function_name(args…)
{   ....................
    // Function Body
    ....................
};
```

- There is a difference between a class template and a template class. While a class template specifies how individual objects can be constructed, the template class, on the other hand, is a generic class which does not know anything about the type of data on which its function will operate.

Program 14.11 Write a program that has a template class array to read and print n numbers.

```
using namespace std;
#include<iostream>
template <class Type>
class Array
{   private:
      Type *arr;
      int size;
    public:
      Array(int n)
      {   arr = new Type [n];
          size = n;
      }
      void read()
      {   for(int i=0;i<size;i++)
            cin>>arr[i];
      }
      void print();
};
template<class Type>
void Array<Type> :: print()
{    for(int i=0;i<size;i++)
      cout<<"\t "<<arr[i];
}
main()
{   Array <int> A(5);
    cout<<"\n Enter the elements for integer array :  ";
    A.read();
    cout<<"\n The array is :  ";
    A.print();
    Array <char> B(7);
    cout<<"\n Enter the elements for character array :  ";
    B.read();
    cout<<"\n The array is :  ";
    B.print();
}
```

OUTPUT

```
Enter the elements for integer array : 1 2 3 4 5
The array is : 1 2 3 4 5
Enter the elements for character array : A B C D E
The array is : A B C D E
```

Program 14.12 Write a program that adds and subtracts two arrays defined as template class.

```
using namespace std;
#include<iostream>
template <class Type>
class Array
{   private:
      Type *arr;
      int size;
    public:
```

```
        Array(int n)
        {   arr = new Type [n];
            size = n;
        }
        void read()
        {   for(int i=0;i<size;i++)
              cin>>arr[i];
        }
        void print()
        {   for(int i=0;i<size;i++)
              cout<<"\t "<<arr[i];
        }
        Array *add(Array Arr2)
        {   for(int i=0;i<size;i++)
              arr[i] += Arr2.arr[i];
           return this;
        }
        Array *sub(Array Arr2)
        {   for(int i=0;i<size;i++)
              arr[i] -= Arr2.arr[i];
           return this;
        }
   };
int main()
{   Array <int> A(5);
    cout<<"\n Enter the elements for integer array :  ";
    A.read();

    Array <int> B(5);
    cout<<"\n Enter the elements for integer array :  ";
    B.read();

    A.add(B);
    cout<<"\n After Addition the array is :  ";
    A.print();

    A.sub(B);
    cout<<"\n After Subtraction array is :  ";
    A.print();
}
```

OUTPUT

```
Enter the elements for integer array : 1 2 3 4 5
Enter the elements for integer array : 2 3 4 5 6
After Addition the array is : 3 5 7 9 11
After Subtraction array is : 1 2 3 4 5
```

Program 14.13 Write a template class Employee with multiple template members to read and print the details of an employee.

```
using namespace std;
#include<iostream>
template <class Type1, class Type2, class Type3, class Type4>
class Employee
```

```
{   private:
      Type1 emp_id;
      Type2 Desig;
      Type3 Salary;
      Type4 Status;
    public:
      void set_data(Type1 eid, Type2 Des, Type3 Sal, Type4 st)
      {   emp_id = eid;
          Desig = Des;
          Salary = Sal;
          Status = st;
      }
      void show_data()
      {   cout<<"\n Employee ID :  "<<emp_id;
          cout<<"\n Designation :  "<<Desig;
          cout<<"\n Salary :  "<<Salary;
          cout<<"\n Status :  "<<Status;
      }
};
int main()
{   int eid = 1;
    char Des[] =  "Manager";
    float Sal = 90000;
    char st = 'P';

    Fmployee <int, char*, float, char> E;
    E.set_data(eid, Des, Sal, st);
    E.show_data();
}
```

OUTPUT

```
Employee ID : 01
Designation : Manager
Salary : 90000
Status : P
```

Program 14.14 Write a program that has a template `Student` to read and print the details of student. Use multiple arguments and at least one default argument.

```
using namespace std;
#include<iostream>
template<class Type1, class Type2, class Type3 = char>
class Student
{   private:
      Type1 ID;
      Type2 name;
      Type3 grade;
    public:
      void get_data()
      {   cout<<"\n Enter the Student_ID :  ";
          cin>>ID;
          cout<<"\n Enter the Name :  ";
          cin>>name;
```

```
        cout<<"\n Enter the Grade :  ";
        cin>>grade;
    }
    void show_data()
    {   cout<<"\n STUDENT ID :  "<<ID;
        cout<<"\n NAME :  "<<name;
        cout<<"\n GRADE :  "<<grade;
    }
};
int main()
{   Student <int,char[10]> S1;
    S1.get_data();
    S1.show_data();

    Student <char, char[10], char[20]> S2;
    S2.get_data();
    S2.show_data();
}
```

OUTPUT

```
Enter the Student_ID : 1
Enter the Name : Niharika
Enter the Grade : O
STUDENT ID : 1
NAME : Niharika
GRADE : O
Enter the Student_ID : 2
Enter the Name : Raju
Enter the Grade : Distinction
STUDENT ID : 2
NAME : Raju
GRADE : Distinction
```

Program 14.15 Write a program that has a template class which has been derived from a non-template class.

```
using namespace std;
#include<iostream>
class Student
{   private:
      int roll_no;
      char name[20];
    public:
      void get_data()
      {   cout<<"\n Enter the roll number :  ";
          cin>>roll_no;
          cout<<"\n Enter the name :  ";
          cin.ignore();
          cin.getline(name, 20);
      }
      void show_data()
      {   cout<<"\n ROLL NUMBER :  "<<roll_no;
          cout<<"\n NAME :  "<<name;
```

```
        }
};
template <class Type>
class Marks : public Student
{   private:
        Type marks[2];
    public:
        void get_details()
        {   get_data();
            cout<<"\n Enter the marks in two subjects :  ";
            cin>>marks[0]>>marks[1];
        }
        void show_details()
        {   show_data();
            cout<<"\n TOTAL :  "<<marks[0] + marks[1];
        }
};
main()
{   Marks <float> M;
    M.get_details();
    M.show_details();
}
```

OUTPUT

```
Enter the roll number : 1
Enter the name : Rashi
Enter the marks in two subjects : 99 100
ROLL NUMBER : 1
NAME : Rashi
TOTAL : 199
```

Program 14.16 Write a class `template` that prints the number of objects created for a class. Hint: Use static data member.

```
using namespace std;
#include<iostream>
template<class Type>
class Counter
{   public:
        static Type count;
        Counter()
        {   count++;
        }
        void print()
        {   cout<<"\n Number of objects :  "<<count;
        }
};
template <class Type>
Type Counter<Type>::count = 0;
main()
{   Counter <int> C1;
```

```
    C1.print();
    Counter <int> C2;
    C2.print();
    Counter <int> C3;
    C3.print();
}
```

OUTPUT

```
Number of objects : 1
Number of objects : 2
Number of objects : 3
```

14.4 CLASS TEMPLATES AND FRIEND FUNCTION

A function can be declared as friend inside a class template. This would allow a non-member function to access the members of the template class. The syntax for defining a friend function inside a class template can be given as follows.

```
template<class Type>
class Myclass
{   private:
        ..................
    public:
        ..................
        friend return_type func(Myclass <Type> Obj)
        {   //code
        }
};
```

Let us consider a program that illustrates the use of `friend` function in class template.

Example 14.4 Merging two array objects

```
using namespace std;
#include<iostream>
template<class Type>
class Array
{ private:
Type *arr;
int size;
public:
Array(int n)
{ arr = new Type [n];
size = n;
}
void read()
{ for(int i=0;i<size;i++)
cin>>arr[i];
}
void print()
{   for(int i=0;i<size;i++)
```

```
cout<<"\t "<<arr[i];
}
friend void merge(Array <Type>&A1 , Array <Type>&A2, Array<Type>&A3)
{
int i=0, j;
for(int j=0;j<A1.size;j++)
A3.arr[i++] = A1.arr[j];
for(j=0;j<A2.size;j++)
A3.arr[i++] = A2.arr[j];
cout<<"\n Elements of the merged array are : ";
for(i=0;i<A3.size;i++)
cout<<"\t"<<A3.arr[i];
}
};
template <class Type>
void merge(Array <Type>&A1, Array <Type>&A2, Array <Type>&A3)
{
int i=0, j;
for(j=0;j<A1.size;j++)
A3.arr[i++] = A1.arr[j];
for(j=0;j<A2.size;j++)
A3.arr[i++] = A2.arr[j];
cout<<"\n Elements of the merged array are : ";
for(i=0;i<A3.size;i++)
cout<<"\t "<<A3.arr[i];
}
main()
{ int num1, num2, num3;
cout<<"\n Enter the number of elements in the first array : ";
cin>>num1;
Array <int> A(num1);
cout<<"\n Enter the elements for integer array : ";
A.read();
cout<<"\n Enter the number of elements in the second array : ";
cin>>num2;
Array <int> B(num2);
cout<<"\n Enter the elements for integer array : ";
B.read();
num3=num1+num2;
Array <int> C(num3);
merge(A,B, C);
}
```

OUTPUT

```
Enter the number of elements in the first array : 5
Enter the elements for integer array : 1 2 3 4 5
Enter the number of elements in the second array : 4
Enter the elements for integer array : 6 7 8 9
Elements of the merged array are : 1 2 3 4 5 6 7 8 9
```

Explanation: In the program, we have a class template array. In `main()`, we make two objects of class array and then call the friend function `merge()` to combine the elements of both the array objects into a single array object.

Besides `friend` functions in template class, C++ also supports a template class to be a friend of a normal class, an ordinary class to be a friend of a template class and a template class being a friend of another template class. The syntax for having a friend class with a template class can be given as follows:

```
template <class Type> class B
class A {
    ..........
    friend class B;
    ..........
};
```

Let us take a sample program to visualize the use of `friend` class with a template class.

Example 14.5 Swapping member of different objects using `friend` template class

```
using namespace std;
#include<iostream>
template <class Type> class Number2;
class Number1
{   public:
      int x;

      void set_x()
      {   x = 10;
      }
      void show_x()
      {   cout<<"\n X =  "<<x;
      }
      template<class Type> friend class Number2;
};
template <class Type>
class Number2
{   private:
      Type y;
    public:
      void set_y()
      {   cout<<"\n Enter a value :  ";
          cin>>y;
      }
      void show_y()
      {   cout<<"\n Y =  "<<y;
      }
      void swap(Number1 &N)
      {   Type temp = y;
          y = N.x;
          N.x = temp;
      }
```

```
};
int main()
{   Number1 N1;
    N1.set_x();
    Number2 <int> N2;
    N2.set_y();
    N1.show_x();
    N2.show_y();
    N2.swap(N1);
    N1.show_x();
    N2.show_y();
}
```

OUTPUT

```
Enter a value : 20
x = 10
y = 20
x = 20
y = 10
```

Explanation: In the program, A is an ordinary class. Class B is a template class that is a friend of class A. the function `swap()` in class B accepts a parameter of type A and uses it to swap A's data with B's data.

14.5 TEMPLATES AND STATIC VARIABLES IN C++

In Chapter 9 on Classes and Objects, we have read about static variables and seen that a static variable is allocated memory only once. All objects of the class share the static variable. Similarly, in function templates, each instantiation of the function has its own local copy of static variables. Let us realize this point with the help of a program.

Example 14.6 Static variable in a function template

```
using namespace std;
#include<iostream>
template <class Type>
void fun(Type data)
{
    static int i = 0;
    i++;
    cout<<"\n Value =  "<<data;
    cout<<"\n The function has been called  "<<i<<" times ";
}
int main()
{
  fun<int>(10);
  fun<float>(20);
  fun<double>(1.1);
  fun<char>('A');
  fun<char*>("Hello");
```

```
}
```

OUTPUT

```
Value = 10
The function has been called 1 times
Value = 20
The function has been called 1 times
Value = 1.1
The function has been called 1 times
Value = A
The function has been called 1 times
Value = Hello
The function has been called 1 times
```

Explanation: In the program, we have a static variable that is initialized to 0. The template function is called five times from `main()` but with parameters of different data types each time. Therefore, with every function instantiation, the value of static variable is incremented and all instantiations share the same copy of static variable.

Let us now consider another program that has a static variable inside a class template.

Example 14.7 Static variable inside a class template

```
using namespace std;
#include<iostream>
template <class Type>
class Sample
{   private:
        Type val;
    public:
        static int count;
        Sample()
        {   count++;
        }
        static void show()
        {   cout<<count;
        }
};
template<class Type>
int Sample<Type>::count = 0;
int main()
{
  Sample <int> I1;
  Sample <int> I2;
  Sample <int> I3;

  Sample <double> D1;
  Sample <double> D2;

  Sample <char> C;
```

```
  cout<<"\n Number of Integer objects =  ";
  Sample<int>::show();

  cout<<"\n Number of Double objects =  ";
  Sample<double>::show();

  cout<<"\n Number of Character objects =  ";
  Sample<char>::show();
}
```

OUTPUT

```
Number of Integer objects = 3
Number of Double objects = 2
Number of Character objects = 1
```

Explanation: In the program, we have a static variable and a static member function with a template class. Recall that you can use only static variables in a static function. Moreover, only a single copy of static variable is created for all the objects of the same class. Therefore, all the objects of the same type share the static variable and hence the result.

14.6 CLASS TEMPLATES AND INHERITANCE

The concept of class templates can be used in conjunction with inheritance to develop hierarchical structures that involves the following:

- Deriving a class template from a base class (template class).
- Deriving a class template from a base class which is a template class and adding more template members to it.
- Deriving a class template from a base class which is a template class but disallowing the derived class and its derivatives to have template features.
- Deriving a non-template base class and adding some template members to it.

The syntax for declaring a derived class from base class which is a template class can be given as follows:

Programming Tip: Templates must be defined in the global section or in a header file because the compiler must have full information about the template before processing a call for it.

```
template<class Type1, class Type 2....>
class Base
{   ------
    // Body of the class
    ------
};

template<class Type1, class Type2 ....>
class Derived : public Base <Type1, Type2, ....>
{   ------
   // Body of the class
    ------
};
```

The class deriving the base class can either be a template class or a non-template class as shown in Fig. 14.3.

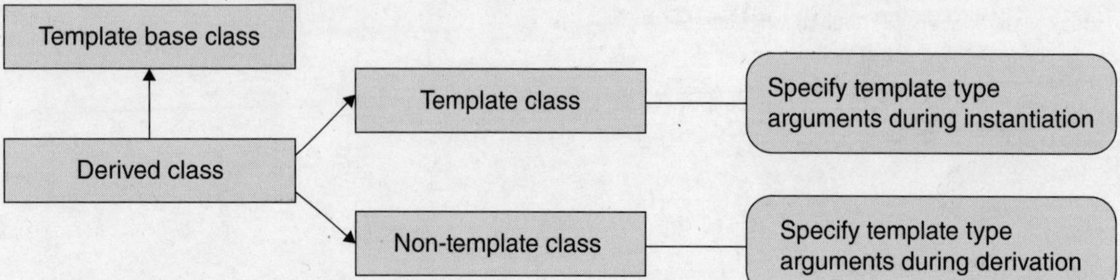

Figure 14.3 Class template and inheritance

In case, the derived class is also a template class, then template arguments type must be specified while making its objects.

If the derived object is an ordinary class, then the template arguments type must be specified during derivation. For example, by writing

```
class Derived : public Base <int, float, ....>
{   ------
    // Body of the class
    ------
};
```

Note A class derived from a template class need not be compulsorily a template class.

Program 14.17 Write a program that uses `friend` function to scale the elements of class array.

```
using namespace std;
#include<iostream>
template<class Type>
class Array;
template<class Type>
Array<Type> scale(Array<Type> &A);
template <class Type>
class Array
{
private:
Type *arr;
int size;
public:
Array(int n)
{ arr = new Type[n];
size = n;
}
void read()
{ for(int i=0;i<size;i++)
cin>>arr[i];
}
```

```
void print()
{ for(int i=0;i<size;i++)
cout<<"\t "<<arr[i];
}
friend Array scale<Type>(Array &A);
};
template <class Type>
Array <Type> scale(Array<Type> &A)
{
for(int i=0;i<A.size;i++)
A.arr[i] += 2;
cout<<"The scaled elements of character array are:";
return A;
}
int main()
{
int num;
cout<<"\n Enter the number of elements in the array : ";
cin>>num;
Array <char> A(num);
cout<<"\n Enter the elements for character array : ";
A.read();
A = scale(A);
A.print();
}
```

OUTPUT

```
Enter the number of elements in the array : 7
Enter the elements for character array : A B C D E F G
The elements of character array are : C D E F G H I
```

Program 14.18 Write a class array that has a friend class EvenOdd. The friend class uses the array class to divide the array elements into two arrays, one that contains even numbers and the other stores the odd elements.

```
using namespace std;
#include<iostream>
template <class Type> class EvenOdd;

template <class Type>
class Array
{   public:
      int *arr;
      int size;
      Array(int num)
      {   size = num;
          arr = new int[size];
      }
      void read()
      {   for(int i=0;i<size;i++)
             cin>>arr[i];
      }
      void print()
```

```
    {   for(int i=0;i<size;i++)
            cout<<"\t "<<arr[i];
    }
    friend class EvenOdd<Type>;
};
template <class Type>
class EvenOdd
{   private:
      Type even_arr[10];
      int size_even;
      Type odd_arr[10];
      int size_odd;
    public:
      void create_arrs(Array <Type> A)
      {   int index1 = 0, index2=0;
          size_even = size_odd = 0;
          for(int i=0;i<A.size;i++)
          {   if(A.arr[i]%2 == 0)
              {   even_arr[index1] = A.arr[i];
                 index1++;
              }
              else
              {   odd_arr[index2] = A.arr[i];
                  index2++;
              }
          }
          size_even = index1;
          size_odd = index2;
       }
       void printevenodd()
       {   cout<<"\n Even elements are :  ";
           for(int i=0;i<size_even;i++)
              cout<<"\t "<<even_arr[i];
           cout<<"\n Odd elements are :  ";
           for(int i=0;i<size_odd;i++)
              cout<<"\t "<<odd_arr[i];
      }
};
int main()
{   Array <int> A(12);
    cout<<"\n Enter the elements of the array :  ";
    A.read();
    EvenOdd <int> EO;
    EO.create_arrs(A);
    EO.printevenodd();
}
```

OUTPUT

```
Enter the elements of the array : 23 56 77 90 85 33 12 11 22 45 63 84
Even elements are : 56 90 12 22 84
Odd elements are : 23 77 85 33 11  45 63
```

Program 14.19 Write a program that inherits template class array to add a function `add()` that appends an element to the existing array.

```
using namespace std;
#include<iostream>
#include<stdlib.h>
template <class Type>
class Array
{   protected:
      Type *arr;
      int size;
    public:
      void read(int n)
      {   size = n;
          arr = new Type [size];
          for(int i=0;i<size;i++)
            cin>>arr[i];
      }
      void print()
      {   for(int i=0;i<size;i++)
          cout<<"\t "<<arr[i];
      }
};

template <class Type>
class Edit_Arr : public Array <Type>
{   public:
    void add(Type Element)
{
                int i;
                this->size++;
                Type *arr1 = new Type[this->size];
                for(i=0;i<this->size-1;i++)
                arr1[i] = this->arr[i];
                arr1[i] = Element;
                delete this->arr;
                this->arr = arr1;
}
};

main()
{
   Edit_Arr <int> A;
   int n;
   cout<<"\n Enter the Size of the Array :  ";
   cin>>n;
   cout<<"\n Enter the elements for integer array :  ";
   A.read(n);
   cout<<"\n The array is :  ";
   A.print();
   int val;
   cout<<"\n Enter the value to be added :  ";
```

```
    cin>>val;
    A.add(val);
    cout<<"\n The modified array is :  ";
    A.print();

    Edit_Arr <char> B;
    cout<<"\n Enter the Size of the Character Array :  ";
    cin>>n;
    cout<<"\n Enter the ielements for the Character array :  ";
    B.read(n);
    cout<<"\n The array is :  ";
    B.print();
    char ch;
    cout<<"\n Enter the character to be added :  ";
    cin>>ch;
    B.add(ch);
    cout<<"\n The modified array is :  ";
    B.print();
}
```

OUTPUT

```
Enter the Size of the Array : 5
Enter the elements for integer array : 1 2 3 4 5
The array is : 1 2 3 4 5
Enter the value to be added : 10
The modified array is : 1 2 3 4 5 10
Enter the Size of the Character Array : 7
Enter the elements for the Character array : A B C D E F G
The array is : A B C D E F G
Enter the character to be added : z
The modified array is : A B C D E F G Z
```

Program 14.20 Write a program that extends template class `Student`. Use multi-level inheritance in such a way that template class `Marks` inherits `Student` and adds another template member. Then, class `Result` is derived from template class `Marks` but does not add any template member to it.

```
using namespace std;
#include<iostream>
template <class Type1, class Type2>
class Student
{   protected:
      Type1 ID;
      Type2 name;
    public:
      void get_data()
      {   cout<<"\n Enter the Student ID :  ";
          cin>>ID;
          cout<<"\n Enter the Name :  ";
          cin>>name;
      }
```

```
    void show_data()
    {   cout<<"\n STUDENT ID :  "<<ID;
        cout<<"\n NAME :  "<<name;
    }
};
template<class Type1, class Type2, class Type3>
class Marks : public Student <Type1, Type2>
{   protected:
    Type3 marks[3];
   public:
    void get_marks()
    {   cout<<"\n Enter the marks in three subjects :  ";
        cin>>marks[0]>>marks[1]>>marks[2];
    }
};
template <class Type1, class Type2, class Type3>
class Result : public Marks <Type1, Type2, Type3>
{   public:
     void get_details()
     { this->get_data();
     this->get_marks();
     }
     void show_details()
     { this->show_data();
     cout<<"\n TOTAL : "<<this->marks[0]+this->marks[1]+this->marks[2];
     }
};
int main()
{   Result <int, char[10], float> R;
  R.get_details();
  R.show_details();
}
```

OUTPUT

```
Enter the Student ID : 1
Enter the Name : Goransh
Enter the marks in three subjects : 98 99 100
STUDENT ID : 1
NAME : Goransh
TOTAL : 297
```

Program 14.21 Write a program that has a template class Employee and a template class Salary. Derive a class with details from both these classes (multiple inheritance) to display the relevant details of the employee.

```
using namespace std;
#include<iostream>
template <class Type1, class Type2>
class Employee
{   protected:
```

```
      Type1 ID;
      Type2 name;
    public:
      void get_data()
      {   cout<<"\n Enter the Employee ID :  ";
          cin>>ID;
          cout<<"\n Enter the Name :  ";
          cin>>name;
      }
      void show_data()
      {   cout<<"\n EMPLOYEE ID :  "<<ID;
          cout<<"\n NAME :  "<<name;
      }
};
template<class Type3>
class Salary
{   protected:
      Type3 sal[4];
    public:
      void get_sal_details()
      {   cout<<"\n Enter the Basic, DA, TA and HRA :  ";
          cin>>sal[0]>>sal[1]>>sal[2]>>sal[3];
      }
};
template <class Type1, class Type2, class Type3>
class Details : public Employee <Type1, Type2>, public Salary <Type3>
{   public:
       void get_details()
       { this->get_data();
       this->get_sal_details();
       }
       void show_details()
       { this->show_data();
       cout<<"\n TOTAL : "<<this->sal[0]+this->sal[1]+this->sal[2]+this->sal[3];
       }
};
main()
{   Details <int, char[10], float> D;
    D.get_details();
    D.show_details();
}
```

OUTPUT

```
Enter the Employee ID : 1
Enter the Name : Meenakshi
Enter the Basic, DA, TA and HRA : 6000 10000 9000 12000
EMPLOYEE ID : 1
NAME : Meenakshi
TOTAL : 37000
```

14.7 CLASS TEMPLATE WITH OPERATOR OVERLOADING

Class templates can also be used with operator overloading functions. This means that we can make the class that defines operator overloaded functions a template class. The syntax for defining the template class is the same as what we have been using until now. Class templates with inheritance and operator overloading features truly allow programmers to extend the language, thereby retaining the readability and maintainability of the code.

Program 14.22 Write a program that has a template class `Complex` which overloads the + operator.

```
using namespace std;
#include<iostream>
template <class Type>
class Complex
{   private:
      Type real, imag;
    public:
      void get_data();
      void show_data();
      Complex operator+(Complex &);
};
template <class Type>
void Complex <Type> :: get_data()
{   cout<<"\n Enter the real and imaginary parts :  ";
    cin>>real>>imag;
}
template <class Type>
void Complex <Type> :: show_data()
{   cout<<real <<  " +  "<<imag<<"i ";
}
template <class Type>
Complex <Type> Complex <Type> :: operator + (Complex <Type>&C)
{   real += C.real;
    imag += C.imag;
    return *this;
}
main()
{   Complex <int> C1, C2, C3;
    cout<<"\n ENTER TWO INTEGER COMPLEX NUMBERS  ";
    C1.get_data();
    C2.get_data();
    cout<<"\n C1 =  ";
    C1.show_data();
    cout<<"\n C2 =  ";
    C2.show_data();
    cout<<"\n C3 = C1 + C2 =  ";
    C3 = C1 + C2;
    C3.show_data();
    Complex <float> C4, C5, C6;
    cout<<"\n ENTER TWO FLOATING POINT COMPLEX NUMBERS  ";
```

```
    C4.get_data();
    C5.get_data();
    cout<<"\n C1 =  ";
    C4.show_data();
    cout<<"\n C2 =  ";
    C5.show_data();
    cout<<"\n C3 = C1 + C2 =  ";
    C6 = C4 + C5;
    C6.show_data();
}
```

OUTPUT

```
ENTER TWO INTEGER COMPLEX NUMBERS
Enter the real and imaginary parts : 2 3
Enter the real and imaginary parts : 4 5
C1 = 2 + 3i
C2 = 4 + 5i
C3 = C1 + C2 = 6 + 8i
ENTER TWO FLOATING POINT COMPLEX NUMBERS
Enter the real and imaginary parts : 2.3 3.4
Enter the real and imaginary parts : 4.5 5.2
C1 = 2.3 + 3.4i
C2 = 4.5 + 5.2i
C3 = C1 + C2 = 6.8 + 8.6i
```

Program 14.23 Write a program that overloads the + operator in a template class `Matrix`.

```
using namespace std;
#include<iostream>
template <class Type1, class Type2 = int>
class Matrix
{   private:
       Type1 mat[2][2];
       Type2 rows, cols;
    public: Matrix(Type2 r, Type2 c)
       {   rows = r;
           cols = c;
       }
       void read_matrix();
       void show_matrix();
       Matrix & operator+(Matrix &);
};
template <class Type1, class Type2>
void Matrix<Type1, Type2> :: read_matrix()
{   for(int i=0;i<rows;i++)
    {   for(int j=0;j<cols;j++)
            cin>>mat[i][j];
    }
}
template <class Type1, class Type2>
void Matrix<Type1, Type2> :: show_matrix()
{   for(int i=0;i<rows;i++)
```

```
    {       cout<<"\n ";
        for(int j=0;j<cols;j++)
            cout<<"    "<<mat[i][j];
    }
}
template <class Type1, class Type2>
Matrix<Type1, Type2>& Matrix<Type1, Type2> :: operator+(Matrix<Type1, Type2>&M)
{       for(int i=0;i<rows;i++)
    {   for(int j=0;j<cols;j++)
          mat[i][j] += M.mat[i][j];
    }
   return *this;
}
int main()
{   int r,c;
    cout<<"\n Enter the number of rows and columns :  ";
    cin>>r>>c;
    Matrix <int> M1(r,c), M2(r,c), M3(r,c);
    cout<<"\n Enter the first Matrix :  ";
    M1.read_matrix();
    cout<<"\n Enter the second Matrix :  ";
    M2.read_matrix();
    M3 = M1 + M2;
    cout<<"\n The Resultant Matrix is :  ";
    M3.show_matrix();
}
```

OUTPUT

```
Enter the number of rows and columns : 2 2
Enter the first Matrix : 1 2 3 4
Enter the second Matrix : 2 3 4 5
The Resultant Matrix is :
3 5
7 9
```

14.8 PROS AND CONS OF TEMPLATES

The advantages of templates are as follows:

- A template not only enhances code reusability but also makes the code short and easy to maintain.
- A single template can handle different types of parameters.

Programming Tip: It is an error to reference a template class without specifying the type.

- Testing and debugging efforts are reduced.
- For non-templated functions or classes, the compiler has to compile all n copies since they are all a part of the source-code. However, with a template, the compiler would compile only for required set of data-types. This means that compilation would be faster if number of different data types actually required during implementation is less than that given in the source code.

Note Templates supports on demand compilation.

The drawbacks are as follows.

- Some compilers provide little support for templates. This reduces the code portability.
- Many compilers do not have clear instructions on when and how to detect a template definition error.
- Even when the compiler detects an error, it takes more time and effort to debug the code and resolve the error.
- Since a separate code is generated for each template type, frequent use of templates can result in larger executables.
- Templates are usually defined in the headers, which exposes the code to the entire program, thereby defeating the concept of information hiding.

Points to Remember

- With templates, programmers can define a family of functions or classes that can operate on different types of data.
- The template function will use generic data types (or general data types) since the exact data types of arguments will be known only at the time of function call.
- Every template data type must be used in the function declaration and/or definition. Failing to do this results in an error and will be treated as an invalid template.
- Class templates specify how individual classes can be constructed so that every individual class supports similar operations on different data types.

Glossary

Class templates Classes that can operate on different data types

Function templates Functions that serve as a pattern for creating other similar functions

Generic programming A technique of programming in which a general code is written first. The code is instantiated only when need arises for specific types (provided as parameters)

Generics Entities such as class or function created using generic programming

Instantiation The process of creating a specific class from a template

Specialization An instantiated object of a templated class

Exercises

Fill in the Blanks

1. Templates fall under the category of ________.
2. Through templates, C++ supports the concept of ________.
3. Entities (like class or function) created using generic programming are called ________.
4. Templates enable programmers to focus on ________ rather than on ________.
5. Function template is also known as a ________.
6. We define the function using placeholder types which are called ________.
7. In case more than one match for a function is found then ________ error is generated.
8. ________ templates cannot be partially specialized.
9. A class created from a template is called a ________.
10. An instantiated object of a templated class is called a ________.
11. Templates support ________ compilation.

State True or False

1. Function templates serve as a pattern for creating other dissimilar functions.
2. The arguments of function template are specified using normal data types.

3. The exact data types are known at the time of function declaration and/or definition.
4. The template declaration and definition must be in the same file.
5. A template function is more efficient than macros.
6. Templates are not type-safe.
7. Macros are compiled inline.
8. At least some template data type must be used in the function declaration and/or definition.
9. The process of creating a specific class from a template is called specialization.
10. C++ allows partial specialization.
11. Programmers must move from an abstract class to a concrete class.
12. Programmers can specify default types for the template class data types.
13. If the derived object is an ordinary class then the template arguments type must be specified during derivation.
14. A class derived from a template class must be a template class.
15. Function template requires more memory space than normal function.
16. An error will be generated if any one of the generic data type specified in the template type list is unused for defining formal parameters.
17. Overloaded operator function can be defined as template function.

Multiple Choice Questions

1. Templates are used to create ______.
   (a) Containers (b) Iterators
   (c) Hash tables (d) All of these
2. The exact data types of template class or function be known only during ______?
   (a) Function declaration
   (b) Function definition
   (c) Function call
   (d) Function return
3. Which keyword informs the compiler that what follows next is a template?
   (a) Generic (b) Template
   (c) General (d) Basic
4. When defining a syntax for the template, TYPE is the name of ?
   (a) Generic parameter
   (b) Generic Function
   (c) Generic class (d) All of these
5. How many copies of the function will be generated if during function calls, two times a generic function is called using `int` as the data types?
   (a) 0 (b) 1
   (c) 2 (d) None of these
6. Template is a model that serves as a pattern for creating which kind of objects?
   (a) Similar (b) Partially similar
   (c) Dissimilar
   (d) Partially dissimilar
7. The compiler looks for any errors only when the class is ______?
   (a) Defined (b) Created
   (c) Declared (d) Instantiated
8. If both the base and the derived classesare template-classed, then template arguments type must be specified whilc ______?
   (a) Making objects of base class
   (b) Making objects of derived class
   (c) During derivation
   (d) All of these
9. Templates are processed by ______?
   (a) Loader (b) Linker
   (c) Compiler (d) Assembler
10. Templates can be used for which data typcs?
    (a) Any data type
    (b) Basic data type
    (c) Derived data type
    (d) User defined data type
11. A template function can accept how many generic parameters?
    (a) 0 (b) 1
    (c) N (d) None of these

Review Questions

1. What do you understand by the term 'template'?
2. Why do we need templates? How does it benefit programmers?
3. Give some uses of templates.
4. What are function templates? Explain with a small program code.
5. Explain the syntax for defining a generic function.
6. Draw a comparison between a template function and a macro.
7. Write a short note on some guidelines that must be followed while defining a function template.
8. Can a generic function be overloaded? Justify your answer with an example.

9. What does a compiler do when it has to call an overloaded function?
10. Does C++ allow recursive template functions? If yes, give a program code to demonstrate it.
11. With the help of a sample code illustrate how the concept of function templates can be combined with function overloading?
12. Can we use user-defined types for template types? If yes, how?
13. Explain the syntax for defining a class template.
14. What do you understand by the term specialization?
15. Does C++ allow programmers to use more than one generic data type in a class template? If no, why? If yes, how?
16. Can we use static members with a template class? If yes, write a program to illustrate.
17. In what ways can we combine the concept of class template and inheritance?
18. Explain the syntax for declaring a derived class from base class which is a template class.
19. With the help of a relevant program code, explain how we can combine the concept of operator overloading with class templates.
20. Give some advantages and disadvantages of using templates.
21. Differentiate between a class template and a template class.

Programming Exercises

1. Write a generic function to calculate `pow(x,y)`.
2. Write a menu-driven program that has template functions to perform addition, subtraction, multiplication, and division of n numbers
3. Write a generic function to perform linear search on an array.
4. Write a generic function to perform binary search on an array.
5. Write a generic function to sort an array using selection sort.
6. Write a recursive generic function to print the Fibonacci series.
7. Write function template to swap the position of the largest and the smallest element in the array.
8. Write a function template to find the second biggest element in an array.
9. Write a function template to encrypt the elements of the array.
10. Write a generic function to reverse the elements of an array.
11. Write a generic class that stores and prints all the information about a product.
12. Write overloaded template functions to calculate the perimeter of a circle, square, rectangle, and a triangle.
13. Create a template class array that reads and prints the elements for which memory is allocated dynamically. Extend the class to perform functions such as merging, searching, sorting, inserting, and deleting on the array.
14. Write a program that has a template class `Product` to display all necessary information about a particular product. Use inheritance to display details.
15. Write a template class `Customer` to print the details about a customer of an online retail shop.
16. Write classes `Product`, `Customer`, and `Bill` to display the information pertaining to the details of the customer bought who bought the product(s), the products purchased and the total bill amount. Use template class(s)and inheritance.
17. Write a menu-driven program that uses class template `Complex` to overload the +, –, *, /,> operators.
18. Write a menu-driven program that uses class template `Matrix` to overload the +, –, *, and!= operators.
19. Write generic classes `Dollar` and `Rupee` and use template functions to convert from one currency to another.
20. Write a function template that returns an absolute value of a number.
21. Write a template class `Set`. Define functions to find the union, intersection, and difference of two sets.
22. Write a generic function that has
    (a) More than one generic type
    (b) A single generic type being used more than once
    (c) Returns a generic type

Find the errors in the following codes

1.
```
template <class Type>
int square(int num)
{   return num*num;
}
```
2.
```
template <class Type>
Type main()
{   Type a=3;
    cout<<a;
}
```
3.
```
template <class Type>
int square(int num)
{   return num*num;
```

```
    }
    void main()
    {   void n = 2;
        square(n);
    }
```

4.
```
template <class Type>
int square(int num)
{   return num*num;
}

int square(Type1 num)
{   Type 1 res = num * num;
return res;
}
```

5.
```
template <class Type1, class Type2>
int square(Type1 num)
{   Type 2 res = num * num;
return res;
}
```

6.
```
template <class Type1, class Type2>
Type3 square(Type1 num)
{   Type 2 res = num * num;
return res;
}
```

7.
```
template <class Type1, class Type2>
int square(Type1 num)
{   Type2 res = num * num;
return res;
}
```

8.
```
template <class Type1, int size=10>
void add(Type1 arr)
{   for(int i=0;i<size;i++)
        arr[i] += 2;
}
```

9.
```
template <class Type1, int Type2>
int square(Type1 num)
{   Type2 res = num * num;
return res;
}
```

10.
```
template <class Type1 = int, class Type2>
Type2 avg(Type1 arr)
{   int sum=0;
    for(int i=0;i<size;i++)
        sum += arr[i];
    return (Type2)sum/size;
}
```

11.
```
template <class Type1, class Type1>
void add(Type1 arr)
{   for(int i=0;i<size;i++)
        arr[i] += 2;
}
```

12.
```
template <class Type>
Type max(Type a, Type b)
{   if(a>b)
        return a;
    else
        return b;
}
main()
{   int x;
    max(x,20);
}
```

13.
```
using namespace std;
#include<iostream>
template<class Type1, class Type2>
class Person
{   private:
        Type1 mt1;
        Type2 mt2;
    public:
        template<class Type1, class Type2>
        Person(Type1 t1, Type2 t2)
        {   mt1 = t1;
            t2 = t2;
            cout<<mt1<<mt2;
        }
};
int main()
{   Person <int, float> P1(1, 3.4);
}
```

Find the output of the following codes

1.
```
using namespace std;
#include<iostream>
template <class Type>
Type Max(Type Var1, Type Var2)
{
    return Var1> Var2 ? Var1:Var2;
}
 int main()
{     cout<<"\n Max(123, 456) =
 "<<Max(123,456);
      cout<<"\n Max('z','B') =
 "<<Max('z','B');
      cout<<"\n Max(12.34,3.45) =
 "<<Max(12.34,3.45);
}
```

2.
```
using namespace std;
#include<iostream>
template<class Type>
void print(Type data)
{   cout<<"\n "<<data;
}
int main()
```

```
{   int i=10;
    float f= 123.456;
    char c = 'A';
    char *s =  "Hello World ";
    print(i);
    print(f);
    print(s);
    print(c);
}
```

3.
```
using namespace std;
#include<iostream>
template <class Type>
class Sample
{   public:
        Sample();
        ~Sample();
        Type Data(Type);
};

template <class Type>
Type Sample<Type>::Data(Type d)
{   return d;
}

template <class Type>
Sample<Type>::Sample()
{   cout<<"\n In Constructor ";
}

template <class Type>
Sample<Type>::~Sample()
{   cout<<"\n In Destructor ";
}
int main()
{   Sample<int> S1;
    Sample<float> S2;
    Sample<char> S3;
    Sample<char*> S4;
    cout<<"\n  "<< S1.Data(11);
    cout<<"\n  "<<S2.Data(12.34);
    cout<<"\n  "<<S3.Data('A');
    cout<<"\n  "<<S4.Data( "Hello World ");
}
```

4.
```
using namespace std;
#include<iostream>
template<type T, type U>
void squareAndPrint(T x, U y)
{
   cout<< x << "   "<< x * x;
   cout<< y <<"   "<<y * y;
}
int main()
{
    int ii = 2;
    float jj = 2.1;
    squareAndPrint <int, float> (ii, jj);
}
```

5.
```
using namespace std;
#include<iostream>
template <class type>
class Test
{
   public:
   type Func(type Var)
      {
         return Var;
      }
};
int main()
{
   Test <int> T1;
   Test <float> T2;
   cout<< T1.Func(200);
   cout<< T2.Func(3.123);
}
```

6.
```
using namespace std;
#include<iostream>
template<class Type>
Type square(Type x)
{
   Type res = x * x;
   return result;
};
int main()
{
   int i = 2, ii;
   float x = 2.2 , xx;
   double y = 2.2, yy;
   ii = square(i);
   cout<< i <<"  "<< ii;
   yy = square(y);
   cout<< y <<"  "<< yy;
}
```

7.
```
using namespace std;
#include<iostream>
class One
{
   public:
      One(int n)
      {
         cout<< n;
      }
};
class Two : public One
{
```

```
    public:
        Two(int n, double d) : One(n)
        {
            cout<< d;
        }
};
class Three : public Two
{
    public:
        Three(int n, double d,
char ch) : Two(n, d)
        {
            cout<<ch;
        }
};
int main()
{
    Three three(5, 4.3, 'R');
}
```

Answers

Fill in the Blanks

1. meta-programming; **2.** generic programming.; **3.** Generics; **4.** Algorithm, data types; **5.** Generic function; **6.** Template-type parameters; **7.** an ambiguity; **8.** function; **9.** template class; **10.** specialization; **11.** on demand

State True or False

1. False **2.** False **3.** False **4.** True **5.** False **6.** False **7.** True **8.** False
9. False **10.** True **11.** False **12.** True **13.** True **14.** False **15.** False **16.** True
17. True

Multiple Choice Questions

1. (d); **2.** (c); **3.** (b); **4.** (a); **5.** (b); **6.** (a); **7.** (d); **8.** (b); **9.** (c); **10.** (a); **11.** (c)

CHAPTER 15

Exception Handling

KEY Concepts

• Try catch block • Multiple catch statements • Catch all exceptions • Stack unwinding • Re-throwing exceptions • Standard exceptions • Exceptions in operator overloaded functions • Exceptions in constructors and destructors • Handling uncaught exceptions

INTRODUCTION

The programs that we write may behave abnormally or unexpectedly because of some errors and/or exceptions as shown in Fig. 15.1. The two common types of errors that we often encounter are syntax errors and logic errors. While logic errors occur due to poor understanding of problem and its solution, syntax errors, on the other hand, arise due to poor understanding of the language. However, such errors can be detected by exhaustive and debugging and testing procedures.

However, many times, we come across some peculiar problems which are often categorized as exceptions. Exceptions are run-time anomalies or unusual conditions such as divide by zero, accessing arrays out of its bounds, running out of memory or disk space, overflow, and underflow that a program may encounter during execution. Like errors, exceptions can also be categorized as synchronous or asynchronous exceptions. While synchronous exceptions—divide by zero, array index out of bound, etc. can be controlled by the program,

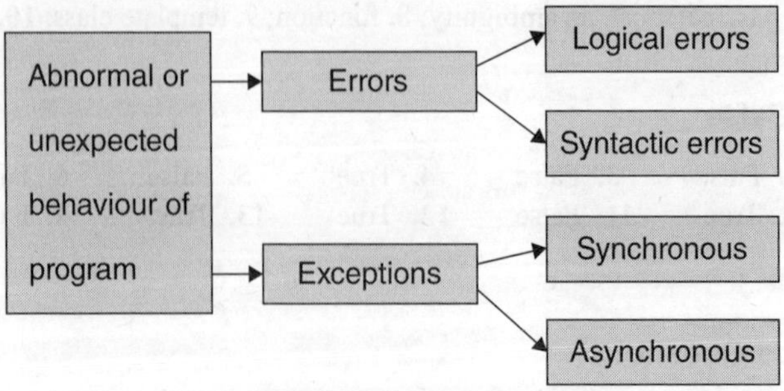

Figure 15.1 Errors and exceptions

asynchronous exceptions—an interrupt from the keyboard, hardware malfunction, and disk failure—are caused by events that are beyond the control of the program.

To handle such exceptional situations, a new feature of exception handling has been added to ANSI C++ that helps the programmers to identify and effectively deal with these run-time errors.

15.1 EXCEPTION HANDLING

Exceptions provide a way to react to exceptional conditions in programs by transferring program control to special functions called handlers.

Exception handling is a newly added feature to C++ that is now almost supported by all compilers. The main aim of exception handling is to detect and report an exceptional condition(s), so that appropriate action can be taken to deal with it.

Note Exceptional handling deals only with synchronous exceptions.

The steps performed in exception handling can be summarized as shown in Fig. 15.2. To hit, catch, throw, and handle the exceptions, the exception handling code comprises two blocks—first to hit and throw the exception and the second to catch and handle it. The first block is called the try block and the second is known as the catch block.

Try block This block is a group of statements that may generate an exception. When an exception is generated, it is thrown using the keyword throw. The throw keyword invokes the exception handling routine.

Catch block This block catches the exception thrown from the try block and handles it in the way specified by the statements in the catch block.

Note `try`, `catch`, and `throw` are specified as keywords. Exception handler is denoted by the keyword, `catch`.

The syntax for the try and catch block can be given as follows:

Programming Tip: No code should be present between the try and catch block

```
--------------------
try
{ -----------------
  throw exception;
  ----------------
}
catch(type arg)
{ ---------------
  ---------------
}
```

According to the syntax, the catch block immediately follows the try block. When the try block throws an exception, the program control leaves the try block and enters the catch block. An exception is an object that transmits information about an unusual condition. The type indicates the type of exception that the catch block handles. `arg` is an optional parameter name. If the type of exception matches with the `arg` type in the catch statement, then the catch block is executed for handling the exception. After executing the exception handler code given in the catch block, the control goes to the statement immediately following the catch block. However, in case the type of `arg` does not match the type specified in the catch statement, the program is aborted by using the `abort()` which is invoked by default. The program flow during a raised exception is shown in Fig. 15.3.

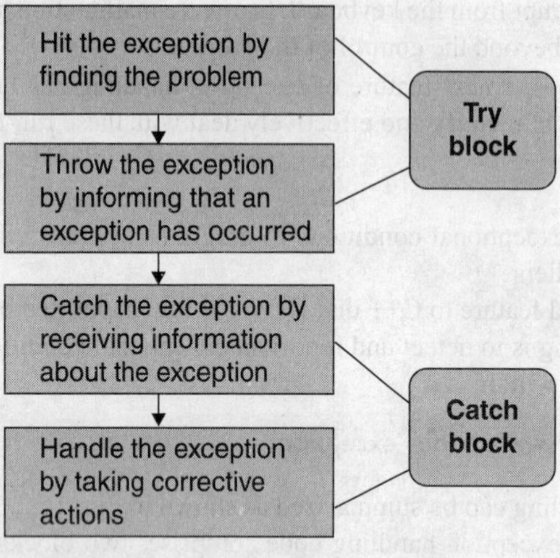

Figure 15.2 Handling exceptions

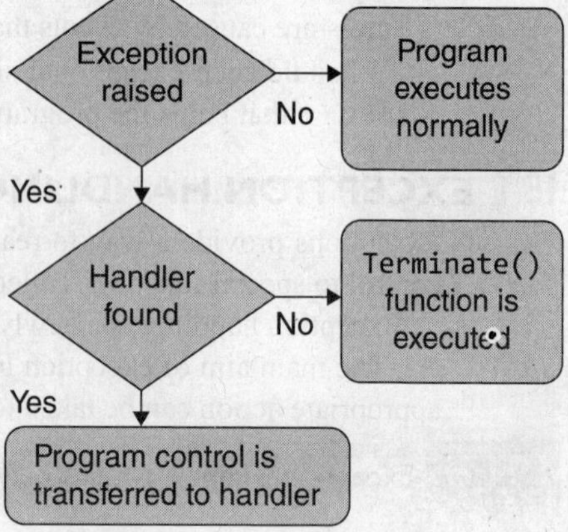

Figure 15.3 Program flow in case of exception

> **Note** If no exception is detected and thrown, then the catch block is not executed. The program control skips the catch block and goes to the statement immediately following the catch block.

Exceptions can be thrown by writing as follows:

```
throw exception;
throw (exception);
throw;
```

The last form of throwing an exception is usually used for rethrowing exceptions, which we will be discussing shortly. The operand exception in other two syntaxes may be of any type including constants. The point at which an exception is thrown is called the throw point. When an exception is thrown, the control never returns to the throw point.

Example 15.1 Consider a simple program that divides a number by zero and see how it behaves in both cases—when the exception does not occur and when it occurs.

```
using namespace std;
#include<iostream>
main()
{  int num1, num2;
   cout<<"\n Enter two numbers : ";
   cin>>num1>>num2;
   try
   {  if(num2!=0)// no exception is thrown
      {  float res = (float) num1/num2;
                          cout<<"\n RESULT = "<<res;
                  }
                  else
                          throw(num2);  //exception thrown
                 }
                 catch(int num2)  // exception caught
                 {  cout<<"\n Divide by zero error encountered";  // exception handled
```

> **Programming Tip:** A rethrown exception cannot be caught in the same function.

```
    }
    cout<<"\n EXITING MAIN()";
}
```

OUTPUT

```
Enter two numbers :9 3
RESULT = 3
EXITING MAIN()
SECOND CASE
Enter two numbers :9 0
Divide by zero error encountered
EXITING MAIN()
```

Explanation: In the first case, when no exception occurs, control passes to the statement following the catch block. In the second case, an exception (using object num2) is thrown from the try block. Since, the exception object, which is of `type int`, matches with the argument specified in the catch block, the catch block is executed.

Note Code within the try block is called protected code.

15.1.1 Multiple Catch Statements

It is possible to associate more than one catch statement with a single try block. This is usually done when a program segment has more than one condition to throw as an exception. In such cases, when an exception is thrown, the exception handlers are searched to find an appropriate match. The first catch block that matches the type of the exception thrown is executed. After execution, the program control goes to the first statement after the last catch block for that try block. This means that all other catch blocks are ignored. However, if no match is found, then the program is terminated using the default `abort()`.

Note In case more than one catch block matches the type of exception thrown, the first catch block that matches the exception is executed.

The syntax for a try block with multiple catch blocks can be given as follows:

Programming Tip: No code should be present between a list of catch statements.

```
--------------------
try
{  ----------------
   throw exception;
   ----------------
}
catch(type1 arg1)
{  ---------------
   ---------------
}
catch(type2 arg2)
{  ---------------
   ---------------
}
----------------------
```

```
catch(typen argn)
{  ----------------
   ----------------
}
```

Example 15.2 Use of multiple catch statements for a single try block

```
using namespace std;
#include<iostream>
main()
{  int num;
   cout<<"\n Enter a positive number : ";
   cin>>num;
   try
   {  if(num==0)
      throw ("Zero");// exception 1
   else if(num<0)
      throw num;  //exception 2
   else
      cout<<"\n NUMBER = "<<num;
   }
  catch(int num)
  {  cout<<"\n"<<num<<" is negative";  // exception 2 caught
  }
  catch(char* msg)
  {  cout<<"\n The number is "<<msg;  // exception 1 caught
  }
  cout<<"\n EXITING MAIN()";
}
```

OUTPUT

```
Enter a positive number : 0
The number is ZERO
```

Note If there is no exception handler for a thrown exception, the program will call the `terminate()`.

15.1.2 Catch all Exceptions

In large software programs, often, it is difficult to anticipate all types of possible exceptional conditions. Therefore, the programmer may not be able to write a different handler (catch block) for every individual type of exception. In such situations, a better idea is to write a handler that would catch all types of exceptions. This is something similar to the default case in a switch statement. The syntax to define a hander (catch block) that would catch every possible exception thrown from the try block is as follows:

```
catch(...)    Catch all exceptions
{
// code to handle all exceptions
}
```

The catch(...) can be used along with other catch handlers, so that some specific types of exceptions are caught and handled by specific handlers and those exceptions that are not handled by those handlers can be handled by the catch(...). However, the default handler must be placed after all other catch blocks because otherwise it would prevent any specific handler to be executed. The first matching catch block is executed and others are ignored.

Example 15.3 Use of catch (...)

```
using namespace std;
#include<iostream>
main()
{  int num;
   cout<<"\n Enter a number (-1, 0, 1): ";
   cin>>num;
   try
   {  if(num==0)
      throw ("Zero"); // exception 1
      else if(num==-1)
      throw num;    // exception 2
      else if(num == 1)
      cout<<"\n NUMBER = "<<num;
else
  throw(float)num;  // exception 3
  }
  catch(int num)  //caught exception 2
  {  cout<<"\n"<<num<<" is negative";
  }
  catch(char* msg)  // caught exception 1
  {  cout<<"\n The number is "<<msg;
  }
catch(...)  // caught exception 3
  {  cout<<"\n No specific code executed";
  }
  cout<<"\n EXITING MAIN()";
}
```

OUTPUT

```
Enter a number (-1, 0, 1): 56
No specific code executed
```

15.1.3 Exceptions in Invoked Function

A large program is usually divided into ‘n’ number of functions. The possibility that the invoked function may generate an exceptional condition cannot be ignored. Figure 15.4 shows the scenario when the function invoked by the try block throws an exception which is handled by the catch block in the calling function. The syntax for such a situation can be given as follows:

```
type function_name(arg list)
{  ----------
   throw (exception);
```

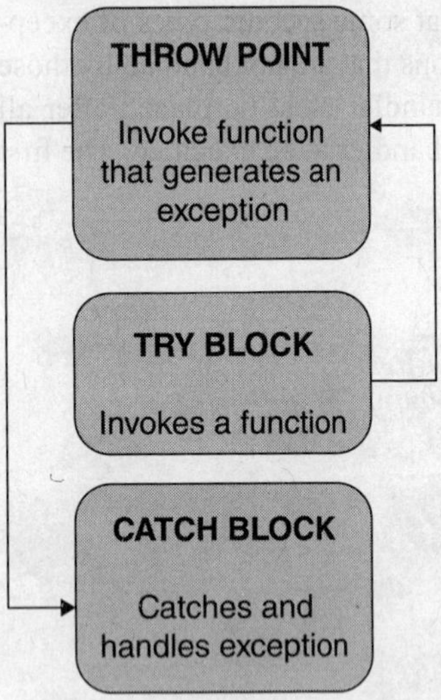

Figure 15.4 Exception in invoked function

```
    ----------
}
-----------------
try
{  -----------
   function_name();    // function call
   -----------
}
catch(type arg)
{  -----------
   // Code to handle exception
   ------------
}
-----------
```

Note Irrespective of the location of the throw point, the try block is always immediately followed by the catch block.

The program given next generates a divide by zero exception from a called function. The `main()` has a try block from which a function `divide()` is invoked. In `divide()`, the exception occurs which is thrown and is caught and handled by the catch block defined in the `main()` immediately followed by the try block.

Example 15.4 Function generating exception

```
using namespace std;
#include<iostream>
void divide(int a, int b)
{  if(b==0)
   throw ("Divide by zero exception");
   else
   {  float res = (float)a/b;
      cout<<"\n RESULT = "<<res;
   }
}
main()
{  int num1, num2;
   cout<<"\n Enter the two numbers : ";
   cin>>num1>>num2;
   try
   {  divide(num1, num2);
   }
   catch(char *mesg)
   {  cout<<"\n"<<mesg;
   }
   cout<<"\n EXITING MAIN()";
}
```

OUTPUT
```
Enter the two numbers : 9 0
Divide by zero exception
EXITING MAIN()
```

Note C++ allows programmers to place the throw point in a deeply nested try block or in a deeply nested function call.

Programming Tip: If the temporary variable is a class object, then destructor of the class is called before function terminates.

15.1.4 Stack Unwinding

Stack unwinding, which is related to exception handling, is the process of removing function entries from function call stack at run time. When an exception is thrown, the function call stack is searched for an exception handler. In this searching process, all the entries before the function with exception handler are removed from the function call stack. Therefore, exception handling performs stack unwinding if the thrown exception is not handled in same function as shown in Fig. 15.5.

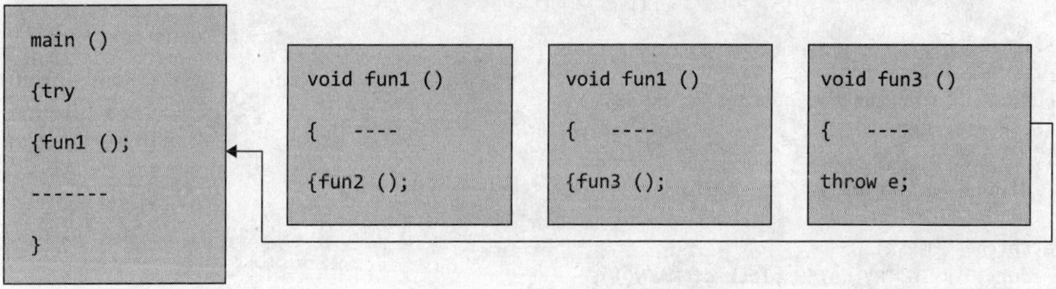

Figure 15.5 Stack unwinding

Note A call stack, function stack, execution stack, run-time stack, or a control stack is used to keep a track of point to which the active function will return after completing its execution.

We have already seen how a function stack is formed in Chapter 4 on Functions. When a function is called, the return address, function arguments any temporary variables are stored on the stack. When the called function completes its execution, the arguments and temporary variables are all cleared and the return address obtained from the stack is used to transfer the control back to the caller.

15.1.5 Rethrowing Exception

In some situations, the exception handler in the catch block may decide to rethrow the exception without processing it. To rethrow an exception, the syntax is as follows:

```
throw;
```

A throw statement without any exception explicitly mentioned causes the current exception to be thrown to the next enclosing try/catch block which catches it and handles it in the specified manner.

Example 15.5 Rethrowing an exception

```
using namespace std;
#include<iostream>
void divide(int a, int b)
{ try
{  if(b==0)
   throw ("Divide by zero exception");
   else
   {  float res = (float)a/b;
      cout<<"\n RESULT = "<<res;
   }
  }
catch(char const*mesg)
  {  cout<<"\n In TRY CATCH block of called function";
     cout<<"\n RE THROWING EXCEPTION";
throw;
  }
}
main()
{  int num1, num2;
   cout<<"\n Enter the two numbers : ";
   cin>>num1>>num2;
   try
   {  divide(num1, num2);
   }
   catch(char *mesg)
   { cout<<"\n In TRY CATCH block of MAIN()";
   cout<<"\n"<<mesg;
   }
   cout<<"\n EXITING MAIN()";
}
```

OUTPUT

```
Enter the two numbers : 9 0
In TRY CATCH block of called function
RE THROWING EXCEPTION
In TRY CATCH block of MAIN()
EXITING MAIN()
```

Note When an exception is rethrown, it will not be caught by the enclosing catch statement. It can be handled only by an appropriate catch statement in the outer try or catch block.

15.1.6 Restricting the Exceptions that can be Thrown

C++ allows programmers to restrict a function to throw only certain specified exceptions. This can be done by adding a throw list clause to the function definition. The syntax of a function explicitly specifying the exceptions that it can throw can be given as follows:

```
type function_name(arg list) throw (type list)
{ ..........
  ..........
}
```

List of exceptions that can be raised

In the syntax, the function header is followed by the keyword `throw` followed by the type list, which specifies the type of exceptions that may be thrown. If the function throws an exception of type not mentioned in the type list, the program will get terminated abnormally.

Example 15.6 Throwing specified exceptions

```
using namespace std;
#include<iostream>
void check_number(int i) throw(int)
{ if(i==0)
       throw(i);  // exception 1
  else if(i==-1)
       throw (float)i;  // exception 2 occurs but not thrown
  else throw (char)i;  // exception 3 occurs but not thrown
}
int main()
{ int num;
  cout<<"\n Enter a number (-1,0 or 1) : ";
  cin>>num;
  try
  {  check_number(num);
  }
  catch(int)
  {  cout<<"\n Caught an integer";
  }
  catch(float)
  {  cout<<"\n Caught a floating point number";
  }
  catch(char)
  {  cout<<"\n Caught a character";
  }
  cout<<"\n Exiting MAIN()";
}
```

OUTPUT

```
Enter a number (-1,0 or 1) : 1
Abnormal Termination
```

In the program, since float type and character type exception was never thrown, they are neither caught nor handled and hence, causes abnormal termination of the program.

Note To prevent a function from throwing any exception, just write `throw();` with an empty `type.list`.

15.1.7 Catching Class Type as Exceptions

It is often more useful to create a class that stores information on exceptions as they occur. Therefore, in addition to throwing exceptions of basic data types, C++ also allows program codes to throw exceptions of user-defined types (like class). In such cases, the code throws an object of a class type. The catch block catches the object of the class and invokes its public method to display the value(s) of its private members, which in turn, stores important information about the exception that has occurred.

Note The header file <exception> includes classes that are used for exception handling. The what( ) method is a frequently used method that is defined in this file. It provides the details of the exceptions generated.

Example 15.7 Creating a class that stores information on exceptions

Programming Tip: A return in catch block forces return from the function that contains the catch block.

```
using namespace std;
#include<iostream>
#include<string.h>
class Exception
{ private:
        int errnum;
        char *err_mesg;
  public:
        Exception(int en, char* em)
        {  errnum = en;
    int len = strlen(em);
    err_mesg = new char[len+1];
    strcpy(err_mesg, em);
  }
  void display()
  {  cout<<"\n ERROR NO. = "<<errno<<"\t ERROR = "<<err_mesg;
  }
};
void divide(int a, int b)
{  if(b==0)
   throw Exception(0, "Divide by Zero Error"); //throwing class type exception
   else
   {  float res = (float)a/b;
    cout<<"\n RESULT = "<<res;
  }
}
int main()
{ int num1, num2;
  cout<<"\n Enter the two numbers : ";
  cin>>num1>>num2;
  try
  {  divide(num1, num2);
  }
  catch(Exception e)  //catching class type exception
  {  e.display();
  }
```

```
  cout<<"\n EXITING MAIN()";
}
```

OUTPUT

```
Enter the two numbers : 9 0
ERROR NO. = 0  ERROR = Divide by Zero Error
EXITING MAIN()
```

Program 15.1 Write a program that throws an exception of index out of bound.

Programming Tip: Exception specifications must be included in function declaration as well definition.

```
          using namespace std;
          #include<iostream>
          class Array
          { private:
                 int *arr;
                 int size;
            public:
            class Error{};
                 Array(int n)
                 {  size = n;
                    arr = new int[size];
       }
       void read()
   {  for(int i=0;i<size;i++)
          cin>>arr[i];
   }
   void display()
   {  for(int i=0;i<size;i++)
          cout<<"  "<<arr[i];
   }
   int &operator[](int index)
   {  if(index<0 || index>=size)
          throw Error();
     else
          return arr[index];
   }
};
int main()
{ int n;
  cout<<"\n Enter the number of elements in the array : ";
  cin>>n;
  Array A(n);
  cout<<"\n Enter the array elements : ";
  A.read();
  cout<<"\n The Array is : ";
  A.display();
  try
  {  A[2] = 20;
     cout<<"\n The Array is : ";
    A.display();
    A[6] = 30;
```

```
    cout<<"\n The Array is : ";
    A.display();
    A[-1] = 40;
    cout<<"\n The Array is : ";
    A.display();
  }
  catch(Array :: Error)
  {  cout<<"\n Out of Bound Exception";
  }
  cout<<"\n EXITING MAIN()";
}
```

OUTPUT

```
Enter the number of elements in the array : 5
Enter the array elements : 1 2 3 4 5
The Array is : 1 2 3 4 5
The Array is : 1 20 3 4 5
Out of Bound Exception
EXITING MAIN()
```

Program 15.2 Write a program that demonstrates the use of throwing a class exception, exception specifications, and multiple catch blocks.

```
using namespace std;
#include<iostream>
class positive{};
class negative{};
class zero{};
void num_type(int num) throw(zero, positive, negative)
{  try
   { if(num==0)
        throw zero();
     else if(num>0)
        throw positive();
     else
        throw negative();
  }
   catch(zero)
   {  cout<<"\n The number is zero";
   }
   catch(positive)
   {  cout<<"\n The number is positive";
   }
   catch(negative)
   {  cout<<"\n The number is negative";
   }
}
main()
{  int num;
   cout<<"\n Enter a number : ";
   cin>>num;
```

Programming Tip: When program throws an exception, control never returns to the *throw point.*

```
   try
{  num_type(num);
   }
   cout<<"\n EXITING MAIN()";
}
```

OUTPUT

```
Enter a number : 7
The number is positive
EXITING MAIN()
```

Program 15.3 Write a program that performs calculator operations and throws exception if an attempt is made to divide a number by zero or if an invalid operator is applied.

```
using namespace std;
#include<iostream>
class Error{ };
int main()
{  int num1, num2, res;
   char op;
   try
   {  cout<<"\n Enter the two numbers : ";
      cin>>num1>>num2;
      cout<<"\n Which operation would you like to perform : ";
      cin>>op;
      switch(op)
      {  case '+':  res = num1 + num2;
                    cout<<"\n RESULT = "<<res;
                    break;
         case '-':  res = num1 - num2;
              cout<<"\n RESULT = "<<res;
                    break;
         case '*':  res = num1 * num2;
              cout<<"\n RESULT = "<<res;
                 break;
         case '/':  try
                    {  if(num2 == 0)
                    throw "Divide by Zero Error";
                    else
                    {  res = num1 / num2;
                       cout<<"\n RESULT = "<<res;
}                            break;
      }
      catch(char *mesg)
                    {  cout<<mesg;
                    }
      default:  throw Error();
             }
}
      catch(Error())
      {  cout<<"\n Invalid Operator";
      }
```

```
    cout<<"\n EXITING MAIN()";
}
```

OUTPUT

```
Enter the two numbers : 9 0
Which operation would you like to perform : =
Invalid Operator
EXITING MAIN()
```

Program 15.4 Write a program that throws an exception raised when memory is not allocated.

```
using namespace std;
#include<iostream>
#include<exception>
int main()
{  int *arr, n, i;
   cout<<"\n Enter the number of elements : ";
   cin>>n;
   try
   {  arr = new int[n];
      cout<<"\n Enter the elements : ";
      for(i=0;i<n;i++)
           cin>>arr[i];
      cout<<"\n The array is : ";
      for(i=0;i<n;i++)
           cout<<" "<<arr[i];
    }
    catch(...)
    {  cout<<"\n Memory Could Not Be Allocated";
       exit(1);
    }
    delete arr;
    cout<<"\n EXITING MAIN()";
}
```

OUTPUT

```
Enter the number of elements : 5
Enter the elements : 1 2 3 4 5
The array is : 1 2 3 4 5
EXITING MAIN()
```

Program 15.5 Write a program that throws an exception raised when memory is not allocated for a two-dimensional array.

```
using namespace std;
#include<iostream>
#include<exception>
int main()
{  int **arr, rows, cols;
   cout<<"\n Enter the number of rows and columns : ";
   cin>>rows>>cols;
   try
   {  arr = new int *[rows];
```

```
        for(int i=0;i<cols;i++)
            arr[i] = new int [cols];
        cout<<"\n Enter the elements : ";
        for(int i=0;i<rows;i++)
        {  for(int j=0;j<cols;j++)
                cin>>arr[i][j];
      }
        cout<<"\n The array is : ";
        for(int i=0;i<rows;i++)
      {  cout<<"\n";
         for(int j=0;j<cols;j++)
              cout<<" "<<arr[i][j];
       }
    }
    catch(...)
    {  cout<<"\n Memory Could Not Be Allocated";
       exit(1);
    }
    for(int i=0;i<rows;i++)
       delete[] arr[i];
       delete[] arr;
    cout<<"\n EXITING MAIN()";
}
```

OUTPUT

```
Enter the number of rows and columns : 2 2
Enter the elements : 1 2 3 4
The array is :
1 2
3 4
```

15.2 EXCEPTIONS IN CONSTRUCTORS AND DESTRUCTORS

The possibility of an exception while initializing the object of a class cannot be ignored. The key concern here is that when an exception occurs while the constructor has not yet fully executed, then it must have had reserved memory for some data members. The allocated memory cannot be freed using destructor because the moment the exception occurs, the program control goes out of the object's context. This may lead to memory leak problems.

To prevent such memory leak problems, the exception handling mechanism must be implemented in the constructor itself. This will enable programmers to free the memory allocated for data members before handling the exception. In case the exception is handled inside `main()`, the `main()` will not be able to deallocate the memory reserved for the private data members of the class.

Note Exception handling must be done in the constructor. After freeing the reserved space for data members, the constructor must rethrow the exception to be handled by `main()`.

As in the case of constructor, the exception handling routine must be defined in the destructor. This is important because an exception may be raised during the execution of the destructor. This may result in memory leak problems when the destructor is unable to release all the reserved space before the exception occurred. This feature helps programmers to write secure operations.

Note: Exception handling in `main()` and not in destructor may lead to abnormal program termination.

Consider the program given here which has three try or catch blocks in `main()`, constructor, and destructor.

Example 15.8 Exception handling in constructor and destructor

Programming Tip: Function calls that you anticipate might produce an exception must be enclosed in braces and preceded by the keyword try.

```
using namespace std;
#include<iostream>
class Divide
{  private:
        int *num1, *num2;
    public:
        Divide()
        {  try
            {
             num1 = new int();
             num2 = new int();
             cout<<"\n Enter the two numbers : ";
             cin>>*num1>>*num2;
            if(*num2==0)
            throw("Divide by zero error will be generated");
            //exception 1 from constructor
        }
        catch(char *mesg)//exception caught
        {  delete num1;
           delete num2;
           throw;  //rethrowing exception
        }
    }
    ~Divide()
    {  try
    {  delete num1;
       delete num2;
    // throw;
        }
    catch(...)
        {  cout<<"\n Exception generated in destructor";
        }
 }
    float division()
    {  return (float)*num1/ *num2;
    }
};
int main()
{  try
   {  Divide D;
      float res = D.division();
      cout<<"\n RESULT = "<<res;
   }
   catch(char *mesg)  // not executed since class exception handler is invoked
   {  cout<<mesg;
   }
```

```
    cout<<"\n EXITING MAIN()";
}
```

OUTPUT

```
Enter the two numbers : 9 0
Divide by zero error will be generated
EXITING MAIN()
```

Explanation: The program has a class `Divide`. It has a try or catch block in the constructor as well as in the destructor. In the constructor, memory is allocated for private data members. If the second number is zero, then an exception is thrown. The catch block of the constructor catches that error, frees memory reserved for private data members, and then rethrows the exception to be handled by `main()`. The code also shows that in case the program executed successfully but if an exception rises during the execution of destructor, then the catch statement of the destructor function itself handles that exception rather than rethrowing it to `main()`.

Moreover, a copy constructor is called in exception handling when an exception is thrown from the try block (as in throw `Error()`). If an exception is thrown from the constructor, destructors are called only for those objects that are completely constructed.

Note If the type of the thrown object is `const` or volatile, then the catch argument must also be a `const` or volatile for a match to occur. However, a `const`, volatile, or reference type catch argument can match a non-constant, non-volatile, or non-reference object type. A non-reference catch argument type can match reference to an object of the same type.

15.3 EXCEPTIONS IN OPERATOR OVERLOADED FUNCTIONS

Programming Tip: Destructors should preferably be written using no exception specification.

Exception handling mechanism can be used with overloaded operator functions to handle system generated or user-specified exceptions. The program code given next has a class `Complex` and overloaded operator += which may throw an exception of class `Error`, if the real parts of both the complex numbers to be added are zero. You could have thrown an exception of any type instead of class `Error`.

Note that in the program, a nameless object of class `Error` is thrown, which is caught and handled by the `catch` block.

Example 15.9 Exception handling in operator overloaded functions

```
using namespace std;
#include<iostream>
class Complex
{  private:
        int real, imag;
   public:
        class Error{};
        Complex(int r, int i)
        {  real = r;
           imag = i;
        }
        void display()
        {  cout<<real<<" + "<<imag<<"i";
        }
```

```
        Complex &operator+=(Complex &C)
        {  if(real == 0 &&C.real == 0)
                throw Error();
           else
           {  real += C.real;
              imag += C.imag;
              return *this;
           }
        }
};
int main()
{  Complex C1(0,2), C2(0,4);
   try
   {
        C1+=C2;
        C1.display();
   }
   catch(Complex :: Error)
   {            cout<<"\n Add Zero Exception";
   }
cout<<"\n Exiting MAIN()";
}
```

OUTPUT

```
Add Zero Exception
Exiting MAIN()
```

15.4 EXCEPTIONS AND INHERITANCE

In this chapter, we have seen that C++ allows programmers to throw classes as exceptions. Since a class can be inherited from another class, let us consider what happens when the inherited classes are used as exceptions. In such a situation, exception handlers will not only match classes of a specific type but will also match classes derived from that specific type. Consider the following program.

Example 15.10 Program using exceptions and inheritance

```
using namespace std;
#include<iostream>
class Base {};
class Derived: public Base
{};
int main()
{  try
   {  throw Derived();
   }
   catch (Base B)
   {
           cout<<"\n Base Class Exception Caught";
   }
```

```
    catch (Derived D)
    {
            cout<<"\n Derived Class Exception Caught";
    }
}
```

OUTPUT

```
Base Class Exception Caught
```

Explanation: In the program, there are two classes, `Base` and `Derived` (which inherits `Base` class). In `main()`, an exception of the derived class is thrown. The first catch block handles the base class exceptions and the second catch block handles the derived class exceptions.

Since a derived class object is compatible with the base class object, it is caught by the first catch block and hence, the result.

If you want that the second catch block to be executed, then place the base class exception handler after the derived class exception handlers. Consider the program here which demonstrates this concept.

Example 15.11 Another program using exceptions and inheritance

```
using namespace std;
#include<iostream>
class Base{};
class Derived: public Base
{};
int main()
{  try
   {  throw Derived();
    }
    catch (Derived D)
    {
            cout<<"\n Derived Class Exception Caught";
    }
    catch (Base B)
    {
            cout<<"\n Base Class Exception Caught";
    }
}
```

OUTPUT

```
Derived Class Exception Caught
```

Note Exception handlers for derived classes should be listed before those for base classes.

15.5 EXCEPTIONS AND TEMPLATES

Exceptions can also be generated in template functions or template class as in case of any other ordinary function or class. Consider the program given next in which an out of bound exception is thrown from the template function.

Example 15.12 Exceptions in template function

```
using namespace std;
#include<iostream>
#include<stdlib.h>
#define MAX 10
template <class Type>
void insert(Type arr[], Type num, int &n)
{  if(n==MAX)
       throw "Exception Thrown";   // Exception thrown
   else
   {  arr[n++] = num;
   }
}
int main()
{  int arr[10], i, num, n;
   cout<<"\n Enter the number of elements : ";
   cin>>n;
   cout<<"\n Enter the array elements : ";
   for(i=0;i<n;i++)
   cin>>arr[i];
  cout<<"\n Enter the number to be inserted : ";
  cin>>num;
  try
  {  insert(arr, num, n);
  }
  catch(...)   // exception caught
  {  cout<<"OUT OF BOUND EXCEPTION";
     exit(1);
  }
  cout<<"\n The Array is : ";
  for(i=0;i<n;i++)
     cout<<"\t"<<arr[i];
}
```

OUTPUT

```
Enter the number of elements : 10
Enter the array elements : 1 2 3 4 5 6 7 8 9 10
Enter the number to be inserted : 11
OUT OF BOUND EXCEPTION
```

Program 15.6 Write a program that has a class Account Holder to store bank's customer(s) name, address, balance and account type. Write functions to print, deposit and withdraw amount. An exception must be thrown if a minimum balance of ₹5000 is not maintained.

```
#include<iostream>
#include<string.h>
#include<exception>
using namespace std;
class Account_Holder
```

```
{  private:
        char *name;
        char *Acc_Type;
        char *address;
        float Balance;
   public:
        Account_Holder(char *n, char *ac, char *add, float bal)
        {  int len = strlen(n);
           name = new char[len + 1];
           strcpy(name, n);
           len = strlen(ac);
           Acc_Type = new char[len + 1];
           strcpy(Acc_Type,ac);
           len = strlen(add);
           address = new char[len + 1];
           strcpy(address, add);
           Balance = bal;
        }
        void Print()
        {  cout<<"\n NAME : "<<name;
           cout<<"\n ACCOUNT TYPE : "<<Acc_Type;
           cout<<"\n ADDRESS : "<<address;
           cout<<"\n BALANCE : "<<Balance;
        }
        void Deposit(float amt)
        {  Balance += amt;
        }
        void Withdraw(float amt)
        {  try
           {
                    Balance -= amt;
                    if(Balance <5000)
                    {  Balance += amt;
                       throw Balance;
                    }
           }
           catch(float f)
           {  cout<<"\n Amount can not be withdrawn as you will be exceeding
your minimum Balance ";
           }
        }
};
int main()
{  Account_Holder AH("Aaditya", "Savings", "Connaught Place", 30000);
  AH.Deposit(10000);
  AH.Print();
  AH.Withdraw(38000);
  AH.Print();
}
```

OUTPUT

```
NAME : Aaditya
ACCOUNT TYPE : Savings
ADDRESS : Connaught Place
BALANCE : 40000
Amount cannot be withdrawn as you will be exceeding your minimum Balance
NAME : Aaditya
ACCOUNT TYPE : Savings
ADDRESS : Connaught Place
BALANCE : 40000
```

Program 15.7 Write a program that throws a named class object when an out of bound exception is raised. The program also throws an exception when the number of elements in the array are either less than 0 or greater than MAX.

```
using namespace std;
#include<iostream>
#define MAX 10
class OverUnderFlow{};
OverUnderFlow ou;
class Array
{  private:
         int *arr;
         int size;
   public:
   class Error{};
         Array(int n)
         {
               try
               {  if(n<0 || n>MAX)
                        throw(ou);
                  else
                  {  size = n;
                     arr = new int[size];
                  }
         }
         catch(OverUnderFlow ou)
         {  throw;
         }
   }
   void read()
   {  for(int i=0;i<size;i++)
         cin>>arr[i];
   }
   void display()
   {  for(int i=0;i<size;i++)
         cout<<"  "<<arr[i];
   }
   int &operator[](int index)
   {  if(index<0 || index>=size)
```

```
            throw Error();
        else
            return arr[index];
    }
};
int main()
{   int n;
    cout<<"\n Enter the number of elements in the array : ";
    cin>>n;
    try
    {   Array A(n);
        cout<<"\n Enter the array elements : ";
        A.read();
        cout<<"\n The Array is : ";
        A.display();
        try
        {   A[2] = 20;
            cout<<"\n The Array is : ";
            A.display();
            A[6] = 30;
            cout<<"\n The Array is : ";
            A.display();
            A[-1] = 40;
            cout<<"\n The Array is : ";
            A.display();
    }
    catch(Array :: Error)
    {   cout<<"\n Out of Bound Exception";
    }
  }
  catch(OverUnderFlow)
  {   cout<<"\n Number of elements can neither be less than 0 nor greater than MAX";
  }
  cout<<"\n EXITING MAIN()";
}
```

OUTPUT

```
Enter the number of elements in the array : 12
Number of elements can neither be less than 0 nor greater than MAX
EXITING MAIN()
```

Program 15.8 Write a program that throws an exception if the candidate is not eligible for applying for the post of Professor. Use classes and inheritance.

```
using namespace std;
#include<iostream>
#include<exception>
#include<typeinfo>
class WRONG_DATA{}:
class Prof_Details
{   protected:
```

```
        char PhD;
        char NET;
        int exp;
   public:
        Prof_Details(char P, char N, int ex)
        {  if(P=='N' || N=='N' || ex<5)
                throw WRONG_DATA();
           else
           {  PhD = P;
              NET = N;
              exp = ex;
           }
        }
        void show_details()
        {  cout<<"\n PhD = "<<PhD;
           cout<<"\n NET = "<<NET;
           cout<<"\n EXPERIENCE = "<<exp;
        }
};
class Acad_Details : public Prof_Details
{  protected:
        int num_papers_published;
        int num_books_published;
   public:
        Acad_Details(char P, char N, int ex, int np, intnb): Prof_Details(P,N,ex)
        {  if(np==0 || nb == 0)
                throw WRONG_DATA();
           else
           {  num_papers_published = np;
              num_books_published = nb;
           }
        }
        void show_details()
        {  Prof_Details::show_details();
           cout<<"\n NO. OF BOOKS PUBLISHED = "<<num_books_published;
           cout<<"\n NO. OF RESEARCH PAPERS PUBLISHED = "<<num_papers_published;
        }

};

int main()
{  char P, N;
   int ex, np, nb;
   cout<<"\n Have you completed your Doctorate (Y/N) : ";
   cin>>P;
   cout<<"\n Have you qualified the NET Examination (Y/N) : ";
   cin>>N;
   cout<<"\n How many years of Experience do you have : ";
   cin>>ex;
   cout<<"\n How many Research Papers have you published : ";
   cin>>np;
```

```
    cout<<"\n How many Books have you published : ";
    cin>>nb;
    try
    {  Acad_Details Prof(P, N, ex, np, nb);
    }
    catch(WRONG_DATA)
    {  cout<<"\n\n The details you have entered are not eligible for applying for
       the post of professor in our university";
       cout<<"\n\n THANK YOU";
       }
    cout<<"\n EXITING MAIN()";
}
```

OUTPUT

```
Have you completed your Doctorate (Y/N) :
Have you qualified the NET Examination (Y/N) :
How many years of Experience do you have :
How many Research Papers have you published :
How many Books have you published :
The details you have entered are not eligible for applying for
the post of professor in our university
THANK YOU
```

Program 15.9 Write a program that has a class `Matrix`, overload the += operator, and throws an exception if number of rows and columns of the two matrices are not equal.

Programming Tip: When the catch statement is reached, all of the automatic variables that are in scope between the throw and catch statements are destroyed in a process known as stack unwinding.

```
using namespace std;
#include<iostream>
#include<exception>
class Error{};
template <class Type>
class Matrix
{   int rows, cols;
    Type mat[5][5];
  public:
    Matrix(int r, int c)
         {  rows = r;
            cols = c;
         }
         void read_matrix()
         {  for(int i=0;i<rows;i++)
              {  for(int j=0;j<cols;j++)
               cin>>mat[i][j];
     }
 }
 void display_matrix()
 {  for(int i=0;i<rows;i++)
      {  cout<<"\n";
         for(int j=0;j<cols;j++)
         cout<<" "<<mat[i][j];
 }
```

```
    }
    Matrix & operator+=(Matrix &M)
    {  if(rows != M.rows || cols != M.cols)
            throw Error();
       else
       {  for(int i=0;i<rows;i++)
          {  for(int j=0;j<cols;j++)
               mat[i][j] += M.mat[i][j];
          }
          return *this;
       }
    }
};
int main()
{  int r, c;
   cout<<"\n Enter the number of rows and columns for the first matrix : ";
   cin>>r>>c;
   Matrix <int> M1(r,c);
   cout<<"\n Enter the elements of the first matrix : ";
   M1.read_matrix();
   cout<<"\n Enter the number of rows and columns for the second matrix : ";
   cin>>r>>c;
   Matrix <int> M2(r,c);
   cout<<"\n Enter the elements of the second matrix : ";
   M2.read_matrix();
   try
   {  M1 += M2;
   cout<<"\n The resultant matrix is : \n";
        M1.display_matrix();
   }
   catch(Error)
   {  cout<<"\n Number of rows and columns must be equal";
   }
   cout<<"\n EXITING MAIN()";
}
```

OUTPUT

```
Enter the number of rows and columns for the first matrix : 2 2
Enter the elements of the first matrix : 1 2 3 4
Enter the number of rows and columns for the second matrix : 2 3
Enter the elements of the second matrix : 5 6 7 8 9 1
Number of rows and columns must be equal
EXITING MAIN()
```

15.6 HANDLING UNCAUGHT EXCEPTIONS

In C++, the following process takes place when an exception occurs in the try block.

- If no exception is generated, all the statements in the try block are executed and the control goes to the statement immediately following the catch block.
- If an exception occurs, it is thrown and then the following steps are taken to handle the exception.

Programming Tip: All errors are exceptions, but not necessarily all exceptions are errors.

- The control goes to the first catch block to check if the exception type matches with that of the catch block.
- If a match is not found, then the control passes to the next catch until a match is found.
- If a match is found then the body of that catch block is executed. In case no match is found, then the compiler looks for a `catch(...)`. If it is present, the block is executed; otherwise, `terminate()` is invoked.

Hence, in C++, all the uncaught exceptions are handled by `terminate()` and `unexpected()`. In addition to these functions, C++ also supports the use of `set_terminate()` and `set_unexpected()`, which are explained in this section.

`terminate()` `terminate()` is invoked when there is no exception handler to handle the raised exception. The `terminate()`, in turn, invokes another function `abort()`, which causes immediate termination of the program being executed. The following program code invokes the `terminate()`, and hence the `abort()` resulting in abnormal termination of the program code.

Example 15.13 Using `terminate()`

```
using namespace std;
#include<iostream>
class Error{};
void main()
{  try
   {  cout<<"\n Throwing Exception";
      throw Error();
   }
catch(int)
   {  cout<<"\n It will never get executed";
   }
}
```

OUTPUT

```
Throwing Exception
Abnormal Program Termination
```

`set_terminate()` C++ allows programmers to modify the way the program will terminate when an exception is raised and is not caught by an exception handler. For this, a function `set_terminate()` is used that invokes a user-defined function rather than invoking the `abort()`. However, the user-defined function must get itself registered with the `set_terminate()`.

The syntax is `set_terminate(terminate_handler)`.

where `terminate_handler` is the function that will be used to `abort()` the program. The following program code illustrates this concept.

Example 15.14 Using `set_terminate()`

```
using namespace std;
#include<iostream>
#include<exception>
```

Programming Tip: catch(...), if included must always be the last catch, unless it is the only catch of the clause.

```
class Error{};
void My_Terminate_Func()  // invoked to handle exception
{  cout<<"\n In My Terminate Function";
   cout<<"\n Abnormal Program Termination";
   exit(1);
}
int main()
{  set_terminate(My_Terminate_Func);
   try
   {  cout<<"\n Throwing Exception";
      throw Error();  // exception thrown
   }
   catch(int)  //exception uncaught
   {  cout<<"\n It will never get executed";
   }
}
```

OUTPUT

```
Throwing Exception
In My Terminate Function
Abnormal Program Termination
```

Explanation: Note that since `set_terminate()` is defined in `except.h`, we have included that file. In `main()`, we have used the `set_terminate()` and registered the `My_Terminate_Func()` with it. Whenever an exception is raised and is uncaught, the user-defined terminate function will execute and not the `abort()`.

In the `My_Terminate_Func(),exit(1)` has been used to end the program.

Note Both user-defined `terminate()` or default `abort()` take no argument and returns nothing.

`unexpected()` The `unexpected()` is automatically invoked when a function throws an exception not listed in its exception specification. The `unexpected()`, in turn, invokes the `terminate()` which invokes the `abort()`. The program code given next invokes the `abort()` through the `terminate()` and the `unexpected()`. The given code demonstrates the situation when `unexpected()` is called.

Example 15.15 Using `unexpected()`

```
using namespace std;
#include<iostream>
class Error{};
int main() throw(int)
{  try
   {  cout<<"n Throwing Exception of class Error Type";
      throw Error();
   }
   catch(int)
   {  cout<<"\n Caught an Exception";
   }
   cout<<"\n EXITING MAIN()";
}
```

OUTPUT

```
Throwing Exception of class Error Type
Abnormal Program Termination
```

`set_unexpected()` The `set_unexpected()` allows a programmer to execute a user-defined function when a function throws an exception not listed in its exception specifications. The user-defined function once registered with the `set_unexpected()`, may involve `abort()`, `exit()`, or `terminate()`. The program code given here illustrates this concept.

Example 15.16 Using `set_unexpected()`

```
using namespace std;
#include<iostream>
#include<exception>
class Error{};
void My_Unexpected()
{  cout<<"\n In My Unexpected Function";
   cout<<"\n Program Terminating Abnormally";
   exit(1);
}
void Func() throw(int)
{     cout<<"\n Throwing Exception of class Error Type";
          throw Error();
}
int main()
{  set_unexpected(My_Unexpected);
   try
   {   Func();
   }
   catch(...)
   {  cout<<"\n Caught an Exception";
   }
   cout<<"\n EXITING MAIN()";
}
```

Programming Tip: A function without an exception specification allows any object to be thrown from the function.

OUTPUT

```
Throwing Exception of class Error Type
In My Unexpected Function
Program Terminating Abnormally
```

15.7 STANDARD EXCEPTIONS

In addition to the user-defined exceptions, C++ also has its own exception handling logic which can be thrown from the try block and handled by the catch block. C++ has an exception class, `std::exception` defined in the exception header file. In this class, seven types of exceptions are defined, of which two most important exceptions are logic and runtime error. While logic errors are related to the logic of the program, run time errors, on the other hand, are error detected during the execution of the program. Table 15.1 gives a summary of the exceptions specified in the `std::exception` class.

It is not uncommon that many times, the cause of the error is not obvious. Therefore, to have a better understanding of what caused an error, the exception class has a public virtual function called `what()` that returns a string that explains the error. The program code given next illustrates the use of `what()`.

Table 15.1 Exceptions in `std::exception`

Type of exception	Position when it was generated
Logic errors • domain_error • invalid_argument • length_error • out_of_range	Logical errors in the program • invalid function argument • invalid arguments in C++ standard functions • length of object exceeds maximum allowable length • array index out of range
Run-time error • range_error • overflow_error • underflow_error	Error during execution • error in standard template library (STL) container • overflow in STL container • underflow in STL container
bad_alloc	Memory could not be allocated
bad_exception	Exception types does not match type of any catch block
ios_base::failure	Error in processing external file
bad_typeid	Error in typeid
bad_cast	Error in dynamic cast

Example 15.17 Using `what()`

```
using namespace std;
#include<iostream>
#include<stdexcept>
int main()
{  try
   {  int * arr = new int[100000000000000000000000000000000000000000000000000];
   cout<<"\n Memory allocated";
   }
catch(exception & e)
  {  cout<<"\n Memory Allocation Failed"<<"\t"<<e.what();
  }
cout<<"\n EXITING MAIN()";
}
```

OUTPUT

```
Memory Allocation Failed  bad_alloc
EXITING MAIN()
```

C++ allows programmers to define their own exceptions by inheriting and overriding exception class functionality. The following program code shows the implementation of programmer defined exception in standard way.

Example 15.18 Programmer defined exception

```
#include<iostream>
#include<stdexcept>
using namespace std;
struct MyException : public exception  // inheriting class exception
{  const char * what () const throw ()
// public virtual and constant member function that is being overridden
  {    return "\n Exception - in what()";
  }
};
main()
{  try
  {
throw MyException();  // throwing customized exception
  }
catch(MyException & e)  //exception caught
  {
cout<< "MyException caught " ;
cout<<e.what() ;
  }
cout<<"\n EXITING MAIN()";
}
```

OUTPUT

```
MyException caught
Exception - in what()
EXITING MAIN()
```

15.8 ADVANTAGES OF EXCEPTION HANDLING

- Exception handling helps programmers develop fault-tolerant systems. A fault-tolerant system enhances reliability by allowing the program to provide service in the presence of one or more faults. To achieve this, exception handling routine detects faults and tries to rectify them.
- Exception handling separates the error handling code from the program code. This makes the code more readable and understandable.
- C++ allows exceptions to be handled outside of the regular code. This eases the task of structuring the program code and enables centralized handling of exceptions.
- Functions can handle any exception they choose. Since a raised exception is passed back up the stack of calling functions, it can be handled at any place. This means that a function can throw many exceptions, but may choose to handle only some of them. Other exceptions which are thrown, but not caught can be handled by caller. If the caller does not catch the thrown exception, it can be handled by caller of the caller.

- With exception handling, the program does not end abruptly. Rather the program terminates gracefully by giving a proper message stating the reason of the exception. If there is any statement after the catch block then instead of terminating the program, it continues to execute the statement.

15.9 WORD OF CAUTION

- To define user-defined exceptions and then incorporate them into pre-existing classes, the engineering effort involved in throwing and handling those exceptions must first be estimated.
- Exception handling many times gives a false impression of security to the programmers. They think that their programs are robust enough to handle the errors while in reality they may be getting even more errors.

Therefore, before implementing exception handling in your program codes, you must take care of the following points:

- Do not throw an exception unless absolutely necessary.
- If an exception is thrown before the execution of constructor is complete, the destructor for that object will not be called.
- Throwing an exception deep inside the nested function(s) should be avoided.

```
Func()
{  //.....
     {  //......
        {  //....
            {  //....
                 {  throw e;
                 }
            }
        }
     }
}// avoid such code
```

- Programmers must keep in mind that in exception handling routines, implicit type conversion does not take place for primitive types. For example, in the following program, "x" is not implicitly converted to int.

```
using namespace std;
#include<iostream>
main()
{  try
   {     throw 'x';
   }
   catch(int)
   {  cout<<"\n Caught an exception";
   }
}
```

- A derived class exception should be caught before a base class exception.

Note C++ library has a standard exception class which is base class for all standard exceptions.

- If an exception is raised, all objects created inside the enclosing try block are destructed before the control is transferred to catch block. The following program code illustrates this concept.

Example 15.19 Sequence of object creation and destruction in try or catch block

```
using namespace std;
#include<iostream>
class Error
{  public:
        Error()
        {  cout<<"\n IN CONSTRUCTOR";
        }
        ~Error()
        {  cout<<"\n IN DESTRUCTOR";
        }
};
main()
{  try
   {  Error E;
      throw "EXCEPTION THROWN";
   }
   catch(char *mesg)
   {   cout<<"\n"<<mesg;
   }
   cout<<"\n EXITING MAIN()";
}

OUTPUT
IN CONSTRUCTOR
IN DESTRUCTOR
EXCEPTION THROWN
EXITING MAIN()
```

- `catch(...)`, if present, must be placed as the last catch block following a try block or else an error occurs because otherwise it would prevent more specific catch blocks from catching exceptions intended for them.
- You can also nest a try block within a catch block.

Points to Remember

- To catch exceptions, a portion of code is placed under exception inspection. This is done by enclosing that portion of code in a try block. When an exceptional circumstance arises within that block, an exception is thrown that transfers the control to the exception handler. If no exception is thrown, the code continues normally and all handlers are ignored.
- While logic errors occur due to poor understanding of problem and its solution, syntax errors, on the other hand, arises due to poor understanding of the language.
- The main aim of exception handling is to detect and report an exceptional condition(s) so that appropriate action can be taken to deal with it.
- It is possible to associate more than one catch statements with a single try block. This is usually done when a program segment has more than one condition to throw as an exception.
- `catch(…)` can be used along with other catch handlers, so that some specific types of exceptions are caught and handled by specific handlers and those exceptions that are not handled by those handlers can be handled by the `catch(…)`.
- Stack unwinding which is related to exception handling is the process of removing function entries from function call stack at run time. When an exception is thrown, the function call stack is searched for an exception handler.
- The exception handler in the catch block may decide to rethrow the exception without processing it using the `throw()`.

- To prevent such memory leak problems, the exception handling mechanism must be implemented in the constructor itself. This will enable programmers to free the memory allocated for data members before handling the exception.
- Exception handling mechanism can be used with overloaded operator functions to handle system generated or user-specified exceptions.
- `terminate()` is invoked when there is no exception handler to handle the raised exception.
- `set_terminate()` is used that invokes a user-defined function rather than invoking the `abort()`.
- `unexpected()` is automatically invoked when a function throws an exception not listed in its exception specification.
- `set_unexpected()` allows a programmer to execute a user-defined function when a function throws an exception not listed in its exception specifications.

Glossary

Catch block The block that catches the exception thrown from the try block and handles it

Exception handlers Exceptions provide a way to react to exceptional circumstances like run-time errors in programs by transferring control to special functions called exception handlers

Exceptions Run-time anomalies or unusual conditions

Throw point The point at which an exception is thrown

Try block A group of statements that may generate an exception

Exercises

Fill in the Blanks

1. Two types of errors are ____ and ____.
2. _____ are run-time anomalies or unusual conditions.
3. Exception handler is denoted by the keyword _____.
4. _____ will prevent a function from throwing any exception.
5. `terminate()` invokes ______, which causes immediate termination of the program being executed.
6. `set_terminate()` is defined in ________ header file.
7. `unexpected()` invokes the ______ which invokes the `abort()`.
8. The ______ allows a programmer to execute a user-defined function when a function throws an exception not listed in its exception specifications.
9. Exception handling helps programmers to develop ________ systems.

State True or False

1. Asynchronous exceptions can be controlled by a program.
2. Exceptions can be thrown from both try as well as the catch block.
3. The try block immediately follows the catch block.
4. If no exception is detected and thrown, then the catch block will still get executed.
5. If no match is found for the exception, then the program is terminated using the `abort()`.
6. A `const`, volatile, or reference type catch argument can match a non-constant, non-volatile, and non-reference type of exception.
7. `terminate()`or the `default abort()` takes only one argument.
8. Functions can handle any exception they choose.
9. We must throw as many exceptions as possible in our code.
10. In exception handling routines, implicit type conversion takes place for primitive types.
11. A derived class exception should be caught before a base class exception.
12. We can have a try block inside a catch block.

Multiple Choice Questions

1. Which errors occur due to poor understanding of problem and its solution?
   (a) Logic (b) Syntactic
   (c) Synchronous (d) Asynchronous
2. Which of the following is an example of a synchronous exception?
   (a) Keyboard interrupt (b) Disk failure
   (c) Hardware malfunction (d) None of these

3. Overflow and underflow conditions are examples of_____ ?
   (a) Logical errors
   (b) Syntactic errors
   (c) Synchronous exception
   (d) Asynchronous exception
4. After handling the exception handler code given in the catch block, the control goes to?
   (a) Throw point
   (b) Statement immediately following the catch block
   (c) try block (d) `main()`
5. In case more than one catch block matches the type of exception thrown, which catch block is executed?
   (a) First (b) Last
   (c) Second (d) All of these
6. The default exception handler must be placed at which location?
   (a) First (b) Last
   (c) Second (d) All of these
7. Which function is automatically invoked when a function throws an exception not listed in its exception specification?
   (a) `terminate()` (b) `set_terminate()`
   (c) `unexpected()` (d) `set_unexpected()`
8. `set_unexpected()`, may invoke which of the following functions?
   (a) `Abort()` (b) `Exit()`
   (c) `Terminate()` (d) All of these

Review Exercises

1. Differentiate between logical and syntactic errors.
2. What do you understand by synchronous and asynchronous exceptions?
3. Define exception. Give some common examples of exception that often occur in our program code.
4. Explain the two types of exceptions.
5. What is exception handling?
6. Explain the significance of try and catch block and give their syntax.
7. Can a try block be nested inside another try block? Give a suitable example to illustrate your answer.
8. When should we go for multiple catch blocks for a single try block?
9. Differentiate between throw and throw exception.
10. Why is it recommended to handle exceptions in class's constructor and destructor?
11. Explain the utility of `set_terminate()` with the help of an example.
12. Explain the utility of `set_unexpected()` with the help of an example.
13. List some advantages of using exception handling routines in your program.

Programming Exercises

1. Write a program that validates user's input.
2. Write a class `Student`. Use exception handling to read the data of 10 students.
3. Write a program that has multiple catch blocks.
4. Write a program that rethrows an exception.
5. Write a program with `catch(...)` handler.
6. Write a program that restricts the type of exceptions that a function can throw.
7. Write a program that throws an exception of class type.
8. Write a program that throws a nameless class object.
9. Write a program in which an exception thrown by one function is handled by another function.
10. Write a program that throws at least two exceptions from a class.
11. Write a program that throws an exception while allocating memory for a string.
12. Write a program that dynamically allocates memory for 50 objects of class student. Throw xalloc-exception if memory could not be allocated.
13. Write a program that has an exception handling block in the class's constructor.
14. Write a program that has an exception handling block in the class's destructor.
15. Write a program that overloads the /= operator in FRACTION class. Throw an exception if a divide by zero exception occurs.
16. Write a program that overloads the -= and /= operators in COMPLEX class. The program must throw an exception if divide by zero exception occurs or if the real parts of the two objects are zero.
17. Write a program that has a class `TIME`. Enter the time when a user started an online test and completed the test. Subtract the two time values and display the duration in which the test was completed. Throw exceptions whenever need arises such as invalid data, or if start time is greater than completion time.
18. Write a program that accepts date of birth along with other personal details of a person. Throw an exception if an invalid date is entered.
19. Write a program that finds square root of a number. Throw an exception if a negative number is entered.

20. Write a template class `Square` that finds the square of a number. Throw an exception if the instead of the number, user enters a character.
21. Write a class `Items_Sold` that stores the `product_code` and price of the item. Throw an exception if either the `product_code` or the price is less than zero.
22. Write a program that calls binary search function. Throw an exception if the array is not sorted.

Find the errors in the following codes

1.
```
using namespace std;
#include<iostream>
class Number
{  int num;
   public:
      Number(int i)
   {  num = 1;   }
      void getnum()
      {  try
         {  switch(num)
            {  case 1:
                  throw ("ONE");
               case 2:
                  throw "TWO";
                  break;
               case 3:
                  throw "THREE";
                  break;
            }
         }
      }
   void operaotr++()
   {  age+=10;
   }
};
int main()
{  Number ob(10);
   ob.getoccu();
   ++ob;
   ob.getnum();
   ++ob;
   ob.getnum();
   getche();
}
```

2.
```
using namespace std;
#include<iostream>
#include<exception>
void main()
{  catch(exception & e)
   {  cout<<"\n Caught an exception";
   }
}
```

3.
```
using namespace std;
#include<iostream>
#include<exception>
main()
{  try
   {  cout<<"\n Throwing an Exception";
   }
}
```

4.
```
using namespace std;
#include<iostream>
#include<exception>
main()
{  catch(Exception & e)
   {  cout<<"\n Caught an Exception";
   }
   try
   {  cout<<"\n Throwing an Exception";
   }
}
```

5.
```
using namespace std;
#include<iostream>
#include<exception>
void main()
{  try
   {  cout<<"\n Throwing an Exception";
   }
   catch(Exception & e)
   {  cout<<"\n Caught anException";
      throw exception();
   }
}
```

6.
```
using namespace std;
#include<iostream>
#include<stdexcept.h>
class Error{};
int main() throw()
{  try
   {  cout<<"\n Throwing an Exception";
      throw Error();
   }
   catch(Exception & e)
   {  cout<<"\n Caught and Exception";
   throw exception();
   }
}
```

7.
```
using namespace std;
#include<iostream>
#include<exception>
class Error{};
int main() throw()
{  try
   {  cout<<"\n Throwing an Exception";
```

```
    throw Error();
}
catch(Exception & e)
{   cout<<"\n Caught an Exception";
}
}
```

8.
```
using namespace std;
#include<iostream>
#include<exception>
class Error{};
void main() throw(int)
{   try
    {   cout<<"\n Throwing an Exception";
        throw Error();
    }
    catch(Exception & e)
    {   cout<<"\n Caught and Exception";
    }
}
```

Find the output of the following codes

1.
```
using namespace std;
#include<iostream>
void func(int i)
{   if(i)
        throw 1;
    else
    throw 0;
}
void func(char *n)
{   try
    {   if(n)
        throw "OK";
    else
    throw "ERROR";
    }
catch(char *name)
    {   cout<<"\n"<<name;
    }
}
int main()
{   try
    {   func("TEST");
    func(1);
    func(0);
    }
catch(int i)
    {   cout<<"\n"<<i;
    }
catch(char *name)
    {   cout<<"\n"<<name;
    }
}
```

2.
```
using namespace std;
#include<iostream>
class A
{   public:
    A()
    {   }
class B{};
class C : virtual public B   {   };
class D : virtual public B { };
voidgetOb()
        {   throw D();
        }
};
main()
{   A a;
    try
    {   a.getOb();
    }
catch(A::B&)
    {   cout<<"\n B";
    }
catch(A::C&)
    {   cout<<"\n C";
    }
catch(A::D&)
    {   cout<<"\n D";
    }
}
```

3.
```
using namespace std;
#include<iostream>
#include<exception>
class Error{};
void Func2() throw(Error)
{   cout<<"\n In Func2";
throw Error();
}
void Func1() throw()
{   try
    {   cout<<"\n In Func1";
    Func2();
    }
catch(…)
    { cout<<"\n In exception handler of
      Func1";
    }
}
int main()
{   try
    {   Func1();
    }
catch(…)
{   cout<<"\n In exception handler of main()";
}
getche();
```

```
}
```

4.
```
using namespace std;
#include<iostream>
int main()
{
    int age =0;
    try
    {
        if(age <0)
            throw"Positive Number Required";
        cout<< age;
    }
    catch(const char*Message)
    {
        cout<<"Error: "<< Message;
    }
}
```

5.
```
using namespace std;
#include<iostream>
int main()
{
    int x =-1;
    char *ptr;
    ptr = new char[256];
    try
    {
        if(x <0)
        {
            throw x;
        }
        if(ptr ==NULL)
        {
            throw" ptr is NULL ";
        }
    }
    catch(...)
    {
        cout<<"Exception occurred";
    }
}
```

6.
```
#include <iostream>
#include <exception>
using namespace std;
void myunexpected ()
{
    cout<<"unexpected called\n";
    throw 0;
}
void myfunction() throw(int)
{
    throw 'x';
}
int main ()
{
    set_unexpected (myunexpected);
    try
    {
        myfunction();
    }
    catch(int)
    {
    cout<<"caught int";
    }
    catch(…)
    {
        cout<<"caught other exception";
    }
}
```

7.
```
using namespace std;
#include<iostream>
main()
{
    try
    {
        throw 1;
    }
    catch(int a)
    {
        cout<<"exception number:  "<< a;
    }
    cout<<"No exception ";
}
```

8.
```
using namespace std;
#include<iostream>
void test(int x)
{
    try
    {
        if(x >0)
            throw x;
        else
            throw'x';
    }
    catch(int x)
    {
        cout<<"integer:"<<x;
    }
    catch(char x)
    {
        cout<<"character:"<< x;
    }
}
int main()
{
    test(10);
    test(0);
}
```

9.
```
using namespace std;
#include<iostream>
void PrintSequence(int StopNum)
{
    int Num = 1;
    while(true)
    {
        if(Num >= StopNum)
            throw Num;
        cout<<Num;
        Num++;
    }
}
int main()
{
    try
    {
        PrintSequence(2);
    }
    catch(int ExNum)
    {
    cout<<"exception: "<< ExNum;
    }
}
```

10.
```
using namespace std;
#include<iostream>
#include<string.h>
int main()
{
    double Op1 =10, Op2 =5, Res;
    char Op;
    try
    {
    if(Op !='+'&& Op !='-'&& Op
    !='*'&& Op !='/')
        throw Op;
    switch(Op)
    {
        case'+':
    Res = Op1 + Op2;
            break;
        case'-':
    Res = Op1 - Op2;
            break;
        case'*':
    Res = Op1 * Op2;
            break;
        case'/':
    Res = Op1 / Op2;
            break;
        }
    cout<<"\n"<< Op1 <<" "<< Op <<"
    "<< Op2 <<" = "<< Res;
  }
    catch(const char n)
    {
        cout<< n <<" is not a
        valid operator";
    }
}
```

11.
```
using namespace std;
#include<iostream>
#include<math.h>
double MySqrt(double d)
{
    if(d<0.0)
        throw "Cannot take sqrt of
        negative number";
    return sqrt(d);
}
int main()
{
    double d =5;
    cout<< MySqrt(d);
}
```

12.
```
using namespace std;
#include<iostream>
class One
{ };
class Two : public One{ };
void Func()
{
    throw Two();
}
main()
{
    try
    {
        Func();
    }
    catch(const OneObj&)
    {
        cerr<<"Caught an exception";
    }
}
```

13.
```
#include<typeinfo>
#include<iostream>
using namespace std;
class One
{
    virtual int  Func() { }
};
main ()
{
    try
    {
        One *one=NULL;
            typeid(*one);
```

```
    }
    catch(std::exception& typevar)
    {
        cout<<"Exception: "<< typevar.
what()<< endl;
    }
}
```

14.
```
using namespace std;
#include<iostream>
int main()
{
int x =-1;
try
{
    if(x <0)
        throw x;
    else
        cout<<x;
}
catch(int x )
{
    cout<<"Exception occurred:
Thrown value is "<< x;
    }
}
```

15.
```
using namespace std;
#include<iostream>
#include <string.h>
int main ()
{
    int num =3;
    string str_bad ="wrong
number used";
try
{
    if( num ==1)
        throw5;
    if( num ==2)
        throw1.1f;
    if( num !=1|| num !=2)
        throw str_bad;
    }
    catch(int a)
    {
        cout<<"Exception is: "<< a;
    }
    catch(float b)
    {
        cout<<"Exception is: "<< b;
    }
    catch(…)
    {
        cout<< str_bad;
    }
}
```

16.
```
#include<typeinfo>
#include<iostream>
using namespace std;
class A
{
    public:
    virtual ~A();
};
main()
{
    A *a = NULL;
    try
    {
        cout<<typeid(*a).name();
    }
    catch(bad_typeid)
    {
        cout<<"Object is NULL";
    }
}
```

Answers

Fill in the Blanks

1. Logical and syntactic; **2.** Exceptions; **3.** Catch; **4.** `Throw()`; **5.** `abort()`; **6.** `except.h`; **7.** `terminate()`; **8.** `set_unexpected()`; **9.** fault tolerant

State True or False

1. False **2.** True **3.** False **4.** False **5.** True **6.** True **7.** False **8.** True
9. False **10.** False **11.** True **12.** True

Multiple Choice Questions

1. (a); **2.** (d); **3.** (c); **4.** (b); **5.** (a); **6.** (b); **7.** (c); **8.** (d)

CHAPTER 16

STL and New Features in C++

KEY Concepts

Containers • Algorithms • Iterators • String class • Boolean data type • Explicit and mutable • RTTI operators • Namespaces

INTRODUCTION

The standard template library (STL) is a collection of classes that provide templated containers, algorithms, and iterators (Fig. 16.1). It contains common classes or algorithms so that programmers can use them without having to write and debug the classes. The STL components, which are now a part of C++ library, are defined in the namespace `std`. Therefore, all programs that make use of STL components must have the directive `using namespace std;`

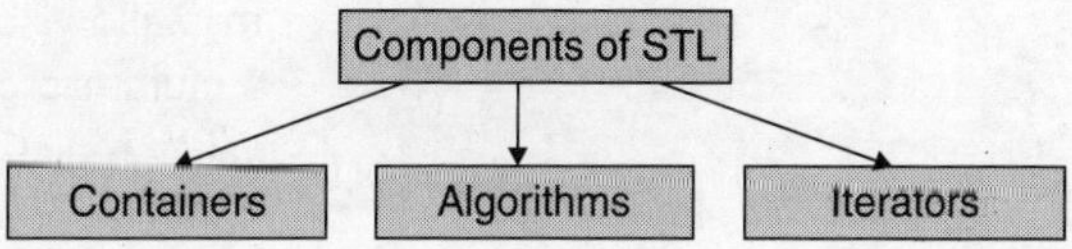

Figure 16.1 Classes in STL

16.1 CONTAINERS

Containers are objects that

- store data
- define the manner in which data will be stored
- are implemented using templates, and can, therefore, store data of different data types

There are three types of containers as shown in Table 16.1. Each container class defines functions to manipulate the data. For example, for manipulating the contents of a vector, the class must have functions to insert, delete, sort, and swap elements.

Table 16.1 Types of containers

Category	Description	Types
Sequence containers	• Data has a linear sequence • Each element is related to other elements by its position along the line • Elements can be accessed using iterator	Vector—Dynamic array that allows insertion/ deletion at the end. Permits direct access to an element. Defined in header file as `<vector>`. List—A bi-direction linear list that allows insertion/deletion at any position. Defined in header file `<list>`. Dequeue—A double-ended queue that allows insertions and deletions at both ends. Permits direct access to any element. Defined in header file `<deque>`.
Associative containers	• Supports direct access to elements using keys • No sequential ordering of elements • Data is sorted while being input • Data is stored using a tree structure • Facilitates fast searching, insertion and deletion • Slow for random access • Not efficient for sorting	Set and multiset—Store multiple data elements and provide functions to manipulate elements using their key values. A multiset is the same as a set, the only difference is that multiset allows duplicate data but a set does not. For example, a set or a multiset may be used to store objects of employee class that are ordered based on their `Employee_ID` as keys. Defined in header file `<set>`. Map and multimap—Stores data as pairs of key and value. While key is used for indexing and sorting, value is used to store data. Allows manipulation of values using keys. Map and multimap are same, the only difference is that map allows only one key for a given value but a multimap permits use of multiple keys for a value. A dictionary is an example of a multimap where, key is the word and value is the meaning of that word. Moreover, a word can have multiple meanings and multiple words can have the same meaning.
Derived containers	• Created from sequence containers • Does not support iterators • Because of no iterator, they cannot be used for data manipulation • Support two member functions—`push()` and `pop()` for inserting and deleting elements	Stack—It is a last in first out (LIFO) data structure (in which data that was last inserted is first to be taken out). Insertion and deletion can be done only at one end. Queue—It is a First in first out (FIFO) data structure (in which data that was first inserted is first to be taken out). Insertion is done at one end and deletion from the other. Priority queue—The first element to be taken out is the highest priority of the element.

16.2 ALGORITHMS

Reinforcing the concept of reusability, STL algorithms consist of functions that programmers can directly use in their code to process data stored in different containers for processing their data. Although each type of container has its own set of functions to perform basic operations, STL defines more than 60 algorithms to facilitate users to perform extended and complex operations. These STL algorithms categorized under five types (Fig. 16.2) are neither declared as member functions of any container class nor are defined as friend functions. They can be accessed by including the header file `<algorithm>`. The utility of these functions are given in Table 16.2.

Retrieve or non mutating	`adjacent_find(), count(), count_if(), equal(), find(), find_end(), find_first_of(), find_if(). for_each(), mismatch(), search(), search_n()`
Mutating	`copy(), copy_backward(), fill(), fill_n(), generate(), generate_n(), iter_swap(), random_shuffle(), remove(), remove_copy(), remove_copy_if(), remove_if(), replace(), replace_copy(), replace_copy_if(), reverse(), reverse_copy(), rotate(), rotate_copy(), swap(), swap_ranges(), transform(), unique(), unique_copy()`
Sorting	`binary_search(), equal_range(), inplace_merge(), lower_bound(), make_heap(), merge(), nth_element(), partial_sort(), partial_sort_copy(), partition(), pop_heap(), push_heap(), sort(), sort_heap(), stable_partition(), stable_sort(), upper_bound()`
Set	`includes(), set_difference(), set_intersection(), set_symmetric_difference(), set_union()`
Relational	`equal(), lexicographical_compare(), max(), max_element(), min(), min_element(), mismatch()`

Figure 16.2 Types of algorithms

Table 16.2 Algorithms in STL

Function	Purpose
• `for_each`	Applies a piece of code to a range of elements
• `count/count_if`	Gives the number of elements that satisfies a specific criteria
• `equal`	Determines if two sets of elements are the same
• `find/find_if/find_if_not`	Finds the first element that meets the given criteria
• `find_end`	Finds the last sequence of elements in a certain range
• `find_first_of`	Searches for any one of a set of elements
• `adjacent_find`	Finds the first two adjacent items that are equal

(Contd)

Table 16.2 (*Contd*)

Function	Purpose
• search	Searches for a range of elements
• search_n	Searches for a sequence of a specified number of similar elements
• copy/copy_if/ copy_n	Copies elements to a new location
• copy_backward	Copies elements in backwards order
• fill	Assigns elements a certain value
• fill_n	Assigns a value to a number of elements
• remove/remove_if	Removes elements
• remove_copy/remove_copy_if	Copies elements after removing certain elements
• replace/replace_if	Replaces elements that matches the condition
• replace_copy/replace_copy_if	Copies elements after replacing with specified value
• swap	Swaps the values of two elements
• swap_ranges	Swaps two ranges of elements
• reverse	Reverses the order of elements
• reverse_copy	Copies elements in reverse order
• rotate	Rotates the order of elements
• rotate_copy	Copies and rotate elements
• random_shuffle/shuffle	Randomly re-orders elements
• unique	Removes consecutive duplicate elements
• unique_copy	Copies after removing duplicate elements
• partition	Divides a range of elements into two groups
• is_sorted	Checks whether a range is sorted into ascending order (function template)
• is_sorted_until (C++11)	Finds the largest sorted subrange (function template)
• sort	Sorts a range into ascending order (function template)
• partial_sort	Sorts the first N elements of a range
• partial_sort_copy	Copies and partially sorts elements in a range
• stable_sort	Sorts a range of elements while preserving order between equal elements
• lower_bound	Finds the first occurrence of a value

(*Contd*)

Table 16.2 (*Contd*)

Function	Purpose
• `upper_bound`	Finds the last occurrence of a value
• `merge`	Merges two sorted sequence of elements
• `includes`	Returns true if one set is a subset of another
• `set_difference`	Finds the difference between two sets
• `set_intersection`	Finds the intersection of two sets
• `set_symmetric_difference`	Finds the symmetric difference between two sets
• `set_union`	Finds the union of two sets
• `max`	Returns the larger of two elements
• `max_element`	Returns the largest element in a range
• `min`	Returns the smaller of two elements
• `min_element`	Returns the smallest element in a range
• `lexicographical_compare`	Returns true if one range is lexicographically less than another
• `adjacent_difference`	Finds the differences between adjacent elements in a range
• `partial_sum`	Finds the partial sum of a range of elements

16.3 ITERATORS

Iterators are pointer-like entities that are used to access the elements stored in the container. Iterators are basically used for traversing the elements of container. This process of traversing from one element to the next is called iterating through the container. All containers provide two main types of iterators as follows:

```
container :: iterator, which provides a read/write iterator
container :: const_iterator, which provides a read-only iterator
```

STL offers five types of iterators (Table 16.3) that can be used with different types of containers. Remember that only sequence containers and associative containers can be used with iterators.

Table 16.3 Types of iterators

Type	Direction	Access type	Function	Ability to be saved
Input	Forward	Linear	Read	No
Output	Forward	Linear	Write	No
Forward	Forward	Linear	Read and Write both	Yes
Bidirectional	Forward backward both	Linear	Read and Write both	Yes
Random	Forward backward both	Random	Read and Write both	Yes

Some overloaded operators that are defined on iterators include the following:

- The dereferencing operator (`*`) that returns the element that iterator is currently pointing at.
- The increment operator (`++`) which moves the iterator to the next element in the container.
- The decrement operator (`--`) which moves the iterator to the previous element in the container.
- The equality (`==`) and the inequality operator (`!=`) to compare two iterators to determine if they are pointing to the same element. However, to compare two iterators, first dereference it and then use the comparison operator.
- The assignment operator (`=`) to assign a new position to the iterator.

Each container class has four basic member functions that can be used with the assignment operator. These functions are as follows:

- `begin()` that returns an iterator to the beginning of the elements in the container.
- `end()` that returns an iterator to the element just past the end of the elements.
- `cbegin()` that is same as `begin()` with a difference that it returns a read-only (`const`) iterator.
- `cend()`that is same as `end()` with a difference that it returns a read-only (`const`) iterator.

16.4 USING CONTAINERS

Although it is impossible to discuss all the containers in this book, we will study about important containers like vectors, maps, and dequeues in this section.

16.4.1 Vector

Vectors are sequence containers that represent dynamic arrays that can change in size. Like arrays, vectors store its elements in contiguous memory locations. The main advantage of vectors is that it may grow in size when number of elements increases and shrink in size when a number of elements are deleted. Let us now write a program which uses the container vector that stores data in contiguous memory locations and provides random access to any element using the overloaded `[]` operator. Since vector is a dynamic array, its size can change at the runtime.

Example 16.1 Using the vector container

```
using namespace std;
#include<iostream>
#include<vector>
int main()
{
int num;
vector<int>vect;
cout<<"\n Enter the elements of the vector : ";
for(int i=0; i<10; i++)
    { cin>>num;
vect.push_back(num); // insert at end of array
    }
cout<<"\n Elements of the vector are : \n";
for(int i=0; i<vect.size(); i++)
cout<<vect[i] << " ";
// iterator points to the first element
vector<int> :: iterator itr = vect.begin();
// inserts one element 25 at the 4th location from the beginning
vect.insert(itr+4,1,25);
//Deleting an element
```

```
vect.erase(vect.begin()+8);    // deletes the 6th element
cout<<"\n Contents after inserting an element at the 4th position and 6th element : \n";
for(int i=0; i<vect.size(); i++)
cout<<vect[i] << " ";
}
```

OUTPUT

```
Enter the elements of the vector : 1 2 3 4 5 6 7 8 9 10
Elements of the vector are : 1 2 3 4 5 6 7 8 9 10
Contents after inserting an element at the 4th position and
8th element : 1 2 3 4 2 5 6 7 9 10
```

Explanation: In the program, we have declared an integer vector and used the `push_back()` to insert an element at the end, `erase()` is used to delete an item, and `insert()` is used to add an element to the vector at the specified location. To delete more than one value in a specified range, use the `erase(m,n)` variant that deletes *m–n* values starting from the *m*th value to the *n*–1th value. For example, `erase(4,8)` deletes the value stored at locations 4,5,6, and 7. Other functions that the container vector supports are given in Table 16.4.

Table 16.4 Functions supported by vector

Function	Purpose
`push_back()`	Adds an element at the end
`erase()`	Deletes elements
`insert()`	Inserts elements
`size()`	Gives the number of elements
`at()`	Gives a reference to the specified element
`back()`	Gives a reference to the last element
`begin()`	Gives a reference to the first element
`capacity()`	Gives the capacity of the vector
`clear()`	Deletes all elements from the vector
`empty()`	Checks if the vector is empty
`end()`	Gives a reference to the end of the vector
`pop_back()`	Deletes the last element
`resize()`	Changes the size of the vector
`swap()`	Interchanges the values stored at specified locations

16.4.2 Dequeue

A dequeue is a double-ended queue that allows insertions and deletions at both ends. The program given next creates adequeue that inserts one element at the end and the other element at the front of the dequeue.

Example 16.2 Using dequeue

```
using namespace std;
#include<iostream>
#include<deque>
int main()
{
int num;
deque<int>deq;
cout<<"\n Enter the elements in the dequeue : ";
for(int i=0; i<5; i++)
  {      cin>>num;
         deq.push_back(num); // insert at end of array
         cin>>num;
         deq.push_front(num); // insert at front of array
  }
    cout<<"\n The contents of the dequeue are : ";
for(int i=0; i<deq.size(); i++)
cout<< "\t"<<deq[i];
}
```

OUTPUT

```
Enter the elements in the dequeue : 1 2 3 4 5 6 7 8 9 10
The contents of the dequeue are : 10 8 6 4 2 1 3 5 7 9
```

16.4.3 List

A list is a container in which element points to the next and previous elements in the list. It supports only sequential or linear access. Therefore, if you want to access the fourth element, you cannot access it directly. You will have to start from the beginning and traverse through the list until the desired element is found.

Let us write a program that makes use of container list. The program will display the elements of the list, sort the list, merge two lists, and also display the elements in reverse.

Example 16.3 Using list

```
using namespace std;
#include<list>
#include<iostream>
#include<stdlib.h>
int main()
{
int num, option;
list<int> L1;
list<int> L2;
list<int> :: iterator itr;
      cout<<"\n Enter the elements in the first list : ";
         for(int i=0; i<5; i++)
             { cin>>num;
                L1.push_back(num); // insert at end of list
```

```
            }
cout<<"\n Enter the elements for the second list : ";
    for(int i=0; i<5; i++)
    {   cin>>num;
        L2.push_back(num); // insert at end of list
    }
    cout<<"\n LIST 1 is : ";
    for(itr = L1.begin();itr!=L1.end();itr++)
        cout<<"\t"<<*itr;
    cout<<"\n LIST 2 is : ";
    for(itr = L2.begin();itr!=L2.end();itr++)
        cout<<"\t"<<*itr;
    L1.reverse();
    cout<<"\n LIST 1 is : ";
    for(itr = L1.begin();itr!=L1.end();itr++)
        cout<<"\t"<<*itr;
    L2.sort();
    cout<<"\n LIST 2 is : ";
    for(itr = L2.begin();itr!=L2.end();itr++)
        cout<<"\t"<<*itr;
    L1.merge(L2);
    cout<<"\n MERGED LIST is : ";
    for(itr = L1.begin();itr!=L1.end();itr++)
        cout<<"\t"<<*itr;
}
```

OUTPUT

```
Enter the elements in the first list : 1 2 3 4 5
Enter the elements in the second list :9 8 7 6 5
LIST 1 is: 1 2 3 4 5
LIST 2 is : 9 8 7 6 5
LIST 1 is : 5 4 3 2 1
LIST 2 is : 5 6 7 8 9
MERGED LIST is :5 4 3 2 1 5 6 7 8 9
```

Explanation: The program uses `push_back()` to insert an element at the end, `sort()` to sort the list, `reverse()` to reverse the list, and `merge()` to join two list objects. Besides these functions, `<list>` also supports all the functions supported by `<vector>` (Table 16.5). However, in addition to all the stated functions, `<list>` adds three more functions as follows:

- `Splice()` which inserts a list into the invoking list
- `Unique()` which deletes the duplicating elements in the list
- `Pop_front()` and `push_front()` to delete from or add an element to the front of the list

Table 16.5 Functions supported by list

Function	Purpose
empty()	Tests whether container is empty
size()	Returns size of the list
max_size()	Returns maximum size of the list

(Contd)

Table 16.5 (*Contd*)

Function	Purpose
`front()`	Accesses the first element
`back()`	Accesses the last element
`push_front()`	Inserts the element at the beginning
`pop_front()`	Deletes the first element
`push_back()`	Inserts the element at the end
`insert()`	Inserts elements
`erase()`	Deletes elements
`swap()`	Swaps elements
`resize()`	Changes the size of the list
`clear()`	Removes all the elements
`remove()`	Removes a specific element
`remove_if()`	Removes element(s) that match a specific condition
`merge()`	Merges two lists
`unique()`	Removes duplicate elements
`sort()`	Sorts the list
`reverse()`	Reverses the list

16.4.4 Maps

Maps are implemented as associative array in which key is specified using the subscript operator as `Scode["Delhi"] = 011`. To insert an entry in the map, write `Scode["Chandigarh"] =0172`. Map supports functions such as `begin()`, `clear()`, `empty()`, `end()`, `erase()`, `find()`, `insert()`, `size()`, and `swap()`.

The program uses two members first and second with the iterator to access the two entries of the map (first for the key and second for the value).

Example 16.4 Using maps

```
using namespace std;
#include<string.h>
#include<iostream>
#include<map>
#include<utility>
int main()
{
   map<int, string> Scode;
   // 1) Assignment using array index notation
   Scode[11] = "New Delhi";
```

```
    Scode[22] = "Mumbai";
    Scode[33] = "Kolkatta";
    Scode[44] = "Chennai";
    cout << "Map size: " << Scode.size() << endl;
    for(map<int,string>::iterator ii=Scode.begin(); ii!=Scode.end(); ++ii)
    {
        cout<< (*ii).first << ": " << (*ii).second << endl;
    }
    cout<< endl << "Reverse Order:" << endl;
    for(map<int,string>::reverse_iterator ii=Scode.rbegin(); ii!=Scode.rend(); ++ii)
    {
        cout<< (*ii).first << ": " << (*ii).second << endl;
    }

}
```

OUTPUT

```
Map size: 4
11: New Delhi
22: Mumbai
33: Kolkatta
44: Chennai

Reverse Order:
44: Chennai
33: Kolkatta
22: Mumbai
11: New Delhi
```

Note that although the entries were not sorted while input but during output the entries are sorted. This is because the list is automatically sorted based on the key.

Program 16.1 Write a program that finds the minimum and the maximum element from a list.

```
using namespace std;
#include<iostream>
#include<list>
#include<algorithm>
int main()
{
    int num;
    list<int> L;
    cout<<"\n Enter the elements of the list : ";
    for(int i=0; i< 10; i++)
    {       cin>>num;
            L.push_back(num);
    }
    list<int>::const_iterator itr;
itr = min_element(L.begin(), L.end());
cout<< "\n The minimum element = "<<*itr;
itr = max_element(L.begin(), L.end());
```

```
cout<< "\n The maximum element = "<<*itr;
}
```

OUTPUT

```
Enter the elements of the list : 1 2 3 4 5 6 7 8 9 10
The minimum element = 1
The maximum element = 10
```

Program 16.2 Write a program that inserts a number before the specified number in the list.

```
using namespace std;
#include<iostream>
#include<list>
#include<algorithm>
int main()
{
  int num;
  list<int> L;
  cout<<"\n Enter the elements of the list : ";
  for(int i=0; i< 10; i++)
  {       cin>>num;
          L.push_back(num);
  }
  cout<<"\n Enter the number before which the new number must be inserted : ";
  cin>>num;
  list<int>::iterator itr;
  itr = find(L.begin(), L.end(), num); // find num in the list
  cout<<"\n Enter the new number to be inserted : ";
  cin>>num;
  L.insert(itr, num); // use list::insert to insert the value 8 before it
  cout<<"\n Contents of the list are : ";
  for(itr = L.begin(); itr != L.end(); itr++) // for loop with iterators
  cout<< "\t"<<*itr;
}
```

OUTPUT

```
Enter the elements of the list : 1 2 3 4 5 6 7 8 9 10
Enter the number before which the new number must be inserted : 8
Enter the new number to be inserted : 0
Contents of the list are : 1 2 3 4 5 6 7 0 8 9 10
```

Program 16.3 Write a program that sorts the contents of the vector and displays it in reverse.

```
using namespace std;
#include<iostream>
#include<vector>
#include<algorithm>
int main()
{
  int num;
  vector<int>vect;
  cout<<"\n Enter the contents of the vector : ";
  for(int i=0;i<10;i++)
  {   cin>>num;
```

```
        vect.push_back(num);
    }
    sort(vect.begin(), vect.end()); // sort the list
    reverse(vect.begin(), vect.end()); // reverse the list
    cout<<"\n Contents of the sorted vector in reverse are : ";
    vector<int>::iterator itr; // declare an iterator
    for(itr = vect.begin(); itr != vect.end(); itr++) // for loop with iterators
    cout<< "\t"<<*itr ;
}
```

OUTPUT

```
Enter the contents of the vector : 9 1 6 2 0 3 7 4 8 -1
Contents of the sorted vector in reverse are : 9 8 7 6 5 4 3 2 1 0 -1
```

16.5 STRING CLASS

Until now, we have been dealing with C-like strings in our program. We were using a string as a sequence of characters terminated by the null character. The string operations were not only complex but also inefficient to use. Therefore, C++ provides its users a string class that has member functions to manipulate the string objects. Moreover, string is treated as a container class. Therefore, all the algorithms that are applicable on containers can also be used with string objects.

To create a string object, the string class has three constructors as follows:

- `String()` that creates an empty string
- `String(const char *str)` that creates a string object from a null-terminated string
- `String(const string &str)` that creates a string object from another object

The functions and operators supported by the string object are shown in Table 16.6.

Note that `capacity()` returns the total number of characters that can be stored in the string, `length()` returns actual number of characters in the string and `maxsize()` returns the maximum possible size of a `string` object in a given system.

Table 16.6 Functions supported by `string` class

Functions	Operators
append(), assign(), at(), begin(), capacity(), compare(), empty(), end(), erase(), find(), insert(), length(), max_size(), replace(), resize(), size(), swap()	=, +, +=, ==, !=, <, <=, >, >=,[ ], <<, >>

Program 16.4 Write a program that performs string operations on an object of class `string`.

```
using namespace std;
#include<iostream>
#include<string.h>
int main()
{ string S1("Hello World");
    int option, pos, num;
  do
```

```
{ cout<<"\n ******** MENU ********";
  cout<<"\n 1. Duplicate a String ";
  cout<<"\n 2. Insert a substring";
  cout<<"\n 3. Delete a substring";
  cout<<"\n 4. Replace a substring";
  cout<<"\n 5. Check for Equality";
  cout<<"\n 6. Concatenate two strings";
  cout<<"\n 7. Find a substring in a string";
  cout<<"\n 8. Find the first and last position of a character";
  cout<<"\n 9. Extract a substring from a string";
  cout<<"\n 10. Swap two strings";
  cout<<"\n 11. Compare substrings from two strings";
  cout<<"\n Enter your option";
  cin>>option;
  if(option==1)
  {   string S2(S1);
      cout<<"\n The duplicate string contains : "<<S2;
  }
  if(option==2)
  {  string substr;
  cout<<"\n Enter the string to be inserted in the main string : ";
  cin>>substr;
  cout<<"\n Enter the position at which substring has to be inserted : ";
  cin>>pos;
  S1.insert(pos, substr);
  cout<<"\n The modified string is : "<<S1;
  }
  if(option==3)
  {   cout<<"\n Enter the position from which substring has to be deleted : ";
      cin>>pos;
      cout<<"\n Enter the number of characters to be deleted : ";
      cin>>num;
      //S1.erase(pos, num);
  }
  if(option==4)
  {   string s2(" Welcome ");
      S1.replace(5,3,s2);       //starting from position 5 3 characters
      will be replaced with s2
      cout<<"\n The modified string is : "<<S1;
  }
  if(option==5)
  {   string S2("Hello");
      if(S1==S2)
           cout<<"\n The two strings are equal";
      if(S1>S2)
           cout<<"\n"<<S1<<" is greater than "<<S2;
      else
           cout<<"\n"<<S2<<" is greater than "<<S1;
  }
  if(option==6)
```

```
    {   string S2(" of Programming");
        S1 += S2;
        cout<<S1;
    }
    if(option==7)
    {       int pos = S1.find("World");
        cout<<"\n World is in "<<S1<<" at position "<<pos;
    }
    if(option==8)
    {  char ch;
        cout<<"\n Which character to be searched : ";
        cin>>ch;
        int pos = S1.find_first_of(ch);
        cout<<"\n The first position of "<<ch<<" in "<<S1<<" at position "<<pos;
        pos = S1.find_last_of(ch);
        cout<<"\n The last position of "<<ch<<" in "<<S1<<" at position "<<pos;
    }
    if(option==9)
    {   cout<<"\n Enter the number of characters to be extracted : ";
        cin>>num;
        cout<<"\n Enter the position from which characters are to be extracted : ";
        cin>>pos;
        string S2;
        S2 = S1.substr(pos,num);
        cout<<"\n The substring is : "<<S2;
    }
    if(option==10)
    {       string S2("C++ Programming");
            cout<<"\n S1 = "<<S1;
            cout<<"\n S2= "<<S2;
            S1.swap(S2);
            cout<<"\n After Swapping";
            cout<<"\n S1 = "<<S1;
            cout<<"\n S2= "<<S2;
    }
    if(option==11)
    {  string S2("Hi and Hello Friends");
            int res = S1.compare(0,5,S2,7,5);
        if(res==0)
    cout<<"\n The two substrings are equal";
    }
  }while(option !=12);
}
```

OUTPUT

```
******** MENU ********
1. Duplicate a String
2. Insert a substring
3. Delete a substring
4. Replace a substring
```

```
5. Check for Equality
6. Concatenate two strings
7. Find a substring in a string
8. Find the first and last position of a character
9. Extract a substring from a string
10. Swap two strings
11. Compare substrings from two strings
Enter your option 5
Hello World is greater than Hello
```

16.6 DATA TYPE BOOLEAN

The Boolean data type is used to declare a variable that can have only one of the two values—true (1) or false (0). To declare a Boolean variable, the `bool` keyword is used. The statement given next declares a Boolean variable and initializes it.

```
bool eligibleToVote = false;
```

Let us write a program that makes use of the Boolean data type. The program accepts the age of a person and determines if he is eligible to vote or not.

Example 16.5 Using Boolean data type

```
using namespace std;
#include<iostream>
int main()
{   int age;
    bool eligibleToVote = false;
    while(1)
    {   cout<<"\n Enter your age : ";
        cin>>age;
        if(age>=18)
        {   eligibleToVote = true;
            cout<<"\n Cast your vote";
        }
        else
        cout<<"\n Sorry, you are not eligible";
    if(age<=0)
        break;
    }
}
```

OUTPUT

```
Enter your age : 33
Cast your vote
Enter your age : 7
Sorry, you are not eligible
Enter your age : 0
```

16.6.1 Uses of Boolean Data Type

Boolean constant(s) can be used to check if the state of a variable, expression, or a function is true or false.

Boolean variables are used in conditional expressions. Consider the following example:

```
if(cond_expr)
    statement_block1;
else
    statement_block2;
```

Boolean variables can be used as the return values for functions that check whether something is true or not. Such functions are usually named starting with the word `Is`.

For example, the program given next checks whether a given number is even or odd.

Example 16.6 Check even or odd

```
using namespace std;
#include<iostream>
bool IsEven(int num)
{   if(num%2==0)
        return true;
    else
    return false;
}
int main()
{   int n;
    cout<<"\n Enter a number : ";
    cin>>n;
    bool flag = IsEven(n);
    if(flag)
    cout<<"\n"<<n<<" is Even.";
    else
    cout<<"\n"<<n<<" is Odd.";
    }
```

OUTPUT

```
Enter a number : 100
100 is Even.
```

16.6.2 Applications of Operators

Negation

```
!false == true
!true == false
```

Prefix or postfix operator (++) When the increment operator is applied to a Boolean variable, it is set to true. Therefore,

```
bool flag = false, passed = true;
flag++, ++passed;    // value of flag and passed will be true
```

Postfix or prefix decrement operator (--) Applying decrement operator on a Boolean type variable is not permissible. Therefore,

```
bool flag = false;
--flag;          // is not allowed
```

Type conversion A Boolean variable that appears on the right size of the assignment operator (as *r*-value) can be converted into an integer type. In such a case, false is written as zero (0) and true is treated as one (1).

Alternate way of assignment In the previous paragraph, we have read only one way of assigning value to a Boolean type variable—`bool eligibleToVote = false`. An alternate way to do the same task is `bool eligibleToVote(false);`we could have also written as `bool eligibleToVote(!true);`

Printing value of Boolean variable When Boolean variables are evaluated, they do not evaluate to be true or false. Rather, they evaluate to the numbers as in 0 for false and 1for true. Therefore, when the value of a Boolean variable is printed, it is printed as either 0 or 1. For example, the statement given here will print 0 on the screen.

Consequently, when we print their values with cout, it prints 0 for false, and 1 for true.

```
bool eligibleToVote = false;
cout<<eligibleToVote;
```

16.7 `wchar_t` DATA TYPE

Until now, we know that a variable of char type occupies a single byte. However, ANSI C++ supports another data type, `wchar_t` that is used to store a wide character. This means that a variable of `wchar_t` reserves two bytes or 16 bits of memory instead of one byte. On some systems, it may also reserve four bytes.

The `wchar_t` data type was mainly incorporated to write programs for international distribution. Earlier, eight bits in a character was unable to support languages that have more than 255 characters. Therefore, to support languages that have a wider character set like Japanese, the `wchar_t` data type was introduced.

Example 16.7 Using `wchar_t` data type

```
using namespace std;
#include<iostream>
int main()
{ wchar_t wch;
  char ch;
  wch = L'R';
  ch = 'R';
  cout<<"\n The value of character is : " <<ch;
  cout<<"\n Size of the wide char is :" <<sizeof(wch);
  cout<<"\n Size of the char is :" <<sizeof(ch);
  }
```

OUTPUT

```
The value of character is : R
Size of the wide char is : 2
Size of the char is : 1
```

Note that in the program we have written,

```
wch = L'R';
```

This is because the wide character literals begin with the letter L.

16.8 RUN-TIME TYPE INFORMATION

Run-time type information (RTTI) is a mechanism to decide the type of the object at runtime. For this, we have different operators (refer to Fig. 16.3), some of which are discussed in this section.

alignas (since C++11)	enum	return
alignof (since C++11)	explicit	short
and	export (1)	signed
and_eq	extern	sizeof
asm	false	static
auto (1)	float	static_assert (since C++11)
bitand	for	static_cast
bitor	friend	struct
bool	goto	switch
break	if	template
case	inline	this
catch	int	thread_local (since C++11)
char	long	throw
char16_t (since C++11)	mutable	true
char32_t (since C++11)	namespace	try
class	new	typedef
compl	noexcept (since C++11)	typeid
const	not	typename
constexpr (since C++11)	not_eq	union
const_cast	nullptr (since C++11)	unsigned
continue	operator	using (1)
decltype (since C++11)	or	virtual
default (1)	or_eq	void
delete (1)	private	volatile
do	protected	wchar_t
double	public	while
dynamic_cast	register	xor
else	reinterpret_cast	xor_eq

Figure 16.3 New operators

16.8.1 `static_cast` Operator

The `static_cast` operator is used for the following reasons:

- To convert one type into another
- To convert a pointer to a base class to a pointer to a derived class (although such conversions are not always safe)
- To convert enumerated data types to integers and vice versa
- To convert from `void*` to any pointer type

The syntax for using the `static_cast` operator is as follows:

```
static_cast<type>(expression);
```

Here, type specifies the destination data type of the expression. For example, to convert an integer into a floating point value, we need to write,

```
double result = static_cast<double>(total/5);
```

Note `static_cast` operator converts a null pointer value to the null pointer value of the destination type.

Drawbacks

A `static_cast` can be used to convert an integer to a character but the resulting char may not have enough bits to hold the entire integer value.

A `static_cast` is not always a safe type of conversion, as it does no run-time type checking. This problem is more prominent when a static cast to an ambiguous pointer is made.

For example, consider the program given here. Ideally, the cast should not be done but since `static_cast` does not perform type checking, the conversion will be done and may result in a run-time error or some disastrous results.

```
using namespace std;
#include<iostream>
class Base
{
    // class members and their definition
};
class Derived : public Base
{
    // class members and their definition
};
int main()
{   Base *b;
    Derived *d;
    b = static_cast<Base*>(d);          // Safe conversion
    d = static_cast<Derived*>(b);       // Unsafe conversion
}
```

In this program, a derived class pointer can point to a base class pointer because the derived class will contain all the members of the base class but vice versa should not be done because the derived class can have additional data members and member functions which are otherwise not present in the base class.

Even if the code gets executed, the base class pointer would point to an incomplete object of the class and would result in runtime errors, if de-referenced.

The `static_cast` operator can be used to convert an integer value to an enumeration type but if the value of the integer does not lie within the range of enumeration values, the resulting enumeration value is undefined.

Therefore, in these cases, it is left to the programmer to verify that the results of a `static_cast` conversion are safe.

The `static_cast` operator cannot cast `const`, volatile, or unaligned attributes.

16.8.2 `const_cast` Operator

In the previous section, we have seen that a variable or a pointer to any data can be converted into any another type but with the exception of `const`, `volatile`, and `__unaligned` qualifiers. To perform conversions for these exceptional variables, the `const_cast` operator is used.

The `const_cast` operator overrides or in simpler terms removes the variable's constant, volatile, or unaligned status to perform the cast. The syntax for using the `const_cast` is same as that of `static_cast` and is given as follows:

```
const_cast<type>(expression);
```

However, an important point to note here is that the type and the type of expression must be the same. They must only differ in their const and volatile qualifiers.

`const_cast` operator is applied at the compile time. Moreover, a `singleconst_cast` expression may remove any number of const or volatile modifiers.

The program given here demonstrates the use of the `const_cast` operator.

Example 16.8 Using `const_cast` operator

```
using namespace std;
#include<iostream>
int main()
{  int num=10;
   const int *cptr = &num;
   int *ptr = const_cast<int *>(cptr);
   cout<<"\n Number = "<<*ptr;
}
```

OUTPUT

```
Number = 10
```

The process of using `const_cast` to remove the `const` qualifier of an expression is called casting away constness.

Note `const_cast` operator is used to remove the constness of object pointed by a pointer.

16.8.3 `reinterpret_cast` Operator

The `reinterpret_cast` operator allows any pointer to be converted into any other pointer type. For example, with `reinterpret cast` operator, `char *` can be converted into `int*` and vice versa. It is mainly used for performing the following tasks:

- To convert any integral value into any pointer type
- To convert any pointer type into any integral value
- To convert a pointer to one class into a pointer to another class, which may be entirely unrelated to each other. Therefore, it is unsafe
- To convert a null pointer value to the null pointer value of the destination type
- To convert an enumeration type to a pointer
- To convert a pointer to a function into a pointer to a function of a different type
- To convert a pointer to a member of a class into a pointer to a member of a different class

The syntax for using the `reinterpret_cast` operator is

```
reinterpret_cast<<type>>(expression)
```

Drawbacks

- Misuse of the `reinterpret_cast` operator can be unsafe so as a good programming habit, it should be avoided until and unless very necessary.
- The `reinterpret_cast` operator cannot cast the variables with const, volatile, or unaligned qualifiers.

Thus, `reinterpret_cast` operator should be used only to cast back a pointer to its original type. This operator is usually used in a hash function that maps a value to an index in such a way that two distinct values rarely comes up with the same index. The program code given next converts an integer pointer to void pointer and then converts the void pointer into an integer pointer.

Example 16.9 Using `reinterpret_cast` operator

```
using namespace std;
#include<iostream>
int main()
{   int num=10;
   int *ptr = &num;
   cout<<"\n Number with *ptr = "<<*ptr;
   void *vptr = reinterpret_cast<void*>(ptr) ;
   cout<<"\n Integer pointer is now Void *";
   int *ptr2 = reinterpret_cast<int*>(vptr);
   cout<<"\n Number with *ptr2 = "<<*ptr2;
}
```

OUTPUT

```
Number with *ptr = 10
Integer pointer is now Void *
Number with *ptr2 = 10
```

Note A `reinterpret_cast` operator handles conversions between unrelated types.

16.8.4 `dynamic_cast` Operator

The `dynamic_cast` operator is used for safe conversion. For this, it ensures that the result of type conversion points to a valid complete object of the destination pointer type. This means that `dynamic_cast` operator can be used for upcast as well as downcast polymorphic classes. `dynamic_cast` operator is also used to perform all permissible conversions on the following:

- pointers
- null pointers
- pointers to different classes (even between unrelated classes)
- pointer of any type to a void* pointer.

The syntax for the `dynamic_cast` operator is

```
dynamic_cast<type>(expression);
```

The operator returns a pointer to specified type, if successful, or returns null pointer to indicate failure when it is unable to cast a pointer because it is not a complete object of the required class. However, if it fails to convert a reference type then it throws an exception of type `bad_cast`.

Drawbacks

The `dynamic_cast` operator can be only used with pointers and references to classes.

Let us write a small program that demonstrates the use of `dynamic_cast` operator. In the program, we will see that a pointer to an object of derived class can be safely converted into a pointer to object of base class but the reverse of this will not be a safe conversion.

```
using namespace std;
#include<iostream>
class Base { };
class Derived: public Base{ };
```

```
int main()
{   Base *bptr;
    Derived *dptr;
    bptr = dynamic_cast<Base *>(dptr);     // Ok
    dptr = dynamic_cast<Derived *>(bptr);    //Compilation error
}
```

The second statement with `dynamic_cast` operator will result in compilation error because base to derived conversion is not allowed with `dynamic_cast` unless the base class is polymorphic. Let us rewrite the same program in such a way that the base class becomes a polymorphic class and analyses the result.

Example 16.10 Using `dynamic_cast` operator

```
using namespace std;
#include<iostream>
#include<exception>
class Base
{  virtual void show()
   {  cout<<"\n In Base Class";
 }
};
class Derived: public Base{ };
int main()
{
   try
 { Base *bptr;
      Derived *dptr;
      bptr = dynamic_cast<Base *>(dptr);
      dptr = dynamic_cast<Derived *>(bptr);
if(dptr==0)
   cout<<"\n Null pointer on dynamic cast";
 }
catch(...)
 { cout<<"\n Exception";
 }
}
```

OUTPUT

```
Null pointer on dynamic cast
```

Note Whenever a class is polymorphic, `dynamic_cast` will perform a special check during execution to ensure that the expression is a valid and a complete object of the requested class will be obtained.

16.8.5 `typeid` Operator

The `typeid` operator is used to determine the type of an object at the run-time. For this, it retrieves the actual derived type of the object referred to by a pointer or a reference. It is usually used when it is difficult to determine the object type with the static information provided, for example, when working with reference to a class or pointers. To use the `typeid` operator, the programmers must include the `<typeinfo>` header file in their programs.

Note typeid operator and dynamic cast operator are used for RTTI.

The syntax for typeid operator is

```
typeid(type); or typeid(expression)
```

- If type is specified, then the typeid operator returns the type of type.
- If expression is specified, then it evaluates the expression and returns type of value. In both cases, the actual type is known at the compile time and thus no run time overhead is caused. However, if the expression is a polymorphic object or if it evaluates to a zero, then the actual type of the class is queried dynamically with some runtime overhead.

Consider the program given here which uses the typeid operator on an integer and floating point variable.

Example 16.11 Using typeid operator

```
using namespace std;
#include<iostream>
#include<typeinfo>
int main() {
int num = 0;
float *ptr;
cout<<"\n Type ID of num = "<<typeid(num).name();
cout<<"\n Type ID of ptr = "<<typeid(ptr).name();
return 0;
}
```

OUTPUT

```
Type ID of num = int
Type ID of ptr = float *
```

Note When typeid operator is used on a polymorphic class, the result is the type of the most derived complete object.

The following program uses typeid operator on a polymorphic class.

Example 16.12 Using typeid operator on a polymorphic class

```
using namespace std;
#include<iostream>
#include<typeinfo>
#include<exception>
class Base
{  virtual void func()
   {}
};
class Derived : public Base
{};
int main ()
{
```

```
try
 { Base B;
   Derived d;
   Base *bptr = &B;
   cout<< "\n Type of b = " <<typeid(B).name();
   cout<< "\n Type of d = " <<typeid(d).name();
   cout<< "\n Type of *bptr = " <<typeid(*bptr).name();
   Derived *dptr = &d;
   cout<< "\n Type of *dptr = " <<typeid(*dptr).name();
   bptr = &d;
   cout<< "\n Type of *bptr = " <<typeid(*bptr).name();
   cout<< "\n Type of bptr = " <<typeid(bptr).name();
 }
catch (...)
{ cout<< "\n Exception Caught";
 }
}
```

OUTPUT

```
Type of b = 4Base
Type of d = 7Derived
Type of *bptr = 4Base
Type of *dptr = 7Derived
Type of *bptr = 4Derived
Type of bptr = P4Base
```

Explanation: If the expression specified to the `typeid` operator is preceded with a * (dereference operator) and evaluates to zero or a null value, then `typeid` throws a `bad_typeid` exception. In case the pointer does not point to a valid object, then a __ `non_rtti_object` exception is thrown.
From the program's output, we can note the following points:

- If the expression points to a base class type but holds the address of a derived class object, then the resultant type is of derived class.
- The expression must point to a polymorphic type (one that has virtual functions).
- The pointer (bptr) must be dereferenced (as in *bptr) so that the object it points to is used. If we write only bptr (without dereferencing the pointer), the result will be the type of the pointer, not what it points to.

Note C++ allows comparing two types as in if `(typeid(int_num) == typeid(float_num)){ //code }`.

16.9 `explicit` KEYWORD

We have read that constructors are functions with the same name as that of the class and are used to create the object of the class. While C++ provides a default constructor for every class, users can also define their own constructors.

The explicit keyword is used with a single parameter constructor to prevent implicit conversion to take place. For example,

```
using namespace std;
#include<iostream>
class Sample
```

```
{   private:
    int data;
public:
    Sample(int num)
    {   data = num;
    }
};
int main()
{
    Sample S = 99;
}
```

In the program, when we write Sample S = 99, an implicit conversion takes place and the data of S is assigned value 99. To avoid such implicit conversion, the explicit keyword is used. The explicit keyword forces the compiler not to perform any kind of implicit conversion and throw an error when an attempt is made to do such conversion. This means that with explicit, programmers are forced to use the correct syntax of initializing the object as in Sample S(99).

Note The `explicit` keyword is used only for the constructors. This keyword is also used to prevent constructor conversion.

Let us rewrite the same program that uses the explicit keyword.

```
using namespace std;
#include<iostream>
class Sample
{   private:
    int data;
public:
    explicit Sample(int num)
    {   data = num;
    }
};
int main()
{   Sample S(99); // right
    Sample S = 99; //error - cannot convert int to Sample
}
```

Therefore, with explicit keyword, unexpected results obtained by implicit conversion can be avoided. However, any value can be now typecast explicitly. For example, by writing,

```
Sample S = (Sample)99;   // explicit type cast as we do with built-in data types.
```

Note the keyword explicit has no effect on a multiple argument constructor because such constructors do not involve implicit conversions. One exception to it is a multiple argument constructor that has a default value for all arguments except one.

For example, constructors 1 and 2 will have the effect of explicit keyword but constructors 3 and 4 will have no effect.

Constructor 1 explicit Sample `(int a, float b = 7.9, char c = 'A');`
Constructor 2 explicit Sample `(int a = 5, float b, char c = 'A');`
Constructor 3 explicit Sample `(int a, float b, char c);`
Constructor 4 explicit Sample `(int a, float b, char c = 'A');`

16.10 MUTABLE KEYWORD

Until now, we have read that a constant member function cannot change the data values. But sometimes we may need to modify one or more data members of class or structure from within a constant function. In such a situation, when we want to modify only few data members (not all), we can prefix the data member declaration with the keyword `mutable`. The syntax for using declaring a variable as mutable is given as follows:

```
mutable datatype variable_name;
```

Mutable allows a data member to be modified from within a constant member function. The second use of keyword mutable is to change the value of data member of a constant object. Recall that the data members of a constant object cannot be modified. The program given here demonstrates the use of mutable keyword in both the stated situations. In the program, we have a class Employee that has name, ID, experience, and salary as its members. Member function `show_data()` is constant that by definition does not allow values of data members to be altered. Since salary has been defined as mutable, its value can change.

Note Keyword mutable cannot be used with data declared as static, or const, or reference.

Example 16.13 Using keyword `mutable`

```
using namespace std;
#include<iostream>
#include<string.h>
class Employee
{   private:
        char name[20];    // data member
        int emp_id;
        int exp;
        mutable float salary;    //mutable data member
    public:
        Employee(char n[], int id, int years, float sal)
    {.  strcpy(name, n);
        emp_id = id;
        exp = years;
        salary = sal;
    }
void show_data() const   // constant member function
    {   cout<<"\n EMPLOYEE ID : "<<emp_id;
        cout<<"\n NAME : "<< name;
        if(exp>5)
          salary += 5000;   //give loyalty bonus   // no other data except salary can be modified
        cout<<"\n SALARY : "<<salary;
    }
};
int main()
{       cout<<"\n\n With mutable data on a constant function";
        Employee e1("Richa Raina", 101, 7, 80000);
        e1.show_data();
```

```
        cout<<"\n\n With mutable data on a constant object";
        const Employee e2("Aditya Roy", 297, 6, 70000);   // constant object
        e2.show_data();
}
```

OUTPUT

```
With mutable data on a constant function
EMPLOYEE ID : 101
NAME :Richa Raina
SALARY : 85000
With mutable data on a constant object
EMPLOYEE ID : 297
NAME : Aditya Roy
SALARY : 75000
```

16.11 NAMESPACES

Consider a situation in which two people have the same name in an organization. One way to identify them is by specifying the department name along with the employee name. Similarly, in our programs, sometimes we may need to have data members, classes, or functions with same name as of another data, class, or function either defined in header file or in our own program. For example, we may need to define our own String class but String is a class already defined in `<string>`. In such cases, the compiler has no way to determine which version of the class is referred in the program code. For this, C++ uses the concept of namespaces.

A namespace provides additional information to differentiate variables, classes, or functions from others with the same name available in different libraries. This means that namespace defines a scope that allows programmers to define the context in which names are defined. The syntax for defining a namespace is given as follows:

```
namespace namespace_name
{   // variable, class or function declaration
}
```

For example,

```
namespace My_space
{   bool flag = 1;
    void show()
    {   cout<<"\n FLAG = "<<flag;
    }
}
```

The code defines a namespace that has a variable flag and a function `show()`. Now, to use the variable or function there are two options available to the programmer.

- Prefix the name of the namespace with the name of the variable or function as in, `My_space::flag` and `My_space::show()`.
- The directive informs the compiler that the subsequent code uses names specified in that particular namespace. For example, we have often used using namespace `std;` `statement` in our program. Therefore, the general syntax of using directive is

```
using namespace namespace_name;
```

Let us write a sample program that demonstrates the use of multiple namespaces.

Example 16.14 Using multiple namespaces

```
using namespace std;
#include<iostream>
namespace Myfirst_namespace
{   void show()
    {   cout<<"\n In First name space";
}
}
namespace Mysecond_namespace
{   void show()
    { cout<<"\n In Second name space";
}
}
int main()
{   Myfirst_namespace :: show();
    using namespace Mysecond_namespace;
    show();
}
```

OUTPUT

```
In First name space
In Second name space
```

Note A namespace defined in several parts consist of the sum of its separately defined parts.

16.11.1 Nested Namespaces

C++ allows programmers to have nested namespaces in which one namespace is defined inside another namespace. The syntax for defining a nested namespace can be given as follows:

```
namespace namespace_name1
{   // variable, class or function declaration
    namespace namespace_name2
    {   // variable, class or function declaration
    }
}
```

To access a member of nested namespace, write

```
using namespace namespace_name1 :: namespace_name2;   OR
namespace_name1 :: or namespace_name2 :: function_name;
```

Consider the program given next which demonstrates the use of nested namespaces.

Example 16.15 Using nested namespaces

```
using namespace std;
#include<iostream>
namespace Myfirst_namespace
{   void show()
```

```
    {   cout<<"\n In First name space";
}
    namespace Mysecond_namespace
    {   void show()
        { cout<<"\n In Second name space";
    }
    }
}
int main()
{   Myfirst_namespace :: show();
    using namespace Myfirst_namespace :: Mysecond_namespace;
    show();
}
```

OUTPUT

```
In First name space
In Second name space
```

Therefore, we see that namespaces allows programmers to group named entities that otherwise would have global scope into narrower scopes. With namespaces, the same identifier can be independently defined in multiple blocks to allow programmers to associate same or different meaning in each block. C++ also allows namespace aliasing in which existing namespaces can be aliased with new names using the following syntax:

```
namespace new_name = current_name;
```

Note Variables, types, constants, and functions of the standard C++ library are declared within the `stdnamespace`.

16.11.2 Unnamed Namespaces

C++ also allows programmers to define unnamed namespaces. By definition, an unnamed namespace is one that is specified without any name. It is primarily used to define global static members that are accessible in all scopes following its declaration. The syntax for defining an unnamed namespace is given as follows:

```
namespace
{   // variable, class or function declaration
}
```

The members of such an unnamed namespace are accessed without using any qualification as illustrated in the program here.

Example 16.16 Using unnamed namespace

```
using namespace std;
#include<iostream>
namespace
{ int num  =  10;
   void show()
   {   cout<<"\n In Unnamed namespace";
```

```
    }
}
int main()
{   cout<<"\n NUMBER = "<<num;
    show();
}
```

OUTPUT

```
NUMBER = 10
In Unnamed namespace
```

16.11.3 Similarity and Dissimilarity with Classes

Like classes and structures, namespaces make it easier to divide a program into logical groups that perform their own function(s). However, unlike classes and structures, namespaces do not require instantiation. This means that programmers need not create objects of namespaces to use them. Rather, to use any member of a namespace, you just require to prefix the namespace followed by the scope operator (::). Moreover, unlike classes, definition of a namespace is not terminated with a semi-colon.

16.11.4 Classes within Namespaces

C++ allows users to define classes within a namespace. This means that a program can have two classes having the same name provided they are in different namespaces.

The program given here demonstrates the use of classes within namespaces.

Example 16.17 Using classes within namespaces

```
using namespace std;
#include<iostream>
#include<string.h>
namespace Student
{   class RollNumber   // class within a namespace
    {   private:
            int num;
        public:
            RollNumber(int n)
        {   num = n;
        }
        void show()
            {   cout<<"\n ROLL NUMBER = "<<num;
            }
 };
class Name
 {  private:
        char n[10];
    public:
    Name(char str[])
    {   strcpy(n, str);
    }
void show()
    {   cout<<"\n NAME = "<<n;
    }
```

```
    };
}
int main()
{   Student::RollNumber Number(10);
// create object of a class within Student namespace using scope resolution operator
    Number.show();
    using namespace Student;
// using keyword to create an object of a class within a namespace
    Name name("Sarthak");
name.show();
}
```

OUTPUT

```
ROLL NUMBER = 10
NAME = Sarthak
```

Explanation: The standard C++ library is declared within the `std namespace`.

Note Namespaces cannot be defined inside any function. They should be global.

16.12 OPERATOR KEYWORDS

To enhance readability of programs, ANSI C++ has added operator keywords which are shown in Table 16.7.

Table 16.7 Operator keywords

Operator	Operator keyword	Usage
&&	and	res = a and b
||	Or	res = a or b
!	Not	res = a not b
!=	not_eq	res = a not_eq b
&	Bitand	res = a bit and b
|	Bitor	res = a bit or b
^	Xor	res = a x or b
&=	and_eq	res and_eq a
!=	or_eq	res or_eq a
^=	xor_eq	res xor_eq a

Table 16.8 Header files

Old name	New name
<assert.h>	<cassert>
<ctype.h>	<cctype>
<float.h>	<cfloat>
<limits.h>	<climits>
<math.h>	<cmath>
<stdio.h>	<cstdio>
<stdlib.h>	<cstdlib>
<string.h>	<cstring>
<time.h>	<ctime>

16.13 SPECIFYING HEADER FILES

ANSI C++ has laid out a new way of including the header files. Besides supporting the old way `#include<iostream.h>` it also supports the new way as `#include<iostream>`. Moreover, some file-names have also been renamed as specified in Table 16.8.

Points To Remember

- The STL components, which are now a part of C++ library, are defined in the namespace `std`.
- Containers are objects that store data and define the manner in which data will be stored.
- STL algorithms consist of functions that programmers can directly use in their code to process data stored in different containers for processing their data.
- Maps are implemented as associative array in which key is specified using the subscript operator.
- List supports only sequential (or linear) access.
- C++ provides its users a string class that has member functions to manipulate the string objects.
- The Boolean data type is used to declare a variable that can have only one of the two value—true (1) or false (0).
- ANSI C++ supports `wchar_t` data type to store a wide character. This means that a variable of `wchar_t` reserves two bytes or16 bits of memory instead of one byte.
- The `const_cast` operator overrides or in simpler terms removes the variable's constant, volatile, or unaligned status to perform the cast.
- The `reinterpret_cast` operator allows any pointer to be converted into any other pointer type.
- The `dynamic_cast` operator is used for safe conversion.
- The `typeid` operator is used to determine the type of an object at the run-time.
- The explicit keyword is used with a single parameter constructor to prevent implicit conversion
- A constant member function cannot change the data values. But sometimes, we may need to modify one or more data members of class or structure from within a constant function. In such a situation when we want to modify only few data members (not all) we can prefix the data member declaration with the keyword mutable.
- Namespace defines a scope that allows programmers to define the context in which names are defined.

Glossary

Casting away constness The process of using `const_cast` to remove the const qualifier of an expression

Dequeue A double ended queue that allows insertions and deletions at both ends

Downcasts Converting a pointer to a base class object to make it a pointer to the derived class

Iterator Pointer-like entities that are used to access the elements stored in the container

List A bi-direction linear list that allows insertion/deletion at any position

Map Stores data as pairs of key and value

Priority queue The first element to be taken out is the highest priority of the element

Polymorphic classes Classes that have virtual functions as their members

Queue It is a FIFO data structure. Insertion is done at one end and deletion from the other end

Set Store multiple data elements and provide functions to manipulate elements using their key values

Stack It is a LIFO data structure. Insertion and deletion can be done only at one end.

Standard template library A collection of classes that provide templated containers, algorithms, and iterators

`static_cast` It can perform conversions between pointers to related classes

Upcasts Converting a pointer to derived class object to make it a pointer to the base class

Vector Dynamic array that allows insertion/deletion at the end

Exercises

Fill in the Blanks

1. STL is a collection of classes that provide _______, _______, and _______ containers, algorithms, and iterators.
2. STL is defined in namespace _______.
3. _______ is a dynamic array.
4. In _______ container, data is sorted while being input.

5. ______ are used for traversing the elements of container.
6. Iterators can be used with ______ and ______ containers.
7. The value of a Boolean variable can be either ______ or ______.
8. Static cast can convert from ______ `void*` to any pointer type.
9. ______ cast can be used to cast constants.
10. ______ operator allows any pointer to be converted into any other pointer type.
11. On failure, `dynamic_cast` throws an exception of type ______.
12. The `dynamic_cast`operator can be only used with ______ and ______.
13. ______ allows a data member to be modified from within a constant member function.
14. ______ defines a scope that allows programmers to define the context in which names are defined.
15. `Cin` and `cout` are defined in ______ namespace.

State True or False

1. STL is implemented using templates.
2. STL supports code reusability.
3. List supports insertion/deletion only at the end.
4. Derived containers stores data using key values.
5. STL algorithms are either declared as member functions of any container class or defined as friend functions.
6. List supports both random and sequential access.
7. String is a container class.
8. Boolean variables can be used as the return values for functions.
9. Static cast cannot convert enumerated data types to integers and vice versa.
10. `Reinterpret_cast` can convert an enumeration type to a pointer.
11. `dynamic_cast` operator can be used for upcast as well as downcast polymorphic classes.
12. Dynamic cast can convert a pointer of any type to a `void*` pointer.
13. The `typeid` operator is used to determine the type of an object at the compile-time.
14. Namespace definition can be distributed in several parts.
15. Iterator is a form of a pointer.
16. A set can have two or more elements for the same key.
17. String objects are null terminated.

Multiple Choice Questions

1. Which STL component defines how data will be stored?
   (a) Container (b) Iterator
   (c) Algorithm (d) All of these
2. In which container, each element is related to other elements by its position along the line
   (a) Sequence (b) Associative
   (c) Derived (d) All of these
3. Which sequence container allows insertions or deletions at both the ends?
   (a) Vector (b) List
   (c) Dequeue (d) All of these
4. Which container does not support the use of iterators?
   (a) Sequence (b) Associative
   (c) Derived (d) All of these
5. Example(s) of derived container are ______.
   (a) Stack (b) Queue
   (c) Priority queue (d) All of these
6. The `static_cast` operator cannot cast which type of identifiers?
   (a) Const (b) Static
   (c) Unaligned (d) All of these
7. Const_cast operator is applied at ______.
   (a) Load time (b) Compile time
   (c) Run time (d) All of these
8. Which cast operator handles conversions between unrelated types?
   (a) Const (b) Dynamic
   (c) Static (d) Reinterpret
9. Which cast operator is used for safe conversion?
   (a) Const (b) Dynamic
   (c) Static (d) Reinterpret
10. The explicit keyword is used only for ______.
    (a) Constructor (b) Data member
    (c) Member function (d) All of these
11. Keyword mutable cannot be used with data declared as ______.
    (a) Static (b) Const
    (c) Reference (d) All of these
12. Which among the following is used to define global static members that are accessible in all scopes following its declaration?
    (a) Explicit
    (b) Mutable
    (c) Unnamed namespace
    (d) namespace

13. Which container would you prefer to perform quick insertions at the end?
(a) Vector (b) List
(c) Dequeue (d) All of these
14. For frequent insertions and deletions at both the ends, which type of container is preferred?
(a) Vector (b) List
(c) Dequeue (d) All of these

Review Questions

1. How does the STL support reusability of code?
2. What are containers? Give examples
3. Explain the different types of containers
4. What are different categories of algorithms?
5. What operators can be applied on iterators?
6. How does a map differ from a list?
7. With help of relevant examples explain how we can create objects of String class
8. Give the significance of Boolean variable
9. What will be the result of applying different operators on Boolean variables?
10. Why do we need `static_cast` operator?
11. What are the main drawbacks of `static_cast` operator?
12. Why is `static_cast` not always a safe type of conversion?
13. When should we use the `reinterpret_cast`?
14. How does `typeid` operator work?
15. In what situations does the explicit keyword lose its significance?
16. Explain the significance of mutable keyword
17. Why do we use namespace in our programs?
18. Why is a namespace considered similar to a class definition?
19. How is a namespace different from a class?
20. Differentiate between
(a) Set and multi-set
(b) Map and multi-map
(c) `Capacity()` and `maxsize()`
(d) Character and a wide character
(e) `Static_cast` and `dynamic_cast`

Programming Exercises

1. Write a program that sorts a vector.
2. Write a program that searches a value in a vector.
3. Write a program that inserts an element at the specified position.
4. Write a program that deletes an element from the specified position.
5. Write a program that inserts elements at the front of the dequeue.
6. Write a program that inserts elements at the back of the dequeue.
7. Write a program that deletes specified number of elements from the front of the dequeue.
8. Write a program that deletes specified number of elements from the back of the dequeue.
9. Write a program to insert elements in a list and then display it in sorted order.
10. Write a program that displays first half of the list.
11. Write a program that deletes duplicating elements from a list.
12. Write a program to display the elements of a list in reverse order.
13. Write a program to create a map that stores name of the country and its capital city.
14. Write a program to reverse a string.
15. Write a program that returns a Boolean variable to notify the caller whether the number was prime or composite.
16. Write a program that demonstrates the use of different cast operators.
17. Write a program that has a list of all even numbers from 1–50 and another list containing all odd numbers in the same range. Merge the two lists and display its contents.
18. Write a program that reads the names of 10 students. Sort these names and then display it on screen.
19. Write a program that reads the names of 10 students. Display the names of only those students whose name starts with 'R'.
20. Write a program that enters a line of text. Count the number of R'sin the text.
21. Write a program that replaces a ',' with a '-' in the text.
22. Write a program to check if a given string object is empty or not. Use `empty()`.
23. Write a program to check is the "bcd" is present in string "acdefgcabcdefg". Use `find()`.
24. Write a program to count the number of vowels in a string.
25. Write a program to delete elements from a list. Use `pop_front()` and `pop_back()`.

Find the errors in the following codes

1.
```
using namespace std;
#include <iostream>
class Distance
{   private:
    float kms;
    public:
explicit Distance(float d)
    {   kms = d;
    }
    bool operator== (Distance D)
    {   return (kms == D.kms)? true :
false;
    }
};
int main()
{   Distance D(3.0);
    if (D == 3.0)
    cout<< "Same";
else
cout<< "Not Same";
return 0;
}
```

2.
```
using namespace std;
#include <iostream>
#include <string.h>
main()
{   string S1("abc");
    string S2("abc"+"def");
    cout<<S2;
}
```

3.
```
using namespace std;
#include <iostream>
#include <string.h>
main()
{   string S1("abcdefghijk");
    int len = S1.length();
for(int i=0;i<len;i++)
    cout<<S1.at[];
}
```

4.
```
using namespace std;
#include<iostream>
main()
{   namespace First
    {   void func()
        {   cout<<"\n Inside Namespace";
        }
    }
}
```

Find the output of the following codes

1.
```
using namespace std;
#include <iostream>
#include <exception>
class Base { virtual void dummy() {} };
class Derived: public Base { };
int main()
{
try
{
    Base * b_to_dptr = new Derived;
    Base * b_to_bptr = new Base;
    Derived *dptr;
    dptr = dynamic_cast< Derived *>
    (b_to_dptr);
    if (dptr ==0)
    cout<< "Null pointer on first type-cast" ;
    dptr = dynamic_cast< Derived *>(b_to_bptr);
    if (dptr ==0)
    cout<<"Null pointer on second
    type-cast" <<endl;
}
catch (...)
{   cout<< "Exception: ";
}
    return 0;
}
```

2.
```
using namespace std;
#include <iostream>
class Complex
{   private:
        int real;
        int imag;
    public:
Complex(int r, int i)
    {   real = r, imag = i;
    }
        bool operator == (Complex C) {
return (real == C.real&&imag == C.
imag)? true : false;
    }
};
int main()
{
    Complex C1(4,7), C2(4,7);
if (C1 == C2)
cout<<"Same";
else
cout<<"Not Same";
return 0;
}
```

3.
```
using namespace std;
#include <iostream>
class Distance
{   private:
        int kms;
    public:
        explicit Distance(int d)
    {   kms = d;
    }
        bool operator == (Distance D) {
return (kms == D.kms)? true : false;
    }
};
int main()
{
    Distance D1(4);
if (D1 == (Distance)4)
cout<< "Same";
else
cout<< "Not Same";
return 0;
}
```

4.
```
using namespace std;
#include <iostream>
#include <string.h>
class Customer
{
char name[20];
mutable char food_ordered[50];
mutable float bill;
public:
Customer(char* s, char* f, float b)
    {
      strcpy(name, s);
      strcpy(food_ordered, f);
      bill = b;
    }
void changeOrder(char *f, float b) const
    {
      strcpy(food_ordered, f);
      bill = b;
    }
void display() const
    {
      cout<< "\n Customer name : " << name;
      cout<< "\n Food ordered : " <<food_ordered;
      cout<< "\n Total Amount : " <<bill;
    }
};
int main()
{
const Customer C1("Richa", "Cold
Coffee", 150);
C1.display();
C1.changeOrder("Tea", 100);
C1.display();
return 0;
}
```

5.
```
using namespace std;
#include <iostream>
namespace first
{   void func()
    { cout<< "\n Inside first namespace";
    }
}
namespace second
{   void func()
    { cout<< "Inside second namespace";
    }
}
using namespace first;
int main ()
{ func();
}
```

6.
```
using namespace std;
#include <iostream>
namespace first
{   int x = 5;
    int y = 10;
}
namespace second
{
double x = 4.5;
double y = 5.678;
}
int main ()
{
cout<<"\n First :: x = "<<first::x;
cout<<"\n Second :: y = "<<second::y;
using namespace first;
cout<<"\n Y = "<<y;
using namespace second;
cout<< "\n X = "<<second::x;
return 0;
}
```

7.
```
using namespace std;
#include <iostream>
#include <string.h>
main()
{   string S1("abc");
    string S2(S1+"def");
    cout<<S2;
}
```

8.
```
using namespace std;
#include <iostream>
namespace first
{
```

```
    int var =5;
}
namespace second
{
    double var =3.1416;
}
int main ()
{
    int res = first::var+ second::var;
    cout<< res;
}
```

9.
```
using namespace std;
#include <iostream>
#include <string.h>
template<class type>
type MyMax(const type Var1, const
type Var2)
{
    cout<<"no specialization";
    return Var1 < Var2 ? Var2 : Var1;
}
const char *MyMax(const char *Var1,
const char *Var2)
{
    return(strcmp(Var1, Var2)<0)? Var2 :
    Var1;
}
int main()
{
    string Str1 ="C++", Str2 =
    "Programming";
    const char *Var3 ="C++";
    const char *Var4 ="Programming";
    const char *str = MyMax(Var3, Var4);
    cout<< str;
}
```

10.
```
using namespace std;
#include <iostream>
#include <exception>
#include <typeinfo>
class Myshape
{
    public:
        virtual void Func() const{}
};
class Triangle : public Myshape
{
    public:
        virtual void Func()const{}
};
main()
{
    Myshape shape;
    Myshape &ref_shape = shape;
    try
    {
        Triangle &ref_triangle =
        dynamic_cast<Triangle&>(ref_shape);
    }
    catch(bad_cast)
    {
      cout<<"Can't do the dynamic_cast";
      cout<<"Caught: bad_cast exception.
      Myshape is not Triangle.";
    }
}
```

11.
```
using namespace std;
#include <iostream>
#include <list>
#include <queue>
int main()
{
    queue<char> q;
    q.push('P');
    q.push('Q');
    q.push('R');
    cout<< q.front();
    q.pop();
    cout<< q.front();
    q.pop();
    cout<< q.front();
    q.pop();
}
```

12.
```
using namespace std;
#include <iostream>
#include <deque>
int main()
{
    unsigned int i;
    deque<int> D1(3,100);
    deque<int> D2(5,200);
    D1.swap(D2);
    cout<<"D1 contains:";
    for(deque<int>::iterator it = D1.
    begin(); it != D1.end();++it)
        cout<<' '<*it;
    cout<"D2 contains:";
    for(deque<int>::iterator it = D2.
    begin(); it != D2.end();++it)
        cout<<' '<<*it;
}
```

13.
```
using namespace std;
#include <iostream>
```

```
#include <deque>
int main()
{
   unsigned int i;
   deque<int> D;
   D.push_back(100);
   D.push_back(200);
   D.push_back(300);
   for(deque<int>::iterator it = D.
   begin(); it != D.end();++it)
   {  }
   D.clear();
   D.push_back(110);
   D.push_back(220);
   for(deque<int>::iterator it = D.
   begin(); it != D.end();++it)
   cout<<' '<<*it;
}
```

14.
```
using namespace std;
#include <iostream>
#include <stack>
int main()
{
   stack<int> S;
   cout<<(int) S.size();
   for(int i =0; i <5; i++)
      S.push(i);
   cout<<(int) S.size();
}
```

15.
```
using namespace std;
#include <iostream>
#include <map>
int main()
{
   multimap<char, int> M;
   M.insert(make_pair('A', 100));
   M.insert(make_pair('B', 200));
   M.insert(make_pair('C', 350));
   M.insert(make_pair('D', 500));
   cout<< M.size();
}
```

16.
```
using namespace std;
#include <iostream>
#include <queue>
using namespace std;
int main()
{
   priority_queue<int> P;
   P.push(10);
   P.push(20);
   P.push(15);
   cout<< P.top();
}
```

17.
```
using namespace std;
#include <iostream>
#include <algorithm>
#include <vector>
int main()
{
   vector<int> V;
   for(int i =1; i <6;++i)
      V.push_back(i);
   reverse(myvector.begin(), myvector.
   end());
   for(vector<int>::iterator it =
   myvector.begin(); it != myvector.
   end();++it)
   cout<<' '<<*it;
}
```

18.
```
using namespace std;
#include<iostream>
#include<algorithm>
int main()
{
   int arr[] = { 10, 20, 30, 30, 20,
   10, 10, 20 };
   int *pbegin = arr;
   int *pend = arr + sizeof(arr) /
   sizeof(int);
   pend = remove (pbegin, pend, 20);
   for (int* p = pbegin; p != pend; ++p)
      cout << ' ' << *p;
}
```

19.
```
using namespace std;
#include<iostream>
#include<algorithm>
#include<vector>
int main()
{
   int arr[] = { 10, 20, 30 ,40 };
   int *p;
   p = find (arr, arr + 4, 30);
   --p;
   cout << *p;
}
```

Answers

Fill in the Blanks

1. containers, algorithms, and iterators; **2.** `std`; **3.** vector; **4.** associative; **5.** iterators; **6.** sequence and associative; **7.** 0, 1; **8.** `void*`; **9.** `const`; **10.** `reinterpret_cast`; **11.** `bad_cast`; **12.** pointers and references to classes; **13.** Mutable; **14.** Namespace; **15.** `std`

State True or False

1. True **2.** True **3.** False **4.** False **5.** False **6.** False **7.** True **8.** True
9. False **10.** True **11.** True **12.** True **13.** False **14.** True **15.** True **16.** False
17. False

Multiple Choice Questions

1. (a); **2.** (a); **3.** (c); **4.** (c); **5.** (d); **6.** (d); **7.** (b); **8.** (d); **9.** (b); **10.** (a); **11.** (d); **12.** (c); **13.** (a); **14.** (c)

ANNEXURE 4

Volatile and Restrict Qualifiers

A4.1 VOLATILE QUALIFIER

In C++, a variable or object declared with the `volatile` keyword will not be optimized by the compiler because the compiler must assume that their values can change at any time.

For example, consider the code given here. Here, the value stored in `WAIT` is 0. It then starts to poll that value repeatedly until it changes to 255.

```
static int WAIT;
void func(void)
{
        WAIT = 0;
while(WAIT != 255);
}
```

An optimizing compiler will observe that no other code is changing the value stored in WAIT, and therefore, assumes that it will remain equal to 0 at all times. The compiler will then replace the function body with an infinite loop similar to the one given here.

```
void func_optimized(void)
{
foo = 0;
while(true);
}
```

However, `func` might represent a location that can be changed by other elements of the computer system at any time (for example, a hardware register of a device connected to the CPU). The code would never detect such a change. When the volatile keyword is used, the compiler assumes that the current program is the only part of the system that could change the value. The declaration of `WAIT` is must, therefore, be modified as follows

Now, the compiler will not optimize the loop and the system will detect the change when it occurs. The volatile keyword is basically used to allow access to memory mapped devices and make use of variables in signal handlers.

```
static volatile int WAIT;
void bar(void)
{
        WAIT = 0;
```

```
while (WAIT != 255);
}
```

Points to Remember

- C++ permits declaration and definition of a `volatile` or `const` function, only if it is a non-static member function.
- C++ permits declaration and definition of a function that returns a pointer to a `volatile` or `const` function.
- An object can be both `const` and `volatile`. Such an object cannot be legitimately modified by its own program but can be modified by some asynchronous process.
- If you put more than one qualifier on a declaration, then the compiler will ignore duplicate-type qualifiers.
- `Volatile` keyword indicates to the compiler that a variable may be modified outside the scope of the program. A `volatile` variable is normally used in multitasking (threading) systems, when writing drivers with interrupt service routines, or in embedded systems, where the peripheral registers may also be modified by hardware alone.
- When you use the `volatile` keyword, your program will run slower, due to the extra read operations. The program will be larger since the compiler is not allowed to optimize as thoroughly.

Scope of volatile keyword

A variable must be declared using the volatile type qualifier in the following cases

- A variable is used in more than one context.
- A common variable is used in more than one task or thread.
- A variable is used both in a task and one or more interrupt service routines.
- A variable corresponds to processor-internal registers configured as input.

A4.2 RESTRICT QUALIFIER

The `restrict` type qualifier may only be applied to a pointer. A pointer declaration with restrict keyword establishes a special association between the pointer and the object it accesses, making that pointer and expressions based on that pointer the only ways to directly or indirectly access the value of that object.

We have studied that a pointer is the address of a memory location. More than one pointer can be used to access the same memory location and modify it during the course of a program. The restrict type qualifier indicates the compiler that if the memory addressed by the restrict-qualified pointer is modified, no other pointer will access that same memory. The compiler may choose to optimize code involving restrict-qualified pointers in a way that might otherwise result in incorrect behaviour.

Points to Remember

- If a particular piece of memory is not altered, then it can be aliased using more than one restricted pointer.
- In the absence of `restrict` keyword, other pointers can alias the object.
- Caching the value in an object designated through a restrict-qualified pointer is safe at the beginning of the block in which the pointer is declared, since no pre-existing aliases may also be used to reference that object.

However, the cached value must be restored to the object by the end of the block, where some pre-existing aliases again become available. If new aliases are formed within the block, they can be identified and adjusted to refer to the cached value.

ANNEXURE 5

Smart Pointers

INTRODUCTION

Smart pointers are objects which store pointers to dynamically allocated (heap) objects. They are objects which behave like pointers but do more than a pointer. Smart pointers are flexible as pointers and have the advantage of being an object. Like an ordinary class, they also have constructors and destructors which are invoked automatically. A smart pointer is designed to handle the problems caused by using normal pointers and are hence called smart.

A5.1 FEATURES OF SMART POINTERS

- They are much like built-in C++ pointers except that they automatically delete the object pointed to at the appropriate time.
- They ensure proper destruction of dynamically allocated objects.
- They keep track of dynamically allocated objects shared by multiple owners.
- Smart pointer class templates have a template parameter, T, to specify the type of the object pointed to by the smart pointer.
- The behaviour of smart pointer templates is undefined if the destructor or operator delete for objects of type T throw exceptions.
- Many functions in smart pointer classes have no side effect. This is because when an exception is thrown by an object of one of these classes, the entire program state remains the same as it was prior to the function call which resulted in the exception being thrown.
- Member functions of smart pointer classes neither throw exceptions nor call other functions which may throw exceptions.
- Smart pointers can be used exactly like dumb or raw pointers. The only difference is that pointer arithmetic is not allowed on smart pointers as they may be unsafe. Smart pointers can be mixed with raw pointers; for example, `smartPtr = rawPtr;` `rawPtr = smartPtr;` etc.

  Unlike dumb pointers, smart pointers throw an exception when
  - its value is `NULL`
  - an attempt is made to dereference it
  - it destroys its contents automatically when it goes out of scope.

A5.2 USES OF SMART POINTERS

- Implementing safe programs
- Allocating temporary memory in functions with multiple exit points.
- Guarding against memory leaks when an exception is thrown.
- Writing efficient code.
- Performing garbage collection.
- Performing resource management of objects such as file handles or network sockets.

Note If a language supports automatic garbage collection like Java or C#, then smart pointers are not needed.

CHAPTER 17

Object-Oriented System Analysis, Design, and Development

KEY Concepts

Object-oriented software development methodology • Traditional software development • Building high quality software • Unified Modelling Language (UML) • Diagrams in UML

INTRODUCTION

Systems development refers to the set of activities that need to be carried out for producing an information system. These activities include the following:

- Analysis
- Design
- Coding or implementation
- Testing
- Maintenance

Therefore, a software development methodology is a series of processes that results in the development of an application that achieves the ultimate goal based on system requirements. As software development process is never-ending, the set of activities mentioned will be continuously applied until the system is in operation.

As software development is a dynamic process, it is always subjected to changes. These changes may be needed either due to change in user's requirements or due to change in technology being used. If the reason for change is technology, then the methods and tools to be used will differ significantly from those currently in use. Among a large number of tools and methodologies present in the market, object-oriented (OO) development techniques top the chart of popularity.

OO software development techniques are strikingly different from traditional development techniques; the latter consider software as a collection of functions and isolated data, where a function is a combination of algorithms that are applied on the data structure. However, in OO techniques, a software system is perceived as a set of mechanisms for performing certain action on certain data. Its main focus is on object and not on functions.

17.1 TRADITIONAL SOFTWARE DEVELOPMENT PROCESS

System development is considered to be a process of change, refinement, transformation, or addition to the existing product. Programmers may replace one sub process with a new one, provided the new sub process has the same interface as the old one, so that it fits into the process as a whole. Moreover, in OO development, each sub-process is clearly spelled out, to allow each operation to be performed independently of other sub processes. For this, each sub-process is supported with the following information:

- how it works
- required inputs
- expected output

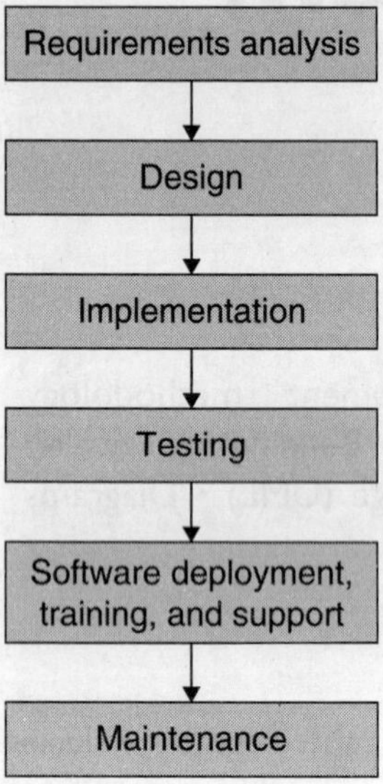

Figure 17.1 Phases in software development life cycle (waterfall model)

In the course of software development, a series of transformation takes place where the output of one transformation becomes the input of the next. These stages of transformation can be given as follows.

First transformation (analysis) The first transformation translates end user's needs into system requirements.

Second transformation (design) The design phase starts with a problem statement and ends with a detailed design that is later used to implement the software system. This transformation details the information regarding how to build the software, its development, and its testing.

Third transformation (implementation) The third transformation refines the detailed design into system deployment that will satisfy the user's needs and ends with embedding the software product within its operational environment.

To carry out these transformations, traditionally, programmers had been using the waterfall model (Fig. 17.1) for software development. However, in real world applications, the problems are not always well-defined. Therefore, the waterfall model has limited utility as the model assumes that the requirements are known before the design begins. In complex applications, requirements may not be clearly understood in the beginning itself and after few months, users may change their requirements. Furthermore, the model neither emphasizes nor encourages the concept of software reusability.

The traditional Software Development Life Cycle (SDLC) model is good for automating existing pen and paper solutions or to update an older software system. The model follows a strict top-down approach in which stepwise refinement leads to a well-defined process.

17.2 BUILDING HIGH-QUALITY SOFTWARE

The software process transforms the user's needs in to a software solution. However, before deploying the software system in a user's environment, the software must be tested to ensure that it is free of bugs. A high-quality software product must not only satisfy user's requirements but also have minimal or no defects. It is always better to correct the errors before delivery to the users than correcting them post-delivery.

The software system must be tested according to how it has been built or, alternatively, what it should do. To ensure this, the software must be checked if it is corrected, verified, and validated. To begin with, the system is validated; it is examined to see how well it matches the needs of the operational environment. Next, the software is verified for its correctness. The major difference between verification and validation is that while verification answers the question, 'Am I building the product right?' Validation, on the other hand, answers the question, 'Am I building the right product?'(refer to Fig. 17.2).

Another major difference between verification and validation is that while validation begins with the start of the project, verification can begin only after a requirement's specification has been finalized. Though these two things may look familiar at this stage, verification and validation are independent of each other. A product may be right according to the requirements but the requirements may be incorrect. For example, a software product may not produce an important report just because it was not included in the original requirements.

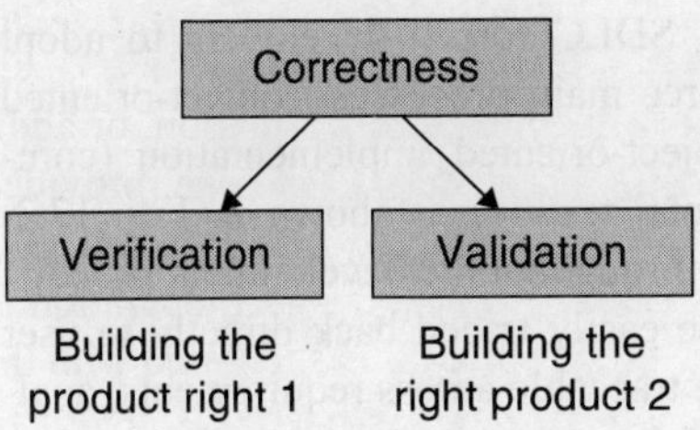

Figure 17.2 Verification and validation

17.3 OBJECT ORIENTED SOFTWARE DEVELOPMENT METHODOLOGY

Unlike the traditional development approach, the OO software development develops a software system by building self-contained objects that can be easily replaced, modified, and reused. For example, the Windows application is composed of Windows objects which are responsible for operations like opening, sizing, and closing itself. Moreover, the Windows object displays another object, say for example, a chart which maintains its data and labels and even draws itself.

OO software development enables programmers to create objects that work together to better model their problem domains than similar systems produced by traditional techniques. Once these objects are defined, they are guaranteed to perform their functions. Therefore, programmers shift their focus on what the objects do rather on how they do. The key advantages of OO techniques over traditional techniques are as follows:

- OO systems are easier to design, code, test, and maintain since programmers need to concentrate only on objects and ignore the rest of the details.
- OO systems easily incorporate changes owing to changed requirements.
- OO software is more robust.
- OO systems support reusability of design and code.
- OO systems offer seamless transition among different phases of software development. In the traditional approach, different styles and methodologies were adopted for each phase of the software development resulting in a complex transition from one phase to the next, which in turn, slows down the development process, increases the project size, and generates more chances of errors. The OO technique, on the other hand, uses the terminology for analysis, design, and implementation. This seamless approach not only reduces the level of complexity and redundancy, but also makes the system clearer and more robust.
- OO development techniques support good programming practices. Programmers design classes. These classes are grouped to form a sub-system in such a way that the individual classes still remain independent. This ensures that changes in one class have no impact on other classes.

17.4 OBJECT-ORIENTED SYSTEMS DEVELOPMENT

OO-SDLC believes that in real world applications, a top down approach cannot be followed. Rather, real world solutions require a partial top-down and a partial bottom-up approach. Another key difference between traditional SDLC and OO SDLC is that design is based on entities (called objects) and not on functions. It is a new discipline that aims to provide faster and cheaper software solutions by reusing existing solutions and focusing on a component based development.

Moreover, traditional SDLC is based on process decomposition that segregates processes from data, making transportation and reuse of code extremely difficult. Besides this, process decomposition focuses on solving a specific business problem. Therefore, the resultant design would be unique, making it difficult to be reused for a generic application.

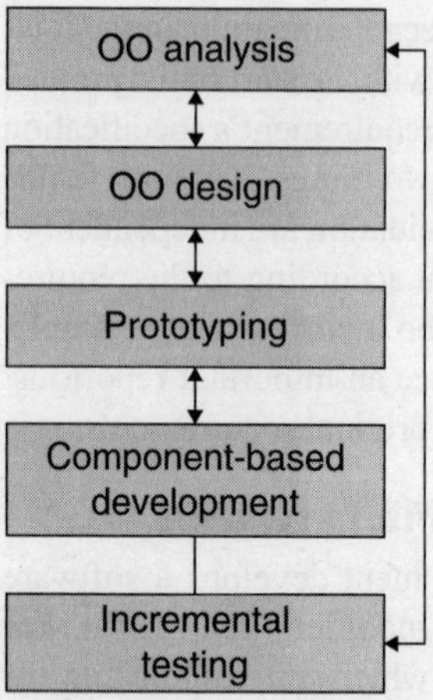

Figure 17.3 Phases in OO software development life cycle

All these shortcomings of traditional SDLC forced developers to adopt the OO-SDLC. OO-SDLC consists of three main processes—object-oriented analysis, object-oriented design, and object-oriented implementation (component based development and incremental testing) as shown in Fig. 17.3. In OO-SDLC, the use case model is used throughout the development process. Moreover, all the design decisions can be easily traced back directly to user requirements. This means that designs are traceable across requirements, analysis, implementation, and testing. OO-SDLC encourages programmers to view the problem as a system of cooperative objects and promotes them to do incremental development.

17.4.1 Object-oriented Analysis

This phase of object-oriented software development determines the system requirements and identifies classes along with their relationship to other classes in the problem domain. For this, the actors and the roles they play in the system are identified.

> **Note** Actors are the people who interact with the system. Their role describes how they use the system.

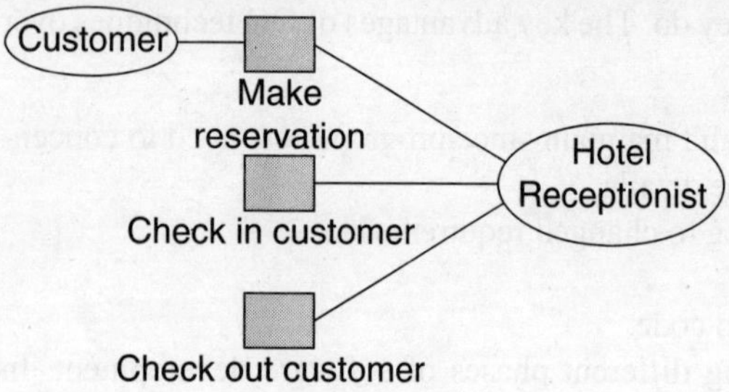

Figure 17.4 Use case model

Like the traditional system development process, the object-oriented system development process also uses scenarios to understand the end user's requirements. However, to ensure that scenarios are completely documented, Ivar Jacobson came up with the concept of the use case, which is another name for a scenario that describes the user computer system interaction. The use case model (Fig. 17.4) has now become the primary element in system development.

Scenarios help analysts understand who does what in interactions among objects and the interrelationships among those objects. The interrelationships demonstrate the role that the objects play. Moreover, the object's roles may intersect to achieve a given goal. This is called collaboration. Analysts use a number of scenarios—those showing usual behaviour or expectations from the system and those showing abnormal behaviour or expectations—to learn about all aspects of the collaboration and potential actions with the system. The steps in OO analysis are shown in Fig. 17.5.

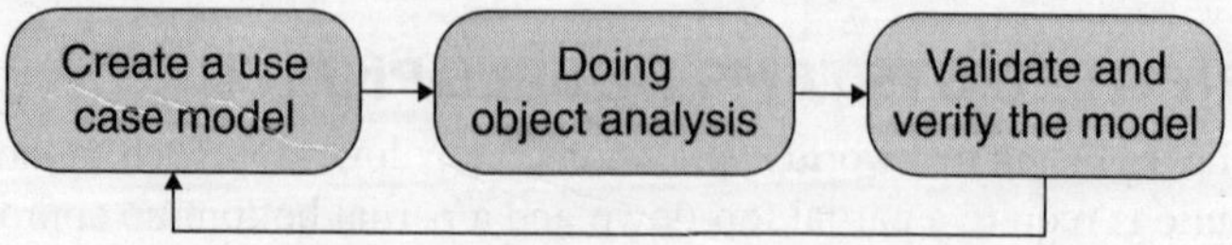

Figure 17.5 Steps in OO analysis

When designing the use case model, analysts capture information for a use case by talking to typical users regarding how they would be using the system For example, in Fig. 17.4, there are two actors—the customer, the hotel receptionist, and three use cases such as make reservation, check-in customer, and check-out customer. While the customer will use the system only for making reservation, the other two use cases will be used by the receptionist as it is his/her responsibility to check-in and check-out a customer.

The technique of expressing these high-level processes and interactions with users in a scenario and analysing them is called use case modelling. The advantages of use case modelling are as follows:

- The use case model represents the user's view of the system or user's needs.
- The process of developing use cases is an iterative process.
- Once a use case is identified, the classes and their relationships are created to establish a workable model.

For example, the objects in the incentive payroll system may include the employee, employer, manager, the pay check, the product being made, the process by which the product has been made, etc. All observations discovered in the analysis phase are documented. However, the documentation should be as short as possible. Generally, the 80-20 rule is used which states that 80 per cent of the work can be done with 20 per cent of documentation. This rule ensures that the 20 per centof documentation is easily accessible to all but the rest of the 80 per cent is available to only those who need to know.

Note Good modelling implies good documentation.

17.4.2 Object-oriented Design

This phase is used to design classes identified in the previous phase and the user interfaces. During the design phase, additional objects and classes that are used for implementing system requirement are identified. For example, additional classes for designing the user interface of the system like Windows, icons, menus, and so on, may be identified and designed.

Although, object-oriented design and analysis are two different disciplines, they can be intertwined. Furthermore, object-oriented development is highly incremental; it enables you to start with analysis, move to its design, and refine and complete the other models of the system. The activities that form a part of object oriented design are shown in Fig. 17.6. First, the classes are designed. All the attributes and functions of the identified classes are defined. In the next step, the object model is created, based on objects and their relationships. The, model is refined in iterations. The relationships that exist between classes are depicted in Fig. 17.6.

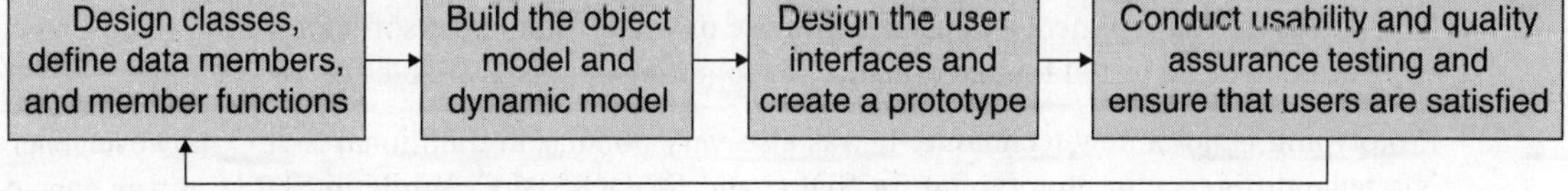

Figure 17.6 Steps in OO design

In the course of refining the model, the classes, attributes, functions, structures, and the association between the classes may be redesigned and refined. Some golden rules that must be followed in the design phase include the following:

- Gain knowledge about the existing classes.
- Reuse existing classes rather than building new ones.
- Design a large number of simple classes, rather than designing a small number of complex classes.
- Design member functions or methods.
- Criticize your own work and if required, go back and refine the classes.

In this phase, software frameworks are also designed where a framework is a generalisation of a system of collaborating objects like a menu, a user-application, a window, etc. While inheritance and polymorphism support reuse at the component-level, frameworks support reuse at the entire system level. For example, the collaborating objects can be generalized to provide new abstractions in class library; for example, an input-event handler or an application routine dispatcher. These generalized concepts can be specialized for new applications.

17.4.3 Prototyping

In the analysis and design phase, system features had been identified and described in detail. The next step is to construct a prototype of some of the key system components. As the saying goes—'A picture is worth a thousand words.' In extension to this, it would not be wrong to say that a prototype is worth a thousand pictures.

A prototype is a version of the software which is developed quite early for specific experimental purposes. While a prototype helps the development team to better understand the system and know whether they are on the right track, the end users, on the other hand, can have a look at it and explain if the product is exactly what they want or there are some deviations from their requirements. Moreover, there may be a case that user's requirements were either wrongly understood or wrongly stated.

In addition to the stated reasons for having a prototype, other benefits of prototyping are as follows:

- Enables users to comment on the usability and usefulness of the user interface design
- Enables the development team to assess the fit between the software tools selected and the functional specification
- Can be used to define the use cases
- Simplifies use case modelling
- Gives the development team an insight into the basic courses of action for developing use cases covered by the prototype
- Provides the development team a means to test and refine the user interface
- Gives a chance to the development team to enhance the usability of the system
- Confirms that the requirements' specification is correct
- Collects information about errors or other problems in the system that can be eliminated in the next prototype
- Gives the management and users a glimpse of what solution the software will provide Can be evaluated and tested for performance if supporting data is available

Prototyping is not a new technique. It was also very popular in traditional SDLC; however, there is a huge difference in prototyping for SDLC and for OO-SDLC. While in SDLC, it was considered to be a quick and dirty way to test the design, user interface, etc. and was usually meant to be thrown away when the actual version of software was developed, in OO-SDLC, on the other hand, the prototype is built with uses-case modelling to design systems that end users would need. This prototype is then refined in increments into the final product. This is done by adding more details to the prototype, testing it, and re-evaluating it until all the application's components work properly within the prototype framework.

There are four types of prototypes (Fig. 17.7), which can be explained as follows.

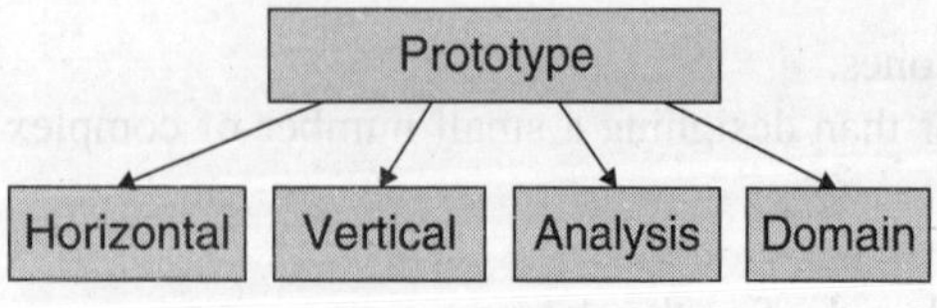

Figure 17.7 Types of prototypes

A horizontal prototype is used to simulate the interface. Such a prototype incorporates the entire user interface that will be in the complete version of the software system. However, it does not contain any functionality, as it is purposely designed to provide an overall feel of the system so that users can evaluate the complexity and usability of the interfaces. No doubt such a prototype can be quickly designed.

A vertical prototype provides a subset of the system features with complete functionality. It is specifically designed so that certain critical features can be tested in great depth.

While both horizontal and vertical prototypes have their own advantages, in building high quality OO software, a hybrid approach that combines features of both is followed. The major portions of the interface are designed and certain features having a high degree of risk are implemented, so that user can get the feel of the system with some knowledge about the functionality.

An analysis prototype is one that is used to explore the problem domain. It is specifically designed to demonstrate the proof of a concept. Hence, it is not used for development and is discarded when it has served its purpose. The analysis prototype provides conceptual knowledge to design the final product.

A domain prototype is used for incremental development of the complete software. It is applied as a tool for the staged delivery of sub-systems. This would enable the development team to demonstrate the feasibility of the implementation. The domain prototype will ultimately evolve into a deliverable product.

The time required to produce a prototype varies from a few days to several weeks, depending on the type and function of prototype. While building the prototype, the development team must be accompanied with representatives from end users and management members to ensure that the prototype meets the requirements established for the overall design.

It would be ideal if the prototype could be developed in parallel with finalizing the requirements specification so that as and when key features are identified, they are prototyped simultaneously to reveal additional features or problems that would not have been obvious until a later stage. Any modifications, if required, can then be easily incorporated in the next prototype.

17.4.4 Objectives of OO Analysis and Design

OO analysis and design enables the software development team to manage complex applications. The modelling language has a direct correspondent with the concepts of programming languages. Therefore, let us try to understand how OO analysis and design would provide a sound domain knowledge to the programmers.

- It gives a better understanding of the problem domain; while undertaking analysis and design, the team, management, and users work together to finalize graphical representations that can be easily interpreted by everyone.
- It describes the problem at a more abstract level that is independent of the programming language.
- It enhances reusability of project.
- It enables users to track whether the software development is on the right track or not.

17.4.5 Tools in OO Analysis and OO Design

Object-oriented analysis and design uses three main tools.

Class diagrams or templates Class diagrams model key entities in the problem domain and their relationships with each other. To develop a class diagram, the first step is to identify candidate classes and objects which may be people, places, things, organizations, concepts, or events. Next, the attributes and functions of each class are then identified and documented.

Object diagrams They are used to model the interactions between objects.

Object state diagrams Object state diagram models the dynamic behaviour within a single object. It shows all the possible states of an object and the allowed transition between the states. This means that the life cycle of each object is formally represented in this diagram.

These tools are the only mechanism through which developers communicate requirements or the design of the system.

Top-down structured design simplifies the development process by decomposing the entire problem into a number of smaller modules where each module denotes a major step in some overall process. In contrast, object-oriented decomposition is based on objects and not algorithms. Object-oriented analysis strives to describe what the system should do in terms of key objects in the problem domain, while object-oriented design strives to describe how the system will work using these objects.

17.4.6 Implementing Component-based Development

Files, functions, classes, executables, etc. are components of C++. We have seen that functions and classes are designed in such a way that they support reusability through the concepts of polymorphism, inheritance, containership, and templates.

These days, the trend in software development is to build the solution from prefabricated components (or classes) that have already been tested. Existing components can be customized based on current requirements and delivered to the users. Component-based manufacturing not only reduces cost but also takes less time to develop. These software components are built and tested in-house using computer-aided software engineering (CASE) tools, which enable the automation of entire SDLC process using a set of integrated tools for modelling and automatic code generation.

Note Components themselves may be constructed from other components.

Although the code generated by CASE tools provides only the skeleton of an application, a lot of code must be added by the programmers to give a complete solution. Whether the components have been re-used or built from scratch, hand-written or automatically generated using CASE tools, these details must be hidden from the users. The key advantages of using a component based development model are as follows:

- Faster product development cycles
- Enhanced flexibility
- Better customization
- Reduced development time and effort
- More efficient systems
- Enables legacy integration through component wrapping.

Existing or legacy applications can be reused. Rewriting such complex and poorly documented applications from scratch is not a good option. Therefore, component wrappers are used to surround the component's code and data, thereby providing an interface that can interact with both the legacy and the new software system.

In object-oriented software development, components are the functional units of a program that are reusable. When requested for a service, the component can either provide its own services or request a service from another component. The components in the system work independently to accomplish a task. The components are completely unaware of the inner details of the other components. A component may depend on other for a particular service but without interfering with each other. The steps in implementing an object-oriented software are summarized in Fig. 17.8.

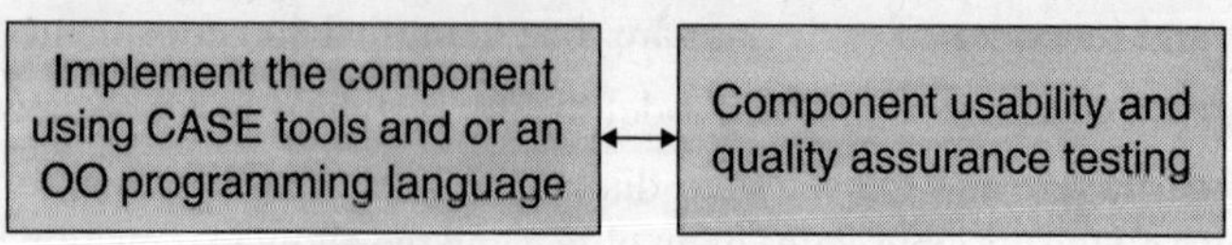

Figure 17.8 Steps in OO implementation

17.5 UNIFIED MODELLING LANGUAGE

Unified modelling language (UML) is an object-oriented system of notation that has finally evolved from the combined efforts of Grady Booch, James Rumbaugh, and Ivar Jacobson. These computer professionals fused their respective technologies into a single, standardized model that has been accepted by the Object Management Group (OMG) as the standard for modelling object-oriented programs.

UML is a general purpose visual modelling language that helps everybody associated with the system to visualize the system and software engineers to specify, construct, and document the software system. This means that UML diagrams are not only used by developers but also for business users and anybody interested to understand the system.

Note UML is not a development method, rather it accompanies with processes to make a successful system.

With UML, any complex system can be easily understood by making some useful diagrams. A single diagram is not enough to cover all aspects of the system. Therefore, UML defines a variety of diagrams to cover most of the aspects of a system. These diagrams include,

17.5.1 Class Diagrams

It is a static diagram that is used for visualizing, describing, and documenting different aspects of a system. The executable code is constructed using these diagrams, as it describes the attributes and operations of a class and also the constraints imposed on the system.

The class diagram also known as a structural diagram (Fig. 17.9) shows a collection of classes, interfaces, associations, collaborations, and constraints.

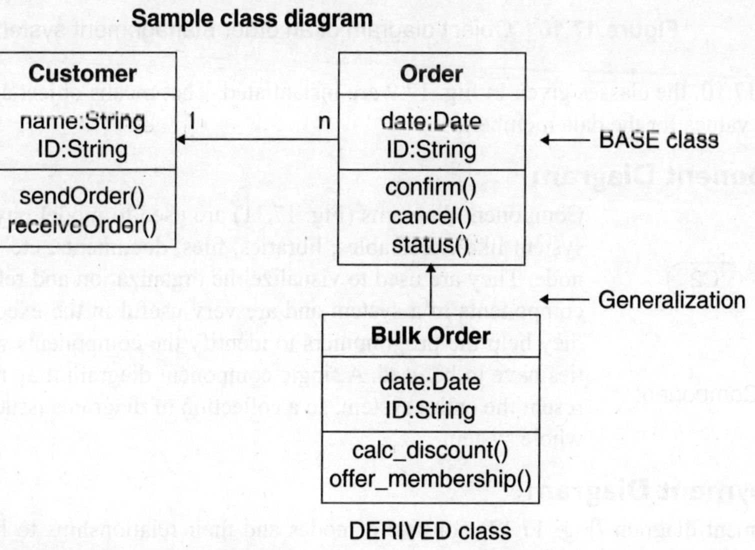

Figure 17.9 Class diagram

There is a class customer, with data members- name and ID, and member functions send order() and receive order(). The class order with data members- date and ID and member functions confirm(), cancel() and status() is derived by another class bulk order. The derived class has members date and ID calc_discount() and offer_membership().

17.5.2 Object Diagram

Object diagrams (Fig. 17.10) are derived from class diagrams to represent an instance of a class diagram. Although the basic concepts of both the diagrams are similar, object diagrams represent the static view of a system at a particular moment. They depict a set of objects and their relationships as an instance.

While the class diagram represents an abstract model consisting of classes and their relationships, object diagram, on the other hand, represents an instance at a particular moment, which is concrete in nature. This means that the object diagram is more close to the actual system behaviour. It not only helps programmers to understand the relationships clearly, but also helps in forward and reverse engineering.

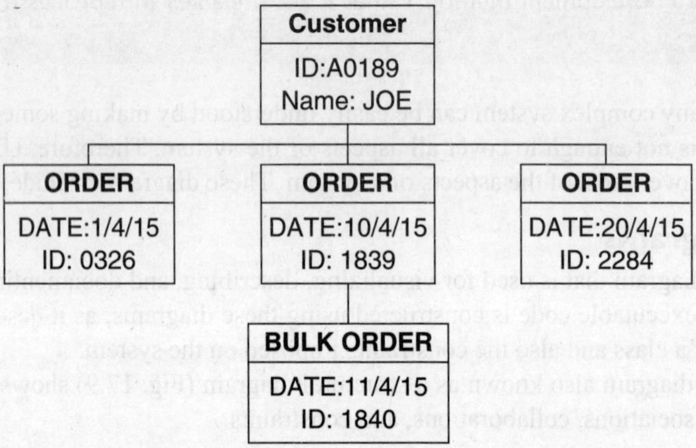

Figure 17.10 Object diagram of an order management system

In Fig. 17.10, the classes given in Fig. 17.9 are instantiated. That means object are made that have specific values for the data members.

17.5.3 Component Diagram

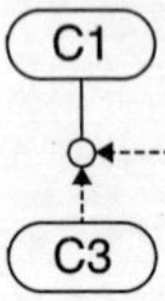

Figure 17.11 Component diagram

Component diagrams (Fig. 17.11) are used to model physical aspects of a system like executables, libraries, files, documents, etc. which reside in a node. They are used to visualize the organization and relationships among components in a system and are very useful in the executable system, as they help the programmers to identify the components whose functionalities have to be used. A single component diagram may not be able to represent the entire system, so a collection of diagrams issued to represent the whole system.

17.5.4 Deployment Diagram

Deployment diagram (Fig. 17.12) consists of nodes and their relationships to help the team visualize the topology of the physical components of a system where the software components are deployed. This means that the diagram describes the hardware components like nodes and connections where software components of the system are deployed. Component diagrams and deployment diagrams are quite similar and related to each other. While the component diagram describes the components to be used, deployment diagrams show how they are deployed in hardware.

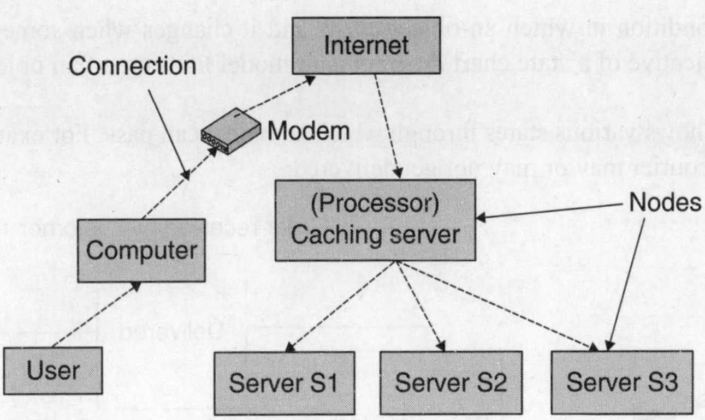

Figure 17.12 Deployment diagram for an order management system

17.5.5 Use Case Diagram

Until now, all diagrams that we had discussed were static diagrams. However, the use case diagram captures the dynamic behaviour of the system. For this, it incorporates some internal or external factors that interact with the system. These internal and external agents are known as actors. A use case diagram is made up of actors, use cases, and their relationships to model the system or subsystem of an application. A single use case diagram captures a particular functionality of a system. Therefore, to model the functionality of the entire system, a number of use case diagrams are used.

Basically, use case diagrams are designed to gather requirements of a system, to get an outside view of a system, identify external and internal agents that interact with the system. We have already seen a use case diagram in Fig. 17.4.

17.5.6 Sequence Diagram

Sequence diagram (Fig. 17.13) is a dynamic diagram that is used to describe some type of interactions among the different elements in the model. For this, it emphasizes on time sequence of messages that are exchanged between system elements. They are used to describe the message flow in the system and describe interaction among objects.

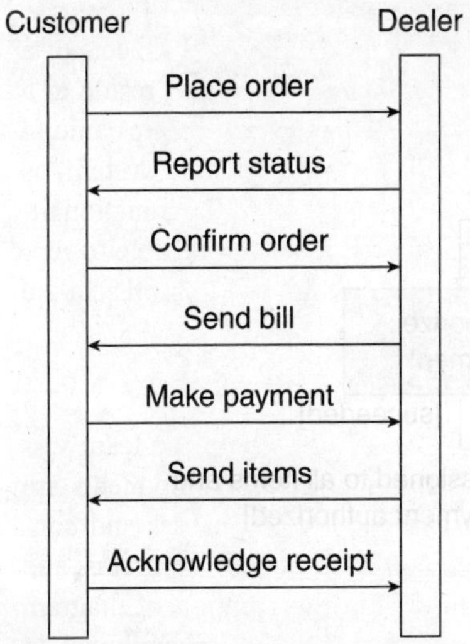

Figure 17.13 Sequence diagram

For example, in Fig. 17.13 the customer places an order is the dealer. The dealer sends a status report to customer that includes availability of items, delivery time, price, etc. The customer confirms the order. The dealer sends him a bill after the customer pays the amount, items are delivered. Finally, the customer acknowledges receipt of items.

17.5.7 State Chart Diagram

As the name implies, a state chart diagram is used to describe different states of a component or object in a system. These states that are controlled by external or internal events vary from one component or object to another and are clearly depicted by the state chart diagram.

State chart diagrams (Fig. 17.14) are useful to model reactive systems (that respond to external or internal events) to describe the flow of control from one state to another state, where a state is defined as a condition in which an object exists and it changes when some event is triggered. Therefore, the objective of a state chart diagram is to model life time of an object from creation to its termination.

Figure 17.14 shows various states through which an object can pass. For example, the order dispatched through courier may or may not get delivered.

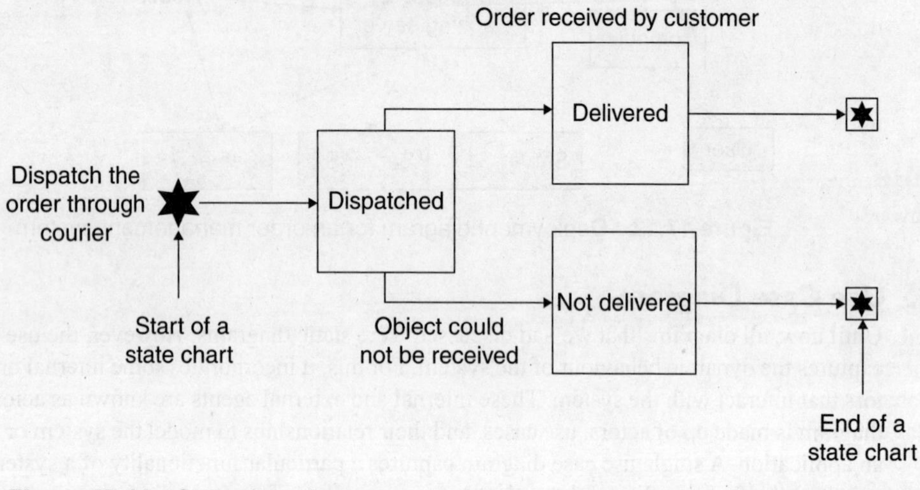

Figure 17.14 State chart diagram

17.5.8 Activity Diagram

Activity diagram (Fig. 17.15) represents the dynamic aspects of the system. It is basically a flow chart to represent the flow from one activity to another activity where an activity means an operation of the system. The flow can be sequential, branched, or concurrent.

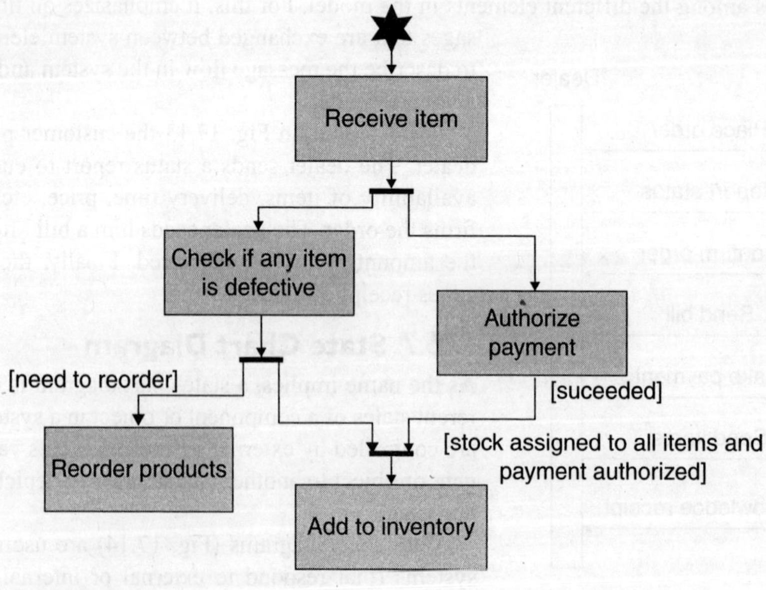

Figure 17.15 Activity diagram

In Fig. 17.15, once an item is recived, it is validated and added to the inventory. Also payment are made for the received items.

Since activities denote the functions the system is supposed to perform, a number of activity diagrams are prepared to capture the entire flow in a system.

Activity diagrams are used to get an idea of how the system will work when executed. The activity diagram shown in the figure continues until everything that needs to be done is done. One drawback of activity diagrams is that they do not make clear which objects execute which activities and what messages they exchange.

However, it is better to draw the activity diagrams as early as possible so that everybody could understand the overall process.

Points to Remember

- Software development is a dynamic and never-ending process that is always subjected to changes.
- Traditional software development techniques consider software as a collection of functions and isolated data.
- Object-oriented software development lays its focus on objects.
- In the traditional approach, different styles and methodologies were adopted for each phase of the software development resulting in a complex transition from one phase to the next which, in turn, slows down the development process, increases the project size, and generates more chances of errors. The OO technique, on the other hand, uses the terminology for analysis, design, and implementation. This seamless approach not only reduces the level of complexity and redundancy but also makes the system clearer and more robust.
- The traditional SDLC model is good for automating existing pen and paper solutions or to update an older software system.
- Before deploying the software system in user's environment, the software must be tested to ensure that it is free of bugs.
- Traditional SDLC is based on process decomposition that segregates processes from data, making transportation and reuse of code extremely difficult.
- OO-SDLC consists of three main processes—object-oriented analysis, object-oriented design, and object-oriented implementation.

Glossary

Prototype A version of the software which is developed quite early for specific experimental purposes

Software development methodology A series of processes that results in development of an application that achieves the ultimate goal based on system requirements

Systems development It refers to the set of activities that needs to be carried out for producing an information system

Use case modelling The technique of expressing high-level processes and interactions with users in a scenario and analysing them

Exercises

Fill in the Blanks

1. Implementation phase follows the ______ phase.
2. Goal is set based on ______.
3. Software may have to be changed due to change in ______ or ______.
4. In traditional approach, software is a combination of ______ and ______.
5. OO software development is centred on ______.
6. Classes are grouped to form ______.
7. ______ translates end user's needs into system requirements.
8. Traditional software development followed ______ model.
9. Software ______ can begin only after a requirements specification has been finalized.
10. In OO-SDLC, the ______ model is used throughout the development process.
11. ______ are the people who interact with the system.

12. ______ is a generalisation of a system of collaborating objects.
13. In OO-SDLC, the prototype is built with ______ to design systems that end users would need.
14. A ______ prototype is used to simulate the interface.
15. The ______ prototype provides conceptual knowledge to design the final product.
16. ______ model key entities in the problem domain and their relationships with each other.
17. ______ are used to model the interactions between objects,
18. In object-oriented software development, ______ are the functional units of a program.

State True or False

1. Testing must start before implementation.
2. The software development process ends after testing the software.
3. Higher cost, more time, and errors are features of traditional software development methodology.
4. The OO technique uses the same terminology for analysis, design, and implementation.
5. Change in one class leads to changes in other classes.
6. The analysis design phase starts with a problem statement.
7. OO software development follows a strict top down approach.
8. Software verification begins with the start of the project.
9. Traditional SDLC is based on process decomposition.
10. OO-SDLC does not support incremental development.
11. Use cases are developed iteratively.
12. A horizontal prototype provides a subset of the system features with complete functionality.

Multiple Choice Questions

1. The first step in system development is ____.
   (a) Design (b) Implementation
   (c) Analysis (d) Coding
2. Software development is a ______ process.
   (a) Static (b) Dynamic
   (c) Persistent (d) Constant
3. System development is considered to be a process of ______.
   (a) Change (b) Refinement
   (c) Transformation (d) All of these
4. Which phase refines the detailed design into system deployment?
   (a) Analysis (b) Design
   (c) Implementation (d) testing
5. OO software development focuses on ______ based development.
   (a) Algorithm (b) Object
   (c) Component (d) Data
6. In OO-SDLC, which phase identifies classes along with their relationship to other classes in the problem domain?
   (a) Analysis (b) Design
   (c) Implementation (d) testing
7. Which prototype is used to explore the problem domain?
   (a) Horizontal (b) Vertical
   (c) Domain (d) analysis
8. The life cycle of each object is formally represented in which diagram?
   (a) Class (b) Object
   (c) Object state (d) Use case

Review Questions

1. List the activities that are performed during system development.
2. What is software development methodology?
3. Why is software development considered to be a dynamic process?
4. How is traditional software development different from object-oriented development?
5. What are the advantages of building a software using objects?
6. How does OO technique provide smooth transitions among different phases?
7. In the course of software development, a series of transformations takes place. Comment on this statement.
8. Why can waterfall model not be applied on real world applications?
9. Explain the significance of testing a software system.
10. Differentiate between software verification and software validation.
11. What are the different phases in OO SDLC? Explain each of them.

12. What is use case modelling? Explain some advantages of using it.
13. What is prototyping? Why is it essential in software development?
14. How is prototyping for traditional SDLC different from that of OO-SDLC?
15. Differentiate between horizontal and vertical prototype.
16. Explain the significance of object orient analysis and design.
17. What are the different tools used in OO analysis and design?
18. What are the advantages of using a component based development model?

Answers

Fill in the Blanks

1. Design; **2.** User's requirements; **3.** Requirements, technology; **4.** Functions, isolated data; **5.** Objects; **6.** Sub systems; **7.** Analysis; **8.** Waterfall; **9.** Verification; **10.** Use case; **11.** Actors; **12.** Framework; **13.** uses-case modelling; **14.** horizontal; **15.** analysis; **16.** Class diagrams; **17.** Object diagrams; **18.** components

State True or False

1. True **2.** False **3.** True **4.** True **5.** False **6.** False **7.** False **8.** False
9. True **10.** False **11.** True **12.** False

Multiple Choice Questions

1. (c); **2.** (b); **3.** (d); **4.** (c); **5.** (c); **6.** (a); **7.** (d); **8.** (c)

APPENDIX A

C++ Standard Library Functions

The C++ standard library offers a huge collection of functions that perform error checking, string manipulations, common mathematical calculations, input/output, character manipulations, and lots of other important operations. These functions make the job of programmers easy by providing many of the much-needed capabilities. The C++ standard library functions (see below table), are included as a part of the C++ programming environment.

> **Note** Old-style header files, which end with .h, have now been superseded by the C++ standard library header files.

C++ standard library header files

C++ standard library header file	Description
<iostream>	It includes function prototypes for the C++ standard input and standard output functions. This header file replaces header file <iostream.h>.
<iomanip>	It comprises function prototypes for stream manipulators that format streams of data. This header file replaces header file <iomanip.h>.
<cmath>	It consists of function prototypes for math library functions. This header file replaces header file <math.h>.
<cstdlib>	It includes function prototypes for conversions of numbers to text, text to numbers, memory allocation, random numbers, and various other utility functions. <cstdlib> replaces header file <stdlib.h>.
<ctime>	<ctime> includes function prototypes and types for manipulating the time and date. This header file replaces header file <time.h>.
<cctype>	It comprises function prototypes for functions that test characters for certain properties, including whether the character is a digit or a punctuation, and function prototypes for functions that can be used to convert lowercase letters to uppercase letters and vice versa. <cctype> replaces header file <ctype.h>.

(Contd)

(*Contd*)

C++ standard library header file	Description
<cstring>	It includes function prototypes for C-style string-processing functions. <cstring> replaces header file <string.h>.
<cstdio>	Containing function prototypes for the C-style standard input/output library functions and information used by them, <cstdio> has replaced header file <stdio.h>.
<fstream>	It includes function prototypes for functions that perform input from files on disk and output to files on disk. This header file replaces header file <fstream.h>.
<climits>	<climits>includes the integral size limits of the system. It replaces header file <limits.h>.
<cassert>	It comprises macros for adding diagnostics that aid program debugging. This replaces header file <assert.h> from pre-standard C++.
<cfloat>	Containing the floating-point size limits of the system, this header file replaces header file <float.h>.
<string>	It includes the definition of class string from the C++ standard library.
<vector>, <list>, <deque>, <queue>, <stack>, <map>, <set>, <bitset>	These include classes that implement the C++ standard library containers that store data during a program's execution.
<typeinfo>	It includes classes for run-time type identification (determining data types at execution time).
<exception>, <stdexcept>	These header files include classes that are used for exception handling.
<memory>	It consists of classes and functions used by the C++ standard library to allocate memory to the C++ standard library containers.
<sstream>	<sstream> includes function prototypes for functions that perform input from strings in memory and output to strings in memory.
<functional>	It comprises classes and functions used by C++ standard library algorithms.
<iterator>	Consists of classes for accessing data in the C++ standard library containers.
<algorithm>	Includes functions for manipulating data in C++ standard library containers.

(*Contd*)

(*Contd*)

C++ standard library header file	Description
`<locale>`	It includes classes and functions normally used by stream processing to process data in the natural form for different languages-for example, sorting strings, monetary formats, character presentation, etc.
`<limits>`	It comprises classes for defining the numerical data type limits on each computer platform.
`<utility>`	Includes classes and functions that are used by many C++ standard library header files.

MATHEMATICAL FUNCTIONS

Some of the important mathematical functions in header file `<cmath>` are shown in table below.

Mathematical functions in header file `<cmath>`

Function	Description
`sin(x)`	Sine of an angle x (measured in radians)
`cos(x)`	Cosine of an angle x (measured in radians)
`tan(x)`	Tangent of an angle x (measured in radians)
`asin(x)`	Sin-1 (x) where x (measured in radians)
`acos(x)`	Cos-1 (x) where x (measured in radians)
`exp(x)`	Exponential function of x (ex)
`log(x)`	Logarithm of x
`log 10(x)`	Logarithm of number x to the base 10
`sqrt(x)`	Square root of x
`pow(x, y)`	x raised to the power y
`abs(x)`	Absolute value of integer number x
`fabs(x)`	Absolute value of real number x

CHARACTER FUNCTIONS

All the character functions require `<cctype>` header file.

Character functions in `<cctype>`

Function	Description
`isalpha(c)`	It returns True, if C is an uppercase letter, and False, if c is lowercase.
`isdigit(c)`	It returns True, if c is a digit (0 through 9), otherwise False.
`isalnum(c)`	It returns True, if c is a digit from 0 through 9 or an alphabetic character (either uppercase or lowercase), otherwise False.
`islower(c)`	It returns True, if c is a lowercase letter, otherwise False.
`isupper(c)`	It returns True, if c is an uppercase letter, otherwise False.
`toupper(c)`	It converts c to uppercase letter.
`tolower(c)`	It converts c to lowercase letter.

APPENDIX B

C++ Interview Questions

How does `void *` differ in C and C++?

C allows a `void*` pointer to be assigned to any pointer type without a cast. However, in C++, it must be explicitly type casted. For example,

```
void *ptr;
int *i = ptr; // allowed in C but not in C++
int *i = (int*) ptr;          // C++ style
```

Example 1 Write a program that produces different results in C and C++.

One example is as follows: character literals are treated differently in C and C++. In C, character literals like 'a' are treated as integers, while in C++, they are treated as characters.

```
using namespace std;
#include<iostream>
int main()
{
  cout<<sizeof('a');
  return 0;
}
In C++, output is 1 byte while in C, it is 2 bytes.
```

Note C++ makes this difference because it supports function overloading. If it treats integer and character literals similarly then overloading will lose its meaning.

Comparison between the use of references with pointers

Similarities

- Both are used to change local variables of one function inside another function.
- Both are used to save memory by preventing copying of objects or variables when passed as function arguments or returned from functions.

Differences

- References are safer to use, as they must be initialized. Problems like wild pointer never occur with references.
- References are easier to use, as to access their value we do not need a dereferencing operator.
- References are less powerful than pointers because once a reference is created, it cannot be later made to reference another object. However, it is possible with pointers.
- References cannot be `NULL` but pointers can be `NULL` to indicate that they are not pointing to any valid value.
- A reference must be initialized when declared, but a pointer may or may not be initialized during declaration.

Due to these limitations, references in C++ cannot be used for implementing data structures like linked list,tree, etc.

There are a few situations in which pointers cannot be used and only references are used. Some such examples are copy constructor argument and arguments in operator overloading functions.

Can references refer to invalid location in C++?

Yes, in some exceptional cases, there can be invalid references. For example,

- Reference to value at uninitialized pointer

```
int *ptr;
int &ref= *ptr;  // Reference to value at some random memory location
```

- Reference to a local variable is returned

```
int &fun()
{  int num = 10;
   return num;
         }
```

Once `fun()` returns, the space allocated to it on stack will be taken back. Therefore, the reference to a local variable will not be valid

Comment on `const` keyword when used with function overloading

If two methods `'void fun() const'` and `'void fun()'` have same signature except that one is const and other is not, then `'const void fun()'` is called on `const` object and `'void fun()'` is called on non-`const` object.

C++ also permits member functions to be overloaded on the basis of `const` type. Such type of overloading often usesone function `const`that returns a const reference or const pointer and the other non-const function that returns non-const reference or pointer. Regarding constant function parameters, C++ allows overloading only if the const parameter is a reference or a pointer.

Can any function be overloaded?

Yes, except the functions in following cases

- Function declarations that differ only in the return type.
- Member function with same name and parameters if one function is static and the other is non-static.
- Parameter declarations that differ only in a pointer (*) versus an array ([]) are equivalent. Therefore, the two declarations given here are equivalent.

```
int fun(int *ptr);
int fun(int ptr[]);
```

- Parameter declarations in which one is a function type and the other is a pointer to the same function type are equivalent.
- Parameter declarations that differ only in the presence or absence of const and/or volatile are equivalent. These specifiers are ignored when determining which function is being declared, defined, or called.
- Parameter declarations that differ only in their default arguments are equivalent.

Can `main()` be overloaded?

No. To have another function `main()`, you may define it as a member of a class

Can a C++ class have an object of self-type?

Yes

What are the constraints on static member function?

- They do not have `this` pointer.
- A static member function cannot be virtual.
- Member functions with the same name and parameters cannot be overloaded, if any of them is a static member function declaration.
- A static member function cannot be declared `const`, `volatile`, or `const volatile`.

What do you understand by delete this?

Programmers should not use the delete operator on the `this` pointer. However, if used, the following points must be remembered:

- `delete` operator works only for objects allocated using *new operator.*
- *Once the object is deleted using delete this, then no attempt should be made to access any of its member.*

What is the type of `this` pointer?

The type of `this` pointer depends upon function declaration as in the following:

- If the member function of a class is declared as `const`, then the type of `this` is `constX*`.
- If the member function is declared `volatile`, the type of this is `volatile X*`.
- If the member function is declared `const volatile`, the type of this is `const volatile X*`.

Is it necessary to define a copy constructor?

If the programmer does not define a copy constructor, then C++ compiler creates a default copy constructor for each class which does a member-wise copy between objects. Therefore, we may skip defining a copy constructor. However, programmers must define a copy constructor if an object has pointers or any run-time allocation of resource like file handle, a network connection,etc

When is a copy constructor called?

A copy constructor is invoked when an object i

- returned by value
- passed by value to a function
- constructed from another object of the same class
- created temporarily

Can a class have more than one destructor?

No, there can only be one destructor in a class.

Is it necessary to define a destructor?

No. In case the programmer does not write a destructor, the compiler creates a default destructor for each class. However, the programmers must define destructors if there are dynamically allocated variables or pointers in the class to avoid memory leak problems

What is the use of private destructor?

To control destruction of objects of a class, a destructor can be made private.

What is copy elision in C++?

Copy elision or copy omission is a compiler optimization technique that avoids unnecessary copying of objects. These days, almost every compiler makes use of this technique.

Differentiate between default constructor and copy constructor?

Default constructor is created by the C++ compiler,if no constructor has been defined. The default constructor has an empty body and does not assign default values to data members. However, the compiler creates a copy constructor if there is no copy constructor in the class. Unlike default constructor, the body of the copy constructor is not empty. It copies all data members of passed object to the object which is being created

If we define a copy constructor, then will the compiler insert a default constructor?

No. The compiler will not create a default constructor if any constructor has been defined

What are static objects in C++?

A static object is declared by using the keyword static as in, static Sample S; The memory for a static object is allocated on the system stack. Like a static variable, the static object is initialized only once and lives until the program terminates.

Is it possible to call constructors and destructors explicitly?

Yes, it is possible to call constructors and destructors explicitly. For example, `Sample();` calls constructor explicitly and `S.~Sample()` calls destructor explicitly

What is object slicing?

When a derived class object is assigned to a base class object, additional attributes of a derived class object are sliced off to form the base class object. This is called object slicing.

Can a static function be declared as virtual?

No. A static function can be neither `virtual`, `const`, nor `volatile`.

Can a virtual function be private?

Yes, a virtual function can be private and can also be overridden by a derived class.

Can a virtual function be inlined?

Virtual functions are used to implement run-time polymorphism. However, the code of an inline function is substituted in the program at the compile time. When a function except a virtual function is defined inside the class definition, it is implicitly treated as an inline function. This is because when a virtual function is invoked using base class pointer, it cannot be inlined because the call will be resolved at run time

When a virtual function is invoked using an object of that class, it can be inlined as it very clearly knows which function to call at the compile time.

Is it necessary to overload the assignment operator?

The answer is same as that for a copy constructor. The C++ compiler automatically creates a copy constructor and assignment operator for a class that does not have pointers or allocates memory dynamically. However, if pointers or dynamically allocated objects are present, then programmers must supply their own definition. Besides this, other situations in which the programmer must explicitly have an overloaded assignment operator include the following:

- When a class has a non-static data member of a const type or a reference type.
- When a class has a non-static data member of a type which has an inaccessible copy assignment operator.
- When a class is derived from a base class with an inaccessible copy assignment operator.

Can we restrict dynamic object creation of a class in `main()` or any other function?

Yes, we can make the new operator function private so that new cannot be called. This can be done as shown here

```
class Sample
{private:
    void* operator new(size_tsize);
    public:
        Sample()    { // code  }
};
int main()
{   Sample *obj=new Sample();  // Error
    Sample S;          //Ok
}
```

Can you print 'Welcome to the world of C++ Programming' without any statement in main()?

Yes, through the following code.

```
using namespace std;
#include<iostream>
class MyClass
{public:
    MyClass()
    {       cout<<"Welcome to the world of C++ Programming";
    }
}Obj;
 void main()
{
}
```

Can you restrict a class to have only static objects?

Yes. For this, make a private destructor in the class. Once it is created, the compiler will generate an error for non-dynamically allocated objects. This is simply because compiler is responsible for removing non-dynamically allocated objects from stack segment once they are not in use. However, the compiler cannot de-allocate dynamically allocated objects. Therefore, it is left as the programmer's job. To call the destructor, use a friend function shown as follows

```
using namespace std;
#include<iostream>
class Sample
{private:
    ~Sample {}
public:
friend void ToDestruct(Sample * );
};
 void ToDestruct(Sample *ptr)
{delete ptr;
}
int main()
{    Sample S;      // Error
     Sample *ptr = new Sample;
               ToDestruct(ptr);
}
```

Can we use function on left side of an expression in C and C++?

Not in C, but it is possible in C++. Look at the code given next, which illustrates how it can be done.

```
using namespace std;
#include<iostream>
int &fun()
{  static int x;
   return x;
}
int main()
{fun() = 100;
cout<<fun();
}
```

Index

About the Author

Reema Thareja is Assistant Professor at Department of Computer Science, Shyama Prasad Mukherji College for Women, University of Delhi. She has completed MCA in Software Engineering, MPhil in Computer, and PhD in the area of improving data warehouse quality. She has around 12 years of teaching experience and specializes in programming languages, operating systems, microprocessors, DBMS, multimedia, and web technologies.

Prof. Thareja has published several research papers in national and international journals of repute. She has done projects on quality monitoring of ATM networks and on steganography in Centre for Development of Telematics (CDoT) and Defence Research and Development Organisation (DRDO), respectively. She is the member of Computer Society of India (CSI).

She is also the author of *Data Warehousing, Data Structures using C, 2e, Python Programming, Data Structures (GTU), Programming in C, 2e, Introduction to C Programming, 2e, Computer Fundamentals and Programming in C, Data Structures for MSBTE, Fundamentals of Computers, Information Technology and its Applications to Business, Course on Computer Concepts (NIELIT),* and *Computer Programming (JNTU-K),* all published by OUP India.